The Cambridge Handbook of Historical Syntax

Change is an inherent feature of all aspects of language, and syntax is no exception. While the synchronic study of syntax allows us to make discoveries about the nature of syntactic structure, the study of historical syntax offers even greater possibilities. Over recent decades, the study of historical syntax has proven to be a powerful scientific tool of enquiry with which to challenge and reassess hypotheses and ideas about the nature of syntactic structure which go beyond the observed limits of the study of the synchronic syntax of individual languages or language families. In this timely handbook, the editors bring together the best of recent international scholarship on historical syntax. Each chapter is focused on a theme rather than an individual language, allowing readers to discover how systematic descriptions of historical data can profitably inform and challenge highly diverse sets of theoretical assumptions.

ADAM LEDGEWAY is Professor of Italian and Romance Linguistics and Chair of the Faculty of Modern and Medieval Languages at the University of Cambridge. His research interests are in the comparative history and morphosyntax of the Romance languages, Italian dialectology, syntactic theory and linguistic change. His recent books include *From Latin to Romance: Morphosyntactic Typology and Change* (2012) and *Diachrony and Dialects: Grammatical Change in the Dialects of Italy* (2014) (co-edited with P. Benincà and N. Vincent).

IAN ROBERTS is Professor of Linguistics at the University of Cambridge. His research interests are in comparative syntax, set against the background assumptions of Universal Grammar argued for by Noam Chomsky. He currently holds a European Research Council Advanced Grant for a project to investigate a hypothesis as to the way in which grammatical options made available by Universal Grammar are organized. His recent publications include *Parametric Variation* (2009) (co-edited with T. Biberauer, A. Holmberg and M. Sheehan) and *Syntactic Variation: The Dialects of Italy* (2010) (co-edited with R. D'Alessandro and A. Ledgeway).

Genuinely broad in scope, each handbook in this series provides a complete state-of-the-field overview of a major sub-discipline within language study and research. Grouped into broad thematic areas, the chapters in each volume encompass the most important issues and topics within each subject, offering a coherent picture of the latest theories and findings. Together, the volumes will build into an integrated overview of the discipline in its entirety.

Published titles

The Cambridge Handbook of Phonology, edited by Paul de Lacy

The Cambridge Handbook of Linguistic Code-Switching, edited by Barbara E. Bullock and Almeida Jacqueline Toribio

The Cambridge Handbook of Child Language, Second Edition, edited by Edith L. Bavin and Letitia Naigles

The Cambridge Handbook of Endangered Languages, edited by Peter K. Austin and Julia Sallabank

The Cambridge Handbook of Sociolinguistics, edited by Rajend Mesthrie

The Cambridge Handbook of Pragmatics, edited by Keith Allan and Kasia M. Jaszczolt

The Cambridge Handbook of Language Policy, edited by Bernard Spolsky

The Cambridge Handbook of Second Language Acquisition, edited by Julia Herschensohn and Martha Young-Scholten

The Cambridge Handbook of Biolinguistics, edited by Cedric Boeckx and Kleanthes K. Grohmann

The Cambridge Handbook of Generative Syntax, edited by Marcel den Dikken

The Cambridge Handbook of Communication Disorders, edited by Louise Cummings

The Cambridge Handbook of Stylistics, edited by Peter Stockwell and Sara Whiteley

The Cambridge Handbook of Linguistic Anthropology, edited by N. J. Enfield, Paul Kockelman and Jack Sidnell

The Cambridge Handbook of English Corpus Linguistics, edited by Douglas Biber and Randi Reppen

The Cambridge Handbook of Bilingual Processing, edited by John W. Schwieter

The Cambridge Handbook of Learner Corpus Research, edited by Sylviane Granger, Gaëtanelle Gilquin and Fanny Meunier

The Cambridge Handbook of Linguistic Multicompetence, edited by Li Wei and Vivian Cook

The Cambridge Handbook of English Historical Linguistics, edited by Merja Kytö and Päivi Pahta

The Cambridge Handbook of Formal Semantics, edited by Maria Aloni and Paul Dekker

The Cambridge Handbook of Morphology, edited by Andrew Hippisley and Greg Stump

The Cambridge Handbook of Historical Syntax, edited by Adam Ledgeway and Ian Roberts

Forthcoming

The Cambridge Handbook of Linguistic Typology, edited by Alexandra Aikhenvald and R. M. W. Dixon

The Cambridge Handbook of Areal Linguistics, edited by Rajmond Hickey

The Cambridge Handbook of Cognitive Linguistics, edited by Barbara Dancggier

The Cambridge Handbook of Historical Syntax

Edited by
Adam Ledgeway and Ian Roberts

CAMBRIDGE
UNIVERSITY PRESS

University Printing House, Cambridge CB2 8BS, United Kingdom

Cambridge University Press is part of the University of Cambridge.

It furthers the University's mission by disseminating knowledge in the pursuit of education, learning and research at the highest international levels of excellence.

www.cambridge.org
Information on this title: www.cambridge.org/9781107049604

First published 2017

Printed in the United Kingdom by Clays, St Ives plc

A catalogue record for this publication is available from the British Library

Library of Congress Cataloguing in Publication data
Ledgeway, Adam, editor. | Roberts, Ian G., editor.
The Cambridge Handbook of Historical Syntax / edited by
Adam Ledgeway and Ian Roberts.
Handbook of Historical Syntax
Cambridge : Cambridge University Press, [2017] |
Series: Cambridge Handbooks in Language and Linguistics |
Includes bibliographical references and index.
LCCN 2016012975 | ISBN 9781107049604 (hardback)
LCSH: Grammar, Comparative and general – Syntax – Handbooks,
manuals, etc. | Grammar, Comparative and general – Grammaticalization –
Handbooks, manuals, etc. | Historical linguistics – Handbooks, manuals, etc. |
BISAC: LANGUAGE ARTS & DISCIPLINES / General.
LCC P291 .C327 2016 | DDC 415–dc23
LC record available at https://lccn.loc.gov/2016012975

ISBN 978-1-107-04960-4 Hardback

Contents

Figures

Tables

Contributors

Henning Andersen, *University of California, Los Angeles*
Theresa Biberauer, *University of Cambridge and Stellenbosch University*
Cedric Boeckx, *ICREA and University of Barcelona*
Kersti Börjars, *The University of Manchester*
Laurel J. Brinton, *University of British Columbia*
James Clackson, *University of Cambridge*
Sonia Cristofaro, *University of Pavia*
Gisella Ferraresi, *University of Bamberg*
Elly van Gelderen, *Arizona State University*
Maria Goldbach, *University of Hamburg*
Cristina Guardiano, *University of Modena and Reggio Emilia*
John Haiman, *Macalester College*
Alice C. Harris, *University of Massachusetts Amherst*
Bernd Heine, *University of Cologne*
Anders Holmberg, *Newcastle University*
Tania Kuteva, *Heinrich Heine University of Düsseldorf*
Adam Ledgeway, *University of Cambridge*
Evelina Leivada, *Cyprus University of Technology*
David W. Lightfoot, *Georgetown University*
Giuseppe Longobardi, *University of York and University of Trieste*
Nerea Madariaga, *University of the Basque Country UPV/EHU*
Pedro Tiago Martins, *University of Barcelona*
Marianne Mithun, *University of California, Santa Barbara*
Heiko Narrog, *Tohoku University*
Susan Pintzuk, *University of York*
Paolo Ramat, *University of Pavia*
Ian Roberts, *University of Cambridge*
Suzanne Romaine, *University of Oxford*
Anna Roussou, *University of Patras*
Ann Taylor, *University of York*

Elizabeth Closs Traugott, *Stanford University*
Nigel Vincent, *The University of Manchester*
George Walkden, *The University of Manchester*
Anthony Warner, *University of York*
Marit Westergaard, *UiT – The Arctic University of Norway and NTNU Norwegian University of Science and Technology*
David Willis, *University of Cambridge*

Abbreviations

*	ungrammatical form or string
#	syllable boundary
1 / 2 / 3	first/second/third person
3R	coreferential third person
↑	the f-structure associated with the mother node
↓	the f-structure associated with this node
A	Agent/Actor, namely subject of a transitive clause
a-structure	argument structure
ABL	ablative
ABS	absolutive (case)
ABSL	Al-Sayyid Bedouin Sign Language
ACC	accusative
AcI	accusative with the infinitive
ADJ	adjunct
ADV	adverbial case
Adv	adverb
agr	agreement
AgrOP	object agreement phrase
AOR	aorist
AP	adjectival phrase
Asp(P)	aspect (phrase)
ASP	aspect(ual)
Aux	auxiliary
Br.Pt.	Brazilian Portuguese
C	(i) consonant
	(ii) head of CP and/or complementizer position
C-I	conceptual-intentional
c-structure	constituent-structure
Cae.	Caesar

B.C.	*de Bello Ciuili*
B.G.	*de Bello Gallico*
Cat.	Catalan
CAUS	causative
CEEC	*Corpus of Early English Correspondence*
CG	Construction Grammar
Ch.	Chinese
CI	conditional inversion
Cic.	Cicero
Diu.	*De diuinatione*
Phil.	*Orationes Philippicae*
CIG	contact-induced grammaticalization
CIL	*Corpus Inscriptionum Latinarum*
CL	clitic
CLat.	Classical Latin
CLF(P)	classifier (phrase)
CM	class marker
CM	Comparative Method
COHA	*Corpus of Historical American English*
COL	collective
ComMod	Comprehensive Model
COMP	(i) complementizer
	(ii) finite clausal complement
COMPL	completive aspect
COND	conditional
CONJ	conjunction
CONT	continuous
COP	copular
CP	complementizer phrase
CSL	cislocative
CUST	customary
D(P)	determiner (phrase)
DAT	dative
DECL	declarative
DEF	definiteness
DEM	demonstrative
Diag	diagnostic
DISTR	distributive
DM	Distributed Morphology
DOEC	*Dictionary of Old English Corpus*
DU	dual
EEBO	*Early English Books Online*
EF	edge feature
EIC	Early Immediate Constituents
EModE	Early Modern English

Eng.	English
EPP	extended projection principle
ERG	ergative (case)
F	feminine
F	feature
F1/2/3	first/second/third factor
(I/U)F	(interpretable/unvalued) feature
f-structure	functional-structure
FDG	Functional Discourse Grammar
FE	feature economy
fem	feminine
FLB	faculty of language in the broad sense
FLN	faculty of language in the narrow sense
FOFC	Final-Over-Final Constraint
FOC	focus
Fr.	French
FUT	future
GB	Government–Binding (Theory)
GEN	genitive
GEND	gender
GER	gerund
Ger.	German
HAB	habitual
i-	interpretable (feature)
i-structure	information structure
IcePaHC	Icelandic Parsed Historical Corpus
IE	Indo-European
IG	Input Generalization
IMP	imperative
IN	inessive
IND	indicative
INDEF	indefinite
I(NFL)	(verbal) inflection
INS	instrumental (case)
INT	interrogative
INTR	intransitive
INV	inversion
IP	inflectional phrase
IPFV	imperfective
IS	information structure
It.	Italian
JUNC	juncture
L2	second language
Lat.	Latin
LF	Logical Form

LFG	Lexical-Functional Grammar
LOC	locative
M	masculine
m-structure	morphological-structure
MaOP	Maximize On-line Processing
MAS	masdar (verbal noun)
MAT	matter
MDL	middle (voice)
ME	Middle English
MED	*The Middle English Dictionary*
MedFa	Medieval Faroese
MGP	Modularised Global Parametrisation
MHG	Middle High German
MiD	Minimize Domains
MiF	Minimize Forms
ML	Model Language
Mod	Modern
Mod(P)	modality (phrase)
ModE	Modern English
ModFa	Modern Faroese
N	neuter
N(P)	noun (phrase)
NAR	narrative
Neg, NEG	negator/negative
NegP	negation phrase
NMZ	nominalizer
nom, NOM	nominative
num, Num(P)	number (phrase)
O	old
Obj, OBJ	object
OBL	oblique
Occ.	Occitan
OCS	Old Church Slavonic
OE	Old English
ON	Old Norse
Op	operator
OPT	optative
OT	Optimality Theory
Ov. *Met.*	Ovid *Metamorphoses*
OV	object–verb (order)
OVS	object–verb–subject (order)
P	(i) object of a transitive clause
	(ii) parameter/property
p-structure	prosodic structure
P&N	person and number

P&P	Principles and Parameters
PART	partitive case
PASS	passive
PAT	patient
PAT	pattern
PCM	Parametric Comparison Method
PERS	person
PF	Phonological Form
PFV	perfect(ive)
PGCH	Performance-Grammar Correspondence Hypothesis
PIE	Proto-Indo-European
PL	plural
PLD	primary linguistic data
POSS	possessive
P(P)	preposition(al phrase)
PPCEME	*Penn–Helsinki Parsed Corpus of Early Modern English*
PPCME2	*Penn–Helsinki Parsed Corpus of Middle English* (2nd edition)
PRED	predicate
PRET	preterite
PRF	perfect
pro	phonologically null pronominal subject
PRO	anaphoric null pronominal
PROG	progressive
PRS	present
PRT	particle
PST	past
Pt.	Portuguese
PTCP	participle
Q	question/interrogative (particle)
Q(P)	quantifier (phrase)
RAH	rich agreement hypothesis
RDP	reduplication
ReCoS	*Rethinking Comparative Syntax*
REFL	reflexive
REL	relative/relativizer
RL	Replica Language
Ro.	Romanian
S	(i) subject of an intransitive clause
	(ii) sentence
Ŝ	non-projecting specifier position
S_0	initial stage of language acquisition
s-structure	semantic structure
SBJ	subject
SBJV	subjunctive
SCL	subject clitic

SF	stylistic fronting
sg, SG	singular
Sic.	Sicilian
SOV	subject–object–verb (order)
Sp.	Spanish
Spec	specifier position
STAT	stative
STR	strong
SUB	subordinate
Subj, SUBJ	subject
SUF	suffix
SVO	subject–verb–object (order)
Swd.	Swedish
t	trace (of moved element)
T(P)	tense (phrase)
TAM	tense, aspect and mood
TEMP	temporal (argument, adjunct)
TLA	triggered learning algorithm
TR	transitive
u-	uninterpretable (feature)
UG	Universal Grammar
UNDG	undergoer
UP	Uniformitarian Principle
v(P)	light (agentive/causative) verb (phrase)
v_i	feature value
(E)V2	(embedded) verb-second (syntax)
V	(i) vowel
	(ii) verb
V(P)	verb (phrase)
VO	verb–object (order)
VOS	verb–object–subject (order)
VSO	verb–subject–object (order)
YCOE	*York–Toronto–Helsinki Parsed Corpus of Old English Prose*
YCOEP	*York–Helsinki Parsed Corpus of Old English Poetry*
WK	weak

SF	stylistic fronting
sg, sc	singular
Sic.	Sicilian
SOV	subject–object–verb (order)
Sp.	Spanish
Spec	specifier position
STAT	stative
STR	strong
SUB	subordinate
subj, subj	subject
suff	suffix
SVO	subject–verb–object (order)
Swd.	Swedish
t	trace (of moved element)
T(P)	tense (phrase)
TAM	tense, aspect and mood
temp	temporal (argument, adjunct)
TLA	triggered learning algorithm
tr	transitive
u-	uninterpretable (feature)
UG	Universal Grammar
u-bc	undergoer
UP	Uniformitarian Principle
vP	light (agentive\causative) verb (phrase)
v	feature value
(E)V2	(embedded) verb-second (syntax)
V	(i) vowel
	(ii) verb
VP	verb (phrase)
VO	verb–object (order)
VOS	verb–object–subject (order)
VSO	verb–subject–object (order)
YCOE	York–Toronto–Helsinki Parsed Corpus of Old English Prose
tCOEP	York–Helsinki Parsed Corpus of Old English Poetry
WK	weak

Introduction

Adam Ledgeway and Ian Roberts

The study of historical linguistics has long been a concern of linguistic theory. Although it has antecedents in the Middle Ages, historical linguistics was not systematically studied until the nineteenth century, when it came to dominate the field. In the past sixty years, the development of both Greenbergian language typology and Chomsky's generative grammar (which has developed an explicitly comparative programme since the early 1980s) has led, at first independently but arguably with growing convergence, to a huge increase in our knowledge of cross-linguistic variation. Our notion of how grammatical systems vary and our ability to provide detailed, sophisticated analyses of this variation across a range of languages and grammatical phenomena is probably greater than it has been at any time in the past. Since synchronic variation reflects and is created by diachronic change, the study of historical syntax has also flourished and continues to do so.

The pioneering work in historical syntax includes, but is not limited to, Kuryłowicz ([1965] 1976), Traugott (1965, 1969), Weinreich, Labov and Herzog (1968), Givón (1971), Andersen (1973), Lehmann (1973, 1974), Li (1975, 1977), Vennemann (1975), Allen ([1977] 1980), Langacker (1977), Timberlake (1977), Moravcsik (1978), Lightfoot (1979) and Lehmann ([1982] 1995). As has often been observed, change appears to be almost an inherent feature of all aspects of language, and syntax is certainly no exception. While the synchronic study of syntax, albeit from a comparative perspective both within and across different language families, does undoubtedly allow us to ask important questions and make insightful and enlightening hypotheses and discoveries about the nature of syntactic structure, the study of historical syntax arguably offers the linguist greater possibilities.

Among other things, through the detailed comparison of different periods of the same language or language family we are able to track and document the individual stages in the development of particular syntactic structures, potentially allowing us to identify, pinpoint and explain the causes – whether endogenous or exogenous – of such changes, their overt reflexes and potential effects on other areas of the grammar, and the mechanisms involved therein. While successive historical stages of individual linguistic varieties are naturally closely related to each other, manifestly displaying in most cases a high degree of structural homogeneity, they often diverge minimally in significant and interesting ways which allow the linguist to isolate and observe what lies behind surface differences across otherwise highly homogenized grammars. By drawing on such historical microvariation, it is possible to determine which phenomena are correlated with particular linguistic options and how such relationships are mapped onto the syntax. In short, the results of the study of historical syntax over recent decades have shown how investigation of structured variation along the diachronic axis can be profitably exploited as a scientific tool of enquiry with which to test, challenge and reassess hypotheses and ideas about the nature of syntactic structure which go beyond the observed limits of the study of the synchronic syntax of individual languages or language families.

Given therefore the central role of syntax and, in turn, historical syntax assumed today within the study of linguistics and the many new and exciting perspectives that it continues to afford us in shaping and informing our theoretical understanding of the nature of language, it seemed timely to the editors to bring together in a single volume a comprehensive and detailed treatment of a number of the key topics and issues in historical syntax. In particular, *The Cambridge Handbook of Historical Syntax* provides an opportunity for some of the foremost scholars in the field to reflect in fresh ways on the major issues in historical syntax in the light of contemporary thinking across a wide variety of syntactic approaches and in relation to a large body of empirical research conducted on a growing number of individual languages and language families. This volume is therefore aimed principally at fellow scholars and researchers in the fields of historical linguistics, and in particular historical syntax and syntactic theory, but will no doubt also be well suited to the needs of advanced undergraduates and postgraduate students specializing in historical linguistics and syntax. Given the enormous surge in interest in historical syntax over the course of the last thirty years which has placed work on syntactic change at the forefront of the research agenda, it is envisaged that the volume will find an extensive international readership.

The *Handbook* aims at originality in two respects. First, we seek, wherever possible, to integrate the results and findings of different theoretical frameworks, models and approaches to changes in syntax. There has been a tendency for different models and approaches to develop separate research agendas and fora (e.g. conferences, journals) and to be pursued by scholars with different types of background and training. The multi-author format of the present *Handbook* allows us to bring together in one place the best of recent international scholarship from across many frameworks and approaches and, through careful editorial intervention, to show how each may cast new and necessary light on the other. While the individual chapters admittedly often embrace a number of quite different perspectives, ranging from the purely descriptive to the more formal (including enlightening analyses of novel data from acquisitional, biolinguistic, emergentist, functionalist and typological perspectives as well as in terms of such frameworks as Cartography, Lexical–Functional Grammar, Minimalism, and Principles and Parameters), this variety of approaches duly reflects the extraordinary breadth and diversity of the issues of interest in historical syntax for the wider linguistic community. We therefore see the eclecticism of the present volume as a strength, insofar as it illustrates how clear and systematic descriptions of the historical data can consistently be exploited to yield and test empirically robust generalizations, as well as profitably inform and challenge highly diverse sets of theoretical assumptions.

Second, the *Handbook* has been conceived in such a way as to break away from a traditional format in which the foci are individual languages or particular grammatical phenomena. By contrast, we have deliberately decided to divide the volume, parts and chapters along complementary thematic lines. In particular, the thirty-one chapters of the present volume variously focus on individual themes, questions and approaches and are arranged in six different parts which specifically deal with I: Types and Mechanisms of Syntactic Change; II: Methods and Tools; III: Principles and Constraints; IV: Major Issues and Themes; V: Explanations; and VI: Models and Approaches. The volume is thus intended to form a coherent whole, in that the rich overview of types and mechanisms of syntactic change critically reviewed in Part I, coupled with the detailed examinations of traditional and new methods and tools of inquiry presented in Part II, provide the necessary broad empirical and theoretical background and context to understand the significance of the discussion of individual principles, constraints, issues and explanations developed in detail in Parts III–V. Finally, the overviews of individual models and approaches to historical syntax presented in Part VI offer the opportunity to see and compare in detail how many of the empirical and theoretical issues and problems explored earlier in the *Handbook* may be approached, interpreted and resolved within a single coherent formal model.

Finally, the editors would like to thank Andrew Winnard of Cambridge University Press for his support and enthusiasm in guiding this project through to completion.

References

Allen, C. L. 1977. 'Topics in diachronic English syntax', PhD thesis, University of Massachusetts (published 1980, New York: Garland).

Andersen, H. 1973. 'Abductive and deductive change', *Language* 49: 765–93.

Givón, T. 1971. 'Historical syntax and synchronic morphology: an archaeologist's field trip', *Chicago Linguistic Society* 7: 394–415.

Kuryłowicz, J. [1965] 1976. 'The evolution of grammatical categories'. Reprinted in J. Kuryłowicz 1976. *Esquisses linguistiques*, vol. 2, Munich: Fink, pp. 38–54.

Langacker, R. 1977. 'Syntactic reanalysis', in C. Li (ed.), *Mechanisms of syntactic change*. Austin: University of Texas Press, pp. 57–139.

Lehmann, C. [1982] 1995. *Thoughts on grammaticalization*. Munich: Lincom Europa.

Lehmann, W. P. 1973. 'A structural principle of language and its implications', *Language* 49: 47–66.

1974. *Proto-Indo-European syntax*. Austin: University of Texas Press.

Li, C. N. (ed.) 1975. *Word order and word order change*. Austin: University of Texas Press.

(ed.) 1977. *Mechanisms of syntactic change*. Austin: University of Texas Press.

Lightfoot, D. 1979. *Principles of diachronic syntax*. Cambridge University Press.

Moravcsik, E. A. 1978. 'Language contact', in J. H. Greenberg, C. A. Ferguson and E. A. Moravcsik (eds.), *Universals of human language*. Stanford University Press, pp. 93–123.

Timberlake, A. 1977. 'Reanalysis and actualization in syntactic change', in Li (ed.), pp. 141–77.

Traugott, E. 1965. 'Diachronic syntax and generative grammar', *Language* 41: 402–15.

1969. 'Toward a grammar of syntactic change', *Lingua* 23: 1–27.

Vennemann, T. 1975. 'An explanation of drift', in Li (ed.), pp. 269–305.

Weinreich, U., Labov, W. and Herzog, M. 1968. 'Empirical foundations for a theory of language change', in W. Lehmann and Y. Malkiel (eds.), *Directions for historical linguistics*. Austin: University of Texas Press, pp. 95–188.

Part I

Types and Mechanisms of Syntactic Change

Part I

Types and Mechanisms of Syntactic Change

1

Grammaticalization

Heiko Narrog and Bernd Heine

1.1 Introduction

Grammaticalization in its broadest sense can be taken as any process that leads to the creation of grammar. We understand it more narrowly here in accordance with the classical definition by Kuryłowicz ([1965] 1976: 52), for whom '[g]rammaticalisation consists in the increase of the range of a morpheme advancing from a lexical to a grammatical or from a less grammatical to a more grammatical status'. While the term 'grammaticalization' as such is relatively young, being generally ascribed to Meillet (1912), the study of the phenomenon can be traced back to the eighteenth century, and is a solid part of the work of nineteenth-century historical linguists such as Bopp, Humboldt and Gabelentz (Lehmann 1982; Heine, Claudi and Hünnemeyer 1991: 6–9). However, when speaking of 'grammaticalization' in current linguistics one usually does not refer to these historical predecessors, but to the work emanating from a new wave of research that started in the 1970s with a seminal paper by Givón (1971), and reached a peak in the 1990s and 2000s. While the original approach to grammaticalization was primarily concerned with the development of morphology, the new wave of research has focused on novel theoretical aspects such as pragmatics, semantics and discourse.

Syntax is an indispensable part of the study of grammaticalization but initially it was backgrounded in comparison to the above-mentioned fields. This has something to do with the intellectual environment in which modern grammaticalization studies emerged. The study of grammaticalization was part of a movement that revolted against the overwhelming dominance of generative linguistics in theoretical linguistics of the 1960s and early 1970s, which seemingly tried to reduce the study of language to the statement of syntactic (and, perhaps, phonological) rules. Generative syntax was perceived as the extreme off-shoot of structuralism, and scholars were looking for paradigms countering or offering an alternative to structuralism and structuralist analysis. The study of gram-maticalization provided such an alternative. The by now classical research of the 1980s and 1990s focused on issues of discourse (e.g. Givón 1975; Hopper 1982, 1987), semantics, especially cognitive semantics (Heine, Claudi and Hünnemeyer 1991; Heine 1997), pragmatics (Traugott 1988) and language processing (Bybee, Perkins and Pagliuca 1994) in grammati-calization. Despite differences in detail, it is fair to say that this classical research shared a number of tenets, in particular the ones listed in (1), which all imply a rejection of generative and even structuralist analysis.

(1)   a. A denial of strict separation between diachrony and synchrony in linguistic analysis. Instead, diachrony is taken to explain synchrony
       b. A denial of a strict distinction between lexical and grammatical categories
       c. The assumption that extra-linguistic factors such as human inter-action, cognition and processing abilities decisively shape lan-guage structure

The rejection of structuralist and generative syntax, and the accompa-nying backgrounding of syntax, however, does not mean that syntax has not played a part in traditional and current mainstream grammaticaliza-tion studies. The role of syntax is practically in-built in the definition of grammaticalization to the extent that it involves the shift from the lexical to the grammatical, even if this shift is now conceptualized as a continuum rather than a categorical jump.

§1.2 of this chapter describes grammaticalization as a framework of its own, where grammaticalization is not only understood as a diachronic phenomenon in grammar, but also as an explanation for synchronic structure. In this case one can rightfully speak of 'grammaticalization theory'. Section §1.3 examines the idea that grammaticalization is subor-dinate to a model of grammar within which it is treated as but one phenomenon. This section is further divided into the study of grammati-calization within both formal and functional models of grammar that posit hierarchical clause structure (§1.3.1), and Construction Grammar (§1.3.2).

1.2 Grammaticalization and Syntax – Grammaticalization on Its Own Terms

While syntax was hardly ever a focal area for grammaticalization studies in the 1980s and 1990s, it was always in their scope and, as was observed in §1.1, it was – implicitly or explicitly – considered to be an indispensable part of these studies. The goal was, and still is, to explain why grammar is structured the way it is, and in accordance with (1c), explanations were sought most of all in human interaction, cognition and/or speech processing (or discourse). Furthermore, the explanations proffered were external rather than internal to language structure, they were diachronic rather than synchronic and they were based on cross-inguistic typological generalizations on grammatical change.

The main goal of the present section is to discuss the approach used and some of the findings made in these studies as far as they contribute to an account of syntactic phenomena. To this end, we will be restricted to clausal subordination, that is, a domain of grammar that intrinsically involves the grammaticalization of syntax. We will be able to do no more than illustrate the main kinds of processes and the main lines of grammaticalization involved; the reader is referred to the works cited for further details.

1.2.1 Introduction

The genesis and development of clausal subordination has been the subject of a wide range of studies (e.g. Givón 1991, 2006; Harris and Campbell 1995; Hopper and Traugott 2003: 175–211; van Gelderen 2004; Diessel 2005; Heine and Kuteva 2007: 210–61; see also the contributions in Bybee, Haiman and Noonan 2001). A major theme in much of this work was to find an answer to the question of how subordinate clauses evolve and why they take the form they do. In the present section we are restricted to a small set of subordinate structures that appear to be cross-linguistically fairly widely distinguished.

From a grammaticalization perspective, Hopper and Traugott (2003: 177–84) propose an alternative classification, distinguishing the three kinds of clause combining listed in (2), which they treat as 'cluster points' along a cline. Paradigm examples of parataxis are provided by juxtaposition and clause coordination by means of 'and', 'but' and 'or'. Hypotaxis includes parenthetical structures such as appositional relatives, adverbial clauses (temporals, causals, conditionals and concessives), while subordination includes restrictive relatives and complement clauses.

(2)   Three types of clause combining according to Hopper and Traugott (2003: 277–84):
        a. Parataxis (relative independence)
        b. Hypotaxis (interdependency)
        c. Subordination (complete dependency)

Hopper and Traugott further hypothesize that the grammaticalization of clause combining is directional, proceeding from (2a) via (2b) to (2c). In the following, we will ignore this hypothesis, mainly for the following reason: the cline proposed aims at an important generalization about syntactic change but, as we will see in §1.2.3 and §1.2.4, it is not always fully supported by the data that we were able to access.

We will therefore be restricted to the distinction between coordination and subordination as the main functional means of clause combining, being aware that there is no clear boundary separating the two, and that in quite a range of languages the distinction between the two is questionable and/or has been discussed controversially. Furthermore, we will refer to markers of clause subordination as subordinators. Subordinators are for the most part short particles or affixes, but they may be complex as well, and they may be discontinuous, being distributed over different parts of a clause.

A survey of works on the grammaticalization of clause subordinators in different parts of the world suggests that there are a number of generalizations that can be proposed, in particular the ones presented in (3) (the terms in parentheses refer to parameters of grammaticalization proposed by Heine and Kuteva 2007: 33–45).

(3)   Generalizations about the grammaticalization of subordinators:
    a. Wherever there is appropriate historical evidence, subordinators are derived from lexical and other linguistic material serving purposes other than that of clause subordination.
    b. When a new subordinator arises, this entails desemanticization, that is, the marker gradually loses its earlier lexical or other function in favour of its new function of signaling clause subordination.
    c. In the transition from non-subordinator to subordinator there is a stage of ambiguity, in that the marker concerned can simultaneously be interpreted with reference to both its earlier and its new function.
    d. With its desemanticization, the subordinator loses morphosyntactic properties characteristic of its earlier grammatical status, being increasingly reduced to marking syntactic relations between clauses (decategorialization).
    e. In addition to external there also may be internal decategorialization: if the marker is morphologically complex it will lose this complexity and turn into a non-compositional, invariable form.
    f. The subordinator may be phonetically and/or prosodically reduced (erosion).

Subordinate clauses are usually divided into relative clauses, complement clauses and adverbial clauses. This division is prototypical rather than discrete in that the boundaries between the three are fluid in many languages and, as we will see below, the three cannot always be neatly separated in their grammaticalization behaviour. Our concern in this section will be with the first two; for space reasons we will not be able to also cover adverbial clauses, which exhibit a wide and a complex field with regard to grammaticalization (but see Hopper and Traugott (2003) and Heine and Kuteva (2007: ch. 5) for discussion of various types of adverbial clauses).

Examples provided below are mostly taken from the English-based creole Sranan. Sranan is a young language. It evolved in Suriname within the last four centuries, and there are historical records that allow one to reconstruct the major lines of its linguistic history from its origin onwards.

1.2.2 A Case Study

The following example from Sranan may illustrate the rise and further development of subordinators (Bruyn 1995a, b, 1996).

There were essentially no formally marked relative clauses in early Sranan, and zero marking of relative clauses continued throughout the nineteenth and twentieth centuries. But for most of the seventeenth century, the demonstrative *disi* 'this' (< English *this*) was functioning both as a nominal modifier and a pronoun. Probably around the end of the seventeenth century, *disi* developed from demonstrative to relativizer within the short period of half a century. In the course of the eighteenth century, *disi* underwent extension as an explicit relativizer. But there was a stage of ambiguity: while *disi* could be understood as a relative clause marker determining the preceding noun, an interpretation as a demonstrative in an independent clause could not be ruled out in most cases. Still, there are also eighteenth-century examples such as (4) where *disi* was already unambiguously a (restrictive) relativizer.

(4)   Sranan (Bruyn 1995a: 168)

Hoe fa   mi zel fom wan   zomma [diesi no   doe ogeri].
Q   manner 1SG FUT beat INDEF.SG person REL   NEG do   harm
'How would I beat someone who didn't do any harm.'

But *disi* underwent a further grammaticalization, namely from relative marker to adverbial clause subordinator (CONJ): in the second half of the eighteenth century, if not earlier, its use was extended to introduce temporal, causal and concessive clauses; see (5a), which illustrates its temporal, and (5b) its causal uses.

(5)   Sranan (Bruyn 1998: 29)

a. ary fadom   trange disi mi de na gron.
   rain fall.down   strong CONJ 1SG be at ground
   'Rain fell heavily when I was in the fields.' (Source from 1765)

b. di   ju brokko mi nefi, ju musse gi   mi wan so srefiwan.
   CONJ 2SG break 1SG knife 2SG must give 1SG a   so same.one
   'Since you've broken my knife, you must give me a similar one.'
   (Source from 1783)

In eighteenth-century sources, the relativizer had the form *disi*; in the course of the nineteenth century, the new relativizer *disi* underwent erosion, that is, it was shortened to *di*, leading to the separation of

Table 1.1 *The grammaticalization of the Sranan demonstrative* disi *'this' to a relative clause marker (based on Bruyn 1995a, b; 1996)*

Stage	Time	Function
0	17th century	Relative clauses are zero marked. *disi* is a demonstrative pronoun meaning 'this'.
1	From end of 17th century	*disi* specializes as a relativizer. There is frequently ambiguity between its demonstrative and relative uses in specific contexts.
2	Mid 18th century	*disi* is extended to also introduce temporal, causal, and concessive adverbial clauses.
3	19th century	*disi* is shortened to *di* as a relativizer, though not as a demonstrative modifier or pronoun.

demonstrative and relative marker. As example (5b) shows, however, instances of erosion of *disi* can be found already much earlier.

The whole process of the rise and development of new forms of clause subordination, however, did not mean that the original zero-marked structure was abandoned; rather, the latter survived to some extent and is still accessible today. The major stages in the development of Sranan *disi* are summarized in Table 1.1.

While not representative in every detail, Sranan *disi* exhibits salient features to be observed in the grammaticalization of subordinators, illustrating most of the generalizations presented in (3): prior to its grammaticalization it served functions other than that of a subordinator, namely that of a spatial deictic (3a); it lost this function in favour of that as a subordinator (desemanticization) (3b); there was a stage of ambiguity (3c); there appears to have been external decategorialization on the way from independent pronoun to relativizer (3d); and there was also erosion (3f).

But this example also illustrates two other points made above. As the example suggests, the function of Sranan *disi* as a relativizer preceded that of an adverbial clause subordinator in time. While the process involved was presumably more complex, it suggests that relative clauses and adverbial clauses are not entirely independent categories but can be part of one and the same pathway of grammaticalization. And it also suggests that the cline hypothesized by Hopper and Traugott (2003: 177–84), leading from parataxis via hypotaxis to subordination, must be taken with care. As was observed above, relative clauses are suggestive of subordination and adverbial clauses of hypotaxis, and if in fact grammaticalization in Sranan proceeded from relative to adverbial clause subordinator, as is suggested by the historical records, then this would be a change in the opposite direction.

1.2.3 Relative Clauses

Our concern is exclusively with restrictive relative clauses, and more narrowly with relative clause markers. Relative clauses in many languages need not be formally marked, at least not obligatorily or in all contexts, but most of them are, and we will look exclusively at the latter in this section.

There is a wide range of structures to be found across languages that speakers have recruited to design relative clause constructions. Presumably the most common way in which new relative clause markers arise is via the grammaticalization of demonstrative pronouns, where either a proximal or a distal demonstrative refers to a noun phrase in the matrix clause. This pathway has been discussed in a number of studies and languages (Heine and Kuteva 2002; 2007: 225–9). There are considerable differences from one language to another depending on the linguistic and sociocultural environment in which this grammaticalization takes place.

We saw an example of this pathway in §1.2.1; the history of English *that* and its predecessors illustrates another example (see e.g. O'Neil 1977; Hopper and Traugott 2003; van Gelderen 2004: 81ff.), and similar grammaticalizations have taken place repeatedly in the history of Chinese (Shi and Li 2002). The process typically involves what in Heine and Kuteva (2007: 224–6) is called integration, whereby two independent clauses are integrated, with one assuming the function of a dependent clause and the demonstrative referring anaphorically to the main clause.

Another pathway that has received extensive treatment concerns the grammaticalization from interrogative forms to relative clause markers (see e.g. Harris and Campbell 1995; Hopper and Traugott 2003: 201–2; Heine and Kuteva 2007: 229). In spite of all the work that has been done on this issue the exact conceptual and syntactic circumstances are not entirely clear. Whether the transition proceeds directly from question marker to clause subordinator or involves some intermediate communicative situation is unclear in most of the languages documented (see Harris and Campbell 1995: 284–5). While this process is widely attested in European and, more generally, in Indo-European languages, it is fairly rare in other regions and language families.

1.2.4 Complement Clauses

There is a wide range of grammaticalization processes leading to the rise of complement clauses. We are restricted here to two pathways which have a fairly wide cross-linguistic distribution. They represent two contrasting patterns of grammatical evolution. The first concerns what is referred to by Heine and Kuteva (2007: 217–24) as expansion, while the second involves the integration of two erstwhile independent clauses.

One common way in which complement clauses arise is via the extension from nominal to clausal structures. The process is described by Givón (2006: 217) as one where 'the complement-clause is treated analogically as a nominal object of the main clause'. The result is that morphological structures associated with noun phrases, such as adpositions, case inflections, gender and definiteness markers, are extended to also mark clausal structures. Thus, in the following example from the Khwe language of Namibia, the accusative case marker 'a is extended from a noun phrase (6a) to also mark complement clauses (6b). This pathway thus accounts for the fact that in a number of languages across the world, complement clauses exhibit features characteristic of nouns or noun phrases; for a five-stage scenario of the pathway, see Heine (2009).

(6)   Khwe (Central Khoisan, Khoisan; own data)
        a. *doá-*   m̀   *'à*   /x̠'ún-   á-   *hān.*
           kudu-   M.SG   ACC   kill-   JUNC-   PRF
           '(They) killed a kudu antelope.'
        b. *xàcí tcà-*   á-   *tè*   *'à*   *tí*   /x̠'ân   *qāámà-*   à-   *tè.*
           she be.sick-   JUNC-   PRS   ACC   I   very   regret-   JUNC-   PRS
           'I am very sorry that she is sick.'

But clearly, in languages worldwide, the most common pathways leading to the rise of complement clauses concern either demonstrative pronouns (see Hopper and Traugott 2003: 190–4 on English *that*-complementation) or verbs, more specifically speech act verbs meaning 'say' or similative verbs meaning 'be like', 'be equal' or 'resemble' (e.g. Hopper and Traugott 2003: 194–6; Heine and Kuteva 2007: 236–40). The construction leading to this grammaticalization involves a speech act or similative verb introducing a direct speech utterance, where the former loses its lexical function in favour of that of a complementizer and the latter gradually turns into a complement clause.

Cross-linguistic evidence suggests that this pathway can be sketched overall as in (7) (see e.g. Lord 1976; Heine, Claudi and Hünnemeyer 1991: 158; Ebert 1991: 87; Frajzyngier 1996; Klamer 2000; Crass 2002).

(7)   Common stages in the evolution from verb for 'say' to clause subordinator (Heine and Kuteva 2007: 236):
        a. Speech act verb 'say'
        b. 'Say' as a quotative marker
        c. Complementizer of object clauses headed by speech-act, perception (e.g. 'see', 'hear'), and cognition verbs (e.g. 'know', 'believe')
        d. Complementizer of subject clauses
        e. Subordinator of purpose clauses
        f. Subordinator of cause clauses

Not all stages are necessarily distinguished in a given case; there are many languages that have not proceeded beyond the quotative or the complementizer stage, and there may be language-specific variation in the sequencing of stages. But it would seem that the general directionality 'say' > quotative > complementizer > subordinator of adverbial clauses is observed in most languages that have made use of this pathway.

The following examples of the verb *taki* 'say' of the creole language Sranan (see §1.2.1) illustrate three stages of this evolution (Plag 1993,

1994, 1995). (8a) represents the quotative stage, dated roughly to the period between 1780 and 1850, while (8b) shows the use of *taki* as a subject complementizer and in (8c), *taki* has acquired the function of an adverbial clause subordinator. Up until the middle of the nineteenth century, *taki* was largely confined to introducing arguments, i.e. quotes and complement clauses, and it is only after 1850 that *taki* came to introduce adjuncts such as purpose clauses (see especially Plag 1995: 130, 134).

(8)   Sranan (Plag 1994: 41; 1995)

      a. Na Papa piki   hem, a **taki** 'Luku, sowan bigi gro mi habi.'
         the father answer him/her 3SG say look   such big field I   have[1]
         'The father answered her; he said "Look, I have so large a field."'
      b. **Taki** Kofi no   kiri Amba meki wi   breyti.
         that Kofi NEG kill Amba make we   happy
         'That Kofi didn't kill Amba made us happy.'
      c. Den de so don   **taki** yu   musu ...
         they be so dumb that you must)
         'They are so dumb that you have to ...'

1.2.5 Conclusions

Our concern in this section was with clause combining as it has been approached in studies of grammaticalization. As the observations made in this section suggest, the cline parataxis > hypotaxis > subordination proposed by Hopper and Traugott (2003: 278) as a major generalization on the syntax of clause combining must be taken with caution. Adverbial clause subordinators, being manifestations of hypotaxis, can be traced back to both relative clause markers (§1.2.2) and complementizers (§1.2.4), both being instances of the notion of subordination as proposed by these authors. This observation might be suggestive of some alternative generalization, but much more research is needed on the evolution of clause combining.

Such research would also need to look into the question of whether the unidirectionality principle of grammaticalization, developed on the basis of regularities in the change of functional categories (see e.g. Heine, Claudi and Hünnemeyer 1991; Bybee, Perkins and Pagliuca 1994; Lehmann [1982] 1995; Hopper and Traugott 2003), is restricted to the evolution of form–meaning units and the associated syntactic features, or whether this principle extends further to the constructions of which these units are a part (see §1.3.2 for a discussion).

Nevertheless, there are a few generalizations on the directionality in the marking of clause subordination, such as the ones listed in (3). For example, there is solid empirical evidence to suggest that demonstrative and

---

[1] Glosses are ours; there are no glosses provided by the author.

interrogative pronouns are pressed into service as markers of clause sub-ordination, or that morphological expressions may lose phonetic substance on the way to developing into subordinators, while there is so far no evidence for a change in the opposite direction of any of these changes.

1.3 Grammaticalization in Syntactic Theories

The previous section dealt with the prevalent approach to grammaticalization, which treats grammaticalization on its own terms. As mentioned in the introduction, the study of grammaticalization developed in the 1970s to 1990s as an alternative to contemporary models of grammar. In fact, as was demonstrated in the previous section, grammaticalization on its own can be taken as an explanation for linguistic phenomena, including those in the area of syntax, and in this case it is legitimate to speak of 'grammaticalization theory'. However, the reverse perspective is also possible, and has become increasingly common in the past decade. Grammaticalization is studied as but one phenomenon among many within the framework of a particular grammatical theory. In this case, two fundamentally different types of theory can be distinguished which lead to strikingly different results. The distinction between these types is not formal vs functional, but between models of grammar that centrally posit hierarchical (i.e. non-relational) constituent structures in the clause, and those that do not. Among the former, it is particularly generative grammar (minimalism) and Functional Discourse Grammar which have served as a theoretical framework for the study of grammaticalization.

1.3.1 Grammaticalization in Syntactic Theories with Hierarchical Clause Structure – Minimalism and Functional Discourse Grammar

If grammaticalization theory developed as an alternative to generative grammar as the dominant paradigm of grammar of the time, and also of today, the initial response from the generative side can best be characterized as disinterest. This reaction results naturally from the perspective of generative grammar, where the ultimate object of study is the (internal) language system of the individual and its acquisition. This basic tenet inevitably relegates diachronic aspects to the periphery of the study of language. Nevertheless, there are some striking and obvious overlaps between empirical observations in grammaticalization studies and structural descriptions in generative grammar which eventually led to a rise in interest in grammaticalization, enhanced by the rise of minimalism. As described by van Gelderen (2011), pioneering work in the early 1990s (e.g. Abraham 1991, 1993; Roberts 1993; van Gelderen 1993) was followed by a distinct surge in research activities in the 2000s.

Within the generative literature on grammaticalization, there is broad agreement about the basic mechanism of grammaticalization, and differences mainly amount to questions about how this mechanism and the presumptive motivations for it are formulated. Sentence structure is analysed as hierarchical tree structure of lexical and functional phrases. The higher nodes in the tree are occupied by functional phrases built around functional heads, while the lower nodes are occupied by lexical phrases built around lexical heads. Grammaticalization, then, is essentially 'climbing up' the tree of a category that was initially merged lower in the tree structure to a higher position. That is, a lexical category can become the realization of a functional (grammatical) category, or a functional category located lower in the tree can become the realization of a functional category located higher in the tree. Roberts and Roussou (2003: 2) thus speak of the 'creation of new functional material'.

In order to eventually 'climb', an item merged lower in the tree must have a feature that was checked at a position higher in the tree. That is, this item originally instantiated features at two or more positions in the tree structure, and underwent Move in order to check a feature at a higher position. If reanalysis (or grammaticalization) takes place, the same feature is merged directly in a higher position. This observation has been formulated as 'structural simplification' by Roberts and Roussou (2003), and as 'economy' by van Gelderen (2004). Van Gelderen (2004) distinguished two Economy Principles, namely (1) the Spec to Head Principle (Head Preference Principle) and (2) the Late Merge Principle. These are motivated by the theory-internal assumptions that (1) checking between two heads is more economical than checking between a specifier and a head, and (2) merging is more economical than moving, since merging is required anyway, but moving comes at additional cost. With respect to 'structural simplification', the structure resulting from grammaticalization is always simpler than the erstwhile structure, if the erstwhile structure implied feature syncretism (i.e. realization of two or more features in one item).

An example is the reanalysis of the numeral classifier *ge* as an indefinite determiner in colloquial Mandarin Chinese (Wu 2004: ch. 2). Example (9) represents the outcome of this change (we assume here that it is not necessary to demonstrate the more common use as a classifier).

(9)   Mandarin Chinese (Wu 2004: 44)
       Ta   he-le   ge san-ping   jiu.
       He   drink-ASP   ge three-CLF   wine
       'He drank three bottles of wine.'

Wu (2004: 44) represents the structure of the object phrase in this sentence as follows:

(10)

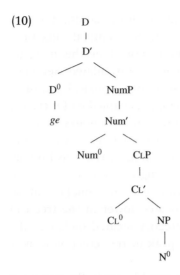

Originally, *ge* is merged as the head of a classifier phrase in CL°. Example
(10) shows that the realization of D in D° cannot be the result of Move
(anymore) since CL° is realized as *ping* 'bottle'. Therefore, *ge* is directly
merged in the DP. According to the analysis by Wu (2004), the structure
in (10) is the result of an intermediate stage at which *ge* was generated in
the CLP but moved to D° position via Num°.

While the descriptive facts so far are rather uncontroversial, the way
they are theoretically framed and motivated differs from researcher to
researcher. Roberts (Roberts and Rousseau 2003; Roberts 2007, and elsewhere) emphasizes that grammaticalization is parameter change, that is,
change in the features associated with a specific lexical or functional item
in the lexicon. Van Gelderen (2004) emphasizes that grammaticalization is
associated with language acquisition. Innate principles of economy cause
the language learner to reanalyse items in the lexicon. More recently, van
Gelderen (2009, 2011) has framed the fundamental idea of economy in
terms of 'feature economy': since it is more economical for an item to have
uninterpretable features, items develop towards having uninterpretable
features.

Hierarchical clause structures are not an exclusive domain of formal
grammars. Functional Discourse Grammar (FDG; formerly 'Functional
Grammar') distinguishes four levels of grammar, the phonological level,
the morphosyntactic level, the representational level and the interperso-
nal level, each of which is in turn organized into layers. Each layer maximally has the following structure:

(11) $\pi \ v_1$: ([head $(v1)_\Phi$]: [$\sigma(v1)_\Phi$])$_\Phi$,

whereby v_1 is the variable of the relevant layer, which is restricted by
a head and (optionally) further by a modifier σ. Head and modifier both
take the variable as their argument. Finally, π (also optional) is an operator

specifying the layer and $_\Phi$ a function relating the layer to other units (Hengeveld and Mackenzie 2008: 14). Crucial to grammaticalization is the Representational Level, which consists of the hierarchical arrangement and realization of semantic categories. This is a purely semantic level which corresponds to syntactic realizations via encoding rules. The layered structure of the Representational Level is given in (12) below in linear order (alternatively to a tree structure representation):

(12) $(p_1: [(ep_1: [(e_1: [(f_1: [(f_2)^n (x_1)_\Phi \ldots (x_1+n)_\Phi] (f_1)) \ldots (f_1+n)(e_1)_\Phi]) \ldots (e1+n)_{[\Phi]}] (ep_1)) \ldots (ep_1+n)_{[\Phi]} (p_1))$

The outermost layer is the proposition (p), which recursively contains episodes (ep), which in turn recursively contain States-of-Affairs (e). These contain Configurational Properties (f_1) that can further contain descriptions of Individuals (x_1) and Lexical Properties (f_2) (Hengeveld and Mackenzie 2008: 15, 181, 215). Also, as mentioned in (12), every layer can have one or more operators, that is, exponents of grammatical categories specifying the layer. In contradistinction to generative grammar, there is no hierarchical relationship between elements of the same layer.

Now, within this model, Hengeveld claimed as early as 1989 that 'diachronic developments in the field of operators tend to follow the direction [from lower layer to higher layer]'[2] (1989: 142). This is probably the first time that a mechanism of grammaticalization was formulated within a specific theory of syntax.

Since FDG is also mainly concerned with synchronic issues, research following up on this observation has remained sparse but includes Boland (2006) and Hengeveld (2011), both primarily concerned with change in the area of tense, aspect and modality (TAM). These are categories for which FDG has traditionally made fine distinctions (see Dik 1997). Different types of tense, aspect and modality are located at different layers of the clause. For example, phasal aspect is located at the layer of Configurational Properties $(f_1$; also labelled as 'Situational Concept' layer), event quantification and relative tense at the State-of-Affairs layer (e), and absolute tense at the Episode layer (ep). The predicted direction of change in the tense/aspect domain is then from phasal aspect to event quantification and relative tense to absolute tense. This is what has actually been observed historically in a number of languages. Hengeveld (2011: 591–2) provides the example of Spanish *haber* 'have' + past participle construction. This construction underwent a development in three stages that can be schematically represented as in Table 1.2.

Subtle distinctions within the domain of TAM have also found an echo in recent approaches to generative grammar, especially the Cartography of

<hr>

[2] According to the model Functional Grammar of that time, this was represented as '$\pi_1 > \pi_2 > \pi_3 > \pi_4$; whereby π_1= predicate operator; π_2=predication operator; π_3=proposition operator; π_4= illocution operator.

Table 1.2 *Grammaticalization of Spanish* haber + *past participle construction in FDG*

	Stage I	Stage II	Stage III
Category	Resultative	Perfect	Past
TA distinction	phasal aspect	relative tense	absolute tense
Layer	f_1	e	ep

Syntactic Structures (Cinque 1999, 2001), where different types of tense, aspect and modality are identified with different functional heads in a finely differentiated hierarchy of functional heads. The hierarchy is presented in (13).

(13) $MoodP_{speech\ act} > MoodP_{evaluative} > MoodP_{evidential} > ModP_{epistemic} > TP_{past} > TP_{future} > MoodP_{irrealis} > TP_{anterior} > ModP_{alethic} > AspP_{habitual} > AspP_{repetitive(I)} > AspP_{frequentative(I)} > ModP_{volition} > AspP_{celerative(I)} > AspP_{terminative} > AspP_{continuative} > AspP_{perfect} > AspP_{retrospective} > AspP_{proximative} > AspP_{durative} > AspP_{progressive} > AspP_{prospective} > AspP_{inceptive(I)} > ModP_{obligation} > ModP_{ability} > AspP_{frustrative/success} > ModP_{permission} > AspP_{conative} > AspP_{completive} > VoiceP > AspP_{repetitive(II)} > AspP_{frequentative(II)} > AspP_{celerative(II)} > AspP_{inceptive(II)} > AspP_{completive(II)} > V$ (see Cinque 2001: 47–8)

Roberts (2010) proposed to associate this hierarchy with grammaticalization. The fundamental idea of 'successive upward reanalysis along the functional hierarchy' (Roberts and Roussou 2003: 202) is the same as before, only that the functional hierarchy is now more fine-grained, leading to more detailed predictions about grammaticalization paths. Concretely, it is possible to predict that any realization of one of the categories lower on this hierarchy can change into a realization of one of the categories higher on the hierarchy.

This idea essentially fits in well with the ideas about hierarchical clause structure and grammaticalization developed in FDG. However, there are two major mismatches. First, while it is assumed in Cartography that every functional head stands in a strictly defined hierarchical relationship to every other head, FDG posits layers within which scope relationships between categories can be flexible. Secondly, the relative positions to which categories are assigned in each hierarchy do not coincide. Both problems are empirical in nature. On the one hand, the question is whether two categories must always stand in the same scope relationship or if they are able to reverse it. On the other hand, it is possible to test the hypotheses about hierarchies on individual languages.

The study presented in Narrog (2009, 2010) is an attempt to test the layering hypotheses on Japanese, a language with a rich inventory of TAM

Table 1.3 *The hierarchy of grammatical categories in Japanese dynamicized (Narrog 2012: 104)*

Non-modal categories	Modal categories
	Illocutionary modification
	Volitive moods (imperative, hortative)
	Epistemic modality 3 (speculative, epistemic mood)
Tense	Evidentiality 3 (reportive)
	Epistemic modality 2 (epistemic possibility)
	Deontic modality 2 (valuative obligation, recommendation)
(Internal) Negation	Evidentiality 2 (inferential evidentials)
	Epistemic modality 1 (epistemic necessity/ expectation)
Perfective/Imperfective aspect	Deontic modality 1 (necessity)
	Evidentiality 1 (predictive appearance)
Phasal aspect	Boulomaic modality
	Dynamic modality
Benefactives	
Voice	

plus evidentiality marking, which is – thanks to the strictly head-final and agglutinative nature of the language – realized relatively regularly in the verbal complex, in contrast to most European languages. With respect to scope flexibility it was found that categories with a similar scope can indeed scope over each other without a change in semantics (see Narrog 2009: §19.4). The findings were further given a historical dimension in Narrog (2012). This is represented in Table 1.3.

The table represents a hypothesis about the hierarchy of verbal categories in Japanese with particular emphasis on modality and evidentiality (non-modal/evidential categories were examined in less detail and are therefore represented separately on the left-hand side of the table). This hierarchy is based on extensive empirical evidence but is neither identical to the FDG hierarchy nor to the hierarchy in Cartography. This fact points to two possibilities: either extant hierarchies need to be further revised, taking into account more empirical evidence such as the one from Japanese, or there is language-specific variation in categories and their mutual scope. Table 1.3 also represents a hypothesis about diachronic change along this hierarchy, namely from categories located lower on the hierarchy, to categories located higher, as represented by the arrow. Additionally, it is hypothesized that there is an accompanying semantic directionality of change towards more speech-act related meanings, which can in turn be broken up into speaker-oriented, hearer-oriented and discourse-oriented meanings.[3] Narrog (2012) presents numerous examples from Japanese and other languages which corroborate this directionality of change.

---

[3] This differs somewhat from Roberts and Roussou (2003) and Roberts (2010), who emphasize semantic bleaching as the basic semantic mechanism accompanying grammaticalization.

1.3.2 Grammaticalization in Construction Grammar

As sketched above, the relationship between grammaticalization and generative grammar has been conflicted. Even in prominent work on grammaticalization within this framework, grammaticalization has been labelled as 'epiphenomenal' (Roberts and Roussou 2003: 2). However, van Gelderen's (2004) association of grammaticalization with the central process of language acquisition indicates that grammaticalization may in fact relate to core properties of language even within a generative framework. In the current alternative to generative grammar, Construction Grammar (CG), the status of grammaticalization has also been controversial, however, for entirely different reasons.

CG is a framework that basically analyses language as the inventory of symbolic combinations of form and meaning, i.e. 'constructions'. This inventory consists of symbolic units of all sizes, from clauses down to the equivalents of traditional morphemes. This has a number of consequences for CG's relationship to grammaticalization. First of all, while for grammaticalization, the distinction between lexical and grammatical, and less vs more grammatical, categories has been definitional, the denial of such a distinction is central to common versions of CG. Thus, Noël (2007: 185) comments that 'grammaticalization, as a change from lexical to grammatical, is not an issue in CG: construction grammatical units can by definition not become more grammatical'. Furthermore, while constituent structure and hierarchical clause structure are compatible with CG in principle, in practice hierarchies have been used only for describing relationships within the inventory of constructions, and not for describing clause structure. Also, the focus in CG has been on identifying and describing individual constructions, especially those apparently not well captured through traditional phrase structures, and not on systematically describing the clause structure (or more generally, the grammatical structure) of any language. Thus, the findings presented in the previous section are in practice irrelevant to current CG.

Nevertheless, attempts to reconcile CG and grammaticalization have recently increased. Such reconciliation is possible if the definition of grammaticalization is adjusted to accommodate constructions on the one hand (e.g. Bybee 2003; Himmelmann 2004), and if CG allows for a counterpart to the distinction between lexical and grammatical, or even less vs more grammatical, on the other hand. The latter is possible if a shift from lexical to grammatical to more grammatical is recast as a shift from more substantive to more schematic constructions (see Gisborne and Patten 2011: 100).

Research bringing together grammaticalization and CG can broadly be divided into two approaches. In one, the change in a construction is investigated from the perspective of grammaticalization. Examples are still sparse but include Traugott's (2008) study of the grammaticalization of 'NP of NP' patterns, Trousdale's (2008) study of the grammaticalization of *give*-gerund CPs and Patten's (2012) study of change in *it*-clefts. What these studies have in common is that they show how the expansion of contexts in the use of a more specific (or 'substantive') construction leads to the development of broader, more abstract constructional schemes. These, in turn, reflect back on the properties of the specific construction, in which individual elements may lose semantic substance. Trousdale (2012) suggests that overall, grammaticalization means an increase in generality, increase in productivity and decrease in compositionality of a construction.

In the other, more common, approach, the focus is on the individual lexical (or grammatical) item, and how it changes within, or together with, a construction. Examples include De Smet's (2010) study of the development of *for* as subject marker, Gisborne's (2011) study of the development of *will* as a future marker and van Bogaert's (2011) study of the grammaticalization of *I think* and similar complement-taking mental predicates. These studies all emphasize how CG improves the analysis of such diachronic developments. A particularly striking case is the recruitment of verbs for grammatical use in Mandarin Chinese in established constructions as described by Bisang (2004, 2010). Since Mandarin Chinese largely lacks morphology, grammaticality and grammatical functions are almost exclusively indicated through the relative position of one item in relation to others. Slots in established constructions appear to have both attractive power for new items and coercive power in imprinting grammatical functions on these new items.

In conclusion, despite some fundamental theoretical problems that cannot be considered as resolved, the intersection between CG and grammaticalization has opened up a rapidly expanding field of study, as did the intersection between generative grammar and grammaticalization.

References

Abraham, W. 1991. 'The grammaticalization of the German modal particles', in Traugott and Heine (eds.), pp. 331–80.

1993. 'Einleitung zum Thema dieses Bandes. Grammatikalisierung und Reanalyse: Einander ausschließende oder ergänzende Begriffe?', *Folia Linguistica Historica* 13(1–2): 7–26.

Bisang, W. 2004. 'Grammaticalization without coevolution of form and meaning: The case of tense-aspect-modality in East and mainland Southeast Asia', in Bisang, Himmelmann and Wiemer (eds.), pp. 109–38.

2010. 'Grammaticalization in Chinese: A construction-based account', in Traugott and Trousdale (eds.), pp. 245–77.

Bisang, W., Himmelmann, N. P. and Wiemer, B. (eds.) 2004. *What makes grammaticalization? A look from its fringes and its components.* Berlin: Mouton de Gruyter.

Boland, J. H. G. 2006. 'Aspect, tense, and modality: Theory, typology, acquisition', unpublished PhD thesis, University of Amsterdam.

Bruyn, A. 1995a. 'Relative clauses in early Sranan', in J. Arends (ed.), *The early stages of creolization.* Amsterdam: John Benjamins, pp. 149–202.

1995b. *Grammaticalization in creoles: The development of determiners and relative clauses in Sranan.* Amsterdam: Institute for Functional Research into Language and Language Use (IFOTT).

1996. 'On identifying instances of grammaticalization in creole languages', in Ph. Baker and A. Syea (eds.), *Changing meanings, changing functions: Papers relating to grammaticalization in contact languages.* London: University of Westminster Press, pp. 29–46.

1998. 'What can this be?', in M. S. Schmid, J. R. Austin and D. Stein (eds.), *Historical linguistics 1997: Selected papers from the 13th International conference on historical linguistics, Düsseldorf, 10–17 August 1997.* Amsterdam: John Benjamins, pp. 25–40.

Bybee, J. 2003. 'Mechanisms of change in grammaticization: The role of frequency', in Joseph and Janda (eds.), pp. 602–23.

Bybee, J. L., Haiman, J. and Noonan, M. (eds.), 2001. *Complex sentences in grammar and discourse: Studies presented to Sandra Thompson.* Amsterdam: John Benjamins.

Bybee, J. L., Perkins, R. D. and Pagliuca, W. 1994. *The evolution of grammar: Tense, aspect, and modality in the languages of the world.* University of Chicago Press.

Cinque, G. 1999. *Adverbs and functional heads.* Oxford University Press.

2001. 'A note on mood, modality, tense and aspect affixes in Turkish', in E. E. Taylan (ed.), *The verb in Turkish.* Amsterdam: John Benjamins, pp. 47–59.

Crass, J. 2002. 'Die Grammatikalisierung des Verbes "sagen" im Beria', unpublished MS, University of Mainz.

De Smet, H. 2010. 'Grammatical interference: Subject marker *for* and the phrasal verb particles *out* and *forth*', in Traugott and Trousdale (eds.), pp. 75–104.

Diessel, H. 2005. *The acquisition of complex sentences* (Cambridge Studies in Linguistics 105). Cambridge University Press.

Dik, S. 1997. *The theory of functional grammar,* part 1: *The structure of the clause,* 2nd rev. edn, ed. K. Hengeveld. Berlin: Mouton de Gruyter.

Ebert, K. 1991. 'Vom Verbum dicendi zur Konjunktion: Ein Kapitel universaler Grammatikentwicklung', in W. Bisang and P. Rinderknecht (eds.), *Von Europa bis Ozeanien – von der Antonymie zum Relativsatz: Gedenkschrift für Meinrad Scheller.* Zurich: Arbeiten des Seminars für Allgemeine Sprachwissenschaft der Universität Zürich, pp. 77–95.

Frajzyngier, Z. 1996. *Grammaticalization of the complex sentence: A case study in Chadic* (Studies in Language Companion Series 32). Amsterdam: John Benjamins.

Gisborne, N. 2011. 'Constructions, word grammar, and grammaticalization', *Cognitive Linguistics* 22(1): 155–82.

Gisborne, N. and Patten, A. 2011. 'Construction grammar and grammaticalization', in Narrog and Heine (eds.), pp. 92–104.

Givón, T. 1971. 'Historical syntax and synchronic morphology: An archaeologist's field trip', *Chicago Linguistic Society* 7: 394–415.

   1975. 'Topic, pronoun and grammatical agreement', in Ch. N. Li (ed.), *Word order and word order change*. Austin: University of Texas Press, pp. 149–88.

   1991. 'The evolution of dependent clause morpho-syntax in Biblical Hebrew', in Traugott and Heine (eds.), pp. 257–310.

   2006. 'Multiple routes to clause union: The diachrony of syntactic complexity', unpublished MS, University of Oregon.

Harris, A. C. and Campbell, L. 1995. *Historical syntax in cross-linguistic perspective*. Cambridge University Press.

Heine, B. 1997. *Cognitive foundations of grammar*. Oxford University Press.

   2009. 'Complexity via expansion', in T. Givón and M. Shibatani (eds.), *Syntactic complexity: Diachrony, acquisition, neuro-cognition, evolution*. Amsterdam: John Benjamins, pp. 23–51.

Heine, B., Claudi, U. and Hünnemeyer, F. 1991. *Grammaticalization: A conceptual framework*. University of Chicago Press.

Heine, B. and Kuteva, T. 2002. *World lexicon of grammaticalization*. Cambridge University Press.

   2007. *The genesis of grammar: A reconstruction*. Oxford University Press.

Hengeveld, K. 1989. 'Layers and operators in Functional Grammar', *Journal of Linguistics* 25: 127–57.

   2011. 'The grammaticalization of tense and aspect', in Narrog and Heine (eds.), pp. 580–94.

Hengeveld, K. and Lachlan Mackenzie, J. 2008. *Functional discourse grammar: A typologically-based theory of language structure*. Oxford University Press.

Himmelmann, N. P. 2004. 'Lexicalization and grammaticalization: Opposite or orthogonal?', in Bisang, Himmelmann and Wiemer (eds.), pp. 21–42.

Hopper, P. J. 1982. *Tense-aspect: Between semantics and pragmatics*. Amsterdam: John Benjamins.

   1987. 'Emergent grammar', *Berkeley Linguistics Society* 13: 139–57.

Hopper, P. J. and Traugott, E. C. 2003. *Grammaticalization*. Cambridge University Press.

Joseph, B. D. and Janda, R. D. (eds.) 2003. *The handbook of historical linguistics*. Malden, MA: Blackwell.

Klamer, M. 2000. 'How report verbs become quote markers and complementisers', *Lingua* 110: 69–98.

Kuryłowicz, J. [1965] 1976. 'The evolution of grammatical categories'. Reprinted in J. Kuryłowicz, *Esquisses linguistiques*, vol. 2, Munich: Fink, pp. 38–54.

Lehmann, Ch. [1982] 1995. *Thoughts on grammaticalization*. Munich: Lincom Europa.

Lord, C. D. 1976. 'Evidence for syntactic reanalysis: From verb to complementizer in Kwa', in S. B. Steever, C. A. Walker and S. S. Mufwene (eds.), *Papers from the parasession on diachronic syntax*. Chicago Linguistic Society, pp. 179–91.

Meillet, A. 1912. 'L'évolution des formes grammaticales', *Scientia (Rivista di Scienza)* 12: 384–400.

Narrog, H. 2009. *Modality in Japanese: The layered structure of clause and hierarchies of functional categories*. Amsterdam: John Benjamins.

    2010. 'The order of meaningful elements in the Japanese verbal complex', *Morphology* 20(1): 205–37.

    2012. *Modality, subjectivity, and semantic change: A cross-linguistic perspective*. Oxford University Press.

Narrog, H. and Heine, B. (eds.) 2011. *The Oxford handbook of grammaticalization*. Oxford University Press.

Noël, D. 2007. 'Diachronic construction grammar and grammaticalization theory', *Functions of Language* 14(2):177–202.

O'Neil, W. 1977. 'Clause adjunction in Old English', *General Linguistics* 17: 199–211.

Patten, A. 2012. *The English it-cleft: A constructional account and a diachronic investigation*. Berlin: Mouton de Gruyter.

Plag, I. 1993. *Sentential complementation in Sranan: On the formation of an English-based creole language*. Tübingen: Niemeyer.

    1994. 'On the diachrony of creole complementizers: The development of Sranan *taki* and *dati*', *Amsterdam Creole Studies* 11: 40–65.

    1995. 'The emergence of *taki* as a complementizer in Sranan: On substrate influence, universals, and gradual creolization', in J. Arends (ed.), *The early stages of creolization*. Amsterdam: John Benjamins, pp. 113–48.

Roberts, I. 1993. 'A formal account of grammaticalization in the history of Romance futures', *Folia Linguistica Historica* 13: 219–58.

    2007. *Diachronic syntax*. Oxford University Press.

    2010. 'Grammaticalization, the clausal hierarchy and semantic bleaching', in Traugott and Trousdale (eds.), pp. 45–73.

Roberts, I. and Roussou, A. 2003. *Syntactic change: A minimalist approach to grammaticalization*. Cambridge University Press.

Shi, Y. and Li, Ch. N. 2002. 'The establishment of the classifier system and the grammaticalization of the morphosyntactic particle *de* in Chinese', *Language Sciences* 24: 1–15.

Traugott, E. C. 1988. 'Pragmatic strengthening and grammaticalization', *Berkeley Linguistics Society* 14: 406–16.

2003. 'Constructions in grammaticalization', in Joseph and Janda (eds.), pp. 624–47.

2008. 'The grammaticalization of NP of NP patterns', in A. Bergs and G. Diewald (eds.), *Constructions and language change*. Berlin: Mouton de Gruyter, pp. 23–46.

Traugott, E. C. and Heine, B. (eds.) 1991. *Approaches to grammaticalization*, vol. 2. Amsterdam: John Benjamins.

Traugott, E. C. and Trousdale, G. (eds.) 2010. *Gradience, gradualness and grammaticalization*. Amsterdam: John Benjamins.

Trousdale, G. 2008. 'Constructions in grammaticalization and lexicalization: Evidence from the history of a composite predicate construction in English', in G. Trousdale and N. Gisborne (eds.), *Constructional approaches to English Grammar*. Berlin: Mouton de Gruyter, pp. 33–67.

2012. 'Grammaticalization, constructions and the grammaticalization of constructions', in K. Davidse *et al.* (eds.), *Grammaticalization and language change: New reflections*. Amsterdam: John Benjamins, pp. 167–98.

van Bogaert, J. 2011. '*I think* and other complement-taking mental predicates: A case of and for constructional grammaticalization', *Linguistics* 49(2): 295–332.

van Gelderen, E. 1993. *The rise of functional categories*. Amsterdam: John Benjamins.

2004. *Grammaticalization as economy*. Amsterdam: John Benjamins.

2009. 'Feature Economy in the linguistic cycle', in P. Crisma and G. Longobardi (eds.), *Historical syntax and linguistic theory*. Oxford University Press, pp. 93–109.

2011. 'Grammaticalization and generative grammar: A difficult liaison', in Narrog and Heine (eds.), pp. 43–55.

Wu, Zoe. 2004. *Grammaticalization and language change in Chinese*. London: Routledge Curzon.

2

Degrammaticalization

David Willis

2.1 Introduction

While grammaticalization represents an extremely common and productive pathway of change, a significant and growing number of examples of historical changes appear to proceed in precisely the opposite direction; that is, formerly functional items unexpectedly acquire lexical status and bound items unexpectedly gain greater freedom. The existence of such changes, termed degrammaticalizations, challenges one of the central claims of much work on grammaticalization, namely that it is fundamentally unidirectional. Furthermore, if degrammaticalization changes exist and turn out to be explicable in terms of particular combinations of familiar processes, this raises questions about the status of grammaticalization. Proponents of grammaticalization have claimed that it is an independent and unitary process of change (Lehmann [1982] 1995: 124) or that it represents 'a bundle of interrelated changes that depend on one another, and operate according to specific principles of historical change' (Hilpert 2008: 23). If degrammaticalization exists, and turns out to result from a combination of well-understood processes such as reanalysis, analogical extension, metaphor and conventionalization of implicature, this invites a similar interpretation of grammaticalization as an all-encompassing term covering a diversity of scenarios involving these same processes (see Campbell 2001). To quote Janda (2001: 293), if degrammaticalization changes exist, this lends support to

> the view that the set of disparate phenomena known by that name [grammaticalization – DW] have a predominant directionality but are countered by a small number of opposite-directional changes which arise from the non-unity and discontinuity inherent in grammaticalization and are relatively infrequent only because they depend for their origin on various accidents of euphemism, homophony, hypercorrection, metonymy, and the like.

Proponents of unidirectionality have tended to dismiss individual instances proposed as examples of degrammaticalization. Lehmann ([1982] 1995: 19), who first coined the term 'degrammaticalisation', did so only to claim that 'no cogent examples of degrammaticalisation have been found'; see also the dismissive comments by Heine (2003: 174f.). Nevertheless, as we shall see, a stubborn core of examples remains, leaving us with the task of identifying a set of instances of degrammaticalization, comparing the processes involved with those typical of grammaticalization, and generalizing across these cases to establish commonalities, thereby building an understanding of why counterdirectional changes occur.

Standard definitions of grammaticalization define it as a historical change which involves movement to the right (downgrading) on hierarchies of functional, formal or semantic integration into the grammar:

(1)   functional (syntactic) hierarchy of grammaticalization
       lexical category (noun, verb, etc.) > functional/grammatical (determiner, tense, aspect, etc.)
(2)   formal (morphophonological) hierarchy of grammaticalization
       free morpheme > clitic > affix
(3)   semantic hierarchy of grammaticalization
       concrete (lexical) meaning > abstract (grammatical) meaning

Conversely, degrammaticalization can be defined as a historical development where an item moves to the left on one or more of these hierarchies (upgrading). Norde (2009: 120; 2010: 126) defines it as 'a composite change whereby a gram in a specific context gains in autonomy or substance on more than one linguistic level (semantics, morphology, syntax, or phonology)'.

This of course does not mean that a given instance of change should have reversed itself to take the language back to its previous historical state (token reversal). Rather we are dealing with general patterns of change that are schematically the inverse of grammaticalization (type reversal) (Norde 2009: 58–61).

2.2 Defining Instances of Degrammaticalization

Before looking at the properties of degrammaticalization changes and attempting to account for them, we need an agreed approach to what falls within the definition of degrammaticalization and what lies outside its scope. Early approaches to degrammaticalization tended to take a Saussurean 'synchronic-slice' approach to determine whether a given item instantiated degrammaticalization; that is, a given item was said to exemplify degrammaticalization if at one point in time it was used in a grammatical function, while at a later point in time an item with similar form was used in a lexical function. This 'diachronic-correspondence' approach fails to consider the process by which the development occurred, and consequently fails to identify a coherent class of changes. More recent approaches have emphasized the diachronic continuity of genuine instances of degrammaticalization, which amounts to 'a construction-internal change' (Norde 2010: 126), and where 'some (or all) of the processes that contribute to grammaticalization must be at work, but must lead to the opposite result from that expected in grammaticalization' (Willis 2007: 273) (see also Haspelmath 2004: 28).

The term 'degrammaticalization' has been used to refer to a variety of diachronic developments in the literature, not all of which belong together. To be of interest for the study of the mechanisms of language change, examples of degrammaticalization need to show continuity between the earlier and later stage, with appropriate intermediate stages where necessary. This strict definition of degrammaticalization has been termed 'antigrammaticalisation' (Haspelmath 1998: 27–9) to distinguish it from looser definitions, although the more firmly established term 'degrammaticalization' will be maintained here. This means we focus on the process of change rather than simply a comparison of two synchronic stages. We can reasonably search for commonalities across a range of examples collected in this way. On this definition, degrammaticalization must not be confused with some other scenarios which yield outputs which appear to be less 'grammatical' historically than their inputs. Notable among things which are not degrammaticalization are zero derivation, metalinguistic upgrading and retraction.

Zero derivation (conversion) is a morphological process where, in some languages, particularly analytical ones, an item may change category (or other properties) without an overt change in form (perhaps reflecting addition of a zero morpheme); where a language permits zero derivation, this process is generally non-directional, and in some cases the input will be a grammatical category and the output a lexical one. Thus, English permits zero derivation of verbs from nouns (consider the verbs *dog*, *cloud*, *water*) and adjectives (consider the verbs *cool*, *blind* and *slow*). Where grammatical categories are the input to this process, the result is a counterdirectional category shift from grammatical to lexical item, as with the English verbs *down* (*down a beer*), *out* (*out a celebrity*), *but* (*don't you but me!*). However, derivation creates a new lexical item, rather than shifting an existing one, and, for this reason, these can be excluded from the definition of degrammaticalization. Instances where inflectional morphology is added to a functional item have also been proposed as cases of degrammaticalization (e.g. the German verb *duzen* 'address using the informal pronoun *du*', formed from pronoun *du* 'you' + epenthetic consonant *-z-* /ts/ plus infinitive ending *-en*). These can be excluded for the same reason.

Similarly, metalinguistic upgrading of bound morphemes (*isms and olo-gies*, *teens*, German *zig* 'umpteen, many'), often a conscious and creative act, is excluded because there is no continuity between the new and old items and there is no intermediate stage. Conversion and metalinguistic upgrading may be treated as sub-types of lexicalization, the creation of new lexical items from whatever source, alongside other derivational morphological processes, including the productive application of existing affixation and compounding, and the creation of new lexical items via loss of boundaries (English *today* < *to day*).

Retraction presents a rather different problem that can be difficult to identify without detailed examination of the historical record. In retraction, an item grammaticalizes by splitting into two items, one the original lexical item and the second, a new functional item ('layering'). The functional item is then lost, leaving only the original lexical item. No individual item in the scenario for retraction develops a less functional, degrammaticalized use, hence there is no actual degrammaticalization. A straightforward example of retraction is the development of the indefinite pronoun *man* 'one, someone' in Middle English. This represents a grammaticalization of Old English *man* 'man, person' (noun > pronoun). In Middle English, both pronoun and noun co-exist, with the pronoun disappearing in the fourteenth or fifteenth century (Rissanen 1997: 520). While on superficial inspection this may seem to exemplify the counter-directional shift pronoun > noun, in practice all that has occurred is the loss of a pronoun. The present-day English noun *man* descends via continuous attestation from the equivalent Old English noun, and has not developed out of the pronoun. The only thing to explain in such cases is therefore the loss of an item, a very common occurrence unrelated to degrammaticalization.

2.3 Degrammaticalization as the Inverse of Grammaticalization

This leaves us with a core of cases which, in some sense or other, reverse grammaticalization, taking it in an unexpected direction. While such cases were once thought to be idiosyncratic exceptions, recent research has attempted, as in other areas of historical linguistics, to generalize across them in the search for commonalities and, hence, an understanding of the processes underlying them. A focus on a narrow and consistent definition helps this search. These changes relate to a mixture of the hierarchies noted above in (1)–(3), mirroring the behaviour of individual instances of grammaticalization, which do not necessarily participate in all of these hierarchies either.

Norde (2009: 133) distinguishes three types of degrammaticalization, namely degrammation, deinflectionalization and debonding, which we now consider in turn.

Degrammation, a term adopted from Andersen (2006), equivalent to 'syntactic lexicalization' (Willis 2007), involves a direct shift from grammatical to lexical content. It is defined as 'a composite change whereby a function word in a specific linguistic context is reanalysed as a member of a major word class, acquiring the morphosyntactic properties which are typical of that word class, and gaining in semantic substance' (Norde 2009: 134). As an example, consider the development of the Middle Welsh preposition *yn ol* 'after', which has split into two items, one developing along a normal grammaticalization path to produce Present-day Welsh *yn ôl* 'according to', and another undergoing degrammation to a lexical verb *nôl* meaning 'fetch'. In the shift from preposition to verb, the item gains a full paradigm of tense, person and number endings in some dialects (in other dialects it remains defective). Degrammations take place within an ambiguous 'bridging context' that allows for reanalysis, this one being facilitated by contexts such as that exemplified in (4). Here, pragmatically, the implicature 'go after something' > 'go after something and bring it back (i.e. fetch)' is available, and, syntactically, two structures could be posited, one with a prepositional phrase, the other with a purpose clause. The reanalysis illustrated in (5) takes us from the former to the latter, involving a counterdirectional category shift, P > V, and increase in structure, PP > IP[VP].

(4)   Middle Welsh (Willis 2007: 294)

Dos   yn ol y   marchawc a   aeth   odyma   y'r
go.IMP after the knight   REL went.3SG from.here to-the
weirglawd...
meadow

'Go after the knight who went away from here to the meadow ...'

(5)   dos [PP [P   yn ol] y   marchawc ...]
go.IMP   after the knight
⇒   dos   [IP y [VP [V nol]   y   marchawc ...]]
go.IMP   to   fetch.INF the knight

Other examples of degrammation are Bulgarian *nešto* 'something' > 'thing' (pronoun > noun) (Willis 2007); Old Irish *ní* 'something' > Scottish Gaelic *nì* 'thing' and Old Irish *nech* 'someone' > Scottish Gaelic *neach* 'person' (pronoun > noun) (Willis 2016); Pennsylvanian German *wotte* 'will' > 'want' (auxiliary > lexical verb) (Burridge 1998); Chinese *děi* 'must' > 'need' (auxiliary > lexical verb) (Ziegeler 2004); Danish *turde* 'dare' auxiliary > lexical verb (Andersen 2008:22); and Welsh *yntau* 'he, him' > 'or else; then' (pronoun > adverb). Degrammation seems to occur via syntactic reanalysis based on semantic indeterminacy (see §2.5 and §2.6 below).

The second type of degrammaticalization is deinflectionalization, defined as 'a composite change whereby an inflectional affix in a specific linguistic context gains a new function, while shifting to a less bound morpheme type' (Norde 2009: 152). In these cases, an item leaves an inflectional paradigm, typically undergoing semantic enrichment to take on a derivational function. This crucially involves both semantic and formal changes, that is, upgrading on both hierarchies (2) and (3) above. In Swedish, the suffix *-er*, originally the nominative masculine singular inflection for adjectives, has developed into a derivational suffix marking nominalizations denoting humans, for instance, *en slarver* 'a messy person' (< *slarv* 'messy') (Norde 2009: 179–81). Another example is the development of the Swedish nominative–accusative plural nominal suffix *-on* to become a suffix denoting berry names (inflection > derivation) (Norde 2009: 181–3). There are few examples of deinflectionalization, and it may be that it should be merged with the next category, debonding, both being (largely) forms of secondary degrammaticalization based on obsolescence and phonological upgrading. The development of English and Mainland Scandinavian possessive *-s* has been treated as an instance of deinflectionalization, and will be discussed in more detail later in this section.

The third type of degrammaticalization in Norde's typology is debonding (cf. 'bond weakening' or 'emancipation', which it resembles; Andersen 2008: 27), a shift in status from bound to free morpheme, hence a counterdirectional shift on the hierarchy in (2). An example is the emergence of the first-person plural pronoun *muid(e)* in Irish, which upgrades from person–number suffix to independent word, with similar but distinct and independent developments in different dialects (Doyle 2002). Irish had full verbal paradigms with contrasting forms for all person–number combinations. These agreeing forms were lost and replaced by an analytic system based on the third-person singular. Where agreement remained rich and distinctive, pronominal subjects were obligatorily null, hence *molfair* 'you will praise (SG)'; but, once agreement was lost, the pronoun became obligatory, hence *molfair* was replaced by *molfaidh tú*, with generalization of the third-person form *molfaidh* followed by the subject pronoun *tú*. The first-person plural future ending survived relatively well, and, in some varieties, was treated as though it was already of the analytic type, hence *molfamaid* [molhəmidʲ] 'we will praise' was reanalysed as though it consisted of the third-person *molfaidh* [molhə] plus a new element *muid* [midʲ]. Under this reanalysis, *muid* had to be a pronoun, and was thus used as such, spreading to other tenses and developing a strong (emphatic) form *muide* [midʲə]. Other examples of debonding include the English and Mainland Scandinavian infinitive markers, which are no longer necessarily proclitic to the verb (Fitzmaurice 2000); the Estonian question particle *es* and emphatic particle *ep* (bound > free) (Campbell 1991); and the Saami abessive case suffix *-taga* > clitic *=taga* > free postposition *taga* 'without' (Kiparsky 2012).

In debonding, the semantics of the element remains essentially unchanged: *muid* denotes first-person plural both before and after the shift. However, its morphophonological status changes. In some cases, this seems to be due to obsolescence of the paradigm of which the item once formed a part. In other cases, the driving force seems to be pragmatic: the item is generalized to convey increasingly intertextual meaning, and, in doing so, gains in scope and hence becomes morpho-phonologically more free. An example of this second possibility is the Japanese connective particle -ga 'although', originally a clause-final clitic, which developed into a freestanding clause-initial connective 'but' (Matsumoto 1988).

Perhaps the best-known example of degrammaticalization is the change in status of the former genitive case suffix -s in English and in most varieties of Mainland Scandinavian to become a phrasal affix (Norde 2001; Allen 2003). In earlier forms of these languages, -s was an obligatory inflection on the head noun, with other elements of the noun phrase also showing genitive inflection, and could only attach to nouns of the relevant declensional classes (most masculine and neuter nouns). Thus we can contrast the early Middle English example in (6), where genitive is marked both on the definite article and the possessor noun, with an equivalent from Present-day English in (7) (the 'group genitive').

(6)   þurh   þæs   arcebiscopes   gearnunge of Cantwerbyrig
       through the.GSG archbishop.GSG desire   of Canterbury
       'through the desire of the archbishop of Canterbury' (*Peterborough Chronicle* 1114.34; Allen 2003: 6)

(7)   the king of England's daughter

As the nominal case system in these languages became obsolescent ('deflexion', obsolescence of inflection), it came to attach to the end of all possessor phrases, leaving the head noun of the possessor phrase, *king* in (7), unmarked. It thus ceased to be an inflection and unexpectedly gained in scope, attaching to a phrase rather than to the head noun alone. Note also that this development follows a very similar course independently in English and in Mainland Scandinavian, suggesting that it is in some way a 'natural' response to the breakdown of the very similar inherited nominal inflectional systems. Germanic languages which have not lost their case system (German, Icelandic) have not undergone this change, suggesting that it is a reaction to obsolescence. Norde treats these developments as examples of deinflectionalization, seeing the shift from genitive to possessive as a semantic shift, since the latter is obligatorily definite. However, the earlier genitive was already effectively restricted to possessive function, in which case the only change is one of status from suffix to phrasal affix, which is debonding.

Alongside this three-way typology, we can also make a distinction between primary and secondary degrammaticalization to parallel the one made by some historical linguists between primary and second-ary grammaticalization (Givón 1995). Primary grammaticalization involves shifts from lexical to grammatical status and secondary

Table 2.1 *Lehmann's parameters of grammaticalization*

	Weight	Cohesion	Variability
Paradigmatic	integrity	paradigmaticity	paradigmatic variability
Syntagmatic	structural scope	bondedness	syntagmatic variability

grammaticalization (also termed regrammaticalization) involves shifts of already functional items to become more functional. Making this same distinction in reverse (Norde 2009: 130), we conclude that degrammation is primary degrammaticalization, taking a functional category and yielding a lexical one; while deinflectionalization and debonding take functional categories and yield other functional categories, but ones that are less integrated into the grammar in the sense of the hierarchies in (2) and (3). They are thus instances of secondary degrammaticalization.

2.4 Parameters of Degrammaticalization

Lehmann ([1982] 1995) suggests that grammaticalization changes are characterized by a decrease in the autonomy of the element undergoing change. This loss of autonomy is reflected in loss of weight and variability and an increase in cohesion, each reflected in two dimensions, paradigmatic and syntagmatic. It is natural to ask whether degrammaticalization changes involve a parallel increase in autonomy (for more detailed discussion, see Norde 2009: 124–32).

The overall schema of parameters is summarized in Table 2.1. Degrammaticalization involves the reverse developments: an increase in the autonomy of the sign, and thus a corresponding gain in weight and variability and a decrease in cohesion. Not all grammaticalizations involve all parameters, and the same holds of degrammaticalization.

The integrity parameter concerns loss of substance or properties, whether semantic, phonological or morphosyntactic. Degrammations involve a gain in lexical semantic content and an adoption of the morphosyntactic properties of the new class. Hence, Welsh *nôl* gains the meaning 'fetch' and adopts the morphology and syntax of a verb when it undergoes the shift from preposition to verb. Deinflectionalization also involves a semantic shift: Swedish *-er* gains the meaning 'person associated with x'. Debonding sometimes involves the development of a less abstract meaning, but the main gain in integrity is phonological, as some items, for instance Irish *muid(e)*, gain the ability to bear stress.

Paradigmaticity is the extent to which the item is integrated into a paradigm, increasing integration being characteristic of grammaticalization. Paradigmaticity is greater if an item belongs to a word class with fewer members (minor word class) or if it expresses a feature of a paradigm. Degrammations involve a shift from a minor to a major word class (preposition to verb, auxiliary to lexical verb, etc.), hence always involve a decrease in paradigmaticity. Deinflectionalization often removes an item from an inflectional paradigm: Swedish -er ceases to expression inflectional features such as case and number and expresses a derivational category instead. Those cases of debonding that involve obsolescence of paradigms inevitably also take an item out of a paradigm; for instance, Irish -muid ceases to be a person–number inflection within the future-tense paradigm of Irish. Other cases of debonding, however, do not involve this parameter.

Paradigmatic variability reflects whether an element is obligatory in relevant semantic contexts: highly grammaticalized categories (e.g. tense inflections) are obligatory, while ungrammaticalized ones (e.g. time adverbs) are not. Lexical items are never obligatory, so degrammation always involves loss of paradigmatic variability. Debonding mostly does not change the status of an item with respect to this parameter.

Structural scope is a difficult parameter. In many cases of grammaticalization, scope decreases. For instance, a preposition has scope over its noun phrase complement. If it develops into an affix, it will have scope only over the head noun. However, other cases that are often included under the umbrella of grammaticalization, such as the development of discourse adverbs (English in fact, hopefully, probably) from manner and other adverbs, involve expansion of scope (Tabor and Traugott 1998). Some cases of degrammaticalization clearly involve scope expansion, notably those involving debonding changes from affix to phrasal affix and beyond (English and Mainland Scandinavian possessive -s, English ish), while others show no clear interaction with scope.

Bondedness straightforwardly decreases in debonding changes, for which it is definitional, with morphophonological boundaries strengthening as affixes become clitics or clitics become free words. In degrammation, bondedness is not relevant, as we are already dealing with free words.

Finally, the parameter of syntagmatic variability refers to the decrease in syntactic freedom, particularly fixing of word order, associated with grammaticalization. Increased syntactic freedom is characteristic of degrammation; for instance, lexical verbs take a greater range of complements than auxiliaries.

Degrammaticalization changes show an overall increase in autonomy in a way broadly comparable and inverse to the decrease in autonomy found in instances of grammaticalization. While not every instance or type of degrammaticalization manifests an increase in autonomy on every parameter, such variability is present in grammaticalizations, which also do not form a fully unitary class.

2.5 Regularities, Pathways and Processes of Degrammaticalization

We have seen that examples of degrammaticalization are not simply idiosyncratic curiosities: they share commonalities among themselves and can be classified into a small number of general types. As elsewhere in linguistics, we need to seek out generalizations in order to understand the underlying processes involved. Degrammaticalization is clearly not a theoretical primitive or mechanism of change in its own right, but instead derives from other well-established processes. We can now turn to consider what processes contribute to the various types of degrammaticalization with a view to understanding why change is sometimes, but by no means always, counterdirectional.

Degrammation changes are the result of syntactic reanalysis based on semantic indeterminacy. It is generally possible to formulate them in terms of conventional reanalysis schemata (see Chapter 4, this volume), as we saw in (5) above. In all cases, the unusual thing about the reanalysis is that it creates more structure. Consider the two types of change that have the best claim to be 'degrammaticalization pathways', patterns found repeatedly in unrelated language histories, namely auxiliary > lexical verb ('deauxiliation') and (indefinite) pronoun > (generic) noun ('depronominalization'). Very schematically, the reanalyses involved in these changes are as follows (subscripts identify individual items across changes in status):

(8) $[_{IP}$ auxiliary$_1$ $[_{VP}$ verb$_2]] =>$ $[_{IP}$ $[_{VP}$ verb$_1$ $[_{CP}$ ... $[_{VP}$ verb$_2]]]]$
(9) $[_{DP}$ pronoun$_1] =>$ $[_{DP}$ ø $[_{NP}$ noun$_1]]$

Deauxiliation in (8) involves reanalysis of a monoclausal structure as biclausal, creating 'space' for other elements (e.g. infinitive markers, a subject for the embedded verb, etc.). The pronoun-to-noun shift involves positing a fully articulated noun phrase, an NP inside a DP in (9), in place of a reduced noun phrase, a DP lacking a complement. In both cases, there is a high degree of semantic and pragmatic indeterminacy, with bidirectional pragmatic inferencing in some cases. Once an item has undergone category shift as the result of reanalysis, it gradually acquires the morphosyntactic properties of its new category: the pronoun that has become a noun in (9) develops plural morphology, may be marked with a definite article and so on.

This all runs against the general pattern of reanalyses, which tend to reduce structure. In degrammation, acquirers posit the absence of something from their experience as accidental, when it is in fact systematic, and create new structure on this basis. Usually in reanalysis, acquirers fail to posit structure which was historically present, as is the case in the more expected development of auxiliaries from lexical verbs ('auxiliation', Kuteva 2001).

This phenomenon has analogues elsewhere in language change: dissimilation, which runs counter to the general trend towards assimilation in sound change, may be attributed to acquirers positing a 'phantom' assimilation process that never happened and reversing it ('hyper-correction', Ohala 1993). In lexical semantic change, some instances of meaning extension (those cases where this is not due to metaphor or metonymy) may be due to acquirers attributing the absence of particular kinds of referent in their experience to chance, cf. the development of English *dog* from 'a breed of large canine' to 'any canine' or of Latin *passer* 'sparrow' to Spanish *pájaro* 'bird'.

Deinflectionalization and debonding, as secondary degrammaticalization, are rather different, and a number of factors may play a role in facilitating them. Obsolescence acts as a catalyst in some cases. Where a particular morphosyntactic subsystem (e.g. case, person–number inflection, etc.) is being lost, surviving instances of that subsystem are susceptible to reanalysis as members of some other category. Thus, as case morphology was being lost on English and Mainland Scandinavian nouns, identification of *-s* as a case inflection became difficult, since the languages no longer offered robust models in the form of other case inflections. The same is true with Irish *muid*, which emerged as Irish was losing person–number inflection on verbs.

Obsolescence may trigger extreme reanalysis, where an item is co-opted for a function completely unrelated to its historical one, because evidence for successful acquisition of the former function is extremely limited under such conditions (Willis 2010; 2016). This is the case with Swedish *-er* (nominal inflection > human nominalization marker). In these cases, degrammaticalization is a form of exaptation (see Narrog 2007), the reuse of 'junk' or obsolescent morphology (Lass 1990; see also §3.1 for fuller discussion).

Even in less extreme cases than this, obsolescence favours degrammaticalization, because, even if transmission of the function of an item is broadly successful, the status it formerly had is no longer available in the language. Thus, once Irish was losing verbal person–number inflection, it made no sense for an acquirer to posit that *-mid* was an inflection, since there was no longer a model in the language to support this hypothesis. Instead acquirers resort to adaptive, analogical hypotheses about what the status of the item is; in this case, the hypothesis that *-mid/muid* was in fact a pronoun found support in the existence of other pronouns in the same morphosyntactic environment.

Kiparsky (2012) has highlighted the role of analogy in degrammaticalization, going so far as to claim that all apparent cases of degrammaticalization are in fact instances of analogy. Analogy clearly plays a significant role in a minority of cases: upgrading of the abessive ('without') case suffix to a clitic in some Balto-Finnic languages, for instance, correlates with the status of the comitative ('with') case in each language; thus the abessive has become a clitic in Seto/Võru and Vepsian, where the comitative is a clitic, while it has remained a suffix in Finnish, where the comitative is a suffix. The case systems in all these languages are robust, so obsolescence clearly plays no role. In other instances of degrammaticalization, analogy is absent: English possessive *-s* shifts from being a suffix to a phrasal affix despite there being no model in the form of an existing phrasal affix with similar meaning. Irish *-mid/muid* is an intermediate case where the syntactic analogy of other person–number combinations is relevant, but where obsolescence is needed to explain why the outcome is not the expected one. We would expect analogical extension of the existing first-person plural pronoun *sinn* into the future tense (i.e. *molfaidh sinn* 'praise.FUT.3SG we (= we shall praise)'), as is indeed the case in many varieties. Acquirers' efforts to make sense of a form they have heard, rendered unparsable through obsolescence, rather than create a new analogical form, is what triggers reanalysis. Thus, analogy is not a general explanation for degrammaticalization.

Finally, a group of debondings is associated not with obsolescence, but rather an increase in scope associated with generalization of meaning. Sometimes there is also increased speaker involvement (subjectification, Traugott 1989), a development normally associated with grammaticalization. Semantic shifts towards more grammatical meanings are generally associated with increased frequency, which may lead to loss of phonetic substance via fast-speech processes and, in some cases, loss of stress. However, increased frequency can in some cases be associated with degrammaticalization, at least in debonding examples. In the case of English possessive *-s*, for instance, generalization of the suffix to all nouns preceded the rise of the group genitive in (7) (Allen 2003), and this loss of allomorphy may have contributed to the shift to clitic status.

Consider further the development of English *-ish*, which undergoes debonding from adjective suffix to clitic and ultimately to independent word. In the course of this development, its meaning generalizes from 'belonging to a particular social or ethnic group' (*Danish*) or 'sharing characteristics of x' (*sheepish*, *goldish*), to 'approximately' (*bluish*). This is an instance of subjectification, since the meaning of the suffix is increasingly grounded in the speaker's evaluation. This new meaning is applicable to many more roots, so the type frequency of the suffix increases. The new words themselves are largely low in frequency, lower in frequency than their roots (e.g. *bluish* and *elevenish* are less frequent that *blue* and *eleven*). Such a relationship encourages on-the-fly parsing of the suffix rather than lexical storage of the entire word (Hay 2002; Hay and Plag 2004), leading to decreasing integration with the root, greater independence and increased scope. The result is that *-ish* degrammaticalizes and can now appear as a phrasal affix (*three o'clockish*) and, recently, as a free adverb taking propositional scope:

(10)   'Trust Davie Morrow.' 'You know him?' 'Ish. He's a regular across the
        road.' (Colin Bateman, *Cycle of violence* vi.94, 1995) (*OED* s.v. *ish*, adv.)

Extension of scope is also relevant to other cases of debonding: Greek
ksana prefix 're-' > independent adverb 'again' (extension of scope from
V to VP) (Méndez Dosuna 1997), Japanese *-ga* 'although' > free adverb 'but'
(extension of scope from within one clause to cover two clauses), English *to*
(extension of scope from V to VP) and so on.

2.6 Barriers to Degrammaticalization

Even proponents of degrammaticalization agree that it is significantly
less common than grammaticalization: Newmeyer (1998: 275) con-
cedes that grammaticalization changes occur at least ten times as
frequently as degrammaticalization, while a more sceptical view is
expressed by Haspelmath (2000: 249), who estimates the disparity
to be a hundred to one. This naturally raises the question of why
degrammaticalization should be so rare in comparison with
grammaticalization.
    Newmeyer explains the disparity by reference to least effort:

> Less effort is required on the part of the speaker to produce an affix than
> a full form ... All other things being equal, a child confronted with the
> option of reanalyzing a verb as an auxiliary or reanalyzing an auxiliary as
> a verb will choose the former.   *(Newmeyer 1998: 276)*

This applies to speakers in production, favouring phonetic reduction
over phonetic strengthening. It could also apply in acquisition, if we
simply assume a least-structure preference by children (cf. the Least
Effort Strategy, Roberts 1993). Such a preference would mean that children
initially prefer to posit a monoclausal structure with auxiliary + lexical
verb, other things being equal, rather than a biclausal structure with
lexical verb + complement clause. Newmeyer suggests that counterdirectional changes require some contrary factor, such as analogy, to counter-
balance the pressure for reduction.
    More broadly, the obvious answer is that the component processes that
make up grammaticalization are themselves largely, although not
entirely, unidirectional (Norde 2009: 89) and there are disparate barriers
to counterdirectional counterparts of these processes.
    In sound change, weakenings such as lenitions are far more fre-
quent than strengthenings. Phonological reductions result from fast-
speech processes and least-effort strategies of speakers. Segments are
more often elided than inserted: epenthesis is relatively rare, attributable largely to specific circumstances such as the coming together of
two vowels in hiatus. This all applies to phonological reduction in

grammaticalization. Furthermore, phonological reduction in grammaticalization is often the result of increase in frequency of grammaticalized items and loss of stress associated with the acquisition of functional status. If degrammaticalization were to involve the acquisition of stress by a previously non-stress-bearing item or a decrease in frequency of a formerly functional item, we might expect a degree of phonological strengthening, or, at least, a barrier to further phonological weakening. These are evidently possible (e.g. the vowel strengthening found in English *the* /ðə/ > /ði/ when it is stressed in the meaning 'the one and only' as in *Are you THE John Malkovich?*; see Norde 2009: 83f.), but require special circumstances, such as contrastive stress on a functional item, and it is not surprising that such circumstances arise only rarely.

The loss or weakening of morphophonological boundaries (e.g. clitic > affix shift) also seems to be largely unidirectional. The 'mistake' of failing to identify a boundary is inherently much more likely that the reverse scenario of wrongly identifying a 'phantom' boundary, although creation of morphological boundaries is not unknown (e.g. English *marathon* > *mara-thon* hence *tele-thon*). Furthermore, weakening of boundaries is often dependent on previous phonological reduction.

Grammaticalization features category reanalysis from lexical to functional. The reverse direction of reanalysis is not impossible, and reanalysis is not generally considered to be unidirectional (Haspelmath 1998: 325). Degrammaticalization involving solely reanalysis (often the case in degrammation, as discussed in §2.5 above) is thus one of the most likely types of counterdirectional shift. Nevertheless, such reanalyses face a number of obstacles. Since functional items form closed classes with few members, there are few regularities of form within these classes. Lexical classes on the other hand are open and contain many members, and, in synthetic and agglutinating languages, membership in these classes is unambiguously established by the presence of distinctive inflectional morphology. Degrammaticalizing reanalyses therefore need bridging contexts (see Evans and Wilkins 2000) where the absence of inflectional morphology is not problematic. Consider the degrammaticalization of the German preposition *zu* 'to' to an adjective 'closed', alongside other prepositions *aus* 'out' > 'finished' and *ab* 'off' > '(switched) off' (Plank 2000: 176–81; Janda 2001: 299f.; Willis 2007: 277f.). This depends crucially on the use of *zu* as a separable verbal prefix, allowing *zu* to appear in contexts where it appeared to contrast paradigmatically with (uninflected) predicative adjectives; consider the parallel of (11) and (12), which facilitated reanalysis of *zu* as an adjective, allowing the innovation of attributive, inflected use, as in (13).

(11) Er   hat   die   Tür   zugemacht. (Ger.)
      He   has   the   door   to.make.PST.PTCP
      'He closed the door.'
(12) Er   hat   die   Hose   kürzer   gemacht. (Ger.)
      he   has   the   trousers shorter   make.PST.PTCP
      'He made the trousers shorter.'
(13) die   zu((e)n)e   Tür (Ger.)
      the   closed.FSG   door
      'the closed door'

A language with elaborate synthetic or agglutinating adjective morphology would be unlikely to make available the relevant environment. Degrammaticalization is thus made easier in languages with analytic morphology in the relevant domain, as with degrammaticalization of Welsh *eiddo* 'his (pronoun)' > 'property' or Bulgarian *nešto* 'something' > 'thing' (Willis 2007), both in languages lacking nominal case morphology.

The semantic and pragmatic processes traditionally associated with grammaticalization are semantic bleaching, metaphor and inference. Early approaches to grammaticalization focused primarily on semantic bleaching, loss of lexical meaning, while more recently various forms of enrichment have been recognized. While some grammaticalizations, such as 'thing' (noun) > 'something' (indefinite pronoun), can usefully be thought of as a loss of the non-logical component of the input, most cases of grammaticalization require some meaning addition, as when deletion of the volitional component of 'want' does not simply yield the meaning 'future'. It is not obvious that the straightforward cases of semantic bleaching are unidirectional: we have already seen cases of 'something' (pronoun) > 'thing' (noun) which do not seem to have been hindered by the need for semantic enrichment. However, the limited role currently envisaged for semantic bleaching in grammaticalization research may limit the practical impact of this observation for degrammaticalization.

Metaphor generally runs from concrete to abstract: the concrete is encountered before the abstract and we conceive and make sense of the unfamiliar in terms of the familiar. Hence temporal prepositions and adverbs develop from spatial ones which themselves develop from concrete nouns. Exceptions exist but are quite limited (Norde 2009: 67–72), and tend to rest on the metaphor 'geographic space as a journey', which gives rise to counterdirectional metaphors expressing space using time (e.g. *The school is after the traffic lights* where the temporal preposition *after* expresses place 'beyond'). It is less obvious that implicature is unidirectional in any meaningful sense. Depending on the circumstances, *I will play tennis tomorrow* may give rise to the degrammaticalizing implicature 'I want to play tennis tomorrow' in much the same way as *I want to play tennis tomorrow* gives rise to the grammaticalizing implicature 'I will play tennis tomorrow'.

2.7 Formal Approaches to Degrammaticalization

Within a generative approach to language change, grammaticalization has been thought of (Willis 2000: 346–7; Roberts and Roussou 2003; Roberts 2010, 2012) as upwards reanalysis, the creation of new functional items in higher clausal positions than before (see §1.3.1). This reanalysis is associated with loss of movement, and, in many cases, also with structural simplification and loss of syntactic structure. For instance, auxiliation, the creation of new auxiliaries from existing lexical verbs, is regarded as loss of structure with an item that formerly moved to an auxiliary position being base-generated there. Thus, the shift in status of an English pre-modal such as *may* from lexical verb to auxiliary involves reanalysis of structure from (14) to (15) (adapted from Roberts and Roussou 2003: 40, 42).

(14)

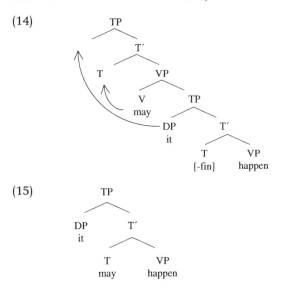

(15)

Such reanalyses are certainly a frequent component of grammaticalization. This naturally leads to the question of whether degrammaticalization can be thought of in inverse terms. Discussion here will be limited to degrammation (primary degrammaticalization), since it most obviously involves a category shift from functional to lexical and is therefore the most purely syntactic type of degrammaticalization. As we saw above in (5), (8) and (9), degrammations typically involve the creation of new syntactic structure, being based on hypercorrect reanalysis, reanalysis that involves the creation of a new structure as a result of wrongly postulating the accidental absence of evidence for that structure. Some, although not all, involve 'downwards reanalysis', the natural inverse of Roberts and Roussou's 'upward reanalysis'. This is fairly clear in the development of lexical verbs from auxiliaries, as in (8) above, and in the development of nouns from indefinite pronouns, as in (9). In both cases, the output of degrammation is an element that occupies a lower clausal position that the input. Whether the two positions are connected via movement is likely to depend on the properties of the individual language concerned: in many languages, lexical verbs move to the auxiliary position (head of TP), in which case degrammation will amount to the creation of a movement operation along with an elaboration of structure. The relative infrequency of such developments is explained in much the same way as before, by the tendency for the component processes to be (mostly) unidirectional. In generative terms, acquirers prefer to posit simpler structures with fewer features: they need positive evidence before they will elaborate the syntactic structure of their language. In degrammation, they do so despite insufficient evidence to justify the elaboration.

2.8 Degrammaticalization and Reconstruction

Finally, we should consider the implications of degrammaticalization for syntactic reconstruction. Grammaticalization has often been proposed as a tool for reconstruction. The disparity in frequency between grammaticalization and degrammaticalization means that, on the whole, where a functional element has a lexical counterpart in the same language or in a related language, it is far more likely that the functional element derives historically from the lexical one, rather than vice versa. However, the existence of degrammaticalization means that we cannot completely exclude the other possibility. Norde (2009: 52) even goes so far as to say that there are so many examples of degrammaticalization that 'grammaticalization is unfit as a tool in reconstruction'. Consider the following data from Slavonic (from Willis 2010):

(16) Serbian (Willis 2010: 24)
      Bi   li   ste   vi   to   učinili?
      COND   Q   be.PRES.2PL   you   that   do.PST.PTCP
      'Would you do that?'

(17) Polish
      Czy   byście   to   zrobili?
      Q   COND.2PL   that   do.PST.PTCP
      'Would you do that?'

In Serbian, *ste* is a clitic auxiliary and can be separated from the conditional marker by other clitics. In Polish, its counterpart *-ście* is a suffix on the conditional marker. Standard assumptions about the unidirectionality of grammaticalization would lead us to conclude that Serbian better represents the ancestral situation, while Polish has grammaticalized *ste* from auxiliary clitic to suffix. However, the textual record in fact shows the reverse: in Serbian *ste* is the result of debonding of an inflection. While this is clearly not the norm, it teaches us to be cautious about using grammaticalization as a tool for reconstruction without additional corroborating evidence.

2.9 Conclusion

Although our body of material for research on degrammaticalization is still quite limited, particularly from languages outside Europe and East Asia, we have seen that it is increasingly possible to classify examples of degrammaticalization, rather than viewing each as an idiosyncratic exception, and that this leads us to ask why degrammaticalizations occur. We have explored some tentative reasons, concerning the partially unidirectional nature of some component processes of grammaticalization, along with interactions with morphological type (analytic vs synthetic/agglutinating), reanalysis, analogy and obsolescence. Degrammaticalization is rare because some of these processes involve loss of material, while material that was previously absent cannot be gained except under exceptional circumstances. While it is clearly far less frequent an occurrence that the changes that have been grouped together under the heading of grammaticalization, its very existence suggests a view of syntactic change in which various processes (notably phonetic reduction, reanalysis, analogical extension, pragmatic inferencing, metaphor) come together in different combinations, sometimes going in unexpected directions, to produce a variety of outcomes.

References

Allen, C. L. 2003. 'Deflexion and the development of the genitive in English', *English Language and Linguistics* 7: 1–28.

Andersen, H. 2006. 'Grammation, regrammation, and degrammation: Tense loss in Russian', *Diachronica* 23: 231–58.

2008. 'Grammaticalization in a speaker-oriented theory of change', in Th. Eythórsson (ed.), *Grammatical change and linguistic theory: The Rosendal papers*. Amsterdam: John Benjamins, pp. 11–44.

Burridge, K. 1998. 'From modal auxiliary to lexical verb: The curious case of Pennsylvania German *wotte*', in R. M. Hogg and L. van Bergen (eds.), *Historical linguistics 1995: Selected papers from the 12th International conference on historical linguistics, Manchester, August 1995*, vol. II. Amsterdam: John Benjamins, pp. 19–33.

Campbell, L. 1991. 'Some grammaticalization changes in Estonian and their implications', in E. C. Traugott and B. Heine (eds.), *Approaches to grammaticalization*. Amsterdam: John Benjamins, pp. 285–99.

2001. 'What's wrong with grammaticalization?', *Language Sciences* 23: 113–61.

Doyle, A. 2002. 'Yesterday's affixes as today's clitics', in I. Wischer and G. Diewald (eds.), *New reflections on grammaticalization*. Amsterdam: John Benjamins, pp. 67–81.

Evans, N. and Wilkins, D. 2000. 'In the mind's ear: The semantic extensions of perception verbs in Australian languages', *Language* 76: 546–92.

Fischer, O., Norde, M. and Perridon, H. (eds.) 2004. *Up and down the cline: The nature of grammaticalization*. Amsterdam: John Benjamins.

Fitzmaurice, S. 2000. 'Remarks on the de-grammaticalisation of infinitival *to* in present-day American English', in O. Fischer, A. Rosenbach and D. Stein (eds.), *Pathways of change: Grammaticalization in English*. Amsterdam: John Benjamins, pp. 171–86.

Givón, T. 1995. *Functionalism and grammar*. Amsterdam: John Benjamins.

Haspelmath, M. 1998. 'Does grammaticalization need reanalysis?', *Studies in Language* 22: 315–51.

2000. 'Why can't we talk to each other?', *Lingua* 110: 235–55.

2004. 'On directionality in language change with particular reference to grammaticalization', in Fischer, Norde and Perridon (eds.), pp. 17–44.

Hay, J. 2002. 'From speech perception to morphology: Affix order revisited', *Language* 78: 527–55.

Hay, J. and Plag, I. 2004. 'What constrains possible suffix combinations? On the interaction of grammatical and processing restrictions in derivational morphology', *Natural Language and Linguistic Theory* 22: 565–96.

Heine, B. 2003. 'On degrammaticalization', in B. J. Blake and K. Burridge (eds.), *Historical linguistics 2001: Selected papers from the 15th International Conference on Historical Linguistics, Melbourne, 13–17 August 2001*. Amsterdam: John Benjamins, pp. 163–79.

Hilpert, M. 2008. *Germanic future constructions*. Amsterdam: John Benjamins.

Janda, R. D. 2001. 'Beyond "pathways" and "unidirectionality": On the discontinuity of language transmission and the counterability of grammaticalization', *Language Sciences* 23: 265–340.

Kiparsky, P. 2012. 'Grammaticalization as optimization', in D. Jonas, J. Whitman and A. Garrett (eds.), *Grammatical change: Origins, nature, outcomes*. Oxford University Press, pp. 15–50.

Kuteva, T. 2001. *Auxiliation: An enquiry into the nature of grammaticalization*. Oxford University Press.

Lass, R. 1990. 'How to do things with junk: Exaptation in language evolution', *Journal of Linguistics* 26: 79–102.

Lehmann, C. [1982] 1995. *Thoughts on grammaticalization.* Munich: Lincom Europa.

Matsumoto, Yo. 1988. 'From bound grammatical markers to free discourse markers: History of some Japanese connectives', *Proceedings of the Fourteenth Annual Meeting of the Berkeley Linguistics Society*, 340–51.

Méndez Dosuna, J. 1997. 'Fusion, fission and relevance in language change: De-univerbation in Greek morphology', *Studies in Language* 21: 577–612.

Narrog, H. 2007. 'Exaptation, grammaticalization, and reanalysis', *California Linguistic Notes* 32: 1–25.

Newmeyer, F. J. 1998. *Language form and language function.* Cambridge, MA: MIT Press.

Norde, M. 2001. 'Deflexion as a counterdirectional factor in grammatical change', *Language Sciences* 23: 231–64.

  2009. *Degrammaticalization.* Oxford University Press.

  2010. 'Degrammaticalization: Three common controversies', in K. Stathi, E. Gehweiler and E. König (eds.), *Grammaticalization: Current views and issues.* Amsterdam: John Benjamins, pp. 123–50.

Ohala, J.J. 1993. 'The phonetics of sound change', in C. Jones (ed.), *Historical linguistics: Problems and perspectives.* Longman: London, pp. 237–78.

Plank, F. 2000. 'Morphological re-activation and phonological alternations: Evidence for voiceless restructuring in German', in A. Lahiri (ed.), *Analogy, levelling, markedness.* Berlin: Mouton de Gruyter, pp. 171–91.

Rissanen, M. 1997. 'Whatever happened to the Middle English indefinite pronouns?', in J. Fisiak (ed.), *Studies in Middle English linguistics.* Berlin: Mouton de Gruyter, pp. 513–29.

Roberts, I. 1993. 'A formal account of grammaticalisation in the history of Romance futures', *Folia Linguistica Historica* 13: 219–58.

  2010. 'Grammaticalization, the clausal hierarchy and semantic bleaching', in E. C. Traugott and G. Trousdale (eds.), *Gradience, gradualness and grammaticalization.* Amsterdam: John Benjamins, pp. 45–73.

  2012. 'Diachrony and cartography: Paths of grammaticalization and the clausal hierarchy', in L. Brugè *et al.* (eds.), *Functional heads: The cartography of syntactic structures*, vol. VII. Oxford University Press, pp. 351–65.

Roberts, I. and Roussou, A. 2003. *Syntactic change: A minimalist approach to grammaticalization.* Cambridge University Press.

Tabor, W. and Traugott, E. C. 1998. 'Structural scope expansion and grammaticalization', in A. Giacalone Ramat and P. J. Hopper (eds.), *The limits of grammaticalization.* Amsterdam: John Benjamins, pp. 229–72.

Traugott, E. C. 1989. 'On the rise of epistemic meanings in English: An example of subjectification in semantic change', *Language* 65: 31–55.

Willis, D. 2000. 'Verb movement in Slavonic conditionals', in S. Pintzuk, G. Tsoulas and A. Warner (eds.), *Diachronic syntax: Models and mechanisms*. Oxford University Press, pp. 322–48.

2007. 'Syntactic lexicalization as a new type of degrammaticalization', *Linguistics* 45: 271–310.

2010. 'Degrammaticalization and obsolescent morphology: Evidence from Slavonic', in K. Stathi, E. Gehweiler and E. König (eds.), *Grammaticalization: Current views and issues*. Amsterdam: John Benjamins, pp. 151–77.

2016. 'Exaptation and degrammaticalization within an acquisition-based model of abductive reanalysis', in M. Norde and F. van de Velde (eds.), *Exaptation and language change*. Amsterdam: John Benjamins, pp. 197–225.

Ziegeler, D. 2004. 'Redefining unidirectionality: Is there life after modality?', in Fischer, Norde and Perridon (eds.), 115–35.

3

Exaptation

John Haiman

3.1 Introduction

A copy of *Moby Dick* can be used to prop up a sofa with a missing leg. The term exaptation was introduced into biological theory by Steven J. Gould and Elizabeth Vrba in 1982, and then imported from biology into linguistics in 1990 by Roger Lass, as a possible label for this kind of functional repurposing. Given all the terms already in use for functional change, why do we need this new label at all? And what does 'this kind of repurposing' mean? We need first of all to define exaptation.

In biology, it is hard to distinguish exaptation from 'pre-adaptation'. Moreover, the term 'pre-adaptation' has teleological overtones, which Gould and Vrba rejected (how can a thing 'adapt in advance' to a non-existent state of affairs?), and if one wants to avoid this, one can coin a neologism: 'accidental pre-apt-ness'. The following two statements are then equivalent:

> *Moby Dick*'s thickness makes it accidentally pre-apt for its present function, which is propping up a specific sofa.
> *Moby Dick* is exapted to prop up said sofa.

A difference between exaptation and pre-apt-ness may reside in the status of the recycled object at the time it takes on its new use. As Lass (1990) suggested in the enormously influential title of his article, exaptation is the recycling of *junk*. Only if nobody is planning to read that copy of *Moby Dick* any more can we speak of its exaptation. Unambiguous cases of pure exaptation may therefore be hard to come by in biology, since even the most apparently useless vestigial organs, like the human appendix, may turn out, like 'junk DNA', to have a possible function of which we are not yet aware. So the notion of 'junk' is unusable in biology.

Another unusable basis for the term is the distinction between 'lower' (read 'more junk-like') and 'higher' ('less junk-like') functions: everyone agrees that being used as a prop is certainly a higher function than not being used at all. And opinions famously differ as to whether propping up a sofa is a higher function than all the works of Melville, etc. One may even call the development of the 'higher uselessness' of Language itself (from originally instrumental acts) a kind of exaptation (see Tinbergen 1952; Wilson 1975; Danto 1983; Boesch 1993). But why should sending a message about nut-cracking be a 'higher' function than cracking a nut? The higher/lower distinction is hard to maintain, at least within biology, for all its intuitive metaphorical appeal, because, on examination, terms like 'the higher functions' usually mean those functions thought to be restricted to human beings, and therefore reek of speciesism.

Closely related to both preadaptation and exaptation is the notion of specialization. In reproducing itself, a cell or another structure may accidentally produce more than one identical copy of itself. Originally the extra copies are redundant (hence eminently junklike), but they may become available for structural modifications and separate specialized functions later on (Mayr 2001: 38; Margulies and Sagan 1997: 168). If this is not exaptation, why not?

This 'junk' criterion may actually be more usable in linguistics than in biology. As proposed by Lass, it allows an easy distinction to be made between two kinds of functional repurposing in language change.

Canonically, the familiar notion of grammaticalization always involves a kind of 'demotion of grammatical status': in terms of Givón's (1979: ch. 5) famous syntacticization trajectory, grammaticalization is the link between two way-stations (words and affixes) on the way between discourse and silence: more generally, grammaticalization includes the transition from words to inflectional and derivational affixes, from 'major' parts of speech like nouns and verbs to 'minor' parts of speech like pronouns, prepositions and auxiliary verbs. There is a sense that 'demotion' should also involve some loss of meaning, but it is not always easy to agree on whether words gain or lose meaning when they are made into grammatical morphemes, and the only thing everyone can agree on is that if something goes from having some meaning to having absolutely none, then the word 'demotion' is appropriate. Not only does the term 'demotion' recall the discredited idea of 'higher and lower' functions: the circularity of the characterization of grammaticalization is blatant in Kuryłowicz's classic definition:

> Grammaticalization consists in the increase of the range of a morpheme advancing from a lexical to a grammatical or *from a grammatical to a more grammatical status.*   (Kuryłowicz [1965]1975: 52; emphasis added)

But it is possible in linguistics to avoid both appeals to metaphor and circularity. A less loaded pair of terms with the same semantic extension as 'major' categories and 'minor' ones is 'class categories whose membership is open or large' and 'class categories whose membership is closed or relatively small'. Demotion of a category is then equivalent to either or both:

- its becoming a member of a class with smaller membership
- its losing all meaning

Grammaticalization is part of a recurrent overall 'compaction trajectory' (Langacker 1977; Givón 1979), wherein syntactic phrases are 'compacted' to lexical compounds, words are further 'compacted' to morphemes, morphemes like the numeral 'one' are compacted to other morphemes like the indefinite article, and all morphemes are ground down to phonemes. Grammaticalization is also often but not always attended by phonetic reduction. Thus the final stage of compaction in Givón's trajectory is the loss of phonemes, a purely phonetic reduction which is formally parallel to the change from words (which typically bear stress and may be polysyllabic), to phonetically less bulky affixes (which typically do not bear stress, and are typically monosyllabic or non-syllabic). In the course of the last stage of compaction, an inflectional language may lose almost all of its inflectional affixes and become an almost entirely isolating one, as has happened most famously with English, which is impressionistically five minutes away from being like Mandarin.

Exaptation on the other hand is one of a number of terms which can then be used to describe various cases of the opposite of grammaticalization: 'grammatical promotion', as it were. The reduction of a word to an affix is grammaticalization; but the morphologization of a phonetic string or the promotion of an affix to word status may be considered exaptation. It is then necessary to distinguish exaptation from two other recognized kinds of promotion:

- degrammaticalization (a change whereby a gram in a specific context gains in autonomy or substance on one or more linguistic levels (semantics, morphology, syntax and phonology))
- at least one kind of lexicalization (controversially defined by Norde (2010) as 'a change where function words or bound morphemes are "taken out of their context", as it were, and upgraded from minor to major word-classes (*pros and cons*, *to up*, *to down*), and derivational affixes are promoted to hypernym nouns (*isms, ologies*)').

Not all cases of Norde's 'lexicalization' can be thought of as upgrading: the nominalization of verbs in expressions like *does and don'ts* is surely an example of the same kind of grammatical decontextualization, yet it only changes verbs to nouns. And this change can surely be thought of as zero derivation – as then, perhaps, can all of Norde's other examples.

And further problems of nomenclature still abound. Assuming that grammaticalization allows us to distinguish not only more and less bonded morphemes, but also higher from lower morphemes along some vertical 'cline', what does one make of countless apparently 'lateral' associational changes, like those based on non-definitional properties (richly exemplified in Darmesteter 1887)? Is the word *horn* not exapted to name a material, or a musical instrument? How about the equally lateral transition from inflectional to derivational affix status, of the sort one can reconstruct for the final *-t* in words like *(pur)suit*?

One possible basis for making a useful distinction between exaptation and all the other varieties of promotion or lateral movement may be the following: all associational changes, lexicalization and degrammaticalization start with grams (that is, meaningful units) of some kind. These changes include not only the passage from one kind of word to another, from inflectional to derivational affixes, from affixes or function words to words (e.g. *-ism* > *ism(s)*; *if* > *if(s)*), but also the passage of affixes to clitics (e.g. the genitive *-s* to the NP-final clitic *-s*).

All cases of functional change which are not clear cases of demotion may be argued to overlap with exaptation. But in this survey, exaptation will be exclusively and non-controversially defined as:

> the promotion of meaningless or redundant material so that it does new grammatical (morphosyntactic or phonological) or semantic work.

3.2   Morphologization of Meaningless Phonetic Strings

When a string of meaningless sounds becomes meaningful, then it is legitimate to speak of exaptation. Possible examples of exaptation in English may then include familiar phonaesthemes like word-initial {gl}, {sl} or word-final {udge}. The partial emergence of these sequences into meaningfulness may have come about through a repetition of accidental associations. To the extent that the recurrent sound associations of {-udge} in words like *sludge, smudge, trudge, grudge, fudge* inspired the neologism *kludge*, 'an awkward inelegant solution to some engineering problem', one may even call the association a productive one.

A more systematic example of this kind of promotion is offered by the genesis of at least one major nearly productive infix in Cambodian (Khmer), an Austroasiatic language. This infix *-Vm(n)-* is apparently not found elsewhere in the family (with the single possible exception of Khmu), and, although derivational affixation is largely moribund in Khmer, this infix seems to border on the productive. Given a verbal mono-syllabic root, it is very frequently possible to make a derived nominal by inserting this infix after the initial consonant, as happens in hundreds of examples like those in (1):

(1) a. *cŋa:j*   'far'   ~ *c-am-ŋa:j*   'distance'
     b. *criang*   'sing'   ~ *c-am-riang*   'song'
     c. *daeu*   'walk'   ~ *d-amn-aeu*   'voyage'
     d. *deung*   'know'   ~ *d-amn-eung*   'knowledge'
     e. *kaeut*   'arise'   ~ *k-amn-aeut*   'birth'
     f. *tlaj*   'be worth'   ~ *d-am-laj*   'value'

It is interesting, however, that this infix may have a variety of other meanings. In a significant number of cases, it acts as a transitivizer or causative morpheme:

(2) a. *slap*   'die'   ~ *s-am-lap*   'kill'
     b. *trev*   'true'   ~ *d-am-rev*   'straighten'
     c. *craeun* 'many'   ~ *c-am-raeun*   'prosper, increase'

In other cases, it provides an idiosyncratic meaning, thus, for example:

(3) a. *neak chw:*
         person ill
         'a sick person'
         neak c-umg-ngw: (with irregular change of [h] to [ŋ])
         person ?sickness
         'a (medical) patient'
     b. *cah* 'old'
         c-amn-ah 'elderly'

Finally, here are a number of cases where it seems to be entirely decorative and have no meaning at all:

(4) a. *cpo:h*   ~   *c-am-po:h*   'towards'
     b. *skoal*   ~   *s-am-koal*   'be acquainted with'
     c. *ksawt*   ~   *k-am-sawt*   'poor, miserable'

Haiman (1998), Haiman and Ourn (2003) and Haiman (2011: ch. 3) argued that the original 'function' of the infix, oddly enough, may be the one that is manifested in the final set of cases. That is, -V*m(n)*- was originally entirely meaningless, hence 'junk-like'. Here is the argument.

Khmer, like most Mon-Khmer languages, is what Matisoff (1973) called 'sesquisyllabic': the canonical word consists of an maximally unstressed introductory or anacrusic initial syllable, followed by a stressed main syllable. Moreover, the anacrusic syllable constantly undergoes further reduction in casual or allegro speech. The obligatory core of the string -V*m(n)*- is a special case of -*VN*-, one of the only two possible rhyme portions of the anacrusic syllable of a sesquisyllabic word (the other one is -*rV*-), and it is precisely this portion of the word – generally, the rhyme portion of this syllable – which is forever elided in the casual pronunciation of sesquisyllabic words by rules of anacrusic syllable reduction (compare formal and increasingly casual pronunciations of English phrases like *good night*). Originally the two pronunciations – one sesquisyllabic, the other monosyllabic – were merely stylistic variants of the same word, as they are in examples like (5):

(5) a. *bamraːm*   ~ *praːm*   'warning'
     b. *bantup*   ~ *p(a)tup*   'room'
     c. *banghaːɲ*   ~ *p(a)haːɲ*   'show'
     d. *kandaːl*   ~ *k(a)daːl*   'middle'
     e. *kanlaeng*   ~ *klaeng*   'place'

(The bracketed graph (a) in the above examples is phonologically ambiguous: an epenthesis rule inserts a schwa between adjacent consonants. There is evidence that the vowel here arises via epenthesis rather than being a retention. Note the devoicing of the initial stop, typologically implausible before a retained vowel.)

A meaningless string of sounds, which tends to disappear in casual pronunciations of sesquisyllabic words, and whose presence thus signals nothing but formality of diction, has been reinterpreted as first, a purely decorative embellishment, and then a meaningful infix in what are now interpreted as monosyllabic words. It can then also be added to inherited and borrowed monosyllabic words.

The evidence in favour of this analysis is fourfold. First, there is the sheer variety of different meanings which the infix may have. It is as if speakers of the language decided to create the infix first, and ask and answer questions about its meaning later.

Second, there is the fact that the infix happens to rebuild precisely the most common elided rhyme of the anacrusic syllable. Only V +nasal and *r*+V occur in the rhyme of this syllable. In Cambodian Khmer, only V+nasal occurs as an infix. However, in Surin Khmer, the variety spoken in northeast Thailand along the Cambodian border, optional infixation of *r*+V occurs regularly with any root, and is as yet completely meaningless (Prakorb 1992: 255). The argument is that at an earlier stage, the -V*m(n)*- infix of Central Khmer was similarly optional and meaningless.

Third, monosyllabic words in Khmer manifest several dozen exotic initial consonant clusters like [l(a)p] (as in [lapav] 'pumpkin'), [t(a)b] (as in [t(a)boːng] 'south') and [k(a)ŋ] (as in [k(a)ngaok] 'goose') which do not occur in the main syllable of sesquisyllabic words. A plausible source for these clusters, which are broken up by phonological epenthesis and morphological infixation, is that they resulted precisely when sesquisyllabic words collapsed into monosyllables via anacrusic syllable reduction in the first place (Pinnow 1978). This is an argument for the antiquity and persistence of the process of anacrusic syllable elision in Khmer.

Finally, there is the fact that infixation still serves always and only to rebuild a sesquisyllabic root from a monosyllabic base: the infix (whether it is meaningful or not) is found to occur on only one polysyllabic verb.

Otherwise it occurs exclusively with monosyllables. If the function of the infix were truly semantic, then this restriction would be an inexplicable gap. If the original function of this process is simply to restore sesquisyllabicity, a favourite phonetic structure, this phonetically characterizable distribution is predicted by definition.

It should be noted in this connection that all hands agree that in at least one particular, the form of this infix is already phonetically motivated: the allomorph -V*m*- occurs when the root begins with a consonant cluster, thus *criang* → *c-am-riang*; the allomorph -V*mn*- when the root begins with a single consonant, thus *daeu* → *d-amn-aeu*. Both allomorphs ensure a maximally unmarked CVx + CVy syllable structure in the sesquisyllabic word (*cam.riang; dam.naeu*), avoiding both typologically aberrant vowel-initial syllables (*[dam.aeu]) and consonant-cluster-initial syllables (*cam.nriang]).

Modelling all this in English: it is as if the casually dropped final {g} of {-ing} were to assume a morphological function. While nothing like this has happened here, Khmer does not seem to be the only language which has morphologized casually elided phonetic strings in exactly this way. In Romanian, up to the beginning of the twentieth century, the inherited infinitival desinence -*re* could be elided in allegro speech (Tiktin 1905). That is, *fi* and *fire* were alternate pronunciations of the infinitive 'to be'. In texts, the -*re* spelling still rendered an infinitive:

(6) și   s-   au   gătit   a sta- re   cu   războiu
     and REFL have prepared to resist-INF with war
     'and they prepared themselves to resist with war' (Hill 2013)

By now, that labile suffix has been reinterpreted exclusively as a derivational nominalizing suffix, hence we observe meaningful contrasts such as

(7) *naște* 'to give birth' vs *naște* +*re* 'birth'
     fi   'to be'   vs *fi*+*re*   'nature, existence'
     ști   'to know'   vs *ști*+*re*   'news'

This nominalizer has been analogically generalized to non-Latinate roots, hence

(8) *iubi* 'to love' vs *iubi*+*re* 'love' < Russian *ljubi-t'*

Derived nouns in -*re*, are now classed as feminine and form plurals in [i]:

(9) convorbir-   i-   le   telephonic- e
     conversation   PL   the.FPL   telephone   FPL
     'the telephone conversations'

And there are examples of this kind of promotional morphologization in other languages. Indeed, if one were to extend the definition of exaptation to include not only 'meaningless' and 'redundant', but also 'automatically conditioned' phonetic material as stuff that is available for promotion, then one could also subsume phonologization with its occasionally attendant morphologization, whereby umlaut becomes ablaut, under this heading, e.g. German *Garten/Gärten* 'garden/gardens'; Piedmontese *os/ös* 'bone/bones'; Neapolitan *russə* 'red' (MSG/PL) vs *rossə* 'red' (FSG/PL). The essential mechanism, of emancipation or decontextualization of a structural process from its original context, is the same as for ritualization (see Jakobson [1931] 1972; Twaddell 1938; Haiman 1994).

3.3   The Lexicalization of Meaningless Phonetic Strings

A sequence of sounds may be created to satisfy some purely ludic or aesthetic imperative. An example is the etymologically unmotivated initial syllable of *ca-boodle*, whose function is to make *boodle* alliterate with *kit* and *cat*. Sometimes such a meaningless sequence may emerge into the lexicon as meaningful word. The best example of this kind of emergence in English may be offered by words like *zigzag*. It is clear that *zigzag* is an example of the kind of reduplication that Marchand (1960) called a 'twin form': rhyming or ablauting pairs of morphemes of which only one (at best) is meaningful. But the moment a speaker says *I zigged when I should have zagged*, a jocular ephemeral meaning has emerged, one which may become institutionalized.

While twin forms like *helter skelter* and *jibber jabber* are a relatively poorly attested phenomenon in English, they are rife in many languages of the world, and frequently signal 'disorderly iteration' (Pott 1862; Wälchli 2005). In particular, twin forms are exceedingly common in languages of mainland Southeast Asia, where they function in a purely decorative way: that is, they do not signal any kind of iteration, or intensification, or pejorification, or anything else other than elegance (see Nguyen 1965; Roffe 1975; Gregerson 1984; Stanford 2007; Ourn and Haiman 2000; Haiman 2011: ch. 4; Williams forthcoming).

In at least one of these languages, Khmer, the originally decorative morphemes in pairs of this kind (known to Khmer grammarians as *bo'ri'va: sap* 'accompanying retinue words') seem to derive from a variety of sources: they may be non-synonyms conscripted to act as retinue words on the basis of euphony (e.g. English compounds *true-blue, loose-y goose-y*), they may be near-synonyms tricked out with extra material to make them conform with their partners (e.g. English *kit, cat* and *ca-boodle*), or they may be produced by rhyme-swap verbal games of the sort which in English produce portmanteaux words like *smog* and Spoonerisms like *tee many Martoonis*. Some of these decorative words may have emerged into the realm of meaning, as, indeed, *smog* has in English. Possibly they appeared first as perfect synonyms of the roots that they accompany, then later as near synonyms (Haiman 2011: ch. 4).

This conjectured development would account for a recurrent puzzling feature of the Khmer lexicon, the enormous number of alliterating near-synonyms like those in (10):

(10) *kantanj*   'short and fat; stocky; broad'
      kantaw: 'small and fat'
      kanthat   'fatty and fat; stocky'
      kanthia   'small and broad'
      kanthok   'obese'
      kanthoc   'fleshy, fat'
      kanthol   'plump, fat, obese'
      kanteunj kantonj   'short, squat, fat'

Obviously, all of these mean something like 'fat' but they are not totally synonymous; and the contention is that most of them originated as decorative accompaniments to one such word that perhaps no longer happens to be attested. Another n-tuple set of such near-synonyms is:

(11) *ravi:k raveu:k*   'twitch, squirm'
      ravi:m raviam   'wriggle; be scarred all over; confused like'
      raviam   'squirm, wriggler'
      ravwc   'wag, swish, flutter'
      ravwc raviam   'bother, annoy'
      raveu:k   'squirm'

Again, it is plain that all of the words above derive from some common source meaning 'squirm'.

If our contention is correct, Khmer provides an example of a language expanding its lexical resources via the exaptation of what was once decorative – originally meaningless – material.

3.4 The Creation of an Auxiliary Verb in English from a Grammatical Cipher

The grammaticalization of the prototypical main verb *do* into the meaningless auxiliary of modern English is one of the most carefully studied grammatical changes in diachronic syntax (Ellegard 1953). In Elizabethan English, the auxiliary was in apparently 'free' variation with its absence (hence meaningless) in positive and negative statements, positive and negative questions, and in positive and negative imperatives (Ellegard 1953: 162). By 1700, however, obligatorification had set in, and the distribution of *do* in statements and questions had become the same as in Present-Day English, as described by the ordered transformational rules of Chomsky (1957). In the theory that Chomsky was creating at the time, the fact that this auxiliary could be introduced as a last resort by a transformational rule of insertion at all was equivalent to its having no meaning. To put it another way, the fact that there are rules that regulate the distribution of *do* constitute one of the most convincing examples of the independence of syntax from semantics.

In imperatives, something different happened. The free variation of *do* versus its absence in Renaissance English, e.g. *Fear not!* vs *Do not fear!*, was exactly comparable to the free variation of *do* versus its absence in positive and negative statements, and in questions. This free variation has given way to the obligatorification of *do* in negative commands, or prohibitives, and its disappearance in non-emphatic positive statements. Given that this meaningless verb was equally infrequent (occurring with a frequency of around 10 per cent according to Ellegård) in both positive statements and prohibitives in 1600, its obligatorification in prohibitives alone by 1700 furnishes a neat example supporting another one of Chomsky's claims: that categorical judgements of grammaticality cannot be predicted from statistical frequency.

But prohibitive *do*, as a number of observers have pointed out (Sadock and Zwicky 1985; Schmerling 1982; Warner 1993), is not the same auxiliary verb whose distribution was famously described by Chomsky, and it is hard to see how any restatement of Chomsky's rules could encompass its idiosyncratic behaviour.

(i) While the meaningless quasi-modal auxiliary of *Syntactic structures* is in complementary distribution with any or all modals, the perfect auxiliary *have*, and *be* in any of its functions, the *do* which occurs in prohibitive imperatives is actually required to co-occur with *be* (13):

(12)   He isn't cruel.   He isn't expecting any favours.
       *He doesn't be cruel.   *He doesn't be expecting any favours.

(13)   Don't be cruel.   Don't be expecting any favours.
       *Be not cruel.   *Be not expecting any favours.

(ii) While the Chomskyan auxiliary's raison d'être was to provide a host of last resort for the unaffixed inflectional *tense+ person* affix occurring in negative statements, emphatic statements and questions, no such raison d'être exists for the prohibitive *do*, since *imperatives are uninflected*. The admittedly minimal evidence for this characterization, given the impoverishment of English inflectional morphology, is provided by the single verb 'to be':

(14)   Be nice!
       *Are nice!

(iii) While the Chomskyan auxiliary is available to 'feed' the transformation which produces confirmation-seeking tags, the prohibitive auxiliary is not available for this function. Observe the contrast in (15):

(15)   You don't really mean that, do you? (Chomskyan *do* feeds tag
       formation)
       *Don't drive so fast, do you? (prohibitive *do* does not feed tag
       formation)

(iv) While the Chomskyan auxiliary undergoes subject–verb inversion in
questions, but not in (most) non-questions, the prohibitive undergoes
obligatory inversion of a kind if the pronoun subject is retained:

(16)   Don't you like me? (subject–verb inversion is ungrammatical in
       statements)
       Don't you step on my blue suede shoes. (This is a prohibition, not
       a question)
       *You don't step on my blue suede shoes. (The absence of
       subject–verb inversion is ungrammatical in prohibitives)

Moreover, this inversion is not the same as the subject–verb inversion
that characterizes questions and 'affective' sentences. In questions, the
negative participates in subject–verb inversion if it is contracted:

(17)   Have you not spoken to him?
       Haven't you spoken to him?

If inversion of the same sort occurred in prohibitives, then both the
following should be grammatical:

(18)   Don't you step on my blue suede shoes
       *Do you not step on my blue suede shoes.

These details lead to the conclusion that between 1600 and 1700, the
meaningless (hence *ex hypothesi*, junk-like) grammatical marker *do*, whose
distribution was seemingly random in Shakespeare's day, has evolved into
two separate morphemes: the first is the meaningless purely grammatical
auxiliary described in Chomsky (1957), and the second is a homophonous
verb subject to different rules which occurs in prohibitives (and, at a later
date, in positive imperatives also). The *don't* of the prohibitive is as different
from *don't* in negative statements and questions as is Latin *noli* from *non* (*noli*
(< *ne* 'not' + *uoli* 'want') in the prohibitive taking as its object complement the
infinitive: e.g. *noli dubita-re* 'do not hesitate.INF'; *non* is the declarative negator
and may simply accompany finite verbs: e.g. *non dubit-ō* 'I do not hesitate').

3.5   From Various Original Functions to Placeholders

A number of languages observe various 'second-position targets' for a class
of migratory words (Wackernagel 1892). Usually these words, often called
clitics, acquire second position by attaching on to the initial word of some
syntactic domain, typically the sentence. Sometimes, however, when an
expected domain-initial 'host' word is missing, another meaningless

cipher will be conscripted to act as a placeholder in its stead. This novel grammatical function of placeholder seems to be confined to languages which have second-position targets for words of various types.

3.5.1   Placeholders in Serbo-Croatian

A number of parts of speech have clitic status in Serbo-Croatian, which should mean that they are attracted to second position. The following presentation ignores both the relative ordering of co-occurring clitics, and the complex subtleties of whether 'second position' is defined syntactically or prosodically (Franks 1998 provides a magisterial summary of recent debates). 'Clitic position' here means only that clitics are prohibited in domain-initial position, a prohibition that distinguishes Serbo-Croatian from Slovenian (Franks 1998). Among the clitics, given in (19) in their ordering, are the polar interrogative marker *li* and the present tense AUX paradigm for the verb 'be', which functions as the copula verb and as the perfect auxiliary: *sam, si, je, smo, ste, su*. The 3sG form *je*, which follows all other clitics when it is itself a clitic, can uniquely also act as a stressed form, and thus begin a sentence (20).

(19)   li > AUX > DAT > ACC > GEN > se > je (from Browne 1974 via Franks 1998)

(20)   Je   li   to   istina?
       be=3sG   whether   that   truth
       'Is that true?'

Although Serbo-Croatian typically allows subject pronouns to be elided, they cannot be if the immediately following word is an AUX clitic, since this would strand the clitic in the prohibited sentence-initial position:

(21)   *(Ja)   Sam   bio   tamo
        I   I=am   been.MSG   there
       'I was there.'

The elision of the subject pronoun is satisfactory, however, if another word stands sentence-initially:

(22)   a.   Bio sam tamo.
            'I was there.'
       b.   Tamo sam bio.
            'I was there.'

Although Serbo-Croatian is basically SVO, word order is far more flexible than English, and other elements besides the subject can be fronted without strong focus or topic associations.

Sometimes, when nothing is available for fronting and satisfaction of the clitic-second target, a now-meaningless word may be recruited to act as a placeholder. Two such elements can be found: the 3sg auxiliary *je* and the complementizer *da*.

There exists a paradigm of 'long' auxiliary forms which *can* occur sentence-initially:

(23)　Je-sam
　　　 Je-si
　　　 Je
　　　 Je-smo
　　　 Je-ste
　　　 Je-su

(24)　Je-sam　bio　　　　tamo
　　　 I=am　 been.msg　there
　　　 'I was there.'

It is clear that the stressed extra initial syllable in the long form is itself the 3sg auxiliary, which, as noted, can act as a stressed form, and, as is apparent from the paradigm above, therefore requires no other longer form. But of course, elsewhere in the long-form paradigm it no longer carries any 3sg meaning, or any other. It has been recycled simply to act as a support for the following clitic.

In polar questions, subject–verb inversion takes place:

(25)　Govorite　li　　　　　(vi)　　　srpskohrvatski?
　　　 speak.2pl　whether　you=all　Serbo-Croatian
　　　 'Do you speak Serbo-Croatian?'

Note that the interrogative marker, as a clitic, is kept in second position by occurring after the verb. If the verb is the AUX, in either function, it must, being sentence-initial, occur in the long form:

(26)　*(Je=)ste　Li　　　　　(vi)　　　bili　　　　tamo
　　　 be=2pl　 whether　you=all　been.mpl　there
　　　 'Have you been there?'

But there is another possibility. The complementizer *da* typically introduces 'that' clauses:

(27)　Izvinite,　　da　　vas　　　　uznemiravam
　　　 excuse.2pl　that　you=acc　I=disturb
　　　 'Excuse me for disturbing you.'

And, when it does, it allows clitics to follow it. That is, it 'counts as' the first element in subordinate clauses:

(28)　Ivan　kaže　da　**mu**　　**je**　　　 knjigu　Marija　dala
　　　 Ivan　says　that　to=him　3sg.aux　book　　Maria　 given.fsg
　　　 'Ivan says that Maria gave him the book.'

But it can also be conscripted to act as a now meaningless sentence-initial placeholder in direct polar questions, in which case, the short clitic forms of the copula are acceptable, and the interrogative marker *li* may precede the verb, in conformity with the clitic-ordering template:

(29) Da   li   ste   bili   tamo
      that whether be=2PL been.MPL there
      'Have you been there?'

3.5.2 'Peg' Syllables in Na-Dene (and Yeniseic)

In most Na-Dene languages, verbs are preceded by a variety of inflectional and derivational prefixes signalling verb class, tense, aspect, mood, subject and object person. An unmarked verb is semantically possible, but formally no verb is allowed to appear without *some* prefix. Eric Weisser (2008: 4) notes, for Na-Dene (see also Rice 1989: 133 on Slave; Faltz 1998: 524 on Navajo; Cook 2004: 14 on Dene):

> Certain verb forms in Navajo, as well as other Na-Dene languages, contain what are known as 'peg syllables' and 'peg consonants'. These morphemes are completely meaningless, and serve only to satisfy morphophonological rules. One such rule states that no Navajo word may begin with a vowel. When a verb's structure is such that it would begin with a vowel, a peg consonant is inserted at the very beginning of the form in order not to violate the rule. When the initial vowel is <i> or <ii>, the peg consonant is y-; when the initial vowel is <o> or <oo>, the peg consonant is w-. Another rule states that all verb forms must contain at least one syllable before the stem. When a verb form would be complete without a syllable before the verb stem, the peg syllable yi- is inserted at the beginning of the form.

Vajda (2010) has reconstructed exactly such a placeholding function in Yeniseic languages as well, arguing thus for a common origin for both families:

> In both families, a peg prefix or other device is normally needed to satisfy the minimum two-syllable requirement in cases where a finite verb form would otherwise be monosyllabic.   *(Vajda 2010: 41)*

Regardless of the exact characterization, all authorities agree that the peg element has a purely placeholding function: the peg is inserted to conform with a commonly occurring paradigm.

3.5.3 Preserving CV Syllables in Olgolo

CV is a typological universal for syllable structures. In the writing systems of a number of languages, among them Hebrew and Khmer, the glottal stop graph acts as an orthographic placeholder for words that begin with a vowel. Dixon (1970) noted that the favourite CV syllable structure of Olgolo, a dying Australian language, was undergoing erosion, as the initial syllable of CVCV words was losing its original consonant. To restore this favourite structure, speakers of Olgolo seemed to be using as initial consonants not the glottal stop, but the remnants of a no-longer active system of nominal classifiers.

3.5.4 When Finite Verbs Are Clitics

Wackernagel famously argued that the finite verb in Indo-European was originally atonic, and it was for this reason that in Germanic the finite verb is such a second-position seeker. Whether or not his thesis that 'verbs in Germanic are second-place because they were originally clitics' is correct (see Kiparsky 1995 for a contrary view), Germanic languages do have a V2 tendency, which is satisfied through SVO word order (avoiding verb-initial order) and through subject–verb inversion in statements with other fronted elements (avoiding verb-third order).

But where a sentential subject is extraposed, the neuter pronoun, now non-referential, could replace it, to conform with the canonical SVX pattern, as Jespersen (1943) recognized:

(30)   It's surprising (that) you should ask.

Or where the subject was indefinite, as in existential sentences, the now-no-longer deictic pronoun *there* could replace it (Breivik 1983):

(31)   There's food in the fridge.

Speaking in favour of this analysis of *it* and *there* as placeholders are a number of facts. First is the fact that in some Germanic languages, the dummy subjects corresponding to English *it* and *there* fail to appear, or appear only optionally, where sentence-initial position is filled by some other constituent. Consider German scene-setting or thetic sentences like:

(32)   Es   schwebt   das   Schiff   auf   glatten   Meereswogen
        It   floats   the   ship   on   smooth   sea.waves

The initial placeholder *es*, emphatically non-referential, is required to maintain V2 order in what is basically a verb-initial sentence. There is no grammatical place for it in sentences which begin with either of the nominal arguments:

(33)   a. Das Schiff   schwebt   (*es)   auf   glatten   Meereswogen.
            the ship   floats   (*it)   on   smooth   sea.waves
        b. Auf   glatten   Meereswogen   schwebt   (*es)   das   Schiff.
            On   smooth   sea.waves   floats   (*it)   the   ship

Table 3.1 *Personal pronouns and imperfective auxiliaries in Papago (Zepeda 1983:18f.)*

	Personal pronouns		Imperfective auxiliaries	
	Singular	Plural	Singular	Plural
1	'a:ñi	'a:cim	añ	'ac
2	'a:pi	'a:pim	'ap	'am
3	hegai	hegam	'o	'o

Second is the fact that not only dummy subjects, but even personal pronoun subjects in so-called non-pro-drop languages, appear obligatorily under the same conditions (Thurneysen 1892 on Medieval French). Third is the fact that the apparently non-pro-drop languages are not a random assortment of say half of the world's languages, but essentially the V2 Germanic languages, and a small number of Romance languages that may have borrowed the V2 target directly from German: in particular, French and Romansch.[1] Indeed, the correlation between V2 and pro-drop still subsists: it is most transparent in Icelandic, partial in German and largely obscured in modern English and French (Haiman 1974). Nor were words meaning 'it' or 'there' the only placeholders. In Medieval Romance, SIC 'thus' > *sì/si* was similarly pressed into service as a simple placeholder to fulfil the V2 constraint (see Fleischman 1992; Ledgeway 2008).

This kind of phenomenon can be recognized in languages outside Germanic. Papago, a Piman language of Arizona, has an Aux/2 target comparable to the Germanic V2 target, as do a number of neighbouring languages of the family (Hill 2005). As can be seen from Table 3.1, the obligatory progressive auxiliary in both first and second persons is a reduced form of the personal pronoun.

The presence of the auxiliary renders the personal pronoun completely redundant and hence optional as a marker of person. Thus, both the following are grammatical:

(34) a. Hegai   'o   cicwi
          3SG   3SG.IPFV   play
          'S/he is/was playing.'
     b. Cicwi   'o
          play   3SG.IPFV
          'S/he is/was playing.'

[1] The editors point out that it is difficult to see how medieval varieties such as Old Neapolitan and Old Sardinian could have borrowed V2 from German; and that, moreover, in Old French/Old Gallo-Romance and Old Italian, when they were V2, pro-drop displayed an asymmetric distribution – pro-drop in root clauses and non-pro-drop in subordinate clauses. The author's response is that these are details. The overarching fact is that the so-called pro-drop languages are geographically restricted to a tiny area of the earth, and that this area is the one where V2 is also a consistent typological feature.

The following, however, is not grammatical, because the auxiliary occupies forbidden initial position:

(35)   *'o   cicwi
       3SG.IPFV   play
       'S/he is/was playing.'

That is, in sentences with S Aux V(O) order, the personal pronoun subject is indeed obligatory, but strictly as a placeholder. In all sentences with other constituents in sentence-initial position, the personal pronoun subject is apparently optional. Thus the distribution of personal pronoun subjects in Papago described in Zepeda (1983) passim is almost exactly the distribution described for personal pronoun subjects in Medieval French by Thurneysen (1892).

3.5.5   INFL as a Clitic in Present-Day English

The last-resort verb *do* in Chomsky's formulation of *do*-insertion is generally identified as an auxiliary verb. It is clear, however, that this meaningless 'auxiliary' does not indicate tense, aspect or mood, or any other semantic category in Present-day English. Consequently it may not be correct to think of it as a grammaticalized auxiliary verb at all, since its actual function is not semantic. So what is its function today? It is notable that the INFL or finite verbal desinence for which it provides a host occupies second position within the verb (as it does for all Indo-European) and that, like a clitic, it migrates into this position (explicitly, in *Syntactic Structures*, from initial position via 'Affix-hopping'). At least in Chomsky's formulation, *do* also functions as a mere placeholder, which prevents the INFL morpheme from remaining stranded and occurring as the initial constituent of the V when this migration is blocked.

In that case, it would be possible to identify both the auxiliary-like functions of this exotic quondam verb (prohibitive marker and placeholder) as exaptations of what was by 1600 meaningless and almost random junk.

(Where this junk itself originated from, what the grammaticalization process was which produced it, is another matter. A number of investigators have identified it as a causative auxiliary; another possibility is that its function as a pro-verb may have provided its original point of entry into the auxiliarization cycle. But that is not our concern in this brief outline.)

3.6   Conclusion

The above survey provisionally suggests that exaptation, in contradistinction to grammaticalization, but very much like other promotion processes such as degrammaticalization and lexicalization, is largely stochastic and opportunistic. While there are well-worn recurrent grooves of grammaticalization (see Bybee, Perkins and Pagliuca 1994; Heine and Kuteva 2002, 2007), functional promotion seems to make do with comparatively random bits of input stuff. With the exception of the various placeholding functions, which are motivated by a drift towards paradigm coherence, and which seem to recur in a variety of languages with canonical word-formation patterns (e.g. consistent syllable structure in Khmer or Olgolo) or syntactic targets (e.g. clitics or verbs second in Indo-European or Papago), the results or output of exaptation are *a priori* unpredictable. That is, except in hindsight there is no real telling what creative uses may be made of junk from one language to the next (see Heine 2003; Haspelmath 2004).

References

Boesch, C. 1993. 'Aspects of transmission of tool use in wild chimpanzees', in K. Gibso and T. Ingold (eds.), *Tools, language, and cognition in human evolution*. Cambridge University Press, pp. 171–83.

Breivik, L. 1983. *Existential there: A synchronic and diachronic study*. Bergen: Department of English, University of Bergen.

Browne, W. 1974. 'The problem of clitic placement in Serbo-Croatian', in R. Brecht and C. Chvany (eds.), *Slavic transformational syntax*, vol. 10. Ann Arbor: Michigan Slavic Materials, pp. 36–52.

Bybee, J., Perkins, R. and Pagliuca, W. 1994. *The evolution of grammar: Tense, aspect and modality in languages of the world*. University of Chicago Press.

Chomsky, N. 1957. *Syntactic structures*. The Hague: Mouton.

Cook, E.-D. 2004. *A grammar of Dene Suline (Chipewyan) (Algonquian and Iroquoian Linguistics Special Athabaskan Number Memoir 17)*. Winnipeg: Algonkian & Iroquoian Linguistics.

Danto, A. 1983. *The transfiguration of the commonplace*. Cambridge, MA: Harvard University Press.

Darmesteter, A. 1887. *La vie des mots étudiée dans leurs significations*. Paris: Delagrave.

Dixon, R. M. W. 1970. 'Olgolo syllable structure and what they are doing about it', *Linguistic Inquiry* 1: 273–6.

Ellegard, A. 1953. *The auxiliary DO: The establishment and regulation of its use in English*. Stockholm: Almkvist & Wiksell.

Faltz, L. 1998. *The Navajo verb*. Albuquerque: University of New Mexico Press.

Fleischman, S. 1992. 'Discourse and diachrony: The rise and fall of Old French *si*', in M. Gerritsen and D. Stein (eds.), *Internal and external factors in syntactic change*. The Hague: Mouton de Gruyter, pp. 433–73.

Franks, S. 1998. 'Clitics in Slavic', paper presented at the Comparative Slavic Morphosyntax Workshop, Spencer, IN, June.

Givón, T. 1979. *On understanding grammar*. New York: Academic Press.

Gould, S. and Vrba, E. 1982. 'Exaptation: A missing term in the science of form', *Paleobiology* 8: 4–15.

Gregerson, K. 1984. 'Pharynx symbolism in Rengao phonology', *Lingua* 62: 209–38.

Haiman, J. 1974. *Targets and syntactic change*. The Hague: Mouton.

　1998. 'Possible sources of infixation in Khmer', *Studies in Language* 22: 595–617.

　1994. 'Ritualization and the development of language', in W. Pagliuca (ed.), *Perspectives on grammaticalization*. Amsterdam: John Benjamins, pp. 3–32.

　2011. *Cambodian: Khmer*. Amsterdam: John Benjamins.

Haiman, J. and Ourn, N. 2003. 'Nouns, verbs, and syntactic backsliding in Khmer', *Studies in Language* 27(3): 505–28.

Haspelmath, M. 2004. 'On directionality in language change with particular reference to grammaticalization', in O. Fischer, M. Norde and H. Perridon (eds.), *Up and down the cline: The nature of grammaticalization*. Amsterdam: John Benjamins, pp. 17–44.

Heine, B. 2003. 'On degrammaticalization', in B. Blake and K. Burridge (eds.), *Historical linguistics 2001*. Amsterdam: John Benjamins, pp. 163–79.

Heine, B. and Kuteva, T. 2002. *World lexicon of grammaticalization*. Cambridge University Press.

　2007. *The genesis of grammar*. Oxford University Press.

Hill, J. 2005. *A grammar of Cupeño*. California: University of California Press.

Hill, V. 2013. 'The stronghold in the Balkans: Early Modern Romanian infinitives', paper presented at the 45th meeting of the Societas Linguistica Europae, Split University.

Jakobson, R. [1931] 1972. 'Principles of historical phonology', in A. Keiler (ed.), *A reader in historical linguistics*. New York: Holt, pp. 121–38.

Jespersen, O. 1943. *A modern English grammar on historical principles*, vols. I–VII. London and Copenhagen: Allen & Unwin.

Kiparsky, P. 1995. 'Indo-European origins of Germanic syntax', in A. Battye and I. Roberts (eds.), *Clause structure and language change*. Oxford University Press, pp. 140–69.

Kuryłowicz, J. [1965] 1975. 'The evolution of grammatical categories', in J. Kuryłowicz (ed.), *Esquisses linguistiques II*. Munich: Wilhelm Fink Verlag, pp. 38–54.

Langacker, R. 1977. 'Syntactic reanalysis', in C. Li (ed.), *Mechanisms of syntactic change*. Austin: University of Texas Press, pp. 57–139.

Lass, R. 1990. 'How to do things with junk: Exaptation in language evolution', *Journal of Linguistics* 26: 79–102.

Ledgeway, A. 2008. 'Satisfying V2 in Early Romance: Merge vs Move', *Journal of Linguistics* 44: 437–70.

Marchand, H. 1960. *Categories and types of English word formation.* Wiesbaden: Harrassowitz.

Margulies, L. and Sagan, D. 1997. *Microcosmos.* Berkeley: University of California Press.

Matisoff, J. 1973. *The grammar of Lahu.* Berkeley: University of California Press.

Mayr, E. 2001. *What evolution is.* New York: Basic Books.

Nguyen, D. Th. 1965. 'Parallel constructions in Vietnamese', *Lingua* 15: 125–39.

Norde, M. 2010. 'Degrammaticalization: Three common controversies', unpublished MS.

Ourn, N. and Haiman, J. 2000. 'Symmetrical compounds in Khmer', *Studies in Language* 24: 483–514.

Pinnow, H.-J. 1978. 'Remarks on the structure of the Khmer syllable and word', *Mon-Khmer Studies* 8: 131–37.

Pott, A. 1862. *Die Doppelung(Reduplikation, Gemination) als eines der wichtigsten Bildungsmittel der Sprache.* NP: Lemgo & Detmold.

Prakorb, C.-n. 1992. 'The problem of aspirates in Central Khmer and Northern Khmer', *Mon-Khmer Studies* 22: 252–6.

Rice, K. 1989. *A grammar of Slave.* Berlin and New York: Mouton de Gruyter.

Roffe, G. E. 1975. 'Rhyme, reduplication, etc. in Lao', in J. G. Harris and J. R. Chamberlain (eds.), *Studies in Tai linguistics in honor of William J. Gedney.* Bangkok: Central Institute of English Language, pp. 285–317.

Sadock, J. and Zwicky, A. 1985. 'Speech act distinctions in syntax', in T. Shopen (ed.), *Typology and syntactic description,* vol. 1: *Clause structure.* Cambridge University Press, pp. 155–96.

Schmerling, S. 1982. 'How imperatives are special and how they aren't', in R. Schneider, K. Tuite and R. Chametzky (eds.), *Papers from the parasession on nondeclaratives.* Chicago Linguistics Society, pp. 202–18.

Stanford, J. 2007. 'Sui adjective reduplication as poetic morpho-phonology', *Journal of East Asian Linguistics* 16(2): 87–111.

Thurneysen, R. 1892. 'Zur Stellung des Verbums im Altfranzösischen', *Zeitschrift für romanische Philologie* 16: 289–307.

Tiktin, H. 1905. *Rumänisches Elementarbuch.* Heidelberg: Carl Winter.

Tinbergen, N. 1952. '"Derived" activities', *Quarterly Journal of Biology* 27: 1–32.

Twaddell, W. F. 1938. 'A note on Old High German umlaut', *Monatshefte für deutschen Unterricht* 37: 177–81.

Vajda, E. 2010. 'A Siberian link with Na-Dene languages', in J. Kari and B. Potter (eds.), *The Siberian–Yeniseian connection.* Fairbanks: University of Abaska, Department of Anthropology, pp. 33–99.

Wackernagel, J. 1892. 'Über ein Gesetz der indogermanischen Wortstellung', *Indogermanische Forschungen* 1: 333–436.

Wälchli, B. 2005. *Co-compounds and natural coordination.* Oxford University Press.

Warner, A. 1993. *English auxiliaries: Structure and history.* Cambridge University Press.

Weisser, E. 2008. 'Ashkii Bizaad: Verbal morphology loss in one young speaker's Navajo', unpublished thesis, Macalester College.

Wiliams, J. (ed.) Forthcoming. *The esthetics of grammar.* Cambridge University Press.

Wilson, E. O. 1975. *Sociobiology (abridged edition).* Cambridge, MA: Harvard University Press.

Zepeda, O. 1983. *A Tohon O'odham grammar.* Tucson: University of Arizona Press.

4

Reanalysis

Nerea Madariaga

4.1 Introduction

Although reanalysis is commonly acknowledged to play a central role in syntactic change, there is no point of agreement about what 'reanalysis' exactly means. Reanalysis is usually defined as the emergence of a new linguistic structure, but this definition leaves open the interpretation of many aspects.

In this chapter, I will test to what extent our theoretical framework and previous assumptions define our view on reanalysis and its properties. The major issues discussed will be the following:

(i) The motivations and triggers of reanalysis, linking to other processes: analogy, grammaticalization, parameter setting, the role of surface ambiguity of the data, and the internal or external character of the initial trigger;
(ii) The nature of reanalysis: whether it is an explanatory mechanism or a real process, gradual or abrupt, and whether it has immediate consequences at a surface level or not;
(iii) The locus of reanalysis: the moment in a speaker's life when reanalysis can happen; during the language acquisition period (in childhood), or once the grammar is already established (in adults).

This chapter is organized as follows: the causes, nature and locus of reanalysis will be discussed together with the major conceptions about reanalysis under different theoretical approaches. In §4.2, I will introduce the classic conception of reanalysis and subsequent redefinitions of it;

I would like to thank the editors of the volume, Adam Ledgeway and Ian Roberts, as well as David Willis, for their comments. This work is part of the VALAL FFI2014-53675-P and FFI2014-57260-P research projects, funded by the Spanish Ministry of Science and Innovation, and has been supported by the research group on linguistics UFI11/14 (funded by the UPV/EHU) and the research group on historical linguistics IT 698–13 (funded by the Government of the Basque Country).

in §4.3, I will review the proposals on reanalysis within functionalist and usage-based models; and finally, §4.4 is devoted to the formal and generative approaches to reanalysis.

I will illustrate the different approaches to reanalysis focusing on a specific syntactic phenomenon in different languages (Finnish, English and Russian), namely, the reanalysis of subjects in non-finite structures. The study of different approaches to similar instances of reanalysis will enable the reader to better understand the divergences and similarities between the existing conceptions.

4.2 The 'Classic' View of Reanalysis

The first definition of syntactic reanalysis was originally borrowed from phonology by Langacker (1977: 58), who characterized it as the 'change in the structure of an expression or class of expressions that does not involve any immediate or intrinsic modification of its surface manifestation'.

In the same book, Timberlake (1977) proposed that syntactic change consists of three successive steps:

– Reanalysis: the rise of new underlying relationships and rules in a grammar;
– Actualization: mapping out the consequences of the reanalysis; and
– Diffusion: the spread of the new analysis throughout a population of speakers.

This hypothesis implies that a given output can be triggered by two different underlying grammars, and that reanalysis is a shift between two of those 'alternative' grammars, i.e. the creation of a new structure on the basis of ambiguous surface data. Actualization is the subsequent manifestation of the new underlying grammar as an innovative output, i.e. the production of new data no longer licensed directly by the original ambiguous data.

Let us briefly present Timberlake's (1977: 143ff.) example: the rise of subject-to-object in Finnish. In older Finnish, case marking on direct objects varied depending on the syntactic construction: the object displayed (i) accusative case encoding with regular active verbs; (ii) partitive case, when the matrix verb was negated; and (iii) nominative case, when the matrix verb was imperative or passive. In older Finnish (in the writings by Agricola, studied by Ojansuu 1909), the subjects of participial clauses also underwent this distribution of cases, as shown in (1a–c), from Timberlake (1977: 145).

(1) a. **seurakunnan** hen lupasi pysyueisen oleuan.
     congregation.ACC he promised long-lasting being
     'He promised the congregation would be long-lasting.'

b. eike lwle **site**   syndic oleuan.
   not   think this.PART sin   being
   'Does one not think this to be a sin?'

c. homaitan se **tauara**   ia   Jumalan **lahia**   poiseleua.
   observed   goods.NOM and God   gift.NOM lacking
   'It is observed that the goods and the gift of God are lacking.'

In Modern Finnish, however, the underlying subject of participial clauses is always in genitive case, no matter whether the matrix verb is active (2a), negated (2b) or passive (2c) (following examples of Modern Finnish from Timberlake 1977: 145–6):

(2) a. Näin **lapsen**   panevan kirjeen taskuunsa.
        saw   child.GEN(ACC) putting   letter   pocket
        'I saw the child putting the letter in his pocket.'

     b. En   sanonut **lapsen**   tulevan.
        not say   child.GEN coming
        'I did not say the child would come.'

     c. **Lapsen**   huomattiin varastavan parhaan hevosen.
        child.GEN observed   stealing   best   horse
        'The child was observed stealing the best horse.'

According to Timberlake (1977), in older Finnish, the underlying subject of the participial clause was analysed by the speakers as the object of the matrix verb, while in Modern Finnish, this underlying subject was reanalysed as the subject of the participle proper.

The first step of the syntactic change at issue was *reanalysis* of certain ambiguous surface data; ambiguity of the data arose in environments like (2a), where a morphological syncretism between the accusative and genitive cases (in singular nouns) took place. After the syncretism, the form *lapsen* 'child' could be parsed as accusative or as genitive case. Therefore, examples such as those in (1a) and (2a), were analysed by the speakers of older Finnish as represented in (3a), whereas in Modern Finnish, after reanalysis, the example given in (2a) was reanalysed as (3b):

(3) a. Grammar 1: [NP-subject matrix-V NP-object [participle-V]] (=1a, 2a)
     b. Grammar 2: [NP-subject matrix-V [NP-subject participle-V]] (=2a)

At this point, the reanalysis represented in (3b) did not affect the surface data. Speakers with Grammar 1 analysed the NP *lapsen* 'child' as the accusative object of the matrix verb (3a), while speakers with Grammar 2 analysed it as the genitive subject of the participial clause (3b). The output, however, remained the same, given the formal coincidence of the genitive and accusative cases on *lapsen* in (2a).

In this conception, *ambiguity of the surface data* in a single environment is enough for a construction to be reanalysed, under the condition that this environment is the unmarked (and most frequent) one. Example (2a) is the appropriate environment for the reanalysis represented in (3b), as it includes the unmarked and most frequent form of the matrix verb (active).

Once reanalysed, the new structure spreads to more marked (and less frequent) environments. This is called *actualization*, the second step of the process of change. In Timberlake's (1977) example, the reanalysis in (3b) spread to negated, imperative and passive environments (2b–c), i.e. more marked contexts which, unlike (2a), were not affected by case syncretism of the accusative and genitive cases. The objects of the matrix verbs in (1b–c) were marked with non-syncretic cases (partitive and nominative, respectively), so they could not display ambiguity of analysis at any point in the process. But after the reanalysis in (3b), speakers 'actualized' all these objects, reinterpreting them as subjects. As a result, all of them started to be marked with genitive case, the only case marking available for underlying subjects in Finnish participial clauses.

A crucial idea in this conception of reanalysis is the dissociation between underlying grammars and the outputs produced by these grammars. This dissociation links to Andersen's (1973) *abduction* principle, which determines the way in which grammar acquisition proceeds between different generations of speakers (see Chapter 14, this volume): first of all, it determines that learners do not have direct access to the grammar of the previous generation, but only to its output, according to the following schema, which goes back to Klima (1965):

(4)   Grammar 1  Grammar 2

       Output 1   Output 2 ...

The abduction principle accounts for the fact itself that reanalysis can take place: abductive inference 'proceeds from an observed result, invokes a law, and infers that something may be the case' (Andersen 1973: 775). The conclusion resulting from such an inference process can be wrong, and it is precisely these flawed conclusions that make language change possible. Otherwise, if language acquisition operated through deductive or inductive inferences, which lead to correct conclusions if the premises are correct, language change would never take place, as the inferences made by learners would make Grammar 2 converge with Grammar 1.

Subsequent elaborated versions of Langacker's/Timberlake's (1977) reanalysis-actualization process are offered in Harris and Campbell (1995) and Andersen (2001), among others. For example, Harris and Campbell (1995) specify and illustrate with detail the different aspects of syntax affected by reanalysis (constituency, hierarchical structure, category labels and grammatical relations). They also detect the reverse process of Langacker's reanalysis, which they call extension, that is, changes in the surface manifestation of a syntactic pattern that do not involve immediate modifications of the underlying structure (see Chapter 5, this volume).

4.3 Reanalysis in Usage-Based Models

The conception of reanalysis in certain authors working within usage-based models can be defined as a 'functional' interpretation of Timberlake's (1977) hypothesis. These authors focus both on the actualization process (the gradual manifestation of a reanalysis in language use) and on the initial data that give rise to reanalysis, because these are the two aspects more clearly affected by language usage, frequency, routinization and related factors (see Hopper and Traugott 2003; Bybee 2007, 2010; Mithun 2011; De Smet 2012). As in synchronic language processes, functional approaches assume that language change too is the result of language usage, of the choices made by a speaker in his/her interaction with an addressee (Traugott 2002).

Such choices are made by adult speakers rather than child learners, so that the *locus of reanalysis* in these models is basically the adult period (Croft 1995). Fischer (2007) proposes that change reproduces, at least in part, certain mechanisms of language acquisition typical of childhood, but specifies that change takes place with the use of language by fluent (adult) speakers, triggered by pragmatic factors, speech errors and the like.

As for the nature of reanalysis, usage-based models do not usually consider potential *ambiguity* of the surface data as a sufficient reason for change. Some scholars within these models (see, among others, De Smet 2009; Garrett 2012; Kiparsky 2012), argue that Langacker's (1977) conception of reanalysis lacks an explanatory force *per se*, in the sense that it describes the way in which change takes place, but does not explain its causes. Instead, most functionalists try to reduce reanalysis to more general explanatory cognitive principles, usually *analogy* and *grammaticalization* (see Chapters 1 and 5, this volume). But, as we will see, this relation is accounted for in different ways, depending on the author.

Reinterpreting Timberlake's (1977) conception of syntactic change, Hopper and Traugott (2003) define as analogical the rule generalization by which a new structure produced by reanalysis spreads to other environments, i.e. they consider analogy as the underlying force in actualization.

Another interpretation of the role of analogy is found in Fischer (2007, 2011), who considers reanalysis not something speakers 'do', at least with reference to language processing, but a concept of the analyst. For her, reanalysis is a vacuous term, and what is usually described as reanalysis can be reduced to diverse metaphorical or metonymic processes (analogy, grammaticalization or other functional mechanisms). According to Anttila

(1989, 2003), based on older ideas, such as Meillet ([1912] 1958) and Kuryłowicz (1964), metaphorical processes in change operate through analogy (the iconic mode of thinking at a paradigmatic level, operating with similarities between objects), while metonymic processes (operating at a syntagmatic level with associations between objects) are realized in grammaticalization and reanalysis. Fischer (2007:121ff.), following Itkonen (2005), argues that analogy is not only a second step after reanalysis (i.e. actualization), but also a condition on it, because the new form that arises is not totally new, but analogical with one that is already in use elsewhere.

The role of analogy in syntactic change is maximized by other authors. De Smet (2009), Garrett (2012) and Kiparsky (2012) consider analogy as the real process of reanalysis, and not as a mere factor playing a role in it. Kiparsky (2012) describes reanalysis as optimization, which stands for the analogical process that eliminates arbitrary complexity from the grammar on the basis of other pre-existing patterns in the language (see Chapter 5, this volume).

De Smet (2009) argues that reanalysis in Langacker's (1977) definition contains a logical flaw, because it implies that a new structure can be created on the only basis of certain ambiguity which, he argues, only exists once change has taken place, i.e. in retrospect. Let us take, for instance, Timberlake's (1977) Finnish example (2a): initially, its only possible parsing was (3a). Only *after* (2a) is reanalysed as (3b), can we speak of ambiguity in parsing the data in (2a). In other words, ambiguity does not precede reanalysis but is created after an alternative analysis of the original data arises (so it cannot be the cause of reanalysis).

What causes reanalysis, then? De Smet (2009) argues that, in order to find out how reanalysis takes place, it must be decomposed into more basic mechanisms of change, namely, semantic change, analogy and automation, all of which are acknowledged mechanisms of synchronic language use, and widely assumed by proponents of usage-based models. He shows reanalysis to be a sort of epiphenomenon with respect to the real processes of syntactic change.

Let us look at a simplified version of one of his examples: the revision of the classic explanation of the development of English infinitive subjects and the emergence of the construction 'for ... to infinitive' (De Smet 2009: 1743ff.), which is parallel to Timberlake's (1977) Finnish example of reanalysis, introduced in §4.2 (following examples from De Smet 2009: 1743):

(5)　　a. It is generally recognized to be [good **for people**] [to own their own houses].

　　　　a′. It is generally recognized to be [good] [**for people** to own their own houses].

　　　　b. In these cases it is [wise] [**for patients** to be taken to casualty first].

Example (5a) illustrates a potentially ambiguous instance, as represented by the different bracketing possibilities in (5a) and (5a′): (5a) stands for a structure, where the PP *for people* depends on the previous adjective *good*, and the whole phrase is followed by an infinitive clause, represented as Grammar 1 in (6a) below. (5a′) represents an alternative analysis, in which the PP is now the syntactic subject of the infinitive clause, Grammar 2 in (6b).

(6)   a. Grammar 1: [[A *for* NP] [*to* infinitive-V]]   (=5a)
       b. Grammar 2: [A [*for* NP-subject *to* infinitive-V]]   (=5a′)

As a second step in the change process, we find (5b), an already reanalysed construction, which displays a single possible analysis, the PP *for patients* being the subject of the infinitive clause; compare the grammaticality and completeness of *This is good for you* with the ungrammatical **This is wise for you*. Then, according to the classic accounts (Fischer 1988; Harris and Campbell 1995: 62), (5a–a′) was the source context of the reanalysis from (6a) into (6b), which spread later to other contexts (5b), yielding Grammar 2 as the only analysis available.

De Smet's (2009: 1746ff.) revision of this classic account goes as follows: drawing from a Middle English corpus (PPCEME), he details the contexts when the first ambiguous and the first reanalysed '*for … to* infinitives' appear. He finds out that the most frequent ambiguous environment in the corpus, the one that allows either (6a) or (6b) as possible interpretations of the data, are extraposed subjects (7a–a′). However, unexpectedly, the most frequent environment of the already reanalysed construction (6b) in the same corpus are not those extraposed subjects, but purpose adjuncts (7b), or verb/noun complements (7c) (following Middle English examples from De Smet 2009: 1744–5):

(7)   a. hit is [a foule þing **for a kyng**] [to iangle moche at þe feste and nouȝt fiȝte in batayle]. (1387, PPCME2)
       a′. hit is [a foule þing] [**for a kyng** to iangle moche at þe feste and nouȝt fiȝte in batayle].
       b. and whan tyme was, the cordes were cutt / and the Trumpetis blew vp, [**for euery man** to do his deuoir]. (1450–99, IMEPC)
       c. the Bysshop of Norwych makyth but delayes in my resonable desyre [**for an eende** to be had in the xxv. marc of Hykelyng]. (1400–49, IMEPC)

This suggests that the environments where the construction '*for … to* infinitive' was ambiguous, and those where it was first reanalysed were different, challenging the classic hypothesis, which proposes that reanalysis originates in a specific initial ambiguous environment.

De Smet's alternative explanation is the following: due to the SOV basic word order in Old English, the object of a *to*-infinitive could precede the infinitive (yielding an OV word order). For independent reasons, the preposition *for* could precede the preposition *to* of the infinitive at that time (8b). As a result of the combination of these two factors, an infinitive object could end up between the prepositions *for* and *to*, followed by an active infinitive, as shown in (8a) (examples of Middle English from De Smet 2009: 1747):

(8)   a. for none envy ne yvel have I drawe this mater togider; but only
          for [goodnesse **to** maintayn], and [errours in falsetees **to** distroy].
          (1400–49, IMEPC)
       b. Ne cam ic noht te ȝiuen ȝew for-bisne ['to set you an example'] of
          mire aȝene wille to donne, ac i cam [**for to** donne mines fader
          wille]. (a1225, HC)

De Smet further argues that, afterwards, SVO word order was fixed in Middle English, but preposed objects as in (8a) still displayed the old OV order ('*for* NP-object *to* infinitive-V'), an irregular and undesirable sequence in a language with VO order. For this reason, grammar exerted such a pressure on these 'irregular' objects that, eventually, they became subjects of a passive infinitive, as in (7c) (e.g. the modern parallel of (8a) would be: *for goodness* **to be maintained**), in accordance with the new SV word order '*for* NP-subject *to* passive-infinitive-V'. This change process involved the following functional mechanisms:

 (i) Analogical reanalysis: it does not imply ambiguity in retrospect, as in Langacker's (1977) model, because the new analysis assigned to a surface sequence is not created out-of-the-blue, but just classifies the sequence as an instance of an already established structure, operating by analogy. In the example introduced here, the original OV structure becomes SV, on the basis of the pre-existing SVO word order.
(ii) Automation: the process by which a specific construction splits from a more general construction through repeated use, and becomes stored independently from its original source. In (8a), the speakers started to store the chunk '*for* NP *to* infinitive', originally a subset of the construction '*for to* infinitive' (8b), as an independent construction. The existence of this model made possible the reanalysis of the original object in (8a) as the subject of a passive infinitive construction, as in (7c).

Garrett (2012) and Kiparsky (2012) also criticize Langacker's 'ambiguity' view on reanalysis, and advocate an account that explains the causes of reanalysis. Garrett (2012) reduces all instances of reanalysis to other acknowledged explanatory devices, namely, analogy or grammaticaliza- tion. Analogy has been already discussed in De Smet's (2009) example, so let us now analyse an example of reanalysis as *grammaticalization* (see Chapter 1, this volume). Grammaticalization, unlike analogy, creates new grammatical categories in an endogenous way, i.e. not necessarily based on previously existing models in the language.

In order to illustrate this, Garrett (2012) offers the example of English 'go-future'. In Garrett's (2012) hypothesis, it is mandatory to have a previous semantic change in a pivot context, within which reanalysis takes place, and from which it spreads to other contexts. In his example, the semantic change was a shift from a meaning of 'motion' in the progressive expression '*be going to* VP' into a prospective future semantics; the pivot context was the one in which *to go* was used as a participal adjunct, followed by an infinitive, as in (9):

(9)   Having [...] two white Leopards and two dragons facing them **as going to engage**, their tounges are done in curiousest wyse. (Register of Riches in *Antiquitates Sarisburienses* (1771) 199 [OED], from Garrett 2012: 67)

According to Garrett (2012), the change in English *go*-future is not a real reanalysis (there is no change in the underlying syntactic structure of the construction), but just the grammaticalization of the verb of motion *go* (in the progressive construction *be going to*) into a prospective future, according to the classic characterization of grammaticalization: a lexical item becomes a grammatical element (here, a regular lexical verb, *to go*, becomes a future auxiliary *be going to*).

4.4   Reanalysis in Formal Approaches

Generative approaches to change usually regard reanalysis as a central mechanism in diachrony (Roberts 2007: 123ff.), in agreement with the proposal about syntactic change put forward by Lightfoot (1979) and subsequent work (1991, 1999, 2006), and widely assumed in the generative linguistic community (Faarlund 1990; Clark and Roberts 1993; Hale 1998; Roberts and Roussou 2003; van Gelderen 2004, 2011; Roberts 2007).

Within this view, reanalysis is not something adult speakers do, i.e. adults do not 'reanalyse' any data or representation of those data. Reanalysis is just a type of 'analysis' of the input a learner receives, a way in which children acquire their grammars. The only difference between 'non-reanalysed' and 'reanalysed' grammars is that, in the case of the former, the learner's grammar converges with the grammar that generated its input, while, in the latter, it does not converge. Non-convergence of grammars is called 'discontinuity or failure of transmission between generations' (see Chapter 24, this volume). Except for that, both converging and non-converging grammars are equal in that they must be acquired afresh, according to the usual procedure of language acquisition, i.e. on the basis of the so-called primary linguistic data (PLD), the input available in a linguistic environment.

From the point of view of an external observer, however, the grammar set by a child who 'reanalysed' has changed, just because it is different with respect to the grammar that generated the input, to which that child was exposed (see Chapter 18, this volume). In this sense, 'syntactic reanalysis' stands for any modification or 'new analysis' within the grammar acquired by a new generation, to the point that 'reanalysis' is often used as a cover term for 'syntactic change'.

Regarding the *locus of reanalysis*, then, formal analyses put syntactic change in childhood, during the language acquisition period, unlike the usage-based models, which locate reanalysis in the adult period. As introduced in §4.1, each approach is bound to different proposals given their prior theoretical assumptions, and this is so also in the case of the locus of reanalysis: in formal linguistics, the 'zero' hypothesis is that our first language syntax is completely acquired in childhood (converging or not with previous grammars), while usage-based models view syntactic change as a result of the expressive necessities of (adult) speakers.

Similarly to the usage-based models, generative diachronic approaches do not support the explanatory force of the *ambiguity of the surface data* in Langacker's (1977) conception of reanalysis. Recall De Smet's (2009) critique of this view: a new structure cannot arise only on the basis of an alleged ambiguity, which is detected once change has taken place, i.e. only after the structure is reanalysed. Admittedly, in cases where a grammar converges with that of the previous generation of speakers, we do not speak of any ambiguity of the PLD.

But even if it cannot be a cause for reanalysis, a certain degree of ambiguity of the data is necessary for change to take place (Roberts 1993, 2007). So how is the ambiguity problem solved in generative grammar? First, by resorting to parameter setting and Universal Grammar – UG (see Chapters 7 and 13, respectively, this volume): UG is understood as the innate system determining possible (and impossible) ways of setting parameters, acquiring structures/features. In this way, UG restricts the range of potential ambiguities in the PLD to those cases, in which different possible parameters can be set during the regular process of language acquisition.

Second, Klima (1965) already noticed that reanalysis takes place not just because a set of data are potentially ambiguous, but because of the accumulation of independent unrelated previous changes, which modify the PLD and complicate them in such a way that reanalysis eventually becomes compulsory. This effect is what Lightfoot (1979) defined later on as 'opacity' of the PLD (see Chapters 15 and 18, this volume).

A further revision of Langacker (1977) concerns the idea that reanalysis goes through a covert rearrangement of the underlying data before it becomes manifest on the surface data. Quite the opposite, generative diachronists claim that reanalysis in a grammar must have *immediate consequences in the output* produced by that grammar. This idea has been made explicit (e.g. in Whitman 2000) after the introduction of the Minimalist Programme, which gave up the idea of the existence of deep and surface levels of syntax.

Related to this, we find the question of the *gradualness* vs *abruptness* of reanalysis, much discussed in the literature about syntactic change (see Chapter 21, this volume). From a formal point of view, reanalysis is essentially abrupt, in the sense that grammars are acquired afresh by each generation of speakers. Reanalysis viewed as the acquisition of a specific structure is itself discrete (Lightfoot 1979, 1991 and later works; see Chapter 6, this volume).

Many alleged instances of gradual change can be reduced to discrete change according to this view: the clearest case is when a reanalysis spreads from speaker to speaker through a linguistic community (Kroch 1989).

Also reanalysis in a specific item/environment can be gradually spread to more items/environments, which was envisaged as successive actualizations in Timberlake's (1977) system, and as new (re)analyses in formal grammar, each of them created anew (Lightfoot 1991: 160ff.).

In general, variation in the surface productions of a language is observable: according to the typological and usage-based models, this is due to the gradual nature of change, but in the generative framework, much of this gradualness has received alternative explanations.

As a general rule, pure optionality (without any phonological or semantic effect, i.e. not detectable at the linguistic interfaces) is not allowed in the generative approach: in the case of syntactic change, a single speaker either acquires a reanalysed variant or not, but cannot acquire both. An explanation for the optionality seen in the texts produced by the speakers of a language is the hypothesis of 'competing grammars' (Kroch 1989; Pintzuk 1999; Yang 2002): when a change is taking place in a language, some speakers have access to two different variants of the same form or structure, an old variant and newly created one. The speakers who display both variants in fact display two different grammars (diglossia), and resort to code-switching while using one or the other, in much the same way as bilinguals do with their different languages.

An alternative, or rather complementary, explanation for a 'diglossia' view on competing grammars is that they can coexist in a speaker because they belong to different linguistic levels. The existence of two variants in the linguistic productions can signal that one of the variants belongs to the linguistic competence (I-grammar) of the speaker, while the other is 'external' to this competence, a variant put to use episodically in the set of utterances produced by a community of speakers, also called E-language (Uriagereka 1997, after Chomsky 1986: 7–8; Lightfoot 1999; Lasnik and Sobin 2000).

Finally, formal diachronic accounts of 'gradience' have succeeded in showing: (i) that the alleged non-discreteness of lexical categories is not real, but seems so because of the fine-grained distinctions that separate one category from another (Roberts 2010); and (ii) that some apparent instances of gradient change can be also accounted for in structural terms (van Gelderen 2010), as separated instances of successive discrete changes in different morphosyntactic conditions, or at different language levels (Madariaga 2012).

An important issue in formal approaches to reanalysis concerns the explanation of what exactly *causes reanalysis*. Most accounts rely on the idea that reanalysis takes place after a series of unrelated changes complicate the grammar, and somehow 'obscure' the PLD a learner receives, resulting in the acquisition of a new grammar/structure (Lightfoot's (1979) 'opacity' principle, already introduced in this section). But what causes those previous changes in the PLD? To answer this question, two distinct views can be distinguished; they do not exclude each other, and are often complementary, but most authors favour one or the other view in their assumptions about reanalysis.

I will term the first view on the causes of reanalysis the 'contingent' view: according to this view, the triggers of reanalysis originate extra-syntactically (externally to I-grammars), in the language performance or E-language (Faarlund 1990; Lightfoot 1991, 1999). This view leaves no space for any endogenous causes of reanalysis: the conditions of language transmission are first altered from the 'outside' by random sociolinguistic or language-usage factors, such as language contact, and linguistic fashions. There are also other 'extrasyntactic', but 'intralinguistic' factors, playing a role in this initial trigger, e.g. phonological erosion or previous morphological changes (Roberts 2007: 126), and the drop of frequency of some portion of the PLD under a threshold that prevents it from being acquired in the way the previous generation did (Lightfoot 1991, 1999; Clark and Roberts 1993). The unpredictability of all these changes in the E-language makes reanalysis itself unpredictable and contingent, requiring a local, case-by-case explanation.

This approach accounts for the so-called '*actuation' problem*, namely, why, if we observe a specific change that takes place in a language at a certain time, we cannot predict that the same change will take place in another language or at another time under similar circumstances (see Chapter 19, this volume). This problem was posited by Weinreich, Labov and Herzog (1968), who wondered whether languages change intrinsically or, on the contrary, only change as a result of language contact and other external sociolinguistic factors. Kroch (2001) argues that it may depend on the language level: for instance, changes in pronunciation can arise spontaneously on the mere basis of language use, while endogenous changes at a syntactic level might not exist.

The weak side of the contingency approach is, as the actuation problem implicitly evidences, that it cannot foresee change, whereas some predictive value is always desirable in science. This empty space is what tries to fill what I will call the 'universality' view which, agreeing with the previous view in many respects, aims to formulate some predictions and find specific regularities in reanalysis at the level of specific structures.

Following this line of thought, Roberts (1993, 2007) tries to predict the structures that learners will acquire, assuming that they acquire the simplest possible option that stems from the available PLD (in a restrictive interpretation of Lightfoot's 'opacity'). In a similar spirit, van Gelderen (2004, 2011) proposes the so-called cycles of grammaticalization, which are not contingent, but universal, and subject to general design constraints, mainly Economy motivations (see Chapter 22, this volume).

The dichotomy between contingency vs universality of syntactic change is founded on the different assumptions regarding language acquisition adopted by the authors. Generative diachronists usually agree in that: (i) acquisition proceeds very accurately, and leaves little room for change; this is called the diachronic 'inertia' of syntax (Longobardi 2001; see Chapter 20, this volume); (ii) reanalysis arises as a result of imperfect learning, according to Andersen's (1973) abductive scheme introduced in §4.2 (see Chapters 14 and 24, this volume).

Most formal accounts agree that imperfect learning can be attributed to the effect of previous changes in the PLD, as the acquisition mechanism is not itself error-driven. However, a conceptual dichotomy with regard to acquisition and change can be distinguished, yielding what I will call a 'bias-based' model vs a 'cue-based' model.

The 'bias-based' model accepts that change can be driven by certain internal biases, which lead the learner to construct an optimal grammar, even if it does not converge with the grammar of the previous generation of speakers. According to van Gelderen (2004, 2011), change is not the mere result of transmission errors, but is driven by a natural tendency towards structure simplification; the causes of change are then internal principles that bias learners towards simpler structures. The observed directionality of change is, in her view, due to Chomsky's (2005) 'third factor': language-independent principles (structural architecture, computational efficiency, data processing) that render language as an optimal solution to the interface (phonological and semantic) conditions (see Chapter 22, this volume).

Another example of the role of Chomsky's (2005) third factor in reanalysis is the model of change as a result of a 'least-effort' learning strategy. In Roberts (2007: 267ff.), Roberts and Holmberg (2010) and Roberts (2012), the syntactic parameters are arranged according to 'hierarchies', which represent a relative complexity or 'markedness' of some options with respect to others, when it comes to acquiring a parameter (see also Chapter 17, this volume). Marked options represent a less desirable option of setting a parameter (and therefore, a less probable result of change), as opposed to less marked, more economical options, which turn out to be more frequent results of change. In order to establish these hierarchies (which allow us to make predictions about change), we must assume the so-called 'uniformitarian' hypothesis (Roberts 2007: 264ff.), which specifies that UG includes a set of parametric options with the same markedness properties across languages and time (see Chapter 16, this volume).

The 'cue-based' model was proposed by Lightfoot (1999, 2006), based on work on language acquisition by, for example, Dresher and Kaye (1990), Fodor (1998) and Dresher (1999). According to this view, the UG specifies a set of parameters, together with a series of 'second-order' data, usually called 'cues' or 'triggers', each one associated with a specific parameter. Learners have direct access to those second-order data or cues which they detect in the PLD, and which help them acquire the corresponding parameter. In this view, there are not marked/ unmarked options that internally bias reanalysis. In accordance with the 'contingent' view introduced above, only external modifications of the PLD (due to sociolinguistic or extrasyntactic factors, or previous independent changes) can be responsible for modifications in the distribution of the relevant cues and, in consequence, drive towards a new way of acquiring a structure.

With respect to other phenomena of syntactic change, most formal approaches consider them a subtype or identify them as instances of 'new analyses' during acquisition. For example, in the generative framework, *grammaticalization* is usually subsumed under this general conception of reanalysis, and characterized as epiphenomenal. This conception is at odds with the functional accounts, e.g. Haspelmath (1998), which consider grammaticalization as a distinct phenomenon requiring a differentiated set of explanations.

The relation between grammaticalization and reanalysis is specifically addressed in Newmeyer (1998: 241ff.). Following previous studies such as Roberts (1993), Newmeyer argues that the standard definition of grammaticalization ('a lexical item becomes grammatical, or a grammatical item becomes "more grammatical"') is a subtype of the definition of reanalysis, if we reword the former as 'an item of a certain category is reanalysed as belonging to another category'.

Roberts and Roussou (2003), van Gelderen (2004) and Wu (2004) analyse classic instances of grammaticalization as 'upwards' or 'up-the-tree' reanalyses, which take place when an element is realized in a higher position in the structure. Grammaticalization is viewed as an instance of upward reanalysis, namely, raising a lexical category to a functional head position, followed by base-generation of the category in the new position.

This is, for instance, Roberts and Roussou's (2003: 37ff.) explanation of the grammaticalization (reanalysis) of the Old and Middle English modal verbal elements (*can, must, shall*, etc.) as auxiliaries, also analysed by Lightfoot (1979). Example (10a) corresponds to the beginning of the fifteenth century, while (10b) illustrates the ungrammaticality of its modern equivalent:

(10) a. but it sufficeth too hem **to kunne** her *Pater Noster* ...   (Lollard sermon 2.325; from Roberts and Roussou 2003: 38)

  b. *But it is sufficient for them **to can** the *Pater Noster*   (Modern English)

Together with many other properties analysed by Lightfoot (1979) and summarized by Roberts and Roussou (2003), the ability of *kunne* (the modern *can*) to function as a regular verb in (10a) shows that such elements initially behaved as verbs and, as regular verbs did in Old English, underwent V-to-T movement, as represented in (11a). Afterwards, an accumulation of previous independent changes 'obscured' the cue necessary to acquire the V-to-T movement of these modals, and they started to be directly merged in the T position (11b), and therefore lost their verbal properties:

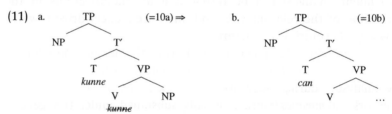

This preference for a learner to analyse an element as directly merged in a certain position, rather than as moved from somewhere else (the principle 'Merge over Move'), is in accordance with the general Economy principles that govern syntactic derivations in the minimalist version of the generative approach. In this view, reanalysis is attributed to Economy motivations, whereby new functional material arises as a result of structural simplification. Other phenomena that fall under the category of 'reanalysis' in formal accounts are changes in categorical features (Whitman 2000, who calls this type of change 'relabelling'; Longobardi 2001), and word-order changes, which basically can be accounted for in terms of loss or gain of features driving movement (Roberts 1993).

As in the previous two sections, I will illustrate the formal approaches to reanalysis with the help of a third example involving non-finite subjects, namely, the loss of overt dative subjects in Old Russian subordinate infinitive clauses, studied in Madariaga (2011).

Old Russian was a 'pro-drop' language, meaning that it licensed non-stressed non-discourse-related null pronominal elements in subject position, as shown in (12a). The pro-drop character was lost in a slow process between the thirteenth and sixteenth centuries, so that nowadays an overt subject is required in Modern Russian, as shown in (12b):

(12)   a. Old Russian (Moscow Chronicle 179v)

       pro Slavenъ   že   bystъ   i   grozenъ.
       glorious   PRT   was.3SG   and   terrible

    b. Modern Russian

       On   byl   slavnym i   groznym.
       he   was.MSG glorious   and   terrible
       'He was glorious and terrible.'

An independent property of Old Russian was that overt (dative case-marked) subjects were licensed in subordinate infinitive clauses in complement function. These overt infinitive subjects could display an effect of disjoint reference i.e. the reference of the embedded subject not being controlled by any element in the matrix clause, as in (13a) or, on the contrary, an element in the matrix clause could control the reference of an embedded pronominal subject (13b):

(13)   a. Old Russian (Pechersk Paterikon 237)

       Bogъ   že   ne   xotja   [ni   **edinomu**   pogybnuti].
       God   PRT   not   wanted not   one.DAT   die.INF
       'God did not want for none of them to die.'

    b. Old Russian (Laurentian Chronicle 170b)

       [Ty   so   mnoju]$_i$ cělovalъ   k(re)stъ   [xoditi **nama**$_i$ po odinoi
       you   with   me   kissed   cross   go.INF we.DAT by one
       dumě   oběma].
       decision both.DAT
       'You and me swore (lit. kissed the cross) to do both the same way.'

In instances of reference control of the embedded subject, also (non-stressed non-discourse-related) null pronouns could be used (14), in complementary distribution with overt pronouns (13b):

(14)   Old Russian (Novgorod Chronicle I, 17)

       I   (oni$_i$)   sdumaša   [jako **pro**$_i$ izgoniti   knjazja   svoego
       and   (they)   though   C   expel.INF   prince   their
       Vsěvoloda].
       Vsevolod
       'And they decided to expel their prince, Vsevolod.'

Overt dative subjects in embedded infinitive clauses were lost approximately in the transition between the sixteenth and seventeenth centuries (Lomtev 1956; Borkovskij 1979: 135). Nowadays, disjoint reference can only be achieved with the help of a finite subordinate CP (15a–b), whereas embedded infinitive clauses force co-reference of the embedded null subject with an element in the matrix clause (15c), as the following Modern Russian examples illustrate:

(15)   a.   Oni   rešili,   [čto knjaz'   **budet**   izgnan].
             they. NOM   decided   C   prince.NOM be.FUT.3SG   expelled
             'They decided that the prince would be expelled.'

       b.   Oni   rešili,   [čtoby knjaz'   sam   **ušël**   s   prestola].
             they.NOM decided C   prince.NOM himself go.PST.MSG from throne
             'They decided in order for the prince to resign himself.'

       c.   **Oni**ᵢ   rešili [tᵢ izgnat'   svoego   knjazja   Vsevoloda].
             they.NOM   decided   expel.INF their   prince   Vsevolod
             'They decided to expel their prince, Vsevolod.'

As argued in Madariaga (2011), Old Russian infinitive structures in complement position, such as (13) and (14), displayed no syntactic control at all (even when the reference of the infinitive subject could be semantically controlled), while the corresponding syntactic environment in Modern Russian, illustrated in (15c), fulfils the control properties, described by Williams (1980) and Hornstein (1999) as 'obligatory control'.

Without entering into much technical detail, the crucial change started from an infinitive structure endowed with a [+tense] feature, which licensed case marking on overt subjects and overt/null pronominal subjects (13), (14); this construction corresponds to Grammar 1, represented in (16a) below. This pattern changed into a control structure with a [−tense] feature, which does not license case marking on its subject. In such constructions, the embedded infinitive subject needs to rise into the matrix clause in order to get case, and leaves a trace in the original position (see Boeckx, Hornstein and Nunes 2010); the result of reanalysis is represented as Grammar 2 in (16b), corresponding to example (15c).

(16)

a. Grammar 1: [NPᵢ matrix-V [(pro / pronoun / NP-subject)ᵢ/ⱼ [infinitive-V]]] (=13, 14)

b. Grammar 2:[NPᵢ matrix-V [tᵢ infinitive-V]] (= 15c)

The change from no control (16a) into obligatory control (16b) in these constructions was triggered by a previous modification in the cue that had been so far necessary for learners to acquire the infinitive structure of Old Russian represented in (16a). This cue was the one responsible for the pro-drop character of Old Russian, that is, the availability of null non-stressed non-discourse-related pronominal subjects in Old Russian (12a), in complementary distribution with overt emphatic pronouns. The same system of overt emphatic pronouns (13a) alternating with null pro (14) was found in embedded infinitive clauses. This cue changed after the loss of the pro-drop character of Old Russian (12b), which produced the result that pro was not an eligible item in a Numeration any more.

This Russian example illustrates the abruptness of reanalysis; the loss of pro as an item available in a Numeration led to the 'catastrophic' restructuring of the Russian subordinate infinitive clauses in complement function: learners could not posit a pro any more in the gap they encountered in this kind of subordinate infinitive sentences. Instead, they started to parse the subject infinitive gap in the alternative way available in languages, i.e. as a NP-trace, and interpret the antecedent in the matrix clause as a moved element. This triggered a shift in the [+tense] feature of the infinitive clause into [−tense], which cancelled the ability of the infinitive to assign case to its subject. This, in turn, disallowed overt dative subjects in non-finite subordinate structures.

Notice that the initial trigger of the change, as expected in the formal approaches to reanalysis, originates 'extrasyntactically'. The loss of pro-drop in Middle Russian was probably due to a drop in frequency of the non-emphatic null pronominal elements in subject position (between the thirteenth and sixteenth centuries), and the corresponding increase of discourse-marked overt pronouns (Borkovskij 1968). Between the fifteenth and sixteenth centuries, the frequency of pro in the Russian PLD dropped under the threshold necessary to acquire the null variant properly, and non-emphatic non-stressed overt pronouns eventually replaced pro.

This Russian example also illustrates the 'contingent' nature of reanalysis: unpredictable factors related to E-language or previous independent changes trigger different types of reanalysis. Theoretically, the Russian infinitive dative subjects could have been reanalysed in a different position in the structure, perhaps as related to the matrix clause (as in Middle English; see §4.2), but they simply disappeared, as a result of the loss of pro-drop.

The example also illustrates other constraints on change and acquisition, such as the principle of 'degree-0 learnability', proposed by Lightfoot (1991, 2012), based on Emonds (1970), who described the properties affecting subordinate clauses as a subset of those affecting matrix clauses (see Chapter 18, this volume). In terms of acquisition, this means that children detect their cues basically in unembedded clauses. The principle of degree-0 learnability is crucial for the change represented in (16), because the cue necessary to acquire (16a), i.e. the presence in the PLD of overt dative subjects and pronouns, was overridden by the evidence from unembedded clauses, which displayed a lack of pro subjects, after the loss of pro-drop.

References

Andersen, H. 1973. 'Abductive and deductive change', *Language* 49: 765–93.
    2001. 'Introduction', in H. Andersen (ed.), *Actualization: Linguistic change in progress*. Amsterdam: John Benjamins, pp. 1–19.

Anttila, R. 1989. *Historical and comparative linguistics*. Amsterdam: John Benjamins.

2003. 'Analogy: the warp and woof of cognition', in B. Joseph and R. Janda (eds.), *The handbook of historical linguistics*. Oxford: Blackwell, pp. 424–40.

Baltin, M. and Collins, C. (eds.) 2001. *Handbook of contemporary syntactic theory*. Oxford: Blackwell.

Boeckx, C., Hornstein, N. and Nunes, J. 2010. *Control as movement*. Cambridge University Press.

Borkovskij, V. I. 1968. *Sravnitel′no-istoričeskij sintaksis vostočnoslavjanskix jazykov. Členy predloženija*. Moscow: Nauka.

1979. *Istoričeskaja grammatika russkogo jazyka: sintaksis – složnoe predloženie*. Moscow: Nauka.

Bybee, J. 2007. *Frequency of use and the organization of language*. Oxford University Press.

2010. *Language, usage and cognition*. Cambridge University Press.

Chomsky, N. 1986. *Knowledge of language: Its nature, origin, and use*. New York: Praeger.

2005. 'Three factors in language design', *Linguistic Inquiry* 36: 1–22.

Clark, R. and Roberts, I. 1993. 'A computational approach to language learnability and language change', *Linguistic Inquiry* 24: 299–345.

Croft, W. 1995. 'Autonomy and functionalist linguistics', *Language* 71: 490–532.

De Smet, H. 2009. 'Analysing reanalysis', *Lingua* 119: 1728–55.

2012. 'The course of actualization', *Language* 88: 601–33.

Dresher, B. E. 1999. 'Charting the learning path: Cues to parameter setting', *Linguistic Inquiry* 30: 27–67.

Dresher, B. E. and Kaye, J. 1990. 'A computational learning model for metrical phonology', *Cognition* 34: 137–95.

Emonds, J. 1970. 'Root and structure-preserving transformations', unpubilshed PhD thesis, MIT.

Faarlund, J. T. 1990. *Syntactic change: Toward a theory of historical syntax*. Berlin and New York: Mouton de Gruyter.

Fischer, O. 1988. 'The rise of the *for NP to V* construction: an explanation', in G. Nixon and J. Honey (eds.), *A historic tongue: Studies in English linguistics in memory of Barbara Strang*. London: Routledge, pp. 67–88.

2007. *Morphosyntactic change: Functional and formal perspectives*. Oxford University Press.

2011. 'Grammaticalization as analogically driven change?', in Narrog and Heine (eds.), pp. 31–42.

Fodor, J. 1998. 'Unambiguous triggers', *Linguistic Inquiry* 29: 1–36.

Galves, C., Cyrino, S., Lopes, R., Sandalo, F. and Avelar, J. (eds.) 2012. *Parameter theory and linguistic change*. Oxford University Press.

Garrett, A. 2012. 'The historical syntax problem: reanalysis and directionality', in Jonas *et al.* (eds.), pp. 52–72.

Hale, M. 1998. 'Diachronic syntax', *Syntax* 1: 1–18.

Harris, A. C. and Campbell, L. 1995. *Historical syntax in crosslinguistic perspective*. Cambridge University Press.

Haspelmath, M. 1998. 'Does grammaticalization need reanalysis?', *Studies in Language* 22: 315–51.

Hopper, P. and Traugott, E. C. 2003. *Grammaticalization*. Cambridge University Press.

Hornstein, N. 1999. 'Movement and control', *Linguistic Inquiry* 30: 69–96.

Itkonen, E. 2005. *Analogy as structure and process*. Amsterdam: John Benjamins.

Jonas, D., Whitman, J. and Garrett, A. (eds.) 2012. *Grammatical change: Origins, nature, outcomes*. Oxford University Press.

Kiparsky, P. 2012. 'Grammaticalization as optimization', in Jonas *et al.* (eds.), pp. 15–51.

Klima, E. 1965. 'Studies in diachronic transformational syntax', unpublished PhD thesis, Harvard University.

Kroch, A. 1989. 'Reflexes of grammar in patterns of language change', *Journal of Language Variation and Change* 1: 199–244.

2001. 'Syntactic change', in Baltin and Collins (eds.), 629–739.

Kuriłowicz, J. 1964. *The inflectional categories of Indo-European*. Heidelberg: Carl Winter.

Langacker, R. 1977. 'Syntactic reanalysis', in Li (ed.), pp. 57–139.

Lasnik, H. and Sobin, N. 2000. 'The *who/whom* puzzle: On the preservation of an archaic feature', *Natural Language and Linguistic Theory* 18: 343–71.

Li, C. (ed.) 1977. *Mechanisms of syntactic change*. Austin: University of Texas Press.

Lightfoot, D. 1979. *Principles of diachronic syntax*. Cambridge University Press.

1991. *How to set parameters: Arguments from language change*. Cambridge, MA: MIT Press.

1999. *The development of language: Acquisition, change and evolution*. Oxford: Blackwell.

2006. *How new languages emerge*. Cambridge University Press.

2012. 'Explaining matrix/subordinate domain discrepancies', in L. Aelbrecht, L. Haegeman and R. Nye (eds.), *Main clause phenomena: New horizons*. Amsterdam: John Benjamins, pp. 159–76.

Lomtev, T. P. 1956. *Očerki po istoričeskomu sintaksisu russkogo jazyka*. Moscow: Izdatel'stvo Moskovskogo Universiteta.

Longobardi, G. 2001. 'Formal syntax, diachronic Minimalism, and etymology: The history of French chez', *Linguistic Inquiry* 32: 275–302.

Madariaga, N. 2011. 'Infinitive clauses and dative subjects in Russian', *Russian Linguistics* 35: 301–29.

2012. 'Formal mismatches and functional advantage in syntactic change: The case of Old and Middle Russian non-verbal predicates', *Diachronica* 29: 231–57.

Meillet, A. 1912 [1958]. *Linguistique historique et linguistique generale*. Paris: Honoré Champion.

Mithun, M. 2011. 'Grammaticalization and explanation', in Narrog and Heine (eds.), pp. 177–92.

Narrog, H. and Heine, B. (eds.) 2011. *The Oxford handbook of grammaticalization*. Oxford University Press.

Newmeyer, F. 1998. *Language form and language function*. Cambridge, MA: MIT Press.

Ojansuu, H. 1909. *Mikael Agricolan kielestä*. Helsinki: Suomalaisen kirjallisuuden seura.

Pintzuk, S. 1999. *Phrase structures in competition: Variation and change in Old English word order*. New York: Garland.

Roberts, I. 1993. *Verbs and diachronic syntax: A comparative history of English and French*. Dordrecht: Kluwer.

    2007. *Diachronic syntax*. Oxford University Press.

    2010. 'Grammaticalisation, the clausal hierarchy and semantic bleaching', in Traugott and Trousdale (eds.), pp. 45–73.

    2012. 'Macroparameters and minimalism: A programme for comparative research', in Galves *et al.* (eds.), pp. 320–35.

Roberts, I. and Holmberg, A. 2010. 'Introduction: Parameters in minimalist theory', in T. Biberauer, A. Holmberg, I. Roberts and M. Sheehan (eds.), *Parametric variation: Null subjects in minimalist theory*. Cambridge University Press, pp. 1–57.

Roberts, I. and Roussou, A. 2003. *Syntactic change. A minimalist approach to grammaticalization*. Cambridge University Press.

Timberlake, A. 1977. 'Reanalysis and actualization in syntactic change', in Li (ed.), pp. 141–77.

Traugott, E. 2002. 'From etymology to historical pragmatics', in D. Minkova and R. Stockwell (eds.), *Studies in the history of the English language: A millennial perspective*. Berlin: Mouton de Gruyter, pp. 19–49.

Traugott, E. and Trousdale, G. (eds.) 2010. *Gradience, gradualness and grammaticalization*. Amsterdam: John Benjamins.

Uriagereka, J. 1997. 'Clarifying the notion "parameter"', *Biolinguistics* 1: 99–113.

van Gelderen, E. 2004. *Grammaticalization as economy*. Amsterdam: John Benjamins.

    2010. 'Features in reanalysis and grammaticalization', in Traugott and Trousdale (eds.), pp. 129–47.

    2011. *The linguistic cycle: Language change and the language faculty*. Oxford University Press.

Weinreich, U., Labov, W. and Herzog, M. 1968. 'Empirical foundations for a theory of language change', in W. Lehmann and Y. Malkiel (eds.), *Directions for historical linguistics*. Austin: University of Texas Press, pp. 95–188.

Whitman, J. 2000. 'Relabeling', in S. Pintzuk, G. Tsoulas and A. Warner (eds.), *Diachronic syntax: Models and mechanisms*. Oxford University Press, pp. 220–40.

Williams, E. 1980. 'Predication', *Linguistic Inquiry* 11: 203–38.

Wu, Z. 2004. *Grammaticalization and language change in Chinese*. London: Routledge.

Yang, C. 2002. 'Grammar competition and language change', in D. W. Lightfoot (ed.), *Syntactic effects on morphological change*. Oxford University Press, pp. 367–80.

5

Analogy and Extension

Alice C. Harris

5.1 Introduction

Analogy is a basic type of human reasoning, and extension one of its
diachronic applications in language. My primary goal in this chapter is to
describe and illustrate change through analogical extension. In addition,
I argue that analogy can play a role in syntactic change of all types, and
I therefore use 'extension' or 'analogical extension' as the name for
a single type of change.

I begin by considering the role of analogy in human cognition and in
synchronic linguistics, in §§5.2 and 5.3. The study of diachronic syntax has
been largely modelled on the study of diachronic phonology and especially
morphology, which was undertaken earlier in history; for this reason it is
important for us to consider briefly how extension applies in morphology
(in §5.4). In §5.5, I examine the way in which analogical extension applies
and, in §5.6, provide examples of extension in syntax. In §5.7, I consider
the role of analogy in diachronic syntax, arguing that analogy may play
a role in changes of all types. In §5.8, I provide a brief summary of the
chapter.

5.2 Analogy in Human Cognition

Many cognitive scientists now recognize analogy as the 'core of cognition', as argued by Hofstadter and Sander (2013, and references cited

Some of the research reported here was supported in part by the International Research and Exchanges Board, under the
ACLS-Academy of Sciences Exchange with the Soviet Union in 1989, and in part by the National Science Foundation
under grants no. SRB-9710085 and BCS-0215523. I am very grateful for this support. I would like to thank my language
consultants, Naira Tsiskarishvili, Luiza Neshumashvili, Dodo Miskalishvili, Nana Agasishvili, Tsatso Chikvaidze, Valya
Broyani, Alvina Matlian-Barxudarashvili and others. I am grateful to Farrell Ackerman and Lyle Campbell for discussion of
analogy.

there). They observe that analogy draws on our past experience to make it possible for us to function; we know how to do things like operate an elevator in a building we have never before entered or navigate through an unfamiliar airport by analogy to our past experiences with elevators or airports. They make the point that we are mostly unaware that we are drawing analogies. Especially relevant to diachronic linguistics is the fact that categories may start small and be extended. For example, the category 'wave' began with a particular motion of water in the ocean. It is extended to 'waves of grain'; America has had 'waves of immigrants'. By analogy, sound occurs in waves, although there are significant differences between waves of water and sound waves. Analogy with sound helped scientists to come to understand light waves. Radio waves are a host that carries sound waves (Hofstadter and Sander 2013: 209–14). I shall adopt a similarly broad view of analogy and its role in linguistic change.

5.3 Analogy in Synchronic Linguistics

Blevins and Blevins (2009) observe that the search for predictability drives us to look for patterns – in language and in life. It is analogy that makes it possible for humans to formulate linguistic generalizations and thus linguistic rules. When a child learns a word, such as *dog*, she generalizes from one animal to another similar one by analogy, sometimes overgeneralizing. When a child learns an affix such as the English plural, by analogy to the first word whose plural she has learned, she extends it to others, in effect creating in her own grammar the rule that plural is -/z/. Syntactic rules, such as *wh*-fronting, must be created by the individual speaker using analogy to sentences heard. Linguistic rules of all kinds are compact statements of analogy.

5.4 Analogy in Diachronic Morphology

Linguists reconstruct syntax on the basis of (by analogy to) the principles used in the reconstruction of sounds and words. Similarly, we understand analogy in syntax on the basis of analogy in diachronic phonology and especially diachronic morphology. Therefore, it is important for us to explore briefly the place of analogy in historical approaches to morphology.

In textbooks we often read examples of the role proportional analogy plays in historical change in morphology. Campbell (1999: 91) provides the following example of proportional analogy from the Finnish word for 'bay'.

(1)   lehden: lehti:: lahden: X, X = lahti

The previous form for the nominative singular for 'bay' was *laksi*, with the genitive singular *lahden*. Under pressure from a different nominative singular/genitive singular pairing, such as *lehti/lehden* 'leaf', the nominative singular of 'bay' was replaced by *lahti*. A problem with the use of four-part analogies in linguistics is that it can give the impression that a single pair of word forms was the analogue, when in fact it is often a large number of such pairs. Similarly, although the implication is that individual lexical items are affected one at a time, it appears that in fact large groups (often whole inflectional classes) may be affected at approximately the same time.

An example of a four-part analogy that applied to a whole class of words is third-person metathesis in Batsbi present and future tense forms of intransitive verbs. Transitive verbs developed a regular metathesis in present and future tense forms, as illustrated by the partial paradigm in (2) (see Harris 2013).

(2)   Batsbi
       y-oʔ-y-o-s   [CM-bring-CM-PRS-1SG][1]   'I will bring her'
       y-oʔ-y-o-(ħ)   [CM-bring-CM-PRS-2SG]   'you will bring her'
       y-oʔ-o-y   [CM-bring-PRS-CM]   's/he will bring her'

The CMs in the gloss are gender-class markers. It is easy to see that the class suffix, *-y-* in this example, metathesizes with the marker of the present tense, *-o* for all transitive verbs. However, at first this applied only to transitive verbs; this situation is preserved in the dictionary, Kadagiʒe and Kadagiʒe (1984), as shown in the last form in (3) below.[2] By analogy, derived intransitives, a very large class that all ended in *-l-a* in the present, replaced *a* with *o* in third person and now also obligatorily undergo metathesis, as shown in (3).

(3)   lečʼqʼ-l-a-s   [hide-INTR-PRS-1SG]   'I hide (INTR)'
       lečʼqʼ-l-a-(ħ)   [hide-INTR-PRS-2SG]   'you hide (INTR)'
       lečʼqʼ-o-l   [hide-PRES-INTR]   's/he hides (INTR)'
       (cf. lečʼqʼ-l-a [hide-INTR-PRS] 's/he hides (INTR)' Kadagiʒe and Kadagiʒe
       1984: 384b)

This could be stated as the proportional analogy in (4).

(4)   **yoʔyos: yoʔoy:: lečʼqʼlas: X, X = lečʼqʼol**   (See (2) and (3) for glosses.)

---

[1] In transcription or transliteration, č is IPA /tʃ/, š IPA /ʃ/, ž IPA /ʒ/, ǰ IPA /dʒ/, ʒ IPA /dz/, c IPA /ts/. Consonants followed by an apostrophe are ejectives, those followed by <:> are long or fortis. Examples from other sources are written with the system used here. In Old Georgian, sources are L Luke, Mk Mark, Mt Matthew, Ad Adiši Gospel, AB Opiza and Tbetʼi Gospels. In Udi, the parts of an interrupted root are each glossed with the same word and with a different subscript number, as in (15a). In Avar, M is masculine (class I), F is feminine (class II), N is neuter (class III). Examples not otherwise attributed are from the author's fieldwork.

[2] Although this dictionary was published in 1984, it was compiled earlier and represents an earlier stage of the language, perhaps the 1930s.

(4) does not seem to capture this change, where two things happen at once (replacement of *a* by *o* and innovation of metathesis). Why is X not *lečʼqʼal*? Why isn't it *lečʼqʼlo*? As with other four-part analogies, from (4) it is not clear that the analogue (on the left) represents a huge class, nor that the affected verb (on the right) also represents a very large class. Both of these are problems with proportional analogy in morphology.

Textbooks also make note of paradigm levelling, a kind of analogical change in which a lexeme may change from one inflectional category to another, usually a more regular one. Garrett (2008), citing Trask(1996), gives the example of the change from the conjugation of the verb 'love' in Old French to the modern equivalent, as in (5).

(5)

	Old French	Modern French	
1SG	aim	aime	'love'
2SG	aimes	aimes	
3SG	aimet	aime	
1PL	amons	aimons	
2PL	amez	aimez	
3PL	aiment	aiment	

The changes we focus on here are in the first and second persons plural, where the Old French stem *am-*, which alternated with *aim-*, is replaced by *aim*, creating a paradigm without stem alternation.

While changes by both proportional analogy and paradigm levelling are frequent in diachronic morphology, analogical extension is not limited to these two types. Fertig (2013) discusses a wide variety of examples of extension through folk etymology. For example, in one type of analogical extension, a hearer assumes that casual speech accurately represents a word; this is buttressed by a folk etymology, as when Ger. *Seelhund* 'seal' (lit. 'seal dog'), which may sometimes have been pronounced with /l/ barely there, is interpreted as *Seehund* 'seal' (literally 'sea dog'). The fact that *See* is 'sea' fits well with a folk etymology, though in this case I would suggest that analogy with such words as *Seewolf* 'wolffish' (lit. 'sea wolf') may also have played a role. On the other hand, a hearer may assume that a careful pronunciation represents casual speech, as when Old English *angnægl* was interpreted as having a suppressed /h/, leading, after loss of the word *ang* 'compressed, tight, painful', to modern *hangnail*. It has long been recognized that borrowed words may be changed to fit a folk etymology, as *woodchuck*, borrowed from Algonquian *otchock*, was.

Another kind of change is discussed by Paul ([1880]1968) (see Fertig 2013:45–7).[3] In Old High German, modals have second-person singular forms ending in -*t*; by reference to other verbs, they

[3] For Paul (1968), analogical change was limited to change by proportional analogy. Most more recent linguists recognize non-proportional analogy, and Hofstadter and Sander (2013) pay little attention to proportional analogy in general cognition.

developed second -person singular forms in -*st*. But because other forms are not shared, it is not possible to state this as a concrete proportional analogy. In (6), the forms on the left of the proportion are forms of *machen* 'make', a non-modal, while those on the right are forms of *dürfen* 'may, can', a modal.

(6)   a. mache 'I make': machst 'you make':: darf: darfst
        b. macht 'he/she/it makes': machst 'you make':: darf: darfst
        c. machen 'we/they make': machst 'you make':: dürfen: darfst

The proportional analogies in (6a–b) fail because the modals had (and have) a conjugational type not shared by other verbs, in which the first person singular is not marked by -*e* nor the third singular by -*t*. (6c) fails because the modal stem undergoes alternation, while the stem of 'make' does not alternate. The change can be expressed as proportional analogy if one uses abstractions, as in (7).

(7)   mach-: -st:: durf-: -st[4]

This may be considered analogical extension, drawing on the broad sense of analogy used in Hofstadter and Sanders (2013) and in most recent work on analogy in linguistics.

Kiparsky ([1978]1982) observes that while analogy (in phonology) often generalizes or extends the range of an earlier rule, in some instances the rule is actually made more complex. The former can be modelled by removing conditions from a rule; the latter must actually add a condition to a rule. For example, the complete loss of word-final devoicing in Yiddish was preceded by a stage at which devoicing was lost except in words ending in -*nd* (Sadock 1973, cited by Kiparsky [1978]1982); thus, this intermediate stage required an added condition on the rule of devoicing. While we must recognize that there are some problems of this kind, most analogical extensions can indeed be expressed as the removal of conditions from a rule.

Historical linguists often divide morphological and syntactic changes internal to a language into two types – reanalysis and analogical extension (e.g. Harris and Campbell 1995). Reanalysis changes the grammatical analysis of a word or construction in a speaker's internal grammar without affecting the surface (see Chapter 4, this volume, for detailed discussion). Analogical extension, on the other hand, changes the surface structure without affecting the analysis. Thus, when the various plurals of Old English (e.g. the -*u* plural in *sċip-u* 'ships' and the -*a* plural in *ġiefa* 'gifts', Campbell 1959: 222–34) are replaced with -*s* plurals, since the structure ROOT-PL remains the same but the sound changes, this is extension (that is, *sċip-u* 'ships' and *ġiefa* 'gifts' change

---

[4] As Fertig (2013) discusses, Paul rejected both the abstract statement in (7) and the idea that this was analogical change.

by analogy to words such as *stān-as* 'stones' which already had this plural). But when *a napron* becomes *an apron*, we have an example of reanalysis. Notice that although analogy to words beginning with a vowel and occurring with *an* must have played a role here, this does not meet the definition of extension, since the surface did not change. Reanalysis and analogical extension may work together, as is generally the case in grammaticalization. Both reanalysis and extension may affect grammatical rules, though they do not always do so.

5.5 How Does Analogical Extension Work?

The issue of what principles guide analogical extension is best studied in languages that are well attested through a long period of time, such as English or some of the Romance languages. Kroch (1989) proposes to account for the nature of extension through the 'constant rate hypothesis', the possibility that a form that occurs with differing frequency in different contexts will spread at a constant rate in all contexts. The most important evidence Kroch adduces is the rise of periphrastic *do* in the history of English. An earlier study by Ellegård (1953) traced the use of *do* in different environments, including affirmative declaratives, negative declaratives, affirmative polar questions, negative polar questions and negative imperatives. Kroch argues that the rate of change in each environment is the same, and that the constant rate hypothesis is thus confirmed.

This claim is challenged by Ogura (1993). Kroch computes the rate of change only for the first seven of Ellegård's periods, that is, until about the middle of the sixteenth century; Ogura argues that all the periods should be used. She finds that when all the data are considered, the plots of the curves do not fit the empirical data for affirmative declaratives. She observes that Kroch omits the negative imperatives without explanation, and that the plots do not fit those empirical data. It is the negative imperatives that started latest and have the sharpest slopes, that is, that do not change at a fixed rate. Ogura argues that Kroch's constant rate approach is wrong and that her empirical studies show that changes that begin earlier have lower rates of change than those that start later.

The role of frequency in the nature of change has long been recognized; Paul ([1880]1968: ch. 5) observed that low-frequency items were the first to undergo morphological levelling (see also Krug 2003: 13f.). In phonology it is often high-frequency items that change first, but several careful studies in morphology and syntax suggest that the issue is more complex in these areas. Cassidy and Ringler (1971: 37, cited by Krug 2003) make the point that more frequent patterns pressure less frequent patterns to regularize; this is the snowball effect, discussed also by Aitchison (1991) and others. Ogura and Wang (1996) argue that in the replacement of English third-person singular present tense -*th* with -*s*, an allomorph previously restricted to northern dialects, change began with a few high-frequency words. After it spread to lower-frequency items, the change went more rapidly; it was a few very high-frequency words, *doth* and *hath*, that were the last to change. Krug (2000) proposes models of analogical extension, taking the emergence of modals as his example; see Krug (2003) for further discussion. While it is widely recognized that frequency plays a role in extensions of this kind, much about the ways that frequency operates is not yet fully understood.

Harris and Campbell (1995) suggest two principles that guide analogical extension. (i) Change spreads from unmarked environments to more marked environments. (ii) Change spreads in such a way that natural classes are created. While each explains some changes, both suffer from a lack of definition, of *marked environment* in the first and of *natural class* in the second. See De Smet (2013: 50–3) for useful discussion; he suggests further that the principal problem of the natural classes principle, (ii), namely the fact that extension often leaves a morphological residue, can be explained as the result of the interaction of this principle and the resistance to change that results from retrieval of frequent words as complete forms (2013: 56f.).[5]

De Smet himself proposes the following principle to explain how extension proceeds:

> The spread of a new pattern from one environment to another is at least in part determined by the linguistic features of the environments and of the spreading pattern itself, in such a way that each diffusional step implements a minimal change to the existing system and maximally avoids clashes between the new pattern and the expectations a given environment raises or the functional constraints it imposes.
>
> *(De Smet 2013: 54; see also p. 61)*

De Smet provides a careful study of the analogical extension of gerunds, participles and *to*-infinitives as complements of verbs in English. This is an important contribution, but much further study is needed to entirely understand the principles that determine and constrain extension.

5.6   A Classic/Traditional View of Extension in Syntactic Change

In the sections below, I provide examples of extension in syntax.

---

[5] On the view that more frequent words are stored as wholes, see Stemberger and MacWhinney (1986) and many other sources. There is more recent evidence that the matter is more nuanced; see for example Baayen, Wurm and Aycock (2007).

5.6.1   Extensions of Case Patterns in Two Kartvelian Languages

Case changes in Laz and Mingrelian (Megrelian) illustrate the loss of a condition on a syntactic rule. These languages are members of the small Kartvelian family, whose other members are Georgian and Svan. Mingrelian and Laz together form a subgroup known as Zan.

Georgian is well known for having three sets of case marking in three different tense-aspect-mood (TAM) categories, known to specialists as Series I, II and III. In Common Zan a similar system existed (See Table 5.1); we will be concerned with only Series I and II. In addition, I simplify here by omitting psych-verbs.

The case distribution reconstructed for Common Zan is attested in Georgian and Svan. Note that this system requires rules like those in (8).

(8)   a. Assign nominative case to the subject, if the verb is in Series I.
        b. Assign dative case to the direct object, if the verb is in Series I.
        c. Assign ergative case to the subject, if (i) the verb is transitive, and (ii) is in Series II.
        d. Assign ergative case to the subject, if (i) the verb is unergative, and (ii) is in Series II.
        e. Assign nominative case to the subject, if the verb is unaccusative.
        f. Assign nominative case to the direct object, if the verb is in Series II.
        g. Assign dative case to an indirect object.

Some linguists would prefer to write these differently, for example, making nominative case the default. Its form is not zero, but this approach could still work; however, we cannot do away with rules (8b, c, d, g). Clearly (8c, d) could be combined, and (8e, f) could be. I will assume all seven rules, but the point would be the same with the smaller set.

Both of the Zan languages made changes in the distribution of cases. Laz remodelled case marking in Series I by analogy to Series II. To do so, the conditions referring to series were eliminated from rules (8c, d, f) (note that (8e, g) are already without conditions that refer to series). The result is the system sketched in Table 5.2 and illustrated in (9–11). This assumes that rules (8a, b) were lost.

Table 5.1 *Case distribution in Common Zan (after Harris 1985)*

	Verb type	Subject case	Direct object case	Indirect object case
Series I	Transitives	Nominative	Dative	Dative
	Unergatives	Nominative	–	–
	Unaccusatives	Nominative	–	Dative
Series II	Transitives	Ergative[a]	Nominative	Dative
	Unergatives	Ergative	–	–
	Unaccusatives	Nominative	–	Dative

[a] *In many works on these languages, the ergative case is referred to as the narrative case.*

Table 5.2 *Case distribution in Laz (after Harris 1985)*

	Verb type	Subject case	Direct object case	Indirect object case
Series I, II	Transitives	Ergative	Nominative	Dative
	Unergatives	Ergative	–	–
	Unaccusatives	Nominative	–	Dative

(9)   Transitives
    a. Series I: k'oči-k   q'vilups γeǰi (Laz)
                man-ERG kill   pig.NOM
                'The man kills a pig.'
    b. Series II: k'oči-k   doq'vilu γeǰi (Laz)
                man-ERG kill   pig.NOM
                'The man killed a pig.'

(10)   Unergative
    a. Series I: aya   k'oči-k   k'ai   ibirs (Laz)
                this   man-ERG well sing
                'This man sings well.'
    b. Series II: bere-k   isteru   γoǰi-s (Laz)
                child-ERG play   yard-DAT
                'The child played in the yard.'

(11)   Unaccusatives
    a. Series I: k'oč-i   γurun (Laz)
                man-NOM die
                'The man is dying.'
    b. Series II: k'oč-i   doγuru (Laz)
                man-NOM die
                'The man died.' (Harris 1985: 52f.)

While Laz remodelled Series I to be like Series II, in Mingrelian Series II was affected by Series I. The effect in Mingrelian was less complete. Other conditions – those referring to verb type (transitive, unergative, unaccusative) – were lost from rule (8c/d). Thus, as in Series I, all subjects are marked with one case – ergative, all direct object with another – nominative, and all indirect objects with yet another – dative, producing the system shown in Table 5.3, illustrated in (12)–(14). This entails that rule (8e) was lost.[6]

(12)   Transitives
    a. Series I: k'oč-i   ?viluns γe-s
                man-NOM kill   pig-DAT
                'The man is killing a pig.'

---

[6] See Harris (1985) for a more complete discussion.

Table 5.3 *Case distribution in Mingrelian (after Harris 1985)*

	Verb type	Subject case	Direct object case	Indirect object case
Series I	Transitives	Nominative	Dative	Dative
	Unergatives	Nominative	–	–
	Unaccusatives	Nominative	–	Dative
Series II	Transitives	Ergative	Nominative	Dative
	Unergatives	Ergative	–	–
	Unaccusatives	Ergative	–	Dative

    b. Series II: k'oč-k(i) do?vilu γej-i

                man-ERG kill   pig-NOM

                'The man killed a pig.'

(13) Unergatives

    a. Series I: (a)te k'oč-i   jgiro ibirs

                this   man-NOM well   sing

                'This man sings well.'

    b. Series II: baγana-k ila?apu ezo-s

                child-ERG play   yard-DAT

                'The child played in the yard.'

(14) Unaccusatives

    a. Series I: k'oč-i   γuru

                man-NOM die

                'The man is dying.'

    b. Series II: k'oč-k   doγuru

                man-ERG die

                'The man died.' (Harris 1985: 56f.)

Thus, from a single set of rules in Common Zan, Laz made one generalization, and Mingrelian another. Laz changed the case marking of Series I by analogy with the pattern in Series II. This is a simple case of extension – simplification of the rules by elimination of conditions. By analogy with the pattern in Series I, Mingrelian extended the case marking of subjects of transitive and unergative verbs in Series II to subjects of unaccusative verbs in that series.

5.6.2 Examples of Extension of Case and Agreement in Two Dialects of Udi

Udi is a language of the Nakh-Daghestanian (Northeast Caucasian) language family. Nineteenth- and very early twentieth-century Udi attests dative case subjects with psych-verbs, such as 'see', 'hear', 'know', 'want' and others, as illustrated in (15).

(15) a. kinbalt'-u-al   a-t'u-k-i   te ...
        industrious-DAT-AND   see₁-INV3SG-see₂-AORI   that
        gogin o-ne   č'e-sa
        green grass-3SG   out-PRES
        'And the industrious one saw that ... green grass was coming
        out.' (Schiefner 1863, text xv, line 47)

     b. gädin-a   i-t'u-bak-i   sa   kolla-qošt'an
        servant-DAT   hear-INV3SG-BE-AORI   one   bush-behind
        sunt'in   ex-ne
        someone.ERG   say-3SG
        'The servant heard someone behind a bush say ... ' (Dirr 1928: 61,
        line 24)

     c. yesir   pasčaγ-a   bu-t'u-q'-sa   ič   ölkinä
        captive king-DAT   want₁-INV3SG-want₂-PRES   self homeland.DAT
        taγa-ne   furuksan ... (Dirr 1928: 67, line 7)
        go-3SG   look.for
        'The captive king wants to go look for his homeland.'

     d. Nikolaj-a   q'a   Sergin-a   gölö   maˤγ-urux-q'o
        Nikolai-DAT   and   Sergei-DAT   many   song-PL-INV3PL
        aba
        Know
        'Nikolai and Sergei know many songs.' (Bouda 1939: 70)

Even at that time, the case of these experiencer subjects was beginning
to change to ergative by analogy with the case of subjects of other transitive verbs. (16) shows ergative subjects with the very same verbs in contemporary Udi.

(16)   Vartašen Udi
     a. ayel-en   a-t'u-k'-e   k'uč'an-ax
        child-ERG   see₁-INV3SG-see₂-AORII   puppy-DAT
        'The child saw the puppy.'

     b. ayel-en   i-t'u-bak-sa   maˤγ
        child-ERG   hear-INV3SG-BE-PRES   song.ABS
        'The child hears a song.'

     c. bäg-en   ene   aba-t'u ...   (Taral)
        nobleman-ERG   already   know-INV3SG
        'The nobleman already knows ... '

This change can also be stated as the removal of a condition on the rule
assigning ergative case. The condition itself could be analysed not as an overt
condition but as a more specific rule, given priority by the Elsewhere
Condition (Kiparsky 1973, among many others). That is, on one analysis,
there was no actual condition on the rule assigning ergative. Rather, the
'condition' that was removed was actually a more specific rule, which
assigned dative to the independent subjects of a particular small set of verbs.

Table 5.4 *Agreement markers and independent pronouns in the Vartašen dialect of Udi* [a]

	Psych verb agreement	Dative of independent pronoun	General subject agreement	Absolutive/ergative of independent pronoun
1SG	-za	za	-zu[b]	zu
2SG	-va	va	-nu	un
3SG	-t'u	met'u, kat'u, šet'u	-ne	meno, kano, šeno/ met'in, kat'in, šet'in
1PL	-ya	ya	-yan	yan
2PL	-va, -vaˁn	vaˁ	-nan	vaˁn, efaˁn
3PL	-q'o	met'oɣo, kat'oɣo, šet'oɣo	-q'un	menor, kanor, šenor/ met'oɣon, kat'oɣon, šet'oɣon

[a] *There are additional markers of agreement, but they are not relevant to the changes discussed here. In the third-person singular and plural 'absolutive/ergative' column, the pronouns are absolutive forms for proximate, medial, distal, followed by the ergative forms in the same order. For a complete treatment of agreement, see Harris (2002).*
[b] *Listed in Table 5.4 are underlying forms. The general markers are sometimes shortened (e.g. first-person singular zu is sometimes shortened to z) or assimilated (for example, the third person assimilates to a preceding /r/ or /l/ as re or le, respectively).*

The examples in (16) are from the Vartašen dialect. As indicated in the glosses, in both (15) and (16) the agreement marker, *-t'u*, is particular to the psych-verb (or 'inversion') construction; the third-person singular agreement marker for other verbs is *-ne*. The other person–number combinations also distinguish between the psych-verb construction and the construction with other verbs, as illustrated in Table 5.4. As shown in the table, the markers in the psych-verb construction are still identical in some person–number combinations to the dative case of the independent pronoun.

Thus, in the psych-verb construction in nineteenth- and early twentieth-century texts, (15), and in the contemporary Vartašen dialect, (16), the agreement marker for subjects is very similar to the dative case form of the independent pronoun. This is especially true in first and second person forms of both numbers. The examples in (17) illustrate some additional person–number combinations.

(17) Vartašen Udi
   a. ma   bu-**va**-q'-sa,   take
      where want₁-2SG-want₂-PRS go.IMP
      'Go wherever you want.' (Jeiranišvili 1971: 170, 1)
   b. šuxo-q'a-**va**   q'iˁbi
      who.ABL-SBJV-2SG fear.PTCP
      'Who should you be afraid of?'
   c. bak-al   te-**za**   s'um   ukes
      can-FUT NEG-1SG bread eat
      'I cannot eat bread (with you).' (Dirr 1928: 61, 4)

Table 5.5 *Agreement markers and independent pronouns in the Nij dialect of Udi*

	General subject agreement	Absolutive/ergative of independent pronoun
1SG	-zu	zu
2SG	-nu	un
3SG	-ne	meno, kano, šeno/ metʼin, katʼin, šetʼin
1PL	-yan	yan
2PL	-nan	vaˤn
3PL	-tʼun	menor, kanor, šenor/ metʼoɣon, katʼoɣon, šetʼoɣon

Note that in Vartašen, (16)–(17), the independent noun subject of a psych-verb is in the ergative case now, but the agreement marker continues to show the older similarity to the dative case of the pronoun.

In a second analogical extension, in the Nij dialect, the agreement markers used in the verb change to those used by general (non-psych) verbs. Thus, we find the agreement markers shown in Table 5.5, without the special markers for the psych-verb construction.

The sentences in (18) use the general agreement markers, while in the Vartašen dialect each requires a special psych-verb ('inversion') marker.

(18) Nij Udi

    a. aˤel-en   güjän-ä   a-**ne**-kʼ-sa
        child-ERG   puppy-DAT   see$_1$-**3SG**-see$_2$-PRS
        'The child sees the puppy.'

    b. yan   ava-**yan**   äš-p-sun
        we.ERG   know-**1PL**   work-DO-MAS
        'We know work.' (Jeiranišvili 1971: 185, 2)

    c. šuxu-**nen**   qʼipsa?[7]
        who.ABL-**2PL**   fear.PRS
        'Who are y'all afraid of?'

    d. Nikolaj-en   qʼa   Sergin-en   gele   maˤɣ-ur-**tʼun**[8]   awa
        Nikolai-ERG   and   Sergei-ERG   many   song-PL-**3PL**   know
        'Nikolai and Sergei know many songs.' (Bouda 1939: 70)

Thus, the Nij dialect has made both the extension made by Vartašen, assignment of the ergative case to the subjects of transitive psych-verbs, and a second extension, assignment of the general set of agreement markers.

---

[7] On the placement of agreement markers in Udi, see Harris (2000b, 2002). In both dialects agreement must be enclitic to focused elements, as in (18c, d). Otherwise it is endoclitic or enclitic to the verb, under specific circumstances.

[8] In Nij, -tʼun corresponds to -qʼun of Vartašen, the general third-person plural subject marker.

We can state the change as an extension of the general marker through the loss of a more specific rule assigning the specific psych-verb markers.

(19) a. Assign one of {*-za*, *-va*, *-t'u*, *-ya*, *-va꞉n*, *-q'o*}[9] according to person–number features of the subject in the environment of a verb {*ak'sun* 'see', ...}.

  b. Assign one of {*-zu*, *-nu*, *-ne*, *-yan*, *-van*, *-q'un*} according to person–number features of the subject.

The loss of the specific (minor) rule (19a) is equivalent to loss of a condition on a rule.

5.6.3 An Example of Extension in Word Order in the History of Georgian

An example of a different type comes from changes in word order. A majority of texts in Old Georgian are translated from Greek, and aspects of Greek grammar may have influenced even texts that are not translated. Because the order of clausal elements S, O and V was very free, the order in the Georgian translation was easily influenced by that of its source. Therefore it is difficult to determine the basic order of major constituents in Old Georgian. The order of other dyads, however, was not very free and hence was not greatly influenced by the orders of the sources.

Old Georgian, which dates from about the fifth century AD, had the dominant orders within dyads listed in (20), among others (Harris 2000a).

(20) NP–Adposition
  Noun–Adjective
  Noun–Genitive
  Noun–Relative clause
  Adjective–Standard of comparison

Among these, all are head-initial orders except the first; postpositional phrases are head-final. In Old Georgian, most adpositions were already postpositions, but a few were still prepositions or ambipositions. Those that were ambipositions occurred most frequently as postpositions. An example of the latter is *zeda* 'on', illustrated in (21).

(21) a. kadagebdit   mas   erdo-eb-sa   **zeda**
      preach.IMP.PL it   roof-COL-DAT on
      'preach it on the housetops' (Mt 10:27Ad)[10]

  b. romeli iq'o **zeda** tav-sa   čemsa
      Which   it.be on   head-DAT   my
      'which was on my head' (Genesis 40:17)

---

[9] Vartašen forms are used here to represent both dialects.   [10] Examples here are from Harris (2000a).

Occasional examples of circumpositions also occur, prepositional and postpositional elements with a single combined meaning. An example is given in (22).

(22) **mi**-mun-dɣe-d-**mde**   romel-sa   ševida   nove   k'idobn-ad
     thither-there-day-ADV-until which-DAT he.enter Noah ark-ADV
     'until the day when Noah entered the ark' (Mt 24:38)

In (22), the meaning of *mi-* and *-mde* is combined. In spite of the occurrence of examples such as (21b) and (22), postpositions, as in (21a), are already dominant in Old Georgian and continue to increase their numbers over time.

In unmarked order, adjectives followed head nouns, and genitives followed head nouns. Both are illustrated below.

(23) siq'mil-i   didi (L 4:25AB)
     famine-NOM   great
(24) ʒe-sa   k'ac-isa-sa
     son-DAT   man-GEN-DAT
     '[the] Son of man' (Mt 8:20)

While the orders Adjective–Noun and Genitive–Noun can be found, they constitute a very small percentage of examples.

The orders of relative clauses and comparatives are essentially uniform, in head-initial order.

(25) mravali bork'il-i   da   ǰač'v-i,   roml-ita šek'rian   igi
     many   fetter-NOM and chain-NOM which-INS they.bind.him him
     'many fetters and chains with which they bound him' (Mk 5:4Ad)
(26) iq'os uk'uanaysk'neli sacturi uʒures p'irvel-isa
     it.be last   error worse first-GEN
     'the last error will be worse than the first' (Mt 27:64)

In (25), the head noun *ǰač'v-i* 'chain' precedes the relative clause 'with which they bind him'; this order is characteristic of this and other kinds of relative clauses in Old Georgian. In (26), the head *uʒures* 'worse' precedes the standard of comparison, *p'irvelisa* 'the first'; this order too is characteristic of this kind of comparative as well as comparatives that make use of the dative.

Eventually, the last two constructions were partially replaced by other constructions with head-final order. The comparative in (26) has almost entirely been replaced; the new comparative seems to have developed out of other constructions whose order it reflects. The relative clause structure illustrated in (25) is mostly restricted now to the literary language, while innovative, more colloquial relatives are head-final.

There are no such explanations for the changes in order undergone by adjective and genitive constructions. Instead, we must assume that they changed by analogy to the head-final order of postpositions (and possibly to the order of major constituents). That is, genitives began to precede their heads (the nouns possessed) by analogy to the fact that NPs already preceded their heads, postpositions.

Because of the problem of stating the order of major constituents (see above in this subsection), I will not try to state the rules for ordering. However, there seems to be no problem in stating this extension in terms of the loss of conditions or of minor rules.

5.6.4   Analogy in the Development of the Greek *θa* Future

The story of the development of the Greek *θa* future is complex and is told effectively in Joseph and Pappas (2002), which I follow in all details. In this section we will look at only one part of this complex development. Early on *θelo* 'I want' came to be used with an infinitive in an auxiliary-like future, (27).

(27)   Θelo   grafein
        I.want   write.INF
        'I will write.'

The word-final *-n* was lost from the infinitive by regular sound change.

(28)   θelo grafei   θelei grafei
        'I will write'   's/he will write'

Loss of final *-n* made the infinitive homophonous with the third-person singular indicative form; both ended in *-ei*, phonetically [i]. At this point, the third-person expression was reanalysed as a combination of two forms, each marked as third person.

(29)   θelei   grafei >   θelei   grafei
        3SG   INF   3SG   3SG

This analysis spread to other person–number combinations by analogy, yielding (30).

(30)   θelo   grafo
        'I will write.'

In this way, analogical extension created a future marking new in the history of Greek. I return to these changes in section 7.

5.6.5   An Example from Bracketing in Avar

Avar is a language of the Nakh-Daghestanian family; like most other languages in the family, it has basic ergative-absolutive case marking and agreement with the absolutive.

(31) ins:u-c:a   ču   b-ec:ula
      father-ERG   horse.ABS   N-praise.PRES
      'Father praises the horse.' (Čikobava and Cercvaӡe 1962: 330)

Avar and a number of other of the Nakh-Daghestanian languages have a participle that may occur as a nominalized clause. Charachidze (1981: 111f.) gives the following examples: *q'ót'-ule-w* [cut-PRS.PTCP-M] 'the one who cuts', *l'á-le-w* [know-PRS.PTCP-M] 'the one (M) who knows', *l'á-le-y* 'the one (F) who knows', future participles, *q'ót'-ile-w* [cut-FUT.PTCP-M] 'the one who will cut', and past participles, *q'ót'-ara-w* [cut-PST.PTCP-M] 'the one who cut'. Many languages of the family, including Avar, have developed a biabsolutive construction; it is not clear whether this construction existed in Proto-Nakh-Daghestanian or whether its development in individual languages was influenced through contact. (32) illustrates the basic biabsolutive in Avar, using the nominalized participle.

(32) emen   [ču   b-ec:ule-w]   w-ugo
      father.ABS   horse.ABS   N-praise-M   M-is
      'Father is (the) one who praises the horse', ' … the praiser of the horse'. (Čikobava and Cercvaӡe 1962: 330; Avar)

A variety of diagnostics show that bracketing like that shown in (33) exists in this construction in several languages (Forker 2012; Gagliardi *et al.* 2014). The participle plus object in (32) represent a reduced clause; the biclausal construction was reanalysed as monoclausal, as in (33), while retaining the biclausal construction.

(33) S [O V$_{PTCP}$] be > S O V$_{PTCP}$ be

At this point, ergative-absolutive marking was extended to the monoclausal construction, producing sentences like (34).

(34) ins:u-c:a   ču   b-ec:ule-b   b-ugo
      father-ERG   horse.ABS   N-praising-N   N-is
      'Father is praising the horse.' (Čikobava and Cercvaӡe 1962: 329)

Agreement confirms that (32) is biclausal and (34) monoclausal (see Harris and Campbell 1995: 187–9 for details).

Extension of the general case marking pattern, ergative-absolutive, here is a clear case of analogical extension (Harris 2014). But note that reanalysis as a single clause is also likely to have been affected by analogy. The biabsolutive was remade as a monoclausal structure by analogy to sentences containing simple tenses, such as (31) above. Thus, analogy exists in changes other than extension, as discussed in greater detail in §5.7.

5.7   Towards a New Understanding of Analogy in Diachronic Syntax

The role of analogy in human cognition is broad, as discussed in §5.2, and it cannot be limited to four-part analogy or any other single model of thought. In linguistic change, too, the effects of analogy are broad; not only can they not be limited to four-part analogy, they cannot even be limited to analogical extension.

When words or expressions are borrowed, it is not like borrowing a book or a cup of sugar. The lending language does not, as a consequence of lending, lose the borrowed word or expression. Instead of taking a word from the lending language, the borrowing language actually recreates the word **by analogy to** the word in the lending language. For example, when English borrowed the word *cosmonaut* from Russian, it became an English word by analogy to the similar word of Russian.

In §5.6 I reviewed seven examples of syntactic change that occurs by extending an existing generalization to new parts of the grammar; these are clearly change by analogy. A pattern or construction previously limited to one part of the grammar begins to appear more generally or throughout the grammar.

Reanalysis, too, often makes use of analogy. Returning to the story of the Greek *θa* future (following Joseph and Pappas 2002), consider the reanalysis in (29), repeated here as (35).

(35)   θelei   grafei >   θelei   grafei
     3SG   INF   3SG   3SG

Recall that the infinitive ending came to be homophonous with the third-person singular ending through a regular sound change that dropped *-n* in word-final position. The resulting infinitive, *grafei* 'to write', was reanalysed in the context of third-person forms in the language, that is, **by analogy to** third-person forms. In another language, with third-person forms with other phonological shapes, *grafei* could not have been reanalysed in this way. If the analogy could not be made, the reanalysis in (35) could not have been made. The same is true of the reanalysis in (33) in Avar as noted in Section 5.6.5. Yet these are not at all the kind of change commonly referred to as analogical change. Thus, reanalysis, too, often involves analogy.

Analogy is such a basic kind of reasoning that it cannot be limited to a single type of change. We can still recognize the three mechanisms of syntactic change – reanalysis, extension and borrowing – while recognizing that analogical reasoning may play a role in any of them.

5.8 Conclusion

I have argued that analogy is basic to human reasoning, and that it is the basis of grammatical generalizations and rules. Analogical extension in morphology provides the model for the study of analogical extension in syntax. Careful studies of richly attested extension such as Los (2005) and De Smet (2013) will help us to discover the principles that govern how extension proceeds in the grammar. A variety of examples from Greek and from languages of the Kartvelian and Nakh-Daghestanian language families illustrate analogical extension, and we can see that extension can generally be expressed as the removing of conditions from a rule or, the equivalent, the loss of a minor rule leaving intact a major rule. Analogy in the broad sense is found in syntactic changes of all kinds, whether borrowing, extension or reanalysis.

References

Aitchison, J. 1991. *Language change: Progress or decay?* London: Fortuna.

Baayen, R. H., Wurm, L. H. and Aycock, J. 2007. 'Lexical dynamics for low-frequency complex words: A regression study across tasks and modalities', *Mental Lexicon* 2: 419–63.

Blevins, J. P. and Blevins, J. 2009. 'Introduction: Analogy in grammar', J. P. Blevins and J. Blevins (eds.), *Analogy in grammar: Form and acquisition.* Oxford University Press, pp. 1–12.

Bouda, K. 1939. 'Beiträge zur Kenntnis des Udischen auf Grund neuer Texte', *Zeitschrift der deutschen morgenländischen Gesellschaft* 93(1): 60–72.

Campbell, A. 1959. *Old English grammar.* Oxford: Clarendon Press.

Campbell, L. 1999. *Historical linguistics: An introduction*, 2nd edn. Cambridge, MA: MIT Press.

Cassidy, F. G. and Ringler, R. N. (eds.) 1971. *Bright's Old English grammar and reader.* New York: Holt, Rinehart & Winston.

Charachidzé, G. 1981. *Grammaire de la langue Avar (langue du Caucase Nord-Est).* Saint-Sulpice de Favières: Jean-Favard.

Čikobava, A. and Cercvaʒe, I. 1962. *Xunzuri ena* [The Avar language]. Tbilisi: Universit'et'i.

De Smet, H. 2013. *Spreading patterns: Diffusional change in the English system of complementation.* Oxford University Press.

Dirr, A. 1928. 'Udische Texte', *Caucasica* 5: 60–72.

Ellegård, A. 1953. *The auxiliary do: The establishment and regulation of its use in English* (Gothenburg Studies in English). Stockholm: Almqvist & Wiksell.

Fertig, D. 2013. *Analogy and morphological change.* Edinburgh University Press.

Forker, D. 2012. 'The bi-absolutive construction in Nakh-Daghestanian', *Folia Linguistica* 46: 75–108.

Gagliardi, A., Goncalves, M., Polinsky, M. and Radkevich, N. 2014. 'The biabsolutive construction in Lak and Tsez', *Lingua* 150: 137–70.

Garrett, A. 2008. 'Paradigmatic uniformity and markedness', in J. Good (ed.), *Linguistic universals and language change*. Oxford University Press, pp. 125–43.

Harris, A. C. 1985. *Diachronic syntax: The Kartvelian case* (Syntax and Semantics 18). New York: Academic Press.

  2000a. 'Word order harmonies and word order change in Georgian', in R. Sornicola, E. Poppe and A. Sisha-Halevy (eds.), *Stability, variation and change of word order patterns over time*. Amsterdam: John Benjamins, pp. 133–63.

  2000b. 'Where in the word is the Udi clitic?', *Language* 76: 593–616.

  2002. *Endoclitics and the origins of Udi morphosyntax*. Oxford University Press.

  2013. 'Origins of metathesis in Batsbi', in T. Lohndahl (ed.), *In search of universal grammar: From Old Norse to Zoque*. Amsterdam: John Benjamins, pp. 221–37.

  2014. 'On the origins of biabsolutive constructions in Avar, Batsbi, and Nakh-Daghestanian languages', presentation at the workshop 'Diachronic Typology of Differential Argument Marking', University of Konstanz, April.

Harris, A. C. and Campbell, L. 1995. *Historical syntax in cross-linguistic perspective*. Cambridge University Press.

Hofstadter, D. R. and Sander, E. 2013. *Surfaces and essences: Analogy as the fuel and fire of thinking*. New York: Basic Books.

Jeiranišvili, E. 1971. *Udiuri ena* [The Udi language]. Tbilisi University.

Joseph, B. D. and Pappas, P. 2002. 'On some recent views concerning the development of the Greek future system', *Byzantine and Modern Greek Studies* 26: 247–73.

Kadagiʒe, D. and Kadagiʒe, N. 1984. *C'ova-tušur-kartul-rusuli leksik'oni* [Tsova-Tush-Georgian-Russian dictionary]. Tbilisi: Mecniereba.

Kiparsky, P. 1973. '"Elsewhere" in phonology', in S. R. Anderson and P. Kiparsky (eds.), *A Festschrift for Morris Halle*. New York: Holt, Rinehart & Winston, pp. 93–106.

  [1978] 1982. 'Analogical change as a problem for linguistic theory', reprinted in *Explanation in phonology*, ed. P. Kiparsky. Dordrecht: Foris, pp. 217–36.

Kroch, A. S. 1989. 'Reflexes of grammar in patterns of language change', *Language variation and change* 1: 199–244.

Krug, M. 2000. *Emerging English modals: A corpus-based study of grammaticalization*. Berlin: Mouton de Gruyter.

2003. 'Frequency as a determinant in grammatical variation and change', in G. Rojdenburg and B. Mondorf (ed.), *Determinants of grammatical variation in English*. Berlin: Mouton de Gruyter, pp. 7–67.

Los, B. 2005. *The rise of the to-infinitive*. Oxford University Press.

Ogura, M. 1993. 'The development of periphrastic <u>do</u> in English: A case of lexical diffusion in syntax', *Diachronica* 10: 51–85.

Ogura, M. and Wang, W. S.-Y. 1996. 'Snowball effect in lexical diffusion: The development of –s in the third person singular present indicative in English', in D. Britton (ed.), *English historical linguistics 1994: Papers from the 8th International Conference on English Historical Linguistics at Edinburgh*. Amsterdam: John Benjamins, pp. 119–41.

Paul, H. [1880] 1968. *Prinzipien der Sprachgeschichte*, 7th edn. Tübingen: Max Niemeyer.

Sadock, J. M. 1973. 'Word-final devoicing in the development of Yiddish', in B. Kachru, R. B. Lees and Y. Malkiel (eds.), *Issues in linguistics: Papers in honor of Henry and Renée Kahane*. Urbana: University of Illinois Press, pp. 790–7.

Schiefner, A. 1863. Versuch über die Sprache der Uden. *Mémoires de l'Académie impériale des sciences de St.-Pétersbourg*, 7th series, 6(8). St Petersburg: Kaiserliche Akademie der Wissenschaften.

Stemberger, J. P. and MacWhinney, B. 1986. 'Frequency and the lexical storage of regularly inflected forms', *Memory and Cognition* 14: 17–26.

Trask, R. L. 1996. *Historical Linguistics*. London: Arnold.

6

Restructuring

David W. Lightfoot

6.1 Introduction

In a sense, 'restructuring' *is* syntactic change: new structures are assigned to expressions as new I-languages develop. Two of the best-understood instances of restructuring are discussed thoroughly in Chapters 18 and 24, this volume. In the early sixteenth century, English I-languages completed a change whereby structures like *Kim* $_{VP}$[$_V$*can* $_{VP}$[*visit Mars*]] were replaced by structures like *Kim* $_{IP}$[$_I$*can* $_{VP}$[*visit Mars*]] for the same sentence, where *can* is now an Infl(ectional) element and no longer a V. We know the form of the restructuring and why children acquired the new I-languages that generated the new structures at the relevant time and in response to relevant primary linguistic data (PLD).

Second, a little later English I-languages ceased to have structures like *Kim* $_{IP}$[$_I$[$_V$~~*saw*~~] $_{VP}$[*saw stars*]], where the verb *saw* moved to a higher Infl(ection) position (as still in most modern European languages), and instead had structures like *Kim* $_{IP}$[$_I$~~*past*~~ $_{VP}$[$_V$*see+past stars*]] for the same sentence, where the Infl(ection) element lowers on to the verb in the VP. Again, we know what the new structure is, how it is generated by the new I-language lacking the V-to-I operation, and why the new system was acquired by children after the seventeenth century.

These are classic cases of restructuring, new structures being assigned for the same sequence of words (Langacker 1977) and triggered by new PLD. Of course, what constitutes restructuring will be shaped finely by broader theoretical considerations. For example, we just noted that a simple modern English subject–verb–object expression *Kim saw stars* had a structure like *Kim* $_{IP}$[~~*past*~~ $_{VP}$[$_V$*see+past stars*]], whereas in earlier English it was *Kim* $_{IP}$[$_I$[$_V$*saw*] $_{VP}$[~~*saw*~~ *stars*]]. However, this depends on assumptions about the nature of an operation raising a verb to a higher Infl(ection) position.

Thinking of such changes as *restructuring* is something of a misnomer. Under the perspective sketched in Chapters 18 and 24 (this volume), children grow an I-language and at a certain time children were exposed to different PLD than earlier members of their speech community and began to develop new I-languages that assigned different structures to particular sentences. Children grow their I-languages when exposed to ambient E-language and quite independently of the I-languages of others, so there is no *restructuring* but just different development. This is not a terminological issue: thinking in terms of I-languages 'changing' or being 'restructured' has misled linguists into postulating *diachronic processes* where one I-language becomes another by some formal operation, and then asking about the nature of those processes, whether they simplify the grammars or make them more efficient or drive them to a different type, etc. (see Andersen 1973 for a critique of this approach). Four instances of this thinking are, first, ideas from the earliest work on syntactic change that there were formal limitations on the ways by which a grammar may change into another grammar (Kiparsky 1968; Klima 1964; Traugott 1969; see Chapter 15, this volume, for discussion); second, approaches to language types that claim that a language undergoing one diachronic change must undergo another particular one later by virtue of a universal diachronic hierarchy of grammars (e.g. Vennemann 1975); third, approaches to grammaticalization that take it to be an explanatory force (Chapter 1, this volume); and, fourth, approaches that seek to derive grammaticalization phenomena from Universal Grammar (UG) 'biases' (Roberts and Roussou 2003; van Gelderen 2011; see also Chapter 13, this volume).

If one deals only with language acquisition, on the other hand, not with a historicist theory of change, and views the acquisition of new I-languages as resulting from exposure to new PLD within a speech community, then there will be new structures but no restructuring as such (Lightfoot 1999, 2006). There may be new structures for the same sequence of words (as in the first two paragraphs here), and there may be new structures that entail new sequences of words and new sentences (e.g. §6.3.1), and the obsolescence of some sentences (e.g. §6.2.1), or even new meanings for some words (e.g. §6.4.1). In this chapter we shall consider the emergence of new structures of a wide range, sometimes yielding different analyses for the same sentences, sometimes new structures that generate different sequences of words, and sometimes new meanings of words and new semantic interpretations. Undoubtedly there are limits on how I-languages may differ for speakers of a certain speech community – for example, it is unlikely that there would be totally different vocabularies or mental lexicons or a brand new fully fledged morphological system – but it is not clear that there are any *formal* limits on the grammars of adjacent generations within one speech community, beyond those of UG; the possibilities for 'restructuring' are those defined by UG and there are no general lower limits that we know.

Unlike the two well-understood, indeed classic cases of restructuring mentioned at the outset, here we shall focus on a wide range of partially understood changes, differing in scale, language and theoretical framework. Certainly one finds a wide range of new systems and we will get a sense of that range over the next pages, and of where new work is needed.

6.2 New Categories

6.2.1 English Quantifiers

Anita Carlson (1976) showed that items like *all, any, both, each, either, every, few, more, none* and *some* have virtually the same distribution in Old English (OE) and in Present-Day English (PDE) but that they were restructured, undergoing a category change, and now function differently with respect to the rest of the grammar.

In PDE quantifiers occupy a unique range of positions and belong to a distinct syntactic category of Quantifier. The corresponding elements in OE freely occupied the same positions (1); see Lightfoot (1979: §4.1), which essentially reproduces Carlson's examples and analysis.

(1) a. Prenominal: OE wið *ealla wundela*, genim þas wyrte. c1000 Sax. Leechd. I 296. PDE 'With all wounds, take this plant.'
     b. Predeterminer: OE ofer *al his rice*. 855 Anglo-Saxon Chronicle (Parker MS). PDE 'Over all his realm.'
     c. Postnominal: OE and *þa scipo alle* geræhton. 885 Anglo-Saxon Chronicle (Parker MS). 'And seized the ships all.'
     d. With a genitive: OE he spræc to *his liornæra sumum*. c875 in OE Texts p178. PDE 'He spoke to some of his disciples.'
     e. Floating: OE *hit* is Adame nu *eall* forgolden. a1000 Gen. (Grein) 756. PDE 'It is now all repaid to Adam.'
     f. Nominal: OE *ælc* hine selfa begrindeþ gastes dugeðum. a1000 Gen. (Grein) 1521. PDE 'Each deprives himself of his soul's happiness.'

However, in OE, unlike in PDE, adjectives could also occur in the same positions and had the same internal morphology (Lightfoot 1979: 172–3). Furthermore, quantifiers occurred in the usual adjective positions. In that case, it is most plausible that OE I-languages had one category, subsuming words that are both quantifiers and adjectives in PDE I-languages, perhaps 'modifiers' (Ledgeway 2012 argues for a similar change in Romance, where adjectives and quantifiers had the same distribution in Latin but differ in the modern languages).

During Middle English and Early Modern English changes affected the distribution and morphology of (non-quantifier) modifiers in such a way that one could view quantifiers as a subset of modifiers but distinct. By the late fifteenth century, quantifiers were exceptional with respect to some general adjectival properties, because adjectives had become more restricted in their distribution. Adjectives (but not quantifiers) could no longer occur *freely* before a determiner, with a genitive, or as a substantive; they did occur in those positions but subject to severe constraints: they occurred before a determiner only if they were numerals or if the expression was a vocative; only comparatives and superlatives occurred with a genitive.

By the end of the sixteenth century, the following changes had taken place.

(2)   a. *all* and *both* first appear with *of* partitives (*all of them at Bristow lost their heads.* 1593 Shakespeare, *Richard II*, III ii 142).

     b. obsolescence of determiner-quantifier-noun (*your some sweete smiles.* 1589 Pottenham, *Eng. Poesie* (Arb.) 235.

     c. obsolescence of multiple quantifiers in sequence (yet would he retain with hym still Silan & Sasilas, all both Lacedemonians. 1571 T. Fortescue, Forest Hist 129).

     d. obsolescence of adjective-determiner-noun (*good my glasse.* 1588 Robert Greene, *Pandosto* 204)

     e. obsolescence of postnominal adjectives (*wadu weallendu.* Beowulf 581).

     f. obsolescence of adjectives used as substantives (*seþe underfehð rihtwisne on rihtwises naman, he onfehð rihtwises mede* 'he that receiveth a righteous (man) in the name of a righteous (man) shall receive a righteous (man)'s reward.' Matt. X 41 Gospels in West Saxon, MS CXL Corpus Christi College, Cambridge).

As adjectives and quantifiers had diverged in their distribution, there was good reason to postulate that they were assigned to different categories and merged into different positions, a restructuring: adjectives were merged with a noun immediately to their right or following a copula verb (3), while quantifiers were merged as the Specifier of a DP or in a Determiner position with a NP or PP complement (4).

(3)   a. $_{NP}[_A\text{red} _{NP}[\text{books}]]$ b. $_{VP}[_V\text{become} _A\text{angry}]$

(4)   a. $_{DP}[_{Spec}\text{all} _{DP}[\text{his apples}]]$ b. $_{DP}[_D\text{both} _{NP}[\text{books about taxes}]]$, $_{DP}[_D\text{all} _{PP}[\text{of the books}]]$

This analysis entails that (2a) will be generated and (2b–f) will not and the restructuring shows the hallmarks of a change in I-languages: the single recategorization is manifested by several new phenomena that emerged at the same time. However, we have no idea *why* the restructuring took place and cannot point to new PLD that triggered I-languages with (3) and (4).

6.2.2   Verb to Preposition in Chinese

The English modal verbs were formerly verbs that were recategorized as Infl(ectional) elements and modern English quantifiers were once modifiers that were recategorized as a distinct category. Similarly, there has been work arguing that serial verbs developed into prepositions or complementizers, notably by Lord (1973, 1976, 1993) for Benue-Kwa languages. The best-studied case of this recategorization is the Chinese *ba* construction, often analysed as the change of an earlier verb into a preposition and studied intensively over a fifty-year period (Wang 1958; Li and Thompson 1974; Peyraube 1985, 1996; Sun 1996).

Wang (1958: 411) cites (5) from Tu Fu, an eighth-century poet, where *ba* functions as a verb meaning 'hold, grasp' and assigning a thematic role to its complement *zhuyu*.

(5)   Zui   ba   zhuyu   zixi   kan
       drunk   take   dogwood   carefully   look
       'Drunk, (I) take the dogwood and look at it carefully.'

However, modern Mandarin *ba* functions as an object marker in sentences like (6), but does not assign a thematic role, and such usages are often regarded as developing from serial verb constructions like (5).

(6)   Zhangsan ba Lisi pian le
       Zhangsan BA Lisi cheat PFV
       'Zhangsan cheated Lisi.'

Ba was used as a serial verb and has become an item that does not have the distribution of a verb, many (but not all) argue. Some specialists have treated modern Mandarin *ba* as a preposition (Li 1990; Peyraube 1996; Sun 1996), but that analysis is disputed, and others argue that modern *ba* is a functional category and some, indeed, a verb. Whitman (2000) gives a clear and judicious account of the controversy and accepts that *ba* is not, in fact, a preposition.

Whitman analyses the earlier serial verb construction (5) as (7) and the modern object marking construction (6) as (8).

(7)

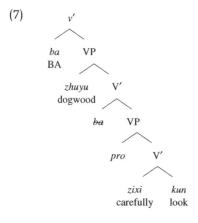

(8)

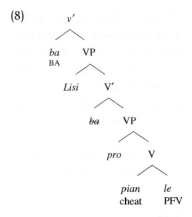

Under this minimalist analysis, as Whitman points out, there is no change in the categorial status or structural position of *ba*. In both cases the NP in the Specifier of the VP complementing *ba* controls an empty NP in the Specifier of its complement. The restructuring is in the properties of *ba*; *ba* assigns a thematic role to the NP beneath it in the earlier (7), but does not in (8).

Djamouri and Paul (2009) enrich this discussion by discussing much data from the thirteenth to eleventh centuries BCE and from modern Mandarin showing that both ancient and modern Chinese have a clear distinction between verbs and prepositions. They discuss why the restructuring of *ba* might have happened, keying their discussion to the assumptions of Longobardi's (2001) inertia and the 'preliminary change' of Roberts and Roussou (2003).

6.3 New Structures

6.3.1 Chinese Word Order

We have just reviewed an example of restructuring in Chinese syntax, where recent work has reformulated the change formerly thought of as a change in category membership but now conceived as a change in the theta-marking properties of *ba*. Let us turn now to changes in Chinese syntax due to a restructuring in the morphological properties of categories.

Diachronic syntacticians have always been intrigued by the relationship between morphology and syntax and by the way in which morphological changes can sometimes be seen to have effects for subsequent syntactic change (Lightfoot 2002 offers several papers on this topic). Recent work on Chinese has sought to link changes in word order to earlier morphological change.

Aldridge has produced a body of work investigating the loss of what she construes as morphological properties in Chinese and the consequences of that loss. In a useful two-part summary, Aldridge (2013) takes (Pre-)Archaic Chinese to be a richly inflected language with morphological distinctions on nouns, pronouns and verbs, either overtly manifested in the logographic writing system or reconstructed. In particular, she argues that the genitive case was lost from noun forms in Early Middle Chinese and that this restructuring had consequences for a number of syntactic constructions.[1]

She notes that the third-person pronoun *zhi* occurred only in accusative case-marked positions in Late Archaic Chinese, functioning as a direct object in (9a). The same form functions as a genitive case marker with a full NP (9b). Meanwhile third-person pronominal possessors were expressed by *qi* (9c).

(9)   a. xue er shi [xi zhi], bu yi yue hu?
         study CONJ time practice 3.ACC not also joy Q
         'To study and periodically practice something, is this not joyful?'
         (Fifth century BCE. *Analects*, Xue'er)

      b. xian wang zhi dao
         former king GEN way
         'ways of the former kings' (Fifth century BCE. *Analects*, Xue'er)

      c. qi zi yan wang?
         3.GEN son where go
         'Where would their sons go?' (Fourth century BCE. *Mencius*, Lilou 1)

Aldridge takes the appearance of genitive pronouns in places where only the accusative could occur earlier as evidence for the loss of the distinctions between accusative and genitive forms. Furthermore, finite embedded clauses were generally expressed as nominalizations with a genitive case marker on their subjects but that ceased and the genitive was lost. (10a) shows the genitive case on a Late Archaic embedded subject, whereas (10b) is a similar sentence from Early Middle Chinese with no genitive case marker on the embedded subject.

(10)   a. [Tianxia zhi wu dao ye] jiu yi.
          world GEN not.have way COP long PERF
          'It is a long time since the world has been without the proper way.' (Fifth century BCE. *Analects*, Bayi)

       b. [Tianxia wu dao] jiu yi.
          world not.have way long PERF
          'It is a long time since the world has been without the proper way.' (First century CE. Shiji, Kongzi Shijia)

---

[1] Bear in mind the logographic character of the Chinese writing system and the fact that *zhi* is an independent morpheme to which Aldridge assigns three distinct functions: third-person accusative pronoun, genitive marker and verb meaning 'go'. If *zhi* may serve as a genitive marker, it is quite different from genitive markers in other languages and not all her examples show the 'genitive' *zhi* linking two DPs. That leads a non-Sinologist to wonder whether other analyses might be proposed, perhaps treating *zhi* as a nominalization particle.

Aldridge points to a striking property of Archaic Chinese, different strategies for forming relative clauses in subject and VP-internal positions: a headless subject relative is followed by the particle *zhe* (11a); in a headed subject relative, the head NP follows the clause and is linked to it by the genitive marker *zhi* (11b); and in a VP-internal relative clause, the particle *suo* appears between the subject and the *v*P, regardless of whether the clause is headed or not (11c). This asymmetry began to break down at the beginning of Middle Chinese: Archaic Chinese had required *suo* at the *v*P boundary in object relatives (11c), but examples without *suo* are found from Early Middle Chinese (11d). Aldridge links the loss of the obligatory *suo* marker in object relatives to the loss of genitive case markers, because the genitive case marker on the subject required the nominalization analysis; once relative clauses are no longer analysed as nominalizations but rather as CP structures, the asymmetry disappeared because an operator could move to the CP from either the subject or object position.

(11)   a. [*e* Yu   zhan zhe] ke wei zhong   yi.
        desire fight ZHE POT say majority ASP
        '(Those) who desire to fight can be said to form the majority.'
        (Fifth century BCE. *Zuozhuan*, Cheng 6)

       b. qi   ruo cong [*e* [bi   shi]   zhi shi]   zai.
        How like follow escape world ZHI scholar EXCL
        'How could that compare to following a scholar who escapes from the world?' (Fifth century BCE. *Analects*, Weizi)

       c. [ren   zhi suo [wei *e*]] bu   ke   bu   wei.
        person GEN SUO fear   not POT not fear
        'What people fear cannot be feared.' (Third century BCE. *Laozi*, 20)

       d. junwang jiang he   [wen zhe] ye?
        majesty will   what ask   ZHE COP
        'What is it that your majesty would like to ask?' (First century BCE. *Zhanguoce*, Chu 1)

Aldridge also links the loss of genitive markers with the loss of two other constructions in Early Middle Chinese, Pronoun Fronting and *Wh*-movement. In Archaic Chinese accusative pronouns moved to a position immediately following a negative (12a) and Aldridge takes the movement to be driven by the case marker: pronouns had to move to acquire case. In Early Middle Chinese, after the loss of case markers, pronouns were no longer fronted (12b).

(12)   a. wu xian   jun yi   mo   zhi   xing ye.
        1 former lord also none 3.ACC do   COP
        'None of our former lords did this either.' (Fourth century BCE. *Mencius*, Tengwen 1)

       b. ren   mo zhi zhi.
        person none knew 3.ACC
        'No one knew it.' (Third century CE. *Sanguozhi*, Wei 11)

This is another instance of a single change, the loss of genitive case, being manifested by a multiplicity of phenomena (see Chapter 18, this volume), because case is taken to drive certain syntactic operations. Aldridge compares that approach to another one that unifies phenomena in a different way. The typological approach views languages as belonging to basic types with Greenberg-style harmonic properties (Greenberg 1966); as a language changes in basic type, so it develops new harmonic properties. Within that approach, Li and Thompson (1974) argued that Chinese underwent a shift in basic word order from subject–verb–object to subject–object–verb, thereby acquiring the harmonic properties of an SOV language instead of those of an SVO language. However, there is little support for postulating a basic SOV order for modern Chinese.

6.3.2 Light Warlpiri

We have written records for forms of English over more than a thousand years and in this chapter we have cited data from Chinese from 2,500 years ago. Very few of the world's languages have such rich records and, even in these cases, there is much that we do not know about the circumstances of the changes we have discussed. Now we will turn to a language that has existed for no more than thirty-five years but has changed a great deal over that brief period. The changes correspond to the kinds of changes that punctuate the histories of more stable languages.

Diachronic linguists, like many evolutionary biologists, political historians, geologists and biological anthropologists, seek not only to understand the present through the past but also to understand the past through the present. By doing the detailed fieldwork that the present sometimes makes possible, we can understand more about changes in language where written records limit what we can deduce about changes taking place two thousand years ago.

Light Warlpiri is a new language spoken by a small community (approximately 600 residents) in a remote area of the Northern Territory of Australia, 600 kilometres from the nearest town and first settled by non-indigenous people in 1948. It is a 'mixed' language that has emerged from Warlpiri, different varieties of English and Kriol. To couch things in terms of the acquisition model sketched in Chapters 18 and 27 (this volume), children acquiring Light Warlpiri were exposed to external language produced by people who had I-languages that yielded forms of quite different types of languages.

Discussion of such mixed languages (for example, Thomason and Kaufman 1988) shows that in contexts of stable multilingualism properties of one language may be adopted by another of the languages with their structures mostly intact. What is striking about Light Warlpiri is that it has developed properties not manifested in the ambient languages. Specifically, Light Warlpiri 'shows radical restructuring of source elements within the verbal auxiliary system, where a formal modal distinction is made that is not found in the source languages' (O'Shannessy 2013: 329). The innovation brings a new syntactic modal (or Infl(ectional)) category of realis/irrealis and O'Shannessy shows 'that the restructuring of the auxiliary system in Light Warlpiri draws selectively from elements of Warlpiri and several varieties and styles of English and/or Kriol, combined in such a way as to produce novel constructions' (2013: 329).

O'Shannessy shows that young children acquiring the new Light Warlpiri I-language were 'sensitive to the presence of multiple sources' and performed the radical restructuring before their late teens. Put differently, those children were influenced by E-language produced by a variety of I-languages. The challenge for generative diachronic syntacticians, as is often the case, is to show which elements of E-language triggered the new elements of the new I-language; in this case the ambient E-language has several sources.

The Light Warlpiri verb system draws properties from the different source languages, Warlpiri, Kriol and Australian English. O'Shannessy goes on to show (2013: 343–6) that the innovative auxiliary system drew a remarkable range of elements and structures from the ambient languages but children restructured selected source elements to create a new system not attested in any of the languages that they were exposed to.

Warlpiri has a realis/irrealis distinction but it is not formally or syntactically marked; Light Warlpiri shows a non-future-realis (actualized) subparadigm in -m that is not found in the source languages, and a future-irrealis-potential subparadigm in -rra, a result of restructuring. The new distinction can be traced to elements in the source languages, which were recombined and reanalysed.

This is not the place to work through the details of O'Shannessy's disentangling of where children do and do not maintain analyses of ambient languages but those details are instructive for understanding how children in the period of Middle English began innovating new inflectional elements, restructuring elements that had been treated as verbs by earlier speakers on exposure to new morphological phenomena as the inflectional properties of verbs came to be greatly simplified (see Chapters 18 and 27, this volume).

6.3.3 Local, Small-Scale Restructuring

Generative work in diachronic syntax over the last forty years has produced a number of cases where we can understand a multiplicity of new phenomena as all stemming from a single change in abstract I-languages. Such cases are particularly enlightening and satisfying but not all change comes in such large-scale 'catastrophes'. One also finds small-scale changes, which also require explanation if they constitute changes in I-languages.

For example, Elenbaas investigated directional *out of* in sentences like *She pushed the box out of the window*. Unlike separable particles in languages like Dutch and German, the particle *out* may appear before or after the complement DP in English: *She pushed out the box* and *She pushed the box out*. However, that variation does not carry over to phrases with *of*: **She pushed out the box of the window*. So it is in Modern English but it was not always thus. Elenbaas (2014) points to examples like (13), which resemble the ungrammatical form of Modern English (citations from the *Penn Corpora of Historical English*).

(13)   a. And he broȝt   out þe water of   þe ston, …
          and he brought out the water from the stone
          'And he brought the water out of the stone, … ' (CMEARLPS, 94.4102)

In Modern English *out* and *of* need to be adjacent but in Old and Middle English they may be adjacent (14) but do not need to be (13, 15).

(14)   And therewith he drew the truncheon of the speare oute of hys body.
      and therewith he drew the fragment   of the spear   out   of his body
      'And with that he drew the fragment of the spear out of his body'
      (CMMALORY, 645.4135)

(15)   a. &   put out his eyen of his heuede.
          and put out his eyes of his head
          'and put his eyes out of his head.' (CMBRUT3, 127.3843)
      b. forto caste oute Sarasynes of þis   lande.
          for-to cast out   Saracens   of this country
          'to cast Saracens out of this country.' (CMBRUT3, 45.1353)

Elenbaas did the corpus work to show that the decrease in non-adjacent directional *out of* examples correlated well with the increase in corresponding adjacent forms.

It is important to bear in mind that in early English the preposition *of* had a directional meaning and one finds forms like (16).

(16)   Hie þa   Demetrias of   þæm rice   adrifon.
      they then   Demetrius from the   kingdom PREFIX-drove
      'Then they drove Demetrius out of the kingdom.' (Orosius *Hist.* (BL Add.) iii. xi. 82)

The online *Oxford English Dictionary* says of *of* that 'the primary sense was "away", "away from", a sense now obsolete, … All the existing uses of *of* are derivative; many so remote as to retain no trace of the original sense, and so weakened as to be in themselves the expression of relatively indefinable syntactic relationships.' Indeed, some speakers have a reduced form of the preposition (*She pushed the box outta the window*) and some do not use *of* at all in these contexts (*She pushed the box out the window*).

Some have treated *of* as 'grammaticized' and Elenbaas treats the change as one of grammaticalization. She argues that *of* is bleached in its meaning and that this led to a syntactic reanalysis of (17), which in turn leads to the possibility of reducing *of* phonologically. She adopts the view of Hopper and Traugott (2003) that grammaticalization always involves reanalysis.

(17) $_{PathP}[_{Path}[out]]$ $_{PathP}[_{Path}[of]$ NP] > $_{PathP}[_{Path}[out]$ $_{PP}[_{P}of$ NP]]

This approach raises the question of why *of* was grammaticalized at this particular time but the syntactic change clearly relates to the properties of *of*; directional phrases with other prepositions are not subject to the adjacency requirement (18).

(18)   She pushed out the box from the window.

There has been recent work on phrase structure and functional categories that bears on the structure of such spatial and directional phrases (notably Cinque and Rizzi 2010; den Dikken 2003; van Riemsdijk and Huybregts 2001; Svenonius 2004). Elenbaas has good discussion of difficulties faced by some of these proposals and I will not attempt to resolve them here. Maybe attending to the diachronic restructuring that has evidently taken place with respect to *out of* in the history of English will help our synchronic colleagues converge on an analysis that will enable diachronic syntacticians to explain why and how I-languages changed in such a way as to cease generating forms where *out* and *of* are separated.

6.4   Semantics

6.4.1   *Like*

Sometimes we find changes in meaning which raise interesting issues for explanation. Meanings may change directly as a function of changes in usage, but sometimes more systematic factors are involved and we can explain the semantic changes through morphological or syntactic restructuring. We shall consider two such examples.

A meaning change that has intrigued historical linguists for over a hundred years concerns psychological verbs such as *like*. The verb *lician* 'like' used to mean 'please', in some sense the 'opposite' of its modern meaning, reversing from 'give pleasure to' to 'receive pleasure from'. So one finds expressions like (19), where 'faithlessness' is the subject of *licode* and carries nominative case.

(19)   Gode   ne licode na   heora geleafleast.
        God [dative]   not liked   their faithlessness [nominative]
        'Their faithfulness did not please God.' (Ælfric, *Homilies* xx 71)

Lician was a common verb, with over 400 citations in the *Concordance to Old English*, and Denison (1990) notes that the type with a dative Experiencer and a nominative Theme made up 'the overwhelming majority, to the extent that it is doubtful whether the others are grammatical at all'.

Nor was this a phenomenon of one isolated verb. In Old English some forty verbs occurred with a dative Experiencer, usually preverbal (20) (see Lightfoot 1979: §5.1).

(20)   a. chance: at last him chaunst to meete upon the way A faithlesse Sarazin.
          'At last he chanced to meet on the way a faithless Saracen.' (1590 Spencer, FQ ɪ ii 12)
       b. motan, 'must': vs muste make lies, for that is nede, Oure-selue to saue..
          'We must tell lies, for that is necessary in order to save ourselves.' (*c.* 1440 York Myst. (Manly, Spec. ɪ) play xxxvɪɪɪ
          (The Carpenteres) 321)
       c. greven: thame grevit till heir his name.
          'It grieves them to hear his name.' (1375 Barbour, *Bruce* xv 541)
       d. lacken: though me lacke to purchase Her worthy thank.
          'I do not have the capacity to gain her worthy gratitude.' (1390 Gower, CA (Morley) 446)

Jespersen (1909–49: III, II.2) noted many such verbs that underwent a parallel reversal in meaning: *ail, repent, become* (= 'suit'), *matter, belong,* etc. So Chaucer could write *it reweth me* and *will it not one day in heaven repent you?*, but later people used personal subjects and said *I rue my ill-fortune* and *Will you not repent (of) it? Rue* and *repent* meant 'cause sorrow' for Chaucer and 'feel sorrow' later.

Visser (1963–73: §34) noted that several of these verbs fell into disuse before or during the Middle English period. However, some new verbs entered the class in early Middle English; Visser lists *him irks, him drempte, him nedeth, him repenteth, me reccheth, me seemeth, me wondreth, us mervailleth, me availeth, him booteth, him chaunced, him deyned, him fell, him happened, me lacketh, us moste,* etc. Van der Gaaf discussed twelve of these Middle English additions and noted that 'a few verbs already in use in OE underwent a more or less radical change in signification, and adopted the A construction [accusative/dative verb]; others were formed from existing stems; others, again, were borrowed from Old French and a few from Old Norse' (1904: 12) and in some cases the borrowing transferred a French or Norse personal verb into the 'impersonal' frame. This indicates that, despite the loss of several of the relevant verbs, the construction with dative Experiencers was still productive in Middle English.

A notable feature of psych-verbs in Old and Middle English is the wide range of syntactic contexts in which they appear – sometimes impersonally with an invariant third-person singular inflection (21a), sometimes with a nominative Theme (21b), sometimes with a nominative Experiencer (21c).

(21) a. Him   ofhreow   þæs   mannes.
         To-him [dative] there-was-pity because-of-the man [genitive]
         'He pitied the man.' (Ælfric, *Catholic Homilies* I, 8.192.16)

      b. Þa   ofhreow   ðam munece þæs hreoflian mægenleast.
         Then brought-pity to-the-monk the leper's   feebleness
         'Then the monk pitied the leper's feebleness.' (Ælfric, *Catholic Homilies* I, 23.336.10)

      c. Se mæssepreost   þæs mannes   ofhreow.
         The priest [nominative] because-of-that man [genitive] felt-pity
         'The priest pitied that man.' (Ælfric, *Lives of Saints* (Oswald) 26. 262)

Adopting the general framework for psych-verbs of Belletti and Rizzi (1988), we can subcategorize verbs to occur with Experiencer and Theme DPs. Two principles are relevant for the mapping of lexical representations into syntactic structures: (a) V assigns structural case only if it has an external argument (an interpretation of *Burzio's Generalization* that a verb case-marks its complement only if it assigns a thematic role to its external argument) and (b) an Experiencer must be projected to a higher position than a Theme DP.[2]

Under that approach, we can postulate two lexical entries that typify several Old English psych-verbs (22), linking DPs with inherent cases.

(22) a. *Hreowan*: Experiencer-dative; (Theme-genitive)
      b. *Lician*: Experiencer-dative; Theme

Hreowan 'pity' and several other verbs sometimes occurred just with an Experiencer DP in the dative case (*Me hreoweþ* 'I felt pity'); or they might assign two inherent cases, yielding surface forms like (21a). *Lician* 'like/please' usually occurred with an Experiencer in the dative and a Theme in the nominative (19). With a lexical entry like (22b), the Theme would receive no inherent case in initial structure. Nor could it receive a structural case from the verb, because verbs assign structural case only if they have an external argument (a nominative subject); this would be impossible, because the Experiencer, having inherent case (dative), could not acquire a second case. Therefore the Theme could receive case only on being externalized, i.e. becoming a subject with nominative case.

Belletti and Rizzi (1988: §4.2) argue that a dative DP may move to a subject position, carrying along its inherent case and therefore not receiving structural case; instead, nominative is assigned to the Theme. This, in turn,

---

[2] A careful analysis of these phenomena requires distinguishing between abstract Case (sic) and morphological, overt case (sic). For the purposes of the discussion here, we can ignore that distinction and think more simply just in terms of morphological case.

suggests that a dative Experiencer could also move to subject position in Old English, and this seems to be true: dative Experiencers could show some subject properties (this has led to chaotic behaviour by editors concerned to 'correct' texts; see Allen 1986 and Lightfoot 1999: 131 for discussion). See also Cardinaletti's (2004) discussion of subject properties.

It is important to recognize that aspects of Belletti and Rizzi's analyses depend on negative data and therefore would be unlearnable by children having access only to positive data; therefore, UG must dictate aspects of the analyses. I-languages along the lines sketched here generate a good sample of the bewildering range of contexts in which psych-verbs may occur in Old English (21, etc.) (Lightfoot 1999: 132); Anderson (1986) gathered a beautiful paradigm, three examples from Ælfric, one showing the verb *hreowan* used impersonally, one with Theme as nominative, and one with Experiencer as nominative (21). Anderson suggested plausibly that (21) represents the typical situation and that verbs that manifest only one or two of the three possibilities in fact reveal accidental gaps in the texts. The writings of some writer might show only the patterns of (21a, b) for a given verb, not (21c), but that does not entail that that writer's I-language could not generate (21c).

Verbs denoting psychological states underwent some striking changes in Middle English and we can understand some aspects of these changes in terms of the loss of the morphological case system (for a fuller account, see Lightfoot 1999: §5.3). A straightforward explanation of the variation and of the syntactic changes affecting psych-verbs lies in the loss of morphological case. If the morphologically oblique cases (dative, genitive) realized abstract, inherent cases assigned by verbs and other heads, their loss in Middle English meant that the inherent cases could no longer be realized in this way. Evidence suggests that as their overt, morphological realization was lost, so inherent cases were lost at the abstract level. DPs that used to have inherent case came to have structural case (nominative, accusative), and this entailed syntactic changes. Loss of inherent case would constitute the relevant restructuring.

An I-language with oblique cases would generate forms like (21a), given a lexical entry (22a). Inherent case would be assigned to the Experiencer and the Theme, realized as dative and genitive respectively. Similarly, it would generate (20a) and (23).

(23) a. Him hungreð
          'He [dative] is hungry.'
      b. Me   thynketh I heare
          me [dative] thinks   I hear
          'I think I hear.'
      c. Mee likes ... go see the hoped   heaven.
          Me pleases   go see the hoped for heaven
          'I like to go and see the heaven hoped for.' (1557 *Tottel's Misc*
          (Arber) 124)

DPs with an inherent case could not surface with a structural case, because nouns have only one case. If a DP has inherent case, it has no reason to move to another DP position.

An I-language with no morphology to realize inherent case lost those inherent cases; consequently the lexical entries of (22) etc. lost the case specifications. Now the DPs had to surface in positions in which they would receive structural case, governed by I, V or P. This entailed that one DP would move to the subject (Specifier of IP) position, where it would be governed by I and receive structural case. A verb may assign structural case (accusative) only if it has an external argument. So the Experiencer DPs in (20a, 23), which formerly had inherent case realized as dative, came to occur in nominative position: *He chanced ...*, *He hungers*, *I think ...*, *I like*, etc. With a verb assigning two thematic roles, as one moved to subject (nominative) position, so the other could be assigned structural accusative (governed by V), generating forms like *The priest* [nominative] *pitied the man* [accusative].

Consider now the verb *like* and its lexical entry (22b) yielding Experiencer [dative]–verb–Theme [nominative]. A child lacking morphological dative case would analyse such strings as Experiencer–verb–Theme, with no inherent cases. Since the Experiencer often had subject properties (Lightfoot 1999: 131) and was in the usual subject position to the left of the verb, the most natural analysis for our new, caseless child would be to treat the Experiencer as the externalized subject, hence with nominative case. The reanalysis of the Experiencer as a subject would permit the verb to assign accusative case to the Theme. And if the Experiencer is now the subject, *like* would have to 'reverse' its meaning, now 'receive pleasure from'.

New I-languages spread through a population of speakers. There were I-languages with and without morphological case. That kind of variation entails that once some people have systems with no oblique morphological case, one might find any psych-verb with nominative and accusative DPs. As dative case ceased to be attested, one finds no verbs lacking a nominative subject.

The loss of the old patterns was gradual. The morphological case system was lost over the period from the tenth to the thirteenth century, so the two I-languages coexisted for several hundred years. The first nominative–accusative forms are found in late Old English, but impersonal verbs without nominative subjects continue to be attested until the mid sixteenth century. The gradualness of the change is expected if the loss of inherent case, the restructuring, is a function of the loss of morphological dative.

There is more to be said about these changes and the reader is referred to Lightfoot (1999: §5.3); Allen (1995), Bejar (2002) and Roberts (2007: 153–61) provide good discussion relating the restructuring to the loss of morphological case but implementing the change somewhat differently and linking the change in *like* and other psych-verbs to changes in indirect passives like *Susan was given the book*, not discussed here. Meanwhile we can see how changes in the meaning of *like* (and several other phenomena) can be explained through the loss of inherent case, an automatic consequence of the loss of oblique morphological cases, and an instance of restructuring.

6.4.2   Verbs with Results

Let us end with a mystery, briefly addressing another case of semantic change reflecting a new morphosyntactic structure. Burnett and Troberg (2013) draw attention to the distinction between (24a) and (24b), where English combines a manner-of-motion verb with a preposition to yield a 'telic' meaning, indicating the result, an end point of the floating, and the French equivalent does not.

(24) a. The bottle floated under the bridge for five minutes/in five minutes. (Eng.)
      b. La bouteille a flotté sous le pont pendant cinq minutes/*en cinq minutes. (Fr.)

They show that Latin manner-of-motion verbs with prefixes may allow the resultative, end-point interpretations that English shows (25), and they point to the Classical alternations between *tacui* 'have been silent' versus the prefixed and telic *conticui* 'have fallen silent' and other such pairs.

(25) a. Caprarum-que uberibus   ad-volant.
         goats.GEN-and udders.DAT   at-fly
         'And they fly onto the udders of the goats.' (Pliny *Nat.* 10, 115)
      b. Inspectum   vulnus   abs-terso   cruore.
         examined.PTCP wound.ACC away-wiped.PTCP blood.ABL
         ' ... that the wound had been examined after the blood was wiped off' (Livy 1, 41, 5)

Telic interpretations of prefixed manner-of-motion verbs continue to be productive in Medieval French. Burnett and Troberg point to *porter* 'carry' indicating an activity, while the prefixed *a-porter* indicates an accomplishment 'bring'; *penser* means 'think', while *apenser* has the telic interpretation 'realize'. Martin (2001) discusses hundreds of similar verbs with the prefix *a(d)-*, showing alternations demonstrating the aspectual force of the prefixed forms, and Burnett and Troberg add other prefixes (26).

(26) *amer* 'love'; *en-amer* 'fall in love'
      aler 'go'; *por-aler* 'go all around'
      voler 'fly'; *tres-voler* 'fly across'

However, the directional/aspectual prefixes that were productive in Classical Latin and Medieval French are no longer productive in Modern French (*a-*, *sous-*, *par-*, *en-*, etc.); the only productive prefixes in Modern French are iterative *re-* and 'change-of-state' *de-*. Furthermore, manner-of-motion verbs may not carry a telic interpretation (24b), (27).

(27) a. *Jean a/est marché à Paris en deux heures.
         Jean aux walked in Paris in two hours

      b. #L'oiseau a volé sur la branche.
         'The bird flew around over/on the branch' (NOT 'The bird flew
         onto the branch.')

Similarly, Medieval French (but not Latin) shows resultative adjectives,
which are not possible in Modern French (28).

(28) a. que mort ne   l'acraventet.
         that dead not him-crush
         'So that it didn't crush him dead.' (*La Chanson de Roland* 285.3930)

      b. Une colder   trencha par   mi,   tute quarree la fendi.
         a   hazel.tree sliced   through middle all   square it cut
         'He sliced a hazel tree through the middle, he cut it right square.'
         (Marie de France, *Lais*, p. 183)

In summary, the telic interpretations of Medieval French appear to be
keyed to the syntactico-semantic properties of prepositional elements; the
way prepositional elements interact with the abstract property PATH
changed and, as a consequence, the telic interpretations ceased to be
available. Burnett and Troberg discuss various possible explanations for
these correlations, invoking Talmy's (2000) typological distinction
between satellite-framed and verb-framed languages, but it is quite
unclear why the new structures emerged.

6.5 Conclusion

We have discussed a wide range of new structures, where the analyses unify
phenomena that seem to be changing at the same time. Unlike the two
classic cases with which we started, the analyses are not fully understood
and in no case can we point to new PLD that trigger them in a convincing
way. Understanding such restructuring is central to work in diachronic
syntax and hopefully future work will yield richer understanding.

References

Aldridge, E. 2013. 'Survey of Chinese historical syntax', *Language and
    Linguistics Compass* 7(1): 39–77.
Allen, C. 1986. 'Reconsidering the history of *like*', *Journal of Linguistics* 22:
    375–409.
    1995. *Case marking and reanalysis: Grammatical relations from Old to Early
    Modern English*. Oxford University Press.
Andersen, H. 1973. 'Abductive and deductive change', *Language* 48: 765–94.

Anderson, J. M. 1986. 'A note on Old English impersonals', *Journal of Linguistics* 22(1): 167–77.

Bejar, S. 2002. 'Movement, morphology and learnability', in D. W. Lightfoot (ed.), *Syntactic effects of morphological change*. Oxford University Press, pp. 307–25.

Belletti, A. and Rizzi, L. 1988. 'Psych-verbs and theta theory', *Natural Language and Linguistic Theory* 6(3): 291–352.

Burnett, H. and Troberg, M. 2013. 'Changes at the syntax-semantics interface: From Late Latin to Modern French', paper presented at DiGS15, University of Ottawa. https://sites.google.com/site/heathersusanburnett.

Cardinaletti, A. 2004. 'Toward a cartography of subject positions', in L. Rizzi (ed.), *The structure of CP and IP: The cartography of syntactic structures*, vol. 2. Oxford University of Press, pp. 115–65.

Carlson, A. 1976. 'A diachronic treatment of English quantifiers', unpublished MA thesis, McGill University, Montreal.

Cinque, G. and Rizzi, L. (eds.) 2010. *Mapping spatial PPs: The cartography of syntactic structures*, vol. 6. Oxford University Press.

Denison, D. 1990. 'The OE impersonals revived', in S. Adamson, V. Law, N. Vincent and S. Wright (eds.), *Papers from the Fifth International Conference on English Historical Linguistics*. Amsterdam: John Benjamins, pp. 111–40.

Dikken, M. den 2003. 'On the syntax of locative and directional adpositional phrases', MS, City University of New York.

Djamouri, R. and Paul, W. 2009. 'Verb-to-preposition reanalysis in Chinese', in P. Crisma and G. Longobardi (eds.), *Historical syntax and linguistic theory*. Oxford University Press, pp. 194–211.

Elenbaas, M. 2014. 'Directional *out of* in the history of English: Grammaticalization and reanalysis', *Journal of Germanic Linguistics* 26(2): 83–126.

Greenberg, J. H. 1966. 'Some universals of grammar with particular reference to the order of meaningful elements', in J. H. Greenberg (ed.), *Universals of language*. Cambridge, MA: MIT Press, pp. 73–113.

Hopper, P. and Traugott, E. C. 2003. *Grammaticalization*. Cambridge University Press.

Jespersen, O. 1909–49. *A modern English grammar on historical principles*, vols. 1–7. London: Allen & Unwin.

Kiparsky, P. 1968. 'Tense and mood in Indo-European syntax', *Foundations of Language* 4: 30–57.

Klima, E. 1964. 'Relatedness between grammatical systems', *Language* 40: 1–20.

Langacker, R. 1977. 'Syntactic reanalysis', in C. N. Li (ed.), *Mechanisms of syntactic change*. Austin: University of Texas Press, pp. 57–139.

Ledgeway, A. 2012. *From Latin to Romance: Morphosyntactic typology and change*. Oxford University Press.

Li, C. N. and Thompson, S. 1974. 'An explanation of word order change SVO > SOV', *Foundations of Language* 12: 201–14.

Li, Y. H. A. 1990. *Order and constituency in Mandarin Chinese*. Dordrecht: Kluwer.

Lightfoot, D. W. 1979. *Principles of diachronic syntax*. Cambridge University Press.

1999. *The development of language: Acquisition, change and evolution*. Oxford: Blackwell.

(ed.) 2002. *Syntactic effects of morphological change*. Oxford University Press.

2006. *How new languages emerge*. Cambridge University Press.

Longobardi, G. 2001. 'Formal syntax, diachronic Minimalism, and etymology: The history of French *chez*', *Linguistic Inquiry* 32: 275–302.

Lord, C. 1973. 'Serial verbs in transition', *Studies in African Linguistics* 4: 269–96.

1976. 'Evidence for syntactic reanalysis: From verb to complementizer in Kwa', in S. Steever, C. Walker and S. Mufwene (eds.), *Papers from the parasession on diachronic syntax*. Chicago Linguistic Society, pp. 179–91.

1993. *Historical change in serial verb constructions* (Typological Studies in Language no. 26). Amsterdam: John Benjamins.

Martin, R. 2001. 'Le prefixe *a-/ad-* en moyen français', *Romania* 119: 289–322.

O'Shannessy, C. 2013. 'The role of multiple sources in the formation of an innovative auxiliary category in Light Warlpiri, a new Australian mixed language', *Language* 89: 328–53.

Peyraube, A. 1985. 'Les structures en 'ba' en chinois medieval et moderne', *Cahiers de linguistique Asie Oriental* 14: 193–213.

1996. 'Recent issues in Chinese historical syntax', in C.-T. J. Huang and Y.-H. Li (eds.), *New horizons in Chinese linguistics*. Dordrecht: Kluwer, pp. 161–213.

Riemsdijk, H. van and Huybregts, M. A. C. 2001. 'Location and locality', in M. van Oostendorp and E. Anagnostopoulou (eds.), *Progress in grammar*. Roccade: Amsterdam and Utrecht, pp. 1–23.

Roberts, I. G. 2007. *Diachronic syntax*. Oxford University Press.

Roberts, I. G. and Roussou, A. 2003. *Syntactic change: A minimalist approach to grammaticalisation*. Cambridge University Press.

Sun, C. 1996. *Word-order change and grammaticalization in the history of Chinese*. Stanford University Press.

Svenonius, P. 2004. 'Slavic prefixes inside and outside VP', in P. Svenonius (ed.), *Nordlyd 32: Special issue on Slavic prefixes*. Tromsø: CASTL, pp. 205–53.

Talmy, L. 2000. *Toward a cognitive semantics*. Cambridge, MA: MIT Press.

Thomason, S. G. and Kaufman, T. 1988. *Language contact, creolization, and genetic linguistics*. Berkeley: University of California Press.

Traugott, E. 1969. 'Toward a grammar of syntactic change', *Lingua* 23: 1–27.

van der Gaaf, W. 1904. *The transition from the impersonal to the personal construction in Middle English*. Heidelberg: Winter.

van Gelderen, E. 2011. *The linguistic cycle: Language change and the language faculty*. Amsterdam: John Benjamins.

Vennemann, T. 1975. 'An explanation of drift', in C. N. Li (ed.), *Word order and word order change*. Austin, TX: University of Texas Press, pp. 269–305.

Visser, F. Th. 1963–73. *An historical syntax of the English language*, vols. 1–3b. Leiden: Brill.

Wang, L. 1958. *Hanyu shi gao* (zhong) [A draft history of Chinese (Part II)]. Beijing: Kexue chubanshe.

Whitman, J. 2000. 'Relabelling', in S. Pintzuk, G. Toulas and A. Warner (eds.), *Diachronic syntax: Models and mechanisms*. Oxford University Press, pp. 220–38.

7
Parameter Setting

Theresa Biberauer and Ian Roberts

7.1 Introduction

Lightfoot (1979) integrated the concerns of historical syntax with those of generative grammar by postulating that language change is driven by abductive reanalysis of primary linguistic data (PLD) in first-language acquisition such that the outcome may be a new generation with a new grammar for a given language. This pioneering work predates the introduction of the Principles-and-Parameters notion of comparative (and diachronic) syntax in Chomsky (1981), but nonetheless the central ideas can be adapted to this model.

One of the leading ideas in Lightfoot (1979) was the Transparency Principle (see Chapter 15, this volume). This was the idea that transformational derivations were limited in the degree of 'opacity' they could induce. If a grammar became too opaque, the Transparency Principle forced a reanalysis. Lightfoot saw the Transparency Principle as a principle of grammar, a general condition on the nature of derivations. Given the nature of the theory at that time, this was an almost inevitable move, since the only other alternative would have been to ascribe it to some aspect of the PLD, which would have been highly implausible. Below we will reconsider the locus of what, in Principles-and-Parameters terms, we could call 'conditions on parameter setting'.

In terms of a Principles-and-Parameters approach, syntactic change involves the 'resetting' of parameter values. Adapting the general approach in Lightfoot (1979) to this model, it is usually thought that parameters are 'reset' in the course of first-language acquisition, presumably on the basis of reanalysis of PLD by language acquirers.

In these terms, one of the key questions for the theory of syntactic change is how this 'resetting' of parameters can happen. Since, from the perspective of the language acquirer, the parameters are not 'reset', but simply set, parameter-setting clearly becomes a central issue. The goal of this chapter is to provide a brief overview of the kinds of answer to this question that have been attempted in the literature since the 1980s, and to suggest a new, and, we believe, highly promising way of addressing this question in terms of an 'emergentist' view of the nature of parameters which relies on Chomsky's (2005) distinction among the three factors of language design.

7.2   Approaches to Parameter Setting

A useful way to think about the various approaches to parameter setting that have been put forward is in terms of Chomsky's (2005) three factors of language design. These are as follows:

(1)   a. The innate endowment: Universal Grammar (Factor 1)
      b. Experience: the primary linguistic data (Factor 2)
      c. Non-domain-specific cognitive optimization principles (Factor 3)

As Chomsky notes, these three conditions are arguably relevant to the development of any biological system. In generative linguistics, the first two factors are familiar (for discussion, see Chapters 6, 13 and 18, this volume). The third has assumed greater prominence in recent work in the Minimalist Programme, and as we will see below, may play an important role in the theory of parameters.

In these terms, the Transparency Principle, as a principle of grammar in Lightfoot's original formulation, would be part of Factor 1. If acquisition is seen as simply setting parameters on the basis of experience, then the role of a condition such as the Transparency Principle is somewhat unclear. This, combined with the fact that it was never properly formalized, led to the abandonment of the Transparency Principle as a principle of grammar. Nonetheless, it has been widely acknowledged that there must be some constraint on the relationship between the PLD and the language acquirer. This can be seen in two ways: on the one hand, the crucial notion may be seen as the complexity of the representations the acquirer is capable of postulating on the basis of given PLD; on the other, it can be articulated in terms of the general idea that only subparts of the PLD are accessible to the child. The general notion of 'trigger' or 'cue', which has been proposed in a variety of different guises as we shall see below, falls under this second heading. In this section, we will look at various approaches of this second kind that followed the abandonment of the Transparency Principle.

7.2.1   Degree-0 Learnability

Lightfoot (1991) was the major study in which a strong constraint on the structural domains accessible to the acquirer was proposed and motivated on the basis of diachronic data. As Lightfoot (1991: 13) points out, 'not every experience is a trigger'. He goes on to formulate a 'degree-0 learn-ability' constraint, based on the earlier 'degree-2 learnability' proposal of Wexler and Culicover (1980). Here the 'degree' refers to the degree of clausal embedding. Hence the degree-0 constraint means that only main-clause material can count as PLD for parameter setting. In fact, Lightfoot (1991: 31–2) argues that the restriction just to main clauses is both arbitrary from a theoretical point of view (since the notion 'clause' is epiphenomenal to UG) and too restrictive: the correct notion is main clause, plus the complementizer and subject position of a complement infinitival.[1]

Very importantly, Lightfoot stresses that the 'claim that children are degree-0 learners ... reflects a property of their "learning" capacity and not of Universal Grammar' (1991: 40). Here Lightfoot seems to be anticipating a notion of third-factor constraint on learning, since the degree-0 con-straint itself cannot be part of the PLD, although it radically affects how the acquirer can interact with the PLD.

Lightfoot's principal diachronic argument for degree-0 learning comes from word-order change from OV to VO in the history of English. It is well known that surface VO orders appeared in main clauses earlier than in embedded clauses, mainly due to the effects of productive 'verb-second'. Of course, the same is true of Modern Dutch and Modern German, but, Lightfoot argues, these languages have various non-embedded 'signposts' which unambiguously indicate the underlying final position of the verb. These signposts include particles of various kinds which indicate the base position of the verb (i.e. *pick the book* **up** *pick*, where strike-through signals the lower trace of the verb). In Old English, however, these signposts were insufficiently robust to cause acquirers to postulate an OV grammar on the basis of main-clause PLD alone. Embedded clauses show systematic OV order in OE, but this is where the degree-0 idea becomes crucial: embedded PLD is not accessible. As Lightfoot says: 'if parameter setting were sensitive to embedded material, there would have been plenty of robust data to warrant object–verb order' (Lightfoot 1991: 43).

A further consequence of degree-0 learning is summed up by the follow-ing quotation: '[m]y general argument is that changes affecting embedded clauses were an automatic by-product of certain changes in unembedded Domains' (Lightfoot 1991: 43). The claim is that once main clauses were reanalysed as VO, the relevant parameter changed, causing all clauses to become VO. To quote Lightfoot again, 'when the new verb order began to affect embedded clauses, it did so rapidly and catastrophically, showing a very different pattern from that observed in main clauses' (Lightfoot 1991: 68). Lightfoot dates the parameter change to the twelfth century.

One major difficulty with this account of word-order change in English (which is shared with others, e.g. van Kemenade 1987) is that it is not

[1] This is formulated in terms of a particular construal of the notion of binding domain.

possible to locate a single date or period in which this change took place. As Pintzuk (1991) and others have shown, Old English shows evidence for VO order independent of verb-second, alongside OV order (this observation led Pintzuk to argue for a competing-grammars approach, which we will discuss in §7.2.3). Moreover, there is clear evidence that OV orders, at least in certain contexts such as infinitives (in particular where the object is negative, or quantified), survived until as late as the fifteenth century; see Fischer, van Kemenade, Koopman and van der Wurff (2000), Moerenhout and van der Wurff (2005) and Taylor and Pintzuk (2012). While the difficulty in pinning down a precise date for a catastrophic change of the kind implied by parameter-resetting would seemingly apply to any parameter-based account, the evidence of OV order in infinitives in late ME is particularly problematic for the degree-0 approach which, as we have seen, predicts that all embedded clauses must change uniformly. We will return to the question of the relation between gradualness and parameter change below (§7.2.3).

7.2.2 Cue/Trigger-Based Approaches

What cue- and trigger-based approaches to parameter-setting share is the idea that only certain parts of the PLD are accessible to the acquirer; in fact, these approaches explicitly define the relation between certain components of the PLD and parameter setting.

Let us consider cue-based approaches first. Dresher and Kaye (1990), which was on phonological acquisition, was the earliest work on cues. This idea was developed in later work by Dresher; Dresher (1999) proposes that all parameters are specified for a marked and a default setting, as well as the cue for the marked setting. Lightfoot (1999, 2006) takes up this notion in relation to syntax and to syntactic change. He takes a stronger view than Dresher, and argues that 'there are no independent "parameters"; rather, some cues are found in all grammars, and some are found only in certain grammars, the latter constituting the points of variation' (Lightfoot 1999: 149). Some examples of cues in this sense are given in §21.2.2. The PLD expresses cues, while a cue is 'an element of I-language' (Lightfoot 1999: 161). For example, the cue for V-to-T movement (at least in earlier English), was [I V], which was unambiguously expressed through subject–verb inversion: this cue 'is expressed robustly if there are many simple utterances which can be analysed by the child only as [I V]' (Lightfoot 1999: 161). On this view, changes in PLD add or remove cues and thereby effect parametric change (see also Chapter 21, this volume; Lightfoot and Westergaard 2007).

One problem with this view is that the status of cues as abstract entities is rather unclear. Cues are I-language elements and determined by UG; they are abstract aspects of linguistic representations. It is therefore unclear how they can be added or removed by changes in PLD, unless some notion of 'cue activation' is entertained. We will return to a more general version of this problem in §7.3.

Clark and Roberts (1993), building on earlier work on language acquisition by Clark (1992), define a notion of trigger in terms of P(arameter)-expression as follows (this formulation is taken from Roberts and Roussou 2003):

(2)   a. Parameter expression: a substring of the input text S expresses
          a parameter p_i just in case a grammar must have p_i set to a definite
          value in order to assign a well-formed representation to S.
       b. Trigger: a substring of the input text S is a trigger for parameter p_i
          if S expresses p_i.

Clark and Roberts apply this idea in an account of certain well-known syntactic changes in the history of French, involving the development of subject clitics, the loss of verb-second and the loss of null subjects. Combined with a Fitness Metric, they argue that verb-second in particular was inadequately triggered at a certain stage, while a non-verb-second grammar was preferred by the Fitness Metric (in effect, the Fitness Metric was an attempt to define the notion of 'tipping point' discussed in recent work by Yang 2013). A variant of these ideas was developed in Roberts and Roussou's (2003) account of grammaticalization (see Chapters 1 and 4, this volume). For criticism, see Dresher (1999: 54–8). An important underlying issue, not fully addressed by Clark and Roberts, concerns the link between the abstract UG property, the value of p_i in (2), and the concrete property of the PLD, the 'expression' of the parameter. More generally, the question of the connection between a feature of PLD and an abstract UG property, known as the Linking Problem (C. L. Baker 1979; Pinker 1984), remains open. We return to this below.

Gibson and Wexler (1994) propose the Triggered Learning Algorithm (TLA). Here the role of trigger is rather different from that defined in (2). The TLA takes the PLD to be a string of categories, and parameter setting starts from a random setting. Learning proceeds as, with each failure to recognise the input string, one parameter value is changed. Gibson and Wexler show two things. First, if more than parameter value is allowed to change at a time, the search space becomes intractably large, and, second, that the model only works if an ordering is imposed on the parameters to be set (see also i.a. Clark 1992; Frank and Kapur 1996; Fodor 1998; Fodor and Sakas 2004; Evers and van Kampen 2008; Sakas and Fodor 2012). Another important idea, which may be directly relevant to parameter change, is that of local maxima. A local maximum is reached when the system gets 'stuck' in an incorrect grammar which can only be repaired by changing more than one parameter value simultaneously (the unreachable target grammar is the absolute maximum). If the learner fixates on a system which does not correspond to that underlying the PLD, this could be a model for change. However, the types of changes discussed are rather implausible (e.g. non-verb-second to verb-second) and must also, crucially, be catastrophic in nature, and catastrophic changes are not the norm in syntactic change. We take up the question of the ordering among parameters in §7.4.1.

7.2.3 Competing Grammars

An approach which is compatible with a parametric approach and with the observed gradualness of many syntactic changes is the competing-grammars model developed by Kroch (1989), Santorini (1989, 1992), Taylor (1990), Pintzuk (1991) and others. The gradualness of a change such as the one from OV to VO in English discussed above could, in principle, be made compatible with a parametric approach if the population dynamics of change are taken into consideration, i.e. if the individuals making up a speech community undergoing change vary as to the parameter setting in their individual grammars, some having the 'innovative' value and others having the 'conservative' value (see Niyogi and Berwick 1995 for an approach of this kind). Kroch (2001: 722), however, criticizes this approach, on the grounds that variation can be found in single texts by one individual. He therefore argues that individuals must have a form of 'covert multilingualism', i.e. they can have more than one mental grammar for what is, in sociocultural terms, the 'same language' or register. This is crucially distinct from an approach like Niyogi and Berwick's, and from what is assumed more generally in Chomskyan linguistics about the I-languages of individual speakers, namely that these may not be entirely identical, but that they nevertheless overlap substantially, and that native competence in a language is defined by a unique I-language. On this view, different registers of 'the same' language which a single speaker may have mastered may, given sufficient phonological, morphological, lexical and/or syntactic differences between them, justify the postulation of more than one I-language, along the lines standardly assumed for bilinguals (see, for example, MacSwan 2000; and see also Roberts 2007: 324–31 for discussion of scenarios where it might be justified to extend such a bilingual model to speakers of 'one language'). For Kroch, however, a single speaker of English can have more than one 'English' I-language even in the absence of such multiple I-language-signalling cues, and they can use these distinct I-languages in the same sociolinguistic or register context.

Pintzuk (1991) applied this approach to word-order change in English, arguing that the OE textual corpus gives evidence of individuals with competing grammars, specifically an OV and a VO language and an 'I-final' and an 'I-medial' one: both pairs of grammars reflecting distinct parameter settings. These grammars remain in competition for several centuries, with the I-final grammar disappearing earlier than the OV one. This approach offers an interesting account of the considerable variation in word order through most of the OE period, and later work by Kroch and Taylor (2000), Pintzuk and Taylor (2006), Taylor and Pintzuk (2012) similarly accounts for some of the variation seen in ME. The competing-grammars framework has also been applied to OV/VO word-order change in the history of Yiddish by Santorini (1989, 1992) and Wallenberg (2009), in Ancient Greek by Taylor (1990), in German by Speyer (2008), in Icelandic by Rögnvaldsson (1996) and Thráinsson (2003) and in Scandinavian more generally by Heycock and Wallenberg (2013), and also to the loss of verb-second in Spanish by Fontana (1993). Furthermore, Yang (2002) shows that the acquisition of competing grammars can be successfully modelled.

However, a number of questions remain unanswered concerning this approach. First, there is the fact that, if this view is correct, individuals can 'code-switch' between grammars in consecutive lines of a single text with no apparent register-related or sociolinguistic correlate, and without any observable phonological, morphological, semantic or lexical correlate. Kroch (1994) discusses the question of 'syntactic doublets', pointing out that true doublets should not persist; they will be ascribed 'social value' by acquirers in the speech community. However, in the case of OE, there is no evidence for this, although the apparent doublets would have had to persist for centuries to account for the attested within-text variation.

There are also empirical concerns. If there are two independent parameters in OE, one governing the order of V and O and the other the order of I and VP, as Pintzuk assumes, and both able to underlie different grammars in competition, then we have a total of four grammars underlying the OE corpus. This predicts that the VO grammar and the 'I-final' grammar should combine, giving the order V>O>Aux in certain cases. However, this order is unattested in OE and elsewhere; indeed, according to Biberauer, Holmberg and Roberts (2014), this order instantiates a universally absent syntactic configuration (see also Fuß and Trips 2002). The competing-grammars system appears to be excessively powerful.

Moreover, the competing-grammars approach is incompatible with parameter-setting approaches like Gibson and Wexler's TLA. Gibson and Wexler assume that acquirers are only able to target a single grammar; if we add the possibility of retaining one value of a parameter alongside its counterpart value (assuming parameters to be binary), then the search space for parameter resetting becomes vastly larger, and, correspondingly, the likelihood of reaching local maxima. So the competing-grammars approach creates problems for any account of how parameter setting works.

A final issue concerns the assumptions made about parameters. Much of the work in this approach deals with word-order change, as we saw above, and assumes simple parameters of the general form of head parameters, i.e. 'X precedes/follows its complement'. However, since Kayne (1994) different approaches to word-order change have been explored, and there is evidence from much cross-linguistic work that head parameters do not represent the optimal way to describe word-order variation and change. In particular, if surface head-final order derives from leftward movement of complements around the head, then standard movement options, such as pied-piping vs stranding of various kinds, come into play, and offer an alternative approach to the variation and change (see Biberauer and Roberts 2005; Biberauer and Richards 2006).

7.2.4   The Subset Condition

A different approach to the parameter-setting question relates to the third factor in (1): non-domain-specific cognitive optimization principles. One such principle may be the Subset Condition, originally put forward by Dell (1981) for phonology and Berwick (1985) for syntax. This can be formulated as follows:

(3)   The learner must guess the smallest possible language compatible with the input at each stage of the learning procedure. (Clark and Roberts 1993: 304–5)

The attractive feature of the Subset Condition is that it prevents learners, who by assumption do not have access to negative evidence (see Brown and Hanlon 1970; Newport, Gleitman and Gleitman 1977; Marcus 1993), from getting caught in 'superset traps', i.e. postulating grammars which generate sentences which are not part of the target but which cannot be perceived as ungrammatical by the acquirer. To the extent that it instantiates a form of computational conservatism on the part of the learner, the Subset Condition can be seen as a third-factor optimization principle. It is therefore neither part of UG nor the PLD.

Biberauer and Roberts (2009) exploit the Subset Condition in relation to parameter setting and syntactic change in two ways. First, they exploit the options afforded by a complement-movement account of surface head-final orders of the kind alluded to at the end of the previous section to formulate an account of the word-order variation attested in OE. The Subset Condition, combined with the technical options regarding this leftwards movement (essentially pied-piping vs 'stranding' again) has the consequence that a system formerly allowing both options will change into one which allows only one of them; all other things being equal as regards the input, this will be the stranding option (since this is the option which moves only the essential part of the complement). They argue that this change happened in ME, thereby explaining the variation between OV and VO orders (and in subject positions and subject realization) found in OE and Early ME in contrast with what is found in later ME.

The reason the Subset Condition has the consequences just described is that it will tend to, all other things being equal, eliminate optionality which is not robustly attested in the PLD from the grammar, since it is clear that a grammar allowing two options in a given case generates a superset of the sentences compared to a grammar allowing only one of the options. In this respect, this approach differs from a competing-grammars approach, in that optionality in a single grammar is allowed, but must be robustly triggered. If the trigger becomes infrequent or ambiguous in some way, then only one option survives. As in the OE/ME word-order case sketched above, the set of formal options available makes it possible to predict which option will survive in the usual case. In this way, pathways of change can be defined (see Biberauer and Roberts 2008 for a more detailed illustration of this).

7.3 An Emergentist View of Parameters

Before presenting our own view of parameter setting, we should first clarify the general minimalist view of the nature of parameters as put forward in Chomsky (1995). Chomsky adopts and adapts an earlier conjecture due to Borer (1984), namely that parametric variation is restricted to lexical items (see also Fukui 1986). More precisely, Chomsky suggests that parametric variation is restricted to the subpart of the lexicon in which the formal features of functional heads are specified. Since Baker (2008), this has become known as the 'Borer–Chomsky Conjecture'. The formal features of functional heads are such items as φ-features, abstract Case features, categorial features and movement-triggering features. For example, on this view, the classical null-subject parameter (Rizzi 1982, 1986) may be formulated, rather than as a variant condition on licensing an empty category such as *pro*, as a feature or feature bundle associated with finite T which interacts with the feature specification of pronouns (for discussion, see Holmberg 2005, 2010; Roberts 2010). This view also implies that parameters like the Head Directionality Parameter (Travis 1984; Koopman 1984) cannot be formulated, but must be revised so as to require the involvement of a functional head, or as aspects of the mapping to PF rather than being part of the 'narrow syntax' (for discussion, see Biberauer 2008; Richards 2008).

In the remainder of this chapter, we will present a new view of the nature of parameters, one which represents a major departure from the 'classical' view, and which is compatible with minimalist assumptions, as well as being in certain respects more compatible with functionalist views on language acquisition and change. This is the 'emergentist' theory of parameters; see Dresher (2009, 2013) for a parallel view of phonological parameters. In this section, we outline this approach. In §7.4, we look at its consequences for parameter setting in syntactic change.

The central idea in the emergentist view of parameters is that the parameters of UG are **not** pre-specified in the innate endowment; in other words, they are not part of Factor 1. Instead, they emerge from the interaction of all three factors. UG itself simply leaves certain options underspecified. These gaps must be filled in order for a grammar to exist, and they are filled in by the acquirer, interacting with PLD and equipped with certain domain-general acquisition strategies. More precisely, we follow the general characterization of parameters in Chomsky (1995): parametric variation lies in variation in the formal features (e.g. Case, person, number, gender, etc.) of functional heads such as determiners, complementizers, auxiliaries, etc. A further important kind of formal feature triggers movement dependencies. As far as UG is concerned, formal-feature variation arises from underspecification for the relevant features: UG simply 'doesn't mind'. Beyond this, and a general format permitting the two primary syntactic relations, Agree and Merge, there is no specification of the nature of parametric variation at the UG level.

The precise nature of this underspecification should be clarified. In fact, on this point, two views are possible. A first, more conservative, view is that languages make a 'one-time selection' (Chomsky 2001: 10) of features from a UG-given inventory, and that the properties of these features are underspecified, e.g. their presence/absence, bundling, values, association with movement triggers ('strength', EPP/Edge Features), etc. A second, more radical view, is that the features themselves are emergent, and that UG simply specifies a general format for them, e.g. [iF, uF] or, in attribute-value terms, [F:__].

Turning to the second of the three factors, the PLD, it is important to stress that this should not be seen as an undifferentiated mass consisting of the totality of the linguistic events to which the child is exposed (the 'text' in classical learnability-theoretic terms deriving from Gold 1967). Instead, PLD designates those aspects of experience to which the acquirer is sensitive and which facilitate the setting of parameters, i.e. 'intake' rather than 'input' (see, for example, the discussion in Evers and van Kampen 2008). We crucially take these to include those aspects of the input which depart from a straightforward one-to-one form–meaning mapping, e.g. agreement (two forms, one meaning), structural Case (form without meaning), multifunctional morphemes (one form, several meanings), elliptical and other empty elements (no form, but meaning) and movement (assuming Chomsky's 2000: 120–1 notion of duality of semantics, 'extra' meaning). These aspects of the input indicate to the acquirer that the system being acquired consists of more than form (phonology) and meaning (semantics), but must involve formal features in the sense of Chomsky (1995).

Any account of how the PLD triggers parameter setting must deal with the Linking Problem mentioned above (see §7.2.2): the question of how the acquirer maps the relevant aspects of the input onto the featural options given by UG. On the conservative 'one-time selection' approach, this can be handled in one of two ways. A first possibility is a cue-based approach of the kind described in Chapter 21; we highlighted some difficulties with cues in our discussion in §7.2.2. In addition to these, in the context of a minimalist approach, specifying cues for parameters looks stipulative, and, in particular, it involves greater enrichment of UG, running counter to the spirit of the Minimalist Programme. A second possibility would be to see the properties listed above as departures from one-to-one form–meaning mapping (agreement, etc.) as triggering parameter setting, in the sense of the underspecified properties of formal features.

On the radical emergentist view, on the other hand, exactly these same properties (i.e. agreement, etc.) can be posited as guiding the acquirer's intake and determining the inventory of features *and* their properties at the same time. Hence this view is more parsimonious than the conservative view in that it requires the same learning mechanisms (see below), the same PLD, but ascribes less to UG itself. We take this to be in line with Chomsky's (2007) project of 'approaching UG from below'.

Let us now turn to the third-factor principles that are relevant to parameter setting. Recall that these are non-domain-specific cognitive optimization principles. These principles guide the acquirer in its use of intake,[2] and thereby create biases both in acquisition and change. We will look at the precise nature of these principles in the following subsections. For now, two points are important. First, following Chomsky's (2005) conception of the third factor in language design, these principles are not domain-specific, i.e. they are not part of the language faculty, but represent general cognitive principles which interact with the language faculty. In our terms, one aspect of this interaction is the role they play in guiding the construction of the feature inventory and hence parameter setting. Second, these principles did not play any explicit role in earlier accounts of parameter setting, although general notions of conservativity and economy such as Clark and Roberts' (1993) Fitness Metric, Roberts and Roussou's (2003) Feature Economy, van Gelderen's (2004) Head Preference and Late Merge principles, and possibly Lightfoot's (1979) Transparency Principle (see Chapter 15, this volume) could be seen, with hindsight, as principles of this kind. Explicitly formulating such principles in a way which relates them to general cognition, and clarifying their relation to both UG and PLD, as the three-factors approach permits, leads to much

[2] Since we regard the acquirer as an algorithm (which takes text as input and produces a grammar as output), we refer to it with the neuter pronoun; see Clark and Roberts (1993).

greater conceptual clarity. It also gives rise to a more principled account of the intuitively appealing notion of 'conservativity'.

7.3.1   Feature Economy

Two conditions that we propose amount together to a general strategy of making maximal use of minimal means. The first of these is Feature Economy (FE), which we formulate as follows:

(4)   Given two structural representations R and R′ for a substring of input text S, R is preferred over R′ iff R contains fewer formal features than R′. (Adapted from Roberts and Roussou 2003: 201)

There is a clear conceptual connection between this idea and the feature-counting Evaluation Metric of Chomsky and Halle (1968: ch. 9). It is important to stress, however, that we see FE as an acquisition bias: learners will only postulate features when confronted with unambiguous evidence in the PLD for their presence. We therefore see the effect of the Evaluation Metric as deriving in part from this acquisition strategy, unlike Chomsky and Halle, who postulated the Evaluation Metric as a separate entity. FE is clearly a strategy which minimizes computation, and may be an instance of general computational conservatism on the part of the learner.

At this point it is necessary to clarify which features are subject to FE. Here of course we limit our attention to the features relevant to syntax (for differing views on the acquisition of phonological distinctive features, see Dresher 2009; Hale and Reiss 1998, 2003). In line with the Borer–Chomsky Conjecture introduced in §7.3, we take the features relevant to parameter setting to be the formal features of functional heads. Hence FE applies to the acquisition of those features.

We described above the emergentist view of parameters we adopt. In line with that view, then, we see the acquisition of formal features, which constitutes the setting of parameters, as a process of 'filling in the gaps' in the underspecified UG. The PLD provides evidence of formal features (it expresses them, slightly extending the definition in (2)), and FE simply amounts to the claim that features must be unambiguously expressed by the PLD or they will not be postulated. FE is therefore defeasible by the PLD. To put this another way, the second factor (PLD) can outrank the third (FE) (see §7.4.3 for discussion of cases where this does not hold). But what determines the inventory of formal features which are open to acquisition and parameter setting?

On this point, two views are possible, as in the case of underspecification of UG as discussed in §7.3 above. A more conservative view is that acquirers make their 'one-time selection' from a predetermined set of features. On this view, FE amounts to selecting the smallest set of formal features consistent with the PLD. A different, more radical view is that the formal features themselves are an emergent property of the interaction of the three factors. In these terms, too, FE constrains the set of formal features acquired to the smallest set compatible with the PLD, but there is no selection from a predetermined list. Instead, the PLD directly triggers both the nature and the quantity of features acquired. This latter view is simultaneously more in line with the overall goals of the Minimalist Programme (as it attributes less content to UG) and more empirically adequate, in that it allows for more flexible feature interaction within the constraints of a narrowly defined feature template. Furthermore it is not subject to the Linking Problem discussed above.

The obvious diachronic consequence of FE is that feature loss is a natural mechanism of change. Since movement triggers are formal features, movement loss is natural in terms of FE, and can take place where a string is ambiguous between showing movement or not (e.g. in many examples of finite-verb placement in Early Modern English, which were ambiguous between a representation involving V-to-T movement and one not showing this movement; see Roberts 2007: 134f. for discussion).

Roberts and Roussou (2003) developed this idea in their account of grammaticalization (although assuming a different conception of parameters and features). On their view, grammaticalization is categorial reanalysis either of lexical categories as functional categories or of hierarchically lower functional categories as higher ones. Since lexical categories inherently have a richer feature specification than functional ones and lower functional heads, they argue, have a richer feature specification than higher ones, this kind of 'upwards grammaticalization' is predicted by FE. Again, movement loss is at work here: an earlier structure where X had a feature attracting Y (and perhaps also one Agreeing with Y) and where X c-commanded Y becomes a structure where Y is first-merged as X. Hence Y changes category (grammaticalization) as features of X are lost. Roberts and Roussou give examples of this kind of change from the C-system, the T-system and the D-system in support of their approach (see §1.3.1 for further discussion).

This approach naturally raises the question of the limits to feature loss. It must be possible for formal features to be innovated as well as lost. In fact, FE can predict this too. Take for example the stage of Jespersen's Cycle at which a former reinforcing element becomes a categorically required formal negation element (for overview discussion, see §22.2.1; Ingham and Larrivée 2011). At this stage, a new formal feature is introduced. We see this as a transition from a lexical item (a minimizer or a generic noun) to a functional item which, despite the introduction of a formal feature (presumably [Neg]), at the same time involves the elimination of a certain degree of lexical content. For example, the n-word *personne* ('nobody') in Modern French originates by grammaticalization from the noun *personne*, which means 'person', but lacks the interpretable φ-features (person, number and gender features) of the noun.

7.3.2 Input Generalization

The second third-factor mechanism that we consider is the Input Generalization (IG). This can be formulated as follows (adapted from Roberts 2007: 275):

(5)   If a functional head sets parameter p_j to value v_i then there is a preference for similar functional heads to set p_j to value v_i.

IG can be seen as a further kind of optimization strategy in acquisition, in that it requires the learner to exploit the features triggered by the PLD to the maximum extent. Hence any formal feature for which there is unambiguous evidence is generalized to the greatest available extent. If, for example, the property of head-finality is detected in the system and if this property is encoded by a formal feature (see Biberauer, Holmberg and Roberts 2014 for a proposal along these lines), then IG requires that this feature be generalized to all lexical items.

Like FE, IG is defeasible by the PLD. So, to pursue the example just given, if having generalized the head-final feature to all lexical items, unambiguous evidence for a head-initial category is detected, then the PLD forces a retreat from the maximal generalization that IG otherwise requires. This retreat divides lexical items into two classes, those with the feature and those without it, thereby creating two categories of lexical items.

FE and IG interact in a way which gives rise to a particular view of the nature of the learning path. The initial hypothesis, which fully satisfies FE and vacuously satisfies IG, is to assume the absence of formal features in the system. The PLD is, of course, guaranteed to disconfirm this maximally simple and general hypothesis by presenting the acquirer with unambiguous evidence for the existence of distinct syntactic categories, i.e. formal features. This requires at least a minimal retreat from FE, and IG now has the effect of generalizing the features posited as far as possible. If the PLD provides unambiguous evidence against the maximal generalization of features, then there is a retreat from IG and a further distinction is made.

We can summarize this interaction by saying that, for a given formal feature F, the initial hypothesis simply does not postulate F (*no* F), in line with FE and IG. Once the PLD triggers the postulation of F – by means of, for example, agreement, structural Case, multifunctional morphemes, elliptical and other empty elements, and movement, as pointed out in §7.3 – F is generalized to all elements (*all* F), in line with IG and a minimal violation of FE. Then, if the PLD provides evidence that not all heads have F, the heads are divided into those which have F and those which don't (*some* F), in line with FE, but with a minimal violation of IG. This process of postulating no F, all F and then some F can be iterated for successive subcategories of F, leading ultimately to a feature system which (nearly) replicates that of the parent generation, which may involve a potentially rich and complex feature system.

We can summarize the learning process just described as follows (for F a formal feature and h a class of lexical items):

(6)   (i) default assumption: $\neg\exists h \ [F(h)]$

     (ii) if F(h) is detected, generalize F to all relevant cases $(\exists h \ [F(h)] \rightarrow \forall h \ [F(h)])$;

     (iii) if $\exists h \ \neg[F(h)]$ is detected, restrict h and go back to (i);

     (iv) if no further F(h) is detected, stop.

The interaction of FE and IG in fact constitutes what might be thought of as a minimax algorithm, since FE minimizes features while IG maximizes their distribution. In other words, the learner makes maximal use of minimal means.

7.3.3 The Subset Condition in the Context of Minimalism

The learning procedure that we have just outlined would seem to contradict the Subset Condition given in §7.2.4, in that it appears that learners start off with very large categories and have to retreat to smaller categories (see Hale and Reiss 2003, who explicitly argue that the Subset Condition requires acquirers to start off with an *over*specified grammar – including all the universally available formal features – which they subsequently refine by 'losing'/'switching off' features not required in the target grammar). As we saw above, the Subset Condition prevents learners from falling into 'superset traps', i.e. postulating grammars which generate sentences which are not part of the target, but which cannot be perceived as ungrammatical by the acquirer. As noted above, a largely accepted key assumption in the acquisition literature is that acquirers have no access to negative evidence, i.e. evidence of ungrammatical sentences (but see Clark and Lappin 2011 for an approach to acquisition which allows negative evidence of a limited type). At first sight, our learning procedure appears to involve moving from superset to subset categories, which raises the question of how they are able to do so if the usual negative evidence assumption is maintained. However, this question does not in fact arise: the categorial distinctions are created by the learning procedure (at the *some* stage, or (6iii)). Before a given categorial distinction is created, there is no superset–subset relation; making the categorial distinction *creates* the subset. On our approach, then, the Subset Condition emerges as an epiphenomenon. Moreover, our account does not make reference to negative evidence; distinctions are triggered by positive evidence in the PLD, more specifically, by the various deviations from the simplest form–meaning mapping highlighted in §7.3 above. Our procedure thus involves a form of 'learning from ignorance' (Branigan 2012; Biberauer 2011).

In fact, the notion of 'superset trap' which the Subset Condition is designed to allow learners to circumvent simply does not arise on our approach. Distinctions are only made on the basis of positive evidence; if there is no such evidence, no distinction is made, and the superset represents the target system.

In conclusion, although the Subset Condition is a good candidate for a third-factor acquisition strategy, we take it to be epiphenomenal to the learning procedure driven by FE and IG as described in the previous section.

7.4 An Emergentist Approach to Parameter Setting

Above we outlined the general emergentist approach to parameter setting and how, once the key third-factor elements (FE and IG) are identified, this leads to a clear conception of the learning procedure. In this section, we look in more detail at the conception of parametric change that emerges from this view.

7.4.1 Types of parametric change

Biberauer and Roberts (2012) propose the following typology of parameters:

(7)   For a given value v_i of a parametrically variant feature F:
  a. **Macroparameters:** all heads of the relevant type, e.g. all probes, all phase heads, etc., share v_i;
  b. **Mesoparameters:** all heads of a given natural class, e.g. [+V] or a core functional category, share v_i;
  c. **Microparameters:** a small, lexically definable subclass of functional heads (e.g. modal auxiliaries, subject clitics) shows v_i;
  d. **Nanoparameters:** one or more individual lexical items is/are specified for v_i.

Macroparameters have highly pervasive effects on the grammatical system, which are then readily detectable in the PLD. As such, they are unlikely to be subject to reanalysis by language acquirers under normal conditions and hence are diachronically stable. A good example of a macroparameter is harmonic head-initial or head-final order: rigid head-final order is stable in many languages and language families, e.g. Dravidian, Japanese and Korean. Mesoparameters on the other hand, while still pervasive in their effects, are, as the definition in (7b) implies, less system-defining than macroparameters.

Mesoparameters are somewhat conserved diachronically, therefore, but less so than macroparameters. They tend to characterize language groups at the level of what Dryer (1992) calls a genus, i.e. the level of the principal subfamilies of a large family like Indo-European. Examples of mesoparameters in familiar Indo-European genera include VSO in the Celtic languages (found in all contemporary Celtic, and also Old Welsh and Old Irish, although probably absent in Gaulish and Celtiberian), multiple wh-fronting in Slavonic, V2 in Germanic (found in all languages except Gothic and Modern English) and Romance null subjects (found in all Romance varieties except the Northwestern ones including French, many Northern Italian dialects, Raeto-Romansch, and basilectal Brazilian Portuguese). Mesoparameters seem amenable to contact-induced change; for example, the Northwestern Romance languages arguably lost the null-subject property owing to Germanic contact.

Microparameters, as the definition in (7c) states, affect relatively small subsystems of grammars. As such, they are more amenable to change and represent less diachronically stable properties of grammars, and are more likely to be idiosyncratic to a grouping smaller than Dryer's genus. Good examples are the subject-clitic systems of northern Italian dialects, arguably restricted to a subgroup of Italo-Romance and Franco-Provençal, and the auxiliary systems found in most varieties of English (including, of course, Standard English). Microparameters are also relatively diachronically unstable: the subject clitics of northern Italian dialects are just a few centuries old (see Poletto 1995 on Veneto, for example), as are the English auxiliary systems, which appear to be undergoing changes in many varieties of English including Standard British English and many varieties of American English.

Finally, nanoparameters are in a sense peripheral to the overall system, representing just a handful of lexical items, or even just one. These items show the clustering of properties typical of all parameters, and therefore have to be distinguished from lexicalized fossils. Examples include conditional inversion in Modern English (as in *Had I been rich, life would have been great*), which only affects three auxiliaries: *had, should* and, more marginally, *were*, and the feminine singular accusative clitic *o* in Modern Romanian, which is the only clitic to appear in enclisis to a past participle or infinitive in compound tenses, all others being proclitic to the auxiliary (*l-am văzut* 'him=I.have seen', *l-aş vedea* 'him=I.would see.INF' vs *am văzut-o* 'I.have seen=her', *aş vedea-o* 'I.would see.INF=her'). Single-lexical-item nanoparameters should be distinguished from mere lexical fossils: compare English conditional inversion with optative inversion, which in the contemporary language only applies to *may* and typically only in fixed expressions, e.g. *May you rot!* Nanoparameters tend to be highly unstable; Denison (1998: 300) shows that English conditional inversion has restricted its scope to the three modern auxiliaries in the past 150 years, for example, and the extent to which conditional inversion is possible with all three auxiliaries or, indeed, at all varies significantly across modern-day varieties (see Biberauer and Roberts 2014). All other things being equal, nanoparameters must be frequently expressed in the PLD; if they are not, IG will lead them to be eliminated by analogy (note that IG can be seen as the acquisition strategy driving analogical change).

Clearly, the four parameter types given in (7) form a hierarchy. Roberts (2012) proposes that there are at least five such hierarchies. In (8), we reproduce a portion of the hierarchy of parameters connected to word order:

(8)

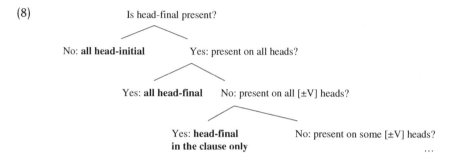

                      Is head-final present?

No: **all head-initial**   Yes: present on all heads?

    Yes: **all head-final**   No: present on all [±V] heads?

        Yes: **head-final**   No: present on some [±V] heads?
        in the clause only   ...

Here 'head-final' may be reduced to a complement-movement feature, following the general approach to word order and phrase structure in Kayne (1994). Clearly, consistent head-finality and head-initiality represent macroparameters, while the lower parameters (governing head-final order in the clause or the nominal) are mesoparameters. In its lower reaches, the hierarchy breaks up into a series of microparameters (e.g. Classical Latin was largely head-final in the clause, but complementizers were head-initial from the earliest stages, i.e. *some* in (8) would distinguish, in featural terms, the categories making up the lower reaches of the clausal extended projection, which were head-final, from those making up the higher parts, which were head-initial; for discussion, see Ledgeway 2012: ch. 5). A nanoparameter governing word order might be, for example, the single complementizer *ki* in Turkish, which takes its TP complement to its right, while Turkish is generally an almost fully harmonic head-final system.

Hierarchies like that in (8), and the associated distinctions among types of parameters given in (7), emerge directly from the learning procedure described in the previous section. In that sense, they are fully emergent properties, and in no sense prespecified in UG. The choice of [±V] as the first distinction once the general options of head-final and head-initial have been disconfirmed by the PLD is purely illustrative here. The emergence of the feature distinguishing nouns from verbs is, however, a good candidate as a first categorial distinction in (8), given the early predicate–argument distinction that children appear to grammaticalize (see, among others, Goldin-Meadow, Butcher, Mylander and Dodge 1994 and much subsequent work by Goldin-Meadow and colleagues; the overview in Gentner and Boroditsky 2001; Fisher 2002; Lidz, Gleitman and Gleitman 2003; Lidz and Gleitman 2004). Ongoing empirical work will determine the exact nature of the featural distinctions which determine the initial choices among disharmonic systems.

To recapitulate, the learning procedure described in the previous section creates parameter hierarchies like that in (8) and the associated typology of parameters given in (7). In diachronic terms, the typology in (7) makes clear predictions regarding diachronic stability. More generally, parameters associated with lower positions in hierarchies will be further along the learning path (requiring more and more iterations of the no>all>some procedure for ever finer-grained featural distinctions) and hence more prone to reanalysis by acquirers, i.e. more prone to change. In the next section, we consider some further diachronic implications of this view.

7.4.2 Consequences of the Emergentist View

Here we briefly consider the consequences of the view of parameters and parameter change sketched above for the Inertia Principle, the role of contact, nanoparametric change and the gradual nature of change.

Consider first the Inertia Principle (see Chapter 20, this volume, for more discussion). Keenan (1998: 3) formulates this as follows (see also Keenan 2002, 2009):

(9)   Things stay as they are unless a force (including decay) acts upon them.

For our purposes, we take (9) to mean that, all other things being equal, the target system is successfully converged on in language acquisition. Longobardi (2001: 278) adopts Keenan's principle, and puts forward the following version of it:

(10)   Syntactic change should not arise, unless it can be shown to be *caused*. (emphasis his)

As Longobardi says, '*syntax*, by itself, is diachronically completely inert' (2001: 277–8). In other words, the core computational operations of the narrow syntax (Merge, Agree) are completely invariant, both synchronically and diachronically. Diachronic invariance corresponds to Inertia (see again Chapter 20, this volume, and Walkden 2012 for a critique).

We can think of the Inertia Principle as asserting that where a definite value v_i is unambiguously expressed for a parameter p_i in the PLD (in the sense of parameter expression given in (2) above) then acquirers will successfully converge on v_i. In other words, the parameter will not change. Longobardi's notion of a cause of change in (10) could be anything that disrupts the PLD so that the expression of p_i is obscured. Such factors include language contact, lexical, phonological or morphological changes and earlier syntactic changes. In the latter case, it is possible for a parametric 'domino effect' to arise; Biberauer and Roberts (2008) discuss one example of a significant cascade of parameter changes in the history of English.

Again, looking at the taxonomy of parameters in (7), it is easy to see that the PLD required for expressing macroparameters is much harder to disturb than that required for mesoparameters, and that the same holds for mesoparameters in relation to microparameters and microparameters in relation to nanoparameters. Hence Inertia applies with the fullest force at the higher levels of the hierarchies. The empirical consequences of this are the observed differences in stability of the different types of parameters as discussed in the previous section.

A major factor that may perturb an otherwise highly inertial system is contact. Extensive contact is probably the only way in which macroparameters can change, and allowing for the possibility of change here does seem to be empirically motivated. Sticking to the example of word order, we have observed that rigidly head-final systems tend to be diachronically very stable, but there are examples of contact-induced changes in this domain. For instance, Biberauer, Sheehan and Newton (2010) discuss the borrowing of head-initial complementizers and question particles into otherwise head-final systems in various Indo-Aryan languages (see also Davison 2007). Biberauer, Sheehan and Newton show that only those systems which have already borrowed an initial complementizer as a consequence of extensive language contact are also able to borrow an initial question particle.

Of course, contact may play a major role in other kinds of change too, but, particularly in the case of micro- and nanoparametric change, endogenous factors, notably grammaticalization (see §7.3.1), are also at work.

Turning now to nanoparametric change, we mentioned in the previous section that nanoparametric specifications of lexical items can only persist if the items are sufficiently frequent in the PLD; otherwise they will be lost, a form of analogical levelling. An interesting aspect of this in our system is that this process of analogical levelling can cause a somewhat marked system to 'revert' to a relatively unmarked state. In the domain of conditional inversion, discussed in §7.4.1, this has happened in a number of 'advanced' varieties of contemporary English, e.g. South African English, in which conditional inversion has completely disappeared along with optative inversion. Other varieties of contemporary English may further be in the process of completely losing subject–auxiliary inversion, including in interrogatives; this seems to be the case in Singlish, for example (Deterding, Low and Brown 2003). The complete loss of subject–aux inversion clearly renders these varieties relatively unmarked in relation to this property of Standard English and earlier stages of the language.

Our approach also leads to a way of potentially reconciling the inherently abrupt and discrete nature of parametric change with the fact that the historical record most often seems to show gradual change. For example, a series of microparametric changes may give the appearance of a gradual mesoparametric change; Roberts and Roussou (2003) make this point in relation to various instances of grammaticalization. Another possibility concerns formal optionality (see §7.2.4): where a given parameter value permits two formal options (e.g. pied-piping or stranding in the case of movement), it is possible that one of the options gradually becomes preferred (because of other changes in the system; see again Biberauer and Roberts 2008 for an example from the history of English). This then leads to a situation in which one option is rare in the PLD, which may render it no longer learnable, with the result that it is fully lost.

7.4.3 Interaction of Second and Third Factors

As we stressed above, the PLD and the third-factor conditions on acquisition, FE and IG, are defeasible. In general, as we have seen, the PLD overrides FE and IG. However, it is possible under certain conditions for the third factors to 'fill in' what is unobtainable in the PLD (this point was made on the basis of somewhat different conceptual assumptions by Clark and Roberts 1993: 314).

Biberauer and Zeijlstra (2012) illustrate this situation in relation to changes in the negation system in contemporary Afrikaans. Following the general approach to negative-concord parameters developed in Zeijlstra (2004), acquirers have to determine whether various negative morphemes have an uninterpretable ([uNEG]) or interpretable ([iNEG]) feature. It is known from the first-language acquisition literature since the pioneering work of Brown (1973) that sentential negation is acquired early. Afrikaans expresses sentential negation by 'doubling' the particle *nie* as in (11):

(11) Ek is **nie** moeg **nie.**
      I   am not   tired not
      'I am not tired.'

As we pointed out in our discussion of the acquisition of formal features in §7.3, doubled features signal the presence of a formal feature (see also Zeijlstra 2008). In Zeijlstra's system, this must be an uninterpretable feature. So examples like (11), readily found in the PLD, lead to the postulation of [uNEG] for *nie*. IG then causes this feature to be assigned to all negative indefinites as they are acquired, giving rise to a strict negative-concord system (see Giannakidou 2000). Since the PLD can override IG, it is possible in principle for acquirers to assign [iNEG] to a negative indefinite as long as appropriate input is available. In this case, relevant PLD would initially seem to consist of a case where two co-occurring negative indefinites give rise to a double-negation interpretation, as in a Standard English example like *Nobody did nothing*, i.e. a case where doubling of negative elements gives rise to doubled negative meaning. Significantly, however, comparable examples in negative-concord systems, featuring the same 'contradiction-contour' intonation (Liberman and Sag 1974), also always give a double-negation interpretation (see, among others, Corblin, Déprez, de Swart and Tovena 2004). Since this is the usual intonation for such an example in Afrikaans, the PLD is essentially impotent, and IG overrides it. The result is that contemporary spoken Afrikaans systematically permits strict negative concord. This is, however, not the Standard Afrikaans pattern, in terms of which multiple negative indefinites deliver a corresponding number of multiple negative interpretations. Standard Afrikaans, with its [uNEG] sentential negation-marker and its IG-violating [iNEG] negative indefinites, does not appear to be acquirable without prescriptive input; in less normative contexts, systems of this type are predicted to be highly unstable, which appears to be correct for Old High German, a short period of which Jäger (2008) characterizes as instantiating this typologically rare type (see Biberauer and Zeijlstra 2011).

Duguine and Irurtzun (2014) present a further case study highlighting the role of third-factor considerations in the change from obligatory *wh*-movement to optional *wh-in-situ* in Labourdin Basque, spoken in a bilingual Basque-French community whose younger members are now French-dominant. Here a preference for simpler representations (*wh-in-situ* rather than movement) has led to a reanalysis of ambiguous PLD, introducing the *wh-in-situ* option alongside the normatively imposed movement one.

7.5 Conclusion and Future Directions

We can see from the foregoing that the conception of parameters has changed significantly. In fact, it may no longer be accurate to speak of 'parameters of Universal Grammar', since the advantages of an emergentist approach seem evident. Moreover, we have sketched an emergentist conception of formal features here; what we have seen is that this approach is important in understanding diachronic change in that it gives a new picture of the acquisition of formal features. Taking the third-factor components in language design seriously means that we are able to formulate notions such as FE and IG, and these play a central role in accounting for language change. Finally, our system allows us to give formal content to intuitive notions such as 'unstable system' in a way that was impossible on the earlier view of parameters.

References

Baker, C. L. 1979. 'Syntactic theory and the projection problem', *Linguistic Inquiry* 10(4): 533–81.

Baker, M. 2008. 'The macroparameter in a microparametric world', in Biberauer (ed.), pp. 351–74.

Berwick, R. 1985. *The acquisition of syntactic knowledge*. Cambridge, MA: MIT Press.

Biberauer, T. (ed.) 2008. *The limits of syntactic variation*. Amsterdam: John Benjamins.

  2011. 'In defence of lexico-centric parametric variation: Two 3rd factor-constrained case studies', paper presented at the Workshop on Formal Grammar and Syntactic Variation: Rethinking Parameters, Madrid.

Biberauer, T., Holmberg, A. and Roberts, I. 2014. 'A syntactic universal and its consequences', *Linguistic Inquiry* 45(2): 169–225.

Biberauer, T., Holmberg, A., Roberts, I. and Sheehan, M. (eds.) 2010. *Parametric variation: Null subjects in minimalist theory*. Cambridge University Press.

Biberauer, T. and Richards, M. 2006. 'True optionality: When the grammar doesn't mind', in C. Boeckx (ed.), *Minimalist essays*. Amsterdam: John Benjamins, pp. 35–67.

Biberauer, T. and Roberts, I. 2005. 'Changing EPP-parameters in the history of English: Accounting for variation and change', *English Language and Linguistics* 9(1): 5–46.

  2008. 'Cascading parameter changes: Internally driven change in Middle and Early Modern English', in Th. Eythórsson (ed.), *Grammatical change and linguistic theory: The Rosendal papers*. Amsterdam: John Benjamins, pp. 79–113.

  2009. 'The return of the subset principle', in Crisma and Longobardi (eds.), pp. 58–74.

  2012. 'Towards a parameter hierarchy for auxiliaries: Diachronic considerations', in J. Chancharu, X. Hu and M. Mitrović (eds.), *Cambridge Occasional Papers in Linguistics* 6: 209–36.

  2014. 'Conditional inversion and types of parametric change', paper presented at the 40th Incontro di grammatica generativa, Trento.

Biberauer, T., Sheehan, M. and Newton, G. 2010. 'Impossible changes and impossible borrowings: The Final-over-Final Constraint', in A. Breitbarth, C. Lucas, S. Watts and D. Willis (eds.), *Continuity and change in grammar*. Amsterdam: John Benjamins, pp. 35–60.

Biberauer, T. and Zeijlstra, H. 2011. 'Negative concord in Afrikaans: Filling a typological gap', *Journal of Semantics* 29(3): 345–71.

2012. 'Negative changes: Three factors and the diachrony of Afrikaans negation', in Galves, Cyrino, Sândalo, Lopes and Avelar (eds.), pp. 237–63.

Borer, H. 1984. *Parametric syntax: Case studies in Semitic and Romance languages.* Dordrecht: Foris.

Branigan, P. 2012. 'Macroparameter learnability: An Algonquian case study', unpublished MS, Memorial University, Newfoundland.

Brown, R. 1973. *A first language: The early years.* Cambridge, MA: Harvard University Press.

Brown, R. and Hanlon, C. 1970. 'Derivational complexity and order of acquisition in child speech', in J. Hayes (ed.), *Cognition and the development of language.* New York: John Wiley and Sons, pp. 11–53.

Chomsky, N. 1981. *Lectures on government and binding.* Dordrecht: Foris.

1995. *The minimalist program.* Cambridge, MA: MIT Press.

2000. 'Minimalist inquiries: The framework', in R. Martin, D. Michaels and J. Uriagereka (eds.), *Step by step: Essays on minimalist syntax in honor of Howard Lasnik.* Cambridge, MA.: MIT Press, pp. 89–156.

2001. 'Derivation by phase', in M. Kenstowicz (ed.), *Ken Hale: A life in language.* Cambridge, MA.: MIT Press, pp. 1–53.

2005. 'Three factors in language design', *Linguistic Inquiry* 36(1): 1–22.

2007. 'Approaching UG from below', in H.-M. Gärtner and U. Sauerland (eds.), *Interface + Recursion = Language? Chomsky's minimalism and the view from syntax and semantics.* Berlin: Mouton de Gruyter, pp. 1–29.

Chomsky, N. and Halle, M. 1968. *The sound pattern of English.* New York: Harper & Row.

Clark, A. and Lappin, S. 2011. *Linguistic nativism and the Poverty of the Stimulus.* Malden, MA: Blackwell.

Clark, R. 1992. 'The selection of syntactic knowledge', *Language Acquisition* 2 (2): 83–149.

Clark, R. and Roberts, I. 1993. 'A computational model of language learnability and language change', *Linguistic Inquiry* 24(2): 299–345.

Corblin, F., Déprez, V., de Swart, H. and Tovena, L. 2004. 'Negative concord', in F. Corblin and H. de Swart (eds.), *Handbok of French semantics.* Stanford, CA: CSLI, pp. 417–52.

Crisma, P. and Longobardi, G. (eds) 2009. *Historical syntax and linguistic theory.* Oxford University Press.

Davison, A. 2007. 'Word order, parameters and the extended COMP projection', in J. Bayer, T. Bhattacharya and M. Veettil Tharayil Hany Babu (eds.), *Linguistic theory and South Asian languages.* Amsterdam: John Benjamins, pp. 175–98.

Dell, F. 1981. 'On the learnability of optional phonological rules', *Linguistic Inquiry* 12(1): 31–7.

Denison, D. 1998. 'Syntax', in S. Romaine (ed.), *The Cambridge History of the English language*, vol. IV: *1776–1997.* Cambridge University Press, pp. 92–329.

Deterding, D., Ling Low, E. and Brown, A. 2003. *English in Singapore: Research on grammar*. Singapore: McGraw-Hill.

Dresher, E. 1999. 'Charting the learning path: Cues to parameter setting', *Linguistic Inquiry* 30(1): 27–67.

    2009. *The contrastive hierarchy in phonology*. Cambridge University Press.

    2013. 'The arch not the stones: Universal Feature Theory without universal features', paper presented at the Conference on Features in Phonology, Morphology, Syntax and Semantics: What Are They?, CASTL, University of Tromsø.

Dresher, E. and Kaye, J. 1990. 'A computational learning model for Metrical Phonology', *Cognition* 34(1): 137–95.

Dryer, M. 1992. 'The Greenbergian word order correlations', *Language* 68: 81–138.

Duguine, M. and Irurtzun, A. 2014. 'From obligatory wh-movement to optional wh-in-situ in Labourdin Basque', *Language* 90(1): e1–e30.

Evers, A. and van Kampen, J. 2008. 'Parameter setting and input reduction', in Biberauer (ed.), pp. 483–515.

Fischer, O., van Kemenade, A., Koopman, W. and van der Wurff, W. 2000. *The syntax of early English*. Cambridge University Press.

Fisher, C. 2002. 'The role of abstract syntactic knowledge in language acquisition: A reply to Tomasello (2000)', *Cognition* 82: 259–78.

Fodor, J. D. 1998. 'Unambiguous triggers', *Linguistic Inquiry* 19(1): 1–36.

Fodor, J. D. and Sakas, W. 2004. 'Evaluating models of parameter setting', *Proceedings of the 28th Annual Boston University Conference on Language Development (BUCLD 28)*. Somerville, MA: Cascadilla Press, pp. 1–27.

Fontana, J. 1993. 'Phrase structure and the syntax of clitics in the history of Spanish', unpublished PhD thesis, University of Pennsylvania.

Frank, R. and Kapur, S. 1996. 'On the use of triggers in parameter setting', *Linguistic Inquiry* 27: 623–60.

Fukui, N. 1986. 'A theory of category projection and its applications', unpublished PhD thesis, MIT.

Fuß, E. and Trips, C. 2002. 'Variation and change in Old and Middle English – on the validity of the double base hypothesis', *Journal of Comparative Germanic Linguistics* 4: 171–224.

Galves, C., Cyrino, S., Sândalo, F., Lopes, R. and Avelar, J. (eds.) 2012. *Parameter theory and linguistic change*. Oxford University Press.

Gentner, D. and Boroditsky, L. 2001. 'Individuation, relational relativity and early word learning', in M. Bowerman and S. Levinson (eds.), *Language acquisition and conceptual development*. Cambridge University Press, pp. 215–56.

Giannakidou, A. 2000. 'Negative ... Concord?', *Natural Language and Linguistic Theory* 18: 457–523.

Gibson, E. and Wexler, K. 1994. 'Triggers', *Linguistic Inquiry* 25(3): 407–54.

Gold, E. M. 1967. 'Language identication in the limit', *Information and Control* 10: 447–74.

Goldin-Meadow, S., Butcher, C., Mylander, C. and Dodge, M. 1994. 'Nouns and verbs in a self-styled gesture system: what's in a name?', *Cognitive Psychology* 27: 259–319.

Hale, M. and Reiss, C. 1998. 'Formal and empirical arguments concerning phonological acquisition', *Linguistic Inquiry* 29(4): 656–83.

2003. 'The subset principle in phonology: Why the *tabula* can't be *rasa*', *Journal of Linguistics* 39(2): 219–44.

Heycock, C. and Wallenberg, J. 2013. 'How variational acquisition drives syntactic change: The loss of verb movement in Scandinavian', *Journal of Comparative Germanic Linguistics* 16(2/3): 127–57.

Holmberg, A. 2005. 'Is there a little pro? Evidence from Finnish', *Linguistic Inquiry* 36(4): 533–56.

2010. 'Null subject parameters', in Biberauer, Holmberg, Roberts and Sheehan (eds.), pp. 88–112.

Ingham, R. and Larrivée, P. 2011. *The evolution of negation: Beyond the Jespersen Cycle*. Berlin: Mouton de Gruyter.

Jäger, A. 2008. *History of German negation*. Amsterdam: John Benjamins.

Kayne, R. 1994. *The antisymmetry of syntax*. Cambridge, MA: MIT Press.

Keenan, E. 1998. 'The historical creation of reflexive pronouns in English', unpublished MS, UCLA.

2002. 'Explaining the creation of reflexive pronouns in English', in D. Minkova and R. Stockwell (eds.), *Studies in the history of English: A millennial perspective*. New York: Mouton de Gruyter, pp. 325–55.

2009. 'Linguistic theory and the historical creation of English reflexives', in Crisma and Longobardi (eds.), pp. 17–40.

Koopman, H. 1984. *The syntax of verbs: From verb movement rules in the Kru languages to Universal Grammar*. Dordrecht: Foris.

Kroch, A. 1989. 'Reflexes of grammar in patterns of language change', *Language Variation and Change* 1(3): 199–244.

1994. 'Morphosyntactic variation', in K. Beals, J. Denton, B. Knippen, L. Meinar, H. Suzuki and E. Zeinfeld (eds.), *Proceedings of the thirtieth annual meeting of the Chicago Linguistic Society*, pp. 180–201.

2001. 'Syntactic change', in M. Baltin and C. Collins (eds.), *The handbook of contemporary syntactic theory*. Malden, MA: Blackwell, pp. 629–739.

Kroch, A. and Taylor, A. 2000. 'Verb–object order in early Middle English', in S. Pintzuk, G. Tsoulas and A. Warner (eds.), *Diachronic syntax: Models and mechanisms*. Oxford University Press, pp. 132–63.

Ledgeway, A. 2012. *From Latin to Romance: Morphosyntactic typology and change*. Oxford University Press.

Liberman, M. and Sag, I. 1974. 'Prosodic form and discourse function', *Chicago Linguistics Society* 10: 416–27.

Lidz, J., Gleitman, H. and Gleitman, L. 2003. 'Understanding how input matters: Verb learning and the footprint of universal grammar', *Cognition* 87(3): 151–78.

Lidz, J. and Gleitman, L. 2004. 'Argument structure and the child's contribution to language learning', *Trends in Cognitive Sciences* 8(4): 157–61.

Lightfoot, D. W. 1979. *Principles of diachronic syntax*. Cambridge University Press.

1991. *How to set parameters: Arguments from language change*. Cambridge, MA: MIT Press.

1999. *The development of language: Acquisition, change and evolution*. Oxford: Blackwell.

2006. *How new languages emerge*. Cambridge University Press.

Lightfoot, D. and Westergaard, M. 2007. 'Language acquisition and language change: Interrelationships', *Language and Linguistics Compass* 1(5): 396–416.

Longobardi, G. 2001. 'Formal syntax, diachronic minimalism, and etymology: The history of French *chez*', *Linguistic Inquiry* 32(2): 275–302.

MacSwan, J. 2000. 'The architecture of the bilingual language faculty: Evidence from intrasentential code switching', *Bilingualism: Language and Cognition* 3(1): 37–54.

Marcus, G. 1993. 'Negative evidence in language acquisition', *Cognition* 46: 53–85.

Moerenhout, M. and van der Wurff, W. 2005. 'Object–verb order in early sixteenth-century English prose: An exploratory study', *English Language and Linguistics* 9(1): 83–114.

Newport, E., Gleitman, L. and Gleitman, H. 1977. 'Mother, I'd rather do it myself: Some effects and non-effects of maternal speech style', in C. Snow and C. A. Ferguson (eds.), *Talking to children: Language input and acquistion*. Cambridge University Press, pp. 109–49.

Niyogi, P. and Berwick, R. 1995. 'The logical problem of language change', A.I. Memo no. 1516, MIT Artificial Intelligence Laboratory.

Pinker, S. 1984. *Language learnability and language development*. Cambridge, MA: Harvard University Press.

Pintzuk, S. 1991. 'Phrase structures in competition: Variation and change in Old English word order', unpublished PhD thesis, University of Pennsylvania.

Pintzuk, S. and Taylor, A. 2006. 'The loss of OV order in the history of English', in A. van Kemenade and B. Los (eds.), *The handbook of the history of English*. Oxford: Blackwell, pp. 249–78.

Poletto, C. 1995. 'The diachronic development of subject clitics in North-Eastern Italian dialects', in A. Battye and I. Roberts (eds.), *Clause structure and language change*. Oxford University Press, pp. 295–324.

Richards, M. 2008. 'Two kinds of variation in a minimalist system', in F. Heck, G. Müller and J. Trommer (eds.), *Varieties of competition: Linguistische Arbeitsberichte*. Leipzig University, pp. 133–62.

Rizzi, L. 1982. *Issues in Italian Syntax*. Dordrecht: Foris.

1986. 'Null objects in Italian and the theory of pro', *Linguistic Inquiry* 17: 501–57.

Roberts, I. 2007. *Diachronic syntax*. Oxford University Press.

    2010. 'A deletion analysis of null subjects', in Biberauer, Holmberg, Roberts and Sheehan (eds.), pp. 58–87.

    2012. 'Macroparameters and minimalism: A programme for comparative research', in Galves, Cyrino, Sândalo, Lopes and Avelar (eds.), pp. 320–35.

Roberts, I. and Roussou, A. 2003. *Syntactic change: A minimalist approach to grammaticalisation*. Cambridge University Press.

Rögnvaldsson, E. 1996. 'Word order variation in the VP in Old Icelandic', *Working Papers in Scandinavian Syntax* 58: 55–86.

Sakas, W. and Fodor, J. D. 2012. 'Disambiguating syntactic triggers', *Language Acquisition* 19: 83–143.

Santorini, B. 1989. 'The generalization of the verb-second constraint in the history of Yiddish', unpublished PhD thesis, University of Pennsylvania.

    1992. 'Variation and change in Yiddish subordinate clause word order', *Natural Language and Linguistic Theory* 10: 595–640.

Speyer, A. 2008. 'On the interaction of prosody and syntax in the history of English, with a few remarks on German', unpublished PhD thesis, University of Pennsylvania.

Taylor, A. 1990. 'Clitics and configurationality in Ancient Greek', unpublished PhD thesis, University of Pennsylvania.

Taylor, A. and Pintzuk, S. 2012. 'Rethinking the OV/VO alternation in Old English: The effect of complexity, grammatical weight, and information status', in E. C. Traugott and T. Nevalainen (eds.), *The Oxford handbook of the history of English*. Oxford University Press, pp. 835–45.

Thráinsson, H. 2003. 'Syntactic variation, historical development, and minimalism', in R. Hendrick (ed.), *Minimalist syntax*. Oxford: Blackwell, pp. 152–91.

Travis, L. 1984. 'Parameters and effects of word order variation', unpublished PhD thesis, MIT.

van Gelderen, E. 2004. *Grammaticalization as economy*. Amsterdam: John Benjamins.

van Kemenade, A. 1987. *Syntactic Case and morphological case in the history of English*. Dordrecht: Foris.

Walkden, G. 2012. 'Against Inertia', *Lingua* 122(8): 891–901.

Wallenberg, J. 2009. 'Antisymmetry and the conservation of c-command: scrambling and phrase structure in synchronic and diachronic perspective', unpublished PhD thesis, University of Pennsylvania.

Wexler, K. and Culicover, P. 1980. *Formal principles of language acquisition*. Cambridge, MA: MIT Press.

Yang, C. 2002. *Knowledge and learning in natural language*. Oxford University Press.

2013. 'Tipping Points', talk given at the 36 Generative Linguistics in the Old World (GLOW36) Conference, Lund.

Zeijlstra, H. 2004. 'Sentential negation and negative concord', unpublished PhD thesis, Amsterdam University.

2008. 'On the syntactic flexibility of formal features', in Biberauer (ed.), pp. 143–73.

8

Contact and Borrowing

Tania Kuteva

8.1   Introduction

When two languages come into contact, that is, when language speakers use two languages, this may lead to transfer of linguistic material from one contact language to the other. Such linguistic transfer constitutes contact-induced language change and encompasses a number of distinct phenomena, syntactic and morphosyntactic change being two of them.

Our goal in the present chapter is to place syntactic and morphosyntactic change resulting from language contact within the global picture of contact-induced linguistic transfer. For this purpose we will first propose a comprehensive model of contact-induced linguistic transfer, for which we will use the term 'Comprehensive Model' (ComMod) as shorthand. First attempts at a model of contact-induced phenomena have been made already, e.g. in Heine and Kuteva (2006), as well as Matras and Sakel (2007) (see discussion below). Notice, however, that in both of these models the authors focus on transfer of linguistic structures whereby no phonetic substance is involved but rather the transfer of patterns, structural templates, i.e. concepts rather than their material encodings (for a critical assessment of both models, see Wiemer and Wälchli 2012). What remains largely under-represented in the literature are types and subtypes of linguistic transfer involving also phonological material transferred from one contact language to the other. Fleshing out a general model of contact-induced linguistic transfer encompassing both types – and their subtypes – of contact-induced change is therefore our first goal in the present chapter.

The author wishes to thank Adam Ledgeway and Ian Roberts for their insightful suggestions and all their help. Deep gratitude is also due to the Endangered Languages Academic Programme at SOAS, University of London, the English Department of UCL, University of London, as well as the Alexander von Humboldt Research Foundation for the stimulating scientific atmosphere and the generous financial support.

As a second step, it is our ultimate goal to establish the place syntactic and morphosyntactic change have in the ComMod proposed here.

We will assume that not only are contact-induced syntactic and morphosyntactic change distinct types of linguistic transfer in a language contact situation, but that language contact can be regarded as an independent mechanism of these types of change (see also Harris and Campbell 1995:150). This mechanism, we will further assume, is on a par with other mechanisms, which have figured prominently in the literature on historical syntax such as typological drift/shift (Lehmann 1973; Harris 1984), abduction (Andersen 1973; Timberlake 1977), phonological and morphological renewal (Harris 1978, 1984; Lightfoot 1991), reanalysis of linguistic structures whereby transparency comes to replace opacity (Langacker 1977; Lightfoot 1991).

The chapter is structured as follows. §8.2 introduces the basic theoretical constructs used here. The following section describes the two ways in which the notion of borrowing has been employed and gives an overview of the universals and principles of borrowing formulated in the literature on language contact so far. §8.4 proposes what is termed a *Comprehensive Model of Contact-Induced Linguistic Transfer* and points out the role syntactic and morphosyntactic change play within such a model. §8.5 presents the conclusions of this chapter.

8.2 Theoretical Preliminaries

Here we will be using terminology that goes back to Weinreich (1953), and has been later adopted by a number of students of language contact (Heine and Kuteva 2003, 2005, 2006, among others). Accordingly, one of the contact languages is the source, or the Model Language (ML), of a particular linguistic structure x, (MLx), that gets transferred from ML to the receiving contact language, or the Replica Language (RL), as the new linguistic structure in R, (RLx).

As pointed out above, we assume – along with Harris and Campbell (1995: 150), among others – that language contact constitutes a distinct, independent mechanism of grammatical change. This assumption is directly relevant to the Integrative Model of grammaticalization – as part of grammatical change – where language contact is seen not only as an accelerating but also as a propelling force triggering language change (Kuteva and Heine 2012).

8.3 Borrowing

Borrowing has been used in two different senses in the literature on language contact, in a broad sense, and in a narrow sense. Since the former constitutes the traditional understanding of the term, it will be the first one to be discussed in the present section.

8.3.1   Borrowing: The Traditional View

The traditional use of the term borrowing follows from a rather general definition of this process, namely the adoption by one language of linguistic elements from another language. Notice that on this definition what is meant by 'linguistic elements' remains maximally unspecified, and the term borrowing itself stands for any type of linguistic transfer in a language contact situation. In this broad sense of the term, there are two major results of the way languages can influence each other in a contact situation, lexical borrowing and structural borrowing.

What has been traditionally understood under lexical borrowing are:

(a) loanwords, e.g. Ger. *Espresso* (from It. *espresso*);
(b) loan translations/calques, i.e. whole phrases/idiomatic expressions acquired through a word-for-word translation into native morphemes, e.g. It. *grattacielo* from Eng. *skyscraper*.

The term structural borrowing, on the other hand, has been used to refer to the transfer from one contact language to the other of:

(a) phonetic/phonological features, e.g. the sound [ʒ] in English from French, or the Latinate English alternation whereby root-final [k] > [s] as in *electric/electricity*;
(b) morphological features, e.g. the productive derivational suffixes *-able/-ible* into English from French;
(c) syntactic features (i.e. the ordering requirements of surface elements involving sentence word order, order of modifier and its head, etc.), e.g. the adoption of SOV word order in Asia Minor Greek dialects under the influence of Turkish.

The organizing principle of the above taxonomy of types of linguistic transfer is a static one: it involves the result of the transfer, and one of two domains of RL affected by the transfer. If it is the domain of the lexicon that is affected, then we are dealing with lexical borrowing; if it is the area of phonology, or morphology or syntax (or any combination of them), then it is structural borrowing. The tacit assumption here is that the domain of grammar encompasses phonology and morphosyntax; hence the frequent interchangeable use of the terms structural borrowing and grammatical borrowing.

Using as a starting point the above broad definition of borrowing, both lexical and structural, students of contact linguistics have proposed a number of universals and principles of borrowing. Even though the following is not an exhaustive list of them, it still includes the most common ones:

1. *Structural borrowing is always preceded by lexical borrowing* (Moravcsik 1978: 110; see also Winford 2003: 61);
2. *Bound morphemes (such as clitics, affixes) are borrowed only after free forms that these bound morphemes are proper parts of have been borrowed* (Moravcsik 1978: 110);
3. *Nouns are borrowed first and foremost* (Moravcsik 1978: 111);
4. *'A lexical item whose meaning is verbal can never be included in a set of borrowed properties'* (Moravcsik 1978: 111);
5. *Free-standing grammatical forms are more easily borrowed than bound morphemes* (Weinreich 1953: 41; Heath 1978: 72);
6. *Inflectional affixes can only be borrowed from a language after derivational ones have been borrowed* (Moravcsik 1978: 111);
7. *Grammatical items (such as conjunctions and adpositions) are borrowed from a language only in accordance with their original word order arrangements* (Moravcsik 1978: 112);
8. *Word order changes are due above all to language contact* (Smith 1981: 52);
9. *Structural borrowing is only possible between languages with similar/compatible systems* (Weinreich 1953: 25; Allen [1977] 1980: 380).

Over the last decades of research on language contact it has been shown that there exist counterexamples to each of the above universals and principles, so that – at worst – they have been proven to be wrong, e.g. (4) above, and – at best – they have been shown to manifest tendencies rather than strict universals or principles in any absolute sense, e.g. (3), (7).

8.3.2   Borrowing: The Present View

Following Heine and Kuteva (2003, 2005, 2006, 2008; see also, among others, Matras and Sakel 2007; Kuteva and Heine 2012), in the present chapter we will use the term borrowing in a narrow sense: the adoption by one language of sounds or form:meaning pairings (e.g. morphemes, words or larger units) from another language. Under this definition, borrowing concerns – crucially – phonetic substance/phonological material. Accordingly, all transfers of sounds and phonological rules, words with both their form and meaning (i.e. loanwords), and morphological as well as morphosyntactic structures involving both form and meaning are cases of borrowing on the present understanding. On the other hand, calques/loanshifts (which concern the structural pattern but not phonological material/phonetic substance), as well as syntactic features such as word order (which involve the ordering requirements of meaningful elements but not the material substance of the elements themselves), fall outside the scope of borrowing.

8.3.3   Three More Principles of Linguistic Transfer

Adopting the above narrow definition of borrowing, we will now take a closer look at three more principles, which have been at the centre of lively debate in the literature on language contact over the last decades: (i) grammatical gaps; (ii) replacement/renewal vs creation of form and function; and (iii) structural simplification. Notice that borrowing – in the narrow sense in which we use it here – is only one type, even though a major one, of contact-induced linguistic transfer; hence, in what follows we will resort to the umbrella term *linguistic transfer* to also refer to what has been traditionally called – in a very broad sense – borrowing.

8.3.3.1 Grammatical Gaps

It has been argued that transfer of grammatical structures in language contact situations has 'therapeutic' value: if a language has a structural gap somewhere in its system, it will transfer structure from a contact language in order to fill in the gap (Vachek 1972: 221f.; Winford 2003: 96). This claim has also run under the name of functional need explanation of language change and has been made both with respect to contact and non-contact-related language change. For non-contact-related language change, there have been a number of studies arguing that new grammatical structures come into existence not because they are functionally needed; they evolve historically rather than because they are 'needed'. Even if at first sight it is intellectually tempting to assume that individual grammatical structures arise to fill a gap in the grammatical system, there have been a number of studies arguing that the rise of grammatical structures in non-contact-related situations does not entail need as a triggering factor (Comrie and Kuteva 2005, among others).

When it comes to contact situations, however, the picture is more complex. On the one hand, it is an undisputable fact that a grammatical structure can be transferred from ML to RL even if in the latter there exists a grammatical structure encoding the same function already (Moravcsik 1978: 104–6). For instance, Yaqui (Uto-Aztecan) has borrowed the Spanish subordinate complement clause marker *ke* (Sp. *que* 'that', used clause-initially) even though its own, indigenous complementizer suffix *-kai* (used clause-finally) is alive and well in the language. This can be illustrated by the following examples from Spanish and Yaqui:

(1)   Spanish (Moravcsik 1978: 105)
       Es   muy   bueno   **que**   esa   mujer   cante.
       is   very good   that   this   woman   sings
       'It is very good that this woman sings.'

(2)   Yaqui (Moravcsik 1978: 105)
       a. Tuisi tu'i   hu   hamut   bwika-**kai**
          very   good   this woman   sing- that
          'It is very good that this woman sings.'
       b. Tuisi tu'i   **ke**   hu   hamut   bwika.
          very   good   that   this woman   sing
          'It is very good that this woman sings.'

In other words, a structural gap in RL is not a necessary prerequisite for the transfer of a grammatical structure from ML.[1] On the other hand, the following observation made in Heine and Kuteva (2003, 2005, 2006) across a sizable body of language contact situations supports – rather than refutes – the 'grammatical gaps' principle. Let us first recall that there exist three theoretical possibilities, if in a language contact situation ML has a grammatical structure x, and RL lacks a comparable grammatical structure x, i.e. RL has a structural gap in that area of its grammar: (i) RL will acquire x, given sufficient intensity and duration of contact; (ii) RL will not acquire x (i.e. RL will maintain its structural gap); and (iii) ML will lose x. Now, it turns out that of these three possibilities the first one is the most likely to materialize and the third one the most unlikely one.

To conclude, more research is needed on the significance of structural/ grammatical gaps as a triggering factor in contact-induced change.

8.3.3.2   Replacement/Renewal of Form vs the Creation of a New Structure

According to another principle of contact-induced language change proposed in the literature, the transfer of a morpheme from one contact language to another usually involves the replacement – or the renewal – of a native morpheme by one from another language rather than the creation of a new morphological category filled by a transferred morpheme (Weinreich 1953: 31–7; Heath 1978: 73). This relates directly to what has been referred to as the principle of 'diachronic stability of grammatical categories': diachronically, there exists a tendency for grams to redevelop into categories that were present at earlier stages of the same language, and not to develop into categories for which that language did not already have grammatical expression (for a detailed discussion, see Kuteva 2001). For instance, a language like English has no grams expressing hodiernal or hesternal pasts, and – according to the diachronic stability principle – it is unlikely that such grams will develop in English, simply because English does not happen to have either a hodiernal or hesternal past gram in its earlier historical stages. The argument usually employed in support of this extreme view of linguistic determinism is the observation made in language change studies about the persistence with which the same grammatical category may re-emerge in a given language, as in Bantu, for instance, where several different lexical morphemes, each of which has 'finish' as its initial semantics, developed into the same grammatical category, i.e. the perfective.

---

[1] Adam Ledgeway (p.c.) points out that if the language were moving (had already largely moved) towards a head-initial setting, then the 'need' (= gap) for a new head-initial complementizer would be very real (and could not be filled by a suffixal head-final *kai*). However, this is all speculation and will depend on the (changing) general word-order patterns in this language.

If the diachronic stability of grams were a universally valid principle, then one would expect – indeed – that when a grammatical structure is transferred from ML to RL, this would be in order to replace/renew a grammatical category already existing in RL. There have been a number of studies, however, showing that grammatical structures may be transferred from ML to RL whereby a new grammatical category is *created* in RL. Examples of grammatical structures that are created anew in RL as a result of linguistic transfer from ML – and not the recurrent tendency to continue diachronically the presence of an already existing gram – are not hard to come by. We can illustrate this by means of an example from Bulgarian, discussed in Kuteva (2001). Bulgarian (Slavonic) is well known for having a grammatical structure for non-witnessed events, traditionally called the *evidential.* It indicates that the relation between the speaker and the event reported is not direct but mediated by a third party; what the speaker is reporting is hearsay information. Thus along with the set of verbal forms for events which are reported as 'first hand' in very much the same way as in most Indo-European languages, Bulgarian has a special grammatical set of forms encoding the fact that the event, denoted by the verb, is presented as hearsay and not as something which has been witnessed directly by the speaker. A comparison between the first example in the declarative and the second one in the evidential below illustrates this difference:

(3) Bulgarian (Kuteva 2001: 127)
     Ne   iskaš   da   í   pišeš.
     not want.2sg.prs   to   her write.2sg.prs
     'You don't want to write to her.'

(4) Bulgarian (Kuteva 2001: 127)
     Ne   **si**   **iskal**   da   í   pišeš.
     not be.2sg.prs   want.ptcp   to   her write.2sg.prs
     They say, you don´t want to write to her.

Whereas the verb *iskaš* 'want' in the declarative sentence is in its present tense form, the verb form *si iskal* in the corresponding evidential sentence is a complex one consisting of the auxiliary *si* 'be' and the so-called *l*-participle of the main verb, *iskal.*

Given that Bulgarian is one of the few languages in the world with a long-attested history, we are in a position to establish the following important fact about the genesis of the evidential category in that language. Old Bulgarian had no gram for the evidential. Moreover, there is no other Slavonic language in which an evidential gram has been attested either diachronically or synchronically. These facts alone indicate that it is unlikely for the Bulgarian evidential to be a genetically inherited Slavonic feature. A careful investigation of Old and Middle Bulgarian texts reveals – indeed – that the first indications for the existence of this gram in

Bulgarian appear after Turkey established its hegemony on the Balkans at the end of the fourteenth century. What is crucially important for the present discussion is that the Turkish language did have an evidential gram *before* the Ottoman Empire was established, i.e. before the fourteenth century. That the Bulgarian evidential was the result of a linguistic transfer from Turkish (Altaic) is not surprising, especially if we take a closer look at the sociolinguistic particulars of the contact situation involving all the languages of the Balkan *Sprachbund*, with Bulgarian and Turkish being two of them (Kuteva 1999). Thus we can conclude that the evidential in Bulgarian arose as a new category imitating the evidential in Turkish at a time when Bulgaria was strongly colonized by Turkish speakers and a great number of Bulgarian speakers were living in conditions of bilingualism (Mirčev 1963: 208).

To sum up, morphological replacement/renewal due to transfer of a grammatical structure from one contact language to another is one – but not the only – possibility in a language contact situation. The creation of a new category as a result of linguistic transfer is just as viable an alternative.

8.3.3.3 Structural Simplification

It has been the common practice in contact linguistics to assume that linguistic transfer in a language contact situation leads to simplification, more precisely to: (i) decrease in size of phonetically realized inflectional affixes on nouns and verbs; (ii) reduction in redundancy; (iii) filtering out of morphological irregularities; (iv) reduction of grammatical systems such as conjugations, declensions and inflected forms. In other words, the traditional assumption has been that high-contact varieties are characterized by reduced, simplified grammar. An attempt at plausible explanation of this poverty of grammatical structure in high-contact varieties has also been around for quite some time now. Trudgill (1983; see also Trudgill 2001) blames it on 'the lousy language-learning abilities of the human adult' trying to cope with second-language acquisition processes. Whereas these processes present no problem for 'the amazing language-learning abilities of the human child', they can be too much of a challenge for the adult language learner. 'Adult language contact means adult language learning; and adult language learning means simplification . . .This can indeed be seen at its most extreme in pidgins and hence in creoles (Trudgill 1996). But it is not confined to this type of language' (Trudgill 2001: 372).

More recent research on high-contact varieties has shown, however, that structural simplification as a result of linguistic transfer is only half of the story. Thus Heath (1978), Nichols (1992) and, more recently, Aikhenvald (2002), Heine and Kuteva (2005), Kuteva (2008), Kuteva and Comrie (2012), among others, have argued that language contact may well bring about diversification and complexification of grammar.

Trudgill himself has come to modify his initial standpoint: in his recent work he acknowledges that there have been two major types of situation identified according to the type of impact social network structure and stability have on linguistic structure (Trudgill 2004: 437f.), a contact-and-simplification situation and a contact-and-complexification one. The former involves cases where 'simplification may occur in high-contact languages as a result of pidginization, which is what occurs in those situations involving adult and therefore imperfect language acquisition on the part of speakers who have passed the critical threshold ...'. In other words, language contact may cause loss (of phonological material, grammatical structures) (see Trudgill 1983; see also Trudgill 1996; 2001: 372).

The contact-and-complexification situation, on the other hand, involves cases where increased complexification may occur in languages as a result of linguistic transfer, whereby long-term contact and childhood bilingualism are necessary accompanying factors (Trudgill 2004: 437f.). That language contact may well bring about structural complexification rather than simplification becomes clear from a recent study by Kuteva and Comrie (2012) on subject relativization, where one of the language samples analysed encompasses twelve high-contact language varieties; these are examined for the marking of the relative clause construction. In six of them, i.e. in 50 per cent of the sample languages, it is possible to identify more than one marker of the relative clause construction. One of the varieties encodes subject relativization by means of zero, or one, or three markers; five of them by means of two markers. Since the latter varieties (with two markers) are relevant to the present discussion, let us illustrate them with an example from the Saraswat Brahmins Konkani variety (Nadkarni 1975: 680; Heine and Kuteva 2005: 128f.). Konkani is an Indo-Aryan language. The Saraswat Brahmins Konkani variety is in close contact with Kannada, a Dravidian language. In this contact situation, Kannada (ML) – see (5b) below – has two relative clause markers (the question word *yāva* 'which?' and the polar question marker *ō* in the relative clause of a correlative construction). Konkani, on the other hand, has an already existing relative construction which is only marked by one relativization marker, the relative pronoun *jo* (Nadkarni 1975: 678). In the high-contact variety, Saraswat Brahmins Konkani (see (5a) below), however, the new relative construction involves more markers than the old one; in fact, the Saraswat Brahmins Konkani speakers are using an isomorphic relative construction whereby instead of the Kannada question word *yāva*, they are using their own question word *khanco*, and instead of the Kannada polar question marker *ō*, they are using the Konkani polar question marker *ki* (see also Heine and Kuteva 2005: 128f.). In other words, the speakers of Saraswat Brahmins Konkani have increased the marking of their relative construction due to the contact with Kannada:

(5)   Saraswat Brahmins Konkani and Kannada (Nadkarni 1975: 674f.;
       Heine and Kuteva 2005: 128f.)
       a. [**khanco** Mhāntāro pepar vāccat āssa-   **ki**] to   Dāktaru   āssa.
       b. [**yāva**   mudukanu pēpar ōdutta iddān- **ō**] avanu Dāktaranu iddāne.
       which   old.man   paper reading is   Q   that   doctor   is
       'The old man who is reading a newspaper is a doctor.'

The fact that high-contact varieties may exhibit more complex subject
relativization is not particularly interesting if viewed against the background of the sample representative of the languages of the world.
As shown in Comrie and Kuteva (2005) and Kuteva and Comrie (2005),
some of the world's languages exhibit not only two but three, or four or
even five markers of the relative clause construction. However, when the
high-contact varieties in Kuteva and Comrie's (2012) sample are compared
to the respective non-contact varieties involved in each particular language contact situation, the result becomes significant: each high-
contact variety exhibits structural complexity either equal to (with the
same number of relativization markers as) or greater than (with a greater
number of relativization markers than) in one or both of the respective
non-contact varieties. We can then conclude that in language contact
situations, it is possible to observe both structural simplification and
structural complexification.

8.4   Contact-Induced Syntactic and Morphosyntactic Change within the Comprehensive Model

It was as late as in the last decade that attempts were made to explicitly
model the types of linguistic transfer that can be distinguished in language
contact (Heine and Kuteva 2006; Matras and Sakel 2007). The major similarity between these models is that they are both based on a two-way
distinction between: (i) linguistic transfer involving phonological ma-
terial/phonetic substance (referred to as *borrowing* – in the narrow sense –
in Heine and Kuteva's model, and *matter* (MAT) in Matras and Sakel's
model, respectively); and (ii) linguistic transfer involving the transfer of
meanings and the structures associated with them whereby *no* phonological material/phonetic substance is involved (referred to as *replication* in
Heine and Kuteva's model, and *pattern* (PAT) in Matras and Sakel's model,
respectively); see Figures 8.1 and 8.2:
In these two models, recognition was given to the different types of
linguistic units (as static products) that get transferred from one contact
language to the other, and even more so to the very *processes* (as dynamic
phenomena) involved in contact-induced linguistic transfer. Accordingly,
in the former model the emphasis lies on a ubiquitous process type which
occurs under various kinds of linguistic contact, *pivot-matching*. This

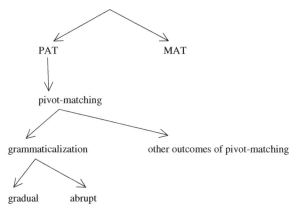

Figure 8.1 PAT vs MAT in structural replication (Matras and Sakel 2007)

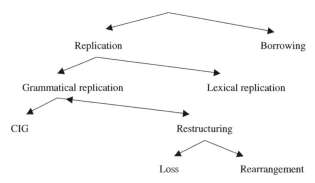

Figure 8.2 Main types of contact-induced linguistic transfer (Heine and Kuteva 2006: 95)

process involves 'identifying a structure that plays a pivotal role in the model construction', and it is matched with 'a structure in the replica language, to which a similar, pivotal role is assigned in a new, replica construction' (Matras and Sakel 2007: 830). In the latter model, it is the process of replication, and contact-induced grammaticalization (CIG) in particular, that is of central interest. While the above models account for a number of contact-induced language change phenomena, there is one area of linguistic transfer that remains beyond their scope of study. Thus both models focus on the distinct subtypes of (ii) replication/pattern (PAT) and leave out of consideration the subdivision of (i) borrowing/matter (MAT) into further subtypes, postponing it as a task for future research. Here we will be using the model proposed in Heine and Kuteva (2006: 95) as our point of departure (for a recent critical assessment of this model, see Wiemer and Wälchli 2012, but also Gast and van der Auwera 2012). Notice that Heine and Kuteva's (2006) model is embedded within the framework of grammatical language change, grammaticalization in particular, as understood from a functional-typological perspective (for pioneering research on grammaticalization in a more formal approach, see Roberts 1993; Roberts and Roussou 2003; and more recently, Ledgeway 2011).

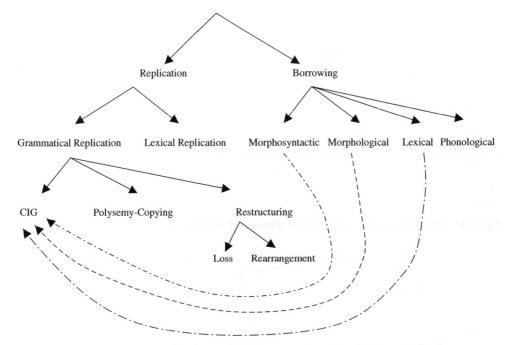

Figure 8.3 Comprehensive Model of Contact-Induced Linguistic Transfer (CM)

The need for elaborating the taxonomy of borrowing (in the narrow sense) on a par with the taxonomy of replication as part of a comprehensive model of contact-induced linguistic transfer has been amply recognized in the specialized literature (see Wiemer and Wälchli 2012, among others). In response to this need, one of our major goals in the present section is to outline such a comprehensive model; having done that, our ultimate goal will then be to identify the role contact-induced syntactic and morphosyntactic change plays within such a model.

8.4.1   ComMod: An Outline

As pointed out already, the ComMod to be outlined here draws on the model proposed in Heine and Kuteva (2006: 95); see Figure 8.2 above. The way in which ComMod differs from its precursor in the latter work is twofold. First, it fleshes out the branch labelled 'borrowing' and – to a lesser degree – the branch labelled 'grammatical replication' in Heine and Kuteva's model. Second, it contains the following unidirectional links, all of which represent dynamic historical processes: (a) *lexical borrowing* – > *CIG*, (b) *morphological borrowing* – > *CIG*, and (c) *morphosyntactic borrowing* – > *CIG*; see Figure 8.3.

8.4.1.1   Taxonomy of Distinct Types of Linguistic Transfer

The backbone of ComMod is – again (like in Matras and Sakel 2007 and Heine and Kuteva 2006) – the major division of contact-induced linguistic transfer in two branches, borrowing (in the narrow sense) and replication.

Unlike the previous two models, however, here borrowing is fleshed out as branching into four subtypes:

(i) lexical borrowing (e.g. Ger. *Website* from Eng. *website*);
(ii) phonological borrowing (/ʒ/ in English from French);
(iii) morphological borrowing (e.g. Nahuatl borrowed from Spanish the plural morpheme -*s*; see Moravcsik 1978: 106);
(iv) morphosyntactic borrowing (e.g. the transfer of the subordinator *ndu* in Media Lengua, a variety of Quechua, from Spanish gerunds ending in -V*ndo*; see Harris and Campbell 1995: 124).

Replication is further subdivided into lexical replication and grammatical replication. Lexical replication concerns the morpheme-by-morpheme translation of a whole phrase or an idiomatic expression from ML into RL, i.e. calquing (Eng. *worldview* from Ger. *Weltanschauung*).

Grammatical replication is a process whereby RL creates a new grammatical structure (RLx) on the model of some structure (MLx) of ML. In Heine and Kuteva's (2006) model, grammatical replication is further subdivided into contact-induced grammaticalization (CIG) and restructuring. Here we propose to include one further subtype of grammatical replication, polysemy copying, as a distinct subtype of grammatical replication.

All three of these subtypes are of major concern for us because, in most cases, they involve contact-induced morphosyntactic change and/or syntactic change. Let us first consider CIG. CIG in our definition is a grammaticalization process that is due to the influence of one language on another. It can be illustrated by means of the following example concerning the grammaticalization development of a *wh*-interrogative word into a relative clause marker. Let us first recall that *wh*-relativization appears to be an areal typological feature specific to Europe; if attested outside Europe, this is primarily in non-European languages that have had some history of contact with European languages. Further on, the historical development of the *wh*-interrogative into relativizer can be represented as a development along a grammaticalization path with three distinct stages: interrogative stage, complementizer stage, relativizer stage (for a detailed description of this grammaticalization path, see Heine and Kuteva 2006: ch. 6). In some language varieties, some *wh*-words have undergone the complementizer and the relativizer stage (e.g. Romance languages); in other varieties, however, we can say that – with respect to some *wh*-interrogatives – only the complementizer stage has been reached. In the Silesian dialect of Polish, for instance, the *wh*-form for animates, *fto* 'who', can only be used as an interrogative and as complementizer, but not as a relativizer (Kocur 2005).

The particular language contact situation we are interested in here involves Balkan Turkish, a high-contact variety of Turkish, spoken on the Balkan Peninsula, where the other languages spoken (Bulgarian, Greek, Albanian, Romanian, Macedonian) belong to the best-studied *Sprachbund* in

the world, the Balkan *Sprachbund*. Now, Standard Turkish consistently
employs the so-called gap relativization strategy, with no overt case-
marked reference to the head noun within the relative clause (Comrie
and Kuteva 2005). What translates English relative clauses in Standard
Turkish are inherited, attributive gerundial constructions preceding the
head noun:

(6)   Turkish (Comrie and Kuteva 2005: 496)
        [kitab- "   al-   an] öğrenci
        book-   ACC buy- PRT student
        'the student who bought the book'

(7)   Turkish (Comrie and Kuteva 2005: 496)
        [öğrenci- nin al- d"ğ- "] kitap
        student-   GEN buy- NMZ- 3SG book
        'the book which the student bought'

Unlike Standard Turkish, Balkan Turkish exhibits a different relative
clause construction. First, it employs a *wh*-form *ne* 'what', which originally
could only be used as an interrogative word, and has only recently taken
on the function of a relativizer. Second, unlike the inherited preposed
gerundial constructions used to mark relativization in Standard Turkish,
the *wh*-form, *ne* 'what', when used as a relative clause marker in Balkan
Turkish, is postposed, just like *wh*-words functioning as relative clause
pronouns in the other Balkan *Sprachbund* languages (and other European
languages). Note that the *wh*-relativization strategy can be used not only
for subject relativization but also for object relativization:

(8)   *Subject relativization*
        Balkan Turkish (Matras 1998: 94)
        şu   araba kimindir   bura ne   duruyor?
        that car   who:GEN:COP   here REL stand:CONT:3SG
        'Whose is that car that is parked here?'

(9)   *Object relativization*
        Balkan Turkish (Matras 1998: 94)
        eski konuşma **ne** onlar   konuşurlar.
        old   speech   REL   3PL:NOM   speak:HAB:3PL
        'It is an old language that they speak.'

Since, as is well established in the typological literature already, *wh*-
relativization is an areal characteristic of European languages, it is perfectly justifiable to regard the exceptional situation of Balkan Turkish
using a *wh*-word as a relativizer as the result of the language contact that
this dialect of Turkish has had with the Balkan *Sprachbund* languages over
centuries. More precisely, as Kuteva and Heine (2012) argue, in this particular variety language contact must have triggered a grammatical innovation, and this innovation – once set in motion – has followed a regular,

cross-linguistically identifiable grammaticalization path. The observations presented in Matras (1998: 94–6) indicate that Balkan Turkish has indeed gone almost – but not fully – the whole way down the grammaticalization path established cross-linguistically for *wh*-relativization. One can say that once the contact with the Balkan *Sprachbund* languages triggered the grammaticalization of the interrogative form *ne* 'what' in Balkan Turkish, this grammaticalizing structure has clearly undergone the complementizer stage; this is indicated by uses going back to Ottoman Turkish (and has parallels in modern Standard Turkish):

(10)   Complementizer stage
       Ottoman Turkish (Matras 1998: 96)
       ekim   siz   dilersenüz   edevüz
       what:CONJ 2PL:NOM wish.COND:2PL   do:OPT:1PL
       'We shall do whatever you wish'

Moreover, it appears to have entered the relativizer stage as well, for the following reasons. First, it can be used as a marker of the relative clause construction with headed relative clauses, as the examples in (8) and (9) above illustrate.

Second, in some contexts it has become an obligatory marker of relativization, with no alternative relative construction marker in the Balkan Turkish dialect. However, as Matras (1998: 94f.) points out, the Balkan Turkish 'relative clause is not yet fully integrated into pre-planned, coherent complex construction'. In other words, in the case of *wh*-relativization in Balkan Turkish we are dealing with a marker of an incipient relativizer stage, that is, a situation where a major part – but not the whole – of a grammaticalization process was replicated, over time, from ML (European Languages spoken on the Balkan Peninsula) into RL (Balkan Turkish).

To sum up, in CIG what is replicated is – usually – part(s) of a grammaticalization process with some kind of a lexical (or less grammatical) linguistic structure at its beginning point and one or more grammatical (or more grammatical) structures along the grammaticalization path that a particular grammaticalization process follows.

Unlike CIG, in the case of polysemy copying, both the lexical (or less grammatical) structure and the grammatical (or more grammatical) structure(s) that the same linguistic expression has given rise to in ML get replicated simultaneously, wholesale, into RL. An example of polysemy copying comes from the contact situation described in Keesing (1991), which involves Oceanic languages (ML) and the English-based pidgin of Vanuatu, Bislama (RL). A number of northern and central Vanuatu languages (ML) have a grammatical structure which constitutes a reduplicated form of the verb 'go' to a marker indicating the passage of time in a narrative (MLx). In Epi (ML), for instance, the reduplicated form *bababa* of the verb of motion *ba* 'go' expresses this meaning. Likewise, in Bislama

(RL), when the verb *go* (< Eng. *go*) is reduplicated as *go-go-go* it is used as a discourse marker which – again – stands for the passage of time in narratives (RLx; see Heine and Kuteva 2005: 100). Thus this is a case where the polysemy of the verb 'go' as a lexical structure (in its spatial meaning) and as a grammatical structure (when reduplicated) has been copied from ML to RL. Notice, however, that unlike CIG, which is characterized by intermediate stages of development, the above example does not appear to involve intermediate stages. Heine and Kuteva (2003: 555f.; 2005: 100–3) explicitly address the issue of polysemy copying (or grammatical copying/grammatical calquing) vs CIG, but given the stage of research on contact linguistics in the previous decade, they conclude that while there are some cases of grammatical replication which can most plausibly be accounted for in terms of polysemy copying, whenever there is sufficient evidence it usually turns out that seeming instances of polysemy copying are actually manifestations of CIG. Since more recent research has brought to light further evidence for both CIG and polysemy copying, in the ComMod here we regard polysemy copying as a branch of grammatical replication distinct from CIG.

The third subtype of grammatical replication is restructuring. It covers those cases of linguistic transfer where, as a result of contact with ML, an existing structure in RL is rearranged or lost. Restructuring is thus further subdivided into loss and rearrangement, which we will exemplify in turn.

Contact-induced loss involves language changes whereby – as a result of language contact – RL loses in categorical distinctions. In other words, RL becomes structurally impoverished in some way vis-à-vis the pre-contact situation in RL. The category that is lost may be morphological, or morphosyntactic or purely syntactic (for examples of all three types of category, see, among others, Heine and Kuteva 2005, 2012). Let us illustrate this by means of an example of a loss of a syntactic category. It comes from the contact situation involving Swiss children bilingual in Schwyzertütsch (ML) and Romansh (RL), as described in Weinreich (1964: 37–9). The category of concern here is agreement between the subject and the predicate adjective. Whereas ML, i.e. Schwyzertütsch, has no agreement, RL, i.e. Romansh, has an obligatory agreement pattern: the predicate adjective is marked for the gender of the subject in Romansh. Now, in the variety of bilingual children in Switzerland, Weinreich (1964: 37–9) observed that they say, in Romansh (RL), /la ʧapeʧa ɛ koʧan/ 'the hat is red', where the subject /la ʧapeʧa/ is marked for the feminine gender (viz. final *-a* on article and noun), but the predicate adjective (/koʧan/) is not on the model of neighbouring Schwyzertütsch, where the pattern of agreement between noun and predicate adjective does not exist.

Rearrangement involves changes in the ordering and/or the syntactic relations of constituents. Contact-induced rearrangement can be straightforwardly illustrated by means of the contact between the Indo-Aryan language Romani (Romanes) and the Balkan languages. Pre-contact Romani is said to have had verb-final (SOV) word order inherited from its Indo-Aryan past. Balkan languages, on the other hand, all have SVO word order. Matras (1996: 64) argues that the word-order change in Romani (RL) is the result of contact with the Balkan languages (ML).

Elaborating the links (a) *lexical borrowing – > CIG*, (b) *morphological borrowing – > CIG*, and (c) *morphosyntactic borrowing – > CIG* represented in ComMod remains beyond the scope of the present chapter. Instead, for an example of (a) we will refer the reader to the discussion of the Finnic lexical borrowing *kansa* 'companion, people' from Germanic, which further grammaticalized into the case marker *-ga* in Estonian with a comitative-instrumental polysemy, in Wiemer and Wälchli (2012: 49). The discussion of the *will*-habitual in New Englishes in Ziegeler (2014) is an example of (b). The link in (c) can be illustrated by the scenario for the development of sentence-final *what* as a general discourse marker of objection in Singlish (Singapore Colloquial English, a nativized, contact dialect of English), proposed in Kuteva (2013). It involves a situation where a sentence-final *what* used as a (now obsolete) marker of solidarity in Standard English (e.g. 1891, *OED: But she's so beastly chic, dontcherknow – eh,* **what***!*) was borrowed from the lexifier, i.e. colonial English (ML) in Singlish (RL). Further on – most likely under the influence of a different set of MLs (mostly the southern Chinese varieties spoken in Singapore), which have a variety of emotive particles used sentence-finally – sentence-final *what* developed into a discourse marker of general objection:

(11)   Singlish (Smith 1985: 110)
        Context: Discussion of a student who is going overseas for one month and missing classes.
        A: He'll never pass the third year.
        B: It's only for one month **what.**

8.4.1.2 The Place of Contact-Induced Syntactic and Morphosyntactic Change in ComMod

That language contact is a key mechanism of (and explanation for) syntactic change has been convincingly argued from different theoretical perspectives. When it comes to word-order change, in particular, some authors have even taken the extreme standpoint that 'word order changes are due above all to language contact, while the other causal factors which have been proposed are of negligible importance' (Smith 1981: 52). For a critical assessment of this view, the reader is referred to Harris and Campbell (1995: 136–41).

The issue that we will address in the present section is syntactic borrowing. This term has been traditionally used in a broad sense in the literature on language contact. For instance, Harris and Campbell (1995: 124) use it in their discussion of the South Asian linguistic area for what on the present understanding constitutes (i) morpho syntactic borrowing; (ii) rearrangement; and (iii) morphological borrowing.

From the previous sections it should have become clear why in the present understanding of borrowing in a narrow sense it is not justifiable to combine 'syntactic' and 'borrowing' in the same terminological expression. On the one hand, if a contact-induced change is syntactic, then it involves the ordering sequence of meaningful elements, i.e. it is only about the ordering requirements and not about the phonological material of meaningful elements. On the other hand, if a contact-induced change constitutes a case of borrowing, then what is involved – crucially – is phonological material and its transfer from ML to RL. Therefore it is a self-contradiction – in the present terminology – to speak of 'syntactic borrowing'. Notice, however, that morphosyntactic borrowing is a felicitous option in our framework: it indicates the transfer of phonological material encoding a grammatical/function morpheme which has a syntactic function as its basic function. That morpheme may well 'drag along' with itself the syntactic characteristics it has in ML (but it does not have to). Or – at least for a transitional period of time – it may well carry with itself its syntactic characteristics from ML and be simultaneously used with its counterpart in RL with the syntactic characteristics of the latter; the result will then be *double marking* of the same function, once with phonological material from ML and its syntactic properties, and then once again with phonological material from RL and its syntactic properties, respectively. Thomason (2001: 152) describes the following case of what in our terminology is a morphosyntactic borrowing of the coordinate conjunction 'and', which involves Siberian Yupic Eskimo. The conventional way of marking phrase coordination in this language is illustrated below:

(12)   Siberian Yupic Eskimo (Thomason 2001: 152f.)
Nunivaym   kijaxtaqut   tiyiyat-**lju**   qawayit-**lju**.
on.the.tundra   live   beasts-with   birds-with
'Beasts and birds live on the tundra.'

After the conjunction *inkam* 'and' was borrowed from Chukchi, Siberian Yupic Eskimo used sentences with both kinds of conjunction (in variation with sentences where just the new conjunction 'and' was used), the native comitative suffix *-lju* 'with' and the new conjunction *inkam*:

(13)   Siberian Yupic Eskimo (Thomason 2001: 152f.)
Nunivaymi   kijaxtaqut   tiyiyat-**lju**   **inkam**   qawayit-**lju**.
on.the.tundra   live   beasts-with   and   birds-with
'Beasts and birds live on the tundra.'

This double marking turns out to be an intermediate stage in the development of the language before the native marking of coordination was completely replaced by the borrowing from Chukchi.

What should have also become clear from the discussion in the previous sections is that within the ComMod, rearrangement is – by definition – a term used for contact-induced syntactic change. Further on, CIG as well as polysemy copying seem to involve – more often than not – morphosyntactic change. For instance, in the CIG of *ne* 'what' into a relativization marker in Balkan Turkish it is both a morpheme for an interrogative element (i.e. a morphological property) and a postposition of the subordinate clause (i.e. a syntactic property) that are replicated from ML to RL.

8.5 Conclusions

Even though recognition of the role of language contact for both purely syntactic and morphosyntactic change goes back at least to the Neogrammarians, Saussure and Meillet, it was as late as the last two decades of the twentieth century that contact-induced language change came to be seen as 'natural'. For the most part of the century the traditional assumption was that a particular grammatical change can either be attributed to universal, cognitive, language-internal processes, or else to language contact. In other words, language-internal change was considered 'natural', whereas contact-induced change, or language-external change, was deemed 'non-natural' (see Trudgill 1983: 102 for explicit articulation of this standpoint). Over the last couple of decades, however, a lot of work has been done within the area of contact linguistics which treats both contact-related and non-contact related language change as equally 'natural' (see Wiemer, Wälchli and Hansen 2012 for a recent example).

In the present chapter we have not dealt with a number of important language-contact phenomena such as pidgins and creoles as an extreme outcome of language contact, which offers a 'window' on syntactic and morphosyntactic change (Bickerton 1981; Roberts 1999), linguistic areas, convergence and divergence (Aikhenvald and Dixon 2001; Haspelmath 2001; Matras, McMahon and Vincent 2006; Kuteva and Heine 2010), borrowability of grammatical forms (Thomason and Kaufmann 1988; Johanson 2002; Matras and Sakel 2007), because they have been given ample recognition in the specialized literature already and the reader is referred to the individual, original works. What we have done here is assess the state-of-the-art in research on language contact focusing on the global picture, i.e. on fleshing out an overall model of distinct types and subtypes of contact-induced linguistic transfer. We have then situated contact-induced syntactic as well as morphosyntactic change within that model.

References

Aikhenvald, A. Y. 2002. *Language contact in Amazonia*. New York: Oxford University Press.

Aikhenvald, A. Y. and Dixon, R. M. W. (eds.) 2001. *A real diffusion and genetic inheritance: Problems in comparative linguistics*. Oxford University Press.

Allen, C. L. [1977] 1980. *Topics in diachronic English syntax*. PhD thesis, University of Massachusetts 1977; published New York: Garland, 1980.

Andersen, H. 1973. 'Abductive and deductive change', *Language* 49: 765–93.

Bickerton, D. 1981. *Roots of language*. Ann Arbor, MI: Karoma.

Comrie, B. and Kuteva, T. 2005. 'Relativization on subjects', in M. Haspelmath, M. Dryer, D. Gill and B. Comrie (eds.), *The world atlas of linguistic structures (WALS)*. Oxford University Press, pp. 494–7.

Gast, V. and van der Auwera, J. 2012. 'What is "contact-induced grammaticalization"? Evidence from Mayan and Mixe-Zoquean Languages', in Wiemer, Wälchli and Hansen (eds.), pp. 381–426.

Harris, A. C. and Campbell, L. 1995. *Historical syntax in cross-linguistic perspective*. Cambridge University Press.

Harris, M. 1978. *The evolution of French syntax: A comparative approach*. London: Longman.

1984. 'On the strengths and weaknesses of a typological approach to historical syntax', in J. Fisiak (ed.), *Historical syntax*. Berlin: Mouton, pp. 183–98.

Haspelmath, M. 2001. 'The European linguistic area: Standard Average European', in M. Haspelmath, E. König, W. Oesterreicher and W. Raible (eds.), *Language typology and language universals: An international handbook*, vol. II (Handbücher zur Sprach- und Kommunikationswissenschaft 20.2). New York: Walter de Gruyter, pp. 1492–510.

Heath, J. 1978. *Linguistic diffusion in Arnhem Land* (Australian Aboriginal Studies Research and Regional Studies 13). Canberra: Australian Institute of Aboriginal Studies.

Heine, B. and Kuteva, T. 2003. 'On contact-induced grammaticalization', *Studies in Language* 27(3): 529–72.

2005. *Language contact and grammatical change*. Cambridge University Press.

2006. *The changing languages of Europe*. Oxford University Press.

2008. 'Constraints on contact-induced linguistic change', *Journal of Language Contact – THEMA* 2: 57–90 (www.jlc-journal.org).

Johanson, L. 2002. 'Contact-induced linguistic change in a code-copying framework', in M. C. Jones and E. Esch (eds.), *Language change: The interplay of internal, external and extra-linguistic factors* (Contributions to the Sociology of Language 86). Berlin: Mouton de Gruyter, pp. 285–313.

Keesing, R. M. 1991. 'Substrates, calquing and grammaticalization in Melanesian Pidgin', in E. C. Traugott and B. Heine (eds.), *Approaches to grammaticalization*, vol. 1. Amsterdam: John Benjamins, pp. 315–42.

Kocur, J. 2005. 'Entwicklung der WH-Relativpronomen im Englischen und Polnischen: Ein Vergleich', unpublished MA thesis, University of Düsseldorf.

Kuteva, T. 1999. 'Languages and societies: The "punctuated equilibrium" model of language development', *Language and Communication* 19: 213–28.

    2001. 'Diachronic stability of grammatical categories and areal grammaticalization', *General Linguistics* 38: 109–32.

    2008. 'On the "frills" of grammaticalization', in M. J. López-Couso and E. Seoane (eds.), in collaboration with T. Fanego, *Rethinking grammaticalization: New perspectives for the twenty-first century* (Typological Studies in Language). Amsterdam: John Benjamins, pp. 189–219.

    2013. 'Sentence-final *what* in Singapore English', paper presented at the Research Colloquium at Institut du Monde Anglophone, Université Sorbonne-Nouvelle Paris 3, Paris, France, May 2013.

Kuteva, T. and Comrie, B. 2005. 'The typology of relative clause formation in African languages', in E. Voeltz (ed.), *African Studies*. Amsterdam: John Benjamins.

Kuteva, T. and Heine, B. 2010. 'Converging grammaticalization processes in Europe: Towards an explanation', in U. Hinrichs (ed.), *Das Handbuch der Eurolinguistik*. Wiesbaden: Harrassowitz, pp. 531–52.

    2012. 'An integrative model of grammaticalization', in Wiemer, Wälchli and Hansen (eds.), pp. 159–98.

Langacker, R. 1977. 'Syntactic reanalysis', in C. N. Li (ed.), *Mechanisms of syntactic change*. Austin: University of Texas Press, pp. 59–139.

Lehmann, W. 1973. 'A structural principle of language and its implications', *Language* 49: 47–66.

Ledgeway, A. 2011. 'Grammaticalization from Latin to Romance', in H. Narrog and B. Heine (eds.), *The Oxford handbook of grammaticalization*. Oxford University Press, pp. 719–28.

Lightfoot, D. 1991. *How to set parameters: arguments from language change*. Cambridge, MA: MIT Press.

Matras, Y. 1996. 'Prozedurale Fusion: Grammatische Interferenzschichten im Romanes', *Sprachtypologie und Universalienforschung* 49(1): 60–78.

    1998. 'Convergent development, grammaticalization, and the problem of mutual isomorphism', in W. Boeder, C. Schroeder and C. H. Wagner and W. Wildgen (eds.), *Sprache in Raum und Zeit: In memoriam Johannes Bechert*, vol. II: *Beiträge zur empirischen Sprachwissenschaft*. Tübingen: Gunter Narr, pp. 89–103.

Matras, Y., McMahon, A. and Vincent, N. (eds.) 2006. *Linguistic areas: Convergence in historical and typological perspective*. Basingstoke: Palgrave Macmillan.

Matras, Y. and Sakel, J. 2007. 'Investigating the mechanisms of pattern replication in language convergence', *Studies in Language* 31: 829–65.

Mirčev, K. 1963. *Istoričeska gramatika na bălgarskija ezik.* Sofia: Nauka i Izkustvo.

Moravcsik, E. A. 1978. 'Language contact', in J. H. Greenberg, C. A. Ferguson and E. A. Moravcsik (eds.), *Universals of human language.* Stanford University Press, pp. 93–123.

Nadkarni, M. V. 1975. 'Bilingualism and syntactic change in Konkani', *Language* 51(3): 672–83.

Nichols, J. 1992. *Linguistic diversity in space and time.* University of Chicago Press.

Roberts, I. 1993. 'A formal account of grammaticalization in the history of Romance futures', *Folia Linguistica Historica* 13: 219–58.

    1999. 'Verb movement and markedness', in M. DeGraff (ed.), *Creolization, diachrony and development.* Cambridge, MA: MIT Press, pp. 287–328.

Roberts, I. and Roussou, A. 2003. *Syntactic change: A minimalist approach to grammaticalization.* Cambridge University Press.

Smith, I. 1985. 'Multilingualism and diffusion: A case study from Singapore English', *Indian Journal of Applied Linguistics* 11(2): 105–28.

Smith, N. V. 1981. 'Consistency, markedness and language change: On the notion of "consistent language"', *Journal of Linguistics* 17: 39–54.

Thomason, S. G. 2001. *Language contact.* Edinburgh University Press.

Thomason, S. G. and Kaufman, T. 1988. *Language contact, creolization, and genetic linguistics.* Berkeley, Los Angeles and London: University of California Press.

Timberlake, A. 1977. 'Reanalysis and actualization in syntactic change', in C. N. Li (ed.), *Mechanisms of syntactic change.* Austin: University of Texas Press, pp. 141–77.

Trudgill, P. 1983. *On dialect: Social and geographical perspectives.* Oxford: Blackwell.

    1996. 'Dual source pidgins and reverse creoles: Northern perspectives on language contact', in H. Jahr Ernst and I. Broch (eds.), *Language contact in the Arctic: Northern pidgins and contact languages.* Berlin: Mouton, pp. 5–14.

    2001. 'Contact and simplification: Historical baggage and directionality in linguistic change', *Linguistic Typology* 5(2/3): 371–4.

    2004. 'The impact of language contact and social structure on linguistic structure: Focus on the dialects of Modern Greek', in B. Kortmann (ed.), *Dialect grammar from across-linguistic perspective.* Berlin: Mouton de Gruyter, pp. 435–52.

Vachek, J. 1972. 'On the interplay of external and external factors in the development of languages', in B. Malmberg (ed.), *Readings in modern linguistics: An anthology.* Stockholm: Läromedelsförlagen, pp. 209–23.

Weinreich, U. [1953] 1964. *Languages in contact.* London, The Hague and Paris: Mouton.

Wiemer, B. and Wälchli, B. 2012. 'Contact-induced grammatical change: Diverse phenomena, diverse perspectives', in Wiemer, Wälchli and Hansen (eds.), pp. 3–63.

Wiemer, B., Wälchli, B. and Hansen, B. (eds.) 2012. *Grammatical replication and borrowability in language contact*. Berlin: Mouton de Gruyter.

Winford, D. 2003. *An introduction to contact linguistics*. Oxford: Blackwell.

Ziegeler, D. 2014. 'Replica grammaticalisation as recapitulation: The other side of contact', *Diachronica* 31(1): 106–41.

Part II

Methods and Tools

Part II

Methods and Tools

9

The Comparative Method and Comparative Reconstruction

James Clackson

9.1 Introduction

It is possible to uncover details about historically prior states of languages through the comparative method (hereafter the CM). The CM operates through comparison of features of genetically related languages to give a picture of their parent language, a process that is termed reconstruction. Generally, the CM is applied to genetic groupings of languages where there is no attested record of the ancestor, but it is also possible to apply the method to language families, such as Romance, where the parent is recorded in writing. Such cases provide guidance on the strengths and weaknesses of the method, and provide an important control for the researcher. Although the reconstruction of a set of phonemes, vocabulary items, morphology or even syntactic rules through the operation of the CM has been taken as 'proof' that a given set of languages are related (this is the assumption that runs through Meillet ([1925] 1967) and can be found in more recent works on Nostratic and other macro-families such as Dolgopolsky (1998), Greenberg (2000–2) and Bomhard (2008)), the CM is not in fact a diagnostic method for assessing the relatedness of languages, but a heuristic device for elucidating the prehistory of a known language family (Nichols 1996).

Despite the widespread acceptance of the CM as a tool of linguistic reconstruction, it is not a 'method' in the same sense as, for example, a statistical procedure (such as the 'method of least squares'). The term 'comparative method', or rather its French equivalent *méthode comparative*, owes its wide currency in historical linguistics, if not its origin, to the title of an influential work by Meillet (1925, translation 1967), originally delivered as lectures to the newly founded Institute for Comparative Research in Human Culture (Instituttet for Sammenlignende Kulturforskning) in Oslo. Although Meillet devoted his opening chapter to a 'Definition of the Comparative Method', in fact the work contains no detailed description of methodology in the same form that can be found in handbooks of historical linguistics (see, for example, Crowley and Bowern 2010: 78–102; Campbell 2013: 107–44; Ringe and Eska 2013: 237–53). Meillet, for whom language was a 'social fact', took the term 'méthode comparative' from Durkheim, who stated in chapter 6 of the second edition of his work on methodology (Durkheim 1937: 124, originally published in 1901) that 'the comparative method is the only method appropriate for sociology'. Contemporaries of Meillet in history departments of francophone universities also discussed the 'méthode comparative' (see Walker 1980). For these historians, as for the nineteenth-century and early twentieth-century historical linguist, the method itself consisted of little more than using comparison as a means to uncover earlier states of affairs. With the advent of more formalist descriptions associated with the school of structuralist linguists, particularly in the United States, the term 'comparative method' became more closely associated with a particular technique of reconstruction. Hoenigswald, who had the benefit of an initial training in Indo-European comparative philology in Germany, Switzerland and Italy followed by an immersion in American structuralist linguistics, was the first scholar to give a complete and rigorous account of the operation of the CM (Hoenigswald 1950, extended in Hoenigswald 1960: 119–43). Hoenigswald exemplifed the ways in which comparison of correspondence sets across several daughter languages could be used to recover the phonemic system of the parent, and elucidate which mergers and splits of phoneme had taken place in daughter languages. Hoenigswald also devoted a short section of his book to the application of the CM to morphology (Hoenigswald 1960: 69–71), although he justified this on the grounds that 'the essence of morphological change is merger', and hence a phonemic approach was justified.

Hoenigswald's work on the CM was to be extraordinarily influential on later historical linguists. But he was limited to the linguistic knowledge available to him at the time, when generative syntactic studies had barely begun. In an entire book on language change and linguistic reconstruction, Hoenigswald only devotes seven lines to the consideration of diachronic syntax (1960: 46), included in a section on 'semantic change', and all he says is that syntactic change can be thought of as the alternation between bounded and free morphs. In the half century since Hoenigswald's book, syntax has undoubtedly been the most studied area within linguistics. But the recent handbook descriptions (Crowley and Bowern 2010; Campbell 2013; Ringe and Eska 2013) go further than Hoenigswald by restricting the CM to phonology alone. Indeed, Ringe and Eska (2013: 253) explicitly state that '[t]here is no method for reconstructing morphology or syntax comparable to the "comparative method" for phonology'.

This restriction of the CM builds on two particular assumptions about phonology and the nature of phonological change. First, the relationship between sound and meaning in the vast majority of vocabulary items is arbitrary, so there is no inherent reason why, for example, the phonetic sequence [kʰæt] should refer to a feline rather than a canid (or indeed be a noun) in English, a point already made by Meillet ([1925: 2] 1967: 14). Secondly, phonological change is largely regular, and almost always independent of semantics or syntax, so that if a dialect speaker of English were to show the change of word-final [t] to glottal stop [ʔ], this affects the word *cat* as well as all other words in which there is a final [t]. For any two or more related linguistic varieties, it should therefore be possible to find phonological correspondences across a significant number of open-class vocabulary items, so long as the two varieties both continue a proportion of the vocabulary of the parent. The amount of discrete data items available allows the construction of sets of correspondences (as I shall show in the next section) from which it is possible to make inferences about the phonology of the parent language. Scholars such as Ringe and Eska argue that only phonological change provides the requisite amount of material from which to build correspondence sets, and the applications of the CM to other domains is doomed to failure.

But others have argued that, although there is no exact analogue to phonological reconstruction in syntax, 'it is nevertheless both possible and appropriate to use the methods of comparative and internal reconstruction to reconstruct syntax' (Harris and Campbell 1995: 344). In this chapter, I shall examine the operation of the CM step by step, comparing at each stage the situation between phonological and syntactic reconstruction (see also the comparisons between the operation of CM in phonology and syntax in Jeffers 1976; Lightfoot 1979: 154–67; Fox 1995: 104–9; Harris and Campbell 1995: 343–78; Roberts 2007: 357–68; Willis 2011; Barðdal and Eythórsson 2012: 261–2; Barðdal 2013: 439–41; Walkden 2013).

9.2 The Steps of the Comparative Method

9.2.1 Creation of Correspondence Sets

'[T]he first law of the comparative method', according to Watkins (1991: 178, see also 1976b: 312), is that 'you have to know what to compare.' Presentations of the operation of the CM across the phonological domain generally illustrate this by the selection of vocabulary items that agree in meaning across related languages (or are presented as doing so), and where there is a correspondence, often immediately evident, between the items. This use of the correspondence set is already introduced early on in Meillet's work ([1925: 3] 1967: 15), albeit briefly, by introducing a series of words of equivalent meaning in the Romance languages, here reproduced as Table 9.1.

Meillet's comparanda are selected to illustrate the point that, although the relation between the three terms for the number 'eight' may not be

Table 9.1 *A correspondence set in Romance (from Meillet 1967)*

Meaning	French	Italian	Spanish
'eight'	huit	otto	ocho
'night'	nuit	notte	noche
'cooked'	cuit	cotto	–
'milk'	lait	latte	leche
'made'	fait	fatto	hecho

Table 9.2 *A correspondence set across Polynesian languages (from Crowley and Bowern 2010)*

Meaning	Tongan	Samoan	Rarotongan	Hawaian
'forbidden'	tapu	tapu	tapu	kapu
'sea'	tahi	tai	tai	kai
'faeces'	taʔe	tae	tae	kae
'side'	tafaʔaki	tafa	taʔa	kaha
'man'	taŋata	taŋata	taŋata	kanaka

apparent at first sight (French *huit* has not a single sound in common with Spanish *ocho*), the correspondence between the sequence represented by <*it*> in French corresponds regularly to the sequence <*ch*> followed by a vowel in Spanish. Meillet, and most of his readers, would have also been aware of the Latin antecedents to these words (respectively *octo*, *noctem*, *coctum*, *lactem* and *factum*), and so the selection of this correspondence set is in this case predicated on prior knowledge of the history of the languages.

For languages without the same time depth as Romance, and without an attested ancestor, operation of the CM can also seem self-evident. Take for example the reconstruction of Proto-Polynesian, on the basis of the comparison of Tongan, Samoan, Rarotongan and Hawaian. It is relatively easy given a set of vocabulary items across the four languages to pull out correspondence sets. Compare the material in Table 9.2 (adapted from Crowley and Bowern 2010: 80), which gives a set of words sharing the correspondence between *t* in Tongan, Samoan and Rarotongan with *k* in the same positions in Hawaian.

In this example, all the members of the correspondence set show the same reflex in each word of the set. As with the Romance correspondences in Table 9.1, the equation between these vocabulary items is immediately obvious. In the absence of the ancestor language, it is up to the historical linguist to work out what the most likely ancestral phoneme is to explain the correspondence (a subject I will return to consider in more detail in §9.2.3). In this case, the preferred reconstruction is **t*, which is made not only on the basis that this is the reflex across the majority of the languages, but also because the change of **t* to *k* is plausible in terms of articulatory and acoustic phonetics.

Table 9.3 *Conditioned sound change in Tongan (from Crowley and Bowern 2010)*

Meaning	Tongan	Samoan
'woman'	*fefine*	*fafine*
'happy'	*fiefia*	*fiafia*
'mountain'	*moʔuŋa*	*mauŋa*

One of the strengths of the CM is that correspondence sets can also be used to identify phoneme splits, that is, cases where a conditioned sound change has led to divergent developments in the daughter languages from a single phoneme in the parent language. An example from the reconstruction of Proto-Polynesian (adapted from Crowley and Bowern 2010: 95–7) can illustrate this point. Tongan and Samoan are both members of the Polynesian language family, and it is possible to draw up correspondence sets for the vowels in the languages (which can be supported by material in related Rarotongan and Hawaian). In the majority of cases, the Tongan vowels *a, e, o* correspond to Samoan *a, e, o* respectively (and the same vowels in Rarotongan and Hawaian). However, there are also a few cases where Tongan *e* and *o* appear to correspond to Samoan *a*, a selection of which are given in Table 9.3. The most economical explanation for these correspondences is not to view them as the reflection of further phonemes of the parent, but the result of a conditioned change, in which an original *a* in the antepenultimate syllable was raised to *e* if followed by the vowel *i* in the penultimate syllable, or to *o* if followed by *u* in the penultimate syllable. The examples of other Tongan words, already given in Table 9.2, such as *tapu* 'forbidden' and *tahi* 'sea', show that this change did not affect the vowel *a* when it was in the penultimate syllable.

The identification of satisfactory correspondence sets may be far less straightforward than the examples from Romance and Polynesian used as illustrations so far. As is well known, the effects of linguistic borrowing can disturb the picture, and this will be the subject of the next section. Semantic change may also lead to the inclusion of material in correspondence sets which do not agree on meaning, and indeed sometimes cognate words can show widely diverging meanings (see Allen 1953: 57–60 for a sustained criticism on the idea of semantic identity in comparisons). To take an example of one such semantic leap necessary for comparison, the Eastern Nilotic language Bari word for 'cloud' *dɨko*, is not connected with the inherited Nilotic terms for 'cloud' but appears to have originated from a root meaning 'coagulated, clotted (of milk)' (Dimmendaal 2011: 122). However, the vagaries of semantic change need not affect the operation of CM; if there are enough lexical matches to arrive at correspondence sets without including those with meanings which are not congruent or overlapping, these items may be left out of consideration in the initial stages of comparison, and then brought into account at a later stage. Thus only when the data set is established to allow the correspondence of Bari *díko* 'cloud' with other Nilotic words referring to 'clotted milk' is it possible to hypothesize possible semantic paths of development.

For the comparative method to work for domains of language other than phonology, it is first necessary to find the analogue to the correspondence sets of phonology (what Roberts 2007: 363, followed by Willis 2011: 411 and Walkden 2013, calls the 'correspondence problem' or 'correspondence set problem'). There have been several solutions proposed for this problem, which I shall explore in turn. In Willis's discussion of the correspondence set problem, he states that the 'obvious answer' is that the correspondence set should consist of cognate sentences, but then rejects this solution on the grounds that it is not isolated sentences that are transmitted from generation to generation, but rather the language grammar (Willis 2011: 411). However, some scholars have argued that, for language families with oral cultures, phrases and sentences were in effect transmitted wholesale, as formulaic utterances, from speaker to speaker. Although such utterances may have been marked against other syntactic patterns in individual languages, their continued use is testament to a structure that is still permitted by the grammatical rules of a daughter language.

This is in effect the thesis proposed for the Indo-European language family by Watkins in both a number of articles (for example Watkins 1976a, b) and later explored at book length (Watkins 1995). Watkins moves between 'the exploration of the syntactic expression of similar thematic contexts in cognate traditions' (1976b: 316) and the fully blown reconstruction of formulaic expressions of Proto-Indo-European verse, proverbs and legal and ritual pronouncements (as in Watkins 1995). However, even if Watkins is right in thinking that these sentences or phrases do reflect inherited formulae, it is not clear how much of the syntactic structure of the parent language is conveyed in these reconstructed formulae, since in their transmission syntactic features, such as word order and co-ordination, have more frequently been disrupted rather than preserved. In Clackson (2007: 180–4) I give the example of a particular formula reckoned to be attested in four early Indo-European languages, Sanskrit, Avestan, Latin and Umbrian, and which is reconstructed by Watkins (1995: 210) as the reflexes of a reconstructed Proto-Indo-European phrase *peh_2- *$w\bar{\i}ro$- *$pek'u$- 'protect men (and) livestock'. Although the lexical roots of this phrase are confidently reconstructed by Watkins, the morphological details (such as verbal inflection, and the number marking of the nouns) are irrecoverable. In the four languages preserving the phrase (or a later variant where one or more of the original lexemes have been replaced), the order of the constituents is also different, with Latin and Umbrian, both members of the Italic branch of Indo-European, placing the verb last, and the other two languages (which belong to the Indo-Iranian branch) placing the verb first. Accordingly, it is impossible to decide which order is original, or even to ascertain whether the phrase existed in Proto-

Indo-European in two variants. However, there is an agreement between two languages in two different branches (Avestan and Umbrian) in the use of asyndeton within the phrase 'man (and) livestock' and this may well reflect an inherited pattern. This may tell us something, but the sceptic can be forgiven for thinking that this is a slender reward for a lot of clever reconstructive footwork. The small returns are unfortunately not untypical for reconstructed Proto-Indo-European formulaic utterances. The Indo-European family has a rich and diverse amount of surviving material that originates from oral poetry or traditional utterances, and these texts have been the object of a great deal of scholarly attention, resulting in excellent editions, commentaries and dictionaries and the like. If the assortment of phrases in Proto-Indo-European reconstructed from this rich material is too patchy to approach anything like a correspondence set, it is unlikely that this enterprise will be any more successful in other language families.

The next solution to the correspondence set problem is the proposition by Harris and Campbell that syntactic patterns can furnish a correspondence set (see, in particular, Harris and Campbell 1995: 343–78; Campbell and Harris 2002; Harris 2008). Harris and Campbell (1995: 347–50) give as an example a discussion of the reconstruction of alignment in proto-Kartvelian syntax, using as a correspondence set the patterns of 'equivalent sentences' in the daughter languages, Georgian, Mingrelian and Laz. They give the following sentences (which in turn are taken from Harris 1985: 52–3, 56) as examples of Mingrelian (1a, 2a, 3a) and Laz (1b, 2b, 3b) comparanda, in each case sharing the same meaning, equivalent tense and aspect categories, and using cognate lexical and morphological material, at least as far as the verbs are concerned.

(1) a. zaza   oškviduans   nodar-s
        Zaza-NOM he.drown.him   Nodar-DAT
     b. zaza-k   oškvidaps   nodari
        Zaza-NAR he.drown.him   Nodar-NOM
        'Zaza drowns Nodar'

(2) a. ate k'oč-i   ǰgiro   ibirs
        this man-NOM well   he.sing
     b. aya k'oči-k   k'ai ibirs
        this man-NAR well he.sing
        'This man sings well'

(3) a. k'oč-i   ɣuru
        man-NOM he.die
     b. k'oči   ɣurun
        man-NOM he.die
        'The man dies'

The assignment of case is, however, different in the two languages, with Mingrelian selecting the nominative case for the subjects of the verb in each sentence, while Laz has a typically active alignment system, with the nominative used to mark the object of transitive verbs and subject of unaccusative verbs, but a different case (here called the narrative, abbreviated NAR) to mark the subject of transitive verbs and unergative verbs. For Harris and Campbell, these examples (together with many others like them) can be said to form 'a set of corresponding sentences' (1995: 348), which can be compared to one another in an analogous way to the lexical lists used in phonological reconstruction. In sentence (3), the correspondence between the Mingrelian nominative and the Laz narrative case found in sentences (1) and (2) no longer holds, but this can be viewed in the same way that a conditioned sound change may disrupt an otherwise regular correspondence set. In this case, the 'conditioning factor' is the semantics of the verb concerned, rather than the immediate syntactic environment. Harris and Campbell do not argue that the sentences themselves are 'inherited', acknowledging the critique (made by Lightfoot 1979 and others) that sentences (except of the formulaic type proposed by Watkins for the Indo-European family) do not get passed down intact from speaker to speaker, but are freshly minted by the internal grammars of speakers in each of the daughter languages. However, sentences such as (1)–(3) can be seen as instantiations of underlying syntactic patterns, just as the initial consonants of the words in the set 'father', 'foot' and 'five' are instantiations of an underlying phoneme /f/ which has no existence outside speakers' mental grammars.

A similar approach to that of Harris and Campbell is taken by those working in the framework of construction grammar (Barðdal and Eythórsson 2012; Barðdal 2013), who take argument-structure constructions to be the basis on which correspondence sets can be built. Working with material in the Indo-European language family, Barðdal (2013) gives as an example the recurrence of the construction of the adverb (or sometimes, as in Modern English, noun) meaning 'woe' in languages of the Germanic branch of Indo-European and the associated construction with the verb meaning 'to be' and a noun in the dative case referring to the experiencer of the woe. Since the same construction is found across the older Germanic languages, she posits that this is a construction that can be taken back to Proto-Germanic, and even further, adducing parallels in Latin and Avestan, to the parent language, Proto-Indo-European. In this analysis (as in many others put forward by those working with reconstruction in the construction grammar model), there are identical structures in the daughter languages to that reconstructed for the parent. Barðdal (2013: 553) argues that reconstructing identical patterns in the parent to those found in the daughters is still an achievement, and adds to our knowledge of what the parent was like, but it is not yet clear how the model deals with cases where there is variation among the daughters. Indeed, this method exemplifies a critique of syntactic reconstruction that Lightfoot had made over thirty years earlier '[r]econstruction will be possible via the comparative method only where the daughter languages show identical constructions either in attested forms or in internally reconstructed abstractions' (1979: 165).

Somewhat different is the work on syntactic reconstruction within a generative framework undertaken by Roberts (2007), Willis (2011) and Walkden (2013). Their preferred solution is to compare not sentences, patterns or constructions, but the grammars of related languages, looking at how individual syntactic features are best accounted for in the cognate languages under discussion, and then attempting to find a path of language change which gives a best fit for explaining the divergent structures. Roberts (2007: 364–7) sketches out how this approach might take place through consideration of variation between syntactic parameters in the different branches of Indo-European: the early IE languages are all null-subject languages, for example, and therefore Proto-Indo-European was most likely also a null-subject language. Willis (2011) gives a more fleshed out account of syntactic reconstruction through tracing the syntax of free relatives in the Brythonic branch of Celtic, and Walkden (2013) gives a minimalist account of the reinterpretation of first- and third-person pronouns as the middle affixes *-mk* and *-sk* in Old Norse. In the latter case the pronouns exist as independent elements in other old Germanic languages (*mik*, *sik* in Gothic, *mih*, *sih* in Old High German and indeed *sik* is also an independent pronoun in Old Norse). The creation of the new middle affixes is the effect of speaker reanalysis of the pronouns when they are adjacent to the verb, with subsequent phonological reduction. Willis and Walkden both take on board the difficulty of finding a syntactic equivalent to phonological correspondence sets, and find shortcomings in both the syntactic patterns and construction grammar solutions to the problem, but do not themselves commit to what a syntactic correspondence *set* (as opposed to a simple correspondence in grammatical structure) would actually look like. Walkden's comparison of, for example, Old Norse *-mk* and *-sk* with their other early Germanic counterparts gives two examples of the same process, but this does not approach the semantic independence that we saw characterized the members of the phonological sets discussed above. The correspondence set problem remains one of the major difficulties for the CM as a tool of syntactic reconstruction and I shall revisit it in the summary to this chapter.

9.2.2 Elimination of the Effects of Language Contact

The reconstruction of phonology by the CM relies upon the fact that the compared material reflects vocabulary inherited from the parent language, rather than the results of interlanguage (or indeed interdialect) transfer. Borrowed vocabulary may disturb the picture, and give invalid correspondence sets; for example, English *p* can be compared to Latin *p* in a number of correspondences such as *paternal: pater* 'father', *pork: porcus* 'pig' and *push: pulsare* 'push', although these all reflect borrowings into English from Latin or French. It is even possible to draw up apparent correspondence sets between words in unrelated languages, such as Arabic, Urdu, Turkish, Swahili and Malay, reflecting the result of large-scale borrowing of Arabic terms reflecting the spread of Arab civilization and Islam, rather than any genetic unity (see Trask and McColl Millar (2007: 273) for an example). Given a sufficiently large number of items included in the comparison, it is usually possible to separate borrowed words from genuine inheritances, since borrowings typically are more prominent in open-class content words, and in some semantic fields, such as body-parts, kinship terms and numerals, borrowing is less common (although not unknown; note the transfer of terms for numerals from Middle Chinese to Thai (Suthiwan and Tadmor 2009: 605)). Since the CM is a heuristic not a diagnostic methodology, the comparison of words in languages for which there is no other reason to suppose a relationship, such as Arabic and Turkish, will inevitably lead to false conclusions, and the success or failure of the CM cannot be judged on such cases.

For the reconstruction of syntax, the problem of separating syntactic changes that have come about due to language contact from those with a language internal motivation is also problematic (Willis (2011: 41) calls this 'the transfer problem'). In the absence of correspondent sets of the same type available for phonology, it is impossible to set contact phenomena apart from other changes so clearly. The example of the 'woe' construction in Indo-European languages discussed in §9.2.1 exemplifies this problem well. To recap, Barðdal (2013: 552–3) argues for the reconstruction of a Proto-Indo-European construction involving an adverb meaning 'woe', a part of the verb 'to be' and an experiencer marked in the dative case, from comparison of a shared lexical item with the meaning 'woe' (for example, Gothic (a Germanic language) *wai*, Latin *uae* and Avestan *auuoi*) and the equivalent structures in Germanic languages, Latin and Avestan. She excludes from consideration, however, the word for 'woe' in other Indo-European languages, in particular the form used in the Greek New Testament, *ouaí*, and the Armenian word *vay*, since in these cases the lexical items 'are assumed to be later developments' (Barðdal 2013: 549). But the Greek and Armenian words are used in the Bible with dative of experiencer and with the verb 'to be', and the same construction is also found in the Gothic Bible. Example (4) gives a biblical verse (Mark 13:17) with the 'woe-construction' found in these three languages, two of which are explicitly excluded from Barðdal's survey.

(4)   a. ouaì dè   taîs   en gastrì ekhoúsais (Greek)
         woe PRT the.DAT.PL in belly   having.DAT.PL

     b. wai þaim   qiþuhaftom (Gothic)
        woe the.DAT.PL pregnant.woman.DAT.PL

     c. vay ic'ê   yłeac'=n (Armenian)
        woe be.3SG.SBJV pregnant.DAT.PL= the
        'Woe to them that are with child'

The Armenian Bible and the Gothic Bible are both translated from the Greek, and so there is a possibility of transfer of the construction from Greek to these languages, except that the Armenian translation shows the inclusion of a form of the verb 'to be' in the translation, which is lacking from the Greek original (and is also not found in the Latin and Old Church Slavonic versions of the same passage). Is this an indication that the Armenian should be included in the correspondence set, despite the doubts over whether the word for 'woe', *vay*, is an element of inherited vocabulary? And is it possible to exclude the possibility that the Gothic, and indeed all the Germanic examples of the construction (which were only written down after the introduction of Christianity) have also been influenced by the language of the Bible, where the 'woe-construction' is well attested? There is no way of knowing, and in any case, in a language with a synchronic dative case with the range of functions inherited from the Indo-European parent language, the selection of the dative for the experiencer is trivial; any Indo-European language which borrowed the word for 'woe' is likely to construe it with the dative.

9.2.3 Reconstruction through Retracing the Effects of Language Change

Once viable correspondence sets, excluding borrowed material, have been established, the next stage of the CM is to form a hypothesis of what is the most likely ancestor to explain the correspondence. Divergent developments across daughter languages need to be explained by the reconstruction of both a likely ancestor, and a plausible scenario of change. In phonological reconstruction, handbooks sometimes set out guidelines, or use examples from real languages in order to enable the reader to follow the steps by which it is possible to arrive at a reconstructed set of phonemes for the parent language (see, for example, the accounts in Crowley and Bowern 2010: 85–92; Ringe and Eska 2013: 228–53). These steps can themselves be reduced to three underlying principles of reconstruction: maximum plausibility of the hypothesized sound changes, maximum plausibility of the reconstructed phonemic system, and maximum efficiency of the model. These principles may work against each other, and there may not be a single reconstruction that strikes a clear balance between all three principles. However, the work of phonological reconstruction is considerably helped through a widespread understanding of what are more plausible phonological changes, on the basis of those which are most widely attested and typological work on different attested phonological systems.

In his discussion of syntactic reconstruction, Jeffers (1976) makes an explicit comparison between the reconstruction of a phonological feature from a correspondence set with the reconstruction of a syntactic feature. He uses the example of a phonological correspondence between *s* in L1 with *r* in L2, where the linguist, knowing that the change of *s* > *r* is common, but the reverse change is exceedingly rare, has little hesitation in reconstructing **s* as the proto-phoneme. Compare this with a situation where there is an equation between a SVO word-order in L1 but SOV word-order in in L2. Here there is no *a priori* reason to suppose that either SVO or SOV, or indeed any other word-order pattern, was the original pattern. Phonological change is thus presented as unidirectional, whereas syntactic change is not, and this makes the reconstruction of syntax less plausible than phonological reconstruction (Willis 2011: 411 refers to this as the 'directionality problem').

Jeffers's criticisms are partly symptomatic of the time he was writing, since most work on syntactic reconstruction was almost entirely concerned with word-order; see for example the two books entitled *Proto-Indo-European Syntax* written in the years immediately before Jeffers's article, Lehmann (1974) and Friedrich (1975), which feature word order either prominently or exclusively. Although some syntactic changes, such as those affecting word-order or alignment (see the Laz example discussed in §9.2.1) may not be unidirectional, in many cases the direction of syntactic change is as clear-cut as some phonological change, for example Walkden's example of an item which acts as an independent pronoun in one language but a grammaticalized morpheme in another. Even with change in constituent order, an increasing sophistication in the syntactic accounts of sentence structure, and a growing awareness of the specific ways in which syntactic reanalysis takes place means that it is perfectly possible to posit a hypothetical constituent-order in the parent language on the basis of the most likely scenario to explain the changes that have taken place in the daughters, and to justify these decisions through evidence from the attested history of languages. Take for example the gradual change from (S)OV word-order to (S)VO (or indeed V(S)O) in Romance. In Ledgeway's (2012) account this is not a simple switch from one order to another, but should be analysed in conjunction with other significant changes, such as the rise in configurationality which led to determiner phrases in Romance (which were lacking in Latin).

The directionality problem seems therefore to be losing its force as an argument against the reconstruction of syntax, especially as accounts take more care to describe the syntax of attested languages accurately, and as a growing body of accurate and theoretically aware descriptions of syntactic changes in attested languages help to build up a typology of syntactic change. There may remain cases where it is not straightforward to find the best fit for a reconstructed ancestor and the syntactic structures attested in the daughter languages, and two or more alternatives are available with little to choose between them. But similar impasses are found for phonological correspondence sets; just consider the notorious case from Indo-European linguistics of 'laryngeal' consonants, which in some accounts, such as Reynolds, West and Coleman (2000) are not reconstructed as consonants at all. The fact that some comparisons give rise to more than a single possible reconstruction does not of itself invalidate the method.

9.2.4   Refining the Reconstructions

Phonological reconstruction by the CM, and indeed the reconstruction of morphemes of inflected languages, does not finish with the identification of reconstructed elements through retracing possible pathways of change. The reconstruction is only complete after the reconstructed system as a whole has been analysed, and this process can lead to the refinement of the results, such as the elimination of any false positives achieved through mistaken comparisons, or the identification of a single phoneme in the parent language which gives rise to two (or more) reflexes in the daughter languages, owing to a conditioned sound-change. Ringe and Eska (2013: 242–51) give an extensive demonstration of these processes through the reconstruction of Proto-Mańśi (an Ob-Ugric language spoken in southwestern Siberia) from comparison of ninety words in two Mańśi dialects, Tavda and Sosva. This example shows how 'the phonological patterns are interlocked; different decisions about consonants, for instance, will lead to increasingly divergent decisions about stressed and unstressed vowels' (Ringe and Eska 2013: 252). Moreover, it is usually possible for the historical linguist to determine whether a reconstruction is inherently plausible or not. Most usually, experienced scholars rely on their own knowledge of attested phonologies and possible diachronic changes in order to test plausibility of alternative explanations. Furthermore, in cases of doubt or disagreement, historical linguists have recourse to typological collections of attested sounds and sound-changes (see, for example, Ladefoged and Maddieson 1996; Kümmel 2007).

It is fair to say that no reconstruction has so far attempted to come up with a complete picture of the syntax of a proto-language. In the previous section we discussed how recent attempts to reconstruct syntax have concentrated on individual features or constructions. It is true that the reconstructions carried out in the minimalist framework have looked at reconstructing parameters (as Roberts 2007), and that the approach of, for example, Willis (2011) and Walkden (2013) involves consideration of the whole grammar of the language rather than a single construction. However, there is still a long way to go from these accounts to anything close to the picture of the phonology of a language gathered from phonological reconstruction. Future research may reveal how the reconstruction of different pieces of the syntactic jigsaw lock together in a particular parent language.

9.3 Conclusion

The CM as presented by Meillet (1925) could in theory apply to phonology, morphology, syntax or the lexicon. Indeed, Hoenigswald (1963: 10) saw the particular merit in Meillet's writings that he extended his consideration of the CM beyond the domain of phonology. But Meillet stressed that reconstruction of a parent language in these areas was a more hazardous affair than for phonology, with reconstruction more dependent 'on the tact, the judgment, and the good sense of linguists' (1967: 125). In effect, even after more than a century of research, a reconstructed parent language, such as Proto-Indo-European, might be said to be a reconstructed phonology only, with no more than a 'hundred-odd words' of vocabulary (Allen 1953: 78), and with morphosyntax largely limited to the identification of certain morphemes. Subsequent works to Meillet in the structuralist tradition, best represented by Hoenigswald (1950, 1960), stressed the most scientific aspects of the CM in an attempt to show that the method was rigorous, self-contained and independent of the researcher. Phonology was the natural domain to exemplify these points, although, as Ringe and Eska (2013: 252) stress, even phonological reconstruction is still partly reliant on the approach taken by the linguist performing the reconstruction, and is not an automatic process.

It is perhaps just a curious accident of the history of linguistics that the most influential work on the CM appeared just too early to take account of the Chomskyan revolution in syntax. Historical syntax has been playing catch-up ever since, seeking to find legitimacy in the appropriation of the methods developed for phonological reconstruction. However, as I hope to have shown in this chapter, phonological and syntactic reconstruction, although not as widely divergent as Jeffers (1976) or Lightfoot (1979, 2002) would make out, cannot operate in the same way, owing to the absence of any meaningful analogue in syntax to the correspondence sets with which the historical phonologist works. The success of the CM in phonological reconstruction is largely dependent on the amount of material it has to work with, which allows the researcher both to eliminate correspondences which might arise through language contact or transfer, and also enables sufficient examples to isolate and identify changes conditioned by context.

Indeed, syntactic reconstruction is a different type of enterprise from phonological reconstruction, a conclusion that is borne out by the comparison of the two. Phonological reconstruction is a 'first-order' reconstruction, in the sense that it is not reliant on any other reconstructed data. Furthermore, although not diagnostic for language relationship, the establishment of correspondence sets in phonology, and the reconstruction of the phonemic system of the parent language, is normally the first test of the viability of a proposed group of languages. The reconstruction of syntax is in contrast a second-order reconstruction, in the same way that the reconstruction of morphology and the lexicon are second-order reconstructions. All rely upon reconstructed phonology, and the established phonological correspondences that exist between the daughter languages. Syntactic reconstruction, like the reconstruction of individual morphemes, goes beyond simple comparison and approaches closer to the techniques of reconstruction associated with the term 'internal reconstruction', that is the hypothesis of the most likely scenario to explain divergent data in a daughter language through reversing commonly attested sound changes. Syntactic reconstruction, as practiced, generally looks at divergent structures in two or more different languages, and looks to reverse recognized processes of syntactic change, such as reanalysis and grammaticalization, in order to arrive at the structure of the parent language. Syntactic reconstruction consequently usually involves weighing up two or more rival explanations, and judging which changes fit better with the picture of the reconstructed language and with what we know of syntactic change. Reconstruction of this type is inevitably even more prone to reflect the judgment of an individual researcher or to accord with the particular theoretical framework in which he or she works, and is liable to be open to criticism or debate (consider the criticism on the construction grammar account of the 'woe is me' construction in Indo-European languages given above). The distinction that has arisen between phonological reconstruction and other types, through the use of the label 'Comparative Method' for phonological reconstruction, is perhaps a useful reminder of the distinctiveness of both phonological change and the data with which it is possible to work. Extending the use of the same label to second-order reconstructions erodes that difference.

All reconstructions are hypothetical. Although the CM gives phonological reconstruction a recognized status within historical linguistics, its results are still hypotheses about the phonology of an unattested and idealized parent language. Indeed, the ascription of phonetic details to the reconstructed phonemes discovered through the CM remains unverifiable; the discovery of a previously unknown written form of a reconstructed parent might be able to confirm the hypothetical phonemic oppositions, but it could not furnish sufficient details to be certain of their phonetic realization. Syntactic reconstruction is certainly feasible and has been attempted at many times for many different language families. Roberts (2007: 361) cites Watkins' view (1976b: 306) that the success of syntactic reconstruction has already been demonstrated by the close correspondence between nineteenth-century predictions of Proto-Indo-European word order and the actual word-order patterns attested in the most archaic IE language, Hittite, which was only deciphered in the early twentieth century. Syntactic reconstruction through comparison of related languages and the formation of explanatory hypotheses for the structure of the parent language seems to work. Perhaps it is time to leave the arguments about methodology to one side, and concentrate on reconstructing syntax.

References

Allen, W. S. 1953. 'Relationship in comparative linguistics', *Transactions of the Philological Society* 52: 52–108.

Barðdal, J. 2013. 'Construction-based historical-comparative reconstruction', in T. Hoffmann and G. Trousdale (eds.), *Oxford handbook of construction grammar*. Oxford University Press, pp. 438–57.

Barðdal, J. and Eythórsson, T. 2012. 'Reconstructing syntax: Construction Grammar and the comparative method', in H. C. Boas and I. A. Sag (eds.), *Sign-based construction grammar*. Stanford, CA: CSLI Publications, pp. 257–308.

Bomhard, A. R. 2008. *Reconstructing Proto-Nostratic: comparative phonology, morphology, and vocabulary*. Leiden: Brill.

Campbell, L. 2013. *Historical linguistics: An introduction*, 3rd edn. Edinburgh University Press.

Campbell, L. and Harris, A. C. 2002. 'Syntactic reconstruction and demythologizing "myths and the prehistory of grammars"', *Journal of Linguistics* 38: 599–618.

Clackson, J. 2007. *Indo-European linguistics*. Cambridge University Press.

Crowley, T. and Bowern, C. 2010. *An introduction to historical linguistics*, 4th edn. Oxford University Press.

Dimmendaal, G. J. 2011. *Historical linguistics and the comparative study of African languages*. Amsterdam: John Benjamins.

Dolgopolsky, A. 1998. *The Nostratic macrofamily and linguistic palaeontology*. Cambridge: McDonald Institute for Archaeological Research.

Durkheim, E. 1937. *Les Règles de la méthode sociologique*. Paris: Presses Universitaires de Paris.

Fox, A. 1995. *Linguistic reconstruction*. Oxford University Press.

Friedrich, P. 1975. *Proto-Indo-European syntax: The order of the meaningful elements* (Journal of Indo-European Studies Monograph Series 1). Butte, MT: Journal of Indo-European Studies.

Greenberg, J. H. 2000–2. *Indo-European and its closest relatives: The Eurasiatic language family*. Stanford University Press.

Harris, A. C. 1985. *Diachronic syntax: The Kartvelian case*. New York: Academic
    Press.
    2008. 'Reconstruction in syntax: Reconstruction of patterns', in
    G. Ferraresi and M. Goldback (eds.), *Principles of Syntactic reconstruction*.
    Amsterdam: John Benjamins, pp. 73–95.
Harris, A. C. and Campbell, L. 1995. *Historical syntax in cross-linguistic perspec-
    tive*. Cambridge University Press.
Hoenigswald, H. M. 1950. 'The principal step in comparative grammar',
    Language 26: 357–64.
    1960. *Language change and linguistic reconstruction*. University of Chicago
    Press.
    1963. 'On the history of the comparative method', *Anthropological
    Linguistics* 5: 1–11.
Jeffers, R., 1976. 'Syntactic change and syntactic reconstruction', in
    W. M. Christie Jr (ed.), *Current progress in historical linguistics:
    Proceedings of the second international conference on historical linguistics*.
    Amsterdam: North-Holland, pp. 1–15.
Kümmel, M. J. 2007. *Konsonantenwandel: Bausteine zu einer Typologie des
    Lautwandels und ihre Konsequenzen für die vergleichende Rekonstruktion*.
    Wiesbaden: Reichert.
Ladefoged, P. and Maddieson, I. 1996. *The Sounds of the world's languages*.
    Malden, MA, and Oxford: Blackwell.
Ledgeway, A. 2012. *From Latin to Romance. Morphosyntactic typology and change*.
    Oxford University Press.
Lehmann, W. P. 1974. *Proto-Indo-European yntax*. Austin: University of Texas
    Press.
Lightfoot, D. W. 1979. *Principles of diachronic syntax*. Cambridge University
    Press.
    2002. 'Myths and the prehistory of grammars', *Journal of Linguistics* 38:
    113–136.
Meillet, A. 1925. *La méthode comparative en linguistique historique*. Oslo:
    Aschehoug.
    1967. *The comparative method in historical linguistics*, trans. Gordon B. Ford.
    Paris: Champion.
Nichols, J. 1996. 'The comparative method as heuristic', in M. Durie and
    M. Ross (eds.), *The comparative method reviewed: Regularity and irregularity
    in language change*. Oxford University Press, pp. 39–71.
Reynolds, E., West, P. and Coleman, J. 2000. 'Proto-Indo-European laryn-
    geals were vocalic', *Diachronica* 17: 351–87.
Ringe, D. and Eska, J. F. 2013. *Historical linguistics: Toward a twenty-first century
    reintegration*. Cambridge University Press.
Roberts, I. 2007. *Diachronic syntax*. Oxford University Press.
Suthiwan, T. and Tadmor, U. 2009. 'Loanwords in Thai', in M. Haspelmath
    and U. Tadmor (eds.), *Loanwords in the world's languages: A comparative
    handbook*. Berlin: Walter de Gruyter pp. 599–616.

Trask, L. and McColl Millar, R. 2007. *Trask's historical linguistics*, 2nd edn. London: Hodder.

Walkden, G. 2013. 'The correspondence problem in syntactic reconstruction', *Diachronica* 30: 95–122.

Walker, L. D. 1980. 'A note on historical linguistics and Marc Bloch's comparative method', *History and Theory* 19: 154–64.

Watkins, C. 1976a. 'Syntax and metrics in the Dipylon vase inscription', in A. Morpurgo Davies and W. Meid (eds.), *Studies in Greek, Italic and Indo-European linguistics offered to Leonard R. Palmer on the occasion of his 70th birthday*. Innsbruck: Institut für Sprachwissenschaft, pp. 431–41.

1976b. 'Towards Proto-Indo-European syntax: Problems and pseudo-problems', in S. B. Steever, C. A. Walker and S. S. Mufwene (eds.), *Papers from the parasession on diachronic syntax, April 22, 1976*. Chicago Linguistic Society, pp. 305–26.

1991. 'Etymologies, equations and comparanda: Types and values, and criteria for judgment', in P. Baldi (ed.), *Patterns of change, change of patterns: Linguistic change and reconstruction methodology*. Berlin and New York: Mouton de Gruyter, pp. 167–82.

1995. *How to kill a dragon: Aspects of Indo-European poetics*. Oxford University Press.

Willis, D. 2011. 'Reconstructing last week's weather: Syntactic reconstruction and Brythonic free relatives', *Journal of Linguistics* 47: 407–46.

10

Internal Reconstruction

Gisella Ferraresi and Maria Goldbach

10.1 Introduction

Internal Reconstruction is an established method in historical linguistic research. Joseph (2010) gives a pretty concise overview of the merits and limits of this method. We can trace it back to the comparative method of historical linguistics in the first part of the nineteenth century (see Baxter 2002, and see Chapter 9, this volume). It concentrates mainly on phonological and morphological changes (or morphophonemic changes) on the basis primarily of written language data. The reasoning is in principle by analogy: in a given language L, if a form A has a grammatical relation to a form A´ and we find a lexical entity B of the same lexical category as A but no corresponding B´, we conclude that there might have been B' in an earlier stage of the language L.

As an illustration, we report Joseph's (2010: 53f.) example of Ancient (Attic) Greek. The masculine noun in the nominative singular *poimé:n* 'shepherd' has the genitive singular form *poiménos*, the feminine noun in the nominative singular *óar* 'wife' has the genitive singular form *óaros*. Now, in Ancient Greek we find the genitive singular form *mélitos* 'of the honey' but in the nominative singular we do not find **mélit* but just *méli* 'honey' (neuter). From this Joseph concludes that in an earlier stage of Ancient (Attic) Greek (or we might even say in its Proto-Indo-European ancestor) most probably there existed **mélit* in the nominative singular and that by regular sound change the final stop underwent apocope. There are several other nouns in Ancient (Attic) Greek which have the same stem allomorphy in their inflectional paradigm: *sô:ma* (neuter NOM.SG) 'body' ~ *sómatos* (GEN.SG). Indeed, in Ancient (Attic) Greek there are no words ending in a voiceless dental (or alveolar) stop. It seems obvious that this language-specific phonological well-formedness constraint on word formation brought about a regular rule, namely the apocope of word final stops. Yet, this regular sound change results in stem allomorphy in the inflectional paradigm of some nouns. This illustrates what is meant by morphophonemic change, or to put it more succinctly, regular phonological change provokes irregularity in inflectional morphology.

But how do we know that there must have been a stage in Ancient Greek where there existed words with final stops if we cannot find any evidence in the data? Well, Joseph (2010: 54) says because we know that inflectional 'paradigms generally start out as perfectly regular, with no allomorphy at the outset'. In other words, the practitioners of the method of Internal Reconstruction presuppose that inflectional paradigms are by default regular and without stem allomorphy such as {méli-} vs {mélit-} and that irregularities, i.e. stem allomorphy, cannot arise other than by phonological sound change. The same assumption is made by Ringe (2003: 249), who gives the following paradigms:

(1) Ancient Greek

	'guard'	'serf'	'black'	'(upon) standing up'
NOM.SG.M	/pʰýlaks/	/tʰéːs/	/mélaːs/	/stáːs/
NOM.PL.M	/pʰýlakes/	/tʰéːtes/	/mélanes/	/stántes/
NOM.SG by internal reconstruction	invariant	*/tʰéːts/	*/mélans/	*/stánts/

According to Ringe, the cumulative case number suffixes /s/ and /es/ are invariable. In the first noun, there is no stem allomorphy, thus there is nothing to reconstruct. The other three nominal categories show stem allomorphy. In the lexeme for 'serf', the voiceless dental (or alveolar) [t] stop is dropped immediately before the homorganic fricative [s]; in the lexeme for 'black', the same happens to the nasal [n]; and in the participle 'standing up', both phonemes are dropped. In the nominative singular of the last two lexemes, the stem vowel is lengthened by what Ringe calls 'second compensatory lengthening'. This means that the loss of the consonants is compensated by lengthening of the stem vowel. Both authors, Ringe (2003) and Joseph (2010), admit that the method of Internal Reconstruction has its limits and must be complemented by external or comparative reconstruction. Thus, to confirm the assumption that in an earlier unattested stage of Ancient (Attic) Greek the nominative singular of the lexeme for 'honey' was *mélit, Joseph (2010: 55) gives the corresponding lexemes in the Indo-European languages Hittite milit and Gothic miliþ. Thus, the reasoning is that since in these cognate Indo-European languages the lexeme for 'honey' is very similar to the Ancient (Attic) Greek méli, and since the Hittite and the Gothic lexemes both end in a voiceless dental obstruent (and Gothic /þ/ for Hittite /t/ is predicted by Grimm's Law), for some proto-Greek period we reconstruct *mélit.

The method of reconstruction started out by being applied to the Indo-European languages, but is not confined just to this language family; for example, Baxter and Sagart (2014) apply it to reconstruct sounds and morpheme shapes in Old Chinese. In the next section we present some critical thoughts concerning this method.

10.2 Critical Aspects of Internal Reconstruction

Let us have a look at the full nominal paradigm of *sô:ma* 'body':

(2) Ancient Greek

		Neuter	'body'
Singular	Nom	/sô:ma/
	Acc	/sô:ma/
	Gen	/só:mat-os/
	Dat	/só:mat-i/
Plural	Nom	/só:mat-a/
	Acc	/só:mat-a/
	Gen	/so:mát-o:n/
	Dat	/sóma-si/

We ignore here the change of stress for our analysis. What has to be explained is the dative plural form. If we follow the reasoning of Ringe (2003) presented above, the dental stop [t] of the stem is dropped if it precedes a homorganic fricative /s/ in the inflectional suffix. Thus, even though the stem of the dative plural appears without the dental stop in its surface form, it can be assumed to have the original form *só:mat* and apocope occurs due to the phonological shape of the inflectional suffix. Presuming this, we count two stems of the paradigm without a dental stop, namely nominative and accusative singular, and six stems with a dental stop, namely the rest of the paradigm. This means the method of Internal Reconstruction tacitly relies on the assumption that the stem allomorph with the widest distribution is the best candidate to be reconstructed. In Ancient (Attic) Greek this assumption is corroborated by quite a large number of nominal lexemes regularly showing this type of stem allomorphy (though we do not know how many there are). And the apocope of word-final stops is a widespread phenomenon; for example, in Modern Italian no native lexeme ends in a stop – therefore this phenomenon is called a regular sound change. But the method of reconstruction relying on the widest distributed stem allomorph reaches its limits when regular sound change is lacking. In (3) we give the present indicative paradigm of the verb *venire* 'to come' in Modern Italian and compare it with its ancestor paradigm in Classical Latin.

(3)		Modern Italian	Classical Latin[1]
	Present Indicative	ve'nire	< we'nire
Singular	1	['vɛŋg-o] <vengo>	'weni-o
	2	['vjɛn-i] <vieni>	'weni-s
	3	['vjɛn-e] <viene>	'weni-t
Plural	1	[ve'n-jamo] <veniamo>	we'ni-mus
	2	[ve'n-ite] <venite>	we'ni-tis
	3	['vɛŋg-ono] <vengono>	'weni-u-nt

In this paradigm we have stem allomorphy consisting of three allo-morphs, /'vɛŋg-/, /'vjɛn-/, /ven-/ and these are evenly distributed over the paradigm cells. Thus, no stem can be singled out for the method of Internal Reconstruction on the basis of frequency of occurrence alone. Several Modern Italian verbs show a similar pattern even though they do not belong to the same inflection class, for example /te'nere/ 'to hold, keep' < CLat. /te'nere/, /so'lere/ 'to be wont to' < CLat. /so'lere/, etc. These verbs are inherited from Latin and did not undergo a strong semantic shift. The Classical Latin ancestor verbs are completely reg-ular in the present indicative. Obviously the Italian verbs experienced non-regular sound changes and thus ended up in a paradigm with three stem allomorphs. In this situation we cannot reconstruct any previous situation and we have no indication that the original stem of ModIt. *venire* is the one found in the plural in the first and second persons. Rohlfs (1968: 259f.) tells us that in Old Italian some of the stems had a palatal sound in their coda ([ɲ, ʎ]) but even this informa-tion cannot be deduced from the Modern Italian paradigms. Thus, the assumption of Joseph (2010) that paradigms generally start out as perfectly regular can only be verified if we take as starting point for the Modern Italian verb stems the Classical Latin ancestors and here we can ask whether this is still Internal Reconstruction or rather external. Already in Old Italian these verbs did not have perfectly regular paradigms and Rohlfs (1968) assumes that verbs with stem allomorphy spread their paradigm pattern to other verbs by analogy. Those types of stem allomorphy have led Aronoff (1994) to propose a special lexical level which he calls morphomic. It seems therefore that Aronoff would reject the assumption of Joseph (2010) that para-digms are perfectly regular by default.

So far we have seen that Internal Reconstruction is challenged when confronted with several stem allomorphs with no candidate showing the widest distribution, and when irregular sound changes occur. Up to now we have only considered inflectional morphology interacting with sound change. But can the method of Internal Reconstruction help us in the case of derivational morphology?

---

[1] Note that the Classical Latin forms given in (3), although accompanied by stress diacritics, are not intended to be read as phonetic transcriptions.

Let us consider the case of the Modern Portuguese suffix {-*agem*}, for example, in (4a–b) in contrast to (4c):

(4)   a. *folhagem* 'foliage'; base noun <folha> 'sheet, leaf'
       b. *crivagem* 'perforation'; base verb <crivar> 'to perforate'
       c. *viagem* 'journey'; simplex, no base

(4a) and (4b) obviously share homonymous suffixes but have different bases. (4c) is borrowed from Provençal *viatge*, which is inherited from Latin UIA-TICUS, an adjective with the meaning 'belonging to the journey/road' (basis: UIA – 'road'; see Infopédia online dictionaries). Thus, even if we took a larger reference set than in (4), we would never be able to internally reconstruct the original function and meaning of the suffix, namely deriving adjectives from nouns, given that the lexemes in (4a) and (4b) are nouns. The same limits of Internal Reconstruction can be found in other affixes as well. Let us take the Modern French masculine noun *ronronnement* 'purring' derived from the base verb *ronronner* 'to purr'. We might be inclined to deduce that the suffix {-*ment*} derives verbs denoting animal sounds. However, we would be on the wrong track in the case of the deverbal event nominalization for the French verb for 'to bark' *aboyer*, because we do not get °*aboiement*,[2] but instead *aboyage* (see Uth 2011, 2012). As soon as we enter into derivational morphology we lose any possibility of predictability and therefore end up with mere speculation, a highly undesirable result from a scientific perspective.

In fact, in Bowern and Evans (2014), who aim 'to reflect both the state of the art and future directions of historical linguistics' (xviii), we do not find a single chapter on Internal Reconstruction and just two items in the index (p. 130 and p. 386, the first of which does not elaborate on the subject of Internal Reconstruction). It seems therefore that Internal Reconstruction lacks some relevance in contemporary research in historical linguistics – and has little prospective in the future. In the same handbook, Koch (2014: 290) tries to reconstruct earlier forms of kin terms in the Australian language Kaurna comparing senior forms with each other, see (5):

(5)   Kaurna

Senior forms	Gloss	Junior form	Gloss
kawawa	'mother's brother'	./.	
kamami	'mother's mother'	*kamilya*	'child of a daughter of a female'
thamamu	'mother's father'	*thamu(tha)*	'son of a daughter of a male'
ngapapi	'father's mother'	*ngapitya*	'child of a son of a female'
matlala	'father's father'	*matlanta*	'child of a son of a male'
ngarrparrpu	'father in law'	*ngarrputya*	'son in law'

---

[2] We use the symbol '°' in the sense of Corbin (1987) for structurally well-formed complex words which are occasionally not attested, that is for accidental lexical gaps.

See Koch's table 12.2 (2014: 290) with the title 'Internal reconstruction of Kaurna reduplicated kin-terms'. Koch suggests that the senior forms are forms of reduplication where the last syllable is the result of morphological reduplication from some previous syllable. His proposal is that the senior forms result from the morphological rule $C_1V_1C_2V_2 \rightarrow C_1V_1C_2V_1C_2V_2$ (see the middle section of 2014: 289). This proposal cannot be right synchronically because it would give the senior form *kamama* for 'mother's mother' and *thamama* for 'mother's father' contrary to the attested forms. Instead of taking any synchronically attested base, Koch presumes an 'earlier (and "well attested" wherever evidence is available) *kami' as the base for the expression of "mother's mother"'. To clarify his method, there is no synchronically available basis for the hypothetical or rather speculative morphological reduplication process proposed by Koch. Without this assumption there is no evidence for any reduplication process in senior kin expressions in Kaurna. Based on the allegedly reduplicated senior forms, Koch proposes proto-forms with total reduplication by Internal Reconstruction (and he proposes that each corresponding proto-form is an expression of both a senior and a junior form, evidence of which comes from other related Australian languages), e.g. *kami-kami* as a designation for 'mother's mother' and 'child of a daughter of a female'. In other words, we have no evidence for this type of Internal Reconstruction.

To us, thus, it seems that the field of Internal Reconstruction abandons the standards and realms of good empirical science. To justify our assessment we cite Sir Karl Popper:

> Some twenty-five years ago I proposed to distinguish empirical or scientific theories from non-empirical ones precisely by defining the empirical theories as the refutable ones and the non-empirical theories as the irrefutable ones … Every serious test of a theory is an attempt to refute it. Testability is therefore the same as refutability, or falsifiability. And since we should call 'empirical' or 'scientific' only such theories as can be empirically tested, we may conclude that it is the possibility of an empirical refutation which distinguishes empirical or scientific theories.
>
> *(Popper 1969: 196f.; see also Dressler 1971: 6 fn.5)*

Anderson (2014) describes several morphological changes, one of which we want to address here in order to try to reconstruct something internally – since this is our task. Anderson (2014: 265) mentions the event nominalization *achievement* derived from the verb *to achieve*, likewise *commencement* from *to commence* and *judgement* from *to judge*. Anderson says that the suffix {-ment} is borrowed from continental Old French and Anglo-French in Middle English by means of adopting a large number of deverbal nouns ending in {-ment}. It is true that perhaps most of these English deverbal nouns are of Old French origin, but not all of them. Thus, if we happen to choose another correspondence set, e.g. *commitment*, *settlement* and *embodiment*, we would be unable to arrive at Anderson's conclusion.

Again, how can we know that *judgement* is an item borrowed from Old French? Not by Internal Reconstruction, but only by (externally) comparing with French *jugement* (first attested around AD 1100; see www.cnrtl.fr), elsewhere by written documents of Middle English. Thus, even in wide parts of morphology the method of Internal Reconstruction fails to be a solid research tool. In the next section we will look at the possibility of applying this method to syntax and syntactic structure.

10.3 Internal Reconstruction Meets Syntax

Barðdal (2014) writes about 'Syntax and syntactic reconstruction'. Her article has as its starting point Construction Grammar (see Goldberg 1995). Although the author does not explicitly declare anywhere in her article that her method is not strictly applicable language internally, it becomes clear that it relies completely on the (external) comparative method. This is true for Harris (2008) and Lühr (2008) as well, inasmuch as these authors all use the comparative method in syntax with correspondence sets from a variety of languages. However, Dufter (2013) provides an example of successful 'internal reconstruction' in syntax by drawing correspondence sets from different diachronic stages of a given language. Dufter analyses the origin and development of dropping of negative *ne* from Early Modern French to Modern French varieties. The author tries to reconstruct the origin and the grammatical conditions of the omission of the negative particle *ne* by a detailed corpus analysis of literary texts of the eighteenth and nineteenth centuries (in continental French; following example taken from Dufter 2013: 141, citing Collé 1974: 697).

(6) qu' un père   il   peut pas avoir   des   sentiments
     that a   father SCL.3SG can   NEG have.INF some emotions
     plus vifs
     more intense
     'as a father he cannot have more intense emotions'

In (6) the negative particle *ne* is dropped before the modal verb form *peut* in the present indicative. In Modern French *ne* is dropped almost categorically and only appears in an emphatic context. Dufter (2013) confirms that *ne*-dropping is favoured by the presence of subject clitics such as *il* in (6), by the use of auxiliaries or other high-frequency verbs such as the modal *peut* in the present indicative and in the environment of negative intensifiers such as *pas* (< 'step') and *point* (< 'point'). That is, his study reconstructs these three syntactic factors just mentioned which trigger *ne*-dropping.

We see that Dufter's method differs quite obviously from the method of Internal Reconstruction presented in our introduction in §10.1. Another point to be mentioned is that this type of 'internal reconstruction' relies exclusively on written records. Therefore the limits of this method are clear: in languages without written documentation we cannot apply it; this is trivial.

We might therefore ask whether there is any alternative to internally reconstructing a previous syntactic state in any structural area of a given language, even if we cannot reasonably compile correspondence sets in the sense of Internal Reconstruction. Let us take, for example, relative clauses. It would hardly make sense to exhaustively compare the set of relative clauses of a given language in order to find out what their structure was like in an earlier stage of the very same language. Additionally, in order to mimic Ringe's (2003) method reported in (1) more accurately we have to ask what is a deviant or irregular relative clause with respect to the supposedly regular ones. This seems to be quite an unreasonable question in syntax in general. In order to illustrate our reasoning, let us look at the following correspondence set of (bracketed) relative clauses from Modern Brazilian Portuguese (see Castilho 2012: 367).

(7) a. Os   painéis   solares   geram   a   energia [com
        the   cells   solar   generate   the energy   with
        que   ⊘ sempre sonhamos]
        that   always we.dream

     b. Os   painéis   solares   geram   a   energia [que
        the   cells   solar   generate   the energy   that
        ⊘   sempre sonhamos com ela]
              always we.dream with it

     c. Os   painéis   solares   geram   a   energia [que
        the   cells   solar   generate   the energy   that
        ⊘   sempre sonhamos]
              always we.dream
        'These solar cells generate the energy which we have always dreamt of'

If we take these three types of relative clause in Brazilian Portuguese, how could we say which is regular and which is not?

It seems, therefore, that Internal Reconstruction in syntax has to take quite a different perspective than those taken in inflectional morphology. This will be the topic of the next and final section of this chapter.

10.4   Conclusion and Proposal

We start by quoting a sentence from Dressler (1971: 7) which we still consider very relevant: 'Widerspricht eine Rekonstruktion den beobachtbaren Fakten aller lebenden Sprachen der Welt, so ist sie sehr unwahrscheinlich' ['If a reconstruction contradicts the facts found in all living languages of the world it is very improbable']. This quotation leads us directly to the model of Principles and Parameters in Generative

Syntax (see Chomsky 1981, and Chapter 27, this volume). The idea behind this syntactic model implies the assumption of innate universal principles. Thus, a human being does not need to acquire these universals. It is obvious that languages differ from one another and this is captured by the concept of parameters (see §7.1). A parameter is a bundle of structural dependencies in causal relationship – and not just temporal coincidences; see, for example, Rizzi (1982) on the Null Subject Parameter – and these have to be acquired by the child. That is, in order to successfully reconstruct in syntax internally, we have to search for general principles (Universal Grammar principles; see Chapter 14, this volume) and for language-distinctive parameters (see Ferraresi and Goldbach 2008: §3). In contrast to the method of Internal Reconstruction illustrated above for morphology, the search for principles and parameters is testable in Popper's (1969) sense and therefore more appropriate for an empirical science such as syntax. Let us illustrate this idea by a conjecture concerning relative clauses and negation. Many languages exhibit the phenomenon of negative concord (see Rizzi 1982: §2).

(8)   Brazilian
        Ninguém Portuguese num queria   voltar   lá   não.
        nobody   NEG   wanted   return.INF there NEG
        'Nobody would like to go back there.'

In (8) the negative adverbs *num, não* do not reverse the negative polarity induced by the negative quantifier-like element *ninguém*. Rather, its negative value is 'absorbed' in the sense of Haegeman and Zanuttini (1991). However, when we split these negative items by a relative clause the negative concord effect is destroyed.

(9)   Ninguém [que já   tenha   visto Rio de Janeiro] não
        nobody   that already   have.SBJV.3SG   seen Rio de Janeiro   NEG
        queria   voltar.   lá
        wanted   return.INF there
        'Nobody who has ever seen Rio de Janeiro would not like to go back there.'

This means that the relative clause changes the polarity value of the matrix sentence from minus to plus since the negative value of *não* in (9) is no longer absorbed. Of course, sentences such as (9) are always uttered in an emphatic context. In fact (9) emphasizes that *all* people who have ever seen Rio de Janeiro would like to return to this city. Thus, we propose that there is a structural correlation between negative concord and relative clauses. Any language exhibiting negative concord shows the effect of polarity reversal when a relative clause interrupts the negative items. To come back to the topic of internally reconstructed syntax, we might say then that, if we find solid evidence for negative concord in a given language, we can conclude that we get polarity reversal effects such as (9). One might surely debate whether this is the best possible approach to 'internal syntactic reconstruction'. But we believe that our proposal is more suitable for syntactic internal reconstruction than the above reported method of Internal Reconstruction.

References

Anderson, S.R. 2014. 'Morphological change', in Bowern and Evans (eds.), pp. 264–85.

Aronoff, M. 1994. *Morphology by itself: Stems and inflectional classes*. Cambridge, MA: MIT Press.

Barðdal, J. 2014. 'Syntax and syntactic reconstruction', in Bowern and Evans (eds.), pp. 343–73.

Baxter, W. H. 2002. 'Where does the 'comparative method' come from?', in F. Cavoto (ed.), *The linguist's linguist: A collection of papers in honour of Alexis Manaster Ramer*. Munich: Lincom Europa, pp. 33–52.

Baxter, W. H. and Sagart, L. 2014. *Old Chinese: A new reconstruction*. Oxford University Press.

Bowern, C. and Evans, B. (eds.) 2014. *The Routledge handbook of historical linguistics*. Routledge: London.

Castilho, A. T. de 2012. *Nova gramática do português brasileiro*. São Paulo: Contexto.

Chomsky, N. 1981. *Lectures on government and binding*. Dordrecht: Foris.

Collé, C. 1974. 'La vérité dans le vin, ou les désagrémens de la galanterie', in J. Truchet (ed.), *Théâtre du XVIIIe siècle* (Bibliothèque de la Pléiade), vol. 2. Paris: Gallimard, pp. 599–655.

Corbin, D. 1987. *La morphologie dérivationnelle et structuration du lexique*, 2 vols. Tübingen: Niemeyer.

Dressler, W. 1971. 'Über die Rekonstruktion der indogermanischen Syntax', *Zeitschrift für vergleichende Sprachforschung* 85: 5–22.

Dufter, A. 2013. 'Zur Geschichte der *ne*-Absenz in der neufranzösischen Satznegation', in L. Fesenmeier, A. Grutschus and C. Patzelt (eds.), *L'absence au niveau syntagmatique*. Frankfurt am Main: Klostermann, pp. 131–58.

Ferraresi, G. and Goldbach, M. (eds.) 2008. *Principles of syntactic reconstruction*. Amsterdam: John Benjamins.

Goldberg, A. 1995. *Construction: A construction grammar approach to argument structure*. University of Chicago Press.

Haegeman, L. and Zanuttini, R. 1991. 'Negative heads and the Neg-criterion', *The Linguistic Review* 8: 233–51.

Harris, A. C. 2008. 'Reconstruction in syntax', in Ferraresi and Goldbach (eds.), pp. 73–95.

Joseph, B. D. 2010. 'Internal reconstruction', in S. Luraghi and V. Bubenik (eds.), *The continuum companion to historical linguistics*. London: Continuum, pp. 52–58.

Koch, H. 2014. 'Morphological reconstruction', in Bowern and Evans (eds.), pp. 286–307.

Lühr, R. 2008. 'Competitive Indo-European syntax', in Ferraresi and Goldbach (eds.), pp. 121–59.

Popper, K. 1969. *Conjectures and refutations: The growth of scientific knowledge*, 3rd edn. London: Routledge & Kegan Paul.

Ringe, D. 2003. 'Internal reconstruction', in B. D. Joseph and R. D. Janda (eds.), *The handbook of historical linguistics*. Oxford: Blackwell, pp. 244–61.

Rizzi, L. 1982. 'Negation, wh-movement and the null subject parameter', in L. Rizzi, *Issues in Italian syntax*. Dordrecht: Foris, pp. 117–84.

Rohlfs, G. 1968. *Grammatica storica della lingua italiana e dei suoi dialetti*, vol. II: *Morfologia*. Turin: Einaudi.

Uth, M. 2011. *Französische Ereignisnominalisierungen. Abstrakte Bedeutung und regelhafte Wortbildung*. Berlin: de Gruyter.

   2012. 'The lexicalist hypothesis and the semantics of event nominalization suffixes', in S. Gaglia and M.-O. Hinzelin (eds.), *Inflection and word formation in Romance languages*. Amsterdam: Benjamins, pp. 347–67.

Websites

www.infopedia.pt
www.cnrtl.fr

11

Corpora and Quantitative Methods

Susan Pintzuk, Ann Taylor and Anthony Warner

11.1 Introduction

The use of electronic corpora as a source of data is a relatively new development in diachronic syntax. Traditionally, much historical syntactic research was based on a scholar's knowledge of the language, including sets of collected examples, or on impressions of general patterns, sometimes using individual examples taken from secondary sources (e.g. Canale 1978; Roberts 1985). Another approach was to use a set of examples systematically collected from a sample of texts (e.g. Ellegård 1953; Kohonen 1978; Bean 1983; Pérez Lorido 2009). The availability of syntactically annotated electronic corpora, such as the series covering the history of English produced at the Universities of Pennsylvania and York, in collaboration with Helsinki, has completely transformed the scope, accuracy and speed of such systematic investigations, with benefits also for more qualitative studies.[1]

Corpora are particularly important in historical research, since there is no route to I-language through the judgements of native speakers. The main use of quantitative data in diachronic syntax is the analysis of variation and change. Frequencies, properly underpinned by a careful theoretical/structural analysis, can provide missing evidence, as we demonstrate below. From this perspective, corpora are essentially tools of great power. In order to properly collect, analyse and interpret corpus data, we need a theory of grammar and theory of language change. Without such a basis, it is impossible to know what data to collect and how to analyse and interpret them appropriately.

[1] For annotated corpora, see Kroch and Taylor (2000), Pintzuk and Plug (2002), Taylor, Warner, Pintzuk and Beths (2003), Kroch, Santorini and Delfs (2004), Taylor, Nurmi, Warner, Pintzuk and Nevalainen (2006), Kroch, Santorini and Diertani (2010), Wallenberg, Ingason, Sigurðsson and Rögnvaldsson (2011).

11.2   Building and data extraction

Modern corpora are constructed with the intention of providing a sample which represents the output of the speech community. In historical work, this is rarely possible. For example, the entire extant Old English (OE) corpus consists of about 1.75 million words, of which 1.25 million are included in the syntactically annotated *York–Toronto–Helsinki Parsed Corpus of Old English Prose* (YCOE). The majority of the excluded texts were either poetry (sampled in the *York–Helsinki Parsed Corpus of Old English Poetry* (YCOEP)), or else of limited syntactic interest (such as duplicates and lists). In later periods of English, more texts are available, and corpus builders, such as the Helsinki team, took care to balance genres. But more vernacular registers, including speech, were simply unavailable; in a largely illiterate society, written material was produced by an elite and was restricted in its functions. The investigator needs to be sharply aware of the nature and limitations of the corpus used: different corpora may give different results even when the object of study is the same.

One thing we have learned about corpora is that size matters. Small data sets can be unrepresentative. For instance, Pintzuk (1999), based on a small, manually collected corpus of about 2,300 clauses, calculates the rate of verb (projection) raising in Old English as 11.2 per cent, while the rate when the entire YCOE is sampled is 30.4 per cent (Haeberli and Pintzuk 2011). On the other hand, recent comparisons of the rate of *do*-support in negative declaratives across different, and differently sized (from moderate to extremely large), corpora are startlingly stable (Ecay 2015).

A syntactically annotated corpus makes the technical aspects of data collection quick and easy. If you know what you want, and the corpus has annotated that category in some way, then you can extract all possible examples in seconds. Knowing what data to collect and how to classify them, on the other hand, is not easy and must be informed by an understanding of the syntax of the construction under consideration. You must also understand the coding practice of the annotator, who may well have avoided distinguishing categories because a proper distinction would require a fuller analysis than was possible within the time constraints of annotation.

11.3   Qualitative Research

While corpora particularly lend themselves to quantitative research, they can also be used for qualitative research. A good syntactic analysis makes predictions beyond the construction under consideration. In studies of living languages, these predictions are checked using grammaticality judgements; for dead languages, a search for the construction in a sufficiently large corpus can provide similar confirmation.

It is important to note, however, that the presence/absence of a construction in a corpus does not straightforwardly equate to grammaticality/ungrammaticality. The absence of a construction, in particular, can be difficult to interpret. The crucial construction type may be rare (e.g. parasitic gaps), or unlikely to occur in the text types available, which are necessarily written and restricted in genre. The possibility that a gap is simply accidental is difficult to rule out. The interpretation of absence is always a judgement call on the part of the researcher.

Positive evidence must also be handled with care. A single example may indicate grammaticality, but given the nature of the text production process, it might equally be an error or misinterpreted. For instance, Biberauer and Roberts (2005) rely on the example in (1), extracted from Fischer *et al.* (2000), to support a particular analysis of the change in verb–object order in Middle English (ME); however, a search for the order object–verb–particle in the PPCME2 reveals no further examples of this order; i.e. this is the only example of its type in the corpus. While this does not invalidate its use as evidence, it does call it into question, and knowing it is the only example in a reasonably sized corpus could change a reader's evaluation of its support for this analysis. Even in qualitative studies, therefore, it is important to give some indication of the frequency of crucial examples. This kind of information is impossible to provide when relying on secondary sources, but can easily be extracted from a corpus.

(1) Þe   þ   swuch fulðe speteð ut   in eni encre   eare²
     that.one that such filth spews out in any anchoress's ear
     'the one that spews out such filth in any anchoress's ear'
     (Ancrene Riwle I.35.29; Fischer *et al.*, 2000: 203, 42a)

Using secondary sources as a source of data is, in general, fraught with problems. The first problem is simple accuracy. Although amazing in its coverage, Visser's great work is not always correct in its classification. Lieber (1979), for example, constructs an argument (pace Lightfoot 1981) that the indirect passive was already available in Old English. However, as Mitchell (1979) and Russom (1982) have noted, the four examples of indirect passives Visser gives are all erroneous, and there are no other cases (Mitchell 1979: 539); this lack is confirmed by a search of the YCOE. Visser compounds his error, presenting a seriously misleading estimate of frequency: 'the number of times they [indirect passives before 1500] are used is so considerable that there is no question of rareness of incidence' (p. 2144). Beware of statements about frequency based on secondary sources when true quantitative data are not available! Brinton (1988: 101), for instance, claims that accusative inflection in agreement with the object is inconsistent on perfect participles in

² The gloss/translation given by Fischer *et al.* and used by Biberauer and Roberts (2005) is also misleading. The full sentence makes it clear that this is a left-dislocation, and the *þe*, rather than being a relative pronoun, is the equivalent of OE *se*, i.e. it is a demonstrative.

OE, being 'not uncommon' in conjoined participles with and without inflection. However, a search of YCOE provides only two cases, representing 8 per cent (2/25) of the possible prose examples. Whether 8 per cent is 'common', 'not uncommon' or 'rare' is a judgement made by the author; without reliable quantitative data, it cannot be evaluated by the reader. Corpora make the reporting of actual frequencies and proportions straightforward, giving the reader the information to evaluate an author's claims.

11.4 Quantitative Research

11.4.1 S-curves

While there are different approaches to the modelling of variation and change in I-language (see Chapter 3, this volume; Biberauer and Roberts 2005, among many others), it is clear that the reflex of syntactic change in E-language involves a long period of competition between conservative and innovative variants. The trajectory of such changes over time has been well documented (see, among many others, Kroch 1989a; Pintzuk 1999; Pintzuk and Taylor 2006; Wallenberg 2009) and almost invariably follows an 'S-curve', with a slow introduction of the new variant, a quick rise in the middle period, and then a tailing off as the conservative variant is lost.

11.4.2 Statistical Tools

A large statistical toolbag is available to the historical syntactician. It is important to recognize that the use of such tools requires some mathematical sophistication; taking a relevant course, or discussing what has been read with someone who understands the topic, is important. In some cases simple figures are sufficient to demonstrate a point. Recurrently useful techniques found in historical syntax are chi-square testing, used in §11.5.2 below, and logistic regression, used in §11.5.1 and §11.5.3. The equation used in logistic regression plots an S-curve of increase (or decrease) against time. It is used in biology to model competition between species in an environment with finite resources. There are two coefficients: one defines the steepness of the S-curve (the rate of change), and the other locates the curve on the time axis.

11.5 Case Studies

In the rest of the chapter we present three case studies from the history of Germanic languages, selected to exemplify the crucial value of precise figures based on corpus data, using statistical techniques where relevant, in arguing for abstract analyses of earlier I-language, and for characterizations of change (see also the discussion in §20.4).

§11.5.1 considers whether object–verb order in earlier English is generated by a single I-language process, or by more than one. The analysis of change across time shows that three different processes must be involved. Here corpus data and the technique of logistic regression are used to argue for an aspect of earlier I-language. §11.5.2 examines the predictions of a particular model of acquisition and change, in the light of figures drawn from two Scandinavian languages; the model is shown to make correct predictions. In §11.5.3 the relevance of age to the progress of a change is investigated, and it is shown that in this case the progress of the competition involves the changing usage of adults, rather than a shift at acquisition.

These cases show that the real strength of corpora is that they enable us to quantify and track variation over time. This, in turn, if properly interpreted, can provide evidence for underlying changes in I-language, and for the nature of change itself.

11.5.1   Case Study 1: The Change from OV to VO in the History of English

It is well known that English changed over time from predominantly object–verb (OV) surface order in Old English to surface verb–object (VO) order now standard in Modern English (ModE). A number of explanations of this change have been suggested in the literature (see Taylor and van der Wurff 2005 and references therein). Many early accounts attribute the change in surface order to a change in underlying order in the eleventh–twelfth centuries; that is, there was a reanalysis of the structure of the VP, from head-final to head-initial, at this point and all deviations from OV order before this date and from VO order after this date must be derived in some way (Stockwell 1977; Canale 1978; Lightfoot 1981; van Kemenade 1987; Danchev 1991; Stockwell and Minkova 1991). Subsequent changes in the theory and a better understanding of the empirical facts, largely brought about through the availability of corpora, have produced more nuanced views of the change in recent work. Of particular interest here is the late Middle English period, when the change is almost complete.[3] In this period (late fifteenth century), VO order is the norm, as in (2a), but OV order continues to appear (optionally) in a limited number of contexts, including when the object is quantified (2b) or negated (2c).

---

[3] OV order with non-negative/non-quantified objects actually continues at a very low rate ($<$ 1%) through the Early Modern English period, and is only completely absent from texts after 1700, putting its complete loss rather later than assumed here. The papers discussed in this section were written prior to the completion of the Early Modern English (1500–1700) PPCEME corpus, and therefore it is not surprising that the extremely rare examples of OV order in the EModE period have gone undetected. This fact does not change the argumentation in this section, but simply dates the time of the change slightly later.

(2)   a. ȝef þu   wult   habben   <u>bricht</u>   <u>sichðe</u>   wið   þine   heorte   echnen
         if   you   will   have   bright   sight   with   your   heart's   eyes
         'If you will have bright sight with your heart's eyes … '
         (CMANCRIW, II.73.839)
         (*ȝef þu wult <u>bricht sichðe</u> habben …)

      b. ȝef   ȝe   habbeð   <u>ani</u>   <u>god</u>   don
         if   you   have   any   good   done
         ' … if you have done any good … ' (Ancrene Riwle I.76.310)

      c. þt   he   ne   mai   <u>nan</u>   þing   don   us   buten   godes   leaue
         that   he   NEG   can   no   thing   do   us   without   God's   leave
         ' … that he can do nothing to us without God's leave'
         (CMANCRIW, II.169.2346)

Van der Wurff (1999), writing before the advent of syntactically parsed electronic corpora, gives a very careful and insightful qualitative account of OV order in late Middle English, using the kind of argumentation standard in syntactic studies of modern languages; that is, presence in the texts is equated with grammaticality (the ability of the I-language to generate a surface form) and absence with ungrammaticality (the inability of the I-language to generate a surface form). The frequency at which a particular configuration occurs at any given point in time or its trajectory over time is not considered relevant to the argument.[4]

Van der Wurff, adopting an anti-symmetry model of syntax, attributes the data in (2) to a change in the I-language in the late fifteenth century. He claims that prior to this date all OV order is derived in the same way, i.e. by overt object movement (to AgrOP) from underlying VO. After this date, overt object movement is no longer generally available; the continuing availability of OV order with negative and quantified objects is instead attributed to the availability of alternate strategies for generating these orders, i.e. movement to SpecNegP and Quantifier Raising, respectively. Van der Wurff's account of this change is thus essentially qualitative. At time 1, based on the fact that OV order is attested with all types of objects, it is claimed that the grammar has a single rule for generating OV order, as in (2a), which applies straightforwardly to all objects. At time 2, however, OV order is only attested with negative and quantified objects, and therefore a general purpose object movement rule can no longer generate the attested patterns. A reanalysis is therefore posited between time 1 and time 2 in which children begin to analyse OV order with negative objects as cases of movement to SpecNegP, and with quantified objects as Quantifier Raising, rather than movement to SpecAgrOP in both cases.

Van der Wurff's account, however, is not the only possible one. An alternative, also consistent with the data as presented, is that OV

---

[4] Although van der Wurff did not have the option of including quantitative data in his analysis, since the corpora were not available at the time of his writing, this type of analysis is still fairly common in diachronic syntax (e.g. Biberauer and Roberts 2005; Los 2009).

configurations with the three types of objects have always had different structures, being derived, for example, by movement to SpecAgrOP, movement to SpecNegP and Quantifier Raising, respectively, right back through Old English. Under this account, the change in late ME involves only loss, and not reanalysis as well. Van der Wurff considers this account (1999: 258) and admits that it would produce the same E-language outcome, but also notes that it would be extremely difficult with the data available to differentiate between the two accounts. This is because the kind of qualitative data needed to distinguish movement to SpecAgrOP (A-movement) from movement to SpecNegP and Quantifier Raising (A-bar movement) involves such rare constructions as parasitic gaps, weak crossover and reconstruction after effects and movement crossing clause boundaries. While these kinds of effects can easily be tested with native-speaker intuitions in living languages, the relevant constructions are extremely unlikely to occur in texts, and thus testing is not possible. Van der Wurff also raises the question of whether quantitative data could distinguish these two analyses (1999: 259), but as the data are not available to him, he can only speculate on this point.

Pintzuk and Taylor (2006) address the same question of the derivation of OV order and its loss in the ME period as van der Wurff. This study, however, differs from van der Wurff's in two important ways: first, it was carried out after the completion of both the Middle and Old English corpora (PPCME2 and YCOE), and thus is able to make full use of quantitative data up to 1500, as well as qualitative data, in its argumentation; and second, it assumes a rather direct relation between the frequencies and surface distributions of the different object types found in the texts (E-language) and the abstract structures produced by the underlying grammar (I-language), following the methodology in Kroch (1989a). That is, it assumes that, all other things being equal, structures derived in the same way by the grammar will produce similar patterns in their distribution within texts and crucially will pattern together across time during a period of change.

Pintzuk and Taylor (2006) test van der Wurff's loss and reanalysis account against the alternative, that the differences observed between object types predate late ME; that is, the change involves only loss. Pintzuk and Taylor's (2006) account, carried out within a model incorporating directionality parameters and grammar competition, is fairly complex; however, as the actual derivations are not particularly relevant here, for expository purposes we will treat the derivation of OV order with each type of object as a single process or 'rule'. The difference between Pintzuk and Taylor's (2006) account and van der Wurff's is summarized in Table 11.1. For van der Wurff, the change involves the loss of a movement that affects all objects (indicated by strikeout) and the addition of two movements that affect only negative and quantified objects, respectively. For Pintzuk and Taylor (2006), on the other hand, there is only loss of one out of three original derivations; there is no change at all to the processes which derive OV with negative and quantified objects, which simply continue as previously.

Table 11.1 *A comparison of van der Wurff (1999) and Pintzuk and Taylor (2006)*

	van der Wurff (1999)	Pintzuk and Taylor (2006)
time 1 (~pre late ME)	OV: movement to SpecAgrOP	O_{pos} V O_{neg} V O_{quan} V
time 2 (~post late ME)	~~OV: movement to SpecAgrOP~~ + O_{neg} V: *movement to SpecNegP* + O_{quan} V: *Quantifier Raising*	~~O_{pos} V~~ O_{neg} V O_{quan} V

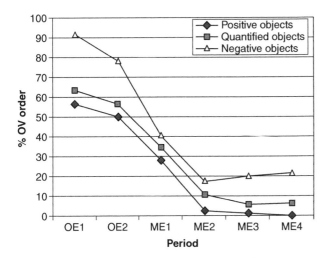

Figure 11.1 The loss of OV order in three types of object

As van der Wurff notes, it is difficult to decide between these two different accounts on the basis of a qualitative analysis alone: in terms of the simple presence/absence of particular surface configurations, they give the same result. However, as Pintzuk and Taylor (2006) show, the distribution of OV order and its frequency with different types of objects over a longer time frame give quite a different picture.

Figure 11.1 (from Pintzuk and Taylor 2006) illustrates the loss of OV order over the early OE to late ME period for all three types of objects. The first point this graph highlights is the now well-known fact that syntactic change progresses gradually with both variants (OV and VO in this case) occurring together in the language over a long period of time.[5] This fact is not straightforwardly reconcilable with the generative understanding of the locus of grammar change as a single reanalysis between one generation and the next. It is difficult, for instance, to identify van der Wurff's point of reanalysis on this graph. Under a grammar competition

---

[5] An even cursory look at any historical data will demonstrate that the variation is at the level of the individual and not the community; that is, individual authors routinely use both forms during such changes.

model of change, on the other hand, change to the underlying grammar (I-language) takes place at two points in time: at the original introduction of the innovative variant to the system, and at the final loss of the conservative variant at the end of the change; in between there is change in the frequency of use of each variant in the E-language, but no change to the I-language. In the OV to VO change under discussion here, the introduction of the innovative VO variant predates extant texts of early Old English prose, as represented in the graph, and the point at which the frequency of OV order reaches zero signifies the loss of the conservative variant. The S-shape of the curve has long been noted to be typical of changes in progress (Weinreich, Labov and Herzog 1968; Bailey 1973; Kroch 1989a; Blythe and Croft 2012): the innovative variant (VO) starts out slowly, picks up speed during the middle of the change and then slowly ousts the conservative variant at the end of the change.

This graph also makes it clear, that, at least as far as frequencies are concerned, the different object types have always behaved somewhat differently, with negative objects consistently most frequent in preverbal position, followed by quantified objects, with positive objects the least frequently preverbal. Nevertheless, this does not by itself indicate a difference in the underlying grammar. It is a commonplace in sociolinguistic studies of change in progress that the innovative variant appears at different frequencies in different contexts, with some contexts favouring the new variant more strongly than others (Labov 1994). This has also been shown to be the case in syntactic changes, as, for example, in the famous case of the rise of *do*-support; *do* is more strongly favoured in yes/no questions than in negative declaratives throughout the period of change (Ellegård 1953; Kroch 1989a).

As the frequencies at any single point in time cannot help us decide whether we are looking at a single derivation affecting all objects differentially (à la van der Wurff) or three different underlying processes, we look rather to the trajectory of the change over time. As initially demonstrated by Kroch (1989a) and confirmed in many later studies (e.g. Santorini 1993; Pintzuk 1999; Cukor-Avila 2002; von Heusinger 2008; Durham *et al.* 2012), different surface manifestations of the loss of a single derivation proceed at the same rate in all environments (the Constant Rate Effect); alternatively, if the rates are different this suggests different underlying derivations.[6]

The rate of change for each object type, represented by the slopes of the lines in Figure 11.2, is significantly different, as shown by the fact that the lines are not parallel. From this we can conclude that OV order is, in fact, lost at different rates for different types of objects across the ME period, and thus that the three object types have different derivations across at least the ME period, and presumably before.

---

[6] The slopes are calculated using logistic regression; see Kroch (1989a, 1994, 2001) for details.

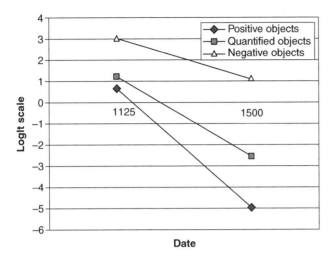

Figure 11.2 Regression lines for three types of object

Note that the quantitative data presented here only tell us that OV order is derived by different process for each object type, not anything about what the derivations actually are. In fact, this data are consistent with two I-language scenarios: (i) OV order with each type of object is generated in a completely separate way, as, for example, by movement to SpecAgrOP, movement to SpecNegP and Quantifier Raising, respectively, and there is no common ground between them; (ii) all types of preverbal objects are affected by a single process (e.g. base-generation in preverbal position in a head-final VP, or overt object movement to SpecAgrOP) which applies at the same rate to each type, with the additional negative and quantified OV tokens the result of some other process which affects only them (e.g. movement to SpecNegP, Quantifier Raising, extraposition). Pintzuk and Taylor (2006) provide further evidence, both qualitative and quantitative, to argue for the second scenario; the reader is referred to the original paper for details.

In conclusion, Pintzuk and Taylor (2006) show that in cases where more than one analysis of a linguistic change is possible on the basis of qualitative data (i.e. the presence/absence of particular constructions), quantitative data extracted from parsed corpora may be the only way to determine which analysis has empirical support.

11.5.2 Case Study 2: Applying a Formal Model of Change to the Loss of V-to-T in Mainland Scandinavian

Many historical linguists agree that acquisition plays at least some role in language change; the rigorous testing of formal models of language acquisition is therefore crucial if we are to make progress in our understanding of language change. However, there have been very few published studies within which a formal model of acquisition has been applied to a documented case of language change so that the predictions of the model can be empirically tested (but see Clark and Roberts 1993). There are many reasons for the absence of these studies: one obvious problem is that they require data that are accessible and suitable for both qualitative and quantitative analysis. With the development and availability of large annotated corpora that are easily searchable, such studies will become more common. In this section we present one such study, Heycock and Wallenberg (2013). They apply the model of Yang (2000) to the loss of verb movement to Tense (V-to-T) in the history of Faroese and the mainland Scandinavian languages. Heycock and Wallenberg (2013) use basic assumptions about Scandinavian syntax to analyse data from four different corpora, and show that Yang's model straightforwardly predicts the patterns in the historical data. Perhaps surprisingly, the corpora that are used are not those of the languages that are in the process of undergoing the loss of V-to-T, but rather languages that exhibit either V-to-T (older stages of Icelandic) or V-*in-situ* (modern Swedish) but not variation between the two. The fact that the Icelandic corpus is composed of historical texts is irrelevant; it was chosen because it contains parsed V-to-T texts that are easily searchable. The use of these corpora enabled Heycock and Wallenberg (2013) to determine the frequencies and distributions of the relevant constructions that are necessary to test Yang's model.

Yang (2000) adapts the learning model of Bush and Mosteller (1951, 1958) to the acquisition of competing grammars. When two competing grammars, G1 and G2, are used by adults to produce primary linguistic data (PLD), and when the child is exposed to this type of mixed PLD, the result is that the language learner acquires both grammars. In the normal case, each grammar generates some sentences that are unambiguous to the learner, i.e. that can be generated and processed by only one of the two grammars, as well as some sentences that are ambiguous, i.e. that can be generated and processed by both grammars. In Yang's model, the child assigns a probabilistic weight to each grammar during the acquisition process and updates the weights as the grammars are being learned. Based on the weights, the child selects a grammar, say G1, to process a sentence. If the sentence is ambiguous, G1 will succeed and be rewarded by an increase in probabilistic weight. If the sentence belongs unambiguously to G1, again G1 will succeed and be rewarded. But if the sentence belongs unambiguously to G2, G1 will fail and will be punished by a decrease in weight. This process is repeated over and over again for the individual learner, with the result that the grammar that is more successful in processing unambiguous sentences will end up with the higher weight. Since the language learners of one generation are the adult speakers of the language of the next generation, the process is also repeated over and over again for each generation. Note that Yang's model is a formal model of language acquisition and language variation and change which relies crucially on one particular form of ambiguity, where sentences produced by one grammar can be produced and processed by a second grammar.

To apply this model to historical data, we start from the basic observation that the grammar that can analyse the higher proportion of sentences that are unambiguous to the learner is the grammar that leads to the production of the higher proportion of unambiguous sentences by the adult speaker. Yang (2000) provides a mathematical proof that if the proportion of unambiguous sentences that G1 produces is greater than the proportion of unambiguous sentences that G2 produces, then G1 will win out at the end of the competition, regardless of the initial weights of G1 and G2 and regardless of the initial frequencies of use of G1 and G2. In other words, once the innovative grammar has been activated and the child hears output from two competing grammars, G1 and G2, the outcome of the competition is fixed, dependent only upon the frequencies of the unambiguous outputs of G1 and G2.

Heycock and Wallenberg (2013) make the following assumptions about Scandinavian syntax:

- All Scandinavian languages exhibit verb-second (V2): in V2 contexts (root clauses and some embedded clauses) the finite verb moves to a position higher than T, probably to a head in the C domain. Icelandic and Swedish examples from Heycock and Wallenberg (2013) are shown below in (3).
- In non-V2 contexts, the position of the finite verb varies: in Icelandic, it usually appears before negation and sentence-medial adverbs; in the mainland Scandinavian languages, it appears after these elements.[7] The standard analysis is that the finite verb moves to T in Icelandic (V-to-T) but remains in situ in mainland Scandinavian (V-*in-situ*). Icelandic and Swedish examples are shown in (4) and (5).
- The linear position of the finite verb can also be affected by Stylistic Fronting (SF), the process which, in the absence of an overt subject, fronts negation and sentence-medial adverbs (among other constituents) to a preverbal position if the verb has moved out of the VP. Icelandic examples are shown in (6).

(3)   a. Icelandic root clause with V2:

    Hún   [c borðar] ekki fisk
    She   eats   not   fish

    'She doesn't eat fish'

    b. Icelandic embedded clause with V2:

    ... að   hún [c borðar] ekki fisk
    ... that she   eats   not   fish

    ' ... that she doesn't eat fish'

---

[7] Negation and sentence-medial adverbs mark the left edge of the VP, and thus serve as diagnostics for verb movement out of the VP to T (or higher). The examples in the text and in Tables 11.2 and 11.3 use negation for illustration; the quantitative data in Heycock and Wallenberg (2013) and here are based on clauses with either negation or a sentence-medial adverb.

    c. Swedish root clause with V2:

      Hon   [c äter]   inte   fisk
      She   eats   not   fish
      'She doesn't eat fish'

    d. Swedish embedded clause with V2:

      ... att   hon   [c äter]   inte   fisk
      ... that   she   eats   not   fish
      ' ... that she doesn't eat fish'

(4)   Icelandic embedded clause, V-to-T:

      ... ef   hún   [T borðar]   ekki   fisk
      ... if   she   eats   not   fish
      ' ... if she doesn't eat fish'

(5)   Swedish embedded clause, V-*in-situ*:

      ... om   hon   [VP inte äter fisk]
      ... if   she   not   eats   fish
      ' ... if she doesn't eat fish'

(6)   a. Icelandic embedded clause with SF of ekki 'not':

      ... sem   ekki   [T borðar]   fisk
      ... C-REL   not   eats   fish
      ' ... who doesn't eat fish'

    b. Icelandic embedded clause without SF:

      ... sem   [T borðar]   ekki   fisk
      ... C-REL   eats   not   fish
      ' ... who doesn't eat fish'

It has been shown that the mainland Scandinavian languages and Faroese independently lost V-to-T during their historical development from an ancestor with a syntax like Icelandic, i.e. V2 and V-to-T (see, for example, Platzack 1988; Falk 1993; Vikner 1997; Sundquist 2002, 2003; Heycock *et al.* 2010). The usual explanation for verb movement is the Rich Agreement Hypothesis (RAH), which comes in two forms, biconditional and one-way conditional: the strong biconditional form is that the finite verb moves out of the VP to T if and only if agreement morphology on the verb is 'rich' (Rohrbacher 1999); the weaker one-way form is that rich agreement morphology forces V-to-T movement, but the lack of rich agreement morphology does not preclude verb movement (Bobaljik and Thráinsson 1998). Thus it can be (and has been) plausibly argued that the loss of V-to-T movement is due to the loss of rich agreement morphology, which seems to account for the situation in the modern Scandinavian languages: Icelandic, with rich agreement morphology on finite verbs, exhibits V-to-T throughout its history and in the modern language; the modern mainland Scandinavian languages, which have lost verbal agreement morphology, are V-*in-situ* languages. Nevertheless, Heycock and Wallenberg (2013) argue that the RAH in both its strong and weak forms makes the wrong predictions about the change. For the strong form, Sundquist's (2002, 2003) detailed work on historical Danish data shows that V-to-T movement persisted several centuries after rich agreement morphology was lost. The weak form of the RAH, under which V-to-T movement can occur with no morphological trigger, fails to explain why V-to-T movement is ever lost, since it can occur regardless of whether the language maintains or loses its rich agreement morphology.

Instead, Heycock and Wallenberg (2013) show that the model of Yang (2000) can explain the loss of V-to-T on the basis of the 'fitness' of the V-to-T vs the V-*in-situ* grammar. They use four corpora to represent the two grammars: the *Icelandic Parsed Historical Corpus* (Wallenberg *et al.* 2011) for the V2 grammar with V-to-T, and three Modern Swedish corpora for the V2 grammar with V-*in-situ*. They distinguish three main syntactic contexts: root clauses, all of which are V2; subordinate clauses that are not affected by embedded V2 (e.g. relative clauses and embedded interrogatives); and subordinate clauses in which embedded V2 (EV2) is possible (e.g. some complement clauses and adverbial clauses). Stylistic fronting in clauses without overt subjects may also apply, affecting the position of the finite verb. Table 11.2, based on the information in Heycock and Wallenberg (2013: 139, figure 2), shows the possible outputs for the two different grammars, V-to-T and V-*in-situ*. For ease of exposition, we have shown only the Modern English glosses of the outputs of the two grammars.

The shaded cells show the outputs that are unambiguous for each grammar. All root clauses and all subordinate clauses with EV2 are

Table 11.2 *Outputs of the V-to-T and V-*in-situ* grammars in various syntactic contexts*

Syntactic context	V-to-T grammar output	V-*in-situ* grammar output
Root clauses (V2)	She eats not fish	She eats not fish
Subordinate clauses, non-EV2		
Overt subject	. . . if she eats not fish	. . . if she not eats fish
Null subject without stylistic fronting	. . . C-rel eats not fish	. . . C-rel not eats fish
Null subject with stylistic fronting	. . . C-rel not eats fish	
Subordinate clauses, possible EV2		
With EV2, overt subject	. . . that she eats not fish	. . . that she eats not fish
With EV2, null subject with/without stylistic fronting	. . . that eats not fish	. . . that eats not fish
Without EV2, overt subject	. . . that she eats not fish	. . . that she not eats fish
Without EV2, null subject without stylistic fronting	. . . that eats not fish	. . . that not eats fish
Without EV2, null subject with stylistic fronting	. . . that not eats fish	. . . that not eats fish

ambiguous, since they can be parsed by both grammars. But the V-to-T grammar cannot parse a subordinate clause with an overt subject and the order Neg > finite verb ('... that she not eats fish'); similarly, the V-*in-situ* grammar cannot parse a non-EV2 subordinate clause with an overt subject and the order finite verb > Neg ('... if she eats not fish').

Table 11.3, based on the data in Heycock and Wallenberg (2013: 143, table 1),[8] contains quantitative data for Table 11.2. The language representing the V-to-T grammar is Older Icelandic; the language representing the V-*in-situ* grammar is Modern Swedish. Note that none of these data come from a language that is in the process of changing from a V-to-T grammar to a V-*in-situ* grammar; instead, the grammars represent the end points of the change. Root clauses are not included in Table 11.3; since all root clauses exhibit V2 and are thus ambiguous (parseable by both grammars), Heycock and Wallenberg (2013) did not include them in their quantitative data. Again, cells that are associated with unambiguous outputs are shaded.[9]

Table 11.3 shows clearly that the frequency of unambiguous clauses, i.e. those that can be processed by one grammar but not by the other grammar, is much higher for the V-*in-situ* grammar, represented by Modern Swedish, than for the V-to-T grammar, represented by older Icelandic: 84.1 vs 34.9 per cent.[10] The difference is statistically significant (chi-square with 1 degree of freedom = 218.611, p <.0001). The quantitative data, when analysed in accordance with Yang's model of variation and change, thus

Table 11.3 *Outputs of V-to-T and V-*in-situ* grammars in various syntactic contexts*

Syntactic context	V-to-T grammar (Older Icelandic)		V-*in-situ* grammar (Modern Swedish)	
	V > Diag ... eats not fish	Diag > V ... not eats fish	V > Diag ... eats not fish	Diag > V ... not eats fish
Subordinate clauses, non-EV2				
Overt subject	379	20	2	147
Null subject	40	122	0	42
Subordinate clauses, possible EV2				
Overt subject	545	7	0	86
Null subject	23	63	0	0
Total unambiguous clauses	419		233	
Total clauses	1199		277	
% Unambiguous clauses	34.9%		84.1%	

[8] For ease of exposition, we have shown counts for only one of the three V-*in-situ* grammars (the Swedish novel), and ignored the counts from the Swedish perfect construction with a non-overt finite auxiliary.

[9] For a discussion of the 27 Diag > V clauses with overt subjects for the V-to-T grammar, see Heycock and Wallenberg (2013: 144, fn.25).

[10] In order for these frequencies to be meaningful, there must be an unexpressed assumption that the two grammars are parallel in all relevant respects, e.g. in the frequencies of EV2, SF, etc.

predict the historical facts: the V-*in-situ* grammar, once introduced in the mainland Scandinavian languages, competes with the V-to-T grammar; and since the 'fitness' of V-*in-situ* is greater than that of V-to-T, the outcome is fixed and V-to-T is lost. Heycock and Wallenberg (2013) show in addition that embedded V2 is necessary for this scenario: if clauses that can be affected by embedded V2 are ignored and only those clauses that cannot be affected by embedded V2 (indirect questions and relative clauses) are considered, the frequency of unambiguous clauses is slightly higher for the V-to-T grammar than for the V-*in-situ* grammar, although not significantly so. In other words, the fitness of the two grammars is about the same; removing clauses with the possibility of embedded V2 eliminated the advantage of the V-*in-situ* grammar. Note here that it is crucial for the researcher to understand how to analyse the clauses that are output by each grammar, and to be able to determine which are ambiguous (i.e. processable by the other grammar) and which are unambiguous (i.e. processable only by the grammar that produces them). In addition, in order to provide a replicable test of Yang's model, or indeed any formal model of language variation and change, it is necessary to use quantitative data from publicly available and easily accessible corpora that are large enough to provide statistically adequate results.

11.5.3 Case Study 3: The Role of Adult Speakers in the Rise of Auxiliary *Do* in Questions

We have just examined two case studies in which differences in the incidence of constructions underpin the analysis of particular changes. In this final section we will outline a distributional argument for a potential property of change by considering an example which apparently shows that the progress of the change is somehow located in use by adults rather than in acquisition by children. It is important for the argument that we have data across an extended period of time, and that we know how old the authors of the texts involved were when they wrote them. We can not only estimate the rate of change shown by the corpus, but also see how this relates to the typical age profile of authors.

The case is the rise of auxiliary *do* in yes/no and adverbial questions. *Do* begins to be used as an auxiliary in Middle English, and in Early Modern English there is variation in direct questions between inversion of finite *do* (as in today's English) and the earlier construction with inversion of the finite verb. Both are shown in the following examples.[11]

(7) Affirmative direct yes/no questions
　　a. Lord, madam, do you know what you do? (324–8)
　　b. Alas, sir, think you the captain has so little wit as to accept of such a poor rascally fellow as I am instead of your son? (229–37)

---

[11] Examples from Thomas Otway *Cheats of Scapin; Friendship in Fashion* 1677 (*Works* 1812).

(8)   Affirmative direct adverbial questions
       a. why do I spend my time in tittle-tattle with this idle fellow?
          (215–8)
       b. Well, madam, how like you it, madam, ha? (301–13)

(9)   Negative direct yes/no questions
       a. did you not hear my lady call you? (327–10)
       b. But seems it not wonderful, that the circumstances of our fortune
          should be so nearly allied, ... ? (233–22)

(10)   negative direct adverbial questions
       a. Why did you not stand farther off? (238–33)
       b. why comes he not forth? (321–13)

At least two I-language changes are involved. The first introduces
a specialized use of *do* as some kind of auxiliary, in which it carries
finiteness, with consequent variation across constructions between finite
do with the infinitive of a lexical verb and the finite form of the lexical
verb. In inverted questions either finite *do* or the finite lexical verb is in
C. The period of variation runs roughly from 1400, with a low proportion
of *do*, to 1800. By this time *do* has largely adopted its modern 'last resort'
distribution, under which lexical verbs are no longer permitted in inverted
questions, and the loss of this option forms part of a further I-language
change. There may also be intermediate I-language changes, in particular
one introducing the 'last resort' distribution in the sixteenth century.
Overall, the change is clearly an example of competition between grammatical options.

We can imagine linguistic variation and change progressing in two
different idealized ways, where a construction is increasing in frequency
over time (as is the case with *do*-questions here), and acquisition includes
the acquisition of the relevant variation. Under the first scenario, the
increase in frequency occurs in acquisition, and once individuals have
acquired their language, their usage remains stable over their lifetime.
If we examine the range of usage in the adult population at any single
point in time, we expect to find a distribution according to age: younger
speakers exhibit a higher frequency of the incoming variant, older speakers a lower. Labov (1994: 84) dubbed this 'generational change' and noted
that it is typically found in phonetic or phonological change.

In the second scenario, the reverse is the case. The increase in use of the
incoming variant does not occur at acquisition, but across a speaker's
lifetime. In this type of change (which Labov 1994: 84 dubbed 'communal
change') 'all members of the community alter their frequencies together'.
If we examine the adult population at a single point in time, a group of
individuals of any set age can be expected to show the same range of
variation as a group of individuals of any other age. Labov has claimed
that syntactic change is typically communal. These two types as we have

presented them are idealized poles. An individual's usage in generational change is not always stable but may show an increase, and there may also be age-related patternings found across individuals more generally, reflecting differences in variation across the lifespan.

In the case of *do* in questions we can ask whether the development found in Early Modern English is more like communal change or generational change, since we know the date of publication of the texts, and the date of birth of most of the authors in the database provided by Ellegård (1953). So we can omit texts for which we do not have the authors' dates of birth, and for the rest we can calculate rates of change across periods of time using logistic regression. We can also see what contribution is made by the age of authors. What is striking is that the coefficients for age are tiny and very far from being significant. This means that, generally speaking, an author's use of *do* increases across his or her lifespan at the same rate as the overall use of *do* increases. This provides evidence for a basic 'communal' change. The traditional account of change within the Chomskyan framework depends on acquisition within the 'critical period' (see Chapter 18, this volume). Since children acquire language independently, interpreting their experience of the data in the light of UG, there is an opportunity for differences between generations at this point. However, if the increase in usage were accounted for at acquisition, we would predict a distribution corresponding to generational change, with a ranking of ages: older individuals would have lower rates of *do*, younger individuals would have higher rates of *do*. But there is no evidence of this (or any element of this) in the case study considered here (and the ages of subjects range from 22 to 76). The figures also give no evidence that there is a role for adolescents here (see Labov 2001: ch. 14; Tagliamonte and d'Arcy 2009). Instead it is clear that adults changed their behaviour, using more *do* as they aged. For details and further argumentation, see Warner (2004). Note that the conclusions here require a sophisticated statistical analysis, involving the interrelation of two numerical factors, and are not simply apparent from the basic data. This discussion has involved only a single case study, but it implies the possible more general relevance of this type of change to syntax. From a theoretical perspective this is a 'mere' change in usage, rather than a change in I-language. But it is the process which links two I-language changes (as noted above), and which indeed means that the initial I-language change is not simply snuffed out. So it has a real importance for the historian of syntax.

Language change is embedded in a context of social, stylistic and internal factors, which are certainly not all retrievable by those dealing with historical data. But it seems reasonable to comment on a couple of possible processes which might underlie adult communal change in syntax. The first is the well-established behavioural principle of accommodation, by which humans (and animals) adapt their behaviour to fit in with their associates. Now suppose that there was some recurrent tendency to misperception, which led hearers into a false estimate of interlocutors' level of use of *do*, in particular that clauses which used the finite form of the main verb were more liable to being misparsed or misheard than forms with auxiliary *do*. Perhaps this would have been a matter of a contextual interpretation without a complete parse. Then instead of perceiving, say, the 40% *do* and 60% finite verb which the interlocutor actually produced, a hearer who 'lost' 5% of the finite verb instances but only 1% of instances with *do*, would perceive 41.4% *do* and 58.6% finite verb, and would tend to accommodate to these figures, increasing the proportion of *do*. If we suppose that the percentage losses are stable, this model has the advantage that the function produced is the logistic, which provides an appropriate fit for change involving competition. This is one of the models of change suggested in Kroch (1989b), and discussed in Sprouse and Vance (1999).

A second possibility is that there is some internal mechanism which impacts on the competition between options. This could perhaps be thought of in terms of priming, that is, the tendency for the use of a form or construction to increase the likelihood of its use in the immediately following context. Suppose that the use in questions of auxiliary *do* and of the lexical finite verb tended to prime further occurrences, but that the priming was not equally balanced. The surface constructions are, after all, quite different, since only one involves the recurrent lexeme *do*, and it would be surprising if the two constructions had the same potential for priming. If *do* had a higher potential, this means that *do* would have become more accessible compared with the finite non-auxiliary form; and if this temporary situation tended to contribute to a permanent level of accessibility, then we would have a recurrent motivation for change.

Other ways of thinking about this are possible. We are not arguing here for a particular model, but noting that there is a serious contribution to change which arguably depends on aspects of interaction or development in adults. It can be deduced from the historical record in the case study considered here, but we need detailed corpora and statistical tools to make appropriate sense of what is going on.

11.6 Conclusion

In this chapter we have presented some aspects of the role of corpora and statistical methods in diachronic syntax, and shown how both quantitative and qualitative research benefit from their use. We then discussed three case studies in which corpus data play a crucial part: the change from OV to VO in the history of English, the loss of V-to-T in mainland Scandinavian and the rise of auxiliary *do* in questions. These case studies illustrate how corpus data and quantitative methods, when combined with a framework of formal syntactic analysis, can be used not only to track variation and change in E-language but also to determine the nature and timing of grammatical competition and change in I-language.

References

Bailey, C.-J. 1973. *Variation and linguistic theory*. Washington, DC: Center for Applied Linguistics.

Bean, M. C. 1983. *The development of word order patterns in Old English* (Croom Helm linguistics series). London: Croom Helm.

Biberauer, T. and Roberts, I. 2005. 'Changing EPP parameters in the history of English: Accounting for variation and change', *English Language and Linguistics* 9: 5–46.

Blythe, R. and Croft, W. 2012. 'S-curves and the mechanisms of propagation in language change', *Language* 88: 269–304.

Bobaljik, J. and Thráinsson, H. 1998. 'Two heads aren't always better than one', *Syntax* 1: 37–71.

Brinton, L. J. 1988. *The development of English aspectual systems: Aspectualizers and post-verbal particles*. Cambridge University Press.

Bush, R. and Mosteller, F. 1951. 'A mathematical model for simple learning', *Psychological Review* 58: 313–23.

  1958. *Stochastic models for learning*. New York: Wiley.

Canale, W. M. 1978. 'Word order change in Old English: Base reanalysis in generative grammar', unpublished PhD thesis, University of Toronto.

Clark, R. and Roberts, I. 1993. 'A computational model of language learnability and language change', *Linguistic Inquiry* 24: 299–345.

Cukor-Avila, P. 2002. '*She say, she go, she be like*: Verbs of quotation over time in African American Vernacular English', *American Speech* 77: 3–31.

Danchev, A. 1991. 'Language change typology and some aspects of the SVO development in English', in D. Kastovsky (ed.), *Historical English syntax*. Berlin: Mouton, pp. 103–24.

Durham, M., Haddican, B., Zweig, E., Johnson, D., Baker, Z., Cockeram, D., Danks, E. and Tyler, L. 2012. 'Constant linguistic effects in the diffusion of *be like*', *Journal of English Linguistics* 40: 316–37.

Ecay, A. 2015. 'Construction and lexical class effects in the history of *do*-support', presentation at *DiGS17*, Reykjavík, Iceland, 29–31 May 2015.

Ellegård, A. 1953. *The auxiliary do: The establishment and regulation of its use in English* (Gothenburg Studies in English). Stockholm: Almqvist and Wiksell.

Falk, C. 1993. 'Non-referential subjects in the history of Swedish', unpublished PhD thesis, University of Lund.

Fischer, O., van Kemenade, A., Koopman, W. and van der Wurff, W. 2000. *The syntax of early English*. Cambridge University Press.

Haeberli, E. and Pintzuk, S. 2011. 'Verb (projection) raising in Old English', in D. Jonas, J. Whitman and A. Garrett (eds.), *Grammatical change: Origins, nature, outcomes*. Oxford University Press, pp. 219–38.

Heycock, C. and Wallenberg, J. 2013. 'How variational acquisition drives syntactic change: The loss of verb movement in Scandinavian', *Journal of Comparative Germanic Linguistics* 16: 127–57.

Heycock, C., Sorace, A. and Hansen, Z.S. 2010. 'V-to-I and V2 in subordinate clauses: An investigation of Faroese in relation to Icelandic and Danish', *Journal of Comparative Germanic Linguistics* 13: 61–97.

Kohonen, V. 1978. *On the development of English word order in religious prose around 1000 and 1200 A.D.: A quantitative study of word order in context.* Meddelanden Fran Stiftelsens for Åbo Akademi Forskningsinstitut, no. 38. Publications of the Research Institute of the Åbo Akademi Foundation. Åbo: Åbo Akademi.

Kroch, A. S. 1989a. 'Reflexes of grammar in patterns of language change', *Language Variation and Change* 1: 199–244.

   1989b. 'Function and grammar in the history of English: Periphrastic *do*', in R. W. Fasold and D. Schiffrin (eds.), *Language change and variation.* Amsterdam: John Benjamins, pp. 132–72.

   1994. 'Morphosyntactic variation', *Proceedings of the 30th Annual Meeting of the Chicago Linguistics Society* 2: 180–201.

   2001. 'Syntactic change', in M. Baltin and C. Collins (eds.), *Handbook of contemporary syntactic theory.* Oxford: Blackwell, pp. 699–729.

Kroch, A., Santorini, B. and Delfs, L. 2004. *The Penn–Helsinki Parsed Corpus of Early Modern English* (PPCEME). Department of Linguistics, University of Pennsylvania. CD-ROM, 1st edn (www.ling.upenn .edu/hist-corpora/).

Kroch, A., Santorini, B. and Diertani, A. 2010. *The Penn–Helsinki Parsed Corpus of Modern British English* (PPCMBE). Department of Linguistics, University of Pennsylvania. CD-ROM, 1st edn (www.ling.upenn.edu /hist-corpora/).

Kroch, A. and Taylor, A. 2000. *The Penn–Helsinki Parsed Corpus of Middle English* (PPCME2). Department of Linguistics, University of Pennsylvania. CD-ROM, 2nd edn (www.ling.upenn.edu/hist-corpora/).

Labov, W. 1994. *Principles of linguistic change*, vol. 1: *Internal factors.* Oxford: Blackwell.

   2001. *Principles of linguistic change*, vol. 2: *Social factors.* Malden, MA, and Oxford: Blackwell.

Lieber, R. 1979. 'The English passive: An argument for historical rule stability', *Linguistic Inquiry* 10: 667–88.

Lightfoot, D. W. 1981. 'Explaining syntactic change', in N. Hornstein and D. W. Lightfoot (eds.), *The logical problem of language acquisition.* London: Longman, pp. 207–40.

Los, B. 2009. 'The consequences of the loss of verb-second in English', *English Language and Linguistics* 13(1): 97–125.

Mitchell, B. 1979. 'F. Th. Visser, *An historical syntax of the English language*: Some caveats concerning Old English', *English Studies* 60: 537–42.

Pérez Lorido, R. 2009. 'Reconsidering the role of syntactic "heaviness" in Old English split coordination', *Studia Anglica Posnaniensia* 45.1: 31–56.

Pintzuk, S. 1999. *Phrase structures in competition: Variation and change in Old English word order*. New York: Garland.

Pintzuk, S. and Plug, L. 2002. *The York–Helsinki Parsed Corpus of Old English Poetry* (YCOEP). Department of Language and Linguistic Science, University of York. Oxford Text Archive, 1st edn (www-users.york.ac .uk/~lang18/pcorpus.html).

Pintzuk, S. and Taylor, A. 2006. 'The loss of OV order in the history of English', in A. van Kemenade and B. Los (eds.), *The handbook of the history of English*. Oxford: Blackwell, pp. 249–78.

Platzack, C. 1988. 'The emergence of a word order difference in Scandinavian subordinate clauses', in D. Fekete and Z. Laubitz (eds.), *McGill Working Papers in Linguistics: Special Issue on Comparative Germanic Syntax*, pp. 215–38.

Roberts, I. 1985. 'Agreement parameters and the development of English modal auxiliaries', *Natural Language & Linguistic Theory* 3: 21–58.

Rohrbacher, B. 1999. *Morphology-driven syntax: A theory of V to I raising and pro-drop* (Linguistik Aktuell, vol. 15). Amsterdam: John Benjamins.

Russom, J. H. 1982. 'An examination of the evidence for OE indirect passives', *Linguistic Inquiry* 13: 677–80.

Santorini, B. 1993. 'The rate of phrase structure change in the history of Yiddish', *Language Variation and Change* 5: 257–83.

Sprouse, A. R. and Vance, B. S. 1999. 'An explanation for the decline of null pronouns in certain Germanic and Romance languages', in M. DeGraff (ed.), *Language creation and language change: Creolization, diachrony and development*. Cambridge, MA: MIT Press, pp. 257–83.

Stockwell, R. 1977. 'Motivations for exbraciation in Old English', in C. N. Li (ed.), *Mechanisms of syntactic change*. Austin: University of Texas Press, pp. 291–314.

Stockwell, R. and Minkova, D. 1991. 'Subordination and word order change in the history of English', in D. Kastovsky (ed.), *Historical English syntax*. Berlin: Mouton, pp. 367–408.

Sundquist, J. D. 2002. 'Morphosyntactic change in the history of the Mainland Scandinavian languages', unpublished PhD thesis, Indiana University.

  2003. 'The rich agreement hypothesis and Early Modern Danish embedded-clause word order', *Nordic Journal of Linguistics* 26: 233–58.

Tagliamonte, S. A. and D'Arcy, A. 2009. 'Peaks beyond phonology: Adolescence, incrementation and language change', *Language* 85(1): 58–108.

Taylor, A., Nurmi, A., Warner, A., Pintzuk, S. and Nevalainen, T. 2006. *The York–Helsinki Parsed Corpus of Early English Correspondence* (PCEEC). Department of Language and Linguistic Science, University of York. Oxford Text Archive, 1st edn (www-users.york.ac.uk/~lang22/PCEEC-manual/index.htm).

Taylor, A. and van der Wurff, W. 2005. 'Special issue on aspects of OV and VO order in the history of English', *English Language and Linguistics* 9(1): 1–4.

Taylor, A., Warner, A., Pintzuk, S. and Beths, F. 2003. *The York–Toronto–Helsinki Parsed Corpus of Old English Prose* (YCOE). Department of Language and Linguistic Science, University of York. Oxford Text Archive, 1st edition (www-users.york.ac.uk/~lang22/ YcoeHome1.htm).

van der Wurff, W. 1999. 'Objects and verbs in modern Icelandic and fifteenth-century English: A word order parallel and its causes', *Lingua* 109: 237–65.

van Kemenade, A. 1987. *Syntactic case and morphological case in the history of English*. Dordrecht: Foris.

Vikner, S. 1997. 'V°-to-I° movement and inflection for person in all tenses', in L. Haegeman (ed.), *The new comparative syntax*. London: Longman, pp. 189–213.

von Heusinger, K. 2008. 'Verbal semantics and the diachronic development of DOM in Spanish', *Probus* 20: 1–31.

Wallenberg, J. 2009. 'Antisymmetry and the conservation of c-command: Scrambling and phrase structure in synchronic and diachronic perspective', unpublished PhD thesis, University of Pennsylvania.

Wallenberg, J., Ingason, A. K., Sigurðsson, E. F. and Rögnvaldsson, E. 2011. *Icelandic Parsed Historical Corpus* (IcePaHC). Department of Linguistics, University of Iceland. Online publication, version 0.9. (www.linguist.is /icelandic_treebank).

Warner, A. 2004. 'What drove DO?', in C. Kay, S. Horobin and J. Smith (eds.), *New perspectives on English historical linguistics. Selected papers from 12 ICEHL*, vol. 1: *Syntax and morphology*. Amsterdam: John Benjamins, pp. 229–42.

Weinreich, U., Labov, W. and Herzog, M. 1968. 'Empirical foundations for a theory of language change', in W. Lehmann and Y. Malkiel (eds.), *Directions for historical linguistics*. Austin: University of Texas Press, pp. 95–189.

Yang, C. 2000. 'Internal and external forces in language change', *Language Variation and Change* 12: 231–50.

12

Phylogenetic Reconstruction in Syntax: The Parametric Comparison Method

Giuseppe Longobardi and Cristina Guardiano

12.1   Introduction

The Parametric Comparison Method (PCM) is a novel tool for studying the historical evolution and classification of languages. The intuition behind it is that purely theoretical advances of linguistics over the past few decades may provide an innovative system for reconstructing language phylogenies.

The possibility of an efficient lexically blind system of syntactic comparison was first suggested in Longobardi (2003). Such suggestions were implemented into the PCM starting with Guardiano and Longobardi (2005), where it was shown that the analysis of a few languages in terms of the PCM could satisfy certain conceptual conditions of adequacy (scattering of language distances, the Anti-Babelic Principle). Longobardi and Guardiano (2009) argued that the PCM provides preliminary taxonomies in good empirical agreement with some independent historical expectation, within and partly outside the Indo-European family. Bortolussi, Longobardi, Guardiano and Sgarro (2011) developed a first argument that the probability of many language distances calculated by the PCM is significant beyond chance, and hence calls for a historical explanation. Longobardi (2012) argued that some apparently paradoxical instances of parallel developments can be readily explained by the structure of the syntactic theory underlying the PCM. Longobardi *et al.* (2013) tested PCM's performance in domains whose genealogy is already known (the phylogeny of Indo-European languages), as well as its ability to reconstruct chronologically deep phylogenies using exclusively modern language

This work was partly supported by the ERC Advanced Grant 295733 LanGeLin (PI: G. Longobardi).

data. Guardiano *et al.* (2016) applied the PCM to the contrastive analysis and historical classification of varieties closely intertwined geographically, genealogically and sociolinguistically, showing that it can successfully analyse microvariation and provide a novel quantitative framework in the study of syntactic dialectology. Longobardi *et al.* (2015, 2016a and b) proved that signals of historical similarity are detectable above family-level, especially between Indo-European and its geographic neighbours, demonstrating that syntactic parameters encode retrievable historical information. These results validate the method as a useful tool for measuring language similarity with precision over long time spans.

12.2   Classification and Historical Explanation in Biology and Linguistics

For nearly two centuries, biological anthropology and historical linguistics have pursued analogous questions, aiming to classify human populations and languages into genealogically significant families, thus explaining their resemblances and charting the paths of their diversification. Beyond the similarity of the problems, it is worth remarking that Darwin himself in *The Origin of Species* had already predicted the eventual emergence of matching phylogenetic results for the two disciplines, which could then reinforce each other in their reconstruction of human past: 'If we possessed a perfect pedigree of mankind, a genealogical arrangement of the races of man would afford the best classification of the various languages now spoken throughout the world; and if all extinct languages, and all intermediate and slowly changing dialects, were to be included, such an arrangement would be the only possible one' (Darwin 1859: ch. 14).

12.2.1   Linguistic and Biological Phylogenies

To test Darwin's claim, one needs a broad amount of information on both linguistic and genetic diversity over the world. Sokal (1988) showed that there are indeed variable degrees of positive correlation between genetic, geographic and linguistic distances in Europe. Cavalli-Sforza *et al.* (1988) claimed to have found a general resemblance between evolutionary trees inferred, respectively, from genetic and linguistic similarities between populations. However, their work has remained controversial, especially among linguists. The crucial linguistic objection was their reliance on highly controversial linguistic superphyla, such as Nostratic or Amerind, produced by quantitatively unsupported and non-replicable taxonomic practices (especially see Ringe's (1996) severe criticism, among others). For, virtually no professional historical linguist unconditionally subscribes to the wide-range language trees used as matches in Cavalli Sforza's experiments, and most of them deny the very possibility of a reliable global classification of languages for serious methodological reasons.

By virtue of recent advances in formal linguistic theory, we feel we are now in a much better position to overcome this objection and successfully readdress the issue bridging the methodological gap between the two disciplines. Indeed, genetics has been able to assess similarities/differences on a global basis, i.e. among very distant populations, and to draw phylogenies by means of exact biostatistical methods; instead, no solid long-range comparison has so far been possible in phylogenetic linguistics and quantitative tools have only recently been adopted (Dyen, Krusal and Black 1992; Ringe, Warnow and Taylor 2002; Gray and Atkinson 2003; McMahon and McMahon 2005). To understand the phylogenetic potential of theoretical developments in linguistics, it will be instructive to consider some aspects of recent work in biological anthropology.

12.2.2 Biological Classifications

Phylogenetic, hence typically *historical*, investigation in biology has undergone a revolution, over the past few decades, on the grounds of purely *theoretical* progress, namely the rise of molecular genetics. Classifications of species, or populations within a species, were traditionally based on externally accessible evidence, the so-called morphological characters (e.g. anthropometric traits such as shape and size of body and skull, colour of skin, hair, eyes, etc.). Such features are not very adequate taxonomic characters because they are highly unstable through time, since they are subject to strong evolutionary selection on the part of the environment. The newly available genetic and molecular evidence has one great advantage: it is less subject to change driven by natural selection and, therefore, is more likely to retain genealogical information.[1] Furthermore, genetic polymorphisms, i.e. the *comparanda* of molecular classifications, exhibit a very useful formal property: they are drawn from a *finite* and *universal* list of *discrete* biological options. Experimental research in this field has led to the discovery of a wealth of deep genetic polymorphisms, able to generate robust phylogenies.

12.2.3 Linguistic Classifications

As in biological classifications, phylogenetic relatedness among languages has been traditionally investigated on the most externally accessible

---

[1] '... the major breakthrough in the study of human variation has been the introduction of genetic markers, which are strictly inherited and basically immune to the problem of rapid changes induced by the environment' (Cavalli Sforza, Menozzi and Piazza 1994: 18).

elements, i.e. sets of words and morphemes (whether roots, affixes or inflections); let us term such entities *lexical* in a broad sense, as they are saliently characterized by Saussurean arbitrariness. Precisely for this reason, lexical items, when resembling each other in form and meaning (e.g. Eng. *thick*, Ger. *dick*), seem able to provide the best probative evidence for relatedness.

However, simply comparing lexical items as such is risky; many word resemblances are due to chance: e.g. English *much*, *day*, *have* and Spanish *mucho*, *dia*, *haber* are false cognates. This risk was successfully overcome by the *classical* comparative method (for further discussion, see Chapter 9, this volume), which focused on more abstract entities (*regular sound correspondences* across vocabularies), whose probability of accidental occurrence ranges below any threshold of significance (Nichols 1996). Etymologies supported by sound correspondences are more reliable entities of inquiry than immediately observable, but deceiving, word resemblances: Eng. *full* and It. *pieno*, or Fr. *(je) fonds* and Ger. *(ich) giesse*, can be proven virtually sound by sound to be cognates, contrary to the English–Spanish similarities above.

The method grounded the study of the Indo-European language family, a breakthrough in the investigation of the human past, particularly of Eurasian (pre-)history, and applied successfully also outside Indo-European. However, the very condition of its success (looking for very improbable, hence necessarily *rare*, agreements) also sets a limit: regular sound correspondences irretrievably disappear in just a few millennia after language separation, leaving little hope of discovering very ancient prehistoric families (say, beyond the time depth of Indo-European, supposedly about 6–7 ky BP). Fascinating questions like 'is Indo-European related to Finno-Ugric and Semitic and, if so, to which one more closely?', 'how many native families exist in the Americas?' remain unanswerable.

12.2.4 Long-Range Comparisons

For a global classification, one should be able to compare any set of languages, no matter how distant in time and space. For this reason, Greenberg (1987, 2000) attempted to resurrect and amend the word resemblance practice. He checked supposedly universal meaning lists for their expression across many languages at a time (*mass* or *multilateral* comparison), guessing common ancestry simply from the gross amount of surface resemblance. This practice has failed to provide precise measures of similarity, let alone of probability of accidental resemblance: indeed, the collation of *comparanda* is intrinsically uncertain and remains heavily in danger of mistaking chance similarities for cognates. Therefore, Greenberg's work met with extremely severe mathematical and empirical critique (Matisoff 1990; Ringe 1992, 1996).

To sum up, the classical method is virtually chance-proof, multilateral comparison is potentially of universal application, but neither enjoys both assets. Furthermore, lexical methods display a common disadvantage, due to the intrinsic non-discreteness of form and meaning differences: they hardly provide precise distance measures to generate mathematically accurate and 'objectively' replicable taxonomies. Therefore, even in important experiments for computing lexical phylogenies (Gray and Atkinson 2003; McMahon and McMahon 2005, among others), such obstacles cannot be completely eliminated (Longobardi and Guardiano 2009; Longobardi *et al.* 2013).

12.3 Syntax as Historical Evidence

Given the time/space limits of the classical method and the vagueness/ unreliability of Greenberg's procedures, the use of taxonomic characters beyond the vocabulary has been advocated (Nichols 1992; Heggarty 2004; Ringe, Warnow and Taylor 2002; Dunn *et al.* 2005). As noted, in biology, the impasse resulting from the limits of morphological traits as taxonomic characters was overcome by accessing more sophisticated evidence, provided by independent theoretical developments of the discipline. *Mutatis mutandis*, analogous theoretical progress has been made in linguistics since the 1950s: the *grammar* of an ever wider array of languages has been investigated since the rise of typology (Greenberg 1963) and of Principles-and-Parameters approaches (Chomsky 1981). In particular, the theory of generative syntax, studying the mind as a system of computation of abstract symbolic entities, has made available a completely new level of evidence, most suitable for comparison and classification (Roberts 1998, 2007).

On the analogy of the theory-induced progress in biological classifications, we think it natural in linguistics to ask if modern syntax can serve genealogical purposes better than lexical methods, namely whether parameters may play a historical role analogous to that played by genetic markers. In this sense, we regard lexical data as resembling the external morphological characters used by more traditional biological taxonomies, while data provided by formal theory may resemble precisely the molecular evidence exploited in population genetic and contemporary biological classifications.

12.3.1 Parametric Linguistics

We regard parametric linguistics as a specific subfield of the formal biolinguistic framework (see Chapter 28, this volume), ranging conceptually from works such as Chomsky (1955, 1965) and Lenneberg (1967) to Kayne (2000), Hauser, Chomsky and Fitch (2002), Lightfoot (2006),

Biberauer (2008), Fitch (2010), Biberauer, Holmberg, Roberts and Sheehan (2010), Di Sciullo and Boeckx (2011), through an exterminate amount of theoretical and empirical work (see Boeckx and Piattelli Palmarini (2005) for the clearest statement of some tenets of this research). Parametric approaches crucially focus on the problem of a formal and principled theory of grammatical diversity, a privileged testing ground for models of the interaction between biologically shaped mental structures and culturally variable information.

Within this framework, the subfield of parametric linguistics can be minimally defined by three fundamental questions (Gianollo, Guardiano and Longobardi 2008):

(1)   a. What are the actual parameters of UG?
        b. What is the form of a possible parameter?
        c. How are parameter values distributed in space and time?

The PCM is first of all an attempt to answer (1c) and to pursue the 'historical' adequacy of linguistic theory, as defined in Longobardi (2003), which should ultimately try to answer a question like (2):

(2)   Why, in the course of cultural history, did precisely the attested variety of human languages arise?

In the specific domain of language, all such questions instantiate much more general issues of anthropology like: 'Why do human cultures vary so noticeably? Why did different cultural features come to be distributed in space and time the way they are?'. In the field of material culture, some of these questions have been most insightfully addressed by groundbreaking works such as Diamond (1998). In the domain of properly cognitive aspects of cultural variation, work is just beginning. Grammatical parameters offer particularly fertile ground for investigation of this kind, owing to certain peculiar features that distinguish them from many other cultural variables. Addressing questions like (1c) is an essentially unprecedented task: it means searching for at least some significant correlation between the distribution of parameter values and some other known geographical or historical variable.

There are two additional reasons to establish syntax as a phylogenetic discipline:

(3)   a. phylogenetic hypotheses yield insights for neighbouring sciences (e.g. the 'New Synthesis') and may thus justify a historical paradigm in syntax as a contribution to general knowledge;
        b. within linguistics proper, success in syntax-based phylogenetic taxonomy could ground all other aspects of diachronic investigation in syntax (see Longobardi 2003: 127).

Meeting these two standards enabled the classical comparative method to establish itself and (historical) linguistics as a full scientific paradigm. The second condition is especially relevant: it would indeed be hard to conceive a theory of etymology and phonological change if the sound shape of the lexicon evolved in so chaotic a way as not to contain salient cues about the phylogenetic relations of languages. Analogously, one might argue that it will only become plausible to expect success from restrictive theories of syntactic change (e.g. Lightfoot (1979) and subsequent work or Keenan's (1994, 2000, 2002) theory of *Inertia*, on which see also Chapter 20, this volume) if the diachronic persistence of syntactic properties is indeed sufficiently robust to carry a detectable phylogenetic signal.

12.3.2   Parameters as a Tool for Historical Investigation

In P&P theory, parameters are conceived as a set of open choices between *discrete* (ideally binary) values, predefined by UG (i.e. universally comparable), closed by each learner on the basis of her/his linguistic environment (*triggers*, in Clark and Roberts' (1993) terms, or *cues*, in Lightfoot's (1991) sense; see further the discussion in Chapters 7, 13 and 27, this volume). Therefore, setting the value of a parameter is an operation of *selection* rather than instruction (Piattelli Palmarini 1989). Open parameters define a variation space for biologically acquirable grammars, closed parameters specify each of these grammars. Thus, grammar acquisition should reduce, for a substantial part, to parameter setting, and the core grammar of every natural language can in principle be represented by a string of binary symbols (e.g. a succession of 0,1 or +, –; see Clark and Roberts 1993), each coding the value of a parameter of UG.

12.3.3   The Implicational Structure of Parametric Diversity

Observable syntactic properties are often not independent of each other: the relation between observable *patterns* (e.g. word order, concord, …) and the actual syntactic *parameters* which vary across languages is quite indirect, somewhat reminiscent of the genotype–phenotype correspondence in biology. Parametric hypotheses intrinsically encode a good deal of the implicational structure of language diversity: P&P theories, inspired by Greenberg's discovery of implicational universals, regard parameters as abstract differences often responsible for wider typological clusters of surface co-variation, often through an intricate deductive structure. In this sense, the concept of parametric data is not to be simplistically identified with that of syntactic pattern. For example, at least the following three surface differences (along with a few minor ones) between e.g. Italian and English appear to systematically cluster together (Longobardi 1994, 1996): (1) in English one says *Ancient Rome was a large city*, not *Rome ancient ..., whereas in Italian it is the opposite (*Roma antica era una grande città*, not *Antica Roma ...); (2) in English one says *Mme Curie discovered radium*, not * ... *discovered the radium*, whereas in Italian one says ... *scoprì il radio*, *not ... *scoprì radio*; (3) in English the order genitive+noun is normal (*John's book*), in Italian impossible: there is nothing like *Gianni*+genitive marker+*libro*. Several other languages behave quite consistently like Italian, others like English. Hence, all these seemingly distinct contrasts appear to derive from a single parametric difference, presumably arisen exactly once in the divergence history of the two languages. Conversely, superficially identical patterns in two languages may be determined by quite different parameter values, distinguishable only by inspecting subtle aspects of such languages, sometimes remote from the pattern under study (Roberts 1998): the same linear and concord pattern *noun–genitive–adjective* in Greek (ίχνη αίματος εμφανή 'clear traces of blood (lit. traces blood clear)') and in Hebrew (*ikvot dam brurim* lit. 'traces blood clear') follow in fact from exactly opposite values in at least two distinct parameters (Longobardi *et al.* 2013).

To sum up, a parameter will be such only if all the grammatical properties supposed to follow from it typologically co-vary; conversely, it will be satisfactorily defined only if no other property significantly co-varies with them. This is a necessary, though not sufficient, condition to ensure that we focus on cognitive structures (i.e. components of I-language, in Chomsky's (1986) terms), not just on generalizations over surface extensions of such structures (parts of E-language). In fact, patterns such as, for example, the traditional N-Gen/Gen-N have already proved at best epiphenomenal at the parametric level: there exist several unrelated types of both constructions and, most importantly, they follow from the combinations of more abstract and independent parameters.

Obviously, in many such cases, counting similarities in visible patterns, rather than in the underlying parameters, might become misleading for mathematically assessing relatedness, no less than relying on superficial lexical resemblances.

Moreover, the potential drawback of building phylogenies on just extensional (though structural) differences, rather than on a more limited set of arguable primitives of syntactic variation, grows substantially when moving from a circumscribed set of similar languages to a more extensive and geographically large-grained scope. For we must compare quite diverse varieties, whose surface properties do not single out immediate points of minimal collation (also see Roberts 1998): remaining on the surface, the risk of missing correspondences, or mistaking pattern similarities for real correspondences, presents itself again. Therefore, on a global scale, where universality and stability are crucial, it is all the more advisable to take a further step in abstraction and use parametric hypotheses as taxonomic characters.

The second implicational aspect of parametric systems, potentially challenging independence of characters, is that parameters form a pervasive network of partial implications (Guardiano and Longobardi 2005, 2016; Longobardi and Guardiano 2009; Longobardi *et al.* 2013): one particular value of some parameter A, but not the other, often entails the irrelevance of parameter B, whose consequences (corresponding surface patterns) become predictable; therefore, B will not be set at all in some languages, representing completely implied information, to be appropriately disregarded in computing language similarity/diversity.

12.4 The Parametric Comparison Method

12.4.1 Formal Properties

Parameters, like genetic markers in biology, form a *universal* list of *discrete* options. Because of these properties, the PCM shares one of the useful formal features of genetic tools and enjoys some advantages over other linguistic taxonomic methods. In particular, it combines the two strengths of the classical comparative method and of multilateral comparison (Guardiano and Longobardi, forthcoming). Like the latter and unlike the former, it is applicable in principle to any set of languages, no matter how different, precisely because parameters are drawn from a universal list. It does not need to search for highly improbable phenomena, and rely on their existence, as a prerequisite to be applied. Like the classical method, the PCM overcomes the intrinsic uncertainty about the appropriate identification of *comparanda* which undermines mass comparison. For, owing again to the universal character of parameters, in the PCM there cannot be any doubt about what is to be compared with what: the value of a parameter in a language must and can be collated with the value of exactly the same parameter in other languages. Of course, agreement in one binary parameter proves nothing by itself; yet, parameters, owing to their discrete nature, lend themselves to precise calculations: the probability of agreements in large numbers of parameters chosen from exactly predefined sets can, in principle, be objectively computed (Longobardi and Guardiano 2009).

12.4.2 Substantive Properties

Parameters are promising characters for phylogenetic linguistics in at least three other respects.

First, like many genetic polymorphisms, they are virtually immune from natural selection and, in general, from environmental factors: e.g. lexical items can be borrowed along with the borrowing of the object they designate, or adapted in meaning to new material and social environments; nothing of the sort seems to happen with abstract syntactic properties.[2]

Second, knowledge of grammar, including parametric values, is largely beyond the grasp of the speakers' *consciousness* (for discussion, see Chomsky 1980: ch. 6), virtually excluding the fact that it may be significantly affected by deliberate individual decisions like other culturally transmitted properties (Cavalli Sforza 2000: 176).

Finally, at least in some obvious cases (e.g. the null subject status of modern Italian or Spanish, apparently inherited unchanged from PIE), parameter values seem able to exhibit 'long-term' historical persistence, somewhat analogous to the *télé-histoires* whose study within different civilizations has been advocated by Braudel (1985), for example. In this sense the *inertial* view of diachronic syntax advocated in Longobardi (2001b) as a specific implementation of Keenan's (1994) original conceptual insights, proposes that formal features (roughly in Chomsky's (1995) terms) are deeper and more stable than lexical semantic and phonological ones, which can be sources of primitive changes; indeed, their change can only be a direct or indirect consequence of some interface innovation, or of some even more external influence on the grammar, such as borrowing. According to such premises, if parameters are properties of formal features, parametric syntax could be among the aspects of a language most apt to preserve traces of original identity, being more conservative than phonology or the lexicon; this is true at least with respect to those parameters which are not primarily set on the grounds of phonological evidence.

12.4.3 Empirical Strategies: The Choice of Parameters

A crucial step in the empirical implementation of the PCM is the choice of the parameters to be compared. Our approach is the historical actualization of the strategy proposed in Longobardi (2003) under the label 'Modularised Global Parametrisation' (MGP); it aims to attain the depth of analysis required by parametric hypotheses and sufficient crosslinguistic coverage (Guardiano and Longobardi 2016). In particular, a sound parametric testing ground should involve:

[2] On syntactic borrowing in general, see Thomason and Kaufman (1988). On syntactic contact and parameter borrowing, see Guardiano *et al.* (2016).

(4)   a. a sufficient number of parameters, possibly subject to reciprocal interactions, but relatively isolated from interaction with parameters external to the set,

       b. a sufficient number of languages,

       c. a sufficiently fine-grained analysis of the data.[3]

In the MGP, these goals can be neared at the cost of narrowing the study to a single syntactic module and trying to be as exhaustive in that. The MGP strategy requires the elaboration of:

(5)   a. a set of parameters, as exhaustive as possible, for the module chosen,

       b. a set of UG principles defining the scope and interactions of such parameters,

       c. a set of triggers for parameter states

       d. an algorithm for parameter setting,

In the execution of the MGP so far used for PCM experiments, the module chosen has been the internal syntax of the Determiner Phrase (DP). The DP may have a further advantage for historical purposes: many syntactic changes have been analysed in the literature as prompted by rapidly changing information structure, which is much richer in sentential than in nominal structure; therefore, nominal structures could be expected to be diachronically more stable than sentences, especially main clauses (Sihler 1995: 238). Furthermore, for the past thirty years, a number of scholars have studied the parametric variation of the internal structure of nominal phrases in several languages; therefore, a good amount of technical and typological literature is now available on DP structure and nominal categories.[4]

The choice of DP-syntax for the first phylogenetic experiment performed through the PCM was successful and is meant to be replicated in refining the parametric probe for wider phylogenetic objectives.

12.4.4   The Parametric Database

The PCM experiments implemented so far have relied on a parametric database consisting of more than 80 binary parameters.[5] Parameters are listed in the third column of a representation format called Table A, reproduced here as Figure 12.1 (from Longobardi *et al.* (2016a), with 75 parameters and 40 languages). In Figure 12.1, each parameter is identified by a progressive number (first column) and by a combination of three capital letters

---

[3] Descriptions in terms of, say, Dixon's (1998) Basic Linguistic Theory are normally insufficient to determine the setting of parametric values.

[4] See Corbett (1991); Giorgi and Longobardi (1991); Fassi Fehri (1993, 2012); Bernstein (2001); Longobardi (1994, 2001a, 2005, 2008); Plank (2003); Alexiadou, Haegeman and Stavrou (2007); Ghomeshi, Paul and Wiltschko (2009); Keenan and Paperno (2012); Longobardi *et al.* (2013), among other valuable works.

[5] A short description of 56 binary DP-parameters used in several PCM experiments is available in Longobardi *et al.*'s (2013) electronic support material (available at https://benjamins.com/#catalog/journals/jhl.3.1.07lon/additional).

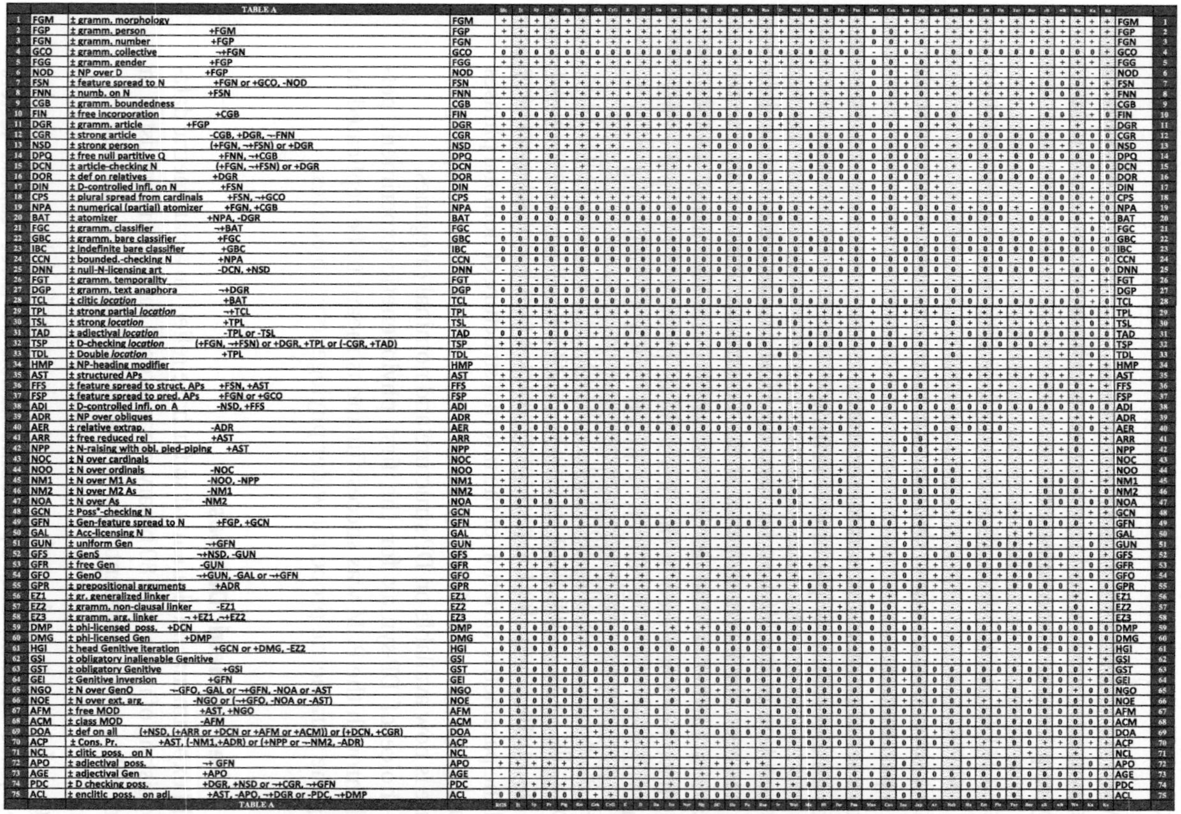

TABLE A

1	FGM	± gramm. morphology		FGM
2	FGP	± gramm. person	+FGM	FGP
3	FGN	± gramm. number	+FGP	FGN
4	GCO	± gramm. collective	¬+FGN	GCO
5	FGG	± gramm. gender	+FGP	FGG
6	NOD	± NP over D	+FGP	NOD
7	FSN	± feature spread to N	+FGN or +GCO, -NOD	FSN
8	FNN	± numb. on N	+FSN	FNN
9	CGB	± gramm. boundedness		CGB
10	FIN	± free incorporation	+CGB	FIN
11	DGR	± gramm. article	+FGP	DGR
12	CGR	± strong article	-CGB, +DGR, ¬-FNN	CGR
13	NSD	± strong person	(+FGN, ¬+FSN) or +DGR	NSD
14	DPQ	± free null partitive Q	+FNN, ¬+CGB	DPQ
15	DCN	± article-checking N	(+FGN, ¬+FSN) or +DGR	DCN
16	DOR	± def on relatives	+DGR	DOR
17	DIN	± D-controlled infl. on N	+FSN	DIN
18	CPS	± plural spread from cardinals	+FSN, ¬+GCO	CPS
19	NPA	± numerical (partial) atomizer	+FGN, +CGB	NPA
20	BAT	± atomizer	+NPA, -DGR	BAT
21	FGC	± gramm. classifier	¬+BAT	FGC
22	GBC	± gramm. bare classifier	+FGC	GBC
23	IBC	± indefinite bare classifier	+GBC	IBC
24	CCN	± bounded.-checking N	+NPA	CCN
25	DNN	± null-N-licensing art	-DCN, +NSD	DNN
26	FGT	± gramm. temporality		FGT
27	DGP	± gramm. text anaphora	¬+DGR	DGP
28	TCL	± clitic *location*	+BAT	TCL
29	TPL	± strong partial *location*	¬+TCL	TPL
30	TSL	± strong *location*	+TPL	TSL
31	TAD	± adjectival *location*	-TPL or -TSL	TAD
32	TSP	± D-checking *location*	(+FGN, ¬+FSN) or +DGR, +TPL or (-CGR, +TAD)	TSP
33	TDL	± Double *location*	+TPL	TDL
34	HMP	± NP-heading modifier		HMP
35	AST	± structured APs		AST
36	FFS	± feature spread to struct. APs	+FSN, +AST	FFS
37	FSP	± feature spread to pred. APs	+FGN or +GCO	FSP
38	ADI	± D-controlled infl. on A	-NSD, +FFS	ADI
39	ADR	± NP over obliques		ADR
40	AER	± relative extrap.	-ADR	AER
41	ARR	± free reduced rel	+AST	ARR
42	NPP	± N-raising with obl. pied-piping	+AST	NPP
43	NOC	± N over cardinals		NOC
44	NOO	± N over ordinals	-NOC	NOO
45	NM1	± N over M1 As	-NOO, -NPP	NM1
46	NM2	± N over M2 As	-NM1	NM2
47	NOA	± N over As	-NM2	NOA
48	GCN	± Poss°-checking N		GCN
49	GFN	± Gen-feature spread to N	+FGP, +GCN	GFN
50	GAL	± Acc-licensing N		GAL
51	GUN	± uniform Gen	¬+GFN	GUN
52	GFS	± GenS	¬+NSD, -GUN	GFS
53	GFR	± free Gen	-GUN	GFR
54	GFO	± GenO	¬+GUN, -GAL or ¬+GFN	GFO
55	GPR	± prepositional arguments	+ADR	GPR
56	EZ1	± gr. generalized linker		EZ1
57	EZ2	± gramm. non-clausal linker	-EZ1	EZ2
58	EZ3	± gramm. arg. linker	¬ +EZ1 ,¬+EZ2	EZ3
59	DMP	± phi-licensed poss.	+DCN	DMP
60	DMG	± phi-licensed Gen	+DMP	DMG
61	HGI	± head Genitive iteration	+GCN or +DMG, -EZ2	HGI
62	GSI	± obligatory inalienable Genitive		GSI
63	GST	± obligatory Genitive	+GSI	GST
64	GEI	± Genitive inversion	+GFN	GEI
65	NGO	± N over GenO	¬-GFO, -GAL or ¬+GFN, -NOA or -AST	NGO
66	NOE	± N over ext. arg.	-NGO or (¬+GFO, -NOA or -AST)	NOE
67	AFM	± free MOD	+AST, +NGO	AFM
68	ACM	± class MOD	-AFM	ACM
69	DOA	± def on all	(+NSD, (+ARR or +DCN or +AFM or +ACM)) or (+DCN, +CGR)	DOA
70	ACP	± Cons. Pr.	+AST, (-NM1,+ADR) or (+NPP or ¬-NM2, -ADR)	ACP
71	NCL	± clitic poss. on N		NCL
72	APO	± adjectival poss.	¬+ GFN	APO
73	AGE	± adjectival Gen	+APO	AGE
74	PDC	± D checking poss.	+DGR, +NSD or ¬+CGR, ¬+GFN	PDC
75	ACL	± enclitic poss. on adj.	+AST, -APO, ¬+DGR or -PDC, ¬+DMP	ACL

TABLE A

Figure 12.1 Table A. 75 parameters and 40 languages: 24 Indo-European; 3 Finno-Ugric; 2 Semitic; 2 Altaic; Basque (2 varieties); Chinese (2 varieties); Inuktitut; Japanese; Kadiweu; Kuikúro; Wolof. For a higher resolution version of this image, please consult the resources section of the book's webpage, which can be found at: www.cambridge.org/9781107049604

(second/fourth column). The order of the parameters is not motivated except for ease of expression of crossparametric dependencies, which are organized to proceed top-down ($p2$ is settable iff $p1$ is set to, '+'; $p3$ is settable iff $p2$ is set to, '+', and so on).

We built a cross-linguistic morphosyntactic difference into Figure 12.1 as a parameter if and only if it entailed any of four types of surface phenomenon (Guardiano and Longobardi 2016): (1) the presence of obligatory formal expression for a semantic or morphological distinction (grammaticalization, i.e. the obligatory presence of a feature in the computation to obtain the relevant interpretation and its coupling with an uninterpretable counterpart); (2) the variable form of a category depending on the syntactic context (selection and licensing); (3) the position of a category (reducible to movement, i.e. overt attraction, triggered by certai features, under a universal base hypothesis); (4) the availability in the lexicon of certain functional features/morphemes.

Within the DP-module, further subdomains can be distinguished: the status of various features typically associated with the functional category that heads nominal structures (D), e.g. Person, Number, Gender and definiteness; the syntactic properties of nominal modifiers (adjectives and relative clauses), of genitival arguments, possessives and demonstratives; the type and scope of 'N-movement' (referring to the movement of the relevant projection headed or characterized by N).

The alternative parameter states are encoded in Figure 12.1 as '+' and '–'. Such symbols have no ontological value; they just have oppositional value. '0' encodes the neutralizing effect of implicational cross-parametric dependencies, i.e. cases in which the content of a parameter is entirely predictable, or irrelevant altogether. The conditions which must hold for each parameter not to be neutralized are indicated in the third column after the name of the parameter itself. They are expressed in a Boolean form, i.e. either as simple states ('+' and '–') of other parameters, or as conjunctions (written ','), disjunctions ('or') or negation ('¬') thereof.[6]

As remarked above, the fact that parameter states are tightly interrelated and that languages fall short of exploiting the entire space of possible grammatical variation due to such implications has often been pointed out as a major formal feature of parameter sets: see Fodor (2001: 735), Baker (2001), Longobardi (2003), Bortolussi *et al.* (2011) Guardiano and Longobardi (2016). But the rich amount of information empirically collected in Figure 12.1 reveals how pervasive the phenomenon of partial interaction among parameters is in a module of grammar of a minimally realistic size. The use of a compact module thus turned out to be helpful for maximizing control of the dependency structure of the parametric system, since the

---

[6] As an example of how to read the notation, the implicational condition of parameter PDC should sound as follows: PDC can be set if and only if parameter DGR is set to + and either parameter NSD is set to + or parameter CGR is not set to + (or both); otherwise it will be neutralized (0). For further discussion on the structure of parametric implications see Guardiano and Longobardi (2016).

consequences of crossparametric implications are more likely to be detectable in close syntactic spaces: at least all the pairs of the parameters of the sample used have been checked conceptually and empirically for the possibility of bearing implications. The huge number of 0s bears witness to the high level of potential redundancy encoded in the database, that must be completely disregarded for taxonomic purposes.

Ideally, the parameter states can be set in languages through the administration of purpose-specific questionnaires (*trigger lists*, i.e. a list of the sets of potential triggers identified for each parameter). Triggers have been formulated using English as a metalanguage. In defining the notion of trigger, we follow Clark and Roberts (1993: 317): 'A sentence s expresses a parameter p_i just in case a grammar must have p_i set to some definite state in order to assign a well-formed representation to s.' Such a sentence (or phrase) s is thus a trigger for parameter p_i. The structural representations of the literal translation(s) of the utterances contained in our questionnaires should be able to set the relevant parameter to a specific state in a given language. So far, two languages have been set to opposite states of a parameter only if their triggers for that parameter differ in structural representation in at least one case, though, owing to the implicational structure, this is not always a logical necessity. For most modern languages, each parameter state assigned in Figure 12.1 and not warranted by reliable literature has been checked with at least one linguistically trained native speaker.

12.5   Quantitative Assessment of Historical Relatedness

The other key factor of progress in evolutionary biology was the introduction of objective mathematical procedures. Their application, indeed, guarantees the replicability of experiments under controlled variable conditions, so allowing one to test the impact of every minimal variation and progressive enrichment of the input data. Furthermore, as stressed by Koyré (1961), in the history of science, the search for accuracy of measurement and a precise mathematical structure of the data has often been an *a priori* methodological decision, eventually rewarded by its empirical success.

The elaboration of phylogenetic hypothesis through bio-statistical methods and computational algorithms has been increasingly improving in recent years: an emerging body of pioneering research on Indo-European[7] and even across language families (Jäger 2013, 2015) has produced improved results in quantifying historical relatedness, though mainly on

[7] See for instance: Lohr (1998); van Cort (2001); Ringe, Warnow and Taylor (2002); Gray and Atkinson (2003); McMahon and McMahon (2003, 2005); Nerbonne and Kretzschmar (2003); the papers collected in Clackson, Forster and Renfrew (2004) and those in *Transactions of the Philological Society* 103(2) (2005).

the basis of lexical datasets such as Dyen, Kruskal and Black's (1992) comparative Indo-European corpus.[8]

12.5.1 Computational Procedures

According to the nature of the input, phylogenetic computational procedures fall into two main types: distance-based and character-based. An extensive list of linguistic implementations of algorithms from the classic PHYLIP package (*Neighbour, Fitch* and *Kitsch*: Felsenstein 1993), all empirically relying on Dyen, Kruskal and Black (1992), is reported in McMahon and McMahon (2005), with the purpose of singling out those most appropriate for linguistic data; they suggest that distance-based algorithms are more viable than character-based ones. In the same vein, Nakhleh, Warnow, Ringe and Evans (2005) and Barbançon *et al.* (2013) discuss various experiments on six reconstruction methods and on four different versions of an Indo-European lexical database.[9]

   In relation to the very nature of our parametric database, character-based algorithms, though more precisely representing language history, must overcome two additional problems. First, the pervasive implications among parameters violate their frequent assumption of character independence. Second, character-based algorithms produce more informative results when the input is supplemented with additional information, especially regarding the directionality of change (e.g. the markedness theory assumed in Ringe's experiments) or the characters' stability (i.e. the possibility of assigning each character a weight, according to its resistance to change). At the present stage, we cannot rely on a solid theory of parameter resetting, therefore no such information has been so far included in the input. Thus, distance-based methods have most often been applied to the PCM database because they minimize the effects of internal dependencies across parameters, and allow phylogenetic hypotheses even in the absence of an appropriate theory of diachronic change.

12.5.2 Empirical Implementations of the PCM: Coefficients and Distances

The first operation in the quantitative elaboration of our data is to compute the number of identities and differences in the parameter settings of each pair of languages (<i;d>, called *coefficients* in Guardiano

---

[8] See for instance: Embleton (1986); Boyd, Bogerhoff-Mulder, Durham and Richerson (1997); Gray and Atkinson (2003); Warnow, Evans, Ringe and Nakhleh (2004); McMahon (2010). As remarked, Dunn *et al.* (2005) and Spruit (2008) use some syntactic data within their structural evidence.

[9] In contrast, some other scholars have applied algorithms directly to linguistic characters, though non-syntactic ones, e.g. in the pioneering work of Ringe, Warnow and Taylor (2002). This work develops a phylogenetic algorithm specifically conceived for the analysis of language relationships, and stresses the practical difficulties in assigning discrete values to lexical correspondences. They adopt taxonomic characters of three types: root correspondences (2002: 333), sound correspondences (2002: 22) and correspondences in inflectional endings (2002: 15), all encoded as binary.

and Longobardi (2005)). As noted, 0s cannot be taken into account for measuring relatedness; therefore, even if only one of the languages of a pair has a 0 for a certain parameter, that correspondence is not counted at all for that pair. For these reasons, the sum of *i* and *d* in a coefficient does not necessarily equal the total amount of parameters compared, and rarely is it the same for different language pairs. As such, coefficients are not a practical measure to rank the distances instantiated by different pairs of languages. Therefore, they must be reduced to a monadic figure (syntactic *distance*). A normalized Hamming distance is obtained by dividing the number of differences by the sum of identities and differences of each pair $(d/(i+d))$: making the differences proportional to the actually compared parameters, it turned out to be most apt in our case, because it almost completely neutralizes many of the numerical drawbacks of pervasive crossparametric dependencies.

The parametric distances between the 40 languages of Figure 12.1 are represented in Figure 12.2.

12.5.3   Empirical Implementations of the PCM: Probabilistic Evaluations

In order for our results to be probative, they must present a plausible distribution of distances. Hence, a first obvious conceptual test is the following:

(6)   The distances in Figure 12.2 should be scattered across different degrees of similarities

For, if all or most pairs were concentrated around the same distance, no significant taxonomic conclusions would be available.

Bortolussi, Longobardi, Guardiano and Sgarro (2011) detailed large-scale computer-run experiment to test the statistical significance of the PCM distances, of which Figure 12.3 is an updated and refined version (Longobardi *et al.* 2016a), consisted of the building of a non-trivial Bayesian algorithm to generate a population of random parameter strings (without any relationship to each other whatsoever), i.e. of *admissible* grammars, out of the possible combinations of parameter states admitted by Figure 12.1, and respecting all their acknowledged crossparametric implications. This was the first step towards understanding implicationally constrained grammatical systems. Using Bortolussi, Longobardi, Guardiano and Sgarro's algorithm, the 75 parameters from Longobardi *et al.'s* (2016a) Table A generated 3.3×10^{15} admissible grammars.[10]

---

[10] A reduction of seven orders of magnitude, compared to the $2^{75} = 3.78 \times 10^{22}$ predicted under total independence (Longobardi *et al.* 2015a). This difference makes it patent that implicational relationships between parameters play a key role in constraining the number of possible languages, and thus can by no means be ignored for a reliable calculation of probability distributions over admissible languages.

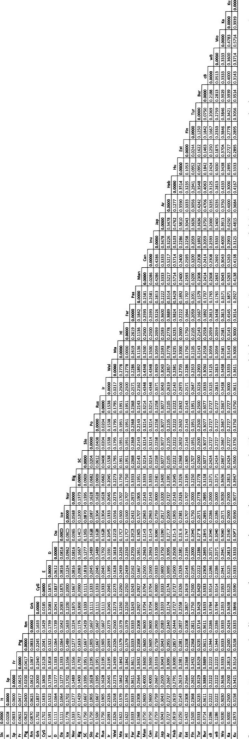

Figure 12.2 Parametric distances between the 40 languages in Figure 12.1. For a higher resolution version of this image, please consult the resources section of the book's webpage, which can be found at: www.cambridge.org/9781107049604

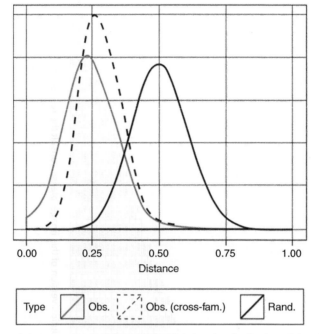

Figure 12.3 A Kernel density plot showing the distribution of the observed distances of Figure 12.2 (grey curve), the observed distances between cross-family pairs in Figure 12.2 (dashed curve), and randomly generated distances (black curve) (from Longobardi *et al.* 2016a)

The density distribution of distances in these random language pairs can then be plotted against that of real-world language pairs from the 40 languages of Figure 12.1; the result (modulo scaling the sizes of the two curves) is the graph represented in Figure 12.3: the actual language distances (solid curve) are clearly scattered across a large space of variability (ranging from 0 to 0.625), and this suggests that the first criterion is in fact met.

A further conceptual test is related to Nichols' (1996) notion of *individual-identifying* evidence:

(7)   The probability of chance resemblance for the most similar languages must attain individual-identifying levels

Longobardi and Guardiano (2009) argued, under elementary binomial evaluations, that the probability of relatedness for the closest language pairs of their Table A fully met Nichols' requirements. Bortolussi *et al.*'s (2011) experiment fully confirmed such a probability as clearly significant, thus proving that actual parametric distances uncover a meaningful amount of relatedness among the languages of Figure 12.1.

A further conceptual test is based on Guardiano and Longobardi's (2005) *Anti-Babelic Principle* (so named with obvious reference to Genesis 11:7–9):

(8)   Anti-Babelic Principle: similarities among languages can be due either to historical causes (common origin or, at least, secondary convergence) or to chance; differences can only be due to chance (no one ever made language diverge on purpose)

In a system of binary equiprobable differences, in order for syntactic distances to display a historically significant distribution, we must expect the following empirical tendencies: pairs of languages known to be closely related should clearly exhibit a distance between 0 and 0.5; other pairs should tend towards distance 0.5; and distances between 0.5 and 1 should tend towards nonexistence. The Anti-Babelic Principle predicts that two completely unrelated languages should exhibit a distance closer to 0.5 than to 1: therefore, a system of parametric comparison producing too huge a number of distances higher than 0.5 is unlikely to correctly represent historical reality. Such expectation could be tested for the first time precisely as an outcome of the PCM, because it has measurable effects only in discrete and universally bounded domains like parametric syntax, hardly in virtually infinite ones like the lexicon. The distribution of the actual syntactic distances correctly meets the expectations above. Indeed, only 8 pairs exceed the median of the random distance distribution (0.5). Most importantly, no real language pair exhibits a distance higher than 0.842, i.e. the distance above which it is very unlikely for a language pair to ever appear, given this set of parameters (its 'Babelic threshold').

These results already lead us to expect that the number of historically wrong taxonomic relations provided by such a parametric sample will be limited.

12.5.4   Empirical Implementations of the PCM: Computational Taxonomies

Starting from Longobardi and Guardiano (2009), various language taxonomies have been produced using parametric distances, with the aid of some distance-based computational algorithms provided in the PHYLIP package (Felsenstein 1993). All the experiments performed so far provided largely correct tree-like phylogenies and networks (Longobardi *et al.* 2013; Guardiano *et al.* 2016).

Figure 12.4 represents a taxonomic tree built from Figure 12.2 using *Kitsch*. Here, most genealogical relations among the 40 languages are correctly represented. As predicted Indo-European is

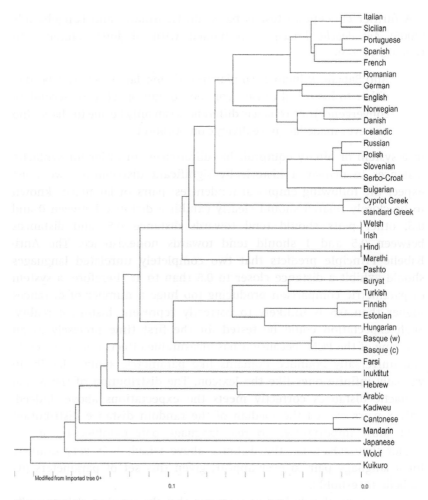

Figure 12.4 *Kitsch* tree from the parametric distances of Figure 12.2

recognized as a unit, with the exception of Farsi.[11] Within Indo-European, all the genealogical subgroupings (Romance, Germanic, Slavic, Greek, Celtic, Indo-Aryan) are correctly identified. Outside Indo-European, an Altaic group and as expected, the clusterings of the three Finno-Ugric languages, the two Semitic and the two Sinitic ones are also recognized. This proves that the PCM succeeds in empirically detecting historical signals within well-established families. A further good result is that the isolates are kept distinct from the core groups and from each other.

---

[11] Farsi turned out to be particularly problematic for classification in many respects, not only for parametric taxonomies (Longobardi *et al.* 2013), but partly also for lexical ones (Dyen, Kruskal and Black 1992).

The genealogical experiment that syntactic parameters encode some non-implausible historical information. These results validate the method as a useful tool for measuring language similarity with high precision, and in turn support parametric grammar as a realistic model of historical language transmission.

12.6 Languages, Genes, Lineages

The encouraging historical results obtained by the PCM make it possible to test its effectiveness for calculating correlations between syntactic and non linguistic variables, such as the biological ones hinted in Darwin's prediction.

To make Darwin's hypothesis empirically testable, it is important to split the issue into (at least) two questions: (1) can a gene–language parallelism indeed be identified? (2) If so, how much of it depends on common demic processes shaping genetic and linguistic diversity together?

12.6.1 Testing Darwin's Prediction in Europe

In Longobardi *et al.* (2015), 15 European languages from 3 different families (Indo-European, Finno-Ugric and Basque) were selected and analysed in terms of the PCM (using the parametric database of Longobardi *et al.* 2013), calculating their syntactic distances. A genetic distance matrix for the 15 corresponding populations, based on 178,000 Single Nucleotide Polymorphisms, was then calculated, along with a matrix of geographical (great circle) distances and one of lexical distances (also reduced to a figure between 0 and 1) drawn from the recent IELex database (Bouckaert *et al.* 2012). Since the IELex database targets only Indo-European languages, maximum distance 1 (no recognized shared etymology) was assigned by default to cross-family language pairs.

Correlations between these four distance matrices were computed according to the Mantel (1967) procedure.[12] The two linguistic matrices were highly correlated (r = 0.850), and, as a consequence, showed very similar levels of correlation with genetic distances (0.60 for syntax and 0.54 for lexicon), both much higher than what we find between genes and geography (0.30). The results hold even when we control for geography: the partial Mantel correlation between syntax

[12] In a *classical* Mantel test, a 0 value means no correlation at all between two numerical variables, 1 fully proportional correlation, −1 fully inverse correlation. A *partial* Mantel test determines the value of these correlations controlling for the effect on the latter of a third variable, e.g. in our case the geographical distance, which might influence at the same time the linguistic and the genetic distance of two populations, so that their correlation would not necessarily speak directly in favour of one and the same historical spread of language and genes.

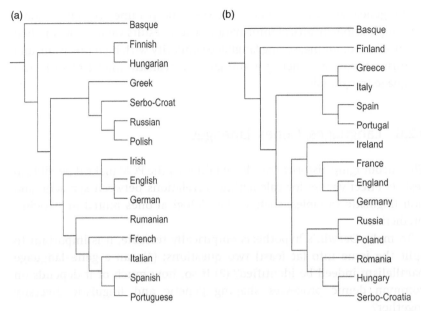

Figure 12.5 Phylogenetic trees drawn from Syntactic (A) and Genetic (B) distances (Longobardi *et al.* 2015)

and genes is still strong (0.57) if we hold geography constant, while the genes–geography correlation is saliently lower (0.20), with syntax held constant. Thus, a gene–language congruence seems to hold at a continent-wide scale (Europe), and to be independent of geographical distances: actually, language, once properly modelled through quantitative tools, proved a better predictor of European genetic diversity than geography (Novembre *et al.* 2008). These results may begin to suggest a possibly positive answer to both subquestions above.

Having reached a preliminary conclusion about the first Darwinian subquestion and gained some promising insight into the second, one can proceed to look in more detail at the demographic history of European populations. Actually, the comparison of the syntactic and biological phylogenetic trees (Figure 12.5) reveals a some significant degree of topological consistency, with some exceptions: the main elements of disagreement in the genomic tree are the positions of Hungarians and Romanians, which cluster genetically with speakers of Serbo-Croatian despite being highly differentiated syntactically. The mismatch is especially salient for Hungarian, whose linguistic distance from IE languages as measured by the PCM is instead expectedly large.

12.6.2 How to Deal with 'Exceptions'

The gene–language mismatch of Hungarians was noticed by Cavalli Sforza, Menozzi and Piazza (1994) and Greenhill (2011), but it was only with the aid of the PCM that it could be quantified. Both ancient and modern genetic evidence presented in the literature has been invoked in Longobardi *et al.* (2015) to suggest that no substantial demographic replacement occurred when a Finno-Ugric language was introduced to what is now Hungary by a group of Asian immigrants during the historical ninth-century invasion. Unsurprisingly, then, the recalculation of the correlations after removing the apparent exception represented by Hungarians led Longobardi *et al.* (2015b) to notice a further increase of that between genetic and syntactic distances ($r = 0.74$), while the correlation with geography remained low ($r = 0.28$). The skew became even sharper in partial Mantel tests ($r = 0.72$ for gene–syntax with geography held constant, while it is $r = 0.093$ for genes–geography with syntax held constant), providing the clearest demonstration to date of a language–biology correlation for the core of Europe.

Longobardi *et al.* (2016b) propose a further test of the ability of such tools to detect special events of demographic history: the Distatis program was used to plot syntactic, genetic and geographic distances into a single multidimensional scaling graph, in order to identify correlation patterns. The results are presented in Figure 12.6. In the graph, it emerges that both genes and syntax are able to identify the two most obvious outliers, Finns and Basques, while their geographical distances ('G') put them closer to their European neighbours. The same appears to be true, to a more reduced extent, for Greeks (Greek, basically an isolate among IE subfamilies, turned out as the linguistic outlier of the IE languages of Europe also in previous experiments, i.e. Gray and Atkinson 2003). Most interestingly, even this test confirms the salient exception exhibited by Hungarians: based on syntactic distances ('S'), they fall close to the other Finno-Ugric population, i.e. Finns, and very far from those speaking Indo-European languages, while, from the viewpoint of biology ('B'), they are indistinguishable from the other Central/Eastern European populations. The gene–language mismatch in Hungary suggests that language replacement there was not due to a radical population replacement. Phenomena of that kind were possible in prehistoric times, but unlikely in more densely populated medieval Europe, i.e. at the time when the migration of Magyars took place (ninth century AD). Such a language replacement is instead compatible with the immigration of a limited group of individuals, whose arrival caused a major cultural shift, without deeply affecting the genetic makeup of the population ('elite dominance' in Renfrew's (1992)

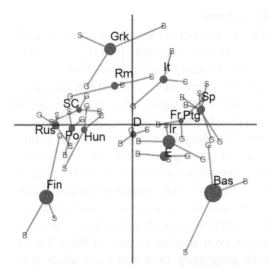

Figure 12.6 A Distatis plot of the (G)eographic, (B)iological/genetic and (S)yntactic distance matrices from Longobardi *et al.* (2016b). The languages are Greek, Romanian, Italian, Russian, Serbo-Croatian, Polish, German (= D), Irish, English, Spanish, French and Portuguese (Indo-European); Finnish and Hungarian (Finno-Ugric); and Basque (a linguistic isolate)

terminology), a situation certainly different from that of more ancient migrations into Europe, irrespective of their controversial dating and routing.

12.6.3   Perspectives for Future Research

The use of a new linguistic tool, able to work across linguistic families and to provide quantitatively measurable conclusions, shows that populations speaking similar languages also tend to resemble each other at the genomic level, suggesting that cultural change and biological divergence have mostly proceeded in parallel in Europe.

A number of previously unaddressable questions can now be put on the research agenda, such as the following:

(9)   a. Do gene–language correlations equally hold on more focused micro-areas (such as smaller areas of Europe or the Mediterranean), or on even wider geographical spaces (e.g. the whole of Eurasia), or, finally, on continents with radically different temporal and social peopling scales (say, the Americas)?

b. Is there a detectable difference between the diffusion of syntax and that of lexicon in space and time?

c. Do various linguistic (syntax, phonology, lexicon) and genetic (subportions of the genome, uniparental markers, etc.) entities correlate with each other in different ways?

For many such inquiries, the novel historical tool offered by syntax with its universal potential has been, and will increasingly be, crucial in allowing comparisons of languages from different families (which by definition are supposed to share no common lexical etymology).

In fact, genetic and syntactic evolution factors seem to correspond well enough to each other: pending further investigation, we suggest that mutation, admixture and genetic drift may be compared to parameter resetting, interference and random change of external language properties, respectively. Further analytical study of each such factor in close comparison to the corresponding biological one may represent the ideal starting point in the attempt to understand cultural evolution along the lines of natural evolution. We are then only left with the significant exception of natural selection, apparently absent from syntactic history.

12.7 Conclusions

The PCM is a new method for classifying languages on the basis of syntactic characters, whose results lend themselves well to mathematical and computational evaluation. It exploits parametric theories to formally measure grammatical diversity and suggests that the taxonomies so derived are likely to have not only typological value, but also some historical significance. Such results may point to three sorts of consequences: for theoretical linguistics, historical linguistics and neighbouring disciplines, respectively.

First, the historical success of the PCM indirectly provides evidence of an unprecedented type for P&P models of grammatical variation, which are in need of strong empirical confirmation (Fodor 2001) although radically alternative models of language acquisition seem *a priori* hard to imagine. Actually, Chomsky's (1995: 7) statement does not seem out of date: 'The P&P model is in part a bold speculation rather than a specific hypothesis. Nevertheless, its basic assumptions seem reasonable ... and they do suggest a natural way to resolve the tension between descriptive and explanatory adequacy.' Phylogenetic success of parameters, especially over less structured models of variation, may represent a critical empirical contribution towards this goal.

Second, the PCM suggests the possibility of a full historical paradigm in formal syntax, beyond the simple study of diachronic syntactic change. Through parametric linguistics, historical concerns may be re-established as central in the study of language and in the wider paradigm of modern cognitive science. Investigation in formal grammar has long since been more or less explicitly modelled after the natural sciences, adopting what Chomsky (1980), borrowing physicist

Steven Weinberg's felicitous expression, termed the 'Galilean style' of inquiry. It would be an extremely suggestive achievement to show that the Galilean style may in some cases be applied to historical research.

Finally, the PCM promises to make a new tool for the investigation of our linguistic past, hopefully able to overcome the limits of the classical comparative method and the issues raised by Greenberg's mass comparison, potentially joining traditional comparative linguistics, archeology and genetics in the 'New Synthesis' approach to the study of human history and prehistory.

References

Alexiadou, A., Haegeman, L. and Stavrou, M. 2007. *Noun phrase in the generative perspective*. Berlin: Mouton de Gruyter.

Baker, M. C. 2001. *The atoms of language*. New York: Basic Books.

Baltin, M. and Collins, C. (eds.) 2001. *The handbook of contemporary syntactic theory*. Oxford: Blackwell.

Barbançon, F. G., Evans, S.N., Nakhleh, L., Ringe, D. and Warnow, T. 2013. 'An experimental study comparing linguistic phylogenetic reconstruction methods', *Diachronica* 30(2): 143–70.

Bernstein, J. 2001. 'The DP hypothesis: Identifying clausal properties in the nominal domain', in Baltin and Collins (eds.), pp. 536–61.

Biberauer, T. (ed.) 2008. *The limits of syntactic variation*. Amsterdam: John Benjamins.

Biberauer, T., Holmberg, A., Roberts, I. and Sheean, M. (eds.) 2010. *Parametric variation: Null subjects in minimalist theory*. Cambridge University Press.

Boeckx, C. and Piattelli Palmarini, M. 2005. 'Language as a natural object; Linguistics as a natural science', *The Linguistic Review* 22(2–3): 447–66.

Bortolussi, L., Longobardi, G., Guardiano, C. and Sgarro, A. 2011. 'How many possible languages are there?', in G. Bel-Enguix, V. Dahl and M. D. Jiménez-López (eds.), *Biology, computation and linguistics*. Amsterdam: IOS Press, pp. 168–79.

Bouckaert, R., Lemey, P., Dunn, M., Greenhill, S. J., Alekseyenko, A. V., Drummond, A. J., Gray, R. D., Suchard, M. A. and Atkinson, Q. D. 2012. 'Mapping the origins and expansion of the Indo-European language family', *Science* 337: 957–60.

Boyd, R., Bogerhoff-Mulder, M., Durham, W. H. and Richerson, P. J. 1997. 'Are cultural phylogenies possible?', in P. Weingart, S. D. Mitchell, P. J. Richerson and S. Maasen (eds.), *Human by nature: Between biology and the social sciences*. Mahwah, NJ: Erlbaum, pp. 355–86.

Braudel, F. 1985. *La Mediterranée*. Paris: Flammarion.

Cavalli Sforza, L. L. 2000. *Genes, peoples, and languages.* Berkeley: University of California Press.

Cavalli Sforza, L. L., Menozzi, P. and Piazza, A. 1994. *The history and geography of human genes.* Princeton University Press.

Cavalli Sforza, L. L., Piazza, A., Menozzi, P. and Mountain, J. 1988. 'Reconstruction of human evolution: bringing together genetic, archeological and linguistic data', *Proceedings of the National Academy of Science USA* 85: 6002–6.

Chomsky, N. 1955. *The logical structure of linguistic theory.* MS, MIT (published in 1975, New York: Plenum).

1965. *Aspects of the theory of syntax.* Cambridge, MA: MIT Press.

1980. *Rules and representations.* New York: Columbia University Press.

1981. *Lectures on government and binding.* Dordrecht: Foris.

1986. *Knowledge of language.* New York: Praeger.

1995. *The minimalist program.* Cambridge, MA: MIT Press.

Clackson, J., Forster, P. and Renfrew, C. (eds.) 2004. *Phylogenetic methods and the prehistory of languages.* Cambridge: McDonald Institute for Archaeological Research.

Clark, R. and Roberts, I. 1993. 'A computational model of language learnability and language change', *Linguistic Inquiry* 24(2): 299–345.

Corbett, G. 1991. *Gender.* Cambridge University Press.

Darwin, C. 1859. *On the origin of species.* London: John Murray.

Diamond, J. 1998. *Guns, germs, and steel: The fates of human societies.* New York: W. W. Norton & Co.

Di Sciullo, A.-M. and Boeckx, C. (eds.) 2011. *The biolinguistic enterprise.* Oxford University Press.

Dixon, R. 1998. *The rise and fall of languages.* Cambridge University Press.

Dunn, M., Terrill, A., Reesink, G., Foley, R. A. and Levinson, S. C. 2005. 'Structural phylogenetics and the reconstruction of ancient language history', *Science* 309(5743): 2072–5.

Dyen, I., Kruskal, J. B. and Black, P. 1992. 'An Indoeuropean classification: A lexicostatistical experiment', *Transactions of the American Philosophical Society* 82(5): 1–132.

Embleton, S. 1986. *Statistics in historical linguistics.* Bochum: Brockmeyer.

Fassi Fehri, A. 1993. *Issues in the structure of Arabic clauses and words.* Dordrecht: Reidel.

2012. *Key features and parameters in Arabic grammar.* Amsterdam: John Benjamins.

Felsenstein, J. 1993. *PHYLIP (Phylogeny Inference Package)* version 3.5c. Distributed by the author. Department of Genetics, University of Washington.

Fitch, T. W. 2010. *The evolution of language.* Cambridge University Press.

Fodor, J. D. 2001. 'Setting syntactic parameters', in Baltin and Collins (eds.), pp. 730–67.

Ghomeshi, J., Paul, I. and Wiltschko, M. (eds.) 2009. *Determiners: Universals and variation*. Amsterdam: John Benjamins.

Gianollo, C., Guardiano, C. and Longobardi, G. 2008. 'Three fundamental issues in parametric linguistics', in T. Biberauer (ed.), *The limits of syntactic variation*. Amsterdam: John Benjamins, pp. 109–41.

Giorgi, A. and Giuseppe, L. 1991. *The syntax of noun phrases: Configuration, parameters and empty categories*. Cambridge University Press.

Gray, R. D. and Atkinson, Q. D. 2003. 'Language tree divergences support the Anatolian theory of Indo-European origin', *Nature* 426: 435–9.

Greenberg, J. 1963. 'Some universals of grammar with particular reference to the order of meaningful elements', in J. Greenberg (ed.), *Universals of language*. Cambridge, MA: MIT Press, pp. 73–113.

1987. *Language in the Americas*. Stanford University Press.

2000. *Indo-European and its closest Relatives: The Eurasiatic language family*. Stanford University Press.

Greenhill, S. J. 2011. 'Levenshtein distances fail to identify language relationships accurately', *Computational Linguistics* 37: 689–98.

Guardiano, C. and Longobardi, G. 2005. 'Parametric comparison and language taxonomy', in M. Batllori, M.-Ll. Hernanz, C. Picallo and F. Roca (eds.), *Grammaticalization and parametric variation*. Oxford University Press, pp. 149–74.

2016. 'Parameter theory and parametric comparison', in I. Roberts (eds.), *The Oxford handbook of Universal Grammar*. Oxford University Press, pp. 377-401.

Forthcoming. 'Formal syntactic methods for establishing language phyogenies', in R.D. Janda, B.D. Joseph and B. Vance (eds.), *The handbook of historical linguistics*, Vol. II. Oxford: Wiley Blackwell.

Guardiano, C., Michelioudakis, D., Ceolin, A., Irimia, M. A., Longobardi, G., Radkevich, N., Silvestri, G. and Sitaridou, I. 2016. 'South by southeast: A syntactic approach to Greek and Romance microvariation', unpublished MS.

Hauser, M. D., Chomsky, N. and Fitch, T. W. 2002. 'The faculty of language: What is it, who has it, and how did it evolve?', *Science* 298: 1569–79.

Heggarty, P. 2004. 'Interdisciplinary indiscipline? Can phylogenetic methods meaningfully be applied to language data – and to dating language?', in Clackson, Forster and Renfrew (eds.), pp. 183–94.

Jäger G. 2013. 'Lexikostatik 2.0', in A. Plewnia and A. Witt (eds.), *Sprachverfall? Dynamik – Wandel – Variation. Jahrbuch 2013 des Instituts für Deutsche Sprache*. Berlin: de Gruyter, pp. 197–216.

2015. 'Support for linguistic macrofamilies from weighted sequence alignment'. *Proceeding of the National Academy of Science* 112(41): 12752-7.

Kayne, R. 2000. *Parameters and universals*. New York: Oxford University Press.

Keenan, E. 1994. 'Creating anaphors: An historical study of the English reflexive pronouns', unpublished MS, UCLA.

2000. 'An historical explanation of some binding theoretic facts in English', unpublished MS, UCLA.

2002. 'Explaining the creation of reflexive pronouns in English', in D. Minkova and R. Stockwell (eds.), *Studies in the history of the English language*. Berlin: Mouton de Gruyter, pp. 325–54.

Keenan, E. and Paperno, D. (eds.) 2012. *Handbook of quantifiers in natural languages*. Dordrecht: Springer.

Koyrè, A. 1961. 'Du monde de l'à peu près' à l'univers de la precision', in *Etudes d'histoire de la pensée philosophique*. Paris: Colin, pp. 311–29.

Lenneberg, E. 1967. *Biological foundations of language*. New York: John Wiley & Sons.

Lightfoot, D. 1979. *Principles of diachronic syntax*. Cambridge University Press.

1991. *How to set parameters*. Oxford: Blackwell.

2006. *How new languages emerge*. Cambridge University Press.

Lohr, M. 1998. 'Methods for the genetic classification of languages', unpublished PhD thesis, University of Cambridge.

Longobardi, G. 1994. 'Reference and proper names', *Linguistic Inquiry* 25(4): 609–65.

1996. 'The syntax of N-raising: A minimalist theory', OTS Working Papers in Linguistics 5, Utrecht.

2001a. 'How comparative is semantics? A unified parametric theory of bare nouns and proper names', *Natural Language Semantics* 9: 335–69.

2001b. 'Formal syntax, diachronic minimalism, and etymology: The history of French chez', *Linguistic Inquiry* 32: 275–302.

2003. 'Methods in parametric linguistics and cognitive history', *Linguistic Variation Yearbook* 3: 101–38.

2005. 'A minimalist program for parametric linguistics?', in H. Broekhuis, N. Corver, R. Huybregts, U. Kleinhenz and J. Koster (eds.), *Organizing grammar: Linguistic studies for Henk van Riemsdijk*. Berlin: Mouton de Gruyter, pp. 407–14.

2008. 'Reference to individuals, person, and the variety of mapping parameters', in A. Klinge and H. Høeg Müller (eds.), *Essays on nominal determination*. Amsterdam: John Benjamins, pp. 189–211.

2012. 'Convergence in parametric phylogenies: Homoplasy or principled explanation?', in C. Galves, S. Cyrino, R. Lopes, F. Sandalo and J. Avelar (eds.), *Parameter theory and language change*. Oxford University Press, pp. 304–19.

Longobardi, G. and Guardiano, C. 2009. 'Evidence for syntax as a signal of historical relatedness', *Lingua* 119(11): 1679–706.

Longobardi, G., Guardiano, C., Silvestri, G., Boattini, A. and Ceolin, A. 2013. 'Toward a syntactic phylogeny of modern Indo-European languages', *Journal of Historical Linguistics* 3: 122–52.

Longobardi, G., Ghirotto, S., Guardiano, C., Tassi, F., Benazzo, A., Ceolin, A. and Barbujani, G. 2015. 'Across language families: Genome diversity mirrors linguistic variation within Europe', *American Journal of Physical Anthropology* 157: 630–40.

Longobardi, G., Ceolin, A., Bortolussi, L., Guardiano, C., Irimia, M. A., Michelioudakis, D., Radkevich, N. and Sgarro, A. 2016a. 'Mathematical modeling of grammatical diversity supports the historical reality of formal syntax', in C. Bentz, G. Jäger and I. Yanovich (eds.), *Proceedings of the Leidon Workshop on Capturing Phylogenetic Algorithms for Linguistics*. University of Tubingen, online publication system, https://publikationen.unituebingen.do/xmlui/handle/10900/68558.

Longobardi, G., Ceolin, A., Ecay, A., Ghirotto, S., Guardiano, C., Irimia, M. A., Michelioudakis, D., Radkevic, N., Luiselli, D., Pettener, D. and Barbujani, G. 2016b. 'Formal linguistics as a cue to demographic history', *Journal of Anthropological Sciences* 94: 1–10..

Mantel, N. 1967. 'The detection of disease clustering and a generalized regression approach', *Cancer Research* 27: 209–20.

Matisoff, J. A. 1990. 'On megalocomparison', *Language* 66: 106–20.

McMahon, A. 2010. 'Computational models and language contact', in R. Hickey (ed.), *The handbook of language contact*. Oxford: Wiley-Blackwell, pp. 31–47.

McMahon, A. and McMahon, R. 2003. 'Finding families: Quantitative methods in language classifying', *Transaction of the Philological Society* 101(1): 7–55.

2005. *Language classification by numbers*. Oxford University Press.

Nakhleh, L., Warnow, T., Ringe, D. and Evans, S. N. 2005. 'A comparison of phylogenetic reconstruction methods on an IE dataset', *Transactions of the Philological Society* 3(2): 171–92.

Nerbonne, J. and Kretzschmar, W. 2003. 'Introducing computational methods in dialectometry', in J. Nerbonne and W. Kretzschmar (eds.), *Computational methods in dialectometry (special issue of Computers and the Humanities* 37(3)), pp. 245–55.

Nichols, J. 1992. *Linguistic diversity in space and time*. University of Chicago Press.

1996. 'The comparative method as heuristic', in M. Durie and M. Ross (eds.), *The comparative method reviewed: Regularity and irregularity in language change*. Oxford University Press, pp. 39–71.

Novembre, J., Johnson, T., Bryc, K., Kutalik, Z., Boyko, A. R., Auton, A., Indap, A., King, K. S., Bergmann, S., Nelson, M. R., Stephens, M. and Bustamante, C. D. 2008. 'Genes mirror geography within Europe', *Nature* 456: 98–101.

Piattelli Palmarini, M. 1989. 'Evolution, selection and cognition: From "learning" to parameter setting in biology and in the study of language', *Cognition* 31: 1–44.

Plank, F. (ed.) 2003. *Noun phrase structure in the languages of Europe*. Berlin: Mouton de Gruyter.

Renfrew, C. 1992. 'Archaeology, genetics and linguistic diversity', *Man* 27 (3): 445–78.

Ringe, D. 1992. 'On calculating the factor of chance in language comparison', *Transactions of the American Philosophical Society* 82(1): 1–110.

1996. 'The mathematics of Amerind', *Diachronica* 13: 135–54.

Ringe, D., Warnow, T. and Taylor, A. 2002. 'Indo-European and computational cladistics', *Transactions of the Philological Society* 100(1): 59–129.

Roberts, I. 1998. 'Review of Harris and Campbell 1995', *Romance Philology* 51: 363–70.

2007. 'The mystery of the overlooked discipline: Modern syntactic theory and cognitive science', available at http://ling.auf.net/lingbuzz/001611.

Sihler, A. 1995. *New comparative grammar of Greek and Latin*. Oxford University Press.

Sokal, R. R. 1988. 'Genetic, geographic, and linguistic distances in Europe', *PNAS* 85: 1722–6.

Spruit, M. R. 2008. *Quantitative perspectives on syntactic variation in Dutch dialects*. Utrecht: LOT.

Thomason, S. G. and Kaufmann, T. 1988. *Language contact, creolization, and genetic linguistics*. Berkeley and Los Angeles: University of California Press.

van Cort, T. 2001. 'Computational evolutionary linguistics: Tree-based models of language change', unpublished PhD thesis, Harvey Mudd College, Pomona, CA.

Warnow, T., Evans, S. N., Ringe, D. and Nakhleh, L. 2004. 'Stochastic models of language evolution and an application to the Indo-European family of languages', in Clackson, Forster and Renfrew (eds.), n.p. (available at www.stat.berkeley.edu/users/evans/659.pdf).

Part III

Principles and Constraints

13

Universal Grammar

Anders Holmberg

13.1 Introduction

When two languages are found to share a grammatical property P, there are four possible reasons: (a) it is accidental; (b) they have a common ancestor language; (c) they have been in contact and one language has taken over P from the other language; (d) P is universal, i.e. all languages have P, not because they all derive from a common source but by necessity, because of 'the nature of language', or in other words, P is determined by Universal Grammar.

The notion of Universal Grammar was introduced into modern linguistics by Noam Chomsky in the early sixties, as part of the generative research programme (Chomsky 1965: 5–8). The idea that all human languages are special instances of a universal format of language has a long history, though, including Roger Bacon and the *modistae* (or speculative grammarians) of the thirteenth and fourteenth centuries, as well as the Port Royal grammarians and the philosophical grammar movement in the seventeenth century, which were particularly important for Chomsky's own project (see Chomsky 1968: 12–19).[1]

The way the idea developed in works by Chomsky and other generative linguists at the time, and the way it came to be understood, is as an innate, cognitive faculty which is crucial for the acquisition and use of human language (see Chapter 18, this volume). Behind all the variation exhibited by the languages of the world, there would be formal properties that are common to all languages because they are determined by genetically encoded properties of our brain, a product of the biological evolution of our cognitive system.

---

[1] Wikipedia's entry on universal grammar mentions that the article on 'Grammar' in the first edition of the *Encyclopædia Britannica* (1771) contains an extensive section entitled 'Of Universal Grammar'.

The notion that there are universal grammatical properties has been advanced on two fronts, though, ever since the early sixties: within generative linguistics and within linguistic typology, emanating from the work of Joseph Greenberg. In linguistic typology there is no commitment to the idea that the universals are ultimately genetically encoded (for discussion, see Chapter 30, this volume). They are generalizations; their explanation may vary from case to case.

In this chapter I will keep distinct two senses of Universal Grammar. One is Universal Grammar in the broad sense, which is all the grammatical properties that are characteristic of human languages, regardless of why they are there. They may be the product of cultural or biological evolution (see Chapter 28, this volume). The other is Universal Grammar in the strict 'Chomskyan' sense, which is the grammatical properties found in all human languages that are ultimately a product of biological evolution. Following tradition, I will refer to the latter sense of Universal Grammar as UG. I will focus mainly on UG, and the development that this theoretical construct has undergone ever since its inception in Chomsky's work in the sixties. As will be shown, it has undergone some considerable changes in the course of its lifetime. As will also be shown, the contribution of Noam Chomsky has been crucial at every turn in this development. I will begin, though, by a short review of the research on universals within linguistic typology.

13.2 Linguistic Typological Universals

Much of the evidence for Universal Grammar in the broad sense comes from cross-linguistic, comparative research. If similarities among languages are discovered which are unlikely to be accidental, and cannot be explained by common origin (see Chapter 9, this volume) or language contact (see Chapter 8, this volume), then, by definition, they belong to Universal Grammar in the broad sense. A very large number of such similarities have indeed been discovered.[2] One line of comparative research with the stated aim of discovering linguistic universals is the typological one (for full discussion, see also Chapter 30, this volume), starting with the work of Joseph Greenberg in the early sixties. On the basis of a sample of 30 languages from a variety of families and locations, Greenberg (1963) proposed a set of 45 cross-linguistic generalizations which he termed universals of language. They are sometimes termed

---

[2] The Konstanz Universal Archive lists about 1,400 linguistic universals. This list includes all universals that have been proposed in the literature, regardless of how hypothetical the basis for them is, and regardless of whether they have since been shown to be spurious. It includes not just absolute universals but also 'statistical universals', that is more or less strong tendencies, following in Greenberg's footsteps. It does not include many universals proposed within the generative tradition, perhaps because they are not typically explicitly referred to as 'universals' in the written sources, even though they are typically assumed, by default, to be universal.

typological universals, to distinguish them from the linguistic universals assumed in the generative tradition. As mentioned, in the case of Greenberg there is no commitment to the idea that the universals are ultimately genetically encoded. The epithet 'universal' has no other significance than that a given generalization, as far as is known, holds true of all languages or 'the overwhelming majority of languages'; in either case there is something to explain. The favoured method within this research programme is comparison of a large set of languages, preferably hundreds, with respect to some grammatical property, where the languages are sampled so as to represent all the major language families and all different corners of the world, in order to avoid genetic bias or areal bias. In practice this means that the data are collected mainly from existing grammatical descriptions of languages.

Within the Greenbergian typological research programme as developed by Lehmann (1973, 1978), Venneman (1974, 1984), Hawkins (1979, 1983), Greenberg, Ferguson and Moravcisk (1978), and later by the linguists associated with the *World Atlas of Language Structures (WALS)* programme (Bernard Comrie, Martin Haspelmath, Matthew Dryer, David Gil, among many others),[3] there has been a strong tendency to favour functional over formal explanations of typological universals, where a functional explanation of a grammatical property P is typically that P makes communication by language more efficient, and therefore all languages have evolved, by cultural evolution, to encompass P; see Newmeyer (1998), and Chapter 31, this volume. A different type of explanation, still functional, would be that P makes language acquisition more efficient, and therefore languages have evolved to encompass P; see Kirby and Hurford (2002) and Kirby and Christiansen (2003) for a particular version of this idea. In Holmberg (forthcoming a) I suggest that there is no logically necessary connection between linguistic typology and functionally based explanation, but that there is a practical connection to do with the methodology. I quote:

> The favoured method in linguistic typological research is comparative surveys on a large scale in order to cover as much as possible of the existing variation and in order to establish, as far as possible, valid global generalizations. This has meant that the grammatical properties that are investigated/compared, are by necessity all easily observable 'surfacy' properties of the kind which are recorded even in sketchy descriptive grammars. One result of this is that the generalizations discovered have been probabilistic, riddled with exceptions, rather than absolute, because surfacy properties are subject to unpredictable variation to a greater extent than more abstract properties ... This disfavours explanations in terms of universal, genetically determined properties of the language faculty, and favours explanations in terms of 'functional pressure', which are expected to allow for exceptions. *(Holmberg forthcoming a)*

---

[3] Bill Croft could also be mentioned as an influential theorist in the typological camp (see Croft 1995, 1999).

Among the universals in Greenberg (1963) which have generated most discussion and most new research are the so-called word-order universals (universals 1 to 25). A subset of them are given here, retaining the numbering in Greenberg (1963):

3. Languages with dominant VSO order are always prepositional.
4. With overwhelmingly greater than chance frequency, languages with SOV order are postpositional.
5. If a language has dominant SOV order and the genitive follows the governing noun, then the adjective likewise follows the noun.
9. With well more than chance frequency, when question particles or affixes are specified in position by reference to the sentence as a whole, if initial, such elements are found in prepositional languages, and, if final, in postpositional.
13. If the nominal object always precedes the verb, then verb forms subordinate to the main verb also precede it
16. In languages with dominant order VSO, an inflected auxiliary always precedes the main verb. In languages with dominant order SOV, an inflected auxiliary always follows the main verb.

These cross-linguistic generalizations have the fascinating property of indicating an underlying pattern, as was observed by Greenberg and formally described in terms of the notions 'harmony' and 'dominance'. Subsequent research led to formulation of the pattern in terms of head–complement order: there is a tendency for phrases to be either head-initial or head-final, across categories; see Dryer (1992).[4] There is a statistical correlation between (S)OV, [NP P], [NP N], [VP Aux] and [IP C] on the one hand, and VO (VSO or SVO), [P NP], [N NP], [Aux VP] and [C IP] on the other hand, even though many (even most) languages exhibit a mixture of head-initial and head-final phrases.[5]

Greenberg's word-order correlations were subsequently tested and, for the most part, confirmed, against a much bigger and more carefully sampled set of 625 languages in Dryer (1992). Dryer's research also demonstrated that some of Greenberg's universals were spurious, being effects of language contact, including Universal 5; see Dryer (1988). The WALS project (Haspelmath, Dryer, Gil and Comrie 2014) has also shown some of Greenberg's universals to be spurious. In spite of these minor objections, Greenberg's research and subsequent typological research has shown persuasively that there is unity, simplicity and some sort of rationality underlying the seemingly unconstrained surface variation, which obviously calls for explanation.

---

[4] Dryer (1992) opted for formulation of the generalization in terms of branching direction: languages tend to be either left-branching or right-branching across categories.

[5] See Baker (2008) for a demonstration that the correlation between head–complement order across categories holds as a universal tendency, in spite of the prevalence of mixed systems.

I will come back to the typological universals, after a discussion of the development of Universal Grammar in the strict sense (UG) in generative linguistic theory.

13.3 Arguments for UG (Strict Sense)

A particularly compelling argument for UG in the strict sense, first expounded in Chomsky (1965), is the argument from 'the poverty of the stimulus'. Insofar as it can be shown that speakers of a language have intuitions about interpretation and grammaticality of constructions that are so complex and/or so rare that the intuitions cannot reasonably be the result of learning purely from experience, i.e. just from exposure to relevant data in conversation, then the intuitions must be based on properties of our cognitive system that are in some sense innate.

The following is an example of this form of argument, from Chomsky (1986). Consider the sentences (1)–(4).

(1) John ate an apple.

(2) John ate.

(3) John is too stubborn to talk to Bill.

(4) John is too stubborn to talk to.

I quote from Chomsky (1986); the example numbers are changed.

> ... sentence (1) means that John ate something or other, a fact that one might explain on the basis of a simple inductive procedure: *ate* takes an object, as in (2), and if the object is missing, it is understood as arbitrary. Applying the same inductive procedure to (3) and (4), it should be that (4) means that John is so stubborn that he (John) will not talk to some arbitrary person, on the analogy of (2). But the meaning is, in fact, quite different: namely, that John is so stubborn that some arbitrary person won't talk to him (John). Again, this is known without training or relevant evidence. *(Chomsky 1986: 8)*

The conclusion is that the interpretation is based on intuitive knowledge of abstract principles of syntax that are inherent to the language faculty, not learnt but only triggered by experience.

One may or may not agree with the premises or the conclusion in the case of this particular example; here, it serves as an illustration of this form of argument. See Berwick, Pietroski, Yankama and Chomsky (2011) for some recent discussion with many more examples.

The argument from the poverty of the stimulus is particularly persuasive when it can be demonstrated that children at a very early age have the relevant intuitions (see also discussion in Chapter 18, this volume). The following example is from de Villiers, Vainikka and Roeper (1990).

(5)   When did the boy tell his father that he hurt himself?

(6)   When did the boy tell his father how he hurt himself?

Sentence (5) is ambiguous: *when* can be about the time of telling (the short-distance reading) or the time of hurting himself (the long-distance reading). (6) is unambiguous: the long-distance reading is unavailable. The reason for this is the intervening question word *how*: the long-distance reading requires movement of *when* out of a clause headed by a *wh*-phrase, which violates the *wh*-island constraint, a universal constraint on movement (Ross 1967; Chomsky 1977) which will be discussed in a little more detail below. Between the ages of three and six, children give long-distance interpretations to questions such as (5) roughly half of the time, but only around 6 per cent for questions such as (6) (de Villiers, Roeper and Vainikka 1990; Pérez-Leroux 1993; Roeper and de Villiers 1994).

It is very unlikely that the children could have acquired these intuitions from experience, i.e. by exposure to relevant data. First, long-distance questions are uncommon in ordinary discourse. Second, learning on the basis of exposure to data that (6) does *not* have a long-distance reading would require exposure to relevant negative data, that is data which indicate that the relevant reading is unavailable. But ordinary discourse does not include such data.[6] If it is not learnt by experience, the relevant intuitions must be based on constraints or principles that are in some sense innate. As such they may be specific to the language faculty or they may derive from more general constraints on cognition. The methodological principle which has been assumed, quite rightly, within generative grammar is that insofar as we are unable to show that the properties have any application outside language, we are entitled to assume that they are specific to the language faculty; see Berwick, Pietroski, Yankama and Chomsky (2011).

13.4 The Content of UG

Chomsky (1965), in the first detailed discussion of UG, proposed making a distinction between substantive and formal universals. Among the substantive universals would be categories characteristic of language: in phonology, vowels and consonants and features such as front vs back, roundedness, nasality, etc.; in syntax, nouns, verbs, adjectives, adpositions, pronouns, negation, tense, aspect, number, etc. Some of these categories are universal in the sense that all languages have them. There is every reason to think that all languages have negation, for example. One

---

[6] Negative evidence does occur: if a form can be expected to occur with some frequency in a language L given general principles and given what is already known by a learner about L, but systematically fails to occur, this may well serve as indirect negative evidence. However, long-distance <k>wh</k>-movement is surely not frequent enough to provide the required indirect negative evidence needed to learn the contrast between (5) and (6) by experience.

of Greenberg's (1963) universals states that all languages have a category of pronouns distinguishing at least three persons and two numbers (see Daniel 2011).[7] But for many of the categories it is controversial whether they occur in all languages. For example, many languages appear not to have adjectives as a category distinct from nouns or verbs (but see Baker 2003, Dixon 2004 for arguments that adjectives are universal), many languages do not have any overt marking for tense (Dahl and Velupillai 2011; Ritter and Wiltschko 2009), many languages do not have any marking for nominal plurality outside the pronominal system (Daniel 2011), and so on. It is not obvious that all languages make even the traditional distinction between noun and verb; see Baker (2003) for discussion.

A widely entertained hypothesis is that UG makes available a pool of categories, from which each language makes a selection. This is the line taken by Chomsky (1995: ch. 4; 2001), for example. Another hypothesis is that all the categories and features are universal, present in all languages, and that the variation is a matter of which of them have morphological realization; see Cinque (1999), Sigurðsson (2004, 2011a,b).

Formal universals are, for example, the fact that syntactic structure is hierarchical, that syntactic rules are recursive, that there is movement, that there is labelling (phrases being labelled by their head), and so on. Though some of them are found in all languages, being constitutive of the grammar of human language, there are other formal properties that are not instantiated in every language. For example, functional heads may be morphologically bound as affixes or clitics, but not all languages make use of this option. There is even some debate whether all languages make use of recursion in the sense of self-embedding (Everett 2005, 2007; Nevins, Pesetsky and Rodrigues 2009a, b; Rodrigues and Sândalo forthcoming).

Another property of UG proposed by Chomsky (1965), but not much elaborated in that work, is what he called an evaluation metric. This would be a set of principles, activated under language acquisition, which would select the most highly valued grammar compatible with the primary data. This is based on the idea that acquisition of a language L, particularly as a first language, is a matter of constructing the grammar of L on the basis of (a) UG and (b) primary data, by a process in which hypotheses are formed by the learner about the mapping between sound and meaning in L, which are then tested and refined in the light of more data, until the grammar of L, which is essentially a theory of L, is complete and able to generate the same range of sentences as the grammars of other people in the linguistic community. However, the formal devices made available by UG are powerful enough to allow for more than one theory which is

---

[7] In a sample of 261 languages, Daniel (2011) found 9 that do not distinguish number in their independent pronoun system, so that part of Greenberg's generalization is too strong.

compatible with the primary data. Movement is a particularly powerful device, in this regard. Consider the following, somewhat trivial example: the embedded question in (7) can be derived by movement of *where* from the PP to initial position, as shown in (8). It can also be derived by movement of the PP, deriving (9a) as an intermediate structure, followed by movement of the preposition back into the VP, deriving (9b), which would be spelled out as (7).

(7)   (I wonder) where it came from.

(8)   where [$_S$ it [$_{VP}$ came [$_{PP}$ from __]

(9)   a. [$_{PP}$ from where] [$_S$ it [$_{VP}$ came __]
        b. [$_{PP}$ __ where] [$_S$ it [$_{VP}$ came from]

   The evaluation metric would prefer the grammar which derives (7) by one movement instead of two: other things being equal, a grammar with shorter derivations is preferred. The evaluation metric may also disprefer the grammar deriving (7) by (9a, b) because it employs downwards movement. Other things being equal, a grammar with fewer formal devices, for instance only upwards movement, is preferred. The evaluation metric of Chomsky (1965) later reappeared in minimalist theory as economy conditions, as will be discussed below in §8 (see also discussions in §7.3.1, §22.4). It also reappeared much sooner, beginning already in the late sixties with Ross (1967) as a forerunner, as conditions on movement, to be discussed in the next section.

13.5   From Conditions on Transformations to Principles-and-Parameters Theory

The Chomskyan theory of UG went through an interesting development in the seventies, culminating in Chomsky's *Lectures of Government and Binding*, published in 1981. The first step was a reorientation from articulating the set of rules deriving all and only the grammatical sentences of a given language, as in the models of Chomsky (1957, 1965), to articulating the formal properties of the rules and the representations derived by them as universal principles, so that the rules themselves could be correspondingly generalized and simplified.

   This approach was pioneered in Ross (1967), where a set of constraints on movement were formulated, prohibiting movement out of certain types of constituents, called islands. Chomsky (1973) proposed some additional constraints on movement, in particular on what would later be identified as A-movement, and on pronominal and anaphoric binding, including (10), which explains, among other things, the contrast between (11a) and (11b).

(10) The Tensed-S condition: No rule can involve X,Y in a structure [...
      X ... [$_\alpha$ ... Y ...]], where α is a tensed sentence.

(11) a. *John seems [$_\alpha$ that __ is tired]
      b. John seems [$_\alpha$ __ to be tired]

Given (10) and certain other conditions like it, the movement rule itself
needs only a very general formulation, at the limit simply 'Move NP'.

The Tensed-S condition would be a property of UG. Given that the
validity of this condition can be observed only on the basis of negative
evidence (such as (11a)), and given that the required negative evidence
does not occur in normal discourse, it cannot be learnt on the basis of
linguistic experience, so the condition has to come from UG.

Chomsky (1977) was another important contribution in the evolution of
the theory in the seventies. In this paper Chomsky showed that a wide
variety of constructions, which up until then had been held to be quite
distinct, each derived by a different set of rules, could be analysed as
derived by one and the same rule, namely *wh*-movement, the application
of which was subject to a locality constraint called Subjacency.

(12) Subjacency: No rule can involve X,Y in a structure [... X ... [$_\alpha$ [$_\beta$ ...
      Y ...]]] where α and β are cyclic nodes.
      Cyclic nodes: S and NP (corresponding to IP and DP in more recent
      theory).

'Cyclic node' was later rephrased as 'bounding node'. Subjacency is
a generalization over a range of island constraints: the *wh*-island constraint, the complex NP constraint, the sentential subject constraint, and
the adjunct island constraint, which were now seen to be instances of the
same condition on movement.

An important complement to the theory of *wh*-movement was Rizzi
(1978) discussing the observation that *wh*-movement appears to allow
violation of Subjacency in certain cases in Italian, as shown in (13).

(13) a. *Your brother, who I wonder which stories they have told to, is
         very worried.
      b. Tuo   fratello, a   cui   mi domando che   storie   abbiano
         your brother   to who me=I.ask   which stories they.have
         raccontato, era   molto preoccupato. (It.)
         told   was   very worried

Rizzi proposed to account for this by assuming a partly different formulation for Subjacency in Italian: the bounding nodes would be CP and
DP, not IP and DP, as in English. In the relative clause in (13b) the *wh*-phrase
a cui has moved across two IP-boundaries, but only one CP boundary.

(14) [$_{CP}$ a cui$_i$ [$_{IP}$ mi domando [$_{CP}$ che storie [$_{IP}$ abbiano raccontato t$_i$]]]]

This pointed to a solution of a major problem for the reorientation from language-specific rules to universal principles, namely how to account for cross-linguistic variation: a universal principle (Subjacency) allowed for variation on a certain point, namely, the identity of bounding nodes.[8]

In the generative grammars of Chomsky (1957, 1965) and subsequent work grammatical variation was accounted for by the system of rules, which was different from language to language. Even though the rules were based on categories drawn from UG and had formal properties dictated by UG, the set of rules could vary indefinitely: a rule could be present or absent in a language, and the formulation of a rule could vary in many ways from language to language (as well as from one period to another) as long as it observed the formal conditions set by UG. Variation was expected. At the same time, however, the system allowed too much variation, failing to capture some of the underlying unity of language, and thereby failing to address 'the logical problem of language acquisition' (also called 'Plato's problem' by Chomsky 1986), namely, how it is possible to acquire such a complex system on the basis of so little evidence.

Once the properties of the constructions/rules were generalized as principles of UG, with the rules correspondingly simplified, the opposite problem arises, which is how to account for the abundant (synchronic and diachronic) cross-linguistic variation. As UG gets more specified, there is correspondingly less room for variation. However, if some principles of UG allow for variation on certain points, which came to be known as parameters, and if the principles are involved in a wide range of constructions, then even very limited variation in the grammar can have far-ranging effects on the language.

A full-blown version of this theory, which came to be known as Principles-and-Parameters theory (see Chapters 7 and 27, this volume), was articulated in Chomsky (1981). The theory at that point encompassed an array of modules/subtheories, each defined by a set of principles, some of which allowed for parametric variation: theta-theory, case theory, binding theory, control theory and bounding theory.

Another influential idea was that grammatical variation would all be lexical in the sense of being a matter of variation with respect to features of functional heads: does I(NFL), the head of IP contain AGR, a set of nominal agreement features, or not? Does C have a feature attracting a verb or not, does definite D attract N or not, and so on. Borer (1984) is usually credited with articulation of this idea (which, incidentally, is not compatible with Rizzi's (1978) subjacency parameter). This is an attractive idea since the lexicon is clearly the locus of much cross-linguistic variation: languages have different words.

---

[8] English and Italian may not, however, be as different as they are made out to be in Rizzi (1978); see Grimshaw (1986).

The outlook at this point was that UG is a rich system of categories and principles, including locality conditions on grammatical relations (with Rizzi's (1990) Relativized Minimality as a particularly interesting development), X-bar theory, and various 'licensing conditions' including conditions on assignment of Case and theta-roles. Discourse-related properties such as topic and focus were also increasingly taken to be elements of grammar, subject to principles and parameters of UG (Horvath 1986; É. Kiss 1987; Rizzi 1997). There were four levels of representation: D-structure, S-structure, PF and LF. The operations were taken to be very simple, possibly because the outputs of the operations were subject to strict well-formedness conditions.

The theory was applied and tested on an increasingly wider range of languages (Baker 1988 could be mentioned as a particularly influential work; also Huang 1982; Baker 1996; McCloskey 1996; Cinque 1999; Kayne 2000). It was applied and tested by experimental work on L1 and L2 acquisition. The prediction was that the principles, with their parameters, would manifest themselves relatively early in L1 acquisition. Some of the results appeared to confirm this prediction (see Chien and Wexler 1990; de Villiers, Vainikka and Roeper 1990; Hyams and Wexler 1993; Guasti 2004), although there were always problems (Fodor 2009). It was applied with success to historical linguistics, in conjunction with Lightfoot's (1979) theory of the role of language acquisition in explaining historical change (see Chapters 6, 15, 18, 24, this volume); Roberts (1993), Heycock and Kroch (1993), Kroch and Taylor (2000).

Another theory which is also based on the idea of a rich UG is Optimality Theory (OT). OT evolved in the early nineties, first as a theory of phonology, but soon also as a theory of syntax; Prince and Smolensky (1993), Legendre, Grimshaw and Vikner (2001). OT is a strictly constraint-based framework, where the grammar is seen as mainly made up of a large set of constraints which are universal but not inviolable. Instead, linguistic variation is modelled as variation in the ranking of the constraints: in a language L, a universal constraint C may be 'ranked higher' than another universal constraint C', and will thereby override constraint C', in a situation where there is a conflict between them. In another language L', C' may instead be ranked higher than C, thus overriding C, in a situation where there is a conflict between them. This will have effects on the output, such that a form which is well-formed in L may be ill-formed in L', and vice versa. OT has had a huge impact in phonology (McCarthy 2001; Prince and Smolensky 1993), less in syntax. There has been a notable rapprochement between OT and Lexical Functional Grammar, though: see Bresnan (2000, 2001), Bresnan and Aissen (2002).

13.6   UG in the Minimalist Programme

The Principles-and-Parameters framework with the associated view of UG has undergone a fairly radical development more recently, starting in the nineties (see also Chapters 7, 27, 28, this volume). One element of this development was Chomsky's so-called Minimalist Programme for linguistic theory articulated in a series of works starting with Chomsky (1993) and including Chomsky (1995, 2000, 2001, 2005, 2008, 2013). It is based on the ambition to approach UG 'from below', that is to ask why UG has the properties it has, as they have unfolded in research over the previous decades. One important idea is that some, perhaps many, of the properties of grammar that have been ascribed to UG are conceptually necessary in any system relating sound to meaning in the fashion of human language, and therefore need not be stipulated as part of UG. The projected outcome of this approach is, therefore, a simpler UG.

The starting point in this approach to grammar and UG is that syntax is a combinatorial system, where the fundamental operation is Merge, an operation which combines two terms, two categories α and β, and yields a new category γ. In the strongest, most provocative formulation of the theory Merge is the only operation needed in syntax (Boeckx 2011). Linguistic expressions can be modelled as constructed bottom-up by Merge, deriving LF, a representation interfacing with the conceptual-intentional system, the 'systems of thought', and, with the help of morphological and phonological rules, deriving PF, a representation interfacing with articulation and perception.[9] Any other devices, categorial distinctions, conditions on well-formedness, levels of representation, etc. that have been employed in order to formally describe the various languages will have to be evaluated in terms of whether they are conceptually necessary or not, and/or whether they are 'interface conditions', not part of syntax proper ('narrow syntax'), but either semantics/pragmatics or phonology/phonetics. Whatever is conceptually necessary does not need to be stipulated as a property of UG. For example, the representations LF and PF are conceptually necessary, but the representations D-structure and S-structure are not. As such they must either be stipulated as elements of UG, or else eliminated from the theory. In the theory of Chomsky (1993; 1995: ch. 4) they are eliminated, as the conditions previously defined in terms of these levels of representation can be met as they appear in the course of the Merge-based derivation.

The theoretical devices needed within this new model, in its present instantiations, include many of the devices that were important in the earlier model(s): the set of functional categories constructing verbal-sentential projections and nominal projections, movement, including

---

[9] This is Chomsky's position. A partly different theory, articulated by Hinzen and Sheehan (2013), is that the syntax *is* the system of thought, the externalized form of which is the spoken or written language.

the distinction between A and A-bar movement, theta-roles, case and agreement. There are some notable differences, though. For example, X-bar theory is no longer included as a stipulation on phrase structure, its properties being instead derived by Merge and labelling, the device which assigns a categorial label to a phrase derived by merge. This is still a source of much debate, though; see Hornstein (2009), Sheehan (2013), Chomsky (2013).

A crucially important issue is, as always, how to model linguistic variation, including variation along the diachronic axis. A radical line is that narrow syntax, that is the derivation of LF, is universal. Linguistic variation would then be all within the derivation of PF, the input to the spoken or signed form of a linguistic expression; see Berwick and Chomsky (2010), Boeckx (2011), Sigurðsson (2011a, b), Hinzen and Sheehan (2013). The alternative is that syntax allows for at least some variation; see Ramchand and Svenonius (2008), Roberts and Holmberg (2010), Holmberg and Roberts (2014).

The idea that Merge is the only operation needed in syntax was helped by a redefinition (first proposed and explored in Chomsky 2004) of syntactic movement as the case when a constituent already merged as part of a tree is merged again. This is 'internal Merge', as opposed to 'external Merge', when a word or phrase is merged the first time.

Standard versions of the theory, however, include another operation: Agree. This is an operation which can link two terms at a distance, provided the right conditions are met. This theoretical device is dependent on the feature theory also articulated by Chomsky (1993, 1995, 2000) and particularly Chomsky (2001). According to this theory certain formal features occur in two forms, an interpretable and an uninterpretable form. An example of an interpretable feature is the number feature on a plural DP. An example of an uninterpretable feature is the number feature on a verb agreeing with a plural DP, which is uninterpretable as it does not affect the semantics of the verb but is just an overt marker of the relation holding between the subject and the predicate. Chomsky (2001) proposes that uninterpretable features enter the syntax unvalued, but need to be assigned a value in the course of the derivation. This is the operation Agree.

Locality is partly redefined in terms of phases, where a phase is a syntactic constituent which is in some sense complete, such that syntactic operations, Agree and internal merge, cannot 'see' into it. Finite clauses, verbal predicates, and DPs are phases. Non-local relations, such as between C, at the head of CP, and a *wh*-phrase inside the sentence would be instances of Agree, subject to locality conditions (relativized minimality, phases), accompanied by movement subject to cross-linguistic variation.

It seems true to say that the most radical pronouncements of the Minimalist Programme are not quite matched by shop-floor practices.

Arguably the theory or theories currently employed to formally describe and explain observed facts in languages investigated, what most linguists do, are not radically different from the mainstream theory or theories of the pre-minimalist period (no doubt with some exceptions). There are some new devices (unvalued features), some reduction (fewer levels of representation, no X-bar theory), and there is a more pronounced ambition to look behind the formal descriptions and explanations, but much of the theory remains essentially the same. One notable difference, though, is in the conception of UG and linguistic variation. I will return to this point at the end of the next section.

13.7 The Evolution of UG

Another interesting development with consequences for the theory of UG is based on research and debate on the evolution of language, a field of inquiry which has attracted a lot of interest in the last two decades.

A notable, highly controversial contribution to this debate is Hauser, Chomsky and Fitch (2002). In this paper, a collaboration between a linguist and two biologists, the authors try to lay the groundwork for fruitful comparative research on human language and non-human communication systems. They make a conceptual distinction between what they call the faculty of language in the broad sense (FLB) and in the narrow sense (FLN). FLB includes all of the capacities that are relevant for language and communication regardless of whether they are specific to language or unique to humans. A number of elements of FLB are discussed in the paper which are shown not to be unique to human language, including vocalization, categorial perception, concept formation and complex communicative behaviour. FLN would then be the part of FLB which is unique to humans and specific to language. As the authors point out (see also Fitch, Hauser and Chomsky 2005), it is an empirical question whether FLN has any content; an alternative idea is that what is unique to humans is a particular, lucky combination of properties that individually are not unique to humans. They put forward the hypothesis that a key component of FLN is the capacity for recursion, making possible the combination of discrete elements (words or morphemes) in infinitely many ways, to form complex meaningful expressions.

How did this capacity evolve? The received view is that what might be called modern human culture, characterized by rapid evolution of technology (see also discussion in §16.3), use of symbolic objects, and migration and adaptation to new environments, is a relatively recent phenomenon, possibly not extending further back than 100,000 years ago (Tattersall 2012; Hauser *et al.* 2014). At some point after this time a change took place, in East Africa, which radically altered the conditions for human existence. It is highly plausible that the crucial change was the birth of modern human language. We know that human language based on UG cannot be the result of just gradual evolution by adaptation and natural selection, simply because there has not been enough time. Our closest relatives in the animal world are chimpanzees and bonobos, members of the *Pan* genus. We know that chimpanzees have a highly limited capacity for concept formation and no capacity for combining concepts in a systematic fashion to form structured expressions (Terrace 1979, 2005; Terrace *et al.* 1979). The time since our last common ancestor with chimpanzees is probably between 6 and 7.5 million years ago (Endicott, Ho and Stringer 2010; Feeney 2014). In this period the capacity for human language must have evolved, and apparently this is not enough time for the evolution of such a specific and complex system to evolve gradually by adaptation and natural selection (Worden 1995; Tattersall 1998).

Taking a broader view, what is minimally needed for human language is the interaction of three distinct components:

(a) a repository of concepts and a capacity for forming new concepts;
(b) a set of operations combining concepts to form structured, complex meanings, particularly forming propositions;[10]
(c) a system for assigning physical form to the concepts and the propositions constructed out of them.

Components (a) and (b) are sufficient for thought. Component (c) is necessary to communicate thought. An idea with some plausibility, compatible with the central position of Merge in Chomsky's minimalist theory, and the comparison of human and non-human language in Hauser, Chomsky and Fitch (2002), is that the capacity for concept formation evolved separately, and also vocalization and other physical expression of meaning evolved separately. The capacity to combine concepts may also have been present in a rudimentary form, but the big change that happened sometime after the 100,000-year mark was a change which resulted in a chance combination of pre-existing elements, probably 'rather minor in genetic terms' (Tattersall 1998), but with hugely advantageous effects, which allowed it to quickly spread in the population. As noted by Hauser, Chomsky and Fitch (2002), it may have been an automatic consequence of increased brain size or it may have been a chance mutation. As suggested in Hauser, Chomsky and Fitch (2002), and developed further in Berwick and Chomsky (2011), the neural change was the capacity for Merge, making possible the construction of an infinite range of propositions by combining words, denoting concepts, in the manner of modern human language, thereby radically altering the conditions of human life.[11]

---

[10] See Hinzen and Sheehan (2013) on the crucial role of propositions in human language and thought.
[11] See Feeney (2014) for a review of recent research on the birth of language, and a partly different idea of how modern language evolved with reference to the theory of language and cognition in Burton-Roberts (2011), Burton-Roberts and Poole (2006).

What does this imply for the idea of UG? The implication of these considerations is that UG, in the strict sense of the innate, genetically encoded capacity for human language, may not be the rich system of syntactic categories, operations, and quite specific principles and conditions (Subjacency, the theta-criterion, the Case Filter, binding principles, the Linear Correspondence Axiom (Kayne 1994), etc.) regulating syntactic operations and defining conditions on representations, with a limited degree of variation permitted by the parameters left open by some of the principles, because consideration of the biological evolution of human language does not allow for evolution of such a rich innate system. This, in turn, implies that the universal properties that have been observed and described in comparative linguistic research may have extra-grammatical explanations more often than used to be acknowledged, at least within mainstream generative linguistics.

13.8 The Three Factors, Linguistic Variation and Underspecification of UG

Chomsky (1995) put forward the following model of the design of human language, often referred to as the 'three factors model' (see also discussion in §7.2):

(15)   Factor 1: the genetic endowment, UG.
        Factor 2: the environment: primary linguistic data for language acquisition.
        Factor 3: General principles of computation and cognition.

A possible case of Factor 3 (henceforth F3) would be the principle of economy of derivation which favours derivation (8) over derivation (9) as discussed earlier (see also discussion in §22.4). This would plausibly not be anything specific to human language, and probably not even to human cognition, but would be a more general property of animal cognition, or even a more general condition on complex systems in the natural world.

F3 would also include general conditions on learning. An example is what is called Input Generalization in Roberts and Holmberg (2010), Holmberg and Roberts (2014), that is the learning strategy which generalizes from observation of one instance of a category to all instances (see also §7.3.2): if you see one white swan, assume all swans are white until further notice. In relation to language acquisition, this might explain the cross-linguistic tendency for word-order generalization across categories, that is the tendency for languages to be either predominantly head-final or head-initial, observed by Greenberg (1963) and discussed in §13.2 above. It would lead the infant learner to generalize from the first instance of a processed head–complement relation to all head–complement relations, with the resulting hypothesis of uniformity across categories subsequently modified in the light of more data. In this perspective, learning a mixed system requires more effort than learning a consistent system, the effort increasing with each counterexample to the first generalization. The prediction is that consistency across categories will be favoured, in a global perspective, which is the case (see Baker 2008). The final output would be the result of F2 (the environment, the grammar used by speakers in the community) but guided by the Input Generalization strategy, an F3 effect.

F2 would include all those properties which (a) exhibit variation across languages, dialects, and individuals, and (b) are learned by exposure to primary linguistic data. There is a logical connection between (a) and (b): for any grammatical property which can vary, it will have to be learnt which value is instantiated in the language being acquired.[12]

F1, finally, is UG proper, universal properties of human language which cannot be reduced to extralinguistic factors. As before, the way to find out what UG consists of is to examine putative universal grammatical features and properties, and consider whether they can be explained in terms of extralinguistic factors. If not, they can be assumed to be part of UG.

As mentioned, the view of UG that is implied within this framework is of a less rich, less specified system, than the view prevalent in classical Principles-and-Parameters theory. This has consequences for the approach to linguistic variation. A partly new approach, articulated and discussed in Biberauer and Richards (2006), Holmberg (2010b), Roberts and Holmberg (2010), is that linguistic variation can be modelled as an effect of underspecification of UG (see also discussion in §7.3). Adapting the words of Biberauer and Richards (2006), variation occurs where 'UG doesn't mind'. In classical Principles-and-Parameters theory variation is modelled as resulting from a set of parameters with specified values, where a language 'chooses' a value for each parameter, or, in slightly less abstract terms, the child in the process of acquiring a language will set each parameter to a value defined by the parameter on the basis of the primary linguistic data encountered (see Chapters 7, 18, 27, this volume). This is learning. In the case of principles without parameters, no learning is required. In the current minimalist perspective there are no specified parameters. Learning is required in every case where no principle or condition, from the F1 or F3 class, determines the form and/or interpretation of a type of expression. This is still typically – or perhaps even by necessity – a matter of choosing among alternatives on the basis of the primary linguistic data, but the alternatives are defined by F1 or F3 factors, or a combination of them. In the case of head–complement order there are

---

[12] This does not exclude the possibility of properties which are universal among human languages but which are nevertheless learnt; see Biberauer, Holmberg, Roberts and Sheehan (2014) for an example.

only two alternatives, the head must either precede or follow the complement, because (a) conditions on selection and labelling require merge of a head α and a complement β (F1), and physical restrictions on articulation and perception dictate that words must be linearized, so α must either precede or follow β (F3).

As pointed out by Roberts and Holmberg (2010), in the case of variation between *wh*-movement and *wh-in-situ*, formulated in Huang's (1982) seminal work as the consequence of a parameter with two specified values, the two alternatives follow if (a) *wh*-movement is universal (F1), and (b) movement either precedes or follows spell out to PF (an F3 effect dictated by the architecture of the grammar). No specification is required over and above (a) and (b). See Holmberg (2010a) for a demonstration that the classical null-subject parameter of Rizzi (1982) can also profitably be viewed as a consequence of underdetermination of UG, in conjunction with F1 and F3 (also Roberts 2010; Holmberg and Roberts 2014).[13]

In a wider perspective there is nothing radically new in the minimalist approach to UG. A generalization, discovered on the basis of comparative research or research on language acquisition, is explained in terms of an innate principle or condition specific to the language faculty, as long as there is no plausible more general principle or other factor which can explain it. This is normal scientific practice. The research agenda may have shifted somewhat, though, within mainstream generative syntactic research, to a more critical attitude towards theoretical devices such as the theta-criterion, the Case Filter, conditions on agreement, anaphoric binding and quantifier-variable relations, standard ingredients of UG ever since Chomsky (1981). The question is if they can be explained in F3 terms, or else can be explained in non-syntactic terms, either semantic or phonological; see Holmberg and Roberts (2014) for some speculations.

Locality conditions, including the notorious island constraints, are particularly good candidates for explanation in F3 terms, particularly in terms of conditions on human processing capacity which are not specific to language. Proposals to this effect have been made in the literature. I will finish by reviewing some interesting recent research testing whether certain island effects can be explained in extralinguistic terms.

---

[13] The fact that the order of a given head–complement pair is typically constant in the language of a speaker does not follow from the factors mentioned above. This would be a consequence of the Input Generalization discussed earlier (assume the maximally general hypothesis compatible with the data, a case of F3) and the one form–one meaning principle, which itself is also possibly the effect of a learning strategy: if variation were allowed, the two alternative orders would tend to be associated with different meanings and/or different classes of lexical items. This is, in fact, what is found in languages where head-complement order can vary; see Holmberg (forthcoming b) on VO order in Finnish.

13.9 Another Look at Constraints on Movement

As mentioned above, the constraints on movement first observed and discussed by Ross (1967) make up a particularly well-established set of universal syntactic constraints. For example, movement out of subjects is much more restricted than movement out of objects.

(16)   a. Which dictator did they make a film about last year?
          b. *Which dictator did a film about appear last year?

Movement out of a finite embedded *wh*-question is much more restricted than movement out of a finite embedded propositional complement.

(17)   a. How did you say [that he fixed the sink <how>]?
          b. *How did you ask [whether he fixed the sink <how>]?

(17a) has a reading where the initial *wh*-word asks for the manner of fixing the sink (as indicated by the copy within angled brackets). (17b) lacks such a reading, being interpretable only as a question about the manner of asking.

It seems *a priori* plausible that the judgements could be explained in terms of a constraint on human processing capacity, which may apply more generally than just in the case of grammar. In terms of Chomsky's three factors, they would be in the F3 class. Proposals to this effect have been made in the literature. Sprouse, Wagers and Phillips (2012) divide these proposals in two categories: one is theories which explain island constraints in terms of independently motivated, non-grammatical constraints on processing capacity. They refer to these as reductionist theories: Givón (1979), Kluender and Kutas (1993), Kluender (1998, 2004), Hofmeister and Sag (2010). The other is theories according to which the constraints are ultimately due to non-grammatical limitations on processing and/or learning capacity, but have been grammaticalized in the course of the cultural evolution of language as grammatical constraints: Fodor (1978, 1983), Berwick and Weinberg (1984), Hawkins (1999) are representatives of this hypothesis. Sprouse, Wagers and Phillips (2012) refer to these as grounded theories of island constraints.

Sprouse, Wagers and Phillips (2012) report a series of experiments to test a prediction made by the reductionist theories, which is that the strength of island effects should vary across speakers as a function of individual differences in processing resources, specifically their working memory capacity. They tested 300 native speakers of English on a set of island constraints, to see if their judgements of the grammaticality correlated with their performance on two different measures of working-memory capacity. They found no correlation. This is consistent with theories according to which island constraints are specific to the faculty of language, including theories according to which they derive from UG, as well as with the grounded theories according to which they are grammatical adaptations to constraints on parsing capacity.

In terms of Chomsky's three factors, classical generative grammar would explain island constraints in terms of UG, i.e. F1. According to the grounded grammatical constraints theory they would be due to F2; they would be acquired by speakers along with other rules of grammar, presumably not as such but as a consequence of acquisition of other properties of structure and movement. According to the reductionist theories they would be F3 effects, being due to non-domain specific constraints on processing capacity. Sprouse, Wagers and Phillips (2012) demonstrate that a particular version of the F3 explanation is untenable. They claim, furthermore, that no other version has been proposed which would be explicit enough to allow testing. See Hofmeister, Staum Casasanto and Sag (2013) and Sprouse, Wagers and Phillips (2012) for discussion.[14]

The moral of this section is that claims about extralinguistic explanations of linguistic generalizations, however plausible they may be, especially within the minimalist conception of UG, still need to be subjected to critical examination. And insofar as they turn out to be wanting, the conclusion we are left with may be that the generalization is due to UG. The minimalist theory of UG, however attractive it may be conceptually and in the light of considerations of language evolution, is still far from established. Even without specified parameters, UG may turn out to be, after all, an irreducibly rich system of categories and conditions on operations and representations which are not learnt by experience and which have no application outside language, and are therefore part of UG.

References

Ambridge, B., Pine, J. M. and Lieven, E. 2014. 'Child language acquisition: Why universal grammar doesn't help', *Language (Perspectives)* 90: 53–90.

Baker, M. 1988. *Incorporation: a theory of function changing.* University of Chicago Press.

1996. *The polysynthesis parameter.* Oxford University Press.

2003. *Lexical categories: Verbs, nouns and adjectives.* Cambridge University Press.

---

[14] See also Ambridge, Pine and Lieven (2014), Pérez-Leroux and Kahnemuyipour (2014), Schütze, Sprouse and Caponigro (2015) for a debate of the grammatical or cognitive basis for certain island constraints. Ambridge, Pine and Lieven (2014) argue that some instances of Subjacency can be explained as effects of a principle of information structure which, they claim, is in principle learnable. In terms of the Chomskyan three factors they would therefore be F2 effects. This is contested by Pérez-Leroux and Kahnemuyipour (2014) and Schütze, Sprouse and Caponigro (2015). The conclusion, if they are right, would be that the island constraints are F1 effects.

2008. The macroparameter in a microparametric world. In T. Biberauer (ed.), *The limits of syntactic variation*. Amsterdam: John Benjamins, 351–74.

Berwick, R. and Chomsky, N. 2011. 'The biolinguistic program: The current state of its development', in A. M. Di Sciullo and C. Boeckx (eds.), *The biolinguistic enterprise: New perspectives on the evolution and nature of the human language faculty*. Oxford University Press, pp. 19–41.

Berwick, R. C., Pietroski, P., Yankama, B. and Chomsky, N. 2011. 'Poverty of the stimulus revisited', *Cognitive Science* 35: 1207–42.

Berwick, R. C. and Weinberg, A. 1984. *The grammatical basis of linguistics performance: Language use and acquisition*. Cambridge, MA: Bradford Books/MIT Press.

Biberauer, T., Holmberg, A., Roberts, I. and Sheehan, M. 2014. 'Complexity in comparative syntax: The view from modern parametric theory', in F. Newmeyer and L. Preston (eds.), *Measuring grammatical complexity*. Oxford University Press, pp. 103–27.

Biberauer, T. and Richards, M. 2006. 'True optionality: When the grammar doesn't mind', in C. Boeckx (ed.), *Minimalist theorizing*. Amsterdam: John Benjamins, pp. 35–67.

Boeckx, C. 2011. 'Approaching parameters from below', in A. M. Di Sciullo and C. Boeckx (eds.), *The biolinguistic enterprise: New perspectives on the evolution and nature of the human language faculty*. Oxford University Press, pp. 205–21.

Borer, H. 1984. *Parametric syntax: Case studies in Semitic and Romance languages*. Dordrecht: Foris.

Bresnan, J. 2000. 'Optimal syntax', in J. Dekkers, F. van der Leeuw and J. van de Weijer (eds.), *Optimality Theory: Phonology, syntax and acquisition*. Oxford University Press, pp. 334–85.

Bresnan, J. 2001. *Lexical-Functional syntax*. Oxford: Blackwell.

Bresnan, J. and Aissen, J. 2002. 'Optimality and functionality: Objections and refutations', *Natural Language & Linguistic Theory* 20(1): 81–95.

Burton-Roberts, N. 2011. 'On the grounding of syntax and the role of phonology in human cognition', *Lingua* 121: 2089–102.

Burton-Roberts, N. and Poole, G. 2006. 'Virtual conceptual necessity, feature dissociation and the Saussurean legacy in generative grammar', *Journal of Linguistics* 42: 575–628.

Chien, Y.-E. and Wexler, K. 1990. 'Children's knowledge of locality conditions in binding as evidence for the modularity of syntax and pragmatics', *Language Acquisition* 1: 225–95.

Chomsky, N. 1957. *Syntactic structures*. The Hague: Mouton.

1965. *Aspects of the theory of syntax*. Cambridge, MA: MIT Press.

1968. *Language and mind*. New York: Harcourt, Brace & World.

1973. 'Conditions on transformations', in S. Anderson and P. Kiparsky (eds.), *A festschrift for Morris Halle*. New York: Holt, Rinehart & Winston, pp. 232–86.

1977. *Essays on form and interpretation.* New York: North-Holland.

1981. *Lectures on government and binding.* Dordrecht: Foris.

1986. *Knowledge of language: Its nature, origin, and use.* New York: Praeger.

1993. 'A minimalist program for linguistic theory', in K. Hale and J. Keyser (eds.), *The view from Building 20: Essays in Linguistics in honor of Sylvain Bromberger.* Cambridge, MA: MIT Press, pp. 1–52.

1995. *The minimalist program.* Cambridge, MA: MIT Press.

2000. 'Minimalist inquiries: The framework', in R. Martin, D. Michaels and J. Uriagereka (eds.), *Step by step: Essays on minimalist syntax in honor of Howard Lasnik.* Cambridge, MA: MIT Press, pp. 89–156.

2001. 'Derivation by phase', in M. Kenstowicz (ed.), *Ken Hale: A life in language.* Cambridge, MA: MIT Press, pp. 1–53.

2004. 'Beyond explanatory adequacy', in A. Belletti (ed.), *Structures and beyond: The cartography of syntactic structures,* vol. 3. Oxford University Press, pp. 104–13.

2005. 'Three factors in language design', *Linguistic Inquiry* 36: 1–22.

2008. 'On phases', in R. Freidin, C. Otero and M.-L. Zubizarreta (eds.), *Foundational issues in linguistic theory.* Cambridge, MA: MIT Press, pp. 133–66.

2013. 'Problems of projection', *Lingua* 130: 33–49.

Cinque, G. 1999. *Adverbs and functional heads: A crosslinguistic perspective.* New York: Oxford University Press.

Croft, W. 1995. 'Autonomy and functionalist linguistics', *Language* 71: 490–532.

1999. *The diversity of human language construction and its influence on the mental development of the human species,* 2nd rev. edn. Cambridge University Press.

Dahl, Ö. and Velupillai, V. 2011. 'The past tense', in Dryer and Haspelmath (eds.), ch. 66.

Daniel, M. 2011. 'Plurality in independent pronouns', in Dryer and Haspelmath (eds.), ch. 35.

de Villiers, J., Roeper, Th. and Vainikka, A. 1990. 'The acquisition of long-distance rules', in L. Frazier and J. de Villiers (eds.), *Language processing and language acquisition.* Dordrecht: Kluwer, pp. 257–97.

Dixon, R. M. W. 2004. 'Adjective classes in typological perspective', in R. M. W. Dixon and A. Aikhenvald (eds.), *Adjective classes: Across-linguistic typological study.* Oxford University Press, pp. 1–49.

Dryer, M. S. 1988. 'Object-verb order and adjective-noun order: Dispelling a myth', *Lingua* 74: 185–217.

1992. 'The Greenbergian word order correlations', *Language* 68: 81–138.

Dryer, M. S. and Haspelmath, M. (eds.) 2011. *The World atlas of language structures online.* Leipzig: Max Planck Institute for Evolutionary Anthropology (available online at http://wals.info).

Endicott, P., Ho, S. Y. W. and Stringer, C. 2010. 'Using genetic evidence to evaluate four paleoanthropological hypotheses for the timing of

Neanderthal and modern human origins', *Journal of Human Evolution* 59: 87–95.

Everett, D. 2005. 'Cultural constraints on grammar and cognition in Pirahã', *Current Anthropology* 46: 621–46.

2007. 'Cultural constraints on grammar in Pirahã: A reply to Nevins, Pesetsky, and Rodrigues (2007)'. Online: http://ling.auf.net/lingBuzz/000427.

Feeney, A. 2014. 'Language evolution: Constraints on conceptions of a minimalist language faculty', unpublished PhD thesis, Newcastle University.

Fitch, T., Hauser, M. and Chomsky, N. 2005. 'The evolution of the language faculty: Clarificatioons and implications', *Cognition* 97: 179–210.

Fodor, J. D. 1978. 'Parsing strategies and constraints on transformations', *Linguistic Inquiry* 9: 427–73.

1983. 'Phrase structure parsing and the island constraints', *Linguistics and Philosophy* 6: 163–223.

2009. 'Syntax acquisition: An evaluation measure after all?', in M. Piatelli Palmarini, J. Uriagereka and P. Salaburu (eds.), *Of minds and language: The Basque Country encounter with Noam Chomsky*. Oxford University Press, pp. 256–77.

Givón, T. 1979. *On understanding grammar*. New York: Academic Press.

Greenberg, J. 1963. 'Some universals of grammar with particular reference to the order of meaningful elements', in J. Greenberg (ed.), *Universals of language*. Cambridge, MA: MIT Press, pp. 58–90. (Reprinted in I. Roberts (ed.), 2007. *Comparative grammar: Critical concepts*, vol. 1. London: Routledge, pp. 41–74.)

Greenberg, J., Ferguson, Ch. A. and Moravcsik, E. A. (eds.) 1978. *Universals of human language*. Stanford University Press.

Grimshaw, J. 1986. 'Subjacency and the S/S' parameter', *Linguistic Inquiry* 17: 364–9.

Guasti, M. T. 2004. *Language acquisition: The growth of grammar*. Cambridge, MA: MIT Press.

Haspelmath, M., Dryer, M. S., Gil, D. and Comrie, B. (eds.) 2014. *The world atlas of language structures*. Munich: Max Planck Digital Library (available online at http://wals.info/).

Hauser, M., Chomsky, N. and Fitch, T. 2002. 'The faculty of language: What is it, who has it, and how did it evolve?', *Science* 198: 1569–79.

Hauser, M., Yang, C., Berwick, R., Tattersall, I., Ryan, M., Watumull, J., Chomsky, N. and Lewontin, R. 2014. 'The mystery of language evolution', *Frontiers in Psychology* 5: 401.

Hawkins, J. A. 1979. 'Implicational universals as predictors of language change', *Language* 55: 618–48.

1983. *Word order universals*. New York: Academic Press.

1999. 'Processing complexity and filler-gap dependencies across grammars', *Language* 75: 244–85.

Heycock, C. and Kroch, A. 1993. 'Verb movement and the status of subjects: Implications for the theory of licensing', *Groninger Arbeiten zur germanistichen Linguistik* 36: 75–102.

Hinzen, W. and Sheehan, M. 2013. *The philosophy of Universal Grammar.* Oxford University Press.

Hofmeister, P. and Sag, I. 2010. 'Cognitive constraints and island effects', *Language* 86: 366–415.

Hofmeister, L., Casasanto, S. and Sag, I. 2013. 'How do individual cognitive differences relate to acceptability judgements? A reply to Sprouse, Wagers, and Phillips', *Language* 88: 390–400.

Holmberg, A. 2010a. 'Null subject parameters', in T. Biberauer, A. Holmberg, I. Roberts and M. Sheehan (eds.), *Parametric variation: Null subjects in minimalist theory.* Cambridge University Press, pp. 88–124.

2010b. 'Parameters in minimalist theory: The case of Scandinavian', *Theoretical Linguistics* 36: 1–48.

Forthcoming a. 'Linguistic typology', to appear in I. Roberts (ed.), *The Oxford handbook of Universal Grammar.* Oxford University Press.

Forthcoming b. 'The Final-over-Final Constraint in a mixed word order language', in M. Sheehan, A. Holmberg and I. Roberts (eds.), *The Final-over-Final Constraint.* Cambridge, MA: MIT Press.

Holmberg, A. and Roberts, I. 2014. 'Parameters and three factors of language design', in C. Picallo (ed.), *Linguistic variation in the minimalist framework.* Oxford University Press, pp. 61–81.

Hornstein, N. 2009. *A theory of syntax: Minimal operations and universal grammar.* Cambridge University Press.

Horvath, J. 1986. *FOCUS in the theory of grammar and the syntax of Hungarian.* Dordrecht: Foris.

Huang, J. 1982. 'Logical relations in Chinese and the theory of grammar', unpublished PhD thesis, MIT.

Hyams, N. and Wexler, K. 1993. 'On the grammatical basis of null subjects in child language', *Linguistic Inquiry* 24: 421–59.

Kayne, R. 1994. *The antisymmetry of syntax.* Cambridge, MA: MIT Press.

2000. *Parameters and universals.* Oxford University Press.

Kirby, S. and Hurford, J. (2002). 'The emergence of linguistic structure: An overview of the iterated learning model', in A. Cangelosi and D. Parisi (eds.), *Simulating the evolution of language.* London: Springer, pp. 121–48.

Kirby, S. and Christiansen, M. H. 2003. 'From language learning to language evolution', in M. Christiansen and S. Kirby (eds.), *Language evolution.* Oxford University Press, pp. 272–94.

É. Kiss, K. 1987. *Configurationality in Hungarian.* Dordrecht: Reidel.

Kluender, R. 1998. 'On the distinction between strong and weak islands: A processing perspective', in P. Culicover and L. McNally (eds.), *Syntax and semantics*, vol. 29: *The limits of syntax.* New York: Academic Press, pp. 241–79.

Kluender, R. 2004. 'Are subject islands subject to a processing account?', *West Coast Conference on Formal Linguistics (WCCFL)* 23: 101–25.

Kluender, R. and Kutas, M. 1993. 'Subjacency as a processing phenomenon', *Language and Cognitive Processes* 8: 573–633.

Kroch, A. and Taylor, A. 2000. 'Verb-Object order in Early Middle English', in S. Pintzuk, G. Tsoulas and A. Warner (eds.), *Diachronic syntax: Models and mechanisms*. Oxford University Press, pp. 132–63.

Legendre, G., Grimshaw, J. and Vikner, S. (eds.) 2001. *Optimality-Theoretic syntax*. Cambridge, MA: MIT Press.

Lehmann, W. 1973. 'A structural principle of language and its implications', *Language* 49: 47–66.

(ed.) 1978. *Syntactic typology: Studies in the phenomenology of language*. Austin: University of Texas Press.

Lightfoot, D. 1979. *Principles of diachronic syntax*. Cambridge University Press.

McCarthy, J. 2001. *A thematic guide to Optimality Theory*. Cambridge University Press.

McCloskey, J. 1996. 'The scope of verb-movement in Irish', *Natural Language and Linguistic Theory* 14: 47–104.

Nevins, A., Pesetsky, D. and Rodrigues, C. 2009a. 'Pirahã exceptionality: A reassessment', *Language* 85: 355–404.

2009b. 'Evidence and argumentation: A reply to Everett (2009)', *Language* 85: 671–81.

Newmeyer, F. 1998. *Language form and language function*. Cambridge, MA: MIT Press.

Pérez-Leroux, A. T. 1993. *Empty categories and the acquisition of wh-movement*. Amherst, MA: GLSA.

Pérez-Leroux, A. and Kahnemuyipour, A. 2014. 'News, somewhat exaggerated: Commentary on Ambridge, Pine, and Lieven', *Language (Perspectives)* 90: 115–25.

Prince, A. and Smolensky, P. 1993. *Optimality theory: Constraint interaction in generative grammar*. Rutgers University Center for Cognitive Science Technical Report 2.

Ramchand, G. and Svenonius, P. 2008. 'Mapping a parochial lexicon onto a universal smantics', in M. T. Biberauer (ed.), *The limits of syntactic variation*. Amsterdam:John Benjamins, pp. 219–45.

Ritter, E. and Wiltschko, M. 2009. 'Varieties of INFL: TENSE, LOCATION and PERSON', in J. van Craenenbroeck (ed.), *Alternatives to cartography*. Berlin: Mouton de Gruyter, pp. 153–201.

Rizzi, L. 1978. 'Violations of the wh-island constraint and the subjacency condition', in C. Dubisson, D. Lightfoot and Y.-C. Morin (eds.), *Montreal Working Papers in Linguistics* 11: 155–90. (Reprinted in Rizzi, L. 1982. *Issues in Italian syntax*. Dordrecht: Foris, pp. 49–76.)

1982. *Issues in Italian syntax*. Dordrecht: Foris.

1990. *Relativized minimality*. Cambridge, MA: MIT Press.

1997. 'The fine structure of the left periphery', in Liliane Haegeman (ed.), *Elements of grammar*. Dordrecht: Kluwer, pp. 281–337.

Roberts, I. 1993. *Verbs and diachronic syntax: A comparative history of English and French*. Dordrecht: Kluwer.

Roberts, I. and Holmberg, A. 2010. 'Introduction', in T. Biberauer, A. Holmberg, I. Roberts and M. Sheehan (eds.), *Parametric variation: Null subjects in minimalist theory*. Cambridge University Press.

Rodrigues, C. and Sândalo, F. Forthcoming. 'Word order as evidence for recursion in Pirahã', to appear in L. Amaral, M. Maia, A. Nevins and T. Roeper (eds.), *Recursion in Brazilian Languages and Beyond*. Berlin: Springer.

Roeper, T. and de Villiers, J. 1994. 'Lexical links in the wh-chain', in B. Lust, G. Hermon and J. Kornfilt (eds.), *Syntactic theory and first language acquisition: Cross-linguistic perspectives*, vol. II: *Binding, dependencies, and learnability*. Hillsdale, NJ: Erlbaum, pp. 357–90.

Ross, J. R. 1967. 'Constraints on variables in syntax', unpublished PhD thesis, MIT.

Schütze, C., Sprouse, J. and Caponigro, I. 2015. 'Challenges for a theory of islands: A broader perspective on Ambridge, Pine, and Lieven', *Language* 91(2): 31–39.

Sheehan, M. 2013. 'Some Implications of a Copy Theory of Labeling', *Syntax* 16: 362–96.

Sigurðsson, H. Á. 2004. 'Meaningful silence, meaningless sounds', *Linguistic Variation Yearbook* 4: 235–59.

2011a. 'On UG and materialization', *Linguistic Analysis* 37: 367–88.

2011b. 'Uniformity and diversity: A minimalist perspective', *Linguistic Variation* 11: 189–222.

Sprouse, J., Wagers, M. and Phillips, C. 2012. 'A test of the relation between working-memory capacity and syntactic island effects', *Language* 88: 82–123.

Tattersall, I. 1998. *Becoming human: Evolution and human uniqueness*. New York: Harcourt Brace.

2012. *Masters of the planet: The search for human origins*. London: Macmillan.

Terrace, H. 1979. *Nim*. New York: Knopf.

2005. 'Metacognition and the evolution of language', in H. Terrace and J. Metcalfe (eds.), *The missing link in cognition: Origins of self-reflective consciousness*. Oxford University Press, pp. 84–115.

Venneman, Th. 1974. 'Topics, subjects, and word order: From SXV to SVX via TVX', in J. Anderson and C. Jones (eds.), *Historical linguistics*. Amsterdam: North-Holland, pp. 339–76.

1984. 'Typology, universals, and change of language', in J. Fisiak (ed.), *Historical syntax* (Trends in Linguistics: Studies and Monographs 23). Berlin: Mouton, pp. 593–612.

Worden, R. P. 1995. 'A speed limit for evolution', *Journal of Theoretical Biology* 176: 137–52.

14

Abduction

Henning Andersen

14.1 Introduction

Abduction is one of the three cognitive operations – the others being
deduction and induction – that explicate the logical relations between
states of affairs and the generalizations that cover them. *Abduction* often
corresponds to the everyday word explanation. 'Abduction consists in
studying facts and devising a theory to explain them' (Peirce 1931–66:
5.145).[1]

If we believe it is possible to explain changes in language, it is because
we assume that there are reasons for them, or, to be more precise, reasons
for the innovations that give rise to changes.

One aim of an explanatory theory of linguistic change, therefore, should
be to reveal the rational structure of the kinds of innovation that occur in
changes and the kinds of premises from which they are derived.

A particular advantage of such a theory is that it turns attention away
from the level of observation where changes are identified as *faits accomplis*
to the finer-grained level of observation where speakers make innovations, create variations with variable conditioning, alter usage, and
thereby rationally, though mainly unwittingly, bring about changes in
their language.

Such a theory might be best served by concepts and terms that are
systematically and explicitly defined in terms of the elementary logical
operations. It is certainly less well served by notions and terms that are
metaphorical, or which were developed for another science, let alone
terms that appear to deny the rational character of linguistic innovations.
Indeed, only a theory of change with an explicitly rational conceptual
apparatus has a chance of corresponding to the phenomena it is intended
to explicate.

---

[1] References to the works of Charles S. Peirce are to the volume and paragraph in his *Collected papers*.

The need for clear concepts does not mean that it is necessary to change standard terminology in historical linguistics. What it does mean is that with a well-defined more general conceptual framework it will be possible to anchor existing terms unequivocally to the specific concepts that have to be represented. This will make it easier to avoid the constant historical changes in meaning that our terms, like all other words, are subject to and hence, unnecessary and irritating misunderstandings.

In the following pages I will present parts of such a theory of change. A central part of it is an explicit description of the kinds of innovation that occur when languages change and the rational structure of each kind. We will see the different roles played by deduction, induction and abduction, and the different types of premisses involved in these operations, structural, typological and universal.

The layout of the exposition is as follows: §14.2 Abduction in logic; §14.3 Abduction in language change; §14.4 Examples of norm change (§14.4.1) and category change (§14.4.2); §14.5 Conclusion.

14.2   Abduction in Logic

The importance of abductive reasoning – in logic, in the sciences, and in human affairs – was first emphasized in modern times by William Whewell (1837), and was a recurrent topic in the writings and lectures of Charles S. Peirce from the 1860s to his death in 1914. Despite the crucial role of abduction in discovery and its obvious relevance for the philosophy of science, most modern logicians have preferred to continue the centuries-long school tradition of recognizing just the two types of inference that are used in logical proof, deduction and induction (Deutscher 2002: 476). Only the relatively recent, growing interest in the work of Peirce has awakened a theoretical interest in abduction among specialists. It is not surprising that *abduction* has not become an everyday word.

A note on usage. In current informal usage abduction is often (unwittingly) referred to by either of its antonyms *deduction* and *induction* or by the hypernym *inference*, which can refer to any one of the three. *Deduction* is also commonly used for induction. The wobbly oral transmission of this terminology is epitomized by the recent innovations replacing the traditional verb *infer* and noun *inference* with the verb *inference* 'infer' and noun *inferencing* 'inference', mostly equivalent to *abduce* and *abduction*. At the same time, in technical usage *deduction* and *induction* continue to be used in their distinct traditional senses, as does *inference*. Most dictionaries ignore the confused informal usage (this is true also of the usage-oriented *American Heritage Dictionary of the English Language* (Soukharov et al. 1992)); they provide only the technical definitions of *deduction* and *induction* and lack a lemma for Peirce's *abduction*, a term he coined to emphasize its relationship with deduction and induction and to give prominence to this neglected but essential mode of inference.

Deduction, induction and *abduction* are the Latin (or Latinate) renderings of the three modes of inference (Gk. *syllogismós* 'reasoning; inference') recognized by Aristotle: *apodeiktikòs syllogismós* 'demonstrative inference, deduction', *epagōgē* 'induction', and *apagōgē* 'abduction', though in Aristotle's scheme of things *epagōgē* and *apagōgē* name kinds of dialogic reasoning; see just below.

Peirce often uses *hypothesis* as a synonym of *abduction*, in both its senses: (i) the process of forming an abductive inference; and (ii) the result of an abductive inference, the proposition (or state of affairs), the CASE in (1). Elsewhere, *hypothesis* may refer to the generalization (or RULE) that is the point of departure in deduction, is verified or invalidated in induction, and is explicitly or implicitly invoked in abduction. In 1898 (Ketner and Putnam 1992: 140) Peirce reports his view, based on supposed parallelisms in Aristotle's descriptions in the *Prior Analytics*, that the proper translation of *apagōgē* is *retroduction*, a term he then prefers to its synonym *abduction*; for the relevant text, see *epagōgē* at 68b15–37, *apagōgē* at 69a20–36 (Ross 1949). The literal meaning of *apagōgē* is 'leading away' (adopted by Smith 1989: 100); this seems opaque, but actually it is no more opaque than *abduction*. Ross (1949: 489) explicates *apagōgē* as 'reduction from one problem to another'. He states that it plays a large role in scientific discovery and was prominent in Greek mathematics. 'In fact it may be said to be the method of mathematical discovery, as distinct from mathematical proof' (1949: 490). Peirce voices the same view in numerous places.

In 1868 (2.623) Peirce illustrates the distinct modes of inference of the figures of the syllogism, employing three identical propositions; see (1). To show the different roles of premisses and conclusion (marked ∴) in each, he labels the propositions *rule, case*, and *result*.[2]

(1)

DEDUCTION	INDUCTION
RULE: All the beans in this bag are white.	CASE: These beans are from this bag.
CASE: These beans are from this bag.	RESULT: These beans are white.
∴RESULT: These beans are white.	∴RULE: All the beans in this bag are white.

HYPOTHESIS (ABDUCTION)
RESULT: These beans are white.
RULE: All the beans in this bag are white.
∴CASE: These beans are from this bag.

In Deduction, what is inferred (RESULT) follows with necessity from the RULE (the major premiss) and the CASE (the minor premiss). If the proposition of the RULE is probable, that of the conclusion is probable as well.

Induction assumes that the particular observed CASE and RESULT (minor premisses) are representative of the entire class to which they belong (see

---

[2] The beans referred to in each CASE are a handful. In the RULES I have replaced Peirce's 'from' with 'in', which makes better sense in contemporary English.

footnote 2) and infers a general RULE. Peirce distinguishes several kinds of induction, primarily quantitative induction, which is based on statistical sampling, and qualitative induction, which is based on the evaluation of practical experiences of different kinds and of varying weight (2.756). Note that both quantitative and qualitative types of induction involve subsidiary premises (assumptions) regarding sample size, weighting, and the like.

Abduction is the process of forming an explanatory hypothesis. It is the only logical operation which introduces any new idea; for Induction does nothing but determine a value (true or false), and Deduction merely evolves the necessary consequences of a pure hypothesis (6.475). Note that the term *hypothesis* is used both about the Abductive conclusion (the CASE) and about the general RULE (major premiss) that is explicitly or implicitly invoked in an abductive conclusion.

Briefly, '[d]eduction proves that something must be; Induction shows that something really is [or is not] so; Abduction merely suggests that something may be. Its only justification is that from its suggestion Deduction can draw a prediction which can be tested by Induction, and that, if we are ever to learn anything or to understand phenomena at all, it must be by Abduction that this is brought about' (5.171).

More often than not abductive inference appears to be based simply on an observed state of affairs. As Peirce puts it: 'The surprising fact C is observed. But if A were the case, C would be a matter of course. Hence, there is reason to suspect that A is true [where A is an antecedent and C, a consequent; H.A.]' (5.189). But behind this Abduction is an implicit RULE: If A, then C.

As an example, consider (2).

(2)   We were driving through Centerville and decided to drop in on our friends on Elm Street. When we got there, to our surprise, there was no light on in their house [C]. Our first thought was that they had gone to bed [A_1]. But it was barely past 9 p.m. They might be out on the town [A_2] or visiting friends [A_3]. Or perhaps they were away on vacation [A_4].

Each of these abductive guesses was a reasonable explanation of the surprising fact C. Each was based on implicit cultural knowledge (RULES). And each introduced into the characters' deliberations some new information, information they had not imagined when they turned down Elm Street, and which was hypothetical and quite insecure.[3]

The example shows some important characteristics of abduction.

First, an abductive conclusion explicitly or implicitly invokes a generalization. But often a given explanandum might be the consequent of any of

---

[3] The reader may find it surprising that the characters in (2) would go visiting at 9 p.m. if they were on their way somewhere else [C] but can probably easily propose a plausible explanation [A].

several antecedents, that is, several other generalizations might be invoked, as here *If A_1 (or A_2, A_3, A_4) then C.* To that extent the abductive conclusion is insecure. It may be a good guess, but one of several possible such. However, each of these Abductions might include premises conducive to making the conclusion more likely right; e.g. A_2 might be strengthened by the premiss that their friends hate cooking or love the vibrant local pub-scene. Conducive premises are important in grammar formation.

Second, an abductive conclusion may be based on an already established generalization, as in (2). But it may also posit a novel connection between an observed state of affairs and a proposed antecedent, in effect positing a new generalization, rule, or law. This may not be so common in everyday human affairs, but all advances in science – and all innovations in the transmission of language – depend on the creativity manifested in such Abductions.

Third, if our characters tried to verify one of the proposed explanatory hypotheses (A_1, A_2, A_3 or A_4), say, by asking their friends' neighbours, they might discover that the dark house, which they took to be a consequent in need of explanation, was in fact an antecedent: their friends had problems with the electrical installations in their house (*A*) and decided to move into a motel for the night (*C*). This last point illustrates an essential feature of both Abduction and Induction, viz. that the first step in both is to decide whether a given particular – here, the dark house – is an antecedent or the consequent. This decision is itself a matter of Abduction, it is an initial procedural assumption, a meta-Abduction, if you will.

In other words, leaving our Centerville example, after a surprising fact is observed, an Abduction posits whether it is an antecedent (CASE) or a consequent (RESULT) and, if the latter, another Abduction hypothesizes an explanatory antecedent (CASE). Deduction applies the implied RULE to new CASES, predicting RESULTS. Induction evaluates whether these are similar to the RESULT that was observed initially. It operates against a background of initial Abductions; see Ketner and Putnam (1992: 67):

> inductive reasoning always requires the presence of assumptions about the general course of the world ... Those assumptions, in Peirce's view, themselves come from Retroduction [Abduction; H.A.], and are thus not knowledge but hypotheses which are 'provisionally adopted'. It is the making of hypotheses and not the empiricist's beloved 'induction' that makes empirical knowledge possible.

In his 1898 Cambridge Lectures Peirce returns to the three figures of the syllogism (1), integrating into a formal account of them the role that is played by probability; for an analysis, see Ketner and Putnam (1992: 60–7). Peirce comments:

> I first gave this theory in 1867, improving it slightly in 1868. In 1878 I gave a popular account of it in which I rightly insisted upon the radical distinction between Induction and Retroduction [Abduction; H.A.]. In 1883,

I made a careful restatement with considerable improvement. But I was led away by trusting to the perfect balance of logical breadth and depth into the mistake of treating Retroduction as a kind of Induction. Nothing I observe is as insidious as a tendency to suppose symmetry to be exact ... In 1892 I gave a good statement of the rationale of Retroduction but still failed to perceive the radical difference between this and Induction, although earlier it had been clear enough to my mind. *(141)*

The key issue in distinguishing Induction and Abduction is whether or to what extent an Inductive conclusion based on observed particulars can legitimately imply or include additional assumptions, i.e. further, hypothetical premises, without being Abductive. Note the powerlessness of strict Induction: From a sample of possible *As* and *Cs* we can inductively conclude only that there is a correlation between two sets of data. It requires an initial abductive guess to regard one set as antecedent and the other as consequent, and even then all we can logically conclude from actual observation is that 'Some *As* have *Cs*', which may not be worth much. If we conclude that 'All *As* have *Cs*', as in Peirce's 1868 example of Induction in (1), we are going way beyond the data. Peirce resolved this issue by noting that Deduction and Induction both refer to determinate proportional universes, and that for both, a degree of probability must be stated. Abduction, by contrast, does not involve probability:

We see three types of reasoning. The first figure embraces all Deduction whether necessary or probable. By means of it we predict the special results of the general course of things, and calculate how often they will occur in the long run. A definite probability always attaches to the Deductive conclusion because the mode of inference is necessary. The third figure is Induction by means of which we ascertain how often in the ordinary course of experience one phenomenon will be accompanied by another. No definite probability attaches to the Inductive conclusion such as belongs to the Deductive conclusion; but we can calculate how often Inductions of a given structure will attain a given degree of precision. The second figure of reasoning is Retroduction [Abduction; H. A.]. Here, not only is there no definite probability to the conclusion, but no definite probability attaches even to the mode of inference. We can only say that Economy of Research prescribes that we should at a given stage of our inquiry try a given hypothesis, and we are to hold to it provisionally as long as the facts will permit. There is no probability about it. It is a mere suggestion that we tentatively adopt.

For example, in the first steps that were made toward the reading of the cuneiform inscriptions, it was necessary to make up hypotheses which nobody could have expected to turn out true, – for no hypothesis positively likely to be true could be made. But they had to be provisionally adopted – yes, and clung to with some degree of tenacity, too, – as long as the facts did not absolutely refute them. For that was the system by which in the long run such problems would quickest find their solution. *(141–2)*

The quotation and its example draw attention to the central role of Abduction in scientific method. Peirce quotes Whewell (1837: 6), who noted that 'progress in science depends upon the observation of the right facts by minds furnished with appropriate ideas' (6.604). He emphasizes the crucial role for the inquiring mind of those ideas that are provided by 'the natural light of reason', what Galileo called '*il lume naturale*' (1.80). This is in essence an instinct (1.630), for '[u]nless man have a natural bent in accordance with nature's, he has no chance of understanding nature at all' (6.477) (see Feibleman 1970 *passim*; Burch 2014 *passim*).

In logical terms, this is tantamount to pointing to the innate major premisses that are tacitly employed in Abductive reasoning, principles for coping with the unforseen that must have evolved through our long association with the world in which we live.

In human culture, and specifically in language transmission, we can assume, these fundamental major premisses are supplemented with more specific ones evolved to enable us to acquire the cultural and linguistic knowledge needed in human societies.

14.3   Abduction in Language

Obviously the transmission of grammar does not depend on newcomers to a speech community having the creative genius of a Galileo.

But it seems right to recognize the creativity of speakers – as innovators who create new signs and devise new uses for existing signs (§14.3.4.1); as participants in the negotiation of community norms of usage, who exercise their free will in following or breaching the norms (§14.3.4.3); and, first and last, as language learners who create mental grammars for themselves and employ them to re-create the usage of their community language (§14.3.4.2) (Andersen 2006: 81–5). These are aspects of language transmission that would not be possible without the speakers' innate capacity for abductive inference.

To appreciate the importance of this creativity for language change one has to look at change in what I call the close-up view (§14.3.3). It brings the observer face to face with details that usually escape attention in the customary wide-angle and basic-level views (§§14.3.1–2.2). Most important of all, the close-up view raises questions about speakers' abductions and the premisses from which they are derived.

14.3.1   The Wide-Angle View: Macrochanges

In the wide-angle view, internally motivated (endogenous) macro-changes such as grammaticalization (see Chapter 1, this volume) or typological drift and externally motivated (exogenous) macrochanges (see Chapter 23, this volume) such as koinéization or the formation of language alliances (*Sprachbünde*) exemplify long-term developmental continuities.

For its interpretation, each such development needs to be resolved into its constituent change events (§14.3.2). Grammaticalization, for instance, consists of a grammation or regrammation that may be followed by morphosyntactic bond-strengthening changes and expression-reduction changes (Heine 2003: 578), types of changes that also occur independently of (re)grammation and of one another (Andersen 2008: 16–31). Typological drift, e.g. the development of head–dependent harmony works its way through the syntax of a language, phrase type by phrase type (Ledgeway 2012). Viewed at this level of resolution, macrochanges only occasionally shed light on aspects of language transmission.

14.3.2 The Basic-Level View: Change Events

In the basic-level view, most typical of language histories, the focus is on the changing grammar. Most often no distinction is made between the covert innovations in grammar and their overt actualizations in speech (see Chapter 19, this volume). As a consequence, changes are portrayed as if consecutive grammars were continuous, and when a change has been defined an explanation for it is sought in the grammar itself.

Some historical linguists operate with the notions reanalysis (see Chapter 4, this volume) and actualization. Thus, in Timberlake's (1977: 141) account, once a reanalysis has occurred, its actualization is 'the gradual mapping out of its structural consequences' in one environment after another. In other words, the reanalysis is actualized in the grammar; similarly Harris and Campbell (1995: 77–81).

In the close-up view, reanalysis is covert, and actualization is overt. When these terms are used to refer to the more abstract basic-level view they will be capitalized as *Reanalysis* and *Actualization*.

14.3.3 The Close-Up View: Subchanges

In this perspective, changes are resolved into the different alterations of grammars and usage by which they come about.

We can distinguish (i) primary innovations and (ii) their actualization in speech; (iii) their adoption by other speakers and (iv) actualization in those speakers' usage; (v) their integration in new learners' grammars and (vi) actualization in the new learners' speech.

The subchanges (i)–(vi) are the categories of innovation through which a change comes about. They are not discrete events, but overlap in time in the sense that a primary innovation may be made by many speakers at different times, and adopted at different times and only with time be acquired by new learners.

The most important parts of this brief formula are the primary innovations (§§14.3.4.1–2), the process of their adoption by other speakers (§14.3.4.3), and that of their integration in the grammars of new speakers (§14.3.4.4).

14.3.4 Primary Innovations

There appear to be three kinds of primary innovation, neologism, extension, and reanalysis.

14.3.4.1 Neologism and Extension

Neologism. Neologism is the creation of new signs or sign elements. Common in lexis, it is perhaps not as unusual in syntax as may appear. Harris and Campbell (1995: 54) recognize neologism under the label 'exploratory constructions'. But they also show that neologisms in sentence syntax arise from 'universally available syntactic constructions', in essence, pragmatic devices that clarify syntactic relations or highlight individual elements of information.

Extension. As a general term, extension is the creation of new uses for existing signs; it increases the semantic breadth of a lexical or grammatical element or its functional scope, or the privileges of occurrence of an element or class of elements. The opposites are semantic narrowing, scope diminution, and curtailment. Extension and curtailment can be complementary processes, as when one member of a paradigm (selectional set) is extended and its counterpart curtailed; common examples are norm changes, where one covariant gains while the other loses extension.

Both neologism and extension innovations presuppose some command of a grammar. This is true even of the neologisms and extensions that occur in children's speech, which exemplify derivation from both universal and language particular premises. In this respect both neologisms and extensions are deductive innovations. But they are created to solve specific communicative problems, which the speaker evaluates abductively; and such a problem might have several more or less felicitous solutions. In this regard neologism and extension are abductive, and with all abductions they share a degree of fallibility.

14.3.4.2 Reanalysis

There are five topics under this heading: reanalysis, actuation, revision, norm change and usage updating.

1. Reanalysis. The term is ambiguous between (i) the fresh analysis of a grammar which is produced by every new speaker and (ii) innovative reanalysis (Timberlake 1977: 142). *Reanalysis* is mostly used in sense (ii), which I adopt here. Where sense (i) is needed I use the neologism *grammanalysis* (§14.3.4.4).

As a primary innovation, reanalysis is the result of abduction. The grounds for reanalysis are typically a surface ambiguity (Andersen 1973: 774; Timberlake 1977: 148; Harris and Campbell 1995: 70) or preliminary, incomplete speech data (Joseph and Janda 2003: 474; see §§14.4.1–3.2). The tradition labels such reanalyses *imperfect learning, misanalysis, misconstrual, misinterpretation, misparsing, misperception*, oblivious to the fact that for the speakers there is no 'correct' analysis, and missing the important insight that every innovation springs from learners' creativity.

Reanalyses reflect the procedures speakers use in grammanalysis, e.g. in syntax, dividing strings of expressions into constituents, assigning content, function, and syntactic properties to constituents, and ranking the identified constructions and elements in their respective paradigms. To the extent that a reanalysis is consistent with already analysed elements of the grammar, the premises from which the abductive conclusion is derived may include structural, typological, or pragmatic properties of the language. In any case, every reanalysis must reflect universal properties of the speakers' 'language acquisition device', the 'laws of language' (Andersen 1973: 78), as well as learners' 'operating principles' (Slobin 1985: 228). Just as a reanalysis may depend on the learners' previous analyses, so young learners' capacity for language is subject to maturation changes. Only the study of reanalysis at this level of observation can clarify the interplay of these diverse premises.

2. Actuation. Reanalysis as described above is the best known source of change. But it is important to recognize that reanalyses can create regularities out of mere fluctuation in usage, as when free variation is interpreted as conditioned (by grammatical or pragmatic variables). Such reanalyses create order where there was none before. They produce grammatical, stylistic, or social indexes; hence their outcome can be understood as a semiotization of variation. The effect of such 'spontaneous innovations' is to actuate change. In phonology, they give rise to subphonemic regularities (allophonic variation), which may eventuate in sound change (Andersen 1989: 21). A syntactic example is mentioned in §14.4.1.

3. Revision. A learner's Inductive observation of additional speech data may motivate (abductive) revision of an initial reanalysis and produce an analysis that enables the speaker to emulate the model usage more closely. Or the initial reanalysis may be retained but supplemented by the (abductive) formation of a usage rule with a similar effect (Andersen 1973: 773; Timberlake 1977: 142; Andersen 2001b: 236; Janda and Joseph 2003: 76). In this case the result is that the unamended primary innovation is not actualized or is not fully actualized in the learners' speech.

This view of reanalysis and revision offers an explanation for the fact that changes can arise in homogeneous speech communities. It allows for the possibility that the same innovation is made by several individuals, and that the innovative primary innovation may be covered up (i.e. remain virtual) or actualized differently in the speech of different speakers. Thus, it may result in a random distribution of innovated elements in learners' usage. Some such fluctuating deviations from regular usage are probably observable at all times.

The account suggested here posits two layers of grammar, (i) a base grammar comprising the system of productive rules and (ii) usage rules that capture current variation (Andersen 1973; Timberlake 1977: 142; Andersen 2001b). The division has observable reflexes in the form of breaches of the norms including hypercorrections. These are deviations from received usage that can be observed, and are experienced by speakers, in every change in progress.

4. Norm change. Usage rules too are subject to reanalysis. Innovations can alter the values (index content) assigned to existing grammatical, stylistic and social variables. These are the values that define individual speakers' perception of (and attitude to) current variation, and which, on a community scale in the long run, determine the fate of variations (Sapir 1921: 155; Andersen 1990; 2001a: 45; 2006: 79).

5. Usage updating. Throughout their lives speakers can revise their usage rules, adjusting to changing ambient usage (perceived norms). In historical documentation such usage adjustments may be reflected in texts written by the same writer at different times; see §14.4.1.

14.3.4.3 Adoption

Reanalysis is covert. It is only when the consequences of a reanalysis are actualized in usage that they, and the reanalysis they imply, can be passively accepted or actively adopted. Adoption is essentially abductive in relation to the observed innovative usage, and its premisses necessarily include elements of the adopting speaker's grammar. It is abductive also in relation to the values that are to be ascribed to the innovation and its covariant(s). Adoption is the type of innovation by which speakers promote and propagate primary innovations in their speech community and, through their various usage, negotiate and collectively determine the conditions of use of given innovated forms (Andersen 1989: 24; Thomsen 2006a: 324).

Traditionally adoption has been explained by differences in prestige, minimally by the different roles played by leaders and followers in social networks (Milroy 1992). A simpler, more general account is Coseriu's (1957: 78), who characterizes 'adoption for use' as speakers learning from one another; like Milroy he emphasizes the communicative-functional aspect of adoption. The rational complexity of adoption is entirely missed by linguists who think it is just a kind of imitation; thus Labov (2001), who cites Tarde (1903).

14.3.4.4 Grammanalysis

Whereas Adoption serves to spread innovations community-wide, the grammanalysis of new speakers integrates innovated elements with received elements in their individual grammars. Such restructurings are grammar innovations that do not produce innovations in usage. Their outcome is a continuity of usage.

14.3.5 Coda

The practice and terminology of historical linguistics suggest several ways of classifying changes: according to the elements that change; according to the kinds of change; according to the layers of structure involved; according to the sociolingual context.

1. The first division distinguishes changes in content (category), content syntax (scope, dependency), expression, and expression syntax (morphosyntax).
2. Second, there are neologisms, extensions, and reanalyses, types of change that are named for the primary innovations (§§14.3.4.1–2) in which they originate.
3. The layers of structure traditionally recognized are the norms (variable rules of usage), the system of productive grammar rules, and the type, the set of typological parameters reflected in the grammatical system.
4. The basic division according to sociolingual contexts is into endogenous and exogenous changes.

   In the preceding sections I have focused on the different perspectives in which we observe and try to account for changes, and especially on what can be observed or inferred in the close-up view.

14.4 Examples

The following pages present two simple examples of syntactic change. Their main purpose is to illustrate the differences between superficial description, structural interpretation, and the close-up view in which one can logically form hypotheses about the rational bases of speakers' contributions to the initiation and advancement of changes.

   In addition the examples illustrate different grounds for reanalysis, the kinds of premises on which reanalyses can be based, and some of the operating principles employed in grammar formation.

14.4.1 Norm Change

Our first example sketches the central part of a development in Polish (Rittel 1975), described from distinct perspectives in Andersen (1987, 1990).

It was initiated before 1500 and has been realized through innumerable minor norm adjustments throughout the subsequent centuries.

Background. In Medieval Polish, the inherited, auxiliated perfect ('be' + '*l*-participle') comes to be used in the functions of the simple preterites, the aorist and imperfect. These go out of use, as does the pluperfect, which had been formed with the imperfect-tense auxiliary. Once the simple preterites are gone, the clitic present-tense auxiliary has no tense function in combination with the *l*-participle; its forms are reanalysed as mere person and number (P&N) markers, and the *l*-participles of the earlier perfect are reanalysed as finite preterite forms ('*l*-forms'), which continue to show subject agreement in gender and number. The P&N clitics are Wackernagel clitics and undergo expression reduction. This is roughly the stage at which the continuous attestation of Polish begins.

Polish at that time had and still has pragmatic word order; hence the information structure of a sentence determined the position of the finite verb. A preterite in sentence-initial position could naturally be directly followed by a clitic P&N marker. If a preterite form was given prominence anywhere else in the sentence, it would tend to host the P&N marker.

The change. The change is a morphosyntactic bond-strengthening (Andersen 2008). From the 1500s to the present, Polish texts show a statistically gradual shift of the P&N markers from the second-position clitic chain to postverbal position anywhere in the clause (see Table 14.1). The P&N markers are agglutinated to preterite forms (a) earlier if first person than if second person; (b) earlier if singular than if plural; (c) earlier in main clauses than in subordinate clauses; (d) earlier in asyndetic clauses than in clauses with a conjunction; and (e) earlier when the first-position constituent is a lexical noun than when it is a pronoun. Each of these gradations is attested (f) earlier and more fully in prose than in poetry; (g) earlier in expository than in artistic prose; (h) more widely in casual than in formal style; and (i) through the 1900s more frequently in speech than in writing (see Table 14.2).

Table 14.1 *Gradual shift of P&N markers from clitic to suffix position: statistics*

	No. tokens	Deviations from 2nd position		Agglutination to l-form	
1500	580	12	2%	130	23%
1600	1303	64	4%	649	49%
1700	1439	62	4%	994	68%
1800	1988	308	15%	1395	80%
1900	3325	503	15%	2817	84%
Expository prose	569	usual		525	92%

Table 14.2 *Gradual shift of P&N markers from clitic to suffix position: conditioning*

		Earlier	Later
(a)	Gramcats	1st person	2nd person
(b)		singular	plural
(c)	Grounding	main clause	embedded clause
(d)		asyndetic	syndetic
(e)		initial lexical noun	initial pronoun
(f)	Genre	prose	poetry
(g)		expository	artistic
(h)	Style	casual	formal
(i)	Medium	speech	writing

Note that of the conditioning categories in this development, (a)–(b) are morphosyntactic categories, (c)–e) are grounding categories, (f)–(g) are genre categories, (h) is a distinction between styles and (i), between media. The only generalization that these data will support appears to be that throughout this long drawn-out development, which began some six hundred years ago, unmarked environments have been hospitable to placement innovations earlier than the corresponding marked environments (Andersen 1990, 2001a). In Modern Polish P&N markers are preterite suffixes. In older styles – familiar to many Poles mainly from literature – the P&N suffixes occasionally occur in *tmesis* ('separation' from the verb), typically as part of the second-position clitic chain.

Structural interpretation. Since the 1500s, there is metrical evidence that *l*-form + (singular) P&N marker combinations had undergone prosodic univerbation (Topolińska 1961: 30). Observe the penultimate stress in the synonymous (3a–b) (stressed vowels underlined).

(3)   a. *wczoraj=em*.1SG   *przyszed-ł*
             yesterday I   arrived
       b. *wczoraj przyszed-ł-em*.1SG

Also since the 1500s there are attestations of innovated preterite forms of obstruent-stem verbs with a P&N marker attached to a bound preterite stem instead of the inherited free stem alternant: inherited combinations of the type *nióstem*.1SG.M 'carried' (i.e. *niós-ł=em*, cf. *niós-ł-Ø*. M.3SG) give way to the modern type *nioslem* (i.e. *nios-ł-em*), which has the same bound stem *nios-ł-* as feminine, neuter, and plural *l*-forms, e.g. *nios-ł-a-*.F.SG *nios-ł-y-*.F.PL. The replacement of free by bound stem alternants is additional evidence that the P&N markers already in the 1500s were evaluated as suffixes that needed a bound stem as host. These innovations make it possible to understand the entire unwavering drift towards suffixation during the many centuries since the 1500s as a structural Actualization.

The close-up interpretation. There are two changes: A. The purely expression-syntactic development from clitic to affix. B. The morphophonemic stem change in obstruent stems.

A. There are three ways of interpreting this change. (a) The inconsistent placement of P&N markers was ambiguous and was reanalysed as suffixation with variant *tmesis*. (b) As soon as the former auxiliaries were reanalysed as P&N markers, they were ambiguous between clitic and suffix whenever they were postposed to an *l*-form, and they were reanalysed as suffixes. The stem + P&N-suffix pattern in other verbal paradigms (present tense, imperative, subjunctive) and perhaps the many other suffixing inflectional categories of the language would be structural premises in such reanalyses and would indicate their status of suffixes. (c) Alternatively, as soon as the former auxiliaries were reanalysed as P&N markers they would be suffixes by typological implication. In any case, generation after generation of speakers would analyse the P&N markers as verbal suffixes and their preposed placement as *tmesis* conditioned by a number of marked features captured by usage rules. Suffixed *l*-forms would naturally receive penultimate stress (see (3)). Cohort after cohort would acquire the synchronic status quo and allow a wider, unmarked placement of the P&N markers in their own usage, producing a gradually increasing use of suffixation and declining use of *tmesis*. There are examples of usage updating (§14.3.4.2.5) from the 1800s in some writers' corrections of manuscripts and proofs of their own work (Rittel 1975: 71).

B. The reanalysis of the P&N markers as suffixes was covert, and it had no observable effect in the preterites of most verb classes. But in the class of obstruent-stem verbs it was actually contradicted by inherited combinations of obstruent-stem + 1sg or 2sg marker: The masculine singular stem underwent a morphophonological rule before clitics ('devoicing sandhi' in north and 'voicing sandhi' in south Polish). The effects of this rule clearly identified such combinations as free form + clitic; see (4a).

(4)   a. OPol. *plótłem*.1sg.m 'braided', *wiódłem*.1sg.m 'led'
        North: *plót-ł=em* [plutem], *wiód-ł=em* [v ʲutem]
        South: *plót-ł=em* [pludem], *wiód-ł=em* [vʲudem]
    b. ModPol. *plot-ł-em* [plotwem], *wiod-ł-em* [vʲodwem]

These inherited combinations were by-passed by innovated word forms of a bound stem variant + suffix; see (4b). This morphosyntactic innovation, an extension of the unmarked stem alternant, has since been repeated for all obstruent-stem verbs. Readily adopted, these unmarked suffixal wordforms have long since been generalized in the dialects on which standard Polish is based.

14.4.2   Category Change and Rebracketing

The typical syntactic Reanalysis is an innovative interpretation of functional categories. Consider the textbook example in (5) (Anttila [1972] 1989: 103; Timberlake 1977: 141–57; Campbell and Harris 1995: 77–9).

The change. There is a phonological change in older Finnish: $m > n$ /—#. As a consequence ACC.SG (earlier -*m*) becomes identical with GEN.SG (-*n*) in nouns; see (5a–c). In object clauses governed by verbs of sensation and thinking, the ambiguous -*n* (earlier ACC.SG) is Reanalysed as GEN.SG (5d). This covert innovation can be inferred from a subsequent change in case marking in pronouns and plural nouns: the Actualization of the change is accompanied by loss of agreement in the participle (5d–e).

(5)   a. **näe-m   poja-m   menevä-m*
      b. *näe-n   poja-n   menevä-n*
          see.1SG boy.ACC.SG go.PTCP.ACC.SG
          'I see the boy go by'
      c. *näe-n   poja-t   menevä-t*
          see.1SG boy.ACC.PL go.PTCP.ACC.PL
      d. *näe-n   poja-n   menevä-n*
          see.1SG boy.GEN.SG go.INV.PTCP
          'I see the boy go by'
      e. *näe-n   pojkien   menevän*
          see.1SG boy.GEN.PL go. INV.PTCP

Structural interpretation. The change is a regrammation (Andersen 2008). The diachronic data set two challenges: how to interpret the grammatical innovation and how to understand its actualization.

In Timberlake's interpretation, which is adopted by Harris and Campbell, Old Finnish had a rule of subject-to-object raising: subjects of certain embedded clauses were treated as matrix clause objects; like all objects they would be in the accusative by default, but in the partitive if the matrix clause was negated, and in the nominative if the clause had no nominative subject; the embedded-clause participle would agree with its object-marked subject. The Reanalysis consisted in changing the object marking to genitive and abandoning participial agreement. Timberlake considers the superficial ambiguity of the case markers (-*n*) a necessary cause of the innovation, but is at a loss to point to a sufficient cause. He ponders whether some superordinate principle would require genitive marking; if so, the change in the grammatical system could be viewed as an Actualization of this higher principle, in line with Coseriu's (1968) – and Sapir's (1921) – understanding that changes in the system of a language may actualize features of its type.

It seems better to take the surface data of Old Finnish at face value, as does Anttila ([1972] 1989: 103). There is no evidence that a subject-to-object rule applied in these embedded clauses. But the matrix verbs in question were transitive, hence direct object nouns would be marked with the requisite object case. The direct object was identical to the subject of a participial clause (a reduced relative clause); this subject was deleted and the active participle was in apposition to and agreed with its head, the direct object. This is a construction well known from other languages, whether with deleted participial subject, or with explicit subject in a relative clause; cf. the former in OCS ... *ašte vidiši človeka ... pridǫšta* 'if you see a man come (lit. coming)' (Vaillant 1964: 343), MHG *ich sah ihn gehend*, OFr. *je le voyois allant*, both: 'I saw him go (lit. going)', and the latter in Fr. *je le voyais qui s'en allait* 'I saw him go (lit. I saw him who was going)'. The two constructions in (5b–c) vs (5d–e) differ in structure. In [*saw → the boy → going*] the participle is in apposition to its direct-object head *the boy*, whereas in [*saw → [the boy's → going*]], the direct object is a determiner phrase with *the boy's* as determiner and *going* a deverbal nominal. The determiner status of the semantic subject is expressed by possessive suffixes in clauses with identical subject in matrix and embedded clause: *Luulee=ko hän$_i$ tulevan-sa$_i$* lit. 'thinks.Q he$_i$ coming-his$_i$' vs *Luulee=ko hän$_i$ hänen$_j$ tulevan* lit. 'thinks.Q he$_i$ his$_j$ coming', both meaning 'does he$_i$ think he$_{i/j}$'ll be coming?'.

The close-up interpretation. It appears this was a premature reanalysis (§14.3.4.2.1), made on the basis of singular nouns alone, before the accusative endings of pronouns and plural nouns were understood or appreciated. If it reveals some bias against these 'adverse' data, maybe it was favoured by analytic assumptions such as these: (i) where possible, assume the semantic subject of a clause is not an immediate constituent of another clause; (ii) where possible, if a functor operates on a whole structure, try to place it external to that structure; (iii) where possible, assume that there is a tight syntactic bond between any semantic subject and its predicate. These three operating principles (Slobin 1985: 228) would explain the reanalysis. For by identifying the ambiguous case as genitive, the reanalysis cast the former main-clause direct object as embedded-clause subject. Thereby the embedded predication as a whole became the main-clause direct object, and the loose apposition was replaced with a tighter determiner phrase.

In any case it appears the reanalysis was made on the basis of singular nouns alone. This forced learners who made or adopted this reanalysis to formulate suitable usage rules to conform to received usage, 'a complicated and detailed list of subrules which matched specific contexts with specific cases' (Timberlake 1977: 152). The effects of these were gradually scaled back as community usage allowed the (unmarked) genitive covariants to occur in more and more environments. Also the agreement in the inflected participle gradually gave way to the uninflected covariant.

Table 14.3 *Variables in the Actualization of the Finnish category change*

	Earlier	Later
Nominals	pronouns	nouns
	singular nouns	plural nouns
	animate nouns	inanimate nouns
	agentive animates	nonagentive animates
Lexical verbs	large, open class	small, closed class

The gradual changes in the norms are reflected across several dimensions. (a) Genitive case marking had already spread to pronouns in the 1600s and spread to plural nouns later, perhaps to animates before inanimates, the Actualization running its course by the end of the 1900s (Timberlake 1977: 153). (b) Already in the 1600s there are examples indicating that as the traditional case usage was replaced with genitive marking, active participles lost agreement and became invariable (Timberlake 1977: 154). (c) The Reanalysis affected not only objects of the large class of verbs of sensation and thinking, but also objects of a small, closed class of verbs including *antaa* 'give, let', *sallia* 'permit', *käskeä* 'order'. In these verbs, the development was slower, genitive having become obligatory in pronouns, but not entirely in plural nouns, where – as recently as the 1970s – it was described as obligatory for agentive, but not for non-agentive nouns (Timberlake 1977: 155). The gradations are summed up by Table 14.3 (Timberlake 1977: 157).

14.5 Conclusion

Additional examples could illustrate a greater variety of grounds for reanalysis, of structural and typological premises, and of the universal premisses expressed as learners' operating principles. Also the grammatical and pragmatic categories that variably condition the gradual process of change could be better exemplified. The number of variables known for these two changes may seem ample, but note that the Polish one does not include information about possible lexical conditioning (some verbs earlier than others), and neither account includes information about the social factors of class, gender and age.

But both examples, especially the long drawn-out change in Polish, illustrate the tug-of-war between grammatical structure and norms that can be presumed in all changes. In the Polish case, suffixation was unmarked in relation to *tmesis*. But at any time during this long development deviations from the established norms might be considered marked. The attested rate of change reflects this speech community's centuries-long tradition of attachment to traditional usage.

References

Andersen, H. 1973. 'Abductive and deductive change', *Language* 49: 567–95.

    1987. 'From auxiliary to desinence', in M. Harris and P. Ramat (eds.), *Historical development of auxiliaries*. Berlin: Mouton de Gruyter, pp. 21–52.

    1989. 'Understanding linguistic innovations', in L. E. Breivik an E. H. Jahr (eds.), *Language change: Contributions to the study of its causes*. Berlin: Mouton de Gruyter, pp. 5–28.

    1990. 'The structure of drift', in H. Andersen and K. Konrad (eds.), *Historical linguistics 1987: Papers from the 8th international Conference on Historical Linguistics*. Amsterdam: John Benjamins, pp. 1–20.

    2001a. 'Markedness and the theory of linguistic change', in Andersen (ed.), pp. 19–57.

    2001b. 'Actualization and the (uni)directionality of change', in Andersen (ed.), pp. 225–48.

    (ed.) 2001c. *Actualization: Linguistic change in progress*. Amsterdam: John Benjamins.

    2006. 'Synchrony, diachrony, and evolution', in Thomsen (ed.), pp. 59–90.

    2008. 'Grammaticalization in a speaker-oriented theory of change', in T. Eythórsson (ed.), *Grammatical change and linguistic theory*. The Rosendal Papers (Linguistik Aktuell/Linguistics Today, 113). Amsterdam: John Benjamins, pp. 11–44.

Anttila, R. [1972] 1989. *Historical and comparative linguistics* (Current Issues in Linguistic Theory 6). Amsterdam: John Benjamins.

Burch, R. 2014. 'Charles Sanders Peirce', in E. N. Zalta (ed.), *The Stanford Encyclopedia of Philosophy* (winter 2014 edition), available at http://plato.stanford.edu/entries/peirce/. Accessed 30 May 2015.

Coseriu, E. 1957. 'Sincronía, diacronía e historia: El problema del cambio lingüístico', *Revista de la Facultad de Humanidades y Ciencias* 15: 201–355. Also as *Sincronía, diacronía e historia: El problema del cambio lingüístico*. Montevideo: Universidad de la Republica, Facultad de Humanidades y Ciencias, Investigaciones y estudios, 1958, 3rd edition. Madrid: Gredos, 1978.

    [1968] 1970. 'Synchronie, Diachronie und Typologie', in U. Petersen, H. Bertsch and G. Köhler (eds.), *Sprache: Strukturen und Funktionen. 12 Aufsätze zur allgemeinen und romanischen Sprachwissenschaft*. Tübingen: Gunter Narr, pp. 91–108. (Translated from 'Sincronía, diacronía y tipología', *Actas del 11 Congreso Internacional de Lingüística i Filología Romanicas*, 1: 269–83. Madrid 1968.)

Deutscher, G. 2002. 'On the misuse of the notion of "abduction" in linguistics', *Journal of Linguistics* 38: 469–85.

Feibleman, J. K. 1970. *An introduction to the philosophy of Charles S. Peirce*. Cambridge, MA: MIT Press.

Harris, A. and Campbell, L. 1995. *Historical syntax in cross-linguistic perspective.* Cambridge University Press.

Heine, B. 2003. 'Grammaticalization', in Joseph and Janda (eds.), pp. 575–601.

Janda, R. and Joseph, B. 2003. 'On language, change, and language change – or, Of history, linguistics, and historical linguistics', in Joseph and Janda (eds.), pp. 3–180.

Joseph, B. and Janda, R. (eds.) 2003. *The handbook of historical linguistics.* Malden, MA, and Oxford: Blackwell.

Ketner, K. L. and Putnam, H. (eds.) 1992. *Reasoning and the logic of things: The Cambridge conference lectures of 1898 of Charles Peirce.* Introduction by K. L. Ketner and H. Putnam. Cambridge, MA: Harvard University Press.

Labov, W. 2001. *Principles of linguistic change*, vol. 2: *Social factors.* Oxford: Blackwell.

Ledgeway, A. 2012. *From Latin to Romance: Morphosyntactic typology and change.* Oxford University Press.

Milroy, J. 1992. *Linguistic variation and change.* Oxford: Blackwell.

Peirce, C. S. 1931–66. *The collected papers of Charles S. Peirce*, ed. C. Hartshorne, P Weiss and A. W. Burks, vols. 1–8. Cambridge, MA: Harvard University Press.

Rittel, T. 1975. *Szyk członów w obrębie form czasu przeszłego i trybu przypuszczającego.* Wrocław: Ossolineum.

Ross, W. D. 1949. *Aristotle. Prior and posterior analytics: A revised text with introduction and commentary.* Oxford: Clarendon Press.

Sapir, E. [1921] 1949. *Language: An introduction to the study of speech.* New York: Harcourt, Brace & World.

Slobin, D. I. 1985. 'The child as linguistic icon maker', in J. Haiman (ed.), *Iconicity in syntax: Proceedings of a symposium on iconicity in syntax, Stanford, June 24–6, 1983* (Typological studies in language, 6). Amsterdam: John Benjamins, pp. 221–48.

Smith, R. 1989. *Aristotle. Prior analytics*, trans., with introduction, notes and commentary. Indianapolis: Hacket.

Soukharov, A. H. *et al.* (eds.) 1992. *The American heritage dictionary of the English language*, 3rd edn. Boston: Houghton Mifflin.

Tarde, G. 1903. *Laws of imitation.* New York: Holt. English translation of Gabriel de Tarde, *Les lois de l'imitation: Étude sociologique.* Paris: F. Alcan, 1873.

Thomsen, O. N. 2006a. 'Towards an integrated functional-pragmatic theory of language and language change. In commemoration of Eugenio Coseriu (1921–2002)', in Thomsen (ed.), pp. 307–38.

   (ed.). 2006b. Competing models of linguistic change. Amsterdam: John Benjamins,

Timberlake, A. 1977. 'Reanalysis and actualization in syntactic change', in C N. Li (ed.), *Mechanisms of syntactic change.* Austin: University of Texas Press, pp. 141–77.

Topolińska, Z. 1961. *Z historii akcentu polskiego od wieku XVI do dziś*. (Prace językoznawcze, 27). Warsaw: Ossolineum.

Vaillant, A. 1964. *Manuel du vieux slave*, vol. 1: *Grammaire*. Paris: Institut d'Études Slaves.

Whewell, W. 1837. History of the inductive sciences, 3rd edition. London: J. W. Parker.

15

Transparency

David W. Lightfoot

15.1 Introduction

Syntactic systems change in a kind of punctuated equilibrium, with occasional phase transitions and discontinuities (see Chapter 24, this volume), and so does the study of those changes. There have been two significant paradigm shifts affecting the study of syntactic change and they are crucial to understanding the emergence and demise of the Transparency Principle, first introduced in Lightfoot (1979), and its later analogues.

The first paradigm shift was the introduction of formal approaches to syntax, beginning with the work of American structuralists in the early twentieth century and then blossoming with the development of the generative transformational analyses of Chomsky (1957). This opened the way for new approaches to syntactic change by Klima (1964), Kiparsky (1968) and Traugott (1965, 1969) in the 1960s, and later by Lightfoot (1979), among others. We will look at this work briefly in §15.2, because it has a very different character from later analyses that followed the second paradigm shift. Crucially, grammars were seen as properties of languages like Japanese and Javanese, not of individual people.

The second paradigm shift came in 1986 with the publication of Chomsky's *Knowledge of Language*, which distinguished external E-language and internal I-languages (see §18.1).[1] This facilitated new explanations for syntactic changes, by encouraging researchers to see change as initially the emergence of a new private, individual language (Lightfoot 1991). Under this view, there may be as many I-languages as there are individuals (indeed the introduction to Jonas, Whitman and Garrett (2012) offers a good account of the early years of generative approaches to diachronic syntax, also emphasizing the I-language innovation). With

---

[1] There is no doubt that the introduction of formal, generative analyses constituted a Kuhnian paradigm shift. The concept of I-languages also constituted a major shift in perspective, although perhaps not fundamental enough for those who wish to reserve 'paradigm shift' for more radical changes.

this shift, grammars, now seen as I-languages, were viewed as properties of individual people and not of whole languages. This entailed analysing the spread of new I-languages by employing the methods of population biology. The move to I-languages was complemented a few years later by Kroch's introduction of coexisting, competing grammars, whereby individuals have more than one I-language and there may be many more I-languages than individuals (Kroch 1989, 1994).

The Transparency Principle was introduced before the second paradigm shift and became unsustainable after that shift for reasons that we shall see. Let us first consider the early generative work on syntactic change, conducted before the emphasis on I-languages.

15.2 Early Generative Analyses of Syntactic Change

Some of the important early work on transformational generative grammar was diachronic in nature. Klima (1964) considered the case markings on pronominal forms, examining four stages of English and arguing that grammars differed in the level at which his Case Marking transformation applied, first on the initial phrase marker ('deep structure') and later after the operation of displacement operations like *wh*-movement; this accounted for the change of forms from *Whom could she see?* to *Who could she see?* Klima actually argued that the Case Marking and *wh*-movement operations were reordered, reflecting a type of change found in phonology (Halle 1962). The second change was a generalization of Case Marking and then, a third change, a lexical reanalysis.

Kiparsky (1968) offered a novel account of the distribution of 'historical present' verbs, verbs in the present tense but with past meaning, extending the discussion to present-tense verbs with future meaning. In the early Indo-European languages, Vedic Sanskrit, Old Irish, early Greek, Latin, etc., the distribution of these tensed presents was syntactically governed: a historical present occurs only after a true past tense (1a); similarly present-tense forms with future meaning occurred only after a true future tense (1b).

(1)   a. *elabon*   de kai to   pʰrourion kai tous pʰulakas *ekballousin*
           they.captured also the fort   and the   guards   out.drive
           'They captured the fort and drove out the guards.' (Thucydides
           VIII 84)
       b. *doulosete*   ... *eremoute*
           you.will.enslave   ... you.lay.waste
           'You will enslave ... will lay waste.' (Thucydides III 58)

As far as one can tell, there is no semantic distinction between these present-tense forms and forms where the second verb is in the past or future tense. Kiparsky postulated an optional rule reducing the form of the second verb to an unmarked form, a kind of conjunction reduction; the unmarked form was the injunctive in Vedic Sanskrit, Celtic and Homeric Greek, and the present indicative in later Greek, Old Irish, Early Latin and Old Icelandic. He then postulated that this conjunction reduction operation was eventually lost and was, in a sense, replaced by a semantic rule interpreting present tenses as 'dramatic'. Kiparsky viewed the change as the loss of a syntactic rule and the development of a new rule of semantic interpretation (see Lightfoot 1979: 26f. for possible alternative accounts) and solved a problem in the internal history of these ancient languages, providing an elegant account of what had changed.

These are two examples of how the earliest generative work on diachrony employed the devices and abstractions of generative grammar to provide accounts of the nature of historical changes in syntactic systems. The idea was that there was a grammar of, say, English or Greek that changed from one generation to another, an object being transmitted between generations and changing its shape in ways defined by the available formalisms, such as rules being reordered or simplified.

The notion that there were formal restrictions on diachronic changes was shared by generativists like Klima and Kiparsky and by the non-generative typologists of the 1970s. The typologists argued that languages might be of a pure or transitional type and that a pure subject–object–verb (SOV) language might develop to a pure subject–verb–object (SVO) one by acquiring the harmonic properties of a SVO language in the order prescribed by a diachronic hierarchy; the diachronic hierarchy defined the sequence of possible changes (so the language acquired Aux–V order and prepositions in the designated order; see Vennemann 1975 and several papers in Li 1975, 1977; for good critical discussion, see the introduction to Jonas, Whitman and Garrett 2012).

In a further example of early generative work, Traugott (1965, 1969) offered a careful study of English auxiliary verbs, arguing that in Old, Middle and Modern English there was a progressive simplification of the phrase structure rules expanding a category Aux (for discussion, see Lightfoot 1979: 28–35). However, she went beyond Klima and Kiparsky and observed that 'a synchronic grammar cannot account for [certain] changes' (Traugott 1965: 412). She went on to advocate a 'diachronic grammar' (Traugott 1969), which contained the 'information' of various synchronic grammars and the *formal* relation between those grammars, where the formal relations included specific instances of rule reordering, simplification, loss, addition, etc. (see Lightfoot and Pires 2013).

The move to a diachronic grammar now looks like a radical move that was not pursued, as far as I know, beyond these publications, but it illustrates an important point and was not so radical at the time. Grammars in the 1960s were generally viewed as systems that generated the sentences of a language, where 'a language' was taken to be a conventional, group notion like English, Spanish or Japanese. For example, at the very beginning of *Syntactic Structures* Chomsky says that a grammar is 'a device of some sort for producing the sentences of the language under analysis' (Chomsky 1957: 11), with many similar comments elsewhere in the book. Taking languages to be sociological entities of this kind raised difficulties about what constitutes linguistic knowledge on the part of individual speakers, because there are incompatibilities; we return to this point in §15.4. In that light, Traugott's move toward a diachronic grammar of English, including information about Old, Middle and Modern English was not a major shift from seeing grammars as including information about a variety of dialects that make up a language. Earlier work had introduced a language's synchronic variation into grammars; Traugott added diachronic variation. In both cases grammars were taken to hold for groups of speakers or for societies, not for individuals (Lightfoot 1995). Grammars before and after the second paradigm shift had quite different properties.

15.3 Transparency Principle

In this context, after the first paradigm shift but before the second, Lightfoot (1979: ch. 2) examined changes whereby certain verbs in Early English came to be recategorized as Infl elements (see Chapters 18 and 24, this volume). In the spirit of the times, in which grammars were devices to generate the sentences of, say, Middle English, the key idea was that the five relevant verbs, *magan, cunnan, motan, sculan* and *willan*, acquired a set of exception features. The idea here, again typical of the times (Lakoff 1970), was that lexical items were annotated with features to indicate which generalizations (transformations, lexical redundancy rules and morphological operations) they were *not* subject to for some speakers.[2] This accounted for individual variation, for the fact that some people at certain times failed to produce sentences with sequences of the relevant verbs (*She shall may visit*), which earlier had been normal. Similarly exception features accounted for the absence for some writers of perfect or progressive participles (*has could, canning*) and the absence of *to* infinitives. Furthermore, as inflections were lost and morphology was simplified radically over the course of Middle English, so the relevant verbs, all formerly members of the preterite-present class, came to have an exception feature indicating that, unlike all other verbs, they lacked any third-person singular ending in *-eþ* or *-s*. Another exceptional property of these verbs was that the past-tense forms, *might, must, could, should* and *would* rarely had past time meaning but instead were a reflex of the

---

[2] These exception features played a significant role in the so-called linguistic wars between lexicalists and transformationalists in the late 1960s, debating where and how exceptions should be treated (Newmeyer 1986: ch 4).

earlier (homophonous) subjunctives with 'subjunctive meanings' (see Chapters 18 and 24, this volume).

So over the course of Middle English, *magan*, for example, developed exception features indicating that, unlike other verbs, it could not be preceded immediately by another verb or by an aspectual marker, that it did not have the usual third-person inflection in *-eþ* or *–s*, that its past-tense form did not convey past-tense meaning. Likewise for *cunnan*, *motan*, *sculan* and *willan*. The language of individuals might be characterized by these exception features, optionally.

Central to this kind of analysis was the assumption that there was a single grammar of Middle English that includes a set of optional exception features that people might use variably. These complicating factors accrued over time and the exception features were the grist for the Transparency Principle.

The claim was that there were two stages to the recategorization of the relevant verbs. First, the exception features, designed to account for individual variation, accumulated gradually in the grammar of the speech community, and then, second, there was 'a sudden, cataclysmic, wholesale re-structuring of the grammar whereby the exceptionality is, in a sense, institutionalized and the derivational complexity is eliminated at a stroke' (Lightfoot 1979: 122). There came a point where the grammar of the language had to undergo a reanalysis whereby these verbs, formerly instances of V, were reanalysed and became instances of T or Infl and the exception features were eliminated. This reanalysis was allegedly provoked by a principle of the theory of grammar, the Transparency Principle. Structural analyses needed to be *transparent*, accessible to the learner, and exception features reduced the transparency of the analysis. 'If the Transparency Principle characterizes the limits to the permitted degree of exceptionality or derivational complexity, then it will follow from this principle that as these limits are approached so some kind of therapeutic reanalysis will be necessary to eliminate the offending complexity' (Lightfoot 1979: 122).

It is important to recognize that the various exception features were postulated because certain writers ceased using the old forms earlier than others (note that the change consisted entirely in the loss of expressions, not in the introduction of new forms; see §18.3); the features were used optionally by individual speakers. They were an artifact of the earlier view of grammars as generating the expressions of a homogeneous language and they constituted an attempt to capture variation between speakers. The last writer to use all the old forms of the modal verbs was Sir Thomas More in the early sixteenth century; the forms are not found after that time, but other writers had ceased using some forms before More. The reanalysis, on the other hand, was not piecemeal: the reanalysis involved a single change at the level of the grammar and the singularity of the change through the abstractions provided by the grammar explained the simultaneity of the phenomena that changed. Once *magan* was recategorized as Infl or T, none of the obsolescent forms could be generated and no particular features were required any longer.

As for why exception features should arise, an important driving force for linguistic change, as often noted, is that language is a means by which group identities are signalled. Young people often identify with others by developing linguistic idiosyncrasies of a type that exception features account for. One can think of exception features as small insults to a system, building up until the system breaks.

The Transparency Principle was intended to *explain* syntactic changes, showing why grammars might become too complex to be sustainable, part of a more general enterprise of explaining changes through first language acquisition (Chapter 18, this volume). The principle was also intended to represent an inductive generalization, resulting from an examination of several radical reanalyses. Other diachronic changes were attributed to the effects of a Transparency Principle.

For a second example, English quantifiers like *all, any, each, both, every, few, more* used to have the same distribution as adjectives in Old and Middle English and therefore belonged to a supercategory that we might label 'modifier'. Future quantifiers and future adjectives could occur prenominally (*Jerry hated all books*), before a determiner (*Jerry burned all his books*), postnominally (*the books all burned*), with a genitive (*some of his books burned*), in a floating position (*the books were all lost*) and as a nominal (*each was insured*). Over the course of time the distribution of quantifiers has remained constant but those modifiers that were to become modern adjectives developed new properties. It is unclear why this happened but the novelties were first expressed through exception features (see §6.2.1; Lightfoot 1979: §4.1). By the end of the fifteenth century pre-adjectives, i.e. modifiers destined to become adjectives, had become more restricted in their distribution: they could no longer occur *freely* before a determiner, with a genitive, or as a nominal (details in §6.2.1). This suggests that the pre-adjective modifiers gradually accrued three exception features precluding such occurrences.

The second stage of the story is that over the next one hundred years, by the end of the sixteenth century, the following changes took place (for examples, see §6.2.1).

(2)   a. *all* and *both* first appear with *of* partitives.
       b. obsolescence of determiner-quantifier-noun.
       c. obsolescence of multiple quantifiers in sequence.
       d. obsolescence of adjective-determiner-noun.
       e. obsolescence of postnominal adjectives.
       f. obsolescence of adjectives used as nominals.

As pre-adjectives and pre-quantifiers had diverged in their distribution, there was good reason for language learners to postulate that they were assigned to different categories: adjectives occurred to the left of a noun or following a copula verb (3), while quantifiers occurred as the Specifier of a DP or in a Determiner position with a NP or PP complement (4).

(3)   a. $_{NP}[_A$red $_{NP}$[books]]
       b. $_{VP}[_V$become $_A$angry]

(4)   a. $_{DP}[_{Spec}$all $_{DP}$[his apples]]
       b. $_{DP}[_D$both $_{NP}$[books about taxes]], $_{DP}[_D$all $_{PP}$[of the books]]

This analysis entails that (2a) will be generated and (2b–f) will not and grammars were restructured: as with the new Infl elements, the single recategorization is manifested by several new phenomena that emerged at the same time. The reanalysis looked like an effect of the Transparency Principle: exception features were eliminated and the new, more transparent analysis yielded more changes (2).

A third example of the effects of a Transparency Principle can be seen in *to* infinitives that were treated as exceptional nouns in Old English and were then later recategorized as verbs. The inflected infinitive in Old English had clear nominal properties and Lightfoot (1979: §4.2) argued that the *(for) to V* infinitive, which replaced the inflected infinitive, had the distribution of a noun in earliest times, occurring after prepositions and in virtually the same environments as a gerund, and that it was later reanalysed as a VP. The occurrence of the *to* infinitive after prepositions, in passive and cleft sentences, and with case endings (the dative *-enne*) clearly indicate nominal status. However, it had exception features: a major feature was that these nominals lacked an appropriate Specifier (never co-occurring with adjectives, articles, demonstratives or possessive modifiers) and *to* infinitives after a preposition, in a passive and cleft construction came to be less common, reflecting exception features barring their distribution there. And the result was a reanalysis in the sixteenth century, whereby *to* infinitives came to be recategorized as VPs. *To* infinitives now could occur with a *for* NP subject, and not as the complement of a preposition, nor as the subject of a passive, nor in a cleft clause, nor with inflectional endings. The exception features became redundant and the analysis more transparent.

A fourth example of a recategorization putatively triggered by the Transparency Principle concerns serial verbs in African languages, notably Kwa. Lord (1973; see also her 1993 book) and Schachter (1974) posited 'serial' VPs for some languages: such verbs share a subject and auxiliary items and the combination of verbs takes on an idiosyncratic meaning, not just the aggregation of the two verbs. The second verb typically lacks inflectional properties, a hallmark of any verb. That suggested that the second of two serial verbs might develop exception features, as they came to be used differently by some speakers. For example, there would be exception features indicating that the verb lacked inflectional properties and combined semantically with the preceding verb to carry a non-compositional meaning. Some evidence indicated that the verb eventually came to be re-categorized as a preposition or a complementizer and that was attributed to the increasing opacity of the verbal nature of the form (Lightfoot 1979: §4.4).

However, the Transparency Principle was never formalized and no precise method was established to quantify degrees of exceptionality in any general way, as noted by Bennett (1979), Fischer and van der Leek (1981) and Romaine (1981). Meanwhile the ground was about to shift.

15.4 The Paradigm Shift and Demise of the Transparency Principle

In the early days of generative grammar, children were seen as acquiring the grammar of Turkish, Tagalog or Tibetan. Languages were group phenomena and an idealization was employed whereby language was seen as developing in an individual in a homogeneous speech community. As Chomsky (1965: 3) put it, the field was 'concerned primarily with an ideal speaker–listener, in a completely homogeneous speech community, who knows its language perfectly and is unaffected by such grammatically irrelevant conditions as memory limitations, distractions, shifts of attention and interest, and errors (random or characteristic) in applying his knowledge of the language in actual performance'. That idealization was linked to the idea that grammars generate the sentences of a speech community or a whole language. Everybody knew that speech communities encompassed much variation but it was a useful idealization to think in terms of a grammar emerging in a speech community and generating the sentences found in that community, with individual variation accounted for by the device of exception features.

All of this changed. Chomsky (1986) essentially abandoned the idealization of speakers in a homogeneous speech community and the paradigm shift had a galvanizing effect on the new field of diachronic syntax and rendered the Transparency Principle redundant, indeed vacuous.

Chomsky postulated a distinction between I-languages and E-language, which were very distinct notions. I-languages, 'I' for internal, individual and intensional, are mental systems that grow in a child, characterize a person's linguistic range, and are represented somehow in the individual's brain; they are biological entities.

I-languages exist in people's brains, but external E-language is part of the outside world. External language is amorphous and not a system. It is language out there in the environment and it includes the kind of things that children hear. This is a function of the various I-languages in a child's environment and of people's *use* of those I-languages and does not reflect any single system. E-language, then, is fluid, in constant flux. No two children hear exactly the same E-language and, as a result, no two people speak in exactly the same way. As a result, because no two people have identical initial experiences, there is always the possibility for new I-languages to emerge, on the assumption (Chapter 24, this volume) that I-languages are triggered by primary linguistic data (PLD), which are part of E-language.

E-language incorporates the kinds of things that groups of people say. 'Spanish', 'Greek', etc. are E-language, group notions, but they are not systematic and their expressions do not and cannot constitute a recursively enumerable set. If one asks whether *She might could do it* is a sentence of English, the answer is Yes in Arkansas but not in Cornwall, and *Bin her happy?* is a sentence of English in Cornwall but not in Arkansas. Since the language of people in Cornwall differs from that of Arkansans, there cannot be a single underlying system.

Under this view, children are exposed to E-language but no two children are exposed to the same E-language. Nonetheless each child grows a private I-language that generates an infinite range of expressions according to the principles of Universal Grammar (UG; see Chaper 13, this volume) and linguists provide an account of *individual* development. Children in Arkansas develop an I-language that generates *She might could do it* but children in Cornwall do not. Linguistic competence now is individualized and group notions like English, Spanish and Greek have no role to play.

Both I-languages and E-language change. I-languages change only when children are exposed to different E-language and therefore hear different things, but E-language changes for various reasons, because of increasingly frequent new topicalization constructions, or because children hear different morphological properties, or because one individual's PLD are truncated in some way, etc. See Chapter 18, this volume, on acquisition and learnability.

If linguists focus on individual development in this way, the whole framework on which the Transparency Principle was predicated evaporates. Now there are no exception features expressing new elements in some speech subcommunity; if there are no exception features, there is no exceptionality to be quantified. Indeed, after the I-language paradigm shift enabled analysts to dispense with the group idealization, Fischer *et al.* (2000: 7) were right to say 'the Transparency Principle has proved to be an undesirable and superfluous addition to the theory of grammar. It is undesirable because it has no possible formal characterization like other principles of grammar' and, after the second paradigm shift, it became superfluous, because we can account for new individual I-languages without appealing to exception features.

Rather, there will be a multiplicity of I-languages developing, some, for example, with *sculan* and *cunnan* categorized as lexical verbs and other I-languages with those words categorized as T or Infl elements. All speakers of very Early English had such words categorized as verbs. However, after the early sixteenth century, all known speakers had I-languages with those words categorized as elements of T or Infl, therefore not generating expressions like *She shall can visit, She had could visit, Canning visit, she stayed long*, etc. In the meantime, there were I-languages of both types coexisting, but no I-languages with the kinds of exception features assumed by Lightfoot (1979). At this point there is variation between different, coexisting I-languages, i.e. variation between two fixed points, but no variation within I-languages through optional features (Lightfoot 2006, 2013; Wallenberg 2013).

Chomsky had now adopted the view of Hermann Paul (1877: 325), who, as we note in Chapters 18 and 24 (this volume), emphasized the individual and biological view of languages, noting 'dass die reelle Sprache nur im Individuum existiert' ('real language exists only in individuals'). In attacking the group psychology of Lazarus and Steinthal, Paul (1880: 31) wrote that 'Wir müssen eigentlich so viele Sprachen unterscheiden als es Individuen gibt' ('we must in fact distinguish as many languages as there are individuals').

As this paradigm shift took place around 1986, the work of Kroch and colleagues on coexisting I-languages took us a step further, arguing that individuals have multiple I-languages and that therefore there are *more* I-languages than individuals (Kroch 1989, 1994; Kroch and Taylor 1997; Pintzuk 1999).

This work on internal multiglossia had considerable methodological impact. For example, it provided a more restricted and more principled way of dealing with variation. Variation now could be seen as oscillation between the fixed points of distinct I-languages and not between the multitude of points defined by arbitrary exception features.

Furthermore, it furnished a new way of thinking about optionality: the apparent optionality of grammatical operations could now be viewed instead as a function of co-existing grammars, with no optional/obligatory distinction internal to individual I-languages. This solved the conceptual problem that a distinction between optional and obligatory operations is not learnable if children are exposed only to occurring speech and are not informed about what cannot occur (see Chapter 24, this volume; Lightfoot 2006; Wallenberg forthcoming).

This work on coexisting I-languages was also facilitated by a technological development, the emergence of partially parsed computerized corpora for historical texts of English and other languages (see Chapter 11, this volume). These corpora have revolutionized our capacity to test hypotheses about, say, thirteenth-century I-languages.

15.5 Modern Analogues to Transparency

Given that grammars/I-languages, under the second paradigm shift, hold for individuals and not for speech communities with inherent variation, children must be assumed to grow the most economical I-languages, which do not contain exception features designed to preclude generating expressions not used by some speakers. Any variation is *between* I-languages and not *within* I-languages (this raises the question of what happens with the apparent mixed systems of bilinguals; much has been written on this topic but there is no clear consensus and there is not a lot of work on the systems of bilinguals in the context of current thinking about I-languages. For some discussion, see Meisel 2011; Lightfoot 2011).

All I-languages grow in children subject to the constraints imposed by UG, being learnable in the usual way in response to the ambient PLD. They encompass the most conservative, economical and learnable structures compatible with UG (Snyder 2007, 2011). For example, they may be subject to the minimalist economy principles of Chomsky (1995). As Battye and Roberts (1995: 9) put it in their introduction, 'acquirers assign the smallest structure possible to the strings with which they are presented, where the constraints on "smallness" are given in part by UG and in part by the trigger experience'. Under this view, individual I-languages are simpler than earlier grammars from the 1960s and 1970s that generated the structures and sentences of a conventional, group language like Navajo and Nubian; individual I-languages do not have exception features or optional devices designed to capture variation between different speakers. If there are no exception features of this type, the Transparency Principle can have no effects and becomes superfluous and vacuous.

However, curiously, analogues to the Transparency Principle have been proposed in recent work, following the second paradigm shift. Clark and Roberts' (1993) Fitness Metric, for example, incorporated the 'elegance' of grammars into their general fitness assessment, where grammars were fitter and more elegant if, other things being equal, they employed fewer active nodes (see Chapter 24, this volume, and, for critical discussion, Lightfoot 1999). Roberts (1993: 156) reformulated this in terms of a Least Effort Strategy: 'Representations assigned to sentences of the input to acquisition should be such that they contain the set of the shortest possible chains (consistent with (a) principles of grammar, (b) other aspects of the trigger experience).' He described this as a strategy of acquisition and not a principle of grammar, 'quite close in spirit to the Transparency Principle of Lightfoot 1979'.

The Transparency Principle was conceived as a principle of grammar, restricting the opacity of syntactic derivations and the amount of exceptionality that grammars could sustain. It therefore was seen as forcing reanalyses when children's experiences had changed, triggering too many exception features in the communal grammar.

Roberts' Least Effort Strategy was a strategy of acquisition with similar effects, encouraging reanalyses. Roberts (1993: 158) postulated that the Least Effort Strategy provoked Diachronic Reanalysis (DR), which he viewed as a formal device relating one set of formal structures to another set, reflecting ideas about grammars being transmitted from one generation to the next with (usually minor) formal changes. An example of a DR is (5) below, corresponding to Roberts' (94) on his p. 295. He described DRs 'as relations between the E-language of one generation (ambiguous trigger experience susceptible of a 'simpler' analysis in the sense defined earlier), and the I-language of a subsequent generation' (1993: 158); see Lightfoot (1994) for critical discussion. He saw DRs as *causes* of parametric shifts.

(5) a. $NP_i [_T do/M_j T^{?-1}] t_j [t_i VP] =>$
     b. $NP [_T did/M] VP$

DRs were said to be provoked by principles of acquisition like the Least Effort Strategy; the Least Effort Strategy led children to reanalyse the structure (5a) as (5b) in the seventeenth century, adopting the analysis of Denison (1985). However, (5a), containing structures and indexed empty elements, is not a piece of E-language but an I-language representation of the relevant E-language string, so DRs relate 'the grammars of successive generations,' as Roberts noted (1993: 154); they do not relate the E-language of one generation to a later I-language. If DRs relate the I-languages of successive generations, then they occur where parametric shifts have already taken place. Roberts notes that 'the notion DR may also prove to be epiphenomenal. All DR's may turn out to be instances of Parametric Change' (1993: 159) and that indeed seems to be the case as a matter of the inherent logic.

In more recent work Roberts (2001: 107–11) points to the loss of verb movement in seventeenth-century English, when verbs ceased to move to a higher functional position like Infl or T and seeks to explain it as following from his Least Effort acquisition strategy: rather than a verb being moved to T, that 'effort' is eliminated from the grammar and yields 'simpler representations for large classes of simple examples' (2001: 109); such phenomena were part of the motivation for the original Transparency Principle (see §15.3).

Roberts and Roussou (2003) adapt the Least Effort Strategy and take eighteen case studies from various languages, showing 'that grammaticalisation involves structural reanalysis so that some new element comes to be merged in a functional position F´ (2003: 234). The structural reanalysis is always simplification as defined by metric (6) (2003: 201):

(6) A structural representation R for a substring of input text S is simpler than an alternative representation R´ iff R contains fewer formal feature syncretisms than R´.

They explain grammaticalization as reflecting a drive towards greater simplicity in I-languages. The greater simplicity comes from the elimination of a movement operation for certain structures, merging the formerly moved element directly in a functional position. For example, they note that what is often referred to as the parade case of grammaticalization, the recategorization of modal verbs during the course of Middle English, no longer involves the movement of a verb to a higher position but instead merges the modal verb directly in the T or Infl position, thereby yielding less complex structures, triggered by the loss of infinitival inflections (see §18.3).

15.6 Prophylaxis, Not Therapy

The general idea behind the various formulations from the 1979 Transparency Principle onwards through Clark and Roberts' elegance, Roberts' Least Effort Strategy, and Roberts and Roussou's precise definition of simplicity is that UG or acquisition strategies weed out less preferred grammars, which may arise in different ways. The idea is that some representations are simpler than others, and therefore intrinsically favoured if other things are equal, and we can understand central elements of diachronic change when representations become simpler over time. The general principles driving these preferences perform a kind of therapy for languages.

It is important to see these ideas in the context of the paradigm shift of the late 1980s. The 1979 Transparency Principle was taken to hold for grammars of socially defined languages, where grammars might incorporate exception features and optional devices capturing variation within the grammar. Roberts' Least Effort Strategy, on the other hand, holds for I-languages, which, in his view, tend to allow simpler representations over time, as disfavoured I-languages cease to be attained by children after some changes in PLD.

All of these principles/strategies provide a way of accounting for a directionality to change but they are all subject to a major problem: if humans have limits to the complexity of attainable systems, why should speech communities develop complex grammars that breach those limits and need to be simplified through the therapeutic effects of the Transparency Principle? Equivalently, why should a Least Effort Strategy be effective in reducing 'effort' in one generation when the previous generation had I-languages that tolerated that degree of effort? Similarly, why has the Least Effort Strategy not simplified the representation of French and Dutch I-languages, rendering the modal verbs as T or Infl elements and eliminating the complex representations resulting from moving verbs to a higher functional position? Similar questions arise for the cyclicity notions of van Gelderen (2011) and other attempts to build 'biases' into theories of UG. The only answer to such questions must lie in the PLD: there must be something robust and unambiguous in the PLD of French and Dutch children precluding an analysis with modal verbs recategorized as Infl elements.

The focus on therapy, incorporating notions of less effort, UG biases, or UG cycles, introduces a kind of indeterminacy for accounts of change and should be contrasted with the approach discussed in Chapter 18 (this volume) on acquisition and learnability, under which new I-languages arise *only* in response to new primary linguistic data in the ambient E-language. Under that view UG imposes limits on biologically possible systems and therefore performs a kind of prophylaxis, preventing logically possible but biologically disfavoured systems from emerging in the first place. If biologically disfavoured grammars are precluded by a good theory of UG, there is no reason for therapeutic principles like Transparency or its more recent analogues. Prophylaxis is enough.

References

Battye, A. and Roberts, I. (eds.) 1995. *Clause structure and language change.* Oxford University Press.

Bennett, P. 1979. 'Observations on the transparency principle', *Linguistics* 17: 843–61.

Chomsky, N. 1957. *Syntactic structures.* The Hague: Mouton.
  1965. *Aspects of the theory of syntax.* Cambridge, MA: MIT Press.
  1986. *Knowledge of language: Its nature, origin and use.* New York: Praeger.
  1995. *The minimalist program.* Cambridge, MA: MIT Press.

Denison, D. 1985. 'The origins of periphrastic do: Ellegård and Visser reconsidered', in R. Eaton *et al.* (eds.), *Papers from the 4th International Conference on Historical Linguistics, Amsterdam, April 10–13, 1985.* Amsterdam: John Benjamins, pp. 45–60.

Fischer, O. C. M. and van der Leek, F. C. 1981. 'Optional vs radical re-analysis: Mechanisms of syntactic change', *Lingua* 55: 301–50.

Fischer, O. C. M., van Kemenade, A., Koopman, W. and van der Wurff, W. 2000. *The syntax of early English.* Cambridge University Press.

Halle, M. 1962. 'Phonology in generative grammar', *Word* 18: 54–72.

Jonas, D., Whitman, J. and Garrett, A. (eds.) 2012. *Grammatical change: Origins, nature, outcomes.* Oxford University Press.

Kiparsky, P. 1968. 'Tense and mood in Indo-European syntax', *Foundations of Language* 4: 30–57.

Klima, E. 1964. 'Relatedness between grammatical systems', *Language* 40: 1–20.

Kroch, A. 1989. 'Reflexes of grammar in patterns of language change', *Language Variation and Change* 1: 199–244.
  1994. 'Morphosyntactic variation', in K. Beals *et al.* (eds.), *Papers from the 30th regional meeting of the Chicago Linguistics Society: Parasession on variation and linguistic theory.* Chicago Linguistics Society, pp. 180–201.

Kroch, A. and Taylor, A. 1997. 'The syntax of verb movement in Middle English: Dialect variation and language contact', in A. van Kemenade and N. Vincent (eds.), *Parameters of morphosyntactic change*. Cambridge University Press, pp. 297–325.

Lakoff, G. 1970. *Irregularity in syntax*. New York: Holt, Rinehart & Winston.

Li, C. N. (ed.) 1975. *Word order and word order change*. Austin: University of Texas Press.

(ed.) 1977. *Mechanisms of syntactic change*. Austin: University of Texas Press.

Lightfoot, D. W. 1979. *Principles of diachronic syntax*. Cambridge University Press.

1991. *How to set parameters: Arguments from syntactic change*. Cambridge, MA: MIT Press.

1994. Review of Roberts 1993, *Language* 70: 571–8.

1995. 'Grammars for people', *Journal of Linguistics* 31: 393–9.

1999. *The development of language: Acquisition, change and evolution*. Oxford: Blackwell.

2006. *How new languages emerge*. Cambridge University Press.

2011. 'Multilingualism everywhere', *Bilingualism: Language and Cognition* 14: 162–4.

2013. 'Types of explanation', *Language* 89.4: e18–e38.

Lightfoot, D. W. and Pires, A. 2013. *Syntactic change*. Oxford: Oxford Bibliographies Online: Linguistics. www.oxfordbibliographies.com.

Lord, C. 1973. 'Serial verbs in transition', *Studies in African Linguistics* 4.3: 269–96.

1993. *Historical change in serial verb constructions* (Typological Studies in Language 26). Amsterdam: John Benjamins.

Meisel, J. M. 2011. *First and second language acquisition: Parallels and differences*. Cambridge University Press.

Newmeyer, F. J. 1986. *Linguistic theory in America: The first quarter-century of transformational generative grammar*, 2nd edn. New York: Academic Press.

Paul, H. 1877. 'Die Vocale der Flexions- und Ableitungssilben in den ältesten germanischen Dialecten', *Beiträge zur Geschichte der deutschen Sprache und Literatur* 4: 314–475.

1880. *Prinzipien der Sprachgeschichte*. Tübingen: Niemeyer.

Pintzuk, S. 1999. *Phrase structures in competition: Variation and change in Old English word order*. New York: Garland.

Roberts, I. 1993. *Verbs and diachronic syntax: A comparative history of English and French*. Dordrecht: Kluwer.

2001. 'Language change and learnability', in S. Bertolo (ed.), *Language acquisition and learnability*. Cambridge University Press, pp. 81–125.

Roberts, I. and Roussou, A. 2003. *Syntactic change: A minimalist approach to grammaticalisation*. Cambridge University Press.

Romaine, S. 1981. 'The Transparency Principle: What it is and why it doesn't work', *Lingua* 55: 93–116.

Schachter, P. 1974. 'A non-transformational account of serial verbs', *Studies in African Linguistics, suppl.* 5: 253–71.

Snyder, W. 2007. *Child language: The parametric approach.* Oxford University Press.

   2011. 'Children's grammatical conservatism: Implications for syntactic theory', in N. Danis *et al.* (eds.), *BUCLD 35: Proceedings of the 35th annual Boston University conference on language development*, vol. 1. Somerville, MA: Cascadilla Press, pp. 1–20.

Traugott, E. C. 1965. 'Diachronic syntax and generative grammar', *Language* 41: 402–15.

   1969. 'Toward a grammar of syntactic change', *Lingua* 23: 1–27.

van Gelderen, E. 2011. *The linguistic cycle: Language change and the language faculty.* Amsterdam: John Benjamins.

Vennemann, T. 1975. 'An explanation of drift', in Li (ed.), pp. 269–305.

Wallenberg, J. Forthcoming. 'Extraposition is disappearing', *Language.*

16

Uniformitarianism

Ian Roberts

16.1 Introduction

In this chapter, after outlining the concept of uniformitarianism, I will first give a very brief overview of the history of this idea (§16.2), and then, in §16.3, look at the consequences of assuming it as a methodological principle for our understanding of linguistic prehistory, drawing particularly on work by Johanna Nichols and Don Ringe, and also an important caveat due to Heggarty (2015: 601). I conclude this section by tentatively distinguishing three phases of human linguistic (pre)history. In §16.4 I will consider how uniformitarianism might be thought of in the context of a formal theory of syntactic variation, contrasting two different versions of principles-and-parameters theory (see also Chapters 7 and 27, this volume).

A good informal definition of uniformitarianism (or the Uniformitarian Principle, UP henceforth) is given by Croft (2003: 233), as follows: 'The languages of the past – at least, those we can reconstruct or find records of – are not different in nature from those of the present.' Stated this way, uniformitarianism entails that, unless we find clear evidence to the contrary, today's phonology is the same in fundamental respects as yesterday's, today's syntax is the same as yesterday's, and so on. Moreover, and very importantly for historical linguistics, it entails that the patterns of language change that we can observe in the attested record are the same as those that must have operated at periods for which we have no records (see Ringe and Eska 2013: 3f. on this point).

16.2 Historical Background and Significance of Uniformitarianism

16.2.1 Uniformitarianism in Western Linguistic Thought

For a long period in the history of linguistic thought in the West, the UP was not assumed. Until the Renaissance, it was thought that the three holy languages, Latin, Greek and Hebrew, were quite different entities from the vernaculars, in particular in that the latter, but not the former, were subject to change (Law 2003: 190, 230).[1] For example, Dante, in the *De vulgari eloquentia*, follows the biblical Babel myth in proposing that language was divided into different idioms, and divides Europe into three linguistic areas, a northern Germanic area (which included Hungarian and Slavic), an eastern Greek-speaking area and a southern Romance-speaking area. He contrasts these vernaculars with 'a secondary form of speech called *grammar* by the Romans' (Law 2003: 190). Not all peoples have this 'secondary form of speech', but he mentions the Greeks (and 'some other nations') as having it. Vernaculars were subject to change, the great merit of Latin and Greek was that they were not. Clearly the UP, as a general principle, has no place here.

The rediscovery of Classical Latin, and in particular Cicero, in the Renaissance led to a change in how Latin in particular was viewed. Here is how Law (2003: 231) recounts it:

> But as Renaissance scholars pondered the writings of classical authors, they realised that the situation was more complicated. Their beloved Cicero described how when he began to write, Latin had been regarded as a rude uncultivated language severely handicapped by a lack of specialised vocabulary for the discussion of technical subjects. Up until then Roman philosophers had always written in Greek because of the inadequacy (they believed) of their native tongue.

It followed from this that 'Latin was subject to change, just like any present-day vernacular' (Law 2003: 231). Nonetheless, the idea that Latin, Greek and Hebrew, as the languages of Holy Scripture, were unchanging was still very much alive in the sixteenth century (see Metcalf 1974: 238).

Clearly, the assumption that Latin and Greek could change was a precondition for the development of any kind of comparative Indo-European historical linguistics, and, as we have seen, this idea is absent prior to the Renaissance. A fascinating question in the history of Western linguistic thought is why this recognition did not directly give rise to the development of comparative philology. The similarities among many of the languages of Europe were known and there was, at least from the time of Salmasius in the mid seventeenth century, an awareness that Sanskrit bore a strong resemblance to Persian and to many European languages (Morpurgo-Davies 1998: 61; Campbell and Poser 2008: 21). As Law (2003: 261) puts it: '[e]verything was thus now in place for the development of a thoroughgoing historical and comparative linguistics, but it didn't happen for nearly 150 years'. In particular, as Law points out in the same

---

[1] Interestingly, there is a sense in which the opposite idea led to the development of the Indian grammatical tradition. The original motivation for the careful phonetic and grammatical description and analysis in this tradition came from the desire to preserve the Vedic hymns from the effects of linguistic change so that they could be accurately recited (Staal 1974: 63; Scharf 2013: 227).

passage, Georg Stiernhielm, in his 1671 edition of the Gospels in Gothic, stated that all languages were subject to change, and indeed this change could be gradual rather than catastrophic. In all but name, then, it seems that the UP was an aspect of seventeenth-century linguistic thought, at least for some scholars.

Although Sir William Jones is arguably given more credit than he deserved as an innovative thinker, and certainly as the 'discoverer' of Indo-European (see Metcalf 1974: 251f.; Morpurgo-Davies 1998: 59–66 and, in particular, Campbell and Poser 2008: chs. 2,3), it is clear that, by the end of the eighteenth century when Jones gave his famous address to the Bengal Asiatic Society, the idea that Latin, Greek and Sanskrit may have had a common origin was known, and hence the idea that Latin or Greek were immutable had been definitively abandoned. Jones certainly did not think in uniformitarian terms (in fact, Campbell and Poser (2008: 40) argue that Jones was interested in reconciling what was being discovered in his time about the languages and peoples of Asia with biblical chronology, which the adoption of the UP in geology completely refuted – see below). The first explicit formulation of the UP in relation to linguistics was in Müller (1864), where, citing the work earlier in the nineteenth century on geology by Charles Lyell (on which see below), he said 'what is real in modern formations must be admitted as possible in more ancient families' (ch. 2).[2]

The UP was widely, but not universally, adopted by nineteenth-century comparative and historical linguists (see Mopurgo-Davies 1998: 190f.). Osthoff and Brugmann (1878) clearly adopt a version of the UP in the Forward to their *Morphologische Untersuchungen*. Christy (1983) argues that the UP was crucial to the neogrammarian project and represented a paradigm shift in nineteenth-century scientific thought. Whitney very clearly adopted the UP (Christy 1983: 78–89; Morpurgo-Davies 1998: 210). The same is true for Scherer (Morpurgo-Davies 1998: 219, 271), Bréal (Morpurgo-Davies 1998: 322) and Steinthal (Morpurgo-Davies 1998: 205). On the other hand, according to Wells (1973: 428), Schleicher's 'organicist' view of language change was anti-uniformitarian (Morpurgo-Davies 1998: 196f.).

16.2.2   Uniformitarianism in Other Disciplines

The concept of uniformitarianism is found in other disciplines. In physics, for example, we assume that the same laws hold in the present and at all times in the past and future (except for certain recent speculative theories in cosmology; see Tegmark 2014). The term was first used by Whewell (1837, 1840), applied retrospectively to the ideas put forward in Lyell (1830–3); Whewell actually suggested that the UP could be applied to the study of language (see Christy 1983: 18–21). The subtitle of Lyell's book,

---

[2] Müller also cites Leibniz's (1710) 'Dissertation on the Origin of Nations'; Christy (1983: 39).

'An attempt to explain the former changes of the Earth's surface by reference to causes now in operation', reveals the basic idea. A key aspect of his thinking, which he took from earlier work by James Hutton, was that since the earth was shaped entirely by forces still in operation today, these forces must act very slowly, and so the earth must be very much older than had previously been thought, and certainly a great deal older than biblical accounts of creation would suggest. This conclusion, now generally accepted, had a huge influence on nineteenth-century thought in many areas, linguistics included (see in particular Christy 1983). Lyell (1863) contained a chapter explicitly about language: 'Origin and development of languages and species compared', where he pointed out analogues between the development of species and languages (mutations, splits) and argued that the one can shed light on the other.

Gould (1965, 1987) criticizes aspects of Lyell's ideas in important ways. Lyell's uniformitarianism is arguably a family of four related propositions (Hooykaas 1963). These are as follows: (i) uniformity of law – the laws of nature are constant across time and space; (ii) uniformity of methodology – the appropriate hypotheses for explaining the past are those with analogues today; (iii) uniformity of kind – past and present causes are all of the same kind, have the same energy, and produce the same effects; (iv) uniformity of degree – geological circumstances have remained the same over time.

Gould argued that (i)–(iv) really reduce to a pair of methodological assumptions and a pair of substantive hypotheses. The methodological assumptions are, first, uniformity of law across time and space: natural laws are constant across space and time. This is now assumed in all scientific discourse (and is empirically confirmed by observations of distant stars and galaxies, as in this case we are directly observing the past). The second assumption is uniformity of process across time and space: natural processes are constant across time and space. This is closest to the UP in linguistics as formulated above, and essentially derives from Occam's Razor: do not invent extra causes to explain the past if those we observe operating in the present will suffice. These two methodological principles are rooted in philosophical views, and are, Gould argues, necessary for the successful pursuit of any science.

The two substantive hypotheses are uniformity of rate across time and space (change is typically slow, steady, and gradual) and uniformity of state across time and space (change is evenly distributed throughout space and time). These are strong empirical hypotheses, somewhat controversial in geology (in fact, Gould argues that they do not hold for geology). In linguistics, they are certainly not universally adopted, and the evidence for or against them is unclear (for discussion of this and other related points concerning the ways in which the UP has been adapted in linguistics, see Janda and Joseph 2003: 26–31). I will briefly consider their possible relevance in the context of a formal theory of syntactic variation in §16.4.

16.2.3   Conclusion

So we see that modern linguistics, since at least the nineteenth century and perhaps earlier, has adopted the UP from more general scientific discourse. As stated in the Introduction in §16.1, it is usually seen as a methodological principle, and as such is fairly uncontroversial (although see §16.3.4). The substantive theses discussed by Gould are of more empirical interest, although it is not clear that they hold for linguistics. I will return to this question below.

16.3   The UP and Linguistic Prehistory

16.3.1   Introduction: Deep Time and Historical Linguistics

The importance of the UP emerges clearly when we consider the time depth at which we can attain information about the languages of the past. The oldest directly attested languages are from around 3000 BC (Sumerian is attested from 3350 BC; Ancient Egyptian from 2690 BC), i.e. roughly 5kya (thousand years ago). Furthermore, it is widely accepted that, beyond a certain degree of temporal separation, which is hard to estimate precisely but is almost certainly less than 10,000 years, techniques of comparative or internal reconstruction are not reliable in that superficial resemblances among possibly cognate forms become increasingly difficult to distinguish from chance similarities, since cognate forms in related languages are replaced over time (Nichols (1997: 365) gives 10kya as the 'fade-out point' for establishing descent and reconstruction in the traditional way; see also Ringe (1992, 1998), the latter illustrating the point vividly in a discussion of the likelihood of an ancient Indo-Uralic unity, and see Bomhard (1998: 20f.) and Greenberg (2005) for a different view). Yet language-possessing humans (modern *homo sapiens*) have been in existence for a very much longer period. Estimates regarding the date of the origin of language vary widely, with anything between 200kya and 50kya being proposed (Tallerman and Gibson 2012: 239–45). It is not necessary to take a view on that date here, since it is clear that, wherever we might situate the date of the origin of language within this range, there are many millennia of unattested languages.[3] How can we be sure that the innumerable languages spoken in the tens of millennia from the origin of language to the earliest date for which we have attested or reconstructed evidence

---

[3] Wells (1973: 427) makes the same point, and also observes that our estimates of the gap between the earliest attestations or reconstructions of languages and the origin of language have grown very significantly since the nineteenth century: 'According to Ussher's chronology [of the events described in Genesis, IR] there would be a gap of about 1,700 years . . . [A]ccording to timetables furnished by the physics and geology of the late nineteenth century, there could be at most a gap of a few thousand years; according to present-day timetables, the gap might be as great as some hundreds of thousands of years'. If – as we will see below – the UP allows us to make inferences about linguistic prehistory back to 50kya, this gap may be less than hundreds of thousands of years, but still most likely several tens of thousands.

were not drastically different from the much more recently attested or reconstructed languages of the past five to ten millennia?

It is precisely in this connection that the UP becomes relevant. As we have seen, the basic idea is that we take it as the null hypothesis that the unobservable distant past was like the observable present and recent past. Ringe (2013) states the point as follows:

> Unless we can demonstrate significant changes in the conditions of language acquisition and use between some time in the past and the present, we must assume that the same types, range and distribution of linguistic structures, variation, changes, etc. existed at that time in the past as in the present.
> *(Ringe 2013: 202)*

Since we have no compelling reason to think that the human language faculty (whatever exactly we might take that to consist in) and, in particular, as Ringe says, 'the conditions of language acquisition and use', are different in the humans which have lived in the past 5,000 years from those who lived in the previous 50,000 or more, then we assume uniformity, and we can extrapolate from our knowledge of the present (and the relatively recent past) to periods of the distant past about which we know nothing from direct evidence. Furthermore, if we have no compelling reason to think that the forces driving language change were different in the distant past from what we can observe regarding change from the recent past to the present, we can extrapolate, assuming the UP, and make inferences regarding patterns of change in the distant past and try to get a picture of the typology and distribution of languages at time depths which exceed both what is directly attested and what is reliably reconstructible. I will return to this point in the context of Principles-and-Parameters theory in §16.4.2 (in this connection, however, we will see that an important caveat is in order, as there may well be compelling reasons to think that in the last few millennia, at least in Eurasia, relatively novel forces have shaped the distribution of languages that were not active at earlier periods – see §16.2.4).

Of course, there is a point in the past when there must have been 'significant changes in language acquisition and use': the time at which the modern human language faculty came into being. As already mentioned, there is little consensus on when this was, and estimates vary widely. Similarly, there is no consensus on what preceded the modern language faculty (no language at all, or perhaps some form of 'proto-language', the latter term being used in the context of discussions of evolutionary linguistics in a way which is significantly different from how it has traditionally been used in historical linguistics, for reasons directly connected to uniformitarianism). Despite our almost total lack of certain knowledge on these questions, we can be sure that there is a point in the past before which the UP does not hold, and after which it does; as Campbell and Poser (2008: 391) point out, this is 'in a sense a definitional demarcation, which says anything else is not human language'. In this connection it is important to distinguish evolutionary linguistics, i.e. the study of genomic changes affecting the language faculty, from diachronic linguistics, the study of changes in instantiations of the language faculty. The UP holds in the latter case but not, since we assume genomic changes are expressed in the phenotype, in the former. The UP can, among other things, act as an important guiding heuristic principle in distinguishing evolutionary linguistics (where little or nothing is really known for certain, beyond the obvious fact that language evolved at some point in the history of our species and, we assume, that this happened through Darwinian descent by modification, i.e. random mutation and natural selection) from diachronic linguistics (where a body of genuine scientific knowledge has accumulated over more than two centuries of research); see again the lucid discussion of these matters in Campbell and Poser (2008: 391f.), and, for an application of UP in the context of evolutionary linguistics, D'Errico and Vanhaeren (2012: 300–2).

16.3.2   Nichols (1990, 1992)

Nichols (1990) observes that the greater linguistic diversity of the New World as compared to the old, which she establishes on several grounds (see below), leads to the conclusion that the view that first settlement of the Americas (generally agreed to have taken place across the Bering Strait from Siberia) must have taken place considerably more than the 12–20kya assumed by standard archaeological models. The best-known such model (although, like all others, it is controversial) is that the first settlers were bearers of the 'Clovis culture', a Paleo-Indian culture named after an archaeological site in Clovis, New Mexico, reliably dated to c. 12kya and often identified with first settlers. Nichols explicitly acknowledges the role of the UP in reaching this conclusion, referring to it as a 'fundamental tenet of science' and defining it as 'the assumption that, although conditions may vary over time, principles do not' (1990: 476). On the basis of the UP, she claims that '[u]nless we can demonstrate very different input conditions, we have no business assuming a tenfold discrepancy in the rate of linguistic differentiation between presently attested language stocks and those that must have existed in the same region in the past' (1990: 476). However, given plausible, and UP-based, assumptions about rates of change and differentiation of linguistic lineages, Nichols argues, exactly this kind of discrepancy arises: a first-settlement date of 12kya simply does not give enough time for the attested linguistic diversity of the New World to arise.

Nichols' conclusions regarding the question of first settlement of the Americas remain controversial (see Nettle 1999 for a critique and Heggarty and Renfrew 2014a for an overview), but, however that may be, they raise three points of interest for historical linguistics.

The first is that these conclusions provide further evidence against Greenberg's (1987) postulated Amerind, one of the three families in his classification of the languages of the Americas, the other two being Proto-Na-Dene and Eskimo-Aleut. Greenberg proposed that Amerind was spoken by the first wave of settlers in the New World, and identified it with Clovis culture. Greenberg arrived at his classification using the method of mass (or multilateral) comparison, i.e. the comparison of sets of forms from putatively related languages and the deduction of actual relationships based on correspondences among any subset of those forms. This methodology has been much criticized, especially in relation to Greenberg's classification of the languages of the Americas; see in particular Campbell (1988), Campbell and Poser (2008) and references given there. Nichols' (1990) critique is of a different kind, however; she says: '[t]he assumptions underlying the method of mass comparison and the procedures usually applied in the search for deep genetic connections are fundamentally mistaken. They presuppose a high degree of genetic elaboration, when that is in fact rare and found only under specific and readily identifiable economic and cultural circumstances' (1990: 492). The reason for this is that mass spread of languages, giving rise to families like Indo-European and Afro-Asiatic, is unusual and directly attributable to cultural and technological developments (see below). Otherwise 'throughout human history most languages have left few descendants, stocks have usually had at most one sister, and at any time about half of the world's lineages have been isolates' (Nichols 1992: 40). It follows, then, that '[t]o assume an Indo-European-like radiation of preagricultural or pre-Neolithic stocks . . . is to violate uniformitarianism' (1990: 492).

Furthermore, Nichols (1990) estimates a likely rate of colonization of the Americas, based on the average time separating the arrival of two historically adjacent stocks (where a 'stock' is the oldest grouping reliably reconstructible using standard techniques, e.g. Indo-European, Eskimo-Aleut, etc.). Based on what is usually thought concerning Eskimo-Aleut and Na-Dene, Nichols estimates the colonization rate for Alaska at one stock per 3,000–5,000 years. But Amerind, as proposed by Greenberg, contains over a hundred stocks. The conclusion is that a 'single pre-Na-Dene entry fits well with the Clovis chronology, where the few millennia between the Na-Dene entry allow just one colonization at the rates established here . . . but genetic unity requires an extremely deep chronology of 50,000 years or more to derive the 140 "Amerind" stocks from a single ancestor' (1990: 513).

A second striking conclusion drawn by Nichols (1990: 504–9) is that (one version of) the Nostratic hypothesis may have more plausibility than Greenberg's Amerind. She begins by noting (1990: 505) that Nostratic (or its 'north Eurasian core': Indo-European, Uralic, Altaic, Kartvelian and possibly Afro-Asiatic) would have to be at least 12,000 years old, hence at least as old as Amerind, if Amerind is associated with Clovis culture. But she shows on the grounds of internal typological diversity, similarity in form of personal pronouns and the ability to recover parts of paradigms (in the case of putative Nostratic personal-pronoun paradigms, 1990: 508) that Amerind looks 'substantially less plausible and substantially older' than Nostratic by all these criteria. This conclusion holds whatever one's view of the general plausibility of this version of the Nostratic hypothesis.

Third, as already adumbrated above, Nichols concludes that large families with multiple sub-branches of the familiar Indo-European kind are the exception rather than the rule in the overall history of the world's languages. This is based on the observation, based on a comparison of a large number of stocks from all over the world, that 'elaboration of lineages [the degree of branching at any given level, IR] appears to proceed at a fairly consistent rate' (1990: 489): most branching is binary and only one to three sub-branches (families) survive per stock. As she points out, Indo-European and Afro-Asiatic are conspicuous counterexamples to this. But, as she further points out, these groups broke up and spread because of 'the development of nomadic or seminomadic stockbreeding, which rapidly increased the scale of the economy' (1990: 498).

This last point is further developed in her discussion in her 1992 monograph:

> The fate of Indo-European, or more generally the fate of a group of typologically similar language families from post-Neolithic inner Asia, has not only distorted theory and method but skewed reality and nature as well. The spread of western Eurasian areal features to cover much of Eurasia has obliterated a great deal of prior linguistic diversity (both genetic and typological) and has skewed world frequencies for structural features . . . Thus our closest perspective on human language comes from the Pacific and the New World, areas relatively unaffected by the vast spreads in the Old World.   *(1992: 281)*

I will take up this last point in the next section.

Nichols (1992) extends her 1990 database and conclusions and represents a major, ground-breaking study of the question of typological variation in the prehistoric past. Her main conclusions are that 'today's linguistic universals are the linguistic universals of the early prehistory of language' (1992: 278), and that she finds 'no evidence that human language in general has changed since the earliest stage recoverable by the method used here. There is simply diversity, distributed geographically. The only thing that has demonstrably changed is the geographical distribution of diversity' (1992: 277). In particular, she concludes that there is evidence for global east–west clines in the distribution of a number of morphosyntactic properties (with Australia and South America at the extreme east and Western Europe at the extreme west) which reflects the original linguistic diversity of the human populations 'at the dawn of human expansion over the globe' (1992: 259), i.e. roughly 60kya. These clines have arisen through 'stabilization of diversity', a process known in population genetics whereby genes tend to approach equilibrium in populations, tending towards 0 or 100 per cent incidence, with equilibrium reached the more quickly the smaller the population. A rough analogy between structurally variant morphosyntactic features and genes leads to the idea that an original slight skewing in the distribution of a given feature could, over many millennia at the global level, give rise to a global cline with distributions at 0 per cent at one end and at 100 per cent at the other (this rough analogy could be made more precise using binary parameters of Universal Grammar; see §16.4). Nichols argues that the incidence of inclusive/exclusive oppositions is a case in point, showing near 0 per cent distribution in Western Europe, at the western extreme of human migration, and nearly 100 per cent in Northern Australia, at the eastern extreme. Although she does not explicitly articulate the UP in the 1992 work, it seems clear that her conclusions are arrived at using the UP as a methodological assumption just as in the 1990 paper, since the typological features that she surveys are assumed to be constant across time and space as structural possibilities of language. In fact, the temporal reach covers a large part of human history, and the spatial reach is global.

Both the 1990 paper and the 1992 book not only assume the UP, but in fact appear to support both the uniformity-of-rate and the uniformity-of-state interpretations of uniformitarianism. The former is supported in the 1990 paper by the empirical observation that elaboration of lineages proceeds at a constant rate and, in the 1992 book, by the idea that stabilization of diversity is a constant function of population size. The latter is supported by the general idea that we can meaningfully compare degrees of diversity, elaboration of lineages, etc., across languages and lineages widely separated in time and space; more specifically, in the 1992 book, it is supported by the idea that variable properties will always tend to equilibrium. For all these reasons, both Nichols' assumptions and conclusions are very important, and testify to the heuristic power of the UP as a methodological principle as well as possibly substantiating the empirical aspects of uniformity isolated by Gould, as discussed in the previous section.

Campbell and Poser (2008: 298–318) criticize several aspects of Nichols' overall programme and conclusions, both in the two works cited here and several others which continue and develop the central ideas in various ways. Their principal criticisms centre on her distinction between 'spread zones' and 'residual/accretion zones', which is not central to her assumption of the UP (although not unconnected from it). They further question both her approach to language sampling and the actual samples chosen in a number of cases. They also question her choice of diachronically stable morphosyntactic typological traits; this would call into question her suggested east–west global clines mentioned above, or at least the instantiations of them she adduces. But it does not call into question the UP as a methodological principle and it leaves open the issue of whether language diversity reflects the population-genetic property of stabilization through diversity, possibly an aspect of uniformity of state. Given the tightly interrelated nature of all these assumptions and choices in Nichols' method and how they jointly inform her conclusions, they conclude that 'we find the overall program so riddled with problems that it offers no reliable insights' (2008: 399). What they do not demonstrate, however, is how actually modifying and 'repairing' some of the assumptions and choices would lead to radically different conclusions. Hence, while their objections (particularly regarding the choice of typological traits) are valid, they do not conclusively demonstrate that her conclusions cannot hold; they simply argue that there are several reasons to doubt them. Moreover, since the UP is a methodological principle and hence not an empirical matter (see the discussion in the previous section), this principle is not invalidated by these objections, although it may be that the empirical claims of uniformity of rate and state do not receive the support that we suggested above; this remains an open question.

16.3.3   Ringe (2013) on Aboriginal Europe

An interesting application of the UP to a specific question in linguistic prehistory is found in Ringe's (2013) paper on the linguistic situation of 'aboriginal Europe', i.e. Europe before the expansion of the Mediterranean classical civilizations of Greece and Rome beginning *c.* 2.5kya. These civilizations were, of course, bearers of Indo-European languages, but it is known that Indo-European languages were spoken in Europe well before the time of their expansion; Celtic especially was spoken over a large area of Western and Central Europe from around 3kya. So, following Ringe, we can look first at the situation as we can reconstruct it, to some extent from classical sources, at the point of Græco-Roman expansion, and then at the situation prior to the arrival of Indo-European in Europe. In both cases, the UP is central to the reasoning.

In dealing with pre-Classical Europe we are dealing with a situation in which there was no state influence on language and language diversity: no government, education system, organized religion or, indeed, any form of centralized power whose effects, over historical time, favour linguistic homogeneity. Hence most of recorded European history does not provide a model for UP-based inferences about the prehistoric situation. Here Ringe's proviso in the comment that '[t]he basic idea behind the UP is that the unobservable past must have been like the observable present, *insofar as relevant conditions have not changed in the meantime'* (Ringe 2013: 202, emphasis original) is crucial. We know that, since the time of the Roman Empire at least, relevant conditions have changed in Europe (at different times in different places of course).

But, as Ringe points out, many parts of the world offer a picture of what prehistoric Europe would have been like, and most of the world (aside from the Near East, Western Asia, India, China and a few other places) prior to European contact in the middle of the last millennium, did. Following Nichols (1990), Ringe takes several geographical factors to condition pre-state distribution of languages. These are latitude (greater density of languages at lower latitudes), littoral (greater density in coastal areas than interiors of continents), rain (less density in arid zones), terrain (greater density in mountainous areas) and scale of the economy (the larger the economy, the less the diversity) (Ringe 2013: 204f., summarizing Nichols 1990: 484–6).

On this basis, we would expect greater linguistic diversity in Mediterranean Europe, particularly Greece and Italy, and also on the Atlantic littoral including the British Isles, with reducing diversity at the higher latitudes; less diversity in the continent's interior, except in the Alps; and little diversity in Scandinavia. Ringe goes on to show that what we know of the languages of the pre-Classical Mediterranean confirms this picture, although of course the record is patchy. As he says, we find 'one substantial family (Italic), two smaller ones [Greek and Celtic, IR] and nine or ten languages that do not belong to any of them' (2013: 207). He adds that 'we might reasonably expect there to have been quite a few other contemporary languages that were never recorded' (2013: 207).

Ringe then goes on to point out that this situation was probably in certain ways atypical, since the spread of a large and complex family such as Indo-European appears to have been quite an unusual event (see the discussion in the previous section and below), and was almost certainly caused by technological or economic advantages associated with speaking that language (not necessarily just the speakers of that language, as Indo-European may have spread through language shift rather than population replacement), e.g. horse-drawn transport and/ or agriculture (see below). So he concludes, still following the UP, that 'the spread of IE languages cannot be expected to have any parallels in the older prehistory of Europe' (2013: 207). Before the arrival of speakers of Indo-European, then, 'a reasonable estimate' for the Mediterranean area 'would be more than thirty languages – possibly many more – grouped into more than twenty families belonging to at least fifteen stocks' (2013: 207). Ringe estimates that the rest of Europe would have altogether shown about as much diversity again, the non-Mediterranean areas all being less intrinsically diverse owing to climate, latitude, topography, inland location, or a combination of these. The total would then have been 'sixty languages in Europe altogether, representing forty language families and thirty stocks' (2013: 208).

Regarding the spread of Indo-European languages into Europe, Ringe (2013: 208f.) argues, again on the basis of the UP, that (a) Proto-Indo-European could never have existed as a single language spoken all over Europe, as this violates the UP-driven scenario just described; (b) Proto-Indo-European must therefore have spread from a much smaller homeland, which (following Anthony 2007) he takes to be 'somewhere in the steppes north of the Black and Caspian Seas'; (c) the spread from that area across Europe to the Atlantic seaboard and the British Isles cannot have taken place through vast population movements or population expansion, again as this is not consistent with the UP; and therefore (d) that Proto-Indo-European spread through what Anthony (2007) terms 'elite recruitment', language shift to a language possibly spoken by a small group of elite migrants driven by the relative political power and/or technological superiority of the latter group. Anthony argues that the power and technological superiority of Indo-European speakers stemmed from domestication of horses and the use of horse-drawn transport. Here again, we see the power of the UP as a heuristic.[4]

16.3.4   A Caveat: Heggarty (2015)

Heggarty (2015: 601) introduces an important caveat to UP-based inferences regarding prehistory. In a section entitled 'A Non-Uniform Prehistory' he states the following:

> Far from appealing to 'uniformitarianism', then, when it comes to the basic forces that shaped human prehistory it is only the very lack of any uniformity in how they applied across time and space that can explain, for example, the glaringly unequal impacts that the societies of Europe and the Americas had upon each other, or those that Bantu-speakers wrought on the populations (and thus languages) of much of Africa. World prehistory is patently not a story of equals and uniformitarianism – so nor is the linguistic panorama that it has shaped.

The point regarding historical divergences in different parts of the world is of course well-taken, but recall Ringe's proviso in his application of the UP in his discussion of prehistoric Europe, quoted above: *'insofar as relevant conditions have not changed in the meantime'*. It seems clear that, probably

---

[4] Ringe, following Anthony, assumes the 'Steppe hypothesis' concerning the location from which Indo-European spread. According to this hypothesis, the proto-language was spoken around 6kya in the steppes north of the Black and Caspian Seas and spread west over Europe and south into Iran, Afghanistan and the Indian subcontinent largely due to the technological advantages afforded by highly mobile horse-based pastoralism. An alternative view, originally proposed in Renfrew (1987), is that the proto-language was originally spoken in Anatolia (modern Turkey) and spread with agriculture from that area across Europe, north to the steppes and south and east into Iran and India (as part of the Neolithic revolution). This latter view entails a much earlier date for the beginning of the spread, probably in the region of 8–10kya. There is little consensus as to which is the correct view, and this is not the place to rehearse the relevant arguments. For a recent overview, see Heggarty and Renfrew (2014a, b).

owing to the development of agriculture and/or to the domestication of horses, relevant conditions did change in Western Eurasia somewhere around 8–12kya. The subsequent history of Western Eurasia, and later the entire world, was indeed non-uniform as a consequence of this.

It is also worth noting that neither Ringe nor Heggarty are discussing structural aspects of languages, but rather likely distributions and densities of languages, language families and stocks. The UP leads us to think that the structural features of prehistoric languages were, all else equal, the same as those of the languages of today and of the documented past, independent of the question of the distribution of languages (and therefore possibly of language types). I will return to this point from a different perspective in §16.4.

16.3.5 Conclusion: Three Phases of Human Linguistic (Pre)History

From the above, we can infer that there have been three major phases in human linguistic history and prehistory. The first phase was prior to the development of the language faculty as we observe it in all present and (documented) past languages, and as we therefore assume, given the UP, it has always existed since whatever evolutionary mechanism led to it arising. As we have mentioned, the date of the emergence of the modern language faculty is much debated, and can be situated at anywhere between 200kya and 50kya. Moreover, what preceded this, either in other hominin species or in archaic *h. sapiens*, is unknown. The concept of proto-language as applied in discussions of language evolution is relevant here, but its utility is uncertain.

The second phase starts from the time of the emergence of the modern language faculty and lasts until roughly 10kya (plus or minus two or three millennia) in Western Eurasia, the time of the emergence and spread of the large language families, arguably disturbing the earlier situation of stable variety due to technological developments, such as agriculture and/or the domestication of the horse. If we accept some version of the Nostratic hypothesis, this would be perhaps as long ago as 12kya. If we leave aside Nostratic, then this would be roughly 8kya (the date of Proto-Afro-Asiatic and, on some reckonings, Indo-European; see footnote 4 on this last point). Ringe's depiction of pre-Indo-European Europe, as well as most of pre-contact America, all of Australia and all of Papua New Guinea, correspond to this situation. As the discussion of Nichols and Ringe above has shown, the UP is central to inferring the nature of this phase. Of course, the linguistic UP does not apply to the articulation from the first to the second phase (see the discussion of Campbell and Poser in §16.2.1).

The third phase involves the spread of major complex families driven by technology (horses, agriculture in Eurasia; boats in Southeast Asia and Taiwan, facilitating the spread of Austronesian). This gives rise to the situation that historical linguists have been able to reconstruct in these parts of the world: large, multiply-branching language families spreading over vast areas of space and time. As Heggarty (2015) points out, it may seem that the UP is not relevant here, but if we take into consideration the effects of what from a linguistic point of view are purely extrinsic technological developments, then perhaps we are here simply observing uniform processes of change, and uniform structural properties, which are differently diffused as compared to the earlier phase owing to the different external conditions (see also Nichols 1990: 475–521).

In this section we have seen the heuristic value of the UP as a methodological principle. It allows us to make plausible inferences regarding what in fact is the greater part of human linguistic history, from the emergence of the modern language faculty to the our earliest reliable reconstructions, i.e. at least 50kya to around 10kya. It also arguably allows us to see that the existence of large language families of the Indo-European type may be a relatively recent phenomenon brought about by extrinsic technological developments. Uniformity of rate and uniformity of state in the sense articulated by Gould and described in §16.2.2 remain unproven, however.

16.4   Uniformitarianism and Universal Grammar

In this section I would like to connect the UP with the Principles-and-Parameters view of syntax. As discussed in Chapters 7 and 27, this volume, the Principles-and-Parameters approach has undergone significant modifications since its inception in Chomsky (1981). Here I will first discuss the 'classical' conception, roughly as put forward in Chomsky (1981) in relation to the UP, and then consider whether the 'emergentist' approach to parametric variation relates to the UP in a different way (see §7.3 for a description of this approach).

16.4.1   Classical Principles-and-Parameters Theory and the UP

The original conception of Principles-and-Parameters theory took Universal Grammar (UG) to consist of a set of principles with parametric options associated with them giving rise to observed variation (for in-depth discussion, see Chapter 13, this volume). For example, UG may determine that a head combines with its complement to form an intermediate (X') projection, but whether the head precedes or follows its complement is a matter of parametric variation.

In terms of this approach to syntax, we can take this to mean that all languages at all times reflect the same basic Universal Grammar and therefore the same set of parametric options. Essentially then, rooting the language faculty in human biology by assuming an innate UG, both the principles and parameters, has the inevitable result that the UP holds. However, uniformity of state and uniformity of rate remain open questions in this context. Concerning uniformity of state, classical principles-and-parameters theory makes no real commitment regarding the distribution of parameter values. If parameters are binary switches, one might expect that the two values of a given parameter would have a roughly 50:50 distribution. For the parameter determining OV vs VO basic word order (however this might be formulated, a matter I leave aside here), this appears correct, as OV and VO languages have roughly the same frequency across the world's languages (Dryer 2013), leaving aside 'minority orders' such VSO, VOS, etc., and the languages for which basic order is hard to discern (Dryer's category of 'no dominant order'). For the null-subject parameter, on the other hand, it appears that the vast majority of the world's languages allow null subjects, with only the Germanic languages, French, some West African languages and a few creoles systematically disallowing them (Newmeyer 2005: 74). Here, of course, markedness may play a role, with the positive value of the null-subject parameter being unmarked (a conclusion reached by Hyams (1986) on the basis of evidence from language acquisition), but no general theory of markedness was developed for this version of principles-and-parameters theory. Concerning uniformity of rate, things are still less clear; see the discussion of parameter resetting as a mechanism of syntactic change in §7.2.

However, although the UP is directly entailed by this view of UG and parametric variation, this conclusion has few clear empirical consequences. One potentially interesting consequence relates to Nichols' proposal that an original slight skewing in the distribution of a given feature could, over many millennia at the global level, give rise to a global cline with distributions at 0 per cent at one end and at 100 per cent at the other, through the process of stabilization of diversity. We can certainly draw an analogy between parameters of UG and genes, thinking of parameters as the unit of linguistic variation and heredity (across generations and through language families), and the surface syntactic phenotype as the expression of the underlying parametric genotype. In that case, perhaps we should expect to find global, or at least areal, clines in the distribution of parametric properties. However, the properties adduced by Nichols (which, as we saw, were criticized by Campbell and Poser 2008) do not lend themselves naturally to an analysis in terms of parameters, at least of the 'classic' kind, and other features such as word order do not appear to show global clines in distribution, although they may show areal ones (e.g. the 'Indosphere' strongly tends to head-finality, object-initial orders are almost entirely restricted to Amazonia, VOS is not found in Europe, etc.). What is needed is more fine-grained investigation combining typological and parametric analysis. Recent refinements of the notion of parameter may be helpful in this connection, and I turn to these in the next section.

16.4.2   Emergent Parameters and the UP

The emergentist approach to parameters is described in detail in §7.3. Here I summarize this approach. The central idea is that the parameters of UG are **not** pre-specified in the innate endowment. Instead, they emerge from the interaction of the three factors in language design identified by Chomsky (2005): the innate endowment, UG (Factor 1), the primary linguistic data of first-language acquisition (Factor 2), and domain-general optimization processes (Factor 3). On this view, one can continue to follow the general characterization of parameters in Chomsky (1995): parametric variation lies in variation in the formal features of functional heads (determiners, complementizers, auxiliaries, etc.), as well as those triggering movement dependencies. Formal-feature variation in UG arises from underspecification for the relevant features. There is thus no specification of the nature of parametric variation at the UG level (although of course UG does specify the invariant properties of language such as Agree and Merge). The third-factor optimization principles are Feature Economy (FE) and Input Generalization (IG), discussed in more detail in §7.3.1 and §7.3.2. Together these principles amount to a form of minimax search and optimization strategy: make maximal use (IG) of minimal means (FE). These principles are not specific to language, although they might represent innate domain-general learning mechanisms (see Biberauer and Roberts 2014).

With this background, we can see that, to the extent that the formal features and the three factors – particularly the third-factor optimization strategies – are innate, then the kinds of parametric options that emerge from their interaction cannot be different in different epochs, as long as the innate endowment is the same. To this extent, then, the emergentist approach does not at first blush appear to offer a dramatically different picture in relation to the UP than the 'classical' principles-and-parameters approach: the strong innateness hypothesis guarantees the UP (across the species).

However, this approach does open up the possibility that the set of formal features subject to UG underspecification and parametrization through interaction with the other two factors may not always have been uniform. The general picture of how parameters emerge could remain entirely consistent with the UP, but this does not commit us to the conclusion that the set of available formal features has not changed over many millennia, or that the set of features accessible in one part of the world may be identical to that available elsewhere. This is particularly clear if we extend the emergentist approach to the array of formal features themselves, as sketched in §7.4 (and see the references given there); if the formal features are not directly given by UG then we are not necessarily committed to the conclusion that this set must always have been uniform (and, again, this does not entail abandoning the UP). This again recalls Nichols' notion of stabilization of diversity giving rise to different kinds of options occurring at 0 per cent in one area and 100 per cent in another (and in fact, her example of clusivity in pronominal systems may be a good candidate for a formal feature, although Campbell and Poser's critique of this specific point is well taken). In particular, we could conjecture that the overall set of formal features may have reduced over time, since certain options may have been winnowed out of the 'feature pool' through being relatively inaccessible to acquisition. Processes of language contact and the spread of large language families in relatively recent millennia, as described in §16.3 above, may have contributed to the reduction of this pool. The result may be that there has been a 'smoothing-out' of the array of available grammatical systems. Hence UG itself and the third-factor acquisition principles do not change, and in fact they cannot change without change to the genome, which we take not to have happened in the time period under consideration, since we are just considering the second and third phases of human linguistic (pre)history discussed in §16.3.5 (i.e. we are concerned with diachrony rather than evolution). The UP is not violated, but at the same time the range of different sets of options actually instantiated in the world's languages may have diminished. In other words, if we think of the set of parameters as defining an abstract space within which grammars can exist, a loss of certain formal-feature options implies that ever smaller pockets of the available space are occupied by actually existing systems. Something like this is certainly possible in principle; whether it has actually happened is an empirical question, albeit a rather difficult one to answer with any certainty. There is perhaps some evidence for something like this from Nichols' observation (1992: 250f.) that the overall level of structural diversity in (some aspects of) grammatical systems is lower in the Old World than in the New World and the Pacific. She points out that '[t]he high diversity there [in the New World and the Pacific – IR] can be regarded as a peripheral conservatism in dialect-geographical terms; these areas, secondarily settled, are far enough from the Old World centers of early spread to have escaped the developments that have lowered genetic density and structural diversity in the Old World' (1992: 250). Here again, of course, the cause may be the external changes which gave rise to the large and complex language families of the Indo-European kind. The intriguing question is whether we can distinguish the effects of large families from possibly independent narrowing of options due to the emergent nature of the factors determining grammatical variation: clearly this would bear significantly on the uniformity of state hypothesis. It may be, then, that as Gould (1965) concluded for geology, substantive uniformitarianism does not hold for linguistics (while methodological uniformitarianism must, as this is a condition for science).

So we see that the emergentist approach to parameters, and *a fortiori* that approach to formal features, may lead to a different view of the relation between the grammatical systems of the present and those of the past as compared to classical principles-and-parameters theory, in particular in relation to the question of uniformity of state. To borrow Newmeyer's (2005) terminology, what is a *possible* language has not changed and cannot change in diachrony (without change to the genome, i.e. evolutionary change), but the array of *probable* languages may be different today from what it was in the second phase of human linguistic (pre)history from at least 50kya to roughly 10kya and not just because of external technological contingencies.

Hence a potential empirical difference between 'classical' and emergentist views of parametric variation arises. Of course, actually verifying this difference is a huge challenge, since we need to know about the typological/parametric variation in languages at a period beyond our earliest attestations and reconstructions. The point may thus seem moot. But, once again, the UP – as a methodological principle – may help us. Specifically, the second methodological principle identified by Gould: do not invent extra causes to explain the past if those we observe operating in the present will suffice (which, as we saw, derives from Occam's Razor). So we should not assume that the forces shaping typological/parametric variation in the distant past were distinct from those at work in the attested recent past. Then we can extrapolate from what we know about typological/parametric change in recorded history to make inferences about what must have gone on in remoter periods. With a sufficiently well-articulated theory of typological/parametric variation, a UP-driven research programme into linguistic prehistory can be descried. Of course, what we lack is an adequate theory of variation. In this connection, a formal theory of parametric variation has the merit of precision, and it is clear from the above that an emergentist theory has the required flexibility (which the 'classical' theory lacks).

16.5 Conclusion

The UP is a fundamental notion in scientific discourse of all kinds, and has been extremely influential in the history of linguistics, although its importance has perhaps not always been fully recognised. Here in §16.2 I briefly sketched the history of the notion within linguistics, noting that it has been central to all modern forms of scientific linguistics, and I tried to briefly to set that against the wider scientific context. In this connection, developments in nineteenth-century biology and geology and the interaction with linguistics were particularly important. In §16.3 I described recent work by Nichols and Ringe which, for all the controversy over certain aspects, clearly shows us the potential power of the UP in allowing known history to shed light on unknown prehistory. Finally, in §16.4, I turned to formal syntactic theory, particularly principles-and-parameters theory, and suggested that the recent emergentist approach to parametric variation may, at least in principle, allow us to make informed inferences about the nature of prehistoric typological/parametric variation.

References

Anthony, D. W. 2007. *The horse, the wheel and language: How Broze Age riders shaped the modern world*. Princeton University Press.

Biberauer, T. and Roberts, I. 2014. 'Contrastive hierarchies in phonology and syntax: The role of third factors (or: Why phonology is *not* different)', MS, University of Cambridge.

Bomhard, A. R. 1998. 'Nostratic, Eurasiatic and Indo-European', in J. C. Salmons and B. D. Joseph (eds.), *Nostratic: Shifting the evidence*. Amsterdam: John Benjamins, pp. 17–50.

Campbell, L. 1988. 'Review of Greenberg (1987)', *Language* 64: 591–615.

Campbell, L. and Poser, W. J. 2008. *Language classification: History and method*. Cambridge University Press.

Chomsky, N. 1981. *Lectures on government and binding*. Dordrecht: Foris.

1995. *The minimalist program*. Cambridge, MA: MIT Press.

2005. 'Three factors in language design', *Linguistic Inquiry* 36(1): 1–22.

Christy, T. C. 1983. *Uniformitarianism in linguistics*. Amsterdam: John Benjamins.

Croft, W. 2003. *Language typology*. Cambridge University Press.

D'Enrico, F. and Vanhaeren, M. 2012. 'Linguistic implications of the earliest personal ornaments', in M. Tallerman and K. Gibson and (eds.), *The Oxford handbook of language evolution*. Oxford University Press, pp. 299–302.

Dryer, M. S. (2013). 'Order of object and verb', in M. S. Dryer and M. Haspelmath (eds.), *The world atlas of language structures online*. Leipzig: Max Planck Institute for Evolutionary Anthropology. (Available online at http://wals.info/chapter/83, accessed on 11 August 2015.)

Gould, S. J. 1965. 'Is uniformitarianism necessary?', *American Journal of Science* 263: 223–8.

1987. *Time's arrow, time's cycle: Myth and metaphor in the discovery of geological time*. Cambridge, MA: Harvard University Press.

Greenberg, J. 1987. *Language in the Americas*. Stanford University Press.

2005. *Genetic linguistics: Essays on theory and method*. Oxford University Press.

Heggarty, P. 2015. 'Prehistory through language and archeology', in C. Bowern and B. Evans (eds.), *The Routledge handbook of historical linguistics*. London: Routledge, pp. 598–626.

Heggarty, P. and Renfrew, C. 2014a. 'Western and Central Asia: Languages', in Renfrew and Bahn (eds.), pp. 1678–99.

2014b. 'Europe and the Mediterranean: Languages', in Renfrew and Bahn (eds.), pp. 1977–93.

Hooykaas, R. 1963. *Natural law and divine miracle: The principle of uniformity in geology, biology, and theology*. Leiden: Brill.

Hyams, N. 1986. *Language acquisition and the theory of parameters*. Dordrecht: Reidel.

Janda, R. and Joseph, B. 2003. 'On language, change, and language change – or, Of history, linguistics, and historical linguistics', in B. Joseph and R. Janda (eds.), *The handbook of historical linguistics*. Malden, MA, and Oxford: Blackwell, pp. 3–180.

Law, V. 2003. *The history of linguistics in Europe: From Plato to 1600*. Cambridge University Press.

Lyell, C. 1830–3. *Principles of geology, being an attempt to explain the former changes of the Earth's surface, by reference to causes now in operation*, vols. 1–3. London: John Murray.

1863. *Geologic evidence of the history of man*. London: John Murray.

Metcalf, G. J. 1974. 'The Indo-European hypothesis in the sixteenth and seventeenth centuries', in D. Hymes (ed.), *Studies in the history of linguistics traditions and paradigms*. Bloomington: Indiana University Press, pp. 233–57.

Morpurgo-Davies, A. 1998. *Nineteenth-century linguistics*, vol. IV of G. Lepschy (ed.), *History of linguistics*. London: Longman.

Müller, F. M. 1864. *Lectures on the science of language*, vol. 2. Reprinted by Cambridge University Press, Cambridge Library Collection, 2013.

Nettle, D. 1999. 'Is the rate of linguistic change constant?' *Lingua* 108: 119–36.

Newmeyer, F. J. (2005). *Possible and probable languages: A generative perspective on linguistic typology*. Oxford University Press.

Nichols, J. 1990. 'Linguistic diversity and the first settlement of the New World,' *Language* 66(3): 475–521.

1992. *Linguistic diversity in space and time*. University of Chicago Press.

1997. 'Modeling ancient population structures and movement in linguistics', *Annual Review of Anthropology* 26: 359–84.

Osthoff, H. and Brugmann, K. 1878. 'Vorwort', in H. Osthoff and K. Brugmann *Morphologische Untersuchungen auf dem Gebiete der indogermanischen Sprachen*, pp. iii-xx. Reprinted by Cambridge University Press. doi:http://dx.doi.org/10.1017/CBO9781139600101.

Renfrew, C. 1987. *Archaeology and language: The puzzle of Indo-European origins.* London: Pimlico.

Renfrew, C. and Bahn, P. (eds.) 2014. *The Cambridge world prehistory*, vol. 3. Cambridge University Press.

Ringe, D. 1992. 'On calculating the factor of chance in language comparison', *Transactions of the American Philological Society* 82(1): 1–110.

1998. 'A probabilistic evaluation of Indo-Uralic', in J. C. Salmons and B. D. Joseph (eds.), *Nostratic: Sifting the evidence.* Amsterdam: John Benjamins, pp. 154–98.

2013. 'The linguistic diversity of Aboriginal Europe', in S.-F. Chen and B. Slade (eds.), *Grammatica et verba, glamor and verve: A festschrift for Hans Henrich Hock.* Beechstave Press, pp. 202–12.

Ringe, D. and Eska, J. F. 2013. *Historical linguistics: Toward a twenty-first-century reintegration.* Cambridge University Press.

Scharf, Peter M. 2013. 'Linguistics in India', in K. Allan (ed.), *The Oxford handbook of the history of linguistics.* Oxford University Press, pp. 227–58.

Staal, J. F. 1974. 'The origin and development of linguistics in India', in D. Hymes (ed.), *Studies in the history of linguistics: Traditions and paradigms.* Bloomington: Indiana University Press, pp. 63–74.

Tallerman, M. and Gibson, K. (eds.) 2012. *The Oxford handbook of language evolution.* Oxford University Press.

Tegmark, D. 2014. *Our mathematical universe: My quest for the ultimate nature of reality.* New York: Knopf.

Wells, R. 1973. 'Uniformitarianism in linguistics', in P. R. Wiener (ed.), *Dictionary of the history of ideas*, vol. 4. New York: Charles Scribner's Sons, pp. 423–31.

Whewell, W. 1837. *History of the inductive sciences, from the earliest to the present times*, 3 vols. London: Parker.

1840. *Philosophy of the inductive sciences founded upon their history*, 2 vols. London: Parker.

17

Markedness, Naturalness and Complexity

Anna Roussou

17.1 Introduction

The terms 'markedness', 'complexity', and 'naturalness' are used, to a large extent, in similar contexts to grasp the need to distinguish between linguistic forms or properties that appear to stand in opposition with each other, may imply some sort of hierarchy, or low vs high frequency in use. In Trubetzkoy's (1931) original analysis, markedness expressed 'privative oppositions', as in the case of voiced vs voiceless, nasalized vs non-nasalized, where the first member of each pair bears a mark, and hence it is 'marked', while the second member lacks it, and hence it is 'unmarked'. Jakobson (1941) extended this view to more abstract properties of lexical and grammatical items; the exemplary case is the perfective vs imperfective aspect in Russian. The former encodes completion while the latter is neutral to the completion or non-completion of an event. Perfective aspect is also morphologically encoded, thus bearing 'formal marking'. The unmarked member in Jakobson's terminology may either be the opposite of the marked or not specified (neutral to one or the other value). Marked forms are also more difficult to learn. So in the Jakobsonian view, markedness correlates with complexity (semantic, formal) and difficulty in terms of learnability.

Since then, the term 'markedness' has expanded to cover a range of relations over different linguistic frameworks both in formal and functional approaches. Battistella (1996) offers a very thorough discussion of how markedness is understood in structuralism (building on Jakobson) and generative grammar. The versatile status of markedness has also led to criticisms. For example, Haspelmath (2006) distinguishes twelve senses of markedness, adding to and elaborating the seven categories of Zwicky (1978), grouped under four main types, namely markedness as *complexity*, as *difficulty*, as *abnormality*, or as a *multidimensional operation*. Haspelmath claims that markedness is a superfluous notion and argues that at least most of the asymmetries attributed to the marked vs unmarked distinction can be captured independently by asymmetries in frequency, or by other factors, such as phonetic difficulty or pragmatic inferences. Markedness as 'complexity' includes Trubetzkoy's notion of opposition in relation to phonemes (e.g. voiceless vs voiced), the opposition in terms of which an element bears a marking (e.g. plural *-s* in English *boys* vs singular *boy*), as well as semantic distinctions (e.g. *dog* denotes both male and female, while *bitch* is only female). Markedness as 'difficulty' involves phonetic properties (e.g. increasing difficulty in the consonantal hierarchy $b > d > g$), morphological (un-)naturalness (e.g. the form *sheep* is not iconic since it stands for both singular and plural, unlike the plural formation *boy-s*), and conceptual properties (e.g. the plural is more difficult to understand). Markedness as 'abnormality' can be textual (e.g. coreference relations), situational (e.g. marked situations invoke more complex expressions), typological, distributional (restricted occurrence under certain conditions which may affect word order for example), and deviating from parameter settings. Finally, markedness as a multidimensional operation expresses a cluster of properties (e.g. the plural is semantically complex, morphologically coded, may not be found in all languages, as opposed to the singular which is simple, not coded, found in all languages, etc.).

Hume (2011) also discusses markedness in a state-of-the-art article, summarizing three types: *descriptive markedness, theoretical markedness* and *markedness constraints*. The first is '[a]n abstract relation holding over members of a set of observations displaying asymmetry, such that one subset is unmarked and the other is marked'; the second is '[a] universal principle or laws that guide language acquisition, loss, inventory structure, processes, rules, etc. toward the unmarked form'; and the third is '[a] technical term in Optimality Theory referring to a category of constraints that evaluate the well-formedness of output structures' (2011: 79). In an earlier paper, Hume (2005) also claims that markedness is a descriptive term, and that the relevant notion to account for the asymmetries observed (focusing on phonology) is that of *predictability*. A form that is more predictable within a system is what qualifies as unmarked; accordingly, the less predictable, the more marked it is. The crucial factor, according to her approach, is linguistic experience. This brings in the role of the learner and the mechanism that allows him/her to sort out the data s/he is exposed to. Furthermore, in Hume's approach, predictability can distinguish between what is language specific (a given grammar) and what is language universal.

The above very brief overview shows that the set of phenomena gathered under markedness have the core property of expressing some sort of asymmetry amongst features, rules/constraints, constructions, or uses. Taking the existence of asymmetries for granted, as the abundance of empirical data manifests, the question is whether 'markedness' serves an explanatory purpose, or whether it is restricted to a descriptive use, as argued by Hume (2005) and Haspelmath (2006) for example. It is important to note that deriving markedness from independent properties does not imply the denial of the attested asymmetries. The crucial question remains what these asymmetries are, what they tell us about the organization of the grammar, and what they tell us about learnability. In the context of the present chapter, the exemplary cases will draw on the view of parameters and their connection with morphosyntactic features. Two issues will be considered: the relevance of 'markedness' within a given grammar and as part of the acquisition/learning process. The combination of these two has also implications for the way we can understand markedness in the context of syntactic change.

The discussion is organized as follows. §17.2 considers markedness in generative grammar and its role in parameter setting. §17. 3 discusses markedness in grammar, showing that the marked vs unmarked distinction can be understood as a language specific property. The definition of formal markedness in the sense of Roberts and Roussou (2003) is relevant here. §17.4 considers markedness from the perspective of a particular grammar, independently of how features are realized (overtly or not) and the role of the learner. The core vs periphery distinction is also relevant here. §17.5 considers markedness in the context of syntactic change. Finally, §17.6 concludes the discussion.

17.2 Markedness and Generative Grammar

17.2.1 Markedness, Evaluation Metric and the Core vs Periphery Distinction

Battistella (1996) offers an interesting and thorough overview of how markedness is understood in the Jakobsonian and the Chomskyan tradition. In Jakobson's view markedness is concerned with binary oppositions and extends from features to semiotics. The opposition in terms of feature values is adopted and elaborated in Chomsky and Halle (1968), where the role of distinctive features in phonology becomes crucial. However, markedness in generative grammar takes different forms at different stages. In the early stages of Transformational Grammar (Chomsky 1965), markedness is associated with an evaluation metric that helps the learner decide which grammar, amongst different ones which can all provide structural description for the available primary linguistic data (PLD), is the optimal one. Chomsky and Lasnik (1977) talk about a 'theory of markedness' which distinguishes between the core grammar (the unmarked case) and the periphery (the marked case). In terms of the evaluation metric, the core grammar is an optimal system.

In Chomsky (1981), the idea of principles and parameters is introduced. Part of the language acquisition process involves fixing parameters.

The simplest setting is the 'default' one, which represents the unmarked case. This has a further implication of allowing marked settings to occur in the core grammar – which are understood as 'preference structures'. In Chomsky's (1981: 7) words:

> When the parameters of UG are fixed in one of the permitted ways, a particular grammar is determined, what I call a 'core grammar'. In a highly idealized picture of language acquisition, UG is taken to be a characterization of the child's pre-linguistic initial state. Experience – in part, a construct based on internal state given or already attained – serves to fix the parameters of UG, providing a core grammar, guided perhaps by a structure of preferences and implicational relations among the parameters of the core theory. If so, then considerations of markedness enter into the theory of grammar.

The availability of possible core grammars derives from the fact that UG makes available a finite set of parameter settings (or more precisely a finite set of parameters, with a finite set of values each). The core vs periphery distinction in relation to markedness is revisited in Chomsky (1986: 147), where three types of markedness are identified: 'core versus periphery, internal to the core, and internal to the periphery'. 'Internal to the core' is what we get in the absence of evidence (the unmarked value of the parameter), while 'internal to the periphery' is what we get in the periphery when certain conditions of the core grammar are relaxed.

In short, moving away from understanding markedness in terms of an evaluation metric that ranks (and constrains) possible grammars brings in the view of markedness as deviation from the core, but also an association with parameter settings. These deviations can be quite regular or highly irregular, which can in turn be treated as exceptions that have to be learnt. An example illustrating this comes from control contexts as in (1) – the controlled subject is represented as PRO, while indices are provided to facilitate readings:

(1)   a. John$_i$ tried [PRO$_i$ to leave].
      b. John$_i$ persuaded Mary$_j$ [PRO$_{*i/j}$ to leave].
      c. John$_i$ promised Mary$_j$ [PRO$_{i/*j}$ to leave].

In (1a) PRO is controlled by the matrix subject, while in (1b) it is controlled by the matrix object, on the assumption that it gets bound by the closest compatible (in phi-features) antecedent. However, in (1c) PRO is controlled by the matrix subject, by-passing the object, contrary to any locality expectations. That *promise* is a subject control predicate is an idiosyncratic property and does not follow from any property of the core grammar. This idiosyncrasy then, which is lexical, has to be learnt and is predicted to be acquired late, as indeed shown by C. Chomsky (1969). Control, as the requirement for a bound reading for the infinitival subject, remains part of the core grammar, and this is obeyed in (1a) and (1b); what differs in (1c) is the choice of controller, in a rather 'unpredictable' and idiosyncratic way.

In the Minimalist Programme (Chomsky 1995), the core vs periphery distinction with the implications it has for markedness does not enter the scene. Parameters are dissociated from principles and are located in the lexicon, very much in the spirit of Borer (1984) and Wexler and Manzini (1987). The distinctions among different levels of syntactic representation, such as S-structure and D-structure, are eliminated and along with them the modular view of grammar. Universal Grammar is minimal and responds to legibility conditions imposed by the interfaces (see Chapter 13, this volume, for discussion). Grammar, or more precisely 'narrow syntax', is understood as a computational system which interfaces with the conceptual-intentional (C-I) system, producing the LF-interface, and the articulatory-perceptual system, producing the PF interface. The two interfaces interact with the corresponding performance systems.

With respect to economy the view is: 'As inquiry has progressed, the presumed role of an evaluation metric has declined, and within the P&P approach, it is generally assumed to be completely dispensable: the principles are sufficiently restrictive so that PLD suffice in the normal case to set the parameter values that determine a language' (Chomsky 1995: 171). Under this view, the evaluation metric, at least in its original sense of guiding the learner to choose from amongst possible grammars, is abandoned. What about parameters then? Are they initially set in the unmarked value and reset to the marked one given sufficient input? Or do they represent open choices at the S_0, that is the initial stage, of language acquisition? In relation to the latter, Chomsky (1995: 213, n. 6) adds '[m]arkedness of parameters, if real, could be seen as a last residue of the evaluation metric'.

It is worth elaborating on the above note. First, despite any potential reservations it leaves open the possibility of having markedness associated with parameters, and second, if this is the case, then the evaluation metric in relation to learnability will also have to be linked to parameters.

17.2.2   Markedness, Parameters and the Lexicon

What the above discussion shows is that the notion of parameters remains crucial in minimalism, where grammar is quite bare. According to Chomsky (1995, 2000, 2001 onwards), narrow syntax as a computational system builds on two primary operations. The first one, Merge, takes two syntactic objects α, β and creates a new syntactic object out of them (labelled as α or β). The recursive application of Merge captures phrase structure. The second one, Agree, establishes a (long-distance) relation between a Probe α and a Goal β, involving feature matching between α and β, which can be construed as members of the same chain. Movement is not a separate operation but an instance of Internal Merge, with β already present in the phrase structure, thus internal – and not external – to the computation. Internal Merge presupposes Agree and leads to displacement of the Goal due to the presence of the EPP (Extended Projection Principle) feature on the Probe. In simple terms, this means that the relation between a Probe α and a Goal β, already established by Agree, further requires merge of the Probe with the Goal. The two different configurations are illustrated in (2) below:

(2)   a. $[_{\alpha P} \alpha [\ldots [_{\gamma P} \gamma .. \beta]]]$ (Agree between α and β)
        b. $[_{\alpha P} \beta \alpha_{EPP} [\ldots [_{\gamma P} \gamma .. \beta]]]$ (Internal merge of α with β)

Whether or not displacement takes place is a matter of language particular properties, and if parametric differences are lexically related, then the options in (2) should be attributed to lexical properties, or more precisely to features associated with lexical items.

In this respect, Roberts and Roussou (2003) take the EPP to be an instruction for spell-out in a higher position, so that the Goal lexicalizes (features of) the Probe as well. So one aspect of parametric variation involves the position where a lexical item is spelled-out, which would in turn give rise to displacement or not. If displacement is more costly because it involves the presence of the EPP feature, second Merge, as well as introduction of an additional copy of β (the Goal), then in terms of complexity, Internal Merge represents a more 'marked' option within a grammar, as opposed to lack of displacement which would then be the 'unmarked' option; in the ranking below, '>' indicates 'more marked than':

(3)   Internal Merge > Agree

Internal Merge then is more marked than *in-situ* configurations which are mediated by Agree only. This picture may look neat but is not complete, since it gives one aspect of parametric variation only, namely the one associated with displacement, derived by a lexical property attributed to the presence of the EPP. Note also that there is a third option in (3), namely 'neither'. This can be understood either as no spell-out for α and β, but still related via Agree for the purposes of interpretation (that is they form a chain which is not spelled-out in either position), or no Agree between the two positions at all, thus α and β do not form a chain. The latter option is obviously not relevant here, as it brings no association between the two elements. In the former case, i.e. Agree with no spell-out, there is essentially no lexical insertion, but only abstract features. That would conform to a formal system which lacks the PF component, a property that is not attested in natural languages though, but this can be a parametric option, as in the case of Agree between v and the direct object in English.

Parametric variation can also arise in the absence of displacement. Consider for example binding relations, as in the case of reflexives where the DP antecedent and the reflexive are both externally merged. Agree in this case ensures that the DP probes for the Goal, i.e. the reflexive, and that they form a chain. The following examples discussed in Wexler and Manzini (1987) illustrate this point with English *himself* vs Icelandic *sig*:

(4)   a. *Jón segir að   [Maria elskar *sig*]
            John said that Mary   loves self
            '*John thinks that Mary loves *himself*'
        b. Jón   segir að   [Maria elski   *sig*]
            John said   that Mary   loves.SBJV self

Wexler and Manzini argue that while both *himself* and *sig* are reflexives obeying Binding Principle A, they have different binding domains; in other words, *himself* requires a local antecedent within its clause, while *sig* can have a long-distance antecedent. More precisely, (4a) is ungrammatical because the reflexive is not locally bound, i.e. within the embedded clause; English and Icelandic behave alike in this example. On the other hand, (4b) is grammatical in Icelandic where the embedded clause has subjunctive inflection, allowing for *sig* to by-pass the embedded subject and take the matrix one as its antecedent; the equivalent English example remains ungrammatical, where in any case there is no subjunctive alternative (see also Koster and Reuland (1991) for wider empirical coverage).

Wexler and Manzini argue that the different binding domains are due to the lexical properties the reflexives *himself* and *sig* have, and argue for the *Lexical Parametrization Hypothesis*:

(5)   'Values for a parameter are associated not with particular lan-
        guages, but with particular lexical items in a language.' (Wexler
        and Manzini 1987: 55)

The lexical parametrization hypothesis gives rise to different binding domains, which stand in a superset–subset relation. In particular, in English the binding domain requires a subject (be that of a finite sentence, a small clause, or a nominal), while in Icelandic it is defined on the basis of inflection (indicative vs subjunctive). The Icelandic value then is a superset of the English one (subset).

The Subset Principle, originally suggested by Berwick (1985), guides learnability in the following way (Wexler and Manzini 1987: 61):

(6)   'The learning function maps the input data to that value of
        a parameter which generates a language: (a) compatible with the
        input data; and (b) smallest among the languages compatible with
        the input data.'

The language learner then starts with what is compatible with the subset grammar and in the light of positive evidence moves on to the superset. The reverse cannot hold, since retreating from a superset to a subset would require negative evidence. The Subset Principle then defines a markedness hierarchy of parameter values viewed from the perspective of the learner.

So far we have identified three types of markedness in relation to parameters: (a) grammar internal as in the case of Internal Merge vs Agree (displacement or not), (b) related to lexical items as in the case of Agree only (e.g. binding), and (c) related to learnability (the Subset Principle). The first two types concern parameters, and should ideally reduce to one another: (a) relates to positions of lexicalization, i.e. the position where a lexical item is spelled out *modulo* the EPP, while (b) relates to properties of lexical items as such. In what follows, I consider markedness in relation to parameters, showing that (a) and (b) reduce to the single property of lexicalization (§17.3), and in relation to the learner (§17.4).

17.3 Formal Markedness and Parametrization

As already discussed, the Minimalist Programme assumes two basic operations, namely Merge and Agree, while the movement operation, which gives rise to displacement of lexical items, reduces to an instance of Internal Merge, following Agree. Let us illustrate the above with some actual examples, starting with *wh*-questions, as in (7):

(7)   a. *Who* did you see _ ?
       b. [*who* [C_{+EPP} did] [you (~~did~~) see ~~who~~] = [[for which x, x a person] did you see x]

The element *who* in (7a) is displaced; syntactically, this is attributed to the presence of an EPP feature associated with a head in the left periphery, here indicated as the interrogative C. According to the configuration in (7b), *who* realizes a scope position consistent with its quantificational force, while the gap (technically a copy of *who*) in the internal argument position of the verb corresponds to a variable; the result is an operator-variable ($Op \ldots x$) chain. The EPP feature then dictates for *who* the scope position where the quantificational (operator) part is lexicalized in the clause structure. Once *who* is displaced, its base position, which is construed as a variable, is not spelled-out. The configuration in (7b) then marks scope via displacement of *who*. This is consistent with Chomsky's (2004) argument that displacement serves legibility conditions at the interface(s), so it is not an imperfection. While the structure in (7b) is transparent in terms of scope marking, it introduces a level of complexity on the morphosyntactic realization of the operator-variable chain, since *who* encodes not only the quantificational part (Op) but also the variable x. In other words, *who* comprises a quantifier feature, namely the *wh*-part, as well as a feature for the variable x, expressed by the vocalic part in this case (cf. also *which*, *what*, *where*, etc.). This is consistent with what Roberts and

Roussou (2003) argue for 'feature syncretism' as a formally marked option: a single lexical item that spells out (lexicalizes) two (or more) positions in the clause-structure has increased feature content, giving rise to a more complex, and in this respect, a more marked output. So whether a feature is 'formally marked' or not corresponds to overt realization (spell-out, lexicalization), which can be derived by a single lexical item encoding different features, or by distinct lexical items.

Chinese, on the other hand, exhibits *wh-in situ*. Cheng (1991) argues that Chinese *wh*-elements are indefinite pronouns, with no inherent quantificational force. As such, they lexicalize the variable part of the *wh*-chain, while scope is computed via binding with a designated Operator in the C position. This is exemplified in (8) below, from Cheng (1991: 112):

(8)   Hufei chi-le   *sheme* (ne)
        Hufei eat-ASP what PART
        'What did Hufei eat?'

In (8) the question particle *ne* may also be present. In this case it spells out the question feature of the clause and marks scope. The *wh*-construction in (8) shows no displacement and the Operator-variable chain is formed by Agree only. According to the markedness hierarchy in (3), this should be a less marked option. In terms of formal markedness, each position can receive its own lexicalization, maximizing the morpho-syntax-LF mapping (one to one). Now, if the question particle is absent, then the scope position receives no lexicalization. In this respect the mapping between morphosyntax and LF is less transparent, allowing for the variable *sheme* to be interpreted either as an interrogative, or an existential quantifier, depending on whether it is bound by the question or the existential operator accordingly.

Agree is also relevant in the binding examples in (4), which exhibit a chain between two argument positions. The two arguments are spelled out independently, thus in terms of formal markedness, the features of each position are independently lexicalized. The anaphoric nature of the reflexive though requires an additional step in terms of interpretation, since the anaphor, in ways similar to the *wh*-variable, has to be bound by a designated argument (an A-chain). The choice of the binder in terms of locality depends on the features the reflexive itself encodes. Thus English *himself* is morphologically complex, comprising the pronoun *him* and the *self* form. The pronominal part *him* dictates obviation from the local subject; on the other hand, *self* suspends this relation and introduces binding by the local subject. Morphologically then, inside the reflexive *him* marks phi-features, while *self* identifies the two distinct arguments as one (simply put, it identifies the Theme with the Agent, thus triggering the reflexive interpretation). Icelandic *sig*, on the other hand, is monomorphemic and has no phi-features, just like *self*. Its morphological make-up then requires that in the absence of any formally marked phi-features, it is compatible with any potential antecedent, subject to locality. Binding by the matrix subject gives rise to a logophoric interpretation (see 4b).

In short, the Internal Merge vs Agree asymmetry can also reduce to lexical properties, with the relevant notion of formal markedness, understood in terms of morphosyntactic realizations. More precisely, in displacement (Internal Merge) the lexical item that qualifies as the Goal is spelled-out in the position of its Probe; so, the same lexical item spells-out two (or more) positions in the clause-structure. If the functional hierarchy defines scope positions, then under displacement, the Goal encodes scope in a transparent way, but at the expense of carrying additional features that allow it to be linked to its base position. This effect is attested with phrases in the *wh*-example considered here, but also includes heads. For example, the auxiliary *did* in (7) spells out the C position, while retaining its inflectional (and verbal) property. So displacement of *did* marks scope over the T (and V) positions. Furthermore, since the verbal part is independently realized by the main verb, we have a chain where V and T/C are independently lexicalized (by the main verb and the auxiliary accordingly), as in Agree relations; in terms of interpretation then both the lexical verb and the auxiliary *did* (which lexicalizes T and interrogative C) are members of the same chain.

If Internal Merge is not at stake, there are two options, as we have seen so far. The first is an *in-situ* configuration where only the Goal is realized; that would be the equivalent of having a *wh-in situ* construction, without a lexicalization of the Probe (no particle in the Chinese case), and therefore no formal marking of the scope position. The second is the case where both the Probe and the Goal are independently realized. In this particular case, the morphosyntactic structure is transparent (distinct realizations for distinct heads), but interpretation at the LF-interface requires the formation of an Agree relation, rendering the two distinct elements part of the same chain; or in other words, forcing matching features to be interpreted as a single syntactic object. Different interpretative effects may arise, depending on further properties of the lexical items involved, as is the case with *himself* vs *sig*.

If parameters are associated with the lexicon, in the sense that lexical items realize features, then the relevant notion is that of formal markedness. A feature is formally marked as a facet of lexicalization (spell-out in minimalism). There are different ways that this can be derived, as we have just seen. Assuming that lexical items (or features) are not interpreted in isolation but in association with other features in the clause structure, they form a chain under the operation of Agree. Internal Merge implies that a lexical item β, as the Goal, realizes features associated with the Probe α (or Probes along the functional hierarchy). Agree comes in two shapes:

either Probe and Goal receive distinct realizations, α and β accordingly, or the Probe is not realized (no α), but the Goal is (via β). The former case, unlike the latter, maximizes the mapping between morphosyntax and LF. What this account implies is that formal markedness in syntax is a property of chains.

Having considered the role of parameters in association with formal markedness as a facet of lexicalization, I next turn to markedness in association with learnability, distinguishing between what is marked or unmarked for a given grammar (reminiscent of the core vs periphery distinction) and what is marked or unmarked for the learner.

17.4   Markedness, Core Grammar and Learnability

One question that arises is whether Universal Grammar predefines parameter settings which are to be understood as the 'unmarked' or 'default' ones. If that is the case, then the acquirer would start from the unmarked, and in the presence of sufficient input data would move to the marked, complying with the adult grammar.

Let us start by considering whether UG already provides an initial setting or not. In order to illustrate this, let us take the null subject (or pro-drop) parameter, which has been extensively discussed in the literature (see also §25.3.3.). The simplest view is that this parameter has a binary setting: a language allows for null finite subjects (pro-drop) or does not (non pro-drop). Italian (and Greek) belong to the former type, while English to the latter, as shown in (9):

(9)   a. Parla Italiano
       b. *Speaks Italian (OK: *He* speaks Italian)

The traditional view (Rizzi 1982, 1986) is that the null subject is an empty pronominal *pro*, which is subject to licensing and identification by an appropriate head (here, finite Tense). Since English does not have the right feature specification on T, *pro* is unavailable. In English we have the reverse situation: the overt DP is required to license and identify the phi-features of finite T (see Ackema 2002).

In this rather simplistic view of the pro-drop parameter, which predicts two types of languages, namely null subject and non-null subject, what is the unmarked setting? Note that this question is close to the Jakobsonian substantive markedness. In her seminal approach to language acquisition as parameter-setting, Hyams (1986) argues that children start with the [+pro-drop] value. This is empirically supported by the fact that early English allows for null referential subjects. Parameter resetting to the [−pro-drop] value of the adult grammar is triggered, according to Hyams, by the realization that an overt subject is required even in contexts where it is not an argument. Expletive subjects then, like *it* and *there*, qualify as cues that force the acquirer to reset the parameter to [–pro-drop].

If the initial state of language acquisition contains the unmarked (or 'default') value of the parameter which is the [+pro-drop] one, this would give rise to the wrong predictions regarding the Subset Principle, since the [+pro-drop] value gives a superset of the [–pro-drop] value (see Smith 1988). So the acquirer would have to start with a superset and move to a subset, for which s/he would need negative evidence, contrary to fact. The picture becomes more complicated once we consider that there are partial pro-drop languages, like Hebrew for example. It is worth pointing out here that parameter settings do not always come in subset–superset relations but quite often give rise to intersective grammars (see Battistella 1996); so perhaps we also need a better understanding of the Subset Principle (see Biberauer and Roberts 2009).

Roberts (2007) takes a different stand on the format of parameters. Assuming for the sake of simplicity that parameters are binary, he formulates the pro-drop parameter as follows (2007: 271):

(10) a. *Parameter*: Finite T {has/does not have} sufficient specification of agreement features φ to bear the subject thematic role/Agree with *pro* in SpecTP.
      b. *Default*: φ is absent.
      c. *Cue/expression*: 'rich' agreement morphology on T- and/or V-elements.

The description of the parameter in (10) is consistent with the current view that parameters are lexical, here expressed in terms of agreement features on finite T. The positive value, namely the availability of null subjects, is triggered by the presence of inflectional agreement on T or V. In this respect then, formal marking plays a role. On the other hand, (10b) implies that there is no initial setting that would favour one or the other type of grammar. If φ is absent, this means that T is unspecified with respect to phi-features. So the language learner will comply with the specification that is compatible with less (or no) features and given the right cues (in the sense of Dresher 1999) will decide about the correct parametric value consistent with the language input. So null subjects in early English grammars will have to be accounted for by some other means. The format in (10) does not only guide language acquisition but can also underlie language change, where a given grammar either reverts to the default (losing null subjects) or develops specified marking (acquiring null subjects along with phi-features on T).

If there is no default initial setting and at the same time parameter settings have to be somehow specified, the learner will assume the less costly option. Roberts (2007) argues that this is in accordance with the absence of phi-features on finite T. Focusing on this, we see the following implication: there is no Agree relation established between T and the subject, but only between T and the verbal head(s) *v*/V. The syntactic subject then is not interpreted in relation to T, carries thematic properties only, cannot be an expletive, and is restricted in referential terms (for example, it cannot have a generic interpretation). How null subjects are represented in early grammars is not clear under this approach.

So, despite potential limitations, the format in (10) raises an important issue, regarding the nature of null subjects in early English vs early Italian/Greek. Indeed, Tsimpli (1996) argues that early subjects in English are not of the *pro*-type but have properties that render them akin to PRO (which due to the nature of child grammars is discourse-bound). The situation is different in Greek for example, where the cue in the form of phi-features is directly available in the language input. As shown in Tsimpli (1996), Greek children are sensitive to inflectional morphology from early on. Thus they do not produce bare forms of the verb, since the verbal stem is bound in Greek, and agreement inflection is present right from the start. The morphological cue then is very prominent in Greek (and Italian) and facilitates parameter setting. On the other hand, the absence of the relevant inflectional morphology in English requires that some other cue, such as word order and/or expletive subjects, is required. So in this case the acquirer would make the simplest assumption (the 'default') consistent with the language input. The obligatory realization of the subject in a fixed position provides the evidence that phi-features in English can only be provided by an overt DP. On this view then, the notion of markedness can also be understood as a device that guides the language learner, who has to figure out the relevant parameter-setting on the basis of the linguistic evidence s/he is exposed to. In other terms, the formulation in (10) is perhaps best understood, not as a UG property, but as one associated with the learner. This has the implication that there are no UG default options, or perhaps less so than originally suggested.

Turning now to the different choices within the same grammar, we observe that the parameter settings go along with different properties associated with the overt or null subject. More precisely, the 'default' choice in Greek or Italian is to have a null subject – this is consistent with the fact that the subject, whether referential or not, is always marked via the inflectional ending on the verb. Since inflection is pronominal, it automatically satisfies the requirement for a syntactic subject, in accordance with the original formulation of the EPP in Chomsky (1982) (see Manzini and Savoia 2007). The realization of a full DP as the subject is not grammatically required, so when present, it can carry additional properties relating to the information structure of the clause, such as topic or focus. On the other hand, the situation in English is the reverse. The DP subject must always be present in finite contexts, since this is the only way for the EPP to be satisfied. So the presence of a DP is grammatically imposed. However, as Haegeman (1990) shows, null subjects in finite clauses in English are possible, but always associated with a certain register, as is the case with diary contexts. In other words, if the grammatical requirement is not fulfilled in the syntax, the interpretation of the null subject is strongly discourse-bound.

The distribution discussed above regarding null subjects in English as opposed to Greek or Italian brings in the core vs periphery distinction in generative grammar. The core in English requires an overt finite subject; null subjects are permitted, but occur in the periphery in the sense that their distribution and interpretation is subject to discourse requirements, and is therefore associated with certain registers. On the other hand, the core in Italian/Greek allows for a null subject with no further requirements. When an overt subject is present it provides additional information. Unlike English though, the overt realization of a subject in these grammars is not associated with certain registers, and in this respect it does not define a property of the periphery in the same way that English null subjects do. So one could say that in Greek/Italian, overt subjects are peripheral within the core grammar. In short, we have a hierarchy viewed from the perspective of a given grammar, as in (11):

(11)   periphery > peripheral to the core > core

The above discussion shows that although it is not so obvious what an unmarked setting provided by UG would look like, it is possible to argue that within a given grammar, certain realizations are more or less marked. Two clarifications are at stake. The notion of markedness invoked here is not that of formal markedness, as both English and Italian/Greek provide an overt realization of the subject, either in terms of an overt DP or in terms of pronominal inflection on the verb. Instead it relates to preferences grammatically (or not) encoded. Second, markedness in the above discussion is associated with specific grammars, or what Tsimpli and Hulk (2013) call a 'linguistic default', namely a property that characterizes options within a specific grammar. They further distinguish the 'learner default', that is the choices the language learner makes. In this respect, the 'default' in (10b) refers to the learner. To make it more precise, for the Greek/Italian learner the 'default' is cued by the presence of inflectional agreement on the verb. As they also point out, in some cases there can be a clash between the grammar and the learner default, causing instability in the system, which may trigger morphosyntactic changes.

We can add more examples of this kind. Consider again the *wh*-parameter exemplified above for English and Chinese. English is a *wh-ex-situ* language, while Chinese is a *wh-in-situ* language, a property which correlates with the fact that Chinese does not have *wh*-pronouns (for an overview, see Cheng 2003a, 2003b). In the format of Roberts (2007: 272), the relevant parameter is as follows:

(12)   a. *Parameter*: [+wh] C {has/does not have} an EPP feature triggering movement of a wh-phrase to its Spec.
    b. *Default*: EPP is absent.
    c. *Cue/Expression*: 'displaced' *wh*-phrases, *wh*-marking on D.

The default according to (12) is that there is no movement; once the learner encounters fronted *wh*-elements or realizes that the DP is morphologically marked as *wh*-, as in English *what, who, which*, etc., the parameter is set to the correct value consistent with the language input.

Once again, this formulation is a bit simplistic, if we are to assume that the early stages of language acquisition exhibit the default value. At least the English and Greek data show that once *wh*-questions are acquired they are formed with displacement (see Tsimpli 2005). So it is rather difficult to maintain the 'UG default' view as the choice for the initial setting that would accordingly lead to instances of *wh-in-situ* in early grammars. If instead, the 'default' concerns the learner, then in the presence of strong cues (relating to formal markedness) in English and Greek for example, the *wh*-parameter is correctly set right from the start, predicting the absence of *in-situ* constructions in the relevant early grammars.

At the same time it is worth pointing out that the language input also contains *wh-in-situ* in both English and Greek (see, among others, Pires and Taylor 2007; Vlachos 2012). Apart from multiple *wh*-constructions of the kind in (13a), we also find constituent questions of the kind in (13b) as information-seeking questions:

(13)   a. *Who* saw *what*?
    b. A: Yesterday, I went to the meeting of the employees.
        B: And you met *who*?

The construction in (13b) is not as uncommon as usually thought. So it exists in the input, along with (13a). However, neither of them qualifies as a cue that would make the acquirer set the parameter to the 'default' value, at least initially. The discussion we had above between the core and the periphery is also relevant here. *Wh-in-situ* constructions of the (13b) type are part of the periphery, in the sense that they belong to certain registers and as such require contextual information; in other words, (13b) cannot be an out-of-the-blue question. Thus although permitted by the grammar, it exhibits different properties in syntax (lack of locality constraints for example; see Vlachos 2012) and the interfaces. In terms of language acquisition, *wh-in-situ* constructions in English would be predicted to come in late in the acquisition process, precisely because they are discourse-oriented and therefore require knowledge which is outside the grammar; in this respect they relate to the acquisition of pragmatics.

17.5   Markedness and Syntactic Change

So far we have considered (a) formal markedness which relates to lexicalization choices, (b) markedness relating to different settings within a given grammar (overt vs null subjects, *ex-situ* vs *in-situ* constructions), and (c) markedeness from the perspective of the learner. In this section we implement the three aspects of markedness with respect to language change, and in particular changes in parameter settings.

Roberts and Roussou (2003) adopt the view that uniformitarianism and connectivity as argued by Croft (1990) underlie diachronic changes, and provide the following formulation in terms of Principles and Parameters (2003: 216) (see Chapter 16, this volume):

(14)   a. Uniformitarianism: the languages of the past conform to the same UG as those of the present;
       b. Connectivity: a grammatical system can change into any other grammatical system given enough time (i.e. all parameters are equally variable).

Given (14), the languages of the past are grammatical systems defined by the operations Merge and Agree which build syntactic objects and relations based on features provided by the lexicon, as well as legibility requirements imposed by the interfaces. As such they are also predicted to exhibit parametric changes which lead to new grammars.

To this we should add the connection between language acquisition and language change, as first pointed out by Lightfoot (1979): a change occurs when a population of language acquirers converges on a parameter setting which differs from the adult grammar. So two issues become relevant: what makes acquirers converge and how parameter resetting takes place. In the context of our discussion, the question is how markedness can affect parameter resetting.

Since parameters are linked to the lexicon, the most relevant notion is that of formal markedness. According to the hierarchy in (3), Internal Merge (lexicalization by displacement) is more marked than lexicalization by Agree. So when a grammatical system moves from the Agree option to the Internal Merge one, it increases in formal markedness. The reverse movement reduces markedness accordingly. As Roberts and Roussou (2003) point out, the question is why grammars do not consistently move towards the less marked option, reaching a stage where Agree does not involve any lexicalization (the third option). As already mentioned, the latter would be the case in a formal system with no PF-interface. Since this is not the case in natural languages, we keep the two options given in (3). As already discussed, there seems to be a trade-off between syntax and the interfaces. In Internal Merge, the same lexical item lexicalizes two positions and also defines the relative scope of the chain. On the other hand, when only Agree is at stake, the two positions receive distinct lexicalizations (or at least the Goal does), which are forced to match as members of the same chain (and thus interpreted as one entity). If the Probe is not lexicalized, scope in a general sense (as an Operator, or an argument in an A-chain) will be computed at the LF-interface only. Thus increase in formal markedness can lead to decrease of complexity in terms of lexical insertion and reading-off the chain at LF.

Consider next 'markedness' as a device that guides the learner. Assuming the conservative nature of the language learner, s/he will take the simplest option compatible with the data. We can illustrate this with the null subject parameter discussed in the previous section. Suppose that a [+pro-drop] language like Greek were to become [–pro-drop] like English. If the null subject in Greek is linked to inflectional morphology, the parametric change would (or could) be expected to relate to loss of inflection. Suppose that inflection, due to phonological or other reasons, became opaque to the acquirer. By 'opaque' we mean that the mapping between the morphosyntactic expression and the features it is meant to encode is not clear. For example, this would be the case where there is no consistent distinction between inflectional endings marking person and number, as is the case with syncretism in morphological paradigms. So either the same piece of inflection is used to express different features (e.g. first and second person, singular or plural) or it is altogether lost.

The first case is more or less what we have with infinitival inflection: the same pronominal ending is compatible with different specifications, thus being compatible with any potential subject; in this respect it can be characterized as a form unspecified for phi-features. Thus there is formal marking of the subject, but the interpretation of the affix is that of a variable. The second case involves complete loss of inflectional endings, leaving no morphological paradigm, as was indeed the case in the history of English (with the exception of third-singular present-tense -s). In this case there is no formal marking provided on the verb. An expected (or possible) consequence of this is the resetting of the null-subject parameter to an option that requires displacement of the subject in order to satisfy the EPP in relation to T (fully for all verbal forms or partially). In principle, the reverse can also take place, namely a grammar can acquire inflectional endings when free-standing pronouns become clitics and further reduce to affixes. This is a change where the syntactic expression of the subject becomes morphosyntactically provided, thus enriching the inflectional paradigm of a given grammar. Changes in formal marking have repercussions in both syntax and the lexicon.

By way of a follow-up on this with respect to markedness within a grammar, it is worth noting that parameter resetting may also affect what counts as unmarked inside the grammar, what we defined as the core vs periphery distinction in broad terms. A grammar that loses null subjects also reverts to a new core where the realization of the overt subject is the basic option. What about the unmarked or default with respect to the learner? As we saw above, the learner plays a crucial role in language change. If the input is opaque or if there is a clash between what is the default in the grammar and what is understood as default (less complex, etc.) by the learner, one expects to find instability in the system which can potentially lead to changes.

For example, Tsimpli and Hulk (2013) discuss the acquisition of gender in Greek and Dutch in order to account for the differences in acquisition in the two grammars. In Greek the 'linguistic' (grammar) and the learner default coincide on the neuter value for gender. In Dutch on the other hand, the picture is more complicated due to the presence of two forms of the definite article, namely *de* (common) and *het* (neuter); *de* is also used in the plural of definite of both common and neuter nouns, while *het* is also the third-person neuter pronoun. As the authors argue, based on formal criteria, *het* is the grammar (linguistic) default, with *de* representing the elsewhere case. However, the acquisition of *het* is very delayed. They then show that *de* is the default for the learner, is not specified for gender but expresses definiteness with both common and neuter nouns. This causes a learnability problem which is enhanced by the fact that pronominal *het* is acquired earlier than other pronouns. Although it is hard to predict any changes, they tentatively suggest that the learnability problem that arises in this case could be an indication that *het* has many chances of becoming obsolete from the nominal system, while remaining in the pronominal one.

In short, markedness in syntactic change plays a role both in terms of formal marking (loss of movement or development of movement, possibly with further consequences for Agree), and in terms of learnability.

17.6 Conclusions

The notion of markedness has received many interpretations and has been used in different frameworks to account for a wide range of empirical data. Its underlying notion is that of opposition. There have also been attempts to reduce markedness as an explanatory tool to a descriptive term, while deriving its consequences from independent properties inside and outside the grammar. Within the Principles and Parameters model, markedness has also received different interpretations. In this chapter I have argued that we can identify three types of markedness: (a) formal markedness, which relates to lexicalization of chains via Internal Merge or Agree only; (b) markedness internal to a given grammar, which relates to parameter settings but also defines grammatical preferences that lead to a core vs periphery distinction; and (c) markedness from the perspective of the learner, which builds on UG properties along with the language input. All three types also enter aspects of diachronic changes.

References

Ackema, P. 2002. 'A morphological approach to the absence of expletive PRO', *UCL Working Papers in Linguistics* 14: 291–319.

Battistella, E. 1996. *The logic of markedness*. Oxford University Press.

Berwick, R. 1985. *The acquisition of syntactic knowledge*. Cambridge, MA: MIT Press.

Biberauer, T. and Roberts, I. 2009. 'The return of the subset principle', in C. Paola and G. Longobardi (eds.), *Handbook of historical linguistics and linguistic theory*. Oxford University Press, pp. 58–74.

Borer, H. 1984. *Parametric syntax*. Dordrecht: Foris.

Cheng, L.L.-S. 1991. 'On the typology of wh-questions', unpublished PhD thesis, MIT.

    2003a. 'Wh-in-situ', *Glot International* 7(4): 103–9.

    2003b. 'Wh-in-situ: Part II', *Glot International* 7(5): 129–37.

Chomsky, C. 1969. *Acquisition of syntax in children 5 to 10*. Cambridge, MA: MIT Press.

Chomsky, N. 1965. *Aspects of the theory of syntax*. Cambridge, MA: MIT Press.

    1981. *Lectures on government and binding*. Dordrecht: Foris.

    1982. *Some concepts and consequences of the theory of government and binding*. Cambridge, MA: MIT Press.

    1986. *Knowledge of language: Its nature, origin, and use*. New York: Praeger.

    1995. *The minimalist program*. Cambridge, MA: MIT Press.

    2000. 'Minimalist inquiries: the framework', in R. Martin, D. Michaels and J. Uriagereka (eds.), *Step by step: Essays on minimalism in honor of Howard Lasnik*. Cambridge, MA: MIT Press, pp. 89–156.

    2001. 'Derivation by phase', in M. Kenstowicz (ed.), *Ken Hale: A life in language*. Cambridge, MA: MIT Press, pp. 1–52.

    2004. 'Beyond explanatory adequacy', in A. Belletti (ed.), *Structures and beyond*. Oxford University Press, pp. 104–31.

Chomsky, N. and Halle, M. 1968. *The sound pattern of English*. New York: Harper and Row.

Chomsky, N. and Lasnik, H. 1977. 'Filters and control', *Linguistic Inquiry* 8: 425–504.

Croft, W. 1990. *Typology and universals*. Cambridge University Press.

Dresher, E. 1999. 'Charting the learning path: cues to parameter setting', *Linguistic Inquiry* 30: 27–68.

Haegeman, L. 1990. 'Understood subjects in English diaries', *Multilingua* 9: 157–99.

Haspelmath, M. 2006. 'Against markedness (and what to replace it with)', *Journal of Linguistics* 42: 25–70.

Hume, E. 2005. 'Deconstructing markedness: A predictability-based approach. *Proceedings of the Annual Meeting of the Berkeley Linguistics Society*, pp. 182–98. Available on line http://elanguage.net/journals/bls/article/viewFile/796/685.

2011. 'Markedness', in M. van Oostendorp, C.J. Ewen, Hume, E. and Rice, K. (eds.), *The Blackwell companion to phonology*, vol. 1. Malden, MA: Wiley-Blackwell, pp. 79–106.

Hyams, N. 1986. *Language acquisition and the theory of parameters*. Dordrecht: Reidel.

Jakobson, R. 1941. *Kindersparche, Aphasie und allgemeine Lautgesetze*. English translation: *Child language, aphasia, and phonological universals*, trans. A. Kiesler. The Hague: Mouton.

Koster, J. and Reuland, E. (eds.) 1991. *Long-distance anaphora*. Cambridge University Press.

Lightfoot, D. W. 1979. *Principles of diachronic syntax*. Cambridge University Press.

Manzini, M. R. and Savoia, L. 2007. *A unification of morphology and syntax: Investigations into Romance and Albanian dialects*. London: Routledge.

Pires, A. and Taylor, H. 2007. 'The syntax of wh-in situ and common ground', *Proceedings from the Annual Meeting of the Chicago Linguistic Society* 43(2): 201–15.

Rizzi, L. 1982. *Issues in Italian syntax*. Dordrecht: Foris.

1986. 'Null objects in Italian and the theory of pro', *Linguistic Inquiry* 17: 501–57.

Roberts, I. 2007. *Diachronic syntax*. Oxford University Press.

Roberts, I. and Roussou, A. 2003. *Syntactic change: A minimalist approach to grammaticalization*. Cambridge University Press.

Smith, A. 1988. 'Language acquisition: Learnability, maturation, and the fixing of parameters', *Cognitive Neuropsychology* 5(2): 235–65.

Trubetzkoy, N. 1931. 'Die phonologischen Systeme', *Travaux du Cercle Linguistique de Prague* 4: 96–116.

Tsimpli, I. M. 1996. *The prefunctional stage of first language acquisition: A crosslinguistic study*. New York: Garland.

2005. 'Peripheral positions in early Greek', in M. Stavrou and A. Terzi (eds.), *Advances in Greek generative syntax*. Amsterdam: John Benjamins, pp. 179–216.

Tsimpli, I. M. and Hulk, A. 2013. 'Grammatical gender and the notion of default: Insights from language acquisition', *Lingua* 137: 128–44.

Vlachos, C. 2012. 'Wh-constructions and the division of labour between syntax and the interfaces', unpublished PhD thesis, University of Patras.

Wexler, K. and Manzini, M. R. 1987. 'Parameters and learnability in binding theory', in T. Roeper and E. Williams (eds.), *Parameter setting*. Dordrecht: Reidel, pp. 41–76.

Zwicky, A. 1978. 'On markedness in morphology', *Die Sprache* 24: 129–43.

18

Acquisition and Learnability

David W. Lightfoot

18.1 Explaining Change through Acquisition and Learnability

In work on syntactic change, one needs good hypotheses for the early stage of the language under investigation and for the late stage, after the change has taken place; one needs a good synchronic analysis at both ends of any changes to be considered. That means that one needs all the ideas marshalled by synchronic syntacticians. However, there is more to describing and explaining changes through time: questions arise that do not typically impinge on synchronic work, different research strategies are called for, and certainly there are different research traditions. Under an approach linking syntactic change to acquisition, work on change casts light on the idealizations used in synchronic work and is instructive for synchronic syntacticians, as I aim to make clear in this chapter.

Historical linguists from the very beginnings of the field in the early nineteenth century have been asking 'why' questions ever since they began discovering the misnamed 'laws' of sound change. Grimm's Law dealt with changes in the Proto-Indo-European consonantal stop system in early Germanic but after colleagues like Hermann Grassmann had begun explaining apparent exceptions to the 'law', Jacob Grimm knew that philologists needed an explanation for why those changes had taken place and turned toward some bad psychology toward the end of his life (Grimm 1848; Lightfoot 2006). There was a great deal of discussion about the explanation of sound changes, usually based on ideas about a universal directionality to change. People generally agreed that there was a directionality to change but there was no agreement on what the directions were. For an account of how historical linguists have sought explanations over the last two hundred years, see Lightfoot (2013).

Over the last decades an approach has developed that links the explanation of syntactic changes to ideas about language acquisition, learnability and the (synchronic) theory of grammar. This linkage is made in two different but not incompatible ways, one seeing change as externally driven and the other as, at least in part, internally driven.

First, Baker and McCarthy (1981) identified the 'logical problem of language acquisition' as one of identifying the three elements of the triplet of (1).

(1)   Primary linguistic data (Universal Grammar → Grammar)

Children are exposed to primary linguistic data (PLD) and, as a result, their initial state characterized as Universal Grammar (UG; for discussion see Chapter 13, this volume) develops into a mature state characterized by a particular individual, internal grammar or, these days, 'I-language' (I use the terms interchangeably). The solution to the logical problem lies in identifying the three items in such a way that links a particular set of PLD to a particular grammar, given particular ideas about UG. Children seek the simplest and most conservative grammar compatible with both UG and with the PLD that they encounter (Snyder 2007).

Under that approach, there can only be one way to explain the emergence of a new grammar: a new grammar will emerge when children are exposed to new PLD such that the new PLD trigger the new grammar. In that sense, it is new PLD that cause the change; principles of UG, so conceived, certainly do not play a causal role in change, as is sometimes said (see Lightfoot 1979 on the Transparency Principle, and Chapter 15, this volume, and Biberauer and Roberts 2009 on the Subset Principle), but provide the outer limits to what kinds of changes may occur.

Crucial to this approach is Chomsky's (1986) distinction between internal and external language, I/E-language, both of which play an essential role in explaining change. E-language is the amorphous mass of language out in the world, the things that people hear. There is no system to it but it reflects the output of the I-language systems of many speakers under many different conditions, modulated by the production mechanisms that yield actual expressions. Internal languages, on the other hand, are mental systems that have grown in the brains of individuals and characterize the linguistic range of each of those individuals; I-languages ('I' for internal and individual) are represented in individual brains and are, by hypothesis, biological entities.

The PLD consist of structurally simple things that children hear frequently, robust elements of their E-language (in fact Degree-0 complex; see Lightfoot 1999). Work in diachrony, therefore, makes crucial use of the E-language/I-language distinction and keys grammatical properties to particular elements of the available PLD in ways that one sees very rarely in work on synchronic syntax. Successful diachronic work distinguishes and links two kinds of changes: changes in PLD (part of E-language) and changes in mature I-languages. The changes are quite different in character, as we will see when we consider some well-understood changes below.

Second, there are other approaches that ascribe to UG not only a means of linking PLD to I-languages but also 'biases' that prefer certain grammars to others independent of the PLD in such a way that they predict how I-languages change over time (Roberts and Roussou 2003; van Gelderen 2011). This revives nineteenth-century and late twentieth-century ideas about universal directions to change and should be kept in mind as a logical possibility: under this view, change is internally driven – a child might be exposed to roughly the same PLD as her mother but converge on a different I-language not because of external forces (new PLD) but because UG has a built-in preference for certain I-languages; somehow UG allows less preferred I-languages to develop and then performs therapy to weed them out, thereby causing change.

Personally, I am sceptical of such explanations and do not believe that a convincing case has been made for them. If UG defines the limits to available I-languages, then it blocks the emergence of other systems, practising a kind of prophylaxis rather than therapy weeding out logically possible but dispreferred systems (see Chapter 15, this volume, for the prophylaxis/therapy distinction). If there is a built-in preference for certain I-languages, one needs something more to explain why relevant changes took place at particular times and under particular circumstances and why they did not take place in languages where they are not attested, and why they did not take place in some speech community one or more generations earlier.

Work on language change, linking changes to language acquisition by children, has been conducted now for some decades and there have been some surprising results that lead us to rethink the relationship between PLD and particular I-languages. Diachronic syntacticians have ideas quite different from those common among their synchronic colleagues about which PLD trigger which particular grammars.

18.2 Models of Acquisition

Work in synchronic syntax has rarely linked grammatical properties to particular triggering effects, in part because practitioners often resort to a model of language acquisition that is flawed and is strikingly unilluminating for work on change. I refer to a model that sees children as *evaluating* grammars against sets of sentences and structures, matching input and evaluating grammars in terms of their overall success in generating the input data most economically, e.g. Clark (1992), Gibson and Wexler (1994), and many others. A fundamental problem with this approach is that I-languages generate an infinite number of structures, and, if children are seen as setting binary parameters, they must, on conservative assumptions that there are only thirty or forty parameters, entertain and evaluate billions or trillions of grammars, each capable of generating an infinite number of structures (for discussion, see Lightfoot 1999 and Chapter 24, this volume).

Beyond these overwhelming issues of feasibility, the evaluation approach raises further problems for thinking about change, because work usually fails to distinguish E-language and I-language changes and encounters problems of circularity: the new grammar is most successful in generating the structures of the new system but that presupposes that the new structures are already available in order to explain the emergence of the new grammar. This is part of a larger problem: if one asks a syntactician how children can learn some grammatical property, she will point to sentences that are generated in part through the effects of the relevant grammatical property, taking those sentences to be the necessary PLD. This circularity will become clear when we discuss specific changes.

A cue-based approach (Fodor 1998; Dresher 1999; Lightfoot 1999) is not subject to the feasibility problems of grammar evaluation and treats children as looking for certain structures *expressed* by the PLD, the cues, i.e. the structures needed in order to parse the sentence. There may be a thousand or more possible cues, provided by UG, but that does not present the feasibility problems of evaluating the success of thirty or forty binary parameters against corpora. Once children have an appropriate set of cues, the resulting I-language generates what it generates and the overall, gross set of structures generated plays no role in triggering or selecting the grammar. This model of acquisition, essentially a *discovery* procedure in the sense of Chomsky (1957; see my introduction to the 2002 second edition of *Syntactic Structures*), keys elements of grammar to particular elements of the PLD and provides good explanations for diachronic shifts and the emergence of new grammars. Under this model, we can link a cue with the PLD that express that cue and this yields some surprising results that force us to think about triggering experiences differently.

So a person's internal language capacity is a complex system that depends on an interaction between learned operations and principles that are conveyed by the genetic material, directly and indirectly. It grows in children in response to the E-language that they encounter, the source of the cues, and becomes part of their biology. If language growth in young children is viewed in this way, then we can explain language change over generations of speakers in terms of the dynamics of these complex systems. In particular, we can explain how languages shift in bursts, in a kind of punctuated equilibrium, and we can explain the changes without invoking principles of history or ideas about a general directionality.

Under this approach, there is no separate theory of change. Sometimes there are changes in E-language such that children are exposed to different PLD that trigger a different I-language. New I-languages, in turn, yield another new set of PLD for the next generation of children in the speech community; that new E-language, stemming in part from the new

I-languages, helps to trigger another new I-language, with further consequences for E-language. In this way we can understand domino effects in language change.

In this chapter we will examine a sequence of three changes in the I-languages/grammars of English speakers, three phase transitions, two of which are well understood; and we will see domino effects in action. In all cases, children are computationally conservative, acquiring the simplest I-language consistent with principles of UG and the ambient E-language and PLD (Snyder 2007); that is all we need to say and we do not need any special principles like Transparency or Least Effort to weed out dispreferred I-languages (see Chapter 15, this volume). One way of keeping children suitably conservative, as proposed by Biberauer and Roberts (2009), is to adopt the Subset Principle of Berwick (1985) as a principle of acquisition forcing children to pick the most conservative grammar consistent with the PLD.

18.3 First Reanalysis

Modern English has forms like (2-6a) but not (2-6b).

(2)   a. He has understood chapter 4
       b. *He has could understand chapter 4

(3)   a. Understanding chapter 4, . . .
       b. *Canning understand chapter 4, . . .

(4)   a. He wanted to understand
       b. *He wanted to can understand

(5)   a. He will try to understand
       b. *He will can understand

(6)   a. He understands music
       b. *He can music

However, earlier forms of English had the (b) forms, which occur in texts up to the writings of Sir Thomas More in the early sixteenth century. More used all the forms of (2)–(6) and the (b) forms occur in nobody's writing after him. (7)–(9) provide examples of the latest occurrences of the obsolescent forms, (7) corresponding to (2b), (8) to (4b), and (9) to (5b).

(7)   If wee **had mought** convenient come togyther, ye woulde rather
       haue chosin to haue harde my minde of mine owne mouthe
       'if we had been able to come together conveniently, ...' (1528,
       More, *Works* 107 H6)

(8)   That appered at the fyrste **to mow** stande the realm in grete stede

'appeared at first to be able to stand the realm in good stead.' (1533, More, *Works* 885 C1)

(9)   I fear that the emperor will depart thence, before my letters **shall may** come unto your grace's hands (1532, Cranmer, *Letters*)

There is good reason to believe that there was a single change in people's internal systems such that *can, could, must, may, might, will, would, shall, should* and *do* were once categorized as lexical verbs but then they were recategorized as Inflectional or T elements in all known grammars of English speakers after the time of More. Before More, verbs like *can* moved to a higher Inflection position, as in (10), and after More they were generated directly as Inflectional elements and occurred in structures like (11), a single shift in the system, which was manifested by the simultaneous loss of the phenomena in (2)–(6b), the phase transition; sentences like (2)–(6b) are not compatible with a system with structures like (11) (if perfective and progressive markers are generated between Infl and V, then they will never occur to the left of Infl as in (2b) and (3b); if there is only one Infl in each clause, then (4b) and (5b) will not be generated). The *singularity* of the change explains the *parallelism* in the loss of phenomena.

(10)
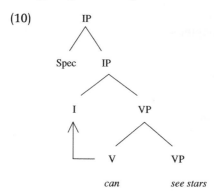

(11)
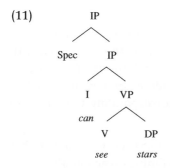

This change occurred only in Early Modern English and nothing comparable happened in any other European language, so it is not satisfactory to say that this change is to be explained by a general tendency to grammaticalize or to recategorize modal verbs as members of a functional category. If there is a general tendency, why has it not yet affected any other European language? In particular, some have revived historicist claims and argued for 'UG biases' as an internal driver to explain grammaticalization phenomena (Roberts and Roussou 2003; van Gelderen 2011). This enables them to unify some phenomena, which provides a level of explanation. The change of category membership for the English modals is a parade case of grammaticalization but saying that it results from an internal drive or a UG bias gives no explanation for why it happened when it did nor under what circumstances, and does not explain why the change has not happened in any other European language.

A critical property of this change is that it consisted entirely in the *loss* of phenomena (2)–(6b) and there were no new forms emerging.[1] Since children converge on their I-language in response to ambient simple expressions and not in response to 'negative data' about what does not occur, the new, more limited data need to be explained by a new abstract system that fails to generate (2)–(6b). There were no new forms in which the modal auxiliaries began to occur, so that the trigger for the new system must lie elsewhere. In this case, the new PLD cannot be the new output of the new grammars, because there are no new forms. Changes like this, which consist only in the loss of expressions, make up a kind of poverty-of-stimulus argument for diachrony: there appear to be no new forms in the PLD that directly trigger the loss of those expressions (see Snyder's (2007, 2011) notion that children are 'grammatically conservative').

If we ask why this or any other I-language change happened, there can only be one answer under this approach: children came to have different primary linguistic data as a result of a prior change in external language. We have a good hypothesis about what the prior E-language change was in this case.

Early English had complex morphological properties. For example, we find *fremme, fremst, fremþ, fremmaþ* in the present tense and *fremed, fremedest, fremede, fremedon* in the past tense of 'do'; *sēo, siehst, siehþ, sēoþ* in the present tense for 'see'; *rīde, rītst, rītt, rīdaþ* for the present tense of 'ride', and *rād, ride, rād* and *ridon* for the past tense. There was a massive loss of verbal morphology in Middle English, beginning in the north of England and due to intimate contact with Scandinavian speakers and widespread English–Scandinavian bilingualism (O'Neil 1978). Again I skip interesting details, but external language that children heard changed such that the modern modal auxiliaries like *can, shall*, etc. came to be morphologically distinct from other verbs, because as the members of the small preterite-present class, they lacked the one surviving feature of present tense verb

---

[1] Lightfoot (1979) notes that *be able to, be used to,* and *be going to* forms are first attested soon after the recategorization, perhaps as a consequence of the change in category membership.

morphology, the -s ending of the third-person singular. Furthermore, their 'past-tense' forms (*could, would, might*, etc.) had meanings that were not past time, reflecting old subjunctive uses (12). The evidence indicates that these modal verbs were recategorized in people's internal systems, because they had become formally distinct from other verbs as a result of the radical simplification of morphology (Lightfoot 1999). So we see domino effects: changes in what children heard, the newly reduced verb morphology, led to a different categorization of certain verbs, which yielded systems (11) that were compatible with (2)–(6a) but not (2)–(6b). This is discussed in greater detail in Chapter 24, this volume.

(12)   They might/could/would leave tomorrow.

More was the last known speaker with the old system. For a period, both systems coexisted: some speakers had (10) and others had (11), the former becoming rarer over time, the latter more numerous. A large literature is now devoted to this kind of sociological variation, changing over time, and we will return to this matter in §18.7.

18.4   Second Reanalysis

A later major change was that English lost (13)–(15a), another phase transition. Such forms occurred frequently in texts up through the seventeenth century, although diminishing over a long period in favour of the *do* forms of (13)–(15b).

(13)   a. *Sees Kim stars?
       b. Does Kim see stars?

(14)   a. *Kim sees not stars
       b. Kim does not see stars

(15)   a. *Kim sees always stars
       b. Kim always sees stars

Again we can understand the parallelism of the three changes in terms of a single change in the abstract system, namely the loss of the operation moving verbs to a higher Inflection position (16). This is another change that did not affect other European languages, whose systems have retained the verb movement operation (apart from Faroese and, perhaps, some Scandinavian systems; see Vikner 1995; Heycock *et al.* 2012). In Present-Day English verbs do not move to the higher position and therefore cannot move to clause-initial position (13a), to the left of a negative (14a), or to the left of certain adverbs (15a). The equivalent movements continue to occur in French, Italian, Dutch and German systems. There has been much recent work refining our understanding of verb movement in various European (and other) languages, which we cannot examine here. But again a contingent explanation is required for the historical change: what was it about English at this time that led to this shift in I-languages? In particular, what were the new PLD that children were exposed to that helped to trigger the new grammar?

(16)

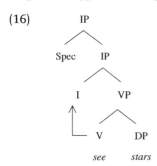

It is reasonable to think that this shift was due to two prior changes and we see another domino effect. The first was the new I-language that we just discussed, involving the recategorization of modal verbs (which occur very frequently in conversational speech); given that words like *can* and *must* were no longer verbs but Infl items, no sentence containing one would have a ₁[V] structure. The second change was the emergence of 'periphrastic' *do* forms as an alternative option for expressing past tense: *John did leave, John did not leave*, etc., instead of *John left* and *John left not* (it has been known since Ellegård (1954) that the new periphrastic *do* forms spread from the West Country, and McWhorter (2009) offers an interesting analysis, attributing the new *do* forms to Cornish influence). Given that *do* forms were instances of Infl, any sentence containing one would not have the ₁[V] structure. As a result of these changes, the Inflection position came to be occupied by modal auxiliaries and by *do* in internal systems and was not available as a target for verb movement in those instances. Thus, lexical verbs did not occur in that position as often as before the days of periphrastic *do* and before modal auxiliaries were no longer verbs, and as a result, the ₁[V] structure was expressed much less and apparently fell below the threshold that had permitted its acquisition by children.

As with the first reanalysis, the two systems coexisted for a while, in fact for a longer period than with the recategorization of the modal verbs: Shakespeare and other writers alternated easily between the coexisting old and new systems, sometimes using the old V-to-I forms and sometimes the new *do* forms, even within the same sentence (17) (*do* in (17c) is the main verb *do*, meaning 'fare').

(17)   a. Where **didst thou** see her? – O unhappy girl! – With the Moor, **say'st thou**?
       b. I **like not** that. // What **dost thou** say?
       c. Alas, what **does this gentleman** conceive? – How **do you**, madam?

Again this is too brief an account (for more on the diffusion of the change, see Chapter 24, this volume) but it should be clear that prior changes in external language, some due to a shift in I-languages, had the effect of reducing enormously children's evidence for the $_1$[V] structure, triggering a new internal system, and that three simultaneous but apparently unrelated changes were a function of a single change in the abstract system.[2]

18.5 Third Reanalysis

There is a third phase transition, resulting in part from the two changes just discussed, observed and analysed by Warner (1995). One way of characterizing the change is that different forms of the verb *be* came to be listed in the mental lexicon as atomic or 'monomorphemic', as Warner puts it.

VP ellipsis is generally insensitive to morphology and one finds cases where the understood form of the missing verb differs from the form of the antecedent (18).

(18) a. Kim slept well, and Jim will [sc. sleep well] too.
      b. Kim seems well-behaved today, and she often has [sc. seemed well-behaved] in the past, too.
      c. Although Kim went to the store, Jim didn't [sc. go to the store].

There is a kind of morphological *sloppy* identity at work here, since *slept* and *sleep* in (18a) are not strictly identical. One way of thinking of this is that in (18a) *slept* is analysed as [past+$_\sqrt{}$*sleep*], and the understood verb of the second conjunct accesses the verb *sleep*, ignoring the tense element.

However, Warner noticed that *be* works differently: *be* occurs in elliptical constructions but only on condition of *strict* morphological identity with the antecedent (19). In (19a–b) the understood form is strictly identical to the antecedent but not in the non-occurring (19c–e).

(19) a. Kim will be here, and Jim will [sc. be here] too.
      b. Kim has been here, and Jim has [sc. been here] too.
      c. *Kim was here and Jim will [sc. be here] too.
      d. *If Kim is well-behaved today, then Jim probably will [sc. be well-behaved] tomorrow.
      e. *Kim was here yesterday and Jim has [sc. been here] today.

This suggests that *was* is not analysed as [past+$_\sqrt{}$*be*], analogously to *slept*, and forms of *be* may be used as an understood form only when precisely the same form is available as an antecedent, as in (19a–b).

---

[2] Many people have contributed to our current understanding of these two phase transitions. Roberts (2007) gives a detailed textbook account of both changes in I-languages.

Warner goes on to note that the ellipsis facts of Modern English *be* were not always so, and one finds forms like (19c–e) in earlier times. Jane Austen was one of the last writers to use such forms, and she used them in her letters and in speech in her novels, but not in narrative prose (20a–b). These forms also occur in eighteenth-century writers (20c), and earlier, when verbs still moved to Infl (20d).

(20)   a. I wish our opinions were the same. But in time they will [sc. be the same]. (1816, Jane Austen, *Emma*, ed. R. W. Chapman (London: Oxford University Press, 1933), p. 471)
       b. And Lady Middleton, is she angry?
          I cannot suppose it possible that she should [sc. be angry]. (1811, Jane Austen, *Sense and sensibility*, ed. R. W. Chapman (London: Oxford University Press, 1923), p. 272)
       c. I think, added he, all the Charges attending it, and the Trouble you had, were defray'd by my Attorney: I ordered that they should [sc. be defrayed]. (1741, Samuel Richardson, *Pamela* (London, 3rd edn), vol. 2, p. 129)
       d. That bettre loved is noon, ne never schal. (*c.* 1370, Chaucer, *A complaint to his lady*, 80, 'So that no one is better loved, or ever shall [sc. be].')

These forms may be understood if *were* in (20a) was analysed as [*subjunctive*+$_V$*be*], and the *be* was accessed by the understood *be* in the following *But* clause. That is, up until the early nineteenth century the finite forms of *be* were decomposable, just like ordinary verbs in Present-Day English.

Warner goes on to show, in addition, that Present-Day English shows quite idiosyncratic restrictions on particular forms of *be*, which did not exist before the late eighteenth century or early nineteenth century. For example, it is only the finite forms of *be* that may be followed by a *to* infinitive (21); only *been* may occur with a directional preposition phrase (22); and *being* is subcategorized as not permitting an *-ing* complement (23).

(21)   a. Kim was to go to Paris.
       b. *Kim will be to go to Paris.

(22)   a. Kim has been to Paris.
       b. *Kim was to Paris.

(23)   a. I regretted Kim reading that chapter.
       b. I regretted that Kim was reading that chapter.
       c. *I regretted Kim being reading that chapter.

Restrictions of this type are stated in the lexicon, and these idiosyncrasies show clearly that *been*, *being*, etc. must be listed as individual lexical entries in order to carry their own individual subcategorization restriction. However, these restrictions did not exist earlier and one finds forms corresponding to the non-occurring sentences of (21)–(23) through the eighteenth century, where (24a) is equivalent to (21b), (24b) to (22b), and (24c–h) to (23c):

(24)   a. You will be to visit me in prison with a basket of provisions ... (1814, Jane Austen, *Mansfield Park*, ed. J. Lucas (London: Oxford University Press, 1970), p. 122)

   b. I was this morning to buy silk. (1762, Oliver Goldsmith, *Cit W*: 158 (meaning 'I went to ...,' not 'I had to ... '))

   c. Two large wax candles were also set on another table, the ladies being going to cards. (1726, Daniel Defoe, *The political history of the devil* (Oxford: Talboys, 1840), p. 336)

   d. ... he being now going to end all with the Queene ... (1661, Samuel Pepys, *Diary*, ii 129.1 (30 June))

   e. One day being discoursing with her upon the extremities they suffered ... (1791, Daniel Defoe, *Robinson Crusoe*, vol. 2, p. 218)

   f. ... and exclaimed quite as much as was necessary, (or, being acting a part, perhaps rather more,) at the conduct of the Churchills, in keeping him away. (1816, Jane Austen, *Emma*, p. 145)

   g. Their being going to be married. (1811, Jane Austen, *Sense and sensibility*, ed. R. W. Chapman (London: Oxford University Press, 1923), p. 182)

   h. The younger Miss Thorpes, being also dancing, Catherine was left to the mercy of Mrs Thorpe. (1818, Jane Austen, *Northanger Abbey*, ed. R. W. Chapman (London: Oxford University Press, 1923), p. 52)

So there were changes in the late eighteenth/early nineteenth century whereby the ellipsis possibilities for forms of *be* became more restricted and particular forms of *be* developed their own idiosyncratic subcategorization restrictions. In fact, another change in the syntax of *be* took place at the same time and is discussed in Lightfoot (1999) and Warner (1995): the first instances of progressives in *is being* begin to appear in the late eighteenth century (*You are being naughty*; *You are being a bore*) and the first of these are in passives: *Everything is being done*; *Susan is being arrested*. It is unclear exactly how this innovation is related to the first changes in *be* that we discussed but those changes strongly suggest that forms of *be* cease to be decomposable.

I-languages perform computational operations on items stored in a mental lexicon and both the operations and the items stored may change over time. There is good reason to believe that decomposable items like [*subjunctive*+$_v$*be*] or [*past*+$_v$*be*] ceased to be stored in that form, replaced by undecomposed, atomic forms like *were*, *was*, *been*, each with its own subcategorization restrictions.

It is natural to view this change as a consequence of the prior two changes discussed. After the loss of rich verb morphology and the loss of the V-to-I operation, the category membership of forms of *be* became opaque. If they were instances of V, then why could they occur where verbs generally cannot occur, to the left of a negative or, even higher, to the left of the subject DP (*She is not here*; *Is she happy?*)? If they were instances of Infl, then why could they occur with another Infl element such as *to* or *will* (*I want to be happy*; *She will be here*)?

In earlier English forms of *be* had the same distribution as normal verbs. After the two phase transitions discussed earlier, they had neither the distribution of verbs nor of Inflection items.[3] The evidence is that from the late eighteenth century children developed I-languages that treated forms of *be* as verbs that have the unique property of moving to higher functional positions but being undecomposed, atomic elements, unlike other verbs.

18.6   Domino Effects

So we see domino effects and we understand them through language acquisition. English underwent massive simplification of its verb morphology, initially under conditions of bilingualism in the northeast. The new primary linguistic data led to a new I-language with about ten former verbs now categorized as Infl items. As a result, the primary linguistic data changed again and along with new periphrastic forms with *do* this led to new I-languages where verbs did not move to a higher Infl position. That, in turn, led to new PLD in which the categorical status of forms of *be* became opaque, leading to the reanalysis described in §18.5.

Amorphous external language and internal *systems* are different in kind and the modern distinction between external and internal language is crucial; both play a role in explaining change (Lightfoot 2006). We see an interplay between changes in E-language (new PLD) and changes in I-languages and changes in both E-language and I-languages are crucial to our account. New E-language leads to new I-languages, new I-languages lead to new E-language, and sometimes we see sequences of changes, domino effects, which we can understand through language acquisition.

When a new I-language (I-language$_p$) develops in one individual, that changes the ambient E-language for others, making it more likely that another child will acquire I-language$_p$; likewise for the next child and so on. As a result, the new I-language spreads through the speech community

---

[3] The same holds for *have* but that story is complicated by significant dialect variation.

quickly; Niyogi (2006) provides a computational model of new language systems spreading through speech communities quickly and the matter is taken up in Chapter 24, this volume.

18.7 Variation

The language capacity is a complex adaptive system. Children are exposed to speech and their biological endowment, a kind of toolbox, enables them to interact with their external linguistic experience, their E-language, thereby growing a private, internal system that defines their linguistic capacity.

Since the systems are complex and adaptive, they involve particular abstractions, categories, and operations and these, not the behaviours themselves, constitute the real points of variation and change. Phenomena do not change in isolation but they cluster, depending on the abstract categories involved. As a result, change is bumpy and takes place in a kind of punctuated equilibrium. We explain the bumps, the clusters of changes, in terms of changes in the abstract system, as we illustrated in the three phase transitions in the history of English. If we get the abstractions right, we explain why phenomena cluster in the way they do.

Everybody's experience varies and people's internal systems may vary, but not linearly. I-languages change over time, and sometimes variation in experience is sufficient to trigger the development of a different internal system. Children are sensitive to variation in initial conditions, in the terminology of chaos theory. In general, we understand change in internal systems through the acquisition process, by virtue of children experiencing different E-language. We explain changes where we can identify changes in the external language that children are exposed to such that the new experiences trigger different internal systems with different categories and operations. For example, after the comprehensive morphological changes of Middle English, young children had different experiences that led them to categorize words like *may* and *must* differently from verbs like *run* and *talk*. Assigning these words to a different category, Infl or T, explains why (2)–(6b) all disappeared in parallel. Similarly, new structures resulting from modal verbs being treated as Infl items and new structures with periphrastic *do* entailed that the $_I[V]$ cue was expressed much less robustly and fell out of use, entailing the obsolescence of (13)–(15b).

Under this approach, change is contingent, dependent on particular circumstances, and we explain why English underwent at this time changes that other European languages have not undergone at any point. English had particular morphological properties that were affected in particular ways by contact with Scandinavian speakers and that led to the new categorization. Other European languages were not affected in that way. If change is contingent like this, then there is no general direction to change and there is no reason to believe that languages all tend to become more efficient, less complex, or less anything else. There are no general principles of history of the kind that nineteenth-century thinkers sought and explanations are local (Lightfoot 2013). There is no reason to revive historicism or invoke principles of history or UG biases, at least not for the changes discussed here.

This approach to syntactic change also provides a new understanding of synchronic variation, along the lines of Labov's discussion of sound change in progress (e.g. Labov 1972). When a phase transition (a 'catastrophe', a rapid, structural shift) takes place, it does not happen on one day. Rather, a new I-language emerges in some children and spreads through the population, taking over from the old I-language, sometimes over the course of a century or more (but typically not for a very long period). Competing grammars (Kroch 1989, 1994) explain the nature of certain variation within a speech community: in this context, one does not find random variation in the texts but oscillation between two (or more) fixed points, two I-languages. In general, writers either have all the forms of the obsolescent I-language or none. Not all variation is to be explained in this way, of course; only variation in I-languages. There is also variation in E-language that has little if anything to do with I-language. In amorphous E-language, variation is endemic: no two people experience the same E-language and, in particular, no two children experience the same primary linguistic data. Since E-language varies so much, there are always possibilities for new I-languages to be triggered.

At a synchronic level, competing grammars also provide a new understanding of apparent optionality of computational operations. If I-language operations may be optional or obligatory, that presents severe learnability problems, because the need for obligatory operations is usually based on precluding what does not occur. That constitutes 'negative data', which are not available to young children. Positing competing grammars enables the elimination of an optional/obligatory distinction within I-languages: rather, there are competing grammars, one allowing an operation, the other not.

A recent development that has revolutionized work in diachronic syntax has been the development of partially parsed corpora of historical prose texts (see Chapter 11, this volume). This began with corpora of texts from various stages of English emanating from the University of Pennsylvania in collaboration with researchers at other universities in other countries. More recently corpora have been developed for other languages, including Portuguese, French, Icelandic, Hungarian and

Early High German. Researchers can search for structures over vast amounts of data.

These corpora open the possibility of searching for coexisting structures and determining whether the coexisting structures cluster in such a way as to manifest competing I-languages, oscillation between two or more fixed points, or whether the variation manifests the randomness of variable E-language. There are different patterns of variation and this, in turn, illuminates the distinction between new I-languages and new E-language that might trigger a new I-language. That enriches our hypotheses about language acquisition, providing data that bear on the distinction between the causes and effects of syntactic change.

18.8   Identifying Triggers

So the major contributions of diachronic work in syntax lie in explaining one kind of variation, due to coexisting I-languages, and in revealing what the E-language trigger might be for any particular property of I-languages.

It is surprising how little discussion there has been among synchronic syntacticians of what triggers what properties, given the explanatory schema of (1). Reducing hypothesis space is an essential part of the enterprise but not sufficient.

Consider the Binding Theory, for example, which postulates that children learn which nouns are anaphors, pronouns, and names (Chomsky 1981, 1986). Given the Binding Theory, once a child has learned that *themselves* is an anaphor, *her* a pronoun, etc., all the appropriate indexing relations follow, with no further learning. Then one must ask how a child learns that *themselves* is an anaphor, *her* a pronoun, and *Kim* a name. Exposure to a simple sentence like (25a), interpreted with *themselves* referring to *they* (coindexed), suffices to show that *themselves* is an anaphor and not a pronoun or name; pronouns and names may not be coindexed with a c-commanding element within its domain.

(25)   a. They$_i$ washed themselves$_i$.
         b. Kim$_i$'s father loves her$_i$.
         c. Kim$_i$ heard $_{DP}$[Bill's speeches about her$_i$].
         d. Kim left.

(25b), interpreted with *her* referring to Kim, shows that *her* is no anaphor and (25c), with *her* referring to Kim, shows that *her* is not a name; the domain of *her* is the DP indicated and *her* is free within that DP. If neither an anaphor nor a name, then *her* is a pronoun. A very simple expression like (25d) shows that Kim is not an anaphor, but there is no positive evidence available to a child showing that Kim is not a pronoun. Analysts know that Kim is not a pronoun, because one does not find sentences of the form *Kim said that Kim left*, with the two Kims referring to the same person, but that is a negative fact concerning something which does not occur, hence unavailable to young children. That suggests a hierarchical organization.

One approach is to say that children initially take every noun as a name, unless there is positive, refuting evidence. If, in a default position, nouns are taken as names, then sentences like (25a) show that *themselves* is an anaphor, and not a pronoun nor a name. And (25c) shows that *her* is not a name, because it is coindexed with the DP Kim, and not an anaphor, because it is not locally coindexed, therefore a pronoun. This yields a satisfactory account. We have a theory of mature capacity that provides the appropriate distinctions and one can show how children learn from environmental data which elements are anaphors and which are pronouns; everything else is a name and no other learning is relevant.

The Binding Theory narrows the hypothesis space and is vastly more simple and elegant than the indexing conventions that preceded it (see the appendix to Chomsky 1980). However, this is not enough and one needs to consider the learning involved and that often involves substantive issues.

We should allow for the possibility that the PLD that trigger a grammatical property may not have any obvious connection with that property. Indeed, our discussion of the recategorization of modal verbs was triggered by new morphological properties.

Niko Tinbergen (1957: ch. 22) once surprised the world of ethologists by showing that young herring gulls' behaviour of pecking at their mothers' mouths was triggered not by the fact that the mother gull might be carrying food but by a red spot. Mothers typically have a red spot under their beak and Tinbergen devised an ingenious series of experiments showing that this was the crucial triggering property. So the chicks would respond to a disembodied red spot and not to a bird carrying food but lacking the strategic red spot. Similarly, gram mars may have certain mechanisms and devices because of properties in the primary data that are not obviously related to those mechanisms, as we saw in our first case study.

People have their own internal system, a grammar, which develops in them in the first few years of life as a result of an interaction between genetic factors common to the species and environmental variation in primary linguistic data. Such a grammar represents the person's linguistic range, the kind of things that the person might say and how he/she may say them. If they hear different things, children may converge on a different system, a new grammar, perhaps the first instance of a particular, new I-language. We want to find out what triggers which aspect of a person's I-language, therefore how new I-languages might emerge.

Many people have claimed that we can discover things about grammars by seeing how they change. In particular, by looking at change one can generate productive hypotheses about what PLD trigger particular properties of I-languages.

18.9   Conclusion and Limits

We may have achieved ideal explanations for certain syntactic changes in terms of how children acquire their I-language: we can identify shifts in I-languages along with prior shifts in the ambient E-language that plausibly triggered the new I-languages. If that is along the right lines, then we have explained diachronic changes in I-languages in terms of language acquisition, alongside a distinction between I-languages and E-language, where each plays a crucial role in our account.

However, it is not clear that this mode of explanation extends to systematic phonological shifts like those of Grimm or Grassmann's Laws. It is unclear how new PLD could have triggered the systematic changes in Germanic consonants and it may be that other forces are at work in phonology, where poverty of stimulus reasoning has not played a major role.[4] Perhaps there are internal forces that drive sound change. For example, many changes can be understood in terms of an internal drive to simplify articulation: Lat. *octo* has become It. *otto*, Swd. *drikka* and *takka* have eliminated the nasal of 'drink' and 'thank', and Eng. *famly* has become *famly*. Listeners sometimes interpret what they hear differently from what was intended and change their pronunciation accordingly, reanalysing the PLD. Often this is influenced by matters of group identity, people adopting new pronunciations as a way of identifying themselves with a group; such factors have not been shown to play a role in syntactic change. Internal drivers may play a role in phonological change but, in general, they are more limited in their explanatory power than the contingent, acquisition-based approach taken here and offer no grammatically based explanation for why the changes take place.

Whether syntax is learned differently from phonology, linking matters of acquisition and learnability to matters of syntactic change permits deep explanations of particular changes and illuminates what experience it takes to trigger elements of I-languages, as a child acquires her mature language capacity. Under this approach, there is no independent theory of change and change is an epiphenomenon. Children acquire their own internal, private I-language when exposed to the ambient E-language and not influenced directly by any ambient I-language. No two children experience the identical E-language and therefore there is always the possibility of a different I-language emerging but nothing is actually transmitted and there is no object that changes.

---

[4] Heinz and Idsardi (2011) offer a recent argument that syntax and phonology are learned differently.

References

Baker, C. L. and McCarthy, J. (eds.) 1981. *The logical problem of language acquisition*. Cambridge, MA: MIT Press.

Berwick, R. 1985. *The acquisition of syntactic knowledge*. Cambridge, MA: MIT Press.

Biberauer, T. and Roberts, I. 2009. 'The return of the subset principle', in P. Crisma and G. Longobardi (eds.), *Historical syntax and linguistic theory*. Oxford University Press, pp. 58–74.

Chomsky, N. 1980. 'On binding', *Linguistic Inquiry* 11: 1–46.

1981. *Lectures on government and binding*. Dordrecht: Foris.

1986. *Knowledge of language: Its nature, origin and use*. New York: Praeger.

[1957] 2002. *Syntactic structures*, 2nd edn. Berlin: De Gruyter.

Clark, R. 1992. 'The selection of syntactic knowledge', *Language Acquisition* 2: 83–149.

Dresher, B. E. 1999. 'Charting the learning path: Cues to parameter setting', *Linguistic Inquiry* 30: 27–67.

Ellegård, A. 1954. *The auxiliary do: The establishment and regulation of its use in English*. Stockholm: Almqvist & Wiksell.

Fodor, J. 1998. 'Unambiguous triggers', *Linguistic Inquiry* 29: 1–36.

Gibson, E. and Wexler, K. 1994. 'Triggers', *Linguistic Inquiry* 25: 407–54.

Grimm, J. 1848. *Geschichte der deutschen Sprache*, vol. 1. Leipzig: Weidmannsche Buchhandlung.

Heinz, J. and Idsardi, W. 2011. 'Sentence and word complexity', *Science* 333 (6040): 295–97.

Heycock, C., Sorace, A., Hansen, Z. S., Wilson, F. and Vikner, S. 2012. 'Detecting the late stages of syntactic change: The loss of V-to-T in Faroese', *Language* 88: 558–600.

Kroch, A. 1989. 'Reflexes of grammar in patterns of language change', *Language Variation and Change* 1: 199–244.

1994. 'Morphosyntactic variation', in K. Beals *et al.* (eds.), *Papers from the 30th regional meeting of the Chicago linguistics society: Parasession on variation and linguistic theory*. Chicago Linguistics Society, pp. 180–201.

Labov, W. 1972. *Sociolinguistic patterns*. Philadelphia: University of Pennsylvania Press.

Lightfoot, D. W. 1979. *Principles of diachronic syntax*. Cambridge University Press.

1999. *The development of language: Acquisition, change and evolution*. Oxford: Blackwell.

2006. *How new languages emerge*. Cambridge University Press.

2013. 'Types of explanation in history', *Language* 89.4: e18–e38.

McWhorter, J. 2009. 'What else happened to English? A brief for the Celtic hypothesis', *English Language and Linguistics* 13: 163–91.

Niyogi, P. 2006. *The computational nature of language learning and evolution.* Cambridge, MA: MIT Press.

O'Neil, W. 1978. 'The evolution of the Germanic inflectional systems: A case study in the causes of language change', *Orbis* 27: 248–85.

Roberts, I. 2007. *Diachronic syntax.* Oxford University Press.

Roberts, I. and Roussou, A. 2003. *Syntactic change: A minimalist approach to grammaticalization.* Cambridge University Press.

Snyder, W. 2007. *Child language: The parametric approach.* Oxford University Press.

2011. 'Children's grammatical conservatism: Implications for syntactic theory', in N. Danis *et al.* (eds.), *BUCLD 35: Proceedings of the 35th annual Boston University conference on language development,* vol. 1. Somerville, MA: Cascadilla Press, pp. 1–20.

Tinbergen, N. 1957. *The herring gull's world.* Oxford University Press.

van Gelderen, E. 2011. *The linguistic cycle: Language change and the language faculty.* Amsterdam: John Benjamins.

Vikner, S. 1995. *Verb movement and expletive subjects in the Germanic languages.* Oxford University Press.

Warner, A. 1995. 'Predicting the progressive passive: Parametric change within a lexicalist framework', *Language* 71: 533–57.

Part IV

Major Issues and Themes

19

The Actuation Problem

George Walkden

19.1 Introduction

The term *actuation problem* was first introduced and defined by Weinreich, Labov and Herzog (1968:102). In their words:

(1) **The actuation problem**
     What factors can account for the actuation of changes? Why do changes in a structural feature take place in a particular language at a particular time, but not in other languages with the same feature, or in the same language at other times?

   This actuation problem is one of five related problems that Weinreich, Labov and Herzog (1968) pose to historical linguists, in an attempt to break down the hows and whys of language change into manageable chunks. It is difficult to overstate the importance that Weinreich, Labov and Herzog accord to the actuation problem: they refer to it as 'the very heart of the matter' (1968: 102). Elaborating on their initial formulation, later in the paper they state:

> ... even when the course of a language change has been fully described and its ability explained, the question always remains as to why the change was not actuated sooner, or why it was not simultaneously activated wherever identical functional conditions prevailed. The unsolved actuation riddle is the price paid by any facile and individualistic explanation of language change. It creates the opposite problem – of explaining why language fails to change.   *(1968: 112)*

   This chapter will provide an overview of the problem in the domain of historical syntax, as well as evaluating a number of potential

I am grateful to Ricardo Bermúdez-Otero, Nigel Vincent, David Willis and the editors of this volume for comments on an earlier draft of this chapter; however, no one but me is responsible for its defects.

solutions.[1] In order to know whether a particular theory or explanatory principle succeeds in solving the 'riddle' of actuation, it is necessary to contrast the actuation problem with the other four key problems that Weinreich, Labov and Herzog outline for a theory of linguistic change; §19.2 serves this purpose, and also relates the actuation problem to questions of prediction and explanation. §§19.3 and 19.4 each survey a family of related proposals in the literature, dealing with 'internal' and 'external' factors respectively. §19.5 concludes.

19.2 The Actuation Problem in Context

19.2.1 Weinreich, Labov and Herzog's Five Problems

Weinreich, Labov and Herzog introduce the actuation problem as the fifth, and toughest, of five problems that must be addressed by any comprehensive theory of language change, alongside the problems of *constraints*, *transition*, *embedding* and *evaluation*. I will outline each in turn.

The *constraints problem* involves formulating 'constraints on the transition from one state of a language to an immediately succeeding state' (Weinreich, Labov and Herzog 1968:100). The type of constraints involved can take a number of forms. One necessary general type of constraint is that no proposed language state should be synchronically impossible; following Lass (1997: 229), I will refer to these as *legality* constraints. To take a concrete example, Holmberg (2000) and Biberauer, Holmberg and Roberts (2007, 2008, 2014) present data motivating a constraint, the Final-over-Final Constraint, which serves to rule out the configuration given in (2), in which a head-final phrase immediately dominates a head-initial phrase.

(2)

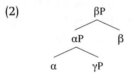

If this constraint exists, then no language should be able to pass through a state in which structures like (2) are found. Biberauer, Newton and Sheehan (2009) argue, based on data from the history of English, Afrikaans and French, that this is correct; see also Ledgeway (2012: ch. 5) for an account of the role of this constraint in word-order change from Latin to Romance).

Lightfoot (1979 and subsequent publications) maintains that legality constraints in this sense are the only type of constraint that should form

---

[1] Some linguists use the term 'actuation problem' in a different sense, to refer to the puzzle of how innovations arise in general, or how change can be rare even when a constant bias is at work (see e.g. Baker, Archangeli and Mielke 2011). I will not address this usage here.

part of a theory of change: 'there is no theory of change to be had independent of theories of grammar and acquisition' (Lightfoot 2002: 127). Another logical possibility is that, independently of legality constraints, there are *process* constraints that restrict possible pathways of change. This type of reasoning has particularly been pursued in the literature on grammaticalization, where certain processes have been characterized as impossible due to unidirectionality (see Chapters 2 and 23, this volume, and Börjars and Vincent 2011, for discussion).

The second of Weinreich, Labov and Herzog's five problems is the *transition* problem, which is discussed only briefly. This is the question of what intervening stages can (or must) be posited between any two forms of a language separated by time. A core instance of the transition problem in syntax is the question of what happens after a change is first innovated but before it has become ubiquitous. Timberlake's (1977) notion of *actualization* is one suggestion: once reanalysis has taken place, a change trickles down through the grammar from one context to another, moving from least to most marked contexts (for a recent reinterpretation, see De Smet 2012). Another influential conception is that of competing grammars. Under this view, due to Kroch (1989, 1994), once innovation has taken place, the new grammar and the old grammar coexist for a period of time, with the new grammar increasing in frequency at the expense of the old. This view is well suited to accounting for Constant Rate Effects (see Kroch 1989; Pintzuk 2003), in which the rate of replacement of the old form by the new form is constant across linguistic contexts.

The *embedding problem* is stated as follows: 'How are the observed changes *embedded* in the matrix of linguistic and extralinguistic concomitants of the forms in question? (That is, what other changes are associated with the given changes in a manner that cannot be attributed to chance?)' (Weinreich, Labov and Herzog 1968: 101; emphasis original). The embedding problem has both a linguistic and a social aspect, which can and should be studied separately (Labov 1982: 28). In both cases, the problem can be approached by the study of correlations: between seemingly independent elements of the linguistic system in the first case, or between linguistic elements and elements of the extralinguistic system of social behaviour in the second case (Labov 1972: 162). Within the study of syntactic change, researchers working in the Principles and Parameters framework have been particularly concerned with the embedding problem, often attempting to relate apparently distinct syntactic phenomena as reflexes of a single parametric change (see Lightfoot 1991, 1999; Roberts 2007; Chapters 7 and 27, this volume).

Finally, the *evaluation problem* deals with the subjective evaluation of a change in progress by members of a speech community, both above and below the level of consciousness (Labov 1982: 28). It is probably fair to say that the evaluation problem, along with the social aspect of the embedding problem, is the least studied of Weinreich, Labov and

Herzog's (1968) five problems as far as syntactic change is concerned: those working on syntactic change often abstract away from the social (see, for example, Hale 1998: 5–6), and the majority of the sociolinguistic literature focuses on sound change (though Naro 1981, Romaine 1982, Cheshire, Adger and Fox 2013 are notable exceptions). This imbalance may not be entirely for sociological reasons: Labov and Harris (1986: 21) suggest that '[a]bstract linguistic structure has little or no social impact on members of the community', perhaps in part because it is rarely consciously evaluated. More recently, Ingason, Sigurðsson and Wallenberg (2012) have put forward a strong Antisocial Hypothesis as regards syntax, suggesting that word order is not socially evaluated unless identified with specific phonological or lexical material. Chapter 25, this volume, explores the issue of social conditioning in much more detail.

It is clear that a solution to the actuation problem will rely on solutions to all of these problems. Yet the actuation problem remains a distinct question: even with a full understanding of (i) the *constraints* governing a change, (ii) the process of *transition* involved, (iii) how the change is *embedded* in other aspects of the language and society and (iv) how it is *evaluated*, we still do not necessarily know why the change took place when and where it did.

19.2.2   Prediction, Explanation and The Actuation Problem

Weinreich, Labov and Herzog (1968: 99f.) distinguish between a 'strong' and a 'weak' theory of language change. A weak theory of language change is essentially coextensive with the problem of *constraints*. A strong theory, on the other hand, is one that is fully predictive: given such a theory and a description of the structure of a language and its speech community at a particular point in time, it should be possible to predict the course of its subsequent development. Solutions to the actuation problem are, of course, an essential component of any such predictive theory.

Weinreich, Labov and Herzog are sceptical: 'Few practicing historians of language would be rash enough to claim that such a theory is possible' (1968: 99). Others have expressed similar views. Meillet (1921: 16) noted that all the laws of linguistic history discovered up to that point were statements of possibility, not of necessity, and that the variable conditions which permitted or catalysed the changes which actually occurred remained to be discovered. The point has been most forcefully made by Lass (1980), who compares explanations proposed in the historical linguistic literature with a gold standard of deductive-nomological explanation, and finds them lacking.[2] Lass's conception of deductive-nomological

---

[2] Lass goes on to conclude that deductive-nomological explanations are *in principle* unavailable in historical linguistics due to the nature of language change (1980: ch. 4). Lass (1997: 336), while acknowledging some weaknesses of his earlier work, remains convinced that it is not the case that 'causal explanations are or ever will be available' in historical linguistics.

explanation, following Hempel and Oppenheim (1948), is said to be one that 'characterizes the physical sciences (or a particular version of them)', and is 'in principle equivalent to a prediction' (1980: 9). Given an explanans – a conjunction of statements specifying both general laws and antecedent conditions – the explanandum (here, the change in question) follows necessarily by the rule of inference *modus ponens*.

The actuation problem and the notion of deductive-nomological explanation are closely related. Specifically, some form of deductive-nomological explanation is a precondition for solutions to individual instances of the actuation problem: if we do not know what the sufficient conditions for a change are, we cannot say why it occurs when and where it does. At the same time, deductive-nomological explanation is not enough to guarantee a solution to the actuation problem. This is because the explanans consists only of conditions that are *sufficient* for the explanandum to occur; these conditions do not have to be *necessary*. A deductive-nomological explanation could then in principle explain why a change had to occur at time t, while the change in fact occurred at time $t - 1$; from the point of view of the actuation problem, this is clearly unsatisfactory.

If a deductive-nomological explanation for a change is not available, then, it follows that the actuation problem has not been solved with respect to that change. It is in this respect that Lass's (1980) arguments against proposed explanations become important in the context of the actuation problem. §19.3 brings out this relevance for individual types of explanation.

19.3 Internal Factors: Speakers, Hearers and Learners

Historical linguists are largely in agreement that the locus of diachronic discontinuity is the gaping chasm between the speaker and the hearer.[3] This is schematized in Figure 19.1, the Z-model of Andersen (1973: 767).

This section focuses on properties of individual language users (speakers, hearers, learners), and whether these properties help us to

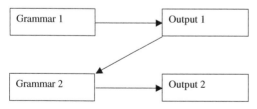

Figure 19.1 Language transmission and change

---

[3] Lass (1997) is a notable exception, arguing that 'we don't gain anything by invoking' speakers and hearers (1997: 377, fn. 42).

solve the actuation problem. A variety of such properties have been suggested to play a causal role in language change. Here I focus first on reanalysis as a commonly assumed mechanism of syntactic change. I then address first-language acquisition and processing-based explanations in turn.

19.3.1 Reanalysis

Langacker (1977: 58) defines reanalysis as 'change in the structure of an expression or class of expressions that does not involve any immediate or intrinsic modification of its surface manifestation' (see also Harris and Campbell 1995:61). Reanalysis on the part of the hearer/learner plays a central role in the historical narratives of linguists of all theoretical persuasions. Roberts (2007: 123), for example, considers reanalysis to be a central mechanism of syntactic change, and 'intimately bound up with parameter change'; Hopper and Traugott (2003: 59) state that 'grammaticalization always involves reanalysis'. Whatever the merits of reanalysis as a mechanism (see Chapter 4, this volume), given its centrality to historical syntax, we can ask: does reanalysis help us to solve the actuation problem?

A prerequisite for reanalysis is string ambiguity: a string has to be amenable to more than one analysis, the 'old' and the 'new' (see Timberlake 1977: 168). Questions arise immediately: why does the new analysis arise when it does? And why is the new analysis adopted at the expense of the old? These are questions to which the concept of reanalysis has no obvious answers in and of itself, though this is of course not to say that the concept is worthless: reanalysis is a mechanism, not an explanation. In order to address these issues, reanalysis needs to be supplemented at the very least with a theory of what the hearer/learner is actually doing: in other words, why one analysis arises and is preferred. This theory can take a number of directions, and the rest of §19.3 is devoted to exploring these directions.

19.3.2 L1 Acquisition Pressures

The idea that the process of first-language (L1) acquisition by children is crucial to understanding language change is generally attributed to Paul (1880), and in recent years has been championed by diachronic syntacticians working in a generative framework (see, for example, Lightfoot 1991, 1999; Roberts 2007). The key notion is that learning may be 'imperfect', in the sense that it does not result in 100 per cent accurate replication of the grammar underlying the input data (see Chapter 24, this volume, for in-depth discussion). Assuming, then, that L1 acquisition plays some role in change: do explanations in these terms allow us to solve the actuation problem?

The first and most essential ingredient that any theory of acquisition needs in order to be in with a chance of solving the problem is that it be deterministic in the sense of Walkden (2012: 894): for any temporally ordered set of sentences (primary linguistic data or PLD), any and all learners exposed to it will converge on the same grammar. The assumption of determinism is necessary because, if the learner's behaviour exhibits randomness, then it is impossible to predict (except stochastically) how a given learner will react to a given set of PLD and consequently impossible to predict when and where an acquisition-driven change will take place. Lightfoot anticipates this point, stating that the ideal theory of grammar and of acquisition, possessed by the acquirer, 'will be so restrictive that for any given language [i.e. set of PLD; GW] there will be only one grammar capable of producing the relevant output in a way consistent with the theory' (1979: 16).

An early and influential proposal for a key component of acquisition is Lightfoot's (1979) Transparency Principle (see Chapter 15, this volume), a 'requirement of the theory of grammar that derivations be of limited complexity' (1979: 344). The Transparency Principle aims to address the problem raised at the end of the last subsection, by supplementing the notion of reanalysis with an acquisition-based explanation for when it will take place and the direction it will take. It is couched in the Extended Standard Theory of the day, and envisages an upper bound on the extent to which transformations can cause surface structure to differ from the initial (base) phrase marker. The idea is that once derivations reach a certain level of opacity and exceptionality, the Transparency Principle will force reanalysis to occur. Lightfoot attributes a high degree of explanatory power to this principle: 'such a principle of grammar will predict the point at which radical re-analyses will take place' (1979: 122), and states that the principle, properly formulated, will provide 'an *explanation* for the re-analysis and for the fact that it took place at this time' (1979: 123; emphasis original), clearly echoing Weinreich, Labov and Herzog's (1968) wording in their formulation of the actuation problem.

The Transparency Principle has been criticized on both an empirical and a conceptual level. See McMahon (1994: 116–29), and Chapter 17, this volume, for an accessible treatment of the proposal and its critics. Even if we assume that the Transparency Principle can be precisely formulated and motivated, however, the principle does not obviously have the explanatory force that Lightfoot attributes to it. This is because its predictions, such as they are, state only that when faced with a particular type of PLD, the acquisition process will take a particular course. In order to predict the time at which a change will take place, an additional ingredient is needed, namely a notion of when this particular triggering experience will arise. Lightfoot clearly acknowledges this limitation in recent work, stating that '[w]hat we cannot explain, in general, is why the linguistic environment should have changed in the first place (as emphasized by Lass 1997 and by others)' (2006: 165). In order to have a truly predictive theory of history which is able to overcome the actuation problem, we need to be able to identify what Lightfoot terms the *local* cause of a change (2006: 166), which is necessarily external. Whether or not this type of explanation is possible will be the focus of §19.4.

The Transparency Principle itself does not feature heavily in more recent work on diachronic syntax. However, the notion that properties of L1 acquisition strategies may play a key role in explaining language change remains alive and well. In particular, Roberts and Roussou (1999, 2003) and van Gelderen (2004, 2009, 2011) have proposed preferences on the part of the acquirer that they suggest explain cross-linguistically observed diachronic pathways of grammaticalization. For Roberts and Roussou, grammaticalization is upward reanalysis, and this follows from (3) (Roberts and Roussou 2003: 201, their (23)).

(3)   Featural Simplicity Metric
       A structural representation R for a substring of input text S is sim-
       pler than an alternative representation R′ iff R contains fewer for-
       mal feature syncretisms than R′.

Van Gelderen (2004, 2009, 2011) proposes two principles which have roughly the same effect: the Head Preference Principle, and the Late Merge Principle. In her recent work she suggests (2009: 186–9) that both follow from a principle of featural economy similar to (3), which prefers uninterpretable features over interpretable features over semantic features.

Lightfoot (2013), however, criticizes the work of Roberts and Roussou (2003) and van Gelderen (2004, 2011) on much the same grounds as I have criticized the Transparency Principle above: 'saying that it [a change; GW] results from an internal drive or a UG bias gives no explanation for why it happened when it did nor under what circumstances' (2013: e35), i.e. it does not solve the actuation problem.[4]

Van Gelderen (2009) explicitly contrasts her perspective with that of Lightfoot (1999, 2006), stating that '[f]or Lightfoot, change can only come from the outside, i.e. triggered by variable data ... I have argued the opposite: that change can come from the inside' (2009:189). However, under her approach, variable data are still required, as otherwise we have no account for why the economy principles take effect when they do. Lohndal (2009: 215), in a discussion of van Gelderen's principles, states that 'unless the external data is such that the principle can kick in, it won't'.

---

[4] However, as we have seen, Lightfoot is willing to recognize this limitation in *any* theory of change (2006: 165f.). It is therefore odd that he should choose to criticize Roberts and Roussou (2003) and van Gelderen (2004, 2011) for not overcoming it.

As we have seen from the examples of the Transparency Principle and of formal approaches to grammaticalization, it is in principle impossible for a theory of change that consists only of a theory of grammar and of acquisition to provide solutions to the actuation problem. This is because acquirers are located in time and space, and are responsive to the PLD they receive: their exact response will depend on these PLD, yet the theory of acquisition by itself says nothing about what these PLD will look like or when they will arrive. At best such a theory can predict what an acquirer will do when faced with a particular set of PLD, and this capacity is likely to turn out to be an important component of any theory of change.

19.3.3 Functional Pressures

Another tradition of explanation that is firmly grounded in the behaviour of individual language users ascribes diachronic change to functional pressures that act indirectly through processes of production and perception to make the language more user-friendly in some respect, typically with regard to its communicative function (see Chapter 31, this volume, for an overview). I will here discuss one paradigm example: Hawkins's (1990, 1994, 2002a, b, 2004) theory of processing efficiency and complexity.

Functional approaches to language are often contrasted with formal approaches: however, this dichotomy is misleading, as functional explanation of the origin of linguistic features and typological tendencies through diachrony is perfectly compatible with a formalist stance on symbolic computation, and with a clear distinction between competence and performance (see Newmeyer 1998; Fischer 2007). The principles proposed by Hawkins, for instance, presuppose some notion of phrase structure similar to that found in X-bar theory. Furthermore, explanations for diachronic change proposed in the 'formalist' literature often have a heavily functional flavour: Lass (1980: 66) observes that the notion of optimization incorporated in King's (1969) classic work on language change and generative grammar is 'nothing if not "therapeutic"'. The same is true of both the Transparency Principle, which Lightfoot explicitly describes as therapeutic (1979: 124), and of Roberts and Roussou's and van Gelderen's simplicity metrics, which serve to eliminate excess complexity in representations. It therefore makes more sense to view functional and acquisition-based explanations of change as the same basic type of explanation: 'internal' – understood as pertaining to speakers, hearers and learners as the (mostly) unconscious agents of change – as opposed to 'external' (on which see §19.4).

Central to Hawkins's work is the Performance–Grammar Correspondence Hypothesis (PGCH) given in (4) (Hawkins 2004: 3).

(4)   Performance–Grammar Correspondence Hypothesis
       Grammars have conventionalized syntactic structures in propor-
       tion to their degree of preference in performance, as evidenced by
       patterns of selection in corpora and by ease of processing in psy-
       cholinguistic experiments.

Evidently, for this to work it is necessary to have an account of what is
preferred in performance. Hawkins's key metric for this is given in (5)
(Hawkins 2004: 107).

(5)   Early Immediate Constituents (EIC)
       The human processor prefers linear orders that maximise PCDs
       [Phrasal Combination Domains; GW] (by maximizing their IC-to-
       nonIC [or IC-to-word] ratios), in proportion to the minimization
       difference between competing orders... The PCD for a mother
       node M and its I(mmediate) C(onstituent)s consists of the smallest
       string of terminal elements ... on the basis of which the processor
       can construct M and its ICs.

EIC creates a preference for harmonic orderings, i.e. those in which the
direction of branching is consistently to the left or consistently to the
right, and a dispreference for centre-embeddings. By the PGCH, then, we
should see transitions away from disharmonic systems, all else being
equal.

Hawkins is mute with regard to actual historical mechanisms that might
underlie the PGCH or explain specific effects, as noted by Aitchison (2003:
742) and Walkden (2009: 69): we have no understanding of exactly how
grammars might conventionalize syntactic structures that the parser prefers. Nevertheless, the idea that they might do so is not implausible.
If a principle like EIC is attributed causal status, though, it is susceptible
to the same kind of arguments adduced by Lass (1980: ch. 3) against
functional pressures in sound change. In brief: if EIC is strong enough to
cause disharmonic branching and centre-embeddings to disappear, then
why does it (a) not cause them to disappear in all cases and all related
languages, and (b) allow them to arise in the first place? To take a concrete
example: early English possessed OV word orders – which for simplicity's
sake we can treat as involving a head-final VP, following van Kemenade
(1987), Pintzuk (1999, 2005) and subsequent work – at the same time as
head-initial structure higher up the tree, for instance in the CP. According
to EIC, this type of word order is dispreferred, since the parser will not be
able to construct the mother node VP until after the verb is encountered.
Therefore, EIC could be said to have played a causal role in the change to
consistently right-branching structure in the history of English. However,
the supposedly problematic word order is maintained in the history of
German until the present day. If EIC is causally active, then why not here as
well, especially given that English and German have a common ancestor?

One possible answer, of course, is that EIC is not the only principle of performance in Hawkins' theory. In his more recent work (2004, 2007), EIC is in fact subsumed under a principle of Minimize Domains (MiD), which operates alongside Maximize On-line Processing (MaOP) and Minimize Forms (MiF). Hawkins views these principles as competing with one another. For instance, in languages that are VO and NRel, MiD and MaOP are acting in unison; in languages which are OV and RelN, MiD defeats MaOP, while in languages which are OV and NRel, MaOP comes out on top (2002b: 221). The retention of OV word order with a head-initial CP in German could, then, potentially be analysed as an instance of another principle trumping MiD.

The prioritization of different functions in different languages is an argument that Lass (1980) anticipates, however, again in relation to an explanation for a sound change proposed by Campbell (1975):

> The trouble with arguments like this is that you can't lose. What Campbell seems to be saying is that 'paradigm conditions' are important except where something else is. To my mind the virtual invulnerability of functional arguments like this strongly militates (to put it weakly) against their acceptability.
>
> *(1980: 70)*

For Hawkins's account, then, the problem is this: why would MiD be ranked above MaOP in one language but not another? Claiming priority for a specific principle in a given language is simply restating the (diachronic) problem: re-ranking of preferences must be possible (see, for instance, Bermúdez-Otero 2006 and the papers in Holt 2000 for diachronic work in Optimality Theory), yet we need an explanation for why and when this would occur.

In sum: functional preferences cannot be both universally active and causal in change, as this leads to a regress problem, but if they are not universally active then we need to know when they are active and when they are not, a question which cannot itself be answered in functional terms.

19.3.4 Internal Factors: Interim Conclusion

So far we have seen that internal approaches to motivations for language change – whether rooted in acquisition, cognition, or language use – are unable to provide satisfactory answers to the actuation problem, at least as long as they involve universal and invariant properties of human cognition or communication. This is not a new realization. Hale (1998) states:

> Numerous 'causes' of change have been cited in the literature. Most mysterious is the frequent claim that various 'constant' factors are the 'cause' of change events. By 'constant' I mean merely factors that can be plausibly assumed to be active in every acquisition event. The fact that these factors were 'active' during the acquisition of the grammar that

serves as the target for a particular acquirer and did not induce a particular change during that earlier acquisition event would seem to preclude attributing changes during the second acquisition event to such factors.

(1998: 8, fn. 9; scare quotes original)

Though stated in terms of acquisition, the same problem arises for any 'constant'-based explanation. Similarly, Labov (2001: 503) formulates a *Principle of Contingency*, asserting that the 'starting point of a historical and evolutionary approach to language change is that one cannot account for change by any universal trait of human beings or of language'; see also Kroch (2000: 699f.), Lightfoot (2006: 165) and Roberts (2007: 126). This is not to say that universal traits are unhelpful in understanding language change: just that, in Weinreich, Labov and Herzog's (1968) terms, they help us to solve the constraints problem and perhaps the transition problem, but not the actuation problem.

There are two obvious responses to this situation, other than giving up. The first is to seek explanations in terms of external factors, such as those which might cause different sets of PLD to be available to different acquirers. The second is to abandon the assumption that the universal traits or preferences are in fact universal, or at least universally ranked. This second direction leads us to the type of competing-motivations approach that has been discussed in §19.3.4 in relation to the work of Hawkins (2002a, b, 2004). But, as observed in that section, this is merely a restatement of the problem, since now we need to account for the differences between individuals in terms of the preferences or rankings. Whichever response we choose, then, we are forced to turn to external factors in order to resolve the situation.

19.4 External Factors: Population Thinking

Lightfoot (1999, 2006, 2013) is not optimistic about the study of external factors. This is not surprising, since it is unlikely that we will ever be able to recover the full details of the PLD for any given acquisition situation. This situation leads Lightfoot (1999) to explore the notion that language change is 'chaotic', in the technical sense: in other words, if it is deterministic, then it is also extremely sensitive to initial conditions, so that we cannot predict the outcome in practice (see also Hale 1998: 9).

Under certain conditions, however, it might be possible to determine what sort of speakers/hearers/learners are present in what sort of situation, or what sort of PLD will be produced. Research in two closely related areas has addressed this question: language contact, and sociolinguistics.

These perspectives require us to abandon the stance that I-language ('individual', 'internal' and 'intensional' language in the sense of Chomsky 1986) is the only coherent object of study, and that a theory of change must reduce to a theory of grammar plus a theory of acquisition (as argued by Lightfoot 1979 and Hale 1998). Instead we must view our I-language-bearing individuals as situated in populations, the composition and distribution of which may change. This population thinking, dominant in evolutionary biology since Darwin, is defined by Lewens (2007) as 'any effort to abstract from a characterisation of individual psychological profiles, in a way that allows an exploration of the consequences of these individual-level dispositions for population-level properties' (see also Mayr 1976: 26–9; 2004; Sober 1980). Importantly, this does not necessitate an abandonment of the insights derived from I-language approaches; in fact, it requires and presupposes a good characterization of the individual, as Lewens's definition makes clear.

19.4.1 Language Contact

Contact has had a chequered history as a type of explanation for change; see Chapter 8, this volume, for a full overview. A common twentieth-century stance has been to ascribe a change to the effects of contact only if there is 'clear and overwhelming evidence' (see Lass 1997: 201), with 'endogenous' explanations to be given priority. This stance has not gone without criticism: see Farrar and Jones (2002) and Filppula (2010: 449) for rejections of this 'if-in-doubt-do-without' methodology. If, as argued in §19.3, internal explanation cannot solve the actuation problem alone, it is worth exploring the explanatory power of contact-based explanations.

If there are speakers possessing two different types of grammar in contact within a population, there are three logical possibilities for the outcome. One is that nothing happens, and stable variation persists. The second possibility is that features of one grammar type are incorporated into the other (which can, of course, happen in both directions simultaneously). Thirdly, the grammar types may change due to contact, but in ways that do not cause them to resemble one another more.

Setting the first possibility aside as uninteresting for the study of the actuation problem, I will refer to the second as *transfer*, following Winford (2003; 2005: 376), who develops ideas first found in van Coetsem (1988, 1995, 2000). Winford develops an approach that might help to predict what type of transfer will occur and in which circumstances. The approach revolves around language dominance, understood in psycholinguistic terms as the language in which the speaker is most proficient. Winford (2005: 376) and van Coetsem (1988: 3) define two types of transfer. The first is *borrowing*, in which material is transferred under what has been called 'recipient language agentivity', i.e. when a speaker dominant in the language that will ultimately receive the feature is actively using features from a different grammar. The second is *imposition*, in which the source language speaker is the agent (source language agentivity).

The distinction between imposition and borrowing is not merely terminological: according to van Coetsem (1988: 25) and Winford (2005: 377), recipient language agentivity and source language agentivity give rise to different types of change. In particular, Winford (2005) argues at length that borrowing standardly involves the transfer of open-class vocabulary items, whereas imposition is more likely to lead to the transfer of phonological or syntactic features. The distinction is not absolute: Winford suggests (2005: 383) that lexical transfer from French into Middle English was mediated by both source and recipient language agents. Similarly, structural transfer may occur under borrowing of lexical items together with their syntactic properties (Winford 2005: 385–8), as seems to be the case with phrase-final prepositions in Prince Edward Island French (King 2000), or it may occur as a result of imposition, as Winford (2005: 394f.) suggests is the case with the argument structure of verbs like *gustar* in Spanish in contact with English, which come to take a nominative experiencer. However, to the extent that it is possible to identify types of transfer characteristic of borrowing and imposition, then, given a characterization of a population in terms of the distribution and psycholinguistic dominance of its individuals, we can approach the question of what features will be transferred, and when and where this transfer will occur. Of course, more work needs to be done on linking different linguistic types of transfer to the two types of agentivity, and on investigating the individual-level processes of production and comprehension they are derived from. Winford (2005: 417–20) takes a step in this direction by looking at production in code-switching, following Myers-Scotton (2002, 2003).

Not all effects of contact are cases of transfer, as Winford recognizes (2005: 376, fn. 3). Lucas (2009) discusses a further type of contact-induced change, which he labels *restructuring* and which corresponds to the third logical possibility mentioned above: 'changes which a speaker makes to an L2 that cannot be seen as the transfer of patterns or material from their L1' (2009: 145; see also Trudgill 2011).[5] Lucas illustrates this possibility using several case studies of L2 acquisition in which systematic deviations from the target grammar have been observed that cannot be interpreted as resulting from the acquirer's L1 (2009: 135–8). Håkansson, Pienemann and Sayehli (2002) show, for example, that speakers of Swedish (a V2 language) learning German (another V2 language) as an L2 regularly produce non-V2 structures in their German output.

---

[5] Van Coetsem (1995: 70) and Winford (2005: 376f.) claim that a speaker is not necessarily psycholinguistically dominant in his/her first or native language, though the two will coincide in the majority of cases. See Lucas (2009: 111–20) for discussion of this issue.

The impact of L2 acquisition, and its potential to lead to contact-induced changes that are not direct transfer, has not been widely studied in the literature on diachronic syntax, though Weerman (1993) is an early exception. Weerman argues for the influence of Old Norse on English in the change from OV to VO (1993: 918–22), despite the fact that both languages were OV, on the grounds that L2 learners of V2 and OV languages tend to assume VO (Clahsen and Muysken 1986). Roberts (2007: 391–9) and Lucas (2009: 145–9, 167–9) provide further discussion. Though this particular example is debated, it is clear that explanations of this *kind* provide something that internal explanations cannot: they can help us identify the reasons that a change took place when and where it did, in population terms. In the case of the change from OV to VO in English, a contact-based explanation has the potential to explain why Dutch and German have not undergone this particular change.

19.4.2 Sociolinguistic Explanations

Of course, not all linguistic changes occur in circumstances in which there are two clearly distinct 'languages' (in the pretheoretical sense) in contact. This is presumably what Lass (1997: 209) has in mind when he states that internal explanations are to be preferred on the grounds that 'endogenous change *must* occur in any case'. Beyond clear cases of language contact, then, can a case be made for external causal factors? The search for such factors is a major part of the work of sociolinguists, in addition to the social embedding problem and evaluation problem as discussed in §19.2 (see also Chapter 23, this volume).

Hale (1998) is sceptical about the role of external factors. He draws a distinction between 'change', i.e. the emergence of a new structural feature, understood simply as a set of differences between two grammars mediated by a single acquisition event, and 'diffusion', whereby additional speakers acquire the new feature. Diffusion, according to Hale, 'represents the trivial case of acquisition: accurate transmission', and no special explanatory principles are required to account for it (1998: 5); furthermore, '"populations" are irrelevant for those interested in studying the properties of I-language' (1998: 6). Diffusion in Hale's sense is indeed irrelevant for the study of the actuation problem, but this does not mean that the structure of populations is also irrelevant. Labov (2007) draws an important, but different, distinction between transmission and diffusion. Transmission, in Labov's sense, refers to an 'unbroken sequence of native-language acquisition by children' (2007: 346), which he argues is likely to be highly accurate; diffusion in Labov's sense, by contrast, involves the attempted replication of linguistic features between adults, often highly inaccurate.

Labov illustrates the difference between transmission and diffusion with reference to the New York short-*a* system (2007: 353–72), among other case studies. He demonstrates that the alternation between tense and lax variants is conditioned by a complex array of factors: function words, for instance, have lax short-*a*, while the vowel is tense in corresponding content words, and there are a number of lexical exceptions to the general phonological rules. The New York system has diffused to other communities, but typically imperfectly: for instance, in New Jersey and Albany the function-word constraint has been lost. Diffusion, according to Labov, normally leads to a 'loss of structural detail' (2007: 357), typical of adult-language acquisition. Note that here we have an event of change, in Hale's terms, but one whose occurrence can be understood in terms of the structure of the population.

The distinction between transmission and diffusion has not been investigated with regard to syntactic change, but the structure of populations plays a similar explanatory role in Kroch's (2000) and Eitler's (2006) accounts of the loss of V2 in English (see also Lightfoot 1999: 151–8). The starting point for these accounts is the observation that Old English had a mixed V2 system, in which the presence or absence of V2 was contingent on properties of the subject and initial adverbs as well as clause type. Northern dialects of English then developed a strict V2 system, comparable to that of present-day Continental Germanic and Scandinavian languages, through contact with speakers of Old Norse (Kroch and Taylor 1997). Speakers of the northern strict V2 and southern mixed V2 varieties would then have come into contact with one another as a consequence of population movements in the Middle English period. Kroch (2000) argues that the non-V2 grammar characteristic of modern English is a consequence of this contact, as northerners hearing surface V3 clauses interpreted the grammar underlying them as non-V2 (rather than mixed V2), and, in accommodating, innovated a non-V2 grammar. Building on Kroch's account, Eitler (2006: ch. 5) demonstrates that this grammar took off first, and fastest, in some London varieties and particularly in the northern and central Midlands. He ascribes this to the heavy immigration and weak social network ties in these areas at the time. These plausibly caused diffusion in Labov's sense/restructuring in Lucas's sense: imperfect acquisition of a grammatical system by adults. Again, if correct, this scenario yields insight into why the change happened when and where it did.

Discussing Milroy's (1992: 10) claim that '[i]n order to account for differential patterns of change at particular times and places, we need first to take account of those factors that tend to maintain language states and resist change', Campbell (2013: 195) queries: 'How can the actuation problem, the question about how changes get started in the first place, be approached with a model based solely on norm maintenance, that is on resistance to change but not on change itself?' Given the discussion in this section, the answer is not too difficult to sketch. According to Milroy, weak ties in social networks are the locus of change. If weak network ties are likely to involve situations of adult language learning and hence lead to diffusion/restructuring, then these nodes in the network may be not only those through which new features are transmitted most rapidly, but also those at which innovations are most likely to take place.

19.4.3 External Factors: Interim Conclusion

Whereas internal factors are inherently incapable of addressing the actuation problem, external factors, i.e. factors to do with population composition and distribution, may have the potential to do so. At least, in contact-based or sociolinguistic explanations, we can gain some insight into why a change happened when and where it did.

This is not to say that particular instances of the actuation problem in the historical record are by any means solved. To pinpoint a precise time and location for a particular innovation, we would need access to detailed information about the PLD available to individual acquirers, and the structure of individual discourses – information which in almost all cases will be beyond our grasp due to the nature of the historical record. The situation is better in studies of change in progress, but not much better, as Lass (1980: 94–6) points out. Here at least we have the potential to observe the moment of actuation directly – but we are unlikely to do so except by accident, and even then we would be unlikely to know what we are observing.

All the potential explanation types given in this section also admit further 'why?'-questions. For instance, with regard to the loss of V2 in English as discussed in §19.4.2: why did the relevant population movements take place during the Middle English period? Why were there weak network ties at just that time and in just that place? So these external factors do not allow us to solve the actuation problem in a completely satisfactory way, even if we had all the relevant historical linguistic data at our disposal. But to the extent that these further questions take us far beyond the domain of language, we are justified in leaving them to our historical and sociological colleagues.

19.5 Conclusion: An Unsolved Riddle

I have argued that internal factors – that is, factors relating solely to the knowledge or behaviour of individuals – are unable to account for the time and place of changes, i.e. to solve the actuation problem. An understanding of these factors is nevertheless crucial, as they form part of the *explanans* for any change, even if they cannot form all of it. External (population-based) factors fare better, as questions such as 'Why did English lose V2 but not German or Dutch?' can in principle be addressed. However, it is all too easy to invoke contact, weak network ties, imperfect learning, etc. as *post hoc* accounts, but much harder to come up with a truly predictive theory, and many of the pieces of the puzzle are still missing. Furthermore, with regard to particular changes in the historical record, the specific details (e.g. PLD) we would need in order to achieve a confidence approaching certainty are essentially always unavailable.

It seems that the 'actuation riddle', if solvable at all, certainly has not yet been solved. Some have argued that the predictive power necessary for a solution to the actuation problem is not a reasonable goal for diachronic linguistics (see McMahon 1994: 44–6; Lightfoot 1999: 253–61; Campbell 2013: 333–5). These authors point to evolutionary biology and its successes as an example of a discipline in which explanation is possible without prediction. The problem is that it then becomes very hard to define what explanation actually is (Lass 1980: 160–9). In any case, in view of some of the proposals mentioned in this chapter, it does not seem necessary to abandon prediction just yet. It is reasonable to assume that a predictive account of language *acquisition* is possible (as discussed in §19.3.2). A predictive account of population dynamics is a much more challenging goal, but some of the results outlined in §19.4 suggest that general, weather-forecast-style predictions and explanations might be possible (see Lightfoot 1999: 267f.). Under this approach, we may not ultimately be successful in pinpointing the solution to the actuation problem for any specific change, but we may be able to narrow down the search space with a reasonable degree of confidence.

References

Aitchison, J. 2003. 'Psycholinguistic perspectives on language change', in B. D. Joseph and R. D. Janda (eds.), *The handbook of historical linguistics*. Oxford: Blackwell, pp. 736–43.

Andersen, H. 1973. Abductive and deductive change, *Language* 49: 765–93.

Baker, J., Archangeli, D. and Mielke, J. 2011. 'Variability in English s-retraction suggests a solution to the actuation problem', *Language Variation & Change* 23: 347–374.

Bermúdez-Otero, R. 2006. 'Phonological change in Optimality Theory', in K. Brown (ed.), *Encyclopedia of language and linguistics*, vol. 9, 2nd edn. Oxford: Elsevier, pp. 497–505.

Biberauer, T., Holmberg, A. and Roberts, I. 2007. 'Disharmonic word-order systems and the Final-over-Final Constraint (FOFC)', in A. Bisetto and F. Barbieri (eds.), *Proceedings of XXXIII incontro di grammatica generativa*, pp. 86–105.

2008. 'Linearising disharmonic word orders: The Final-over-Final Constraint', in J. Y. Yoon and K.-A. Kim (eds.), *Perspectives on linguistics in the 21st Century*. Seoul: Hankook Munhwasa, pp. 301–18.

2014. 'A syntactic universal and its consequences', *Linguistic Inquiry* 45(2): 169–225.

Biberauer, T., Newton, G. and Sheehan, M. 2009. 'Limiting synchronic and diachronic variation and change: the Final-Over-Final Constraint', *Language and Linguistics* 10: 701–43.

Börjars, K. and Vincent, N. 2011. 'Grammaticalization and directionality', in H. Narrog and B. Heine (eds.), *The Oxford handbook of grammaticalization*. Oxford University Press, pp. 163–76.

Campbell, L. 1975. 'Constraints on sound change', in K.-H. Dahlstedt (ed.), *The Nordic languages and modern linguistics*, vol. 2. Stockholm: Almqvist & Wiksell, pp. 388–406.

2013. *Historical linguistics: An introduction*. Edinburgh University Press.

Cheshire, J., Adger, D. and Fox, S. 2013. 'Relative *who* and the actuation problem', *Lingua* 126: 51–77.

Chomsky, N. 1986. *Knowledge of language: Its nature, origin, and use*. Westport, CT: Praeger.

Clahsen, H. and Muysken, P. 1986. 'The availability of universal grammar to adult and child learners: A study of the acquisition of German word order', *Second Language Research* 2: 93–119.

De Smet, H. 2012. 'The course of actualization', *Language* 88: 601–33.

Eitler, T. 2006. 'Some sociolectal, dialectal and communicative aspects of word order variation in late Middle English', unpublished PhD thesis, Eötvös Loránd University.

Farrar, K. and Jones, M.C. 2002. 'Introduction', in M. C. Jones and E. Esch (eds.), *Language change: The interplay of internal, external, and extralinguistic factors*. Berlin: Mouton de Gruyter, pp. 1–16.

Filppula, M. 2010. 'Contact and the early history of English', in R. Hickey (ed.), *The handbook of language contact*. Oxford University Press, pp. 432–53.

Fischer, O. 2007. *Morphosyntactic change: Functional and formal perspectives*. Oxford University Press.

Håkansson, G., Pienemann, M. and Sayehli, S. 2002. 'Transfer and typological proximity in the context of second language processing', *Second Language Research* 18: 250–73.

Hale, M. 1998. 'Diachronic syntax', *Syntax* 1: 1–18.

Harris, A. C. and Campbell, L. 1995. *Historical syntax in cross-linguistic perspective*. Cambridge University Press.

Hawkins, J. A. 1990. 'A parsing theory of word order universals', *Linguistic Inquiry* 21: 223–61.

1994. *A performance theory of order and constituency*. Cambridge University Press.

2002a. 'Symmetries and asymmetries: Their grammar, typology and parsing', *Theoretical Linguistics* 28: 95–149.

2002b. 'Issues at the performance-grammar interface: Some comments on the commentaries', *Theoretical Linguistics* 28: 211–27.

2004. *Efficiency and complexity in grammars*. Oxford University Press.

2007. 'Processing typology and why psychologists need to know about it', *New Ideas in Psychology* 25: 87–107.

Hempel, C. G. and Oppenheim, P. 1948. 'Studies in the logic of explanation', *Philosophy of Science* 15: 135–75.

Holmberg, A. 2000. 'Deriving OV order in Finnish', in P. Svenonius (ed.), *The derivation of VO and OV*. Amsterdam: John Benjamins, pp. 123–52.

Holt, D. E. (ed.) 2000. *Optimality theory and language change*. Dordrecht: Kluwer.

Hopper, P. and Traugott, E. C. 2003. *Grammaticalization*, 2nd edn. Cambridge University Press.

Ingason, A. K., Sigurðsson, E. F. and Wallenberg, J. C. 2012. 'Antisocial syntax: Disentangling the Icelandic VO/OV parameter and its lexical remains', paper presented at *DiGS 14*, Lisbon, 6 July.

King, R. D. 1969. *Historical linguistics and generative grammar*. Englewood Cliffs, NJ: Prentice Hall.

King, R. 2000. *The lexical basis of grammatical borrowing: A Prince Edward Island case study*. Amsterdam: John Benjamins.

Kroch, A. S. 1989. 'Reflexes of grammar in patterns of language change', *Language Variation and Change* 1: 199–244.

1994. 'Morphosyntactic variation', *Proceedings of the 30th Annual Meeting of the Chicago Linguistics Society* 2: 180–201.

2000. 'Syntactic change', in M. Baltin and C. Collins (eds.), *The handbook of contemporary syntactic theory*. Oxford: Blackwell, pp. 629–739.

Kroch, A. S. and Taylor, A. 1997. 'Verb movement in Old and Middle English: Dialect variation and language contact', in A. van Kemenade and N. Vincent (eds.), *Parameters of morphosyntactic change*. Cambridge University Press, pp. 297–325.

Labov, W. 1972. *Sociolinguistic patterns*. Philadelphia, PA: University of Pennsylvania Press.

1982. 'Building on empirical foundations', in W. P. Lehmann and Y. Malkiel (eds.), *Perspectives on historical linguistics*. Amsterdam: John Benjamins, pp. 17–92.

2001. *Principles of linguistic change*, vol. 2: *Social factors*. Malden, MA, and Oxford: Blackwell.

2007. 'Transmission and diffusion', *Language* 83: 344–87.

Labov, W. and Harris, W. A. 1986. 'De facto segregation of Black and White vernaculars', in D. Sankoff (ed.), *Diversity and diachrony*. Amsterdam: John Benjamins, pp. 1–24.

Langacker, R. W. 1977. 'Syntactic reanalysis', in C. N. Li (ed.), *Mechanisms of syntactic change*. Austin: University of Texas Press, pp. 57–139.

Lass, R. 1980. *On explaining language change*. Cambridge University Press.

1997. *Historical linguistics and language change*. Cambridge University Press.

Ledgeway, A. 2012. *From Latin to Romance: Morphosyntactic typology and change*. Oxford University Press.

Lewens, T. 2007. 'Cultural evolution', in *Stanford Encyclopedia of Philosophy*. http://plato.stanford.edu/entries/evolution-cultural/. Accessed 2 November 2012.

Lightfoot, D. W. 1979. *Principles of diachronic syntax*. Cambridge University Press.

1991. *How to set parameters: Arguments from language acquisition.* Cambridge, MA: MIT Press.

1999. *The development of language: Acquisition, change, and evolution.* Oxford: Blackwell.

2002. 'Myths and the prehistory of grammars', *Journal of Linguistics* 38: 113–36.

2006. *How new languages emerge.* Cambridge University Press.

2013. 'Types of explanation in history', *Language (Historical Syntax)* 89: e18–e39.

Lohndal, T. 2009. 'The copula cycle', in E. van Gelderen (ed.), *Cyclical change.* Amsterdam: John Benjamins, pp. 209–42.

Lucas, C. 2009. 'The development of negation in Arabic and Afro-Asiatic', unpublished PhD thesis, University of Cambridge.

Mayr, E. 1976. *Evolution and the diversity of life.* Cambridge, MA: Harvard University Press.

2004. *What makes biology unique? Considerations on the autonomy of a scientific discipline.* Cambridge University Press.

McMahon, A. M. S. 1994. *Understanding language change.* Cambridge University Press.

Meillet, A. 1921. *Linguistique historique et linguistique générale*, 1st edn. Paris: Champion.

Milroy, J. 1992. *Linguistic variation and change: On the historical sociolinguistics of English.* Oxford: Blackwell.

Myers-Scotton, C. 2002. *Contact linguistics: Bilingual encounters and grammatical outcomes.* Oxford University Press.

2003. 'What lies beneath: Split (mixed) languages as contact phenomena', in Y. Matras and P. Bakker (eds.), *The mixed language debate: Theoretical and empirical advances.* Berlin: Mouton de Gruyter, pp. 73–106.

Naro, A. 1981. 'The social and structural dimensions of a syntactic change', *Language* 57: 63–98.

Newmeyer, F.J. 1998. *Language form and language function.* Cambridge, MA: MIT Press.

Paul, H. 1880. *Prinzipien der Sprachgeschichte*, 1st edn. Halle: Max Niemeyer.

Pintzuk, S. 1999. *Phrase structures in competition: Variation and change in Old English word order.* New York: Garland.

2003. 'Variationist approaches to syntactic change', in B. D. Joseph and R. D. Janda (eds.), *The handbook of historical linguistics.* Oxford: Blackwell, pp. 509–28.

2005. 'Arguments against a universal base: Evidence from Old English', *English Language and Linguistics* 9: 115–38.

Roberts, I. 2007. *Diachronic syntax*. Oxford University Press.

Roberts, I. and Roussou, A. 1999. 'A formal approach to "grammaticalization"', *Linguistics* 37: 1011–41.

2003. *Syntactic change: A minimalist approach to grammaticalization*. Cambridge University Press.

Romaine, S. 1982. *Socio-historical linguistics: Its status and methodology*. Cambridge University Press.

Sober, E. 1980. 'Evolution, population thinking, and essentialism', *Philosophy of Science* 47: 350–83.

Timberlake, A. 1977. 'Reanalysis and actualization in syntactic change', in C. N. Li (ed.), *Mechanisms of syntactic change*. Austin: University of Texas Press, 141–77.

Trudgill, P. 2011. *Sociolinguistic typology: Social determinants of linguistic complexity*. Oxford University Press.

van Coetsem, F. 1988. *Loan phonology and the two transfer types in language contact*. Dordrecht: Foris.

1995. 'Outlining a model of the transmission phenomenon in language contact', *Leuvense Bijdragen* 84: 63–85.

2000. *A general and unified theory of the transmission process in language contact*. Heidelberg: Carl Winter.

van Gelderen, E. 2004. *Grammaticalization as economy*. Amsterdam: John Benjamins.

2009. 'Renewal in the left periphery: Economy and the complementiser layer', *Transactions of the Philological Society* 107: 131–95.

2011. *The linguistic cycle: Language change and the language faculty*. Oxford University Press.

van Kemenade, A. 1987. *Syntactic case and morphological case in the history of English*. Dordrecht: Foris.

Walkden, G. 2009. 'Deriving the Final-over-Final Constraint from third factor considerations', *Cambridge Occasional Papers in Linguistics* 5: 67–72.

2012. 'Against inertia', *Lingua* 122: 891–901.

Weerman, F. 1993. 'The diachronic consequences of first and second language acquisition: the change from OV to VO', *Linguistics* 31: 903–31.

Weinreich, U., Labov, W. and Herzog, M. 1968. 'Empirical foundations for a theory of language change', in W. Lehmann and Y. Malkiel (eds.), *Directions for historical linguistics*. Austin: University of Texas Press, pp. 95–189.

Winford, D. 2003. *An introduction to contact linguistics*. Oxford: Blackwell.

2005. 'Contact-induced changes: Classification and processes', *Diachronica* 22: 373–427.

20

Inertia

Ian Roberts

20.1 Introduction

The Inertia Principle was first put forward by Keenan. In Keenan (2002: 2), he formulates it as follows:[1]

(1)   'Things stay as they are unless a force (including decay) acts upon them.'

Longobardi (2001: 278) adopts Keenan's principle, and puts forward the following version of it:

(2)   'syntactic change should not arise, unless it can be shown to be *caused*' (emphasis original)

In other words, as Longobardi says, '*syntax*, by itself, is diachronically completely inert' (2001: 277f.). As pointed out in §7.4.2, Longobardi's notion of a cause of change includes anything that disrupts the primary linguistic data (PLD) for language acquisition: language contact, lexical, phonological or morphological changes and earlier syntactic changes.

In this chapter, I will first argue that the Inertia Principle is fully compatible with the idea that language change is driven by first-language acquisition (see Chapters 6, 15, 17, 18, 21 and 22, this volume, for discussion and illustration of this idea from varying perspectives; this section repeats and develops some of the points made in §7.4.2); in fact, given the perspective on parameters, features and language acquisition outlined in Chapter 7, this volume, it may be that the effects of the Inertia Principle follow. In §20.3 I turn to the critique of the Inertia Principle in Walkden (2012). Finally, in §20.4 I consider the Inertia Principle in relation to the notion of 'drift', showing how that notion can be seen as a cascade of parametric changes; I illustrate this idea by summarizing the key points of Biberauer and Roberts (2008).

---

[1] Keenan (2002) was the first to formulate inertia, although the paper in which he did this was published after Longobardi (2001) owing to the vagaries of publication delays.

20.2   Inertia, Language Acquisition and Language Change

Here I take the general view that syntactic change is parametric change, and that parametric change occurs when a population of acquirers converges on a grammar (i.e. a set of parameter values) which differs in the value of at least one parameter as compared to earlier generations culturally defined as 'speakers of the same language' (see again Chapter 7, this volume, for discussion of this idea, and in particular the issues raised by the Linking Problem in language acquisition). A key notion here is that of P(arameter)-expression, introduced in Clark and Roberts (1993). This notion, and the corollary definition of trigger, were defined as follows in Roberts (2007: 232):

(3)   a. Parameter expression:
             A substring of the input text S expresses a parameter p_i just in case a grammar must have p_i set to a definite value in order to assign a well-formed representation to S.
        b. Trigger:
             A substring of the input text S is a trigger for parameter p_i if S expresses p_i.

From this, (4) follows:

(4)   If a definite value v_i is expressed for a parameter p_i in the PLD, then (a population of) acquirers will converge on v_i.

In other words, given adequate P-expression, inertia will hold. So inertia implies that most of the time change does not happen.

It further follows that change happens when no definite value v_i is expressed for a parameter p_i in the PLD. According to Longobardi's version of Inertia in (2), this lack of robust P-expression must be 'a well-motivated consequence of other types of change (phonological changes and semantic changes, including the appearance/disappearance of whole lexical items) or, recursively, of other syntactic changes' (2001: 278).

Roberts (2007: 233f.) proposes that both ambiguity and 'opacity' of the P-expression are required in order for change to take place. Ambiguity is defined in relation to parametric systems as follows (again these definitions originate in Clark and Roberts (1993), but the formulations given here are from Roberts (2007: 233)):

(5)   a. P-ambiguity:
             A substring of the input text S is strongly P-ambiguous with respect to a parameter p_i just in case a grammar can have p_i set to either value and assign a well-formed representation to S.
        b. A strongly P-ambiguous string may express either value of p_i and therefore trigger either value of p_i.
        c. A weakly P-ambiguous string expresses neither value of p_i and therefore triggers neither value of p_i.

Here I will largely leave aside weak P-ambiguity (but see the discussion in the next section), and focus mainly on strong P-ambiguity (Roberts (2007: 233–5) argues that strong P-ambiguity is required for reanalytical change).

The notion of 'opacity' is now best understood in relation to the third-factor acquisition preferences discussed in §7.3, Feature Economy (FE) and Input Generalization (IG) (see also the discussion of the emergentist approach to parameters given there):

(6) Feature Economy:
     Given two structural representations R and R´ for a substring of input text S, R is less marked than R´ iff R contains fewer formal features than R´. (Roberts and Roussou 2003: 201)

(7) Input Generalization (adapted from Roberts 2007: 275):
     If a functional head sets parameter p_j to value v_i then there is a preference for similar functional heads to set p_j to value v_i.

As stated in §7.3, these two principles are 'non-domain-specific cognitive optimization principles. These principles guide the acquirer in its . . . use of intake, and thereby create biases both in acquisition and change.'

If a given piece of PLD is strongly P-ambiguous, there will be at least two representations for it. Since potentially variant aspects of syntactic representations are created by differences in the incidence, distribution or properties of formal features (see again §7.3) and differences in formal features correspond to different parameter values, strong P-ambiguity entails that the two representations will differ in relation to one or both of FE and IG. All other things being equal, FE and IG will guide the learner to choose the representation that maximally satisfies the two principles. The dispreferred representation will be both opaque (i.e. non-optimal in relation to FE and IG) and ambiguous (by definition). It is thus inaccessible to the learner, i.e. it is effectively unlearnable. In this connection, when we speak of the acquirer 'choosing' a representation, it is not really presented with a choice, but rather led to one of two representations that are compliant both with UG (the first factor) and the PLD (the second factor, i.e. the PLD is P-ambiguous) by the third-factor principles FE and IG. The interaction of the three factors lead the acquirer to posit the optimal, emergent set of parameter settings; under the relevant conditions, this can lead to the emergence of a novel grammar, i.e. a change.

The Inertia Principle comes into this picture in that it implies that strong P-ambiguity cannot arise endogenously (see further also the discussion in Chapter 23, this volume). Following Longobardi then, we might suppose that it arises either from extrasyntactic factors or as the consequence of an independent syntactic change. It is important to see that the situation just described does not guarantee a change, it just suspends inertia. Hence, under these conditions, it is possible that things will not stay as they are. Whether a change actually takes place will depend on the precise nature of the interaction of FE and IG with the PLD. The key point in relation to Inertia Principle is that in order for a change to take place, there must be a change in the PLD. In other words, some extrasyntactic factor, or a syntactic factor independent of the change in question, introduces strong P-ambiguity into the expression of at least one parameter in the PLD.

In this connection, consider the typology of parameters introduced in §7.4.1 and §27.4 (originally in Biberauer and Roberts 2012):

(8)   For a given value v_i of a parametrically variant feature F:
       a. **Macroparameters**: all heads of the relevant type, e.g. all probes, all phase heads, etc., share v_i;
       b. **Mesoparameters**: all heads of a given natural class, e.g. [+V] or a core functional category, share v_i;
       c. **Microparameters**: a small, lexically definable subclass of functional heads (e.g. modal auxiliaries, subject clitics) shows v_i;
       d. **Nanoparameters**: one or more individual lexical items is/are specified for v_i.

As stated in §7.4.1, '[m]acroparameters have highly pervasive effects on the grammatical system, which as such are readily detectable in the PLD. As such, they are unlikely to be subject to reanalysis by language acquirers under normal conditions and hence are diachronically stable.' Mesoparameters are somewhat less salient and less stable, while micro- and nanoparameters are still less salient and therefore more unstable. The Inertia Principle is fully consistent with this view, since it guarantees that as long as the PLD is unambiguous, change will not occur; the informal notion of 'salience' introduced here can be understood as P-unambiguity.

In this section, I have outlined the connection between the Inertia Principle and acquisition-driven change. The Inertia Principle holds because acquisition is largely convergent. Two conditions are relevant to suspension of the Inertia Principle, making a change possible: strongly P-ambiguous PLD and interaction of FE and IG with each other and with the PLD in such a way as to guide the acquirer to a novel representation (in relation to that held by earlier generations) of the ambiguous PLD. Strong P-ambiguity can only be introduced through extrasyntactic factors, e.g. through language contact, morphophonological erosion, or through an independent syntactic change.

So we see two of Chomsky's (2005) three factors at work here: the PLD (Factor 2) and FE/IG (Factor 3). Of course, Factor 1, UG, is also relevant since all representations imposed by the acquirer on the PLD and influenced by IG and FE must be UG-compatible (see further Chapter 13, this volume). So the three factors interact to determine the nature of change. To the extent that this interaction of the three factors, and particularly the role of FE/IG, determines the course and output of language acquisition, both the effects of the Inertia Principle, and of its suspension when change takes place, can be accounted for. Although an extremely useful methodological principle, then, the Inertia Principle need not be postulated as an independent principle, either of language or of general cognition.

20.3 Walkden (2012) on Inertia

Walkden (2012) argues against the specific version of the Inertial Theory of change proposed in Longobardi (2001). It is important to note that Walkden does not argue against the intuition behind inertia as articulated by Keenan and stated in (1). Instead, he argues against the conjunction of three propositions from Longobardi (2001). These are (2), repeated here, and (9a–b):

(2)   'syntactic change should not arise, unless it can be shown to be *caused*'

(9)   a. 'linguistic change proper ... may only originate as an interface phenomenon'
      b. '*syntax*, by itself, is diachronically completely inert' (Longobardi 2001: 277f., emphases original)

Walkden first points out that the Inertia Principle cannot be derived from, and is not naturally compatible with, minimalist assumptions. This is undoubtedly true, but as I suggested at the end of the previous section, it may follow from an emergentist approach to parametric variation and change of the kind sketched there and described in more detail in §7.3.

The core of Walkden's argument against the Inertia Principle as a theoretical principle, or, more precisely, against the conjunction of (2) and (9a–b), is a thought experiment, under the idealization that PLD is provided only by parents, as follows:

> Imagine a child whose parents' grammar ... requires V-to-C movement in *wh*-questions ...[T]he postulation of the presence of this movement requires evidence in the data ... Now let us suppose that the parents never needed or wanted to ask direct questions in the presence of the child and therefore that ... the PLD ... includes no relevant examples. The child therefore fails to acquire V-to-C movement in *wh*-questions in her grammar.   *(Walkden 2012: 895)*

In this scenario, Walkden points out, there is no doubt that a syntactic change has happened. But, he argues, it is not caused in any empirically useful sense. He claims, first, that 'acceptance of non-expression in the PLD as ultimate cause of a change is not conducive to a satisfactorily explanatory model of syntactic change' (2012: 895f.). He then develops the argument by imagining that the child in question's parents were members of a religious cult which forbade asking direct questions. In that case, human intentionality might have to be invoked as a cause, with the consequence that 'the notion of causality must be understood to be so broad as to be entirely vacuous' (2012: 896). He further observes that there is no meaningful sense in which (9a) is satisfied here: non-use of direct questions is not an interface phenomenon in a standard sense.

It is here that the concept of *weak* P-ambiguity, as defined above in (5c), becomes relevant. The thought experiment described by Walkden gives rise to the total absence of a trigger for a parameter: there is simply nothing in the PLD that can trigger V-to-C movement in interrogatives. Walkden is correct in seeing this as a problem for Longobardi's notion of caused syntactic change, and this kind of scenario may be problematic for other approaches to acquisition and change too. However, in terms of the general approach to parameter-setting and change described in §§7.3–4, this is simply the *no* case: the absence of a trigger for V-to-C movement results in a grammar which lacks this operation. This is presumably what happens regarding the non-triggering of classifiers in the acquisition of English, or pronominal clitics in Chinese, etc. From the perspective described there, this is not problematic. Longobardi's thesis (2) holds as the cause is the absence of the trigger, and this approach explicitly allows for absent triggers. In this situation (which can also be thought of as extreme P-ambiguity), the third-factor principles of Feature Economy and Input Generalization interact to guarantee that the relevant features are not acquired. This could be portrayed as saying that a 'negative parameter setting' for V-to-C movement is arrived at, but it would be more accurate to say that *no* parameter-setting is arrived at and hence the phenomena depending on a positive parameter setting are not found. Here, then, there is a meaningful notion of cause, understood in terms of how the second and third factors interact in this kind of case.

In fact, there are arguably real cases where V-to-C movement has been lost in certain varieties of English. Varieties such as Manglish and Singlish, spoken in Malaysia and Singapore respectively, tend to lack (overt) *wh*-fronting and concomitant V-(or T-)-to-C movement in direct interrogatives, as well as using particles borrowed from Chinese to mark yes/no questions. Concerning *wh*-movement, Zhiming (2001: 305) says '[i]n Singapore English, wh-movement is optional … questions in which the wh-elements remain *in situ* are equally grammatical, and common', and gives the following examples:

(10)   a. John must buy what? (Chow 1995: 25)
        b. John must have dinner with who? (Chow 1995: 32)
        c. After that, you went to what? (*International Corpus of English*)

This ongoing loss of (overt) *wh*-movement in Singlish is almost certainly due to contact with the Chinese varieties (Mandarin, Cantonese, Teochew, Hakka and Hokkien) which are widely spoken in the multilingual environment of Singapore. Moreover, Mandarin is an official language of Singapore, along with English, Malay and Tamil. All of the official languages besides English, as well as the unofficial non-Mandarin varieties of Chinese, are *wh-in-situ*. Moreover, the population of Singapore is roughly 75 per cent ethnically Chinese. Hence it is easy to see how a child acquiring English in Singapore may encounter PLD in which the Standard English parameter of *wh*-movement is not robustly triggered; this can happen through multilingualism or through exposure to second-language speakers of English who have retained the *in-situ* setting for *wh*-movement in their interlanguage, thereby significantly modifying the nature of the PLD acquirers are exposed to.

Similarly, in Singlish yes/no questions do not feature V-to-C movement (or T-to-C movement, i.e. Subject–Aux inversion). Instead, particles directly borrowed from the Chinese varieties, e.g. *hah*, *hor*, *meh* and *ar*, are used. Borrowing these lexical items and their associated formal features (e.g. [Q] for interrogativity, although it should be stressed that the discourse uses of these particles are more complex than this simple characterization might suggest) effectively introduces a new parameter setting into Singlish. Again, it is clear how this could have happened given the nature of the PLD many Singaporean acquirers of English are exposed to. Hence we have a real case where V/T-to-C and overt *wh*-movement are being lost, and this clearly complies both with Longobardi's inertial theory and with the emergentist-based understanding of the Inertia Principle sketched above.

So we conclude that the Inertia Principle may be useful as a methodological principle. The exclusion of purely endogenous syntactic change is desirable. In fact, it follows from the emergentist approach that this kind of change is not possible: UG on its own cannot instigate change (in this sense, Longobardi's Inertial Theory is correct). But the interaction of the PLD with UG, and with FE and IG, can and does; in cases of contact and multilingualism of the kind creating Singlish the role of the PLD is very clear.

So we accept Walkden's general critique of Longobardi's (2001) construal of the Inertia Principle, but suggest that there is nonetheless a role for the notion of inertia, although this too may derive from the interaction of the three factors rather than being directly stated as part of UG (certainly undesirable in the context of minimalism, as Walkden correctly pointed out) or as a (somewhat mysterious) third factor. In fact, Walkden points out in a footnote (2001: 899 n. 12), that 'non-occurrence of relevant data in PLD ... leaves us with a form of "weak inertia"'. Weak inertia, in this sense, may be associated with weak P-ambiguity, as defined in (5). Weak P-ambiguity may simply fail to set a parameter, a notion which is incoherent on the standard view of parameters as articulated since Chomsky (1981), but predicted by the emergentist approach sketched here in §§7.3–4.

20.4 Inertia, Drift and Parameters

Here we turn to the question of whether it is meaningful, or even possible, to think of syntactic change as having an inherent direction. The idea that change is directional was stated very influentially, and eloquently, by Sapir (1921: 160f.) in terms of the concept of drift. He says '[l]anguage moves down time in a current of its own making. It has a drift' (1921: 160), and goes on to assert that '[e]very word, every grammatical element, every locution, every sound and accent is a slowly changing configuration, moulded by the invisible and impersonal drift that is the life of language. The evidence is overwhelming that this drift has a certain consistent direction' (1921: 183). Moreover, we can infer the 'drift' of a language from its history: 'The linguistic drift has direction ... This direction may be inferred, in the main, from the past history of the language' (1921: 165f.). He suggests three connected drifts in the history of English: the 'drift toward the abolition of most case distinctions and the correlative drift toward position as an all-important grammatical method' and 'the drift toward the invariable word' (1921: 180). These are all long-term drifts: '[e]ach of these has operated for centuries ..., each is almost certain to continue for centuries, possibly millennia' (1921: 174). Each change is therefore just one in a series of changes, created by what went before and in turn creating the conditions for subsequent changes.

Could we meaningfully entertain a notion of 'parametric drift'? If so, what would the implications be for the Inertia Principle (in any form)? The first question which springs to mind is: if there is such a thing as parametric drift, what causes it? In particular, if grammars are transmitted discontinuously from generation to generation through language acquisition, as we are assuming here (and see again Chapters 6, 7, 15, 17, 18, 21 and 22, this volume) how can acquirers know which way the system they are acquiring is drifting? This point has been very forcefully made by Lightfoot (1979, 1991, 1999). A second question is: if drift does exist, what are the natural directions for it? Third, how does this concept relate to the general idea that syntactic change is subject to the Inertia Principle?

In Roberts (2007: 341f.) I suggested that parametric drift can be thought of as a cascade of changes, a kind of 'domino effect' in the parametric system, whereby an initial, exogenous change destabilizes the system and causes it to transit rather rapidly through a series of marked states until it eventually restabilizes at a relatively unmarked system again. The series of marked states could in principle cover several generations, with each group of acquirers being led to reanalyse different aspects of the PLD which have been rendered marked by an earlier change. This idea of cascading parameter change was taken up and developed much more fully in Biberauer and Roberts (2008), and below I will briefly summarize their proposals.

This approach answers the questions raised above in the following ways: FE and IG (as well as possibly other third-factor principles) may be what underlies parametric drift and determines the natural direction of change; as we saw above, these principles play an important causal role in bringing about parametric change in general (interacting with P-ambiguous PLD and the boundary conditions set by UG), explaining why the Inertia Principle does not always hold.

Typological studies have often emphasized the directional nature of change. In the early days of modern language typology, Lehmann (1973) and Vennemann (1974) proposed long-term typological change in word order, i.e. typological drift. Lehmann (1973: 55) proposed that languages which are not typologically consistent in terms his OV vs VO typology are undergoing change. There is a clear notion of directional change from OV to VO (or *vice versa*). This idea can be applied to the history of English, in that we can observe that English has been drifting from OV to VO since at least the Proto-Germanic period, and has not yet completed the drift in that Present-Day English is not a fully harmonic head-initial language (see further the discussion in §11.5.1). Vennemann's (1974) approach also ran into the difficulty that 'mixed' systems must be regarded as persisting over very long periods.

As already mentioned, Lightfoot has criticized approaches to syntactic change which invoke typological drift as a mechanism. The most detailed and explicit discussion is in Lightfoot (1979: 385–99). He criticizes this general approach to word-order change on three grounds, all of them essentially stemming from the single general point that grammars must be seen as being replicated through language acquisition, rather than transmitted in any direct way (for discussion, see Chapter 18, this volume). The following quotation summarizes Lightfoot's position:

> Languages are learned and grammars constructed by the individuals of each generation. They do not have racial memories such that they know in some sense that their language has gradually been developing from, say, an SOV and towards an SVO type, and that it must continue along that path. After all, if there were a prescribed hierarchy of changes to be performed, how could a child, confronted with a language exactly half-way along this hierarchy, know whether the language was changing from type *x* to type *y*, or vice versa? *(Lightfoot 1979: 391)*

From this he concludes: 'Therefore, when one bears in mind the abductive nature of the acquisitional process, the concept of an independent diachronic universal (i.e. unrelated to the theory of grammar) becomes most implausible.' He identifies three ways in which one could countenance long-term drift against the background of 'the abductive nature of the acquisitional process'. The first is racial memory, which is self-evidently absurd. The second consists in 'mystical metaconditions on linguistic families or goal-oriented clusters of changes' (1979: 395).

Lightfoot objects that such metaconditions amount to diachronic grammars, a notion inherently incompatible with the nature of the language acquisition and, as such, untenable. The third is the kind of typological drift postulated by Lehmann and Vennemann. Here, as is clear from the above quotation, the objection is that there is no way of building such long-term teleology into the language-acquisition process. Moreover, Lightfoot questions the empirical basis for the diachronic generalizations: we have good long-term textual attestation of very few languages, we know that typological shifts can go in different directions and we know that even in Indo-European a fair amount of variation in basic word order can be observed: SVO (English, Romance, etc.), SOV (Indic) and VSO (Celtic). Finally, he observes that many changes do not involve alterations to observed word order: the development of the modal auxiliaries in Early Modern English (discussed in §18.3, §21.3.1, §24.5) did not change the surface order of modals and main verbs, but was arguably nonetheless a significant change in the syntax of English. Despite all these criticisms, Lightfoot does not deny that changes can be 'provoked by earlier changes and in turn themselves provoke others' (1979: 397); this is essentially the 'cascade' idea, which, as we have already seen, is consistent with the Inertia Principle too.

The conceptual underpinning of much of Lightfoot's critique of typological drift is fully valid: the general idea that syntactic change is driven through language acquisition. All Lightfoot's points are well-taken. Lightfoot (1979: 396) does acknowledge, however, that 'implicational sequences of syntactic changes do exist ... there are sets of roughly analogous changes which cluster together in independent languages'. His critique focuses on the facts that the 'implicational sequences of syntactic changes' are something to be explained rather than an explanatory notion in themselves. Again, this point is well taken.

So, how can we understand 'implicational sequences of syntactic changes' in terms of a parametric theory of change and variation? Here, we seem at first sight to be confronted with a paradox, as noted by Roberts and Roussou (2003: 3f.). They point out that one can view the parameters of UG as defining an abstract space of variation. In that case, the natural, and arguably the usual, way of viewing synchronic variation is to see grammars as randomly scattered through this space, while the natural way to think of diachronic change would be to see it as a random 'walk' around this space. This is consistent with the idea that typological drift is an incoherent notion, essentially for the reasons Lightfoot gives. But, in that case, what of 'implicational sequences of syntactic changes' in the diachronic domain, and what of implicational relations in the synchronic domain?

A further point arises from Sapir's original discussion of drift. His concern is to understand why languages differ from each other at all. He observes that social, geographical or even individual variation does not actually provide an explanation. He says that if 'individual variations "on a flat" were the only kind of variability in language, I believe we should be at a loss to explain why and how dialects arise, why it is that the linguistic prototype gradually breaks up into a number of mutually unintelligible languages' (1921: 160). It is in this context that he introduces drift. So, for Sapir, drift explains the very existence of different grammatical systems. Some explanation of this phenomenon is also required even if a parametrized syntax is assumed: why, even if there are different parameters, should there be different systems? Niyogi and Berwick (1995, 1997) and Niyogi (2006) have shown on the basis of computational simulations of the acquisition of parametric systems that variation may spontaneously arise through the interaction of the set of possible grammars, the learning algorithm and fluctuations in the PLD, but Sapir's point is that the variation over time in a group in relation to the 'linguistic prototype' must be centrifugal. Otherwise, as he says '[o]ught not the individual variations of each locality, even in he absence of intercourse between them, to cancel out to the same accepted speech average?' (1921: 160). He proposes drift as the centrifugal force and, arguably, a parametric approach needs something similar.

A final argument in favour of treating diachronic change, seen as parameter change, as something more than a random walk through the range of possibilities defined by UG comes from the observation that the UG-defined space, all other things being equal, is simply too big. The space of grammars defined by 30 binary, independent parameters is 2^{30}, i.e. just over a billion; that defined by a 100 such parameters is 2^{100}.[2] Roberts (2001: 90f.) made this point as follows:

> the fact that on the basis of a small subset of currently-existing languages we can clearly observe language types, and note diachronic drift from one type to another, is simply astonishing ... languages should appear to vary unpredictably and without assignable limits, even if we have a UG containing just 30 or so parameters.

Essentially, uniformitarianism (see Chapter 16, this volume) ought to have no empirical bite at all: there are just too many systems in the space of available variation. So many grammatical systems are available that they could appear to vary wildly, and there would be no way to establish uniformity, even with a restrictive UG and just thirty binary parameters.

So we must add something to the conception that parameters diachronically 'walk' around the parameter space defined by UG. Something must cause grammatical systems to clump together synchronically in certain areas of that space and to drift towards those areas diachronically, i.e. something creates local maxima in that space (these are what we might

---

[2] This exponential expansion of the class of grammars is one of the reasons for introducing parameter hierarchies. Properly constructed, such hierarchies yield a space of parameters n+1, where n is the number of parameters. Independent parameters yield a space of the size 2^n. Given 100 parameters, the first approach yields 101 grammars, while the second gives 1,267,650,600,228,229,401,496,703,205,376. See Sheehan and Roberts (2015).

think of as 'macro-types'). UG cannot be responsible for this; to build such tendencies directly into UG would be against both the letter and the spirit of the Minimalist Programme and might bring us back to something akin to the 'diachronic grammars' Lightfoot warned against. The PLD is self-evidently unable to bring about these local maxima (on its own). Therefore the third factors, FE and IG and perhaps others, must be responsible.

In terms of the theory of dynamical systems, we can think of UG as a state space, a multidimensional space in which each point represents a system-state, i.e. a set of values of parameters, a grammar. FE and IG interact with each other and with the PLD in such a way as to create basins of attraction in this space, points towards which grammars always tend to move. In other words, certain areas of the parameter space attract grammatical systems. There are presumably a number of basins of attraction and hence a number of 'macro-types'; on the emergentist view of parameters (see above and §§7.3–4) these will be connected to the macro-parametric settings of the languages (the notion of 'pleiotropic parameter', briefly introduced in §27.5, may also be relevant here). For present purposes, the notions of attractor, basin of attraction and space of variation can be taken as metaphorical (although a systematic attempt to formulate change and variation in parametric systems in terms of dynamical-systems theory would be very welcome). The central point is that something like Sapir's notion of drift is required on both empirical and conceptual grounds, even given a highly restrictive theory of UG and a relatively small number of binary parameters of variation, and that this notion can be understood in terms of FE and IG.

Perhaps surprisingly, this view is also compatible with the Inertia Principle: essentially if no other force acts on a grammatical system (i.e. no syntax-external contingency radically alters the PLD), a grammar will continue to drift in a given direction. Inertia does not necessarily entail stasis. Furthermore, this idea is compatible with Lightfoot's (1999: 90f.) view that parametric change is chaotic in the sense that it is highly sensitive to very small variations in initial conditions. Again speaking metaphorically, a grammar may only need a very small 'push' in order to start to drift in a direction which may take it, given enough time, a long distance in the state space from its starting point. In other words, a long-term typological change may come about through a cascade of smaller changes all tending the same overall typological direction.

Let us now illustrate these ideas from the history of English, drawing, as already mentioned, on Biberauer and Roberts (2008). It has often been pointed out that English seems to diverge quite radically from the other West Germanic languages. It used to be thought that this had to do with the influence of Norman French, although more recently the effects of Old Norse have sometimes been regarded as responsible for this divergence (a recent very strong statement of the latter idea is Emonds and Faarlund 2014). A series of changes took place in the history of English between 1100 and 1700, which had the net effect of transforming English from a system very close to that found elsewhere in West Germanic into the unusual system of Modern English. This was a cascade of parametric changes. It amounts to what Sapir referred as 'the vast accumulation of minute modifications which in time results in the complete remodeling of the language' (1921: 165).

As summarized by Biberauer and Roberts (2012), a simple, broad-brush summary of developments in the history of English syntax states that Old English was like Modern Dutch, in being underlyingly OV, showing productive verb-second in main clauses and verb-raising and verb-projection raising in subordinate clauses, giving rise to complex verbal clusters. Middle English, on the other hand, was rather like Modern Icelandic: it was VO, still V2, had V-to-T movement (e.g. placing the finite verb in front of the main clausal negation in both main and embedded clauses), object shift (raising direct objects out of VP in contexts of verb-movement, giving orders such as *She saw the man not*) and Transitive Expletive Constructions (widely found in Modern Germanic, of the form *There could no man enter the castle*). Modern English, as is well known, is strikingly unlike its closest Germanic relatives in lacking all the above properties (except VO of course) and having a complex auxiliary system. Modern English is also quite different from other geographically nearby languages such as Celtic and French (although there is reason to think that there has been some limited contact influence from both).

Biberauer and Roberts (2008) propose the following sequence of changes:

(11) a. Loss of VP-to-SpecvP movement (late twelfth/early thirteenth century)
      b. Restriction of object shift to negative and quantified objects (1400)
      c. Loss of vP-movement to SpecTP (early fifteenth century)
      d. Loss of V2 (1450)
      e. Development of lexical T (modals and *do*) (1525)
      f. Loss of V-to-T (1575)
      g. Contraction of negation (1600)
      h. Development of negative auxiliaries (1630s)
      i. Development of *do*-support (later seventeenth century)

It is not possible to describe all these changes in full technical detail here; this is the central goal of Biberauer and Roberts (2008). But it is worth pointing out some fairly clear cross-linguistic similarities and differences. The changes in (11a–c) underlie the surface shift from head-final to head-initial in TP (see Biberauer and Roberts 2005) and as such also happened in North Germanic and probably also in the transition from Latin to Romance (see §27.3 and the references given there) as well as elsewhere in Indo-European.

(11d), the loss of verb second (§21.3.4), has also happened in French (see Adams 1987; Vance 1988, 1997; Roberts 1993) and Welsh (Willis 1998). Change (11f) has also happened in the history of the Mainland Scandinavian languages (Holmberg and Platzack 1995), and may be happening – or have just happened – in some varieties of Faroese (see Heycock, Sorace, Hansen and Wilson 2013; Heycock, Sorace, Hansen, Vikner and Wilson 2011, 2012). So all of the changes prior to the Early Modern period are shared with other languages.

The change in (11e) is unique to English in this form, although it is a case of grammaticalization and as such an instance of a very common kind of change (see Chapter 1, this volume). The changes in (11g–i) are features of Standard English not general to all varieties of English: the syntax of negation is somewhat different in Scottish varieties (see Adger, Heycock, Smith and Thoms 2013), and *do*-support has a different distribution in South-Western dialects (Ihalainen 1991). So Modern Standard English has emerged as a typologically unusual system through a series of changes of varying degrees of generality. In terms of the typology of parameters in (8), (11a–d), exactly those shared with other languages are mesoparametric (although (11a) and (11c) are connected to macroparameters concerning harmonic word-order patterns). Changes (11e, f, h) are microparametric (affecting small subsets of functional elements), while (11g) and (11i) are nanoparametric (affecting just one lexical item in each case). These microparametric changes are unique to English, and the nanoparametric changes found only in certain varieties, notably Standard English. It is also worth pointing out that each change succeeds its predecessor rather rapidly: aside from (11a) to (11b) – an interval of about 200 years – the gap between changes is never more than 75 years, i.e. about three generations. So all the systems, aside perhaps from the first, are somewhat unstable.

The change in (11a), which began the cascade, was caused by the interaction of complex lexical and morphological factors, including the borrowing of many verbs from French in the early Middle English period which reduced the incidence of verb-particle constructions, an important trigger for OV order (see Lightfoot 1991); see again Biberauer and Roberts (2008) for details. These initial changes never affected the rest of West Germanic and so the cascade never took place in those languages.

The original 'roll-up' of VP movement to SpecvP combined with V-to-v movement to give orders in which the complements of the verb always preceded the verb (in non-V2 environments), since the derived structure was as in (12):

(12) $[_{vP} [_{VP} (V) \text{ Obj}] [_v \text{ V } v] (VP)]$

After the loss of VP-movement, surface OV orders were reanalysed as involving object-movement without the associated VP-movement; this movement later became restricted to a certain class of objects, as is typical of object-shift cross-linguistically ('restriction of function' of this kind may be linked to the Subset Condition – a further possible third-factor condition – leading to new formal features being associated with functional heads; see Biberauer and Roberts 2009). Hence (11a) created the conditions for (11b). (11b) meant that there was a much higher incidence of VO orders than formerly in the PLD, and this meant that the earlier way of placing the subject in a position preceding T (achieved by *v*P-movement to SpecTP) was ambiguous with simple DP-movement to SpecTP. The change is schematized in (13):

(13)   a. [$_{TP}$ [$_{vP}$ Subj   [$_v$ V *v*] [$_{VP}$ (V) Obj]] T (*v*P)]   (conservative)
       b. [$_{TP}$ Subj T [$_{vP}$ (Subj)   [$_v$ V *v*] [$_{VP}$ (V) Obj]]]   (innovative)

This change, fed by (11b), in turn led to (11d). This is because the consequence of this change was that finite T was restricted to always and only attracting a DP. Independent evidence for this comes from the development of TP-expletives at this time. In this connection, van Kemenade (1997: 350) observes that '[t]he loss of V2 and the loss of expletive *pro*-drop ... coincide historically'. Biberauer and Roberts (2008: 98) interpret this as showing the development of a requirement for SpecTP always to be filled with a DP. This led to the loss of V2 in that a crucial step in the loss of V2 in English appears to have involved 'decliticization' of subject pronouns (see, for example, van Kemenade 1987; Platzack 1995; Kroch and Taylor 1997; Fuß 1998; Haeberli [1999] 2002; Fuß and Trips 2002). Formerly, the clitic nature of the pronouns had meant that they did not count for the computation of V2 (however that is or was done, a matter I leave aside here). Decliticization (possibly a phonological change in itself) combined with the new DP-only attraction of T meant that subject pronouns were analysed as being in SpecTP. In verb-third main clauses with the order *XP – subject pronoun – V*, formerly analysed as V2 with subject clitics, then, the consequence was that the verb had to be analysed as occupying T rather than C. Hence, over a wide class of cases, V2 was lost. This change is schematized in (14):

(14)   a. [$_{CP}$ XP [$_C$ SCL-[$_C$ [$_v$ V *v*] C]] [$_{TP}$ [$_{vP}$ (SCL) ([$_v$ V *v*])] T *v*P]]
       b. [$_{CP}$ XP C [$_{TP}$ SCL [$_T$ [$_v$ V *v*]]   *v*P]]

In North Germanic, subject pronouns have never been clitics, and concomitantly V3 orders of the kind observed in Old and pre-fifteenth-century Middle English are not found. Hence, although the word-order changes in (11a–c) took place (see in particular Hróarsdóttir (1999, 2000) for documentation of this in the history of Icelandic, although her analysis is somewhat different from Biberauer and Roberts'), V2 has never been lost since the conditions for its loss were absent in those languages. In North Germanic, then, the cascade stopped at this point.

An important consequence of the loss of V2 was that V-to-T movement became a general feature of finite clauses, as can be seen from (14b).

The next change to take place was the lexicalization of T by the reanalysis of modals and *do* as auxiliaries. This most probably happened *c.* 1525–50 (Lightfoot 1979; Roberts 1985, 1993: 310f.; Warner 1997: 382f.; see also §11.5.3). Roberts and Roussou (2003: 40f.) argue that a further factor in this change was the loss of the infinitival ending on verbs, which had the consequence that constructions consisting of modals followed by an infinitive were reanalysed as monoclausal: the absence of the infinitival ending meant that there was no evidence for the lower functional T-*v* system (see §27.2.1 for further discussion of Roberts and Roussou's proposal). Both Denison (1985) and Roberts (1993) suggest that *do* became an auxiliary at the same time as the modals, in the early sixteenth century. Formerly, in Late Middle English, *do* had been a raising or causative verb (see Roberts 1993: 282f.).

The reanalysis of the modals favoured the loss of V-to-T movement. Warner (1997: 382f.) observes that the period 1575–1600 seems to be the crucial one as far as this change is concerned. The development of auxiliaries, and particularly the free availability of 'dummy' *do*, including in positive declaratives, meant that T was frequently lexically filled and that this option was always available.

By now the verb-auxiliary system is rather similar to that of Modern English, and as such very different from the rest of Germanic. The principal feature of Modern English that was yet to arise was *do*-support. As just mentioned, *do* could still be freely inserted in positive declarative clauses, and, conversely, clausal negation could appear without *do*, giving rise to examples with the order *not* – V, and no auxiliary (since V-to-T has been lost):

(15)   a. Or if there were, it not belongs to you.
           (1600: Shakespeare *2 Henry IV*, IV, i, 98; Battistella and Lobeck 1991: 33)
        b. Safe on this ground we not fear today to tempt your laughter by our rustic play.
           (1637: Jonson *Sad Shepherd*, Prologue 37; Kroch 1989)

The development of *do*-support was preceded by the development of contracted negation, which took place around 1600, as the following remark by Jespersen (1909–49, V:429), cited in Roberts (1993: 305), suggests:

> The contracted forms seem to have come into use in speech, though not yet in writing, about the year 1600. In a few instances (extremely few) they may be inferred from the metre in Sh[akespeare], though the full form is written.

Around 1600, then, negation contracted onto T, but since V-to-T movement of main verbs had been lost, only auxiliaries were able to be negative. This gave rise to a new system of clausal negation in which negative auxiliaries were used as the basic marker of clausal negation (it is clear from a range of languages, including Uralic, Latin, Afrikaans, Old English, and others, that negative auxiliaries are a UG option). The new class of auxiliaries included negative modals like *won't, can't, shan't*, etc., but also the non-modal negator and *don't/doesn't/didn't* (see Zwicky and Pullum (1983) for arguments that these are independent lexical items from their positive counterparts).

Once the negative auxiliaries, including *doesn't, don't, didn't*, are established as the unmarked expression of clausal negation (probably by the middle of the seventeenth century; Roberts 1993: 308), the modern system of *do*-support comes into being. In this system, merger of *do* in T depends either on the presence of an 'extra' feature on T, in addition to Tense and φ-features (Q, Neg) or on the presence of a discourse effect, on contexts of emphasis and VP-fronting; see Biberauer and Roberts (2010) for a detailed analysis of the Modern English auxiliary system in these terms. With this final development, the present-day English system is in place.

Each of the changes in (11) is in principle independent of the others (as the cross-linguistic and cross-dialectal observations made above confirm). Taken together, they give rise to a major reorganization of the English clause, and have created a system which is quite unlike anything found elsewhere in Germanic (or Romance), from a starting point in 1100 which was very similar (in fact, at this rather approximate level of analysis, identical) to what we find elsewhere in West Germanic. So we see exactly 'the vast accumulation of minute modifications which in time results in the complete remodeling of the language' Sapir described. These changes can all be described as changes in the features of functional heads, and so we have here a clear example of parametric drift.

What causes the cascade effect? The key idea, due to Lightfoot (1979: 123), is that 'grammars practice therapy, not prophylaxis' (see §15.6). Essentially, each parameter change skews the PLD in such a way that the next is favoured. We have seen in the description above how each successive change was favoured. In general, then, we see that it is possible to maintain a version of the Inertia Principle and at the same time account for an intricate series of related syntactic changes, not all of which have a purely syntax-external cause. There are many details, both technical and empirical, that remain to be clarified in the account of these changes in ME and ENE, but in general terms we can see this as a clear example of parametric drift.

A final quotation from Sapir illustrates a further point:

> The general drift of language has its depths. At the surface the current is relatively fast. In certain features dialects drift apart rapidly. By that very fact these features betray themselves as less fundamental to the genius of the language than the more slowly modifiable features in which the dialects keep together long after they have grown to be mutually alien forms of speech.. The momentum of the more fundamental, pre-dialectic, drift is often such that languages long disconnected will pass through the same or strikingly similar phases.　　*(1921: 184)*

If we think of drift in parametric terms, we can understand this, admittedly rather metaphorical, statement of Sapir's as saying that some parameters are more likely to change than others. This is exactly what the taxonomy of parameters in (5) implies in the diachronic domain, a point developed in more detail in Chapter 27, this volume (see also Biberauer and Roberts 2012).

In this section, we have discussed the possibility of parametric drift, considered its relation to typological drift of the more familiar kind, and Lightfoot's (1979) well-known objections to the latter, and sketched a possible example of this drift from the history of English. If parametric change admits of directionality, as I have suggested (*pace* Lightfoot), that it does, this has important implications for the possibility of syntactic reconstruction (see Chapter 9, this volume, on comparative reconstruction). The obvious question to investigate is whether we can exploit this potential directionality in reconstructing lost parametric systems; I leave this important question aside here.

20.5 Conclusion

In this chapter I have introduced the Inertia Principle and looked at a number of its problems and implications. In §20.2 I showed how the Inertia Principle is compatible with an acquisition-driven approach to change, in that it can be construed as asserting that acquisition is generally convergent, and hence nothing is reanalysed; therefore nothing is changed. I suggested that the emergentist approach to parameters and parameter-setting described in §§7.3–4 was best suited to incorporate the Inertia Principle in an acquisition-driven approach to change. In §20.3 I considered the objections to Longobardi's (2001) construal of the Inertia Principle put forward by Walkden (2012). There I argued that, although valid in relation to Longobardi's proposals, these objections do not apply to the emergentist view of parameters, which can readily accommodate a notion of 'weak inertia' linked to weak P-ambiguity. Finally, §20.4 looked at Sapir's notion of drift, arguing, following Roberts (2007: 341f.) and *pace* Lightfoot (1979: 385–99), that a notion of parametric drift is possible and maybe even desirable. This idea too fits readily into the emergentist conception of parameters.

References

Adams, M. 1987. 'From Old French to the theory of pro-drop', *Natural Language and Linguistic Theory* 5: 1–32.
Adger, D., Heycock, C., Smith, J. and Thoms, G. 2013. 'Remarks on negation in varieties of Scots', paper presented at the workshop 'The Comparative Syntax of English', University of Cambridge, 7 November.

Battistella, E. and Lobeck, A. 1991. 'On verb fronting, inflection movement, and Aux support', *Canadian Journal of Linguistics* 36: 225–67.

Biberauer, T. and Roberts, I. 2005. 'Changing EPP-parameters in the history of English: Accounting for variation and change', *English Language and Linguistics* 9: 5–46.

   2008. 'Cascading parameter changes: Internally-driven change in Middle and Early Modern English', in T. Eythórssen (ed.), *Grammatical change and linguistic theory: The Rosendal papers*. Amsterdam: John Benjamins, pp. 79–114.

   2009. 'The return of the subset principle', in P. Crisma and G. Longobardi (eds.), *Historical syntax and linguistic theory*. Oxford University Press, pp. 58–74.

   2010. 'Subjects, Tense and verb movement', in T. Biberauer, A. Holmberg, I. Roberts and M. Sheehan (eds.), *Parametric variation: Null subjects in minimalist theory*. Cambridge University Press, pp. 263–302.

   2012. 'The significance of what hasn't happened', paper presented at the 14th Diachronic Generative Syntax conference, Lisbon, 4 July.

Chomsky, N. 1981. *Lectures on government and binding*. Dordrecht: Foris.

   2005. 'Three factors in language design', *Linguistic Inquiry* 36(1): 1–22.

Chow, W. H. 1995. 'Wh-questions in Singapore colloquial English', unpublished honours thesis, Department of English Language and Literature, National University of Singapore.

Clark, R. and Roberts, I. 1993. 'A computational model of language learnability and language change', *Linguistic Inquiry* 24(2): 299–345.

Denison, D. 1985. 'The origins of periphrastic do: Ellegård and Visser reconsidered', in R. Eaton, O. Fischer, W. F. Koopman and F. van der Leek (eds.), *Papers from the 4th international conference on historical linguistics, Amsterdam, April 10–13, 1985*. Amsterdam and Philadelphia: John Benjamins, pp. 45–60.

Emonds, J. E. and Faarlund, J. T. 2014. *English: The language of the Vikings* (Olomouc Modern Language Monographs 3). Olomouc: Palacký University.

Fuß, E. 1998. 'Zur Diachronie vom Verbzweit', MA thesis, University of Frankfurt.

Fuß, E. and Trips, C. 2002. 'Variation and change in Old and Middle English: On the validity of the Double Base Hypothesis', *Journal of Comparative Germanic Linguistics* 4: 171–224.

Haeberli, E. 1999. 'Features, categories and the syntax of A-positions. Synchronic and diachronic variation in the Germanic languages', PhD thesis, University of Geneva (published as Haeberli, E. 2002. *Features, categories and the syntax of A-positions. cross-linguistic variation in the Germanic languages*. Dordrecht: Kluwer).

Heycock, C., Sorace, A., Hansen, Z. S. and Wilson, F. 2013. 'Acquisition in variation (and vice versa): V-to-T in Faroese children', *Language Acquisition* 20(1): 5–22.

Heycock, C., Sorace, A., Hansen, Z. S., Vikner, S. and Wilson, F. 2011. 'Residual V-to-I in Faroese and its lack in Danish: Detecting the final stages of a syntactic change', *Working Papers in Scandinavian Syntax* 87: 137–65.

    2012. 'Detecting the late stages of syntactic change: The loss of V-to-T in Faroese', *Language* 88(3): 558–600.

Holmberg, A. and Platzack, C. 1995. *The role of inflection in Scandinavian syntax*. Oxford University Press.

Hróarsdóttir, T. 1999. 'Verb phrase syntax in the history of Icelandic', unpublished PhD thesis, University of Tromsø.

    2000. *Word order change in Icelandic: From OV to VO*. Amsterdam: John Benjamins.

Ihalainen, O. 1991. 'Periphrastic *do* in affirmative sentences in the dialect of East Somerset', in P. Trudgill and J. K. Chambers (eds.), *Dialects of English: Studies in grammatical variation*. London: Longman, pp. 148–60.

Jespersen, O. 1909–49. *A modern English grammar on historical principles I-VII*. London and Copenhagen: Allen and Unwin.

Keenan, E. 2002. 'Explaining the creation of reflexive pronouns in English', in D. Minkova and R. Stockwell (eds.), *Studies in the history of English: A millennial perspective*. Berlin: Mouton de Gruyter, pp. 325–55.

Kroch, A. 1989. 'Reflexes of grammar in patterns of language change', *Language Variation and Change* 1: 199–244.

Kroch, A. and Taylor, A. 1997. 'Verb movement in Old and Middle English: Dialect variation and language contact', in A. van Kemenade and N. Vincent (eds.), *Parameters of morphosyntactic change*. Cambridge University Press, pp. 297–325.

Lehmann, W. 1973. 'A structural principle of language and its implications', *Language* 49: 47–66.

Lightfoot, D. W. 1979. *Principles of diachronic syntax*. Cambridge University Press.

    1991. *How to set parameters: Arguments from language change*. Cambridge, MA: MIT Press.

    1999. *The development of language: Acquisition, change and evolution*. Oxford: Blackwell.

Longobardi, G. 2001. 'Formal syntax, diachronic minimalism, and etymology: The history of French *chez*', *Linguistic Inquiry* 32(2): 275–302.

Niyogi, P. 2006. *The computational nature of language learning and evolution*. Cambridge, MA: MIT Press.

Niyogi, P. and Berwick, R. 1995. 'The logical problem of language change', AI Memo no. 1516, MIT Artificial Intelligence Laboratory.

    1997. 'A dynamical systems model for language change', *Complex Systems* 11: 161–204.

Platzack, C. 1995. 'The loss of verb second and English and French', in A. Battye and I. Roberts (eds.), *Clause structure and language change*. Oxford University Press, pp. 200–26.

Roberts, I. 1985. 'Agreement parameters and the development of English modal auxiliaries', *Natural Language and Linguistic Theory*, 3: 21–58.

1993. *Verbs and diachronic syntax: A comparative history of English and French.* Dordrecht: Kluwer.

2001. 'Language change and learnability', in S. Bertolo (ed.), *Parametric linguistics and learnability*. Cambridge University Press, pp. 81–125.

2007. *Diachronic syntax.* Oxford University Press.

Roberts, I. and Roussou, A. 2003. *Syntactic change: A minimalist approach to grammaticalisation.* Cambridge University Press.

Sapir, E. 1921. *Language.* New York: Harcourt Brace & Co.

Sheehan, M. and Roberts, I. 2015. 'A parameter hierarchy for passives', talk given at the 2015 *Annual Meeting of the Linguistics Association of Great Britain*, University College London, 18 September.

van Kemenade, A. 1987. *Syntactic case and morphological case in the history of English*, Dordrecht: Foris.

1997. 'V2 and embedded topicalization in Old and Middle English', in A. van Kemenade and N. Vincent (eds.), *Parameters of morphosyntactic change*. Cambridge University Press, pp. 326–52.

Vance, B. 1988. 'Null subjects and syntactic change in medieval French', unpublished PhD thesis, Cornell University.

1997. *Syntactic change in medieval French: Verb second and null subjects.* Dordrecht: Kluwer.

Vennemann, T. 1974. 'Topics, subjects, and word order: From SXV to SVX via TVX', in J. Anderson and C. Jones (eds.), *Historical linguistics: Proceedings of the first international congress of historical linguistics, Edinburgh, September 1973*, vol. II. Amsterdam: North-Holland, pp. 339–76.

Walkden, G. 2012. 'Against Inertia', *Lingua* 122: 891–901.

Warner, A. 1997. 'The structure of parametric change, and V movement in the history of English', in A. van Kemenade and N. Vincent (eds.), *Parameters of morphosyntactic change*. Cambridge University Press, pp. 380–93.

Willis, D. 1998. *Syntactic change in Welsh: A study of the loss of verb second.* Oxford: Clarendon Press.

Zhiming, B. 2001. 'The origins of empty categories in Singapore English', *Journal of Pidgin and Creole Languages* 16: 275–319.

Zwicky, A. and Pullum, G. 1983. 'Cliticisation vs. inflection: English *n't*', *Language* 59: 502–13.

21

Gradience and Gradualness vs Abruptness

Marit Westergaard

21.1 Introduction

One of the central issues in historical syntax is whether changes are typically gradual or abrupt, i.e. whether they may span several centuries or whether they appear between one generation of speakers and the next. This is linked to two main theoretical approaches to historical change, a functionalist and a formal (generative) perspective. This question may also have different answers depending on whether change is considered at the level of the speech community or in the grammatical competence of individual speakers, or in the words of Lightfoot (1999: 83), whether we are investigating language change or grammar change.

The next section briefly discusses some central issues related to gradualness vs abruptness in historical change, such as reanalysis, grammar competition and the distinction between I-language and E-language. §21.3 provides some central examples, mainly from the history of English and the Scandinavian languages. §21.4 discusses certain problematic issues and §21.5 outlines some synchronic variation and provides evidence from language acquisition studies that children are sensitive to fine syntactic distinctions from early on. In §21.6 we suggest that the key to understanding variation and change is in identifying the *size* of syntactic rules, and argue that most changes affect very small parts of the grammar. Thus, we indicate that a possible reconciliation of the two perspectives, gradualness vs abruptness, may lie in considering change in terms of micro-steps, micro-parameters or micro-cues (Traugott and Trousdale 2010; Biberauer and Roberts 2012; Westergaard 2009a, b).

21.2   Some Central Issues

21.2.1   Gradience and Gradualness

Traugott and Trousdale (2010) make a distinction between gradience and gradualness, considering the former a synchronic and the latter a diachronic phenomenon. According to Aarts (2007: 97), gradience is typically understood as a 'phenomenon whereby a particular set of elements displays a categorical shading in prototypicality from a central core to a more peripheral boundary'.[1] As an example, Aarts discusses verbs in English and argues that this is a fuzzy category in that there are prototypical members, such as lexical verbs *eat* and *read*, while auxiliaries (*have*, *be* or modals) and semi-auxiliaries (e.g. *be going to*) are more peripheral, as they display a different syntactic behaviour. Other approaches to category membership often treat auxiliaries and lexical verbs as completely separate categories (e.g. Palmer 1990).

Gradualness may to some extent be considered the 'diachronic dimension of gradience' (Traugott and Trousdale 2010: 26). However, as also stated in Roberts (2010: 48), there is only a one-way implicational relationship between the two concepts, as 'synchronic gradience implies diachronic gradualness, but not vice versa'. The reason is that not all linguistic phenomena may be gradient, e.g. word order, but they may nevertheless undergo gradual change.

In this chapter, the focus is on diachronic gradualness. The study of historical texts provides us with considerable evidence that diachronic development is typically gradual. That is, a syntactic change in a speech community may hardly ever be specified as occurring in a specific year or decade, often not even in a specific century. In traditional approaches to syntactic change, this may be considered to reflect a drift in usage frequencies, occasionally leading to a linguistic form falling out of general use. Within a generative account, on the other hand, historical development is considered to be change in the abstract grammars of individual speakers. Diachronic change must therefore be abrupt, reflecting clear differences between the grammar of one generation of speakers and the next.

This means that the question of gradualness vs abruptness in diachronic development is to some extent dependent on our object of study – changes in the speech community or changes in the grammatical representations in the minds of speakers. This also means that abruptness is compatible with gradual change if the latter is considered to be a reflection of the spread of a change across different speakers.

---

[1] Aarts refers to this as subsective gradience, distinguishing it from intersective gradience. We will not be concerned with this distinction in this chapter.

21.2.2   Reanalysis, I-Language Change and Cue-Based Acquisition

Lightfoot (1979) relates historical change to first-language acquisition and argues that children may acquire a different grammar from the previous generation as a result of certain shifts in the input. This process is referred to as *reanalysis*, causing abrupt changes between the grammatical system of one generation and the next.

But variation in historical data is not restricted to differences across texts. There is often considerable variation within texts, indicating that individual speakers/writers have produced a mixture of forms. For this reason, it is crucial for Lightfoot's theory that a distinction is made between E-language and I-language (Chomsky 1986). The former refers to speakers' production (Externalized language) and the latter to linguistic competence (Internalized language). Changes in the E-language may be accidental and appear for various linguistic and non-linguistic reasons, according to Lightfoot (1991: 160–2), while an I-language change affects a speaker's abstract grammar. Many small changes in the E-language may over time lead to children not being able to acquire the same I-language grammar as the previous generation, and this may cause what Lightfoot (1999) refers to as 'catastrophic' or 'saltational' change, typically reflecting a parameter being set to a new value (see Chapters 7 and 27, this volume). Thus, this grammar change is likened to a tipping point in a complex system, having cascading effects.

In Lightfoot (1999, 2006), the idea of change as reanalysis is refined within a cue-based approach to language acquisition and change. A cue is a small piece of abstract syntactic structure in speakers' I-language. The cues are provided by Universal Grammar (UG; see Chapter 13, this volume), and in the acquisition process children scan the input for triggers to these cues. For example, the cues for OV word order, V2 syntax and V-to-I movement are formulated as in (1)–(3). Although Lightfoot (2006: 78) argues that there is no need for parameters in addition to cues, we may note that these cues correspond directly to some major parameters in traditional generative literature.

(1)   Cue for OV word order: $_{VP}$[DP V]   (from Lightfoot 2006: 97)

(2)   Cue for V2 syntax: $_{CP}$[XP $_C$V ...]   (from Lightfoot 2006: 86)

(3)   Cue for V-to-I movement: $_I$[V]   (from Lightfoot 2006: 97)

The input triggering the activation of these cues in a child's I-language grammar is a structure where the object precedes the verb (for OV), a clause where the finite verb appears in second position (for V2), and a structure with the verb appearing in front of adverbs or negation (for V-to-I movement). If the triggers in the input are obscured for some reason, this may result in children being unable to activate the cue, causing loss of the corresponding structure in the language. Lightfoot (1999: 156) also assumes that there is a frequency threshold for the activation of cues, and comparing a count in a Middle English text to the evidence found in present-day V2 languages, he suggests the threshold for V2 syntax to be between 17 and 30 per cent.

21.2.3 Grammar Competition

An alternative generative approach to language change is proposed by Kroch (1989), who points out that most diachronic changes are entirely gradual. In order to explain this, he develops a theory of grammar competition, where two grammars, typically understood as conflicting settings of a parameter, coexist in a speech community as well as in the I-language of individual speakers. The existence of different grammars in a speech community is a result of geographical and sociolinguistic/stylistic variation, while different grammars in individual speakers is referred to as 'syntactic diglossia' (Kroch 2001: 722) and code-switching or register-switching (Pintzuk 1999: 278). In Roeper (1999), the idea of grammar competition is extended to monolingual grammars more generally and referred to as 'universal bilingualism'.

Under this view, gradualness in historical data does not represent fuzziness, but instead two discrete entities in the minds of speakers, one gradually replacing the other. Like Lightfoot, Kroch (1994: 184) relates his theory to language acquisition and argues that a learner 'will postulate competing grammars only when languages give evidence of the simultaneous use of incompatible forms', e.g. both settings of a parameter. Kroch (1994: 185) also states that, in the case of competing forms, 'speakers learn one or the other form in the course of basic language acquisition, but not both'. The other variant will be learned later and have the 'status of a foreign element'. We return to this in §21.5.

21.3 Some Central Examples

21.3.1 The English Modals

One of the main examples referred to by Lightfoot (1979) as an abrupt, sudden development is the category change in the English modals from full verbs to auxiliaries. In Present-Day (Standard) English, the modals behave differently from lexical verbs and other auxiliaries in that they are syntactically and morphologically defective: they have no infinitive, past-tense or participle forms (*to must/*musted/*has musted); see the discussion of gradience in category membership in §21.2. The lack of the infinitive also makes it impossible to stack the modals (*shall must). In Old and Middle English (OE/ME), on the other hand, the modals belonged to the category of full verbs and these forms are therefore abundant in historical texts. Relevant examples are attested as late as the early sixteenth century, as shown by the sentences from Sir Thomas More's writings in (4)–(6), from Lightfoot and Westergaard (2007: 403).

(4)   I fear that the emperor will depart thence, before my letters **shall may** come unto your grace's hands (1532)

(5)   That appered at the fyrste **to mow** stande the realm in grete stede (1533)
        'appeared at first to be able to stand the realm in good stead'

(6)   If wee **had mought** convenient come togyther ... (1528)
        'if we had been able to come together conveniently ....'

This change did not take place in languages closely related to English, e.g. Norwegian, where sentences corresponding to (4)–(6) are still grammatical. According to Lightfoot (1979, 1999, 2006) the reason why the modals changed in English is a massive loss of inflectional morphology during the ME period, leading to a system where the only agreement ending is the 3sg. -s, which became the only distinctive defining property of English verbal morphology. In OE, the modals belonged to a class of verbs called the preterite-presents, which never had the -eth or -s ending. As long as the language had rich verbal morphology, this was just one difference among many, but when the agreement morphology broke down during the ME period, the result was that the modals stood out as a special class morphologically. This had syntactic effects, due to the process of acquisition: modals are quite frequent in children's input, especially in their auxiliary form (e.g. *you* **must/can/may not do** *it*). And since children are so-called 'conservative learners' (more about this in §21.5), not generalizing to all members of a category unless there is clear evidence for this in the input, children exposed to sixteenth-century English interpreted the modals as a special category both morphologically and syntactically. As a result, the modals were no longer considered to belong to the category of full verb, but rather the category of auxiliary. The evidence that this is an abrupt change is that all the forms in (4)–(6) were lost together, reflecting a 'single change at the abstract level' (Lightfoot 2006: 93) at the end of the ME period.

Nevertheless, different views on the development of the modals have been offered. First and foremost, if one takes the gradient view of the verbal category mentioned above (e.g. Aarts 2007), this development does not involve a category change but simply illustrates a loss of certain prototypical verbal properties. It has also been argued that the different full verb properties of modals were in fact not lost simultaneously (e.g. Warner 1982; Roberts 1985). Furthermore, it has been pointed out that the change did not affect all modal verbs at exactly the same time; e.g. Warner (1983) shows that *must* and *shall* were auxiliaries only already before the ME period.

21.3.2   The Loss of V-to-I

Around the same time as the change in the modals, English lost V-to-I movement, the rule that produced a word order where the verb precedes adverbs or negation, illustrated in the first sentence in (7) from Shakespeare's *Othello* (Lightfoot and Westergaard 2007: 406). This word order was produced by verb movement to the Inflection position; cf. the cue in (3) above.

(7)   I **like not** that. // What **dost thou** say?

According to Lightfoot (1999, 2006), this change is due to the cue for V-to-I movement not being expressed frequently enough in the input to children. There are mainly two reasons for this: one is that the (frequent) modals had been reanalysed as always being in the I position, due to the category change outlined in the previous section. Another reason was the increased use of periphrastic *do* in the E-language, which was initially used simply as an alternative to expressing past tense, e.g. *John did leave, John did not leave* instead of *John left, John left not* (Lightfoot and Westergaard 2007: 406). Since the I position was increasingly occupied by a modal or *do*, children acquiring the language failed to identify the cue, and V-to-I movement was lost from their I-language. Since this reflects an abstract grammar change in the minds of individual speakers, this is also necessarily an abrupt change.

However, note that Shakespeare used both options, as shown in the second sentence in (7), sometimes even in the same line, illustrated in (8). This means that in order to explain the loss of V-to-I movement as an abstract and abrupt grammar change, Lightfoot needs to argue that only one of the word orders is produced by the speaker's internalized grammar, while the other is an E-language phenomenon. Which one is which may vary from speaker to speaker, depending on whether the grammar change (loss of the V-to-I cue) has taken place or not.

(8)   Where **didst thou** see her? – O unhappy girl! – With the Moor, **say'st thou**?

An alternative approach to this is offered by Kroch (1989), who argues that the coexistence of different word orders in historical data is the result of two grammars competing with each other and one of them finally winning over the other. In a large study of historical texts, he traces the gradual development of the loss of V-to-I movement and the corresponding rise of *do*-support from 1400 to 1700 in different syntactic contexts (negative declaratives, *wh*-questions, etc.). The result is an S-shaped curve which starts slowly, then picks up speed, and then slowly tapers off towards the completion of the change. Importantly, Kroch (1989) shows that the rate of change is essentially identical in all contexts, and based on this, he develops the concept of the Constant

Rate Effect and argues that a new form replaces a competing form at the same rate in all contexts.

The V-to-I movement operation has also generally been lost in the Mainland Scandinavian languages, but not in Icelandic, while Faroese has been argued to be in the process of change, allowing both word orders (e.g. Jonas 2002). Given that these are all V2 languages, requiring that the finite verb appear in second position in (most) main clauses, the result of V-to-I movement is only visible when V2 does not apply, i.e. in embedded clauses. The difference between present-day Icelandic and Swedish is shown in (9)–(10), while (11) illustrates that the syntax of Old Swedish displayed V-to-I (examples from Holmberg and Platzack 1995: 77).

(9)   að   Jón **hafði raunverulega** keypt   bókina (Icelandic)
      that J   had   probably   bought book.DEF
      'that John had probably bought the book'

(10) at   John **faktisk hade** köpt   boken (Swedish)
      that J   actually had   bought book.DEF
      'that John had actually bought the book'

(11) at   Gudz ordh **kan ey** vara j   honom (Old Swedish)
      that God's word can not be   in him
      'that God't word cannot be in him'

Unlike Lightfoot (1999, 2006), who has a syntactic cue triggering V-to-I movement, it has been common to link V-to-I movement to morphological agreement; i.e. the verb must move to I in order to get (or check) inflectional morphology. Thus, the historical loss of this syntactic movement has been connected to the loss of agreement morphology. According to Holmberg and Platzack (1995), this change took place between the fifteenth and seventeenth centuries in Old Swedish, and referring to historical data investigated in Falk (1993), they claim that the loss of this syntactic operation takes place roughly at the same time as the loss of verbal agreement. Further evidence for this connection is that in Icelandic, where this syntactic change has not occurred, agreement morphology is intact. The change in Mainland Scandinavian is considered to represent a resetting of the V-to-I parameter, i.e. a change in the abstract grammar of individual speakers, and as such to be sudden or abrupt. Nevertheless, Holmberg and Platzack also report that speakers/writers use both word orders in historical texts from this time, with the new word order gradually increasing.

This has also been found in a large study of the development of embedded word order in Norwegian carried out by Vitterso (2004). In her data, the historical texts display virtually only the old word order (V-Adv/Neg) up to 1370, illustrated in (12), from Vitterso (2004: 26).

(12)　ef herra Sughuatr **er æigi** i　dalenom
　　　if sir　　Sughuatr is not　in valley.DEF
　　　'if Sir Sigvat isn't in the valley'

According to Vittersø (2004), the new word order without verb move-ment (Adv/Neg-V) starts out in what she refers to as 'higher levels of society' in Oslo and spreads gradually over the next 200 years with clear geographical and sociolinguistic distinctions. Importantly, the old word order is still attested more than 50 per cent at the end of this period in texts written by authors from 'lower levels of society'. Furthermore, while this period also saw a decline of verbal morphology, Vittersø finds no evidence that the new word order is correlated with lack of agreement.

Recent work has shown that this word-order change may still not be completed, even thought there is no longer any morphological agreement that supposedly triggered V-to-I movement at earlier stages. According to Gregersen and Pedersen (1997), both word orders are still in use in spoken Danish, and Waldmann (2008) shows that this is also the case in Swedish. Furthermore, the 'old' word order has been attested in certain dialects of Norwegian, illustrated in (13) from Bentzen (2005: 156), and the variation seems to be dependent not only on differences in geographical distribu-tion, but also on linguistic factors such as the matrix verb, type of embedded clause, and type of verb and adverb in the embedded clause. We return to this microvariation in §21.5.

(13)　Vi　lurte　　på kem han **lånte vanligvis** penga　til. (North Norwegian)
　　　we wondered on who he　lent　　usually　　money to
　　　'We wondered who he usually lent money to.'

21.3.3　The Change from OV to VO

According to Faarlund (2000: 122), the oldest records of North Germanic have OV word order, as shown by the runic inscription in (14), while VO is found at a slightly later time; see (15). In Old Norse (seventh–fifteenth centuries), VO had become the norm in main clauses, while there was considerable variation in embedded clauses. In fact, although all the present-day Nordic languages are clearly VO, Iversen (1973: 442) shows that OV word order has occasionally been attested in spoken Norwegian as late as the twentieth century, illustrated in (16).

(14)　godagastiz **runo faihido** (Nordic runic inscription, 350–400)
　　　Godagasi　rune painted
　　　'Godagasti painted the rune.'

(15)　ek hagustadaz **hlaaiwido magu minio** (Nordic runic inscription, 450)
　　　I　Hagustada buried　　　son　　my
　　　'I, Hagustada, buried my son.'

(16)   Eg lit   på [at du **so gjerer**] (Norwegian, twentieth century)
       I   trust on that you so do
       'I trust that you will do that.'

This change has also taken place in Icelandic. As shown by Hróarsdóttir (2004), Old Icelandic was predominantly OV, while Modern Icelandic is VO; see examples (17)–(18), from Hróarsdóttir (2004: 140–1). She claims that this change was relatively abrupt, taking place at the beginning of the nineteenth century. However, the mixed word order existed for several centuries before this time, with the percentage of OV in Hróarsdóttir's data maintaining a stable level around 50–60 per cent during the fourteenth to seventeenth centuries, and then dropping to 37.0 per cent in the eighteenth and 15.6 per cent in the nineteenth century.

(17)   að   hann hafi **hana drepið**. (Old Icelandic)
       that he   had her   killed
       'that he had killed her'

(18)   fieir munu aldrei hafa **lesið bókina**. (Modern Icelandic)
       they will   never have read book.THE
       'They will never have read the book.'

In the spirit of Lightfoot's (1999) cue-based approach, Hróarsdóttir (2004) argues that this abrupt development reflects an I-language change, i.e. the loss of the cue for OV (see (1) above). This is a result of certain shifts in the E-language, due to changes in patterns of information structure (IS), heavy objects conveying new information increasingly appearing in postverbal position. Furthermore, the change in the E-language is also argued to be due to certain external factors, most notably increased language contact with Danish as well as a number of epidemics, famines and natural disasters causing major population changes throughout the eigtheenth century.

The change from OV to VO in the history of English has similarly been argued to be an abrupt change by van Kemenade (1987), who dates this parameter resetting to around 1200. However, as pointed out by Pintzuk (1999: 33), citing Allen (1990: 51), OV word order was productive for 200 years after this time. Furthermore, Pintzuk shows that there was considerable variation between VO and OV word orders already in OE, illustrated in (19)–(20), from Pintzuk (2002: 285).

(19)   ðæt   hi   mihton **heora fynd oferwinnen** (OE)
       so-that they could   their foes overcome
       'so that they could overcome their foes'

(20)   ðæt he mot   **ehtan   godra manna** (OE)
       that he might persecute good   men
       'that he might persecute good men'

Pintzuk (1999) also shows that the variation extends throughout the OE period, with the VO word order increasing in frequency until it is categorical at the end of the ME period. She analyses the word-order variation as synchronic competition between two different phrase structure configurations, a VO and an OV grammar. Investigating syntactic evidence from a high number of other constructions interacting with VO/OV word order, Pinzuk (1999: 246) argues that the change from OV to VO was 'a gradual one, proceeding via synchronic variation within the grammars of individual speakers to reach completion hundreds of years after the point of actuation'.

21.3.4 The loss of V2

Finally, we turn to the loss of V2. In the history of English, both V2 and non-V2 word orders existed side by side for several centuries, as illustrated in the OE examples in (21)–(22), from Haeberli (2002: 88–90). According to van Kemenade and Westergaard (2012), the variation is relatively stable in OE and then declines throughout the ME period.

(21) On his dagum **sende Gregorius** us fulluht. (OE)
       in his days   sent   Gregory   us baptism
       'In his time, Gregory sent us Christianity.'

(22) &   fela   ðinga **swa gerad man sceal don**. (OE)
       and many things so wise   man must do
       'And such a wise man must do many things.'

According to Lightfoot (1999), the historical development nevertheless represents an abrupt change in speakers' I-language grammars at the end of ME, reflecting a loss of the cue for V2; see (2) above. This is the result of a shift in language use, causing the frequency of the cue to drop below a critical level for language acquisition. Focusing on the gradualness of the change, on the other hand, Kroch and Taylor (1997) argue that the change is caused by grammar competition, more specifically between a Southern dialect displaying a V2 grammar with verb movement to the I-position and a Northern dialect displaying almost categorical inversion due to influence from Scandinavian.

But it is well known that the word-order variation attested in OE/ME is also dependent on linguistic factors, e.g. clause type, type of initial element and distinctions in terms of IS. It is thus not clear that V2 and non-V2 word orders in different contexts are incompatible and really compete with each other (more about this in §21.5). In van Kemenade and Westergaard (2012) it is also shown that V2 declines at different rates during the ME period depending on linguistic context, e.g. type of initial element, verb type or subject type (see also

Warner 2007).[2] Eitler and Westergaard (2014), investigating four late ME texts written by the same author (John Capgrave) for different audiences (local, regional and national), find that the geographical and sociolinguistic variation in the texts is mixed with syntactic and IS factors.

Turning to a present-day phenomenon, it has also been argued that variable V2 in wh-questions in Norwegian dialects represents an ongoing change (Westergaard 2009a; Westergaard, Vangsnes and Lohndal 2012). There is considerable microvariation across different dialects, with word order being dependent not only on geographical distribution but also linguistic factors such as type of initial element, function of the wh-element (as subject or non-subject) as well as IS (whether the subject conveys given or new and/or focused information). For example, in the dialect spoken in Tromsø, there is a clear difference between short and long wh-elements (heads vs phrases), the latter requiring V2 and the former allowing both word orders, dependent on IS, non-V2 appearing with informationally given subjects (often pronouns); see (23)–(24). Furthermore, subject questions require non-V2 in that the relative complementizer *som* is required in second position, shown in (25).

(23)   Koffer **drikk du**   kaffe? / *Koffer du drikk kaffe? (Norwegian, Tromsø dialect)
        why   drink you coffee
        'Why do you drink coffee?'

(24)   Ka   **drikk de   nye studentan**? / Ka **du drikk**?
        what drink the new students   /what you drink
        'What do the new students drink? /What do you drink?'

(25)   Kem **som drikk** te? / *?Kem drikk te?
        who som drink tea
        'Who drinks tea?'

Simplifying somewhat, the distribution of this microvariation can be outlined in the following way: it is generally the case that non-V2 in subject questions entails non-V2 in non-subject questions, and non-V2 with phrasal wh-elements implies that non-V2 is also allowed with short wh-words. Based on the nature of this geographical and linguistic variation, Westergaard (2009a) and Westergaard, Vangsnes and Lohndal (2012) argue that this is a result of a diachronic development in progress from V2 to non-V2, which (1) starts with subject questions, (2) spreads to non-subject questions with short wh-elements, and then either (3) spreads to

---

[2] The reason for the discrepancy of this finding and Kroch's (1989) Constant Rate Effect may be that V2 affects the C-domain, while Kroch investigated a phenomenon in the I-domain, which is presumably identical in all clause types. See Westergaard and Bentzen (2007) for a similar distinction between the two domains found in acquisition.

the phrasal *wh*-elements in some dialects, or (4) is restricted to short *wh*-elements in subject questions in other dialects.

This means that the development is a step-wise process, where each step is relatively small. Moreover, step 4 shows that it is possible to reverse a historical process; i.e. development is not unidirectional. This has also been pointed out by Sollid (2003), who shows that non-V2 with long *wh*-elements has appeared in a dialect in the north and argues that this is the result of language contact with Finnish and Saami (both non-V2 languages) at the beginning of the previous century. Since the surrounding dialects do not (yet) allow non-V2 in this context, this has become a stigmatized word order and is currently only used by the older population. We are thus seeing a reversal of the historical development in a particular geographical area for sociolinguistic reasons.

21.4 Further Issues

Despite the attractiveness of these syntactic approaches, it has become obvious in the discussion of attested changes in the previous section that there are certain problems and open questions. For example, as pointed out by Harris and Campbell (1995), Croft (2000) and others, Lightfoot's (1979, 1991) theory offers no explanation for why changes occur in language *use*. Furthermore, Harris and Campbell (1995: 40) claim that there is no straightforward way to distinguish 'the "catastrophic" changes ... from the gradually accumulating "environmental" changes'. Here we will add that the distinction between E-language and I-language changes is also not unproblematic from the perspective of first-language acquisition, as it is questionable that massive changes could take place in the E-language without any prior change in speakers' internalized grammars. In work on child language data, a difference in production frequencies is normally assumed to be a reflection of differences in the I-language grammar. For example, arguing against Hyams' (1986) claim that English-speaking children's early null subjects are due to a mis-setting of the pro-drop parameter, Valian (1990, 1991) refers to quantitative and qualitative differences between Italian and English-speaking children: At the relevant stage (around age 2;0), children learning Italian produce about 30 per cent overt subjects, while the percentage for children acquiring English is approximately 70 per cent. English-speaking children also produce a considerable number of pronominal subjects, which are hardly attested at all in the production of Italian children at this stage. These quantitative and qualitative differences are taken to be evidence that the two groups of children have different I-language grammars; i.e. the English-speaking children 'know' that they are learning a non-null-subject language. Furthermore, in a number of studies it has been shown that L1 attrition in adult bilinguals may cause them to produce a different proportion of null vs overt subjects in pro-drop languages such as Italian and Greek; see e.g. Tsimpli, Sorace, Heycock and Filiaci (2004). These shifts in the E-language are thus considered to reflect changes in the internalized grammar.

Similar argumentation is also found in second-language acquisition studies: for example, Bohnacker and Rosén (2007) show that although both Swedish and German are V2 languages, they differ considerably with respect to the type of initial element found in non-subject-initial declaratives, German allowing more objects and informationally heavy elements and Swedish more often displaying lighter elements in initial position, e.g. expletives. Swedish learners of German are shown to be target-consistent with respect to the position of the verb, placing it consistently in second position, but they produce different types of initial elements with the same frequencies as their L1. This is argued to indicate that these learners still have a Swedish I-language grammar in their L2 German.

Roberts (2007) also points out a number of problems with the concept of grammar competition. For example, if speakers can acquire and maintain two grammars in their I-language system, as argued by e.g. Kroch (1994) or Roeper (1999), it is not clear why this will necessarily lead to diachronic change. As we saw in previous sections, some variation is also quite stable across many centuries, e.g. OV/VO in the history of Icelandic or V2/non-V2 throughout the OE period. Moreover, Roberts (2007: 325) argues that Kroch's (1994) and Pintzuk's (1999) claim that grammar competition represents a diglossic situation or code-switching is not supported, as the variation attested in historical texts does not indicate that speakers/writers mix two grammars for social or stylistic purposes (with the exception of clear geographical and sociolinguistic variation such as that found in Eitler and Westergaard (2014) described in the previous section).

As discussed in Westergaard (2008, 2009b), another problem with grammar competition is that it does not recognize the extent to which variation is dependent on linguistic factors, such as fine distinctions in syntax and IS (e.g. with respect to V2). In these cases, variation does not generally seem to represent conflicting evidence to the language-learning child, as we show in the next section. Similarly, investigating complex variation in Old Italian, Poletto (2014) warns that 'dismissing optionality as a competition between two different systems prevents us from looking at more details which reveal an emerging pattern that can be explained within a single grammar'.

Since generative theories of language change rely heavily on language acquisition, it is important to investigate whether there is any support in child language data for the proposed concepts, e.g. parameter setting, grammar competition, cue-based learning, or the suggested input threshold for language acquisition. We turn to this in the next section.

21.5   Synchronic Microvariation and Language Acquisition

It has long been clear that there is hardly any evidence in child language data for abrupt changes in development that would indicate parameter setting. This has led Wexler (1999) to argue for what he refers to as Very Early Parameter Setting, claiming that it occurs even before children start producing relevant utterances. In some areas of child grammar, one sees gradual development, as in the disappearance of so-called optional infinitives or null subjects in non-null-subject languages. Yang (2002, 2010) assumes that the gradualism attested in child language is similar to what is found in historical data and proposes a Variational model of language acquisition that is based on grammar competition. He argues that UG provides the child with all possible human grammars, and the child's task is to select one based on positive evidence in the input. Since some of the input will not give conclusive evidence for a particular grammar (e.g. pro-drop or V2), and some evidence may be contradictory, the child keeps several grammars in the hypothesis space for an extended period of time. The child is also assumed to be a statistical learner, keeping track of frequencies of evidence for the various grammars, until one of them wins out.

Recent studies on syntactic microvariation (e.g. large-scale dialect syntax projects such as ScanDiaSyn in the Nordic countries) have made it clear that children are exposed to considerable variation in the input. One example of this is the variable V2 found in *wh*-questions in many Norwegian dialects, illustrated in (23)–(25) above, where children are exposed to V2 and non-V2 in different contexts. This has led to numerous acquisition studies focusing on how children acquire this variation; see Westergaard (2013) for an overview. The main findings from these studies are that children's production is target-consistent from early on, with appropriate word orders *in the right contexts*. Thus, Norwegian children have no problem with the V2/non-V2 variation in *wh*-questions. With respect to synchronic microvariation in V-to-I movement (see §21.3.3), a particularly convincing example from Swedish child language is provided by Waldmann (2008). He distinguishes between three different types of embedded clause (introduced by *att* 'that', *för (att)* 'for (that)', *så (att)* 'so (that)'), showing that there is a frequency distinction between them with respect to the proportion of V-Neg/Adv word order in the input. Crucially, the children investigated are found to make exactly the same distinctions between the three clause types from early on, showing clear sensitivity to this microvariation. These examples indicate that linguistically conditioned variation does not constitute conflicting input for children, as they seem to easily resolve this variation within a single grammar.

In cases of variation in the input, parameter setting as well as Yang's (2002) competition model would predict overgeneralization of one variant early on, requiring the child to learn exceptions at a later stage (as predicted by Kroch 1994; see §21.3.3). However, Snyder (2007) finds that young children are so-called conservative learners, typically making errors of omission, while the number of errors of commission is negligible in child language data. Westergaard (2009a, 2013) also finds that most errors may be accounted for by a principle of economy; i.e. children will not produce or move an element unless there is clear evidence for this in the input. With respect to V2 or subject–auxiliary inversion, for example, the findings show that children occasionally produce sentences without syntactic movement, illustrated in (26)–(27). Overgeneralization of verb movement, on the other hand, is virtually unattested in child language data.

(26)   der   **Ann har** et. (Ann, age 2;1.28) (Norwegian)
        there Ann has one
        'There Ann has one.'

(27)   Why **he can't** hit? (Adam, age 3;4.01)

Thus, findings from child data show that children are sensitive to variation in the input, distinguishing between clause types, subject types, verb types, types of initial element, etc. Children are also able to acquire infrequent structures both easily and early (e.g. Westergaard 2008), so that the cut-off point for acquisition must be considerably lower than the 17–30 per cent that Lightfoot (1999) suggested. In order to account for these findings, Westergaard (2009c, 2013) has developed a model of micro-cues, which is a generative model where acquisition is argued to result from an interaction between the input, certain third factors (Chomsky 2005) and a somewhat reduced UG (without parameters). Importantly, the formulation of micro-cues includes the linguistic *context* for a particular construction. For example, there is a separate micro-cue for V2 in questions with short *wh*-elements (heads) in Norwegian dialects, formulated as in (28), specifying that verb movement takes place only when the subject conveys new information ([+FOC]), as in example (24) above (cf. Lightfoot's general cue for V2 in (2) above). The model of micro-cues also differs from Lightfoot's (1999, 2006) theory in that the micro-cues are not provided by UG, but are part of a speaker's internalized knowledge of a *specific* language.

(28)   Micro-cue for V2 in *wh*-questions with short *wh*-elements:
        $_{IntP}[_{Int°}[wh] _{TopP}[_{Top°}[V \ldots XP_{[+FOC]} \ldots]]]$

21.6   The 'Size' of Historical Change: Micro-cues, Micro-parameters or Micro-steps

Most of the problems outlined in §21.4 are related to the fact that the changes discussed are of a considerable size, typically involving major parameters such as VO/OV, V2 or V-to-I. The acquisition studies reviewed in §21.5 also indicate that children are not learning by setting major parameters, nor do they seem to be indiscriminately weighing two parameter settings against each other for an extended period of time. Detailed analyses of language change also indicate that change is typically not global, but takes place in smaller steps and at different rates. For example, the studies reported in van Kemenade and Westergaard (2012) or Westergaard, Vangsnes and Lohndal (2012) distinguish between different linguistic contexts for the loss of V2 in ME and present-day Norwegian and show that the decline of V2 is not a completely gradual process, but one that affects one context at a time. For this reason, the micro-cue model of language acquisition has also been used to account for language change; see Westergaard (2009a, b, d). On this view, historical development is *expected* to take place in small steps, affecting one micro-cue at a time. This also means that there is not necessarily a conflict between gradual and abrupt changes, as gradualism may be considered many small I-language changes in succession.

The size of rules is also the focus of Biberauer and Roberts (2012) and related work. Within a framework attempting to revitalize the Principles-and-Parameters theory, they introduce a hierarchy of four distinct types of parameters, depending on the size of the context that the relevant process applies to; e.g. whether they apply to all heads in the language (macro), all heads of a particular category such as N or V (meso), a linguistically relevant subcategory (micro) or one or more lexical items (nano).

This parameter hierarchy makes predictions about historical change. According to Biberauer and Roberts (2012: 288) there is a parametric 'size'–stability correlation, in that the higher levels are more stable than lower levels. Thus, they predict that micro- and nanoparameters will be affected by diachronic change relatively frequently, while macroparameters are stable over millennia. Biberauer and Roberts (2012) show this by reference to considerable synchronic variation in the auxiliary system in a number of New Englishes, changes that have affected a micro- or nanoparameter and that have taken place in a relatively short time span. This is illustrated in (29), showing lack of *wh*-question inversion in Singaporean English, and (30), showing invariant tense–mood–aspect particles in Jamaican Creole (from Biberauer and Roberts 2012: 279–80, originally from Gupta 1994: 8 and Durrleman-Tame 2008: 30).

(29) What **the cruise is** like? (Singaporean English)

(30) Im **wi mos (h)afi** tek dat. (Jamaican Creole)
      s/he will must have-to take that
      'S/he will be obliged to take that.'

On this view, it is not surprising that the category change in the modals discussed in §21.3.1 took place relatively abruptly, given that it affected a small domain (representing a microparameter, perhaps even a nanoparameter if one considers the change to have spread from verb to verb). Also Lightfoot (1999: 88) refers to this as a small-scale change. The rule changing OV syntax to VO, on the other hand, affects a much larger domain (a mesoparameter) and will necessarily be a considerably longer process. When such major changes do take place within a relatively short time span, as in the history of Icelandic (see §21.3.3), it is to be expected that external factors play an important role, e.g. language contact.

The move from major parameters to smaller rules within generative theory not only makes it possible to some extent to reconcile gradualness and abruptness, but also brings generativism closer to functional approaches to language change. Discussing synchronic gradience and diachronic gradualness in relation to grammaticalization, Traugott and Trousdale (2010: 20) argue that 'most instances of change involve small micro-steps', which in themselves are 'discrete and therefore abrupt (in a tiny way)'. They also claim that different parts of a construction may undergo change at different times, but in a larger time perspective the change may seem gradual. That is, diachronic gradualness is, when studied in fine detail, really a number of cognitively abrupt micro-changes in succession. This is of course similar to the micro-cue approach mentioned above, which has been developed to account for language acquisition. Traugott and Trousdale (2010: 24–5) also state that there has been an 'unfortunate … polarization of reanalysis and gradualness', and point out that their abrupt micro-steps are in fact consistent with gradualness in diachronic data.

21.7 Conclusion

The study of historical texts shows us that diachronic development is typically gradual, often spanning several centuries. Nevertheless, children may have different abstract internalized grammars from their parents, indicating that syntactic change is abrupt, taking place from one generation to the next. Discussing some central examples mainly from the history of English and the Scandinavian languages, this chapter suggests that gradualness and abruptness may be reconciled by considering syntactic change as taking place in small but discrete steps.

References

Aarts, B. 2007. *Syntactic gradience: The nature of grammatical indeterminacy.* Oxford University Press.

Allen, C. 1990. 'Review of van Kemenade, *Syntactic Case and morphological case in the history of English*', *Language* 66: 146–52.

Bentzen, K. 2005. 'What's the better move?', *Nordic Journal of Linguistics* 28.2: 153–88.

Biberauer, T. and Roberts, I. 2012. 'Towards a parameter hierarchy for auxiliaries: Diachronic considerations', *Cambridge Occasional Papers in Linguistics* 6: 267–94.

Bohnacker, U. and Christina, R. 2007. 'How to start a V2 declarative clause: Transfer of syntax vs. information structure in L2 German', *Nordlyd* 34(3): 29–56.

Chomsky, N. 1986. *Knowledge of language: Its nature, origin and use.* New York: Praeger.

  2005. 'Three factors in language design', *Linguistic Inquiry* 36: 1–22.

Croft, W. 2000. *Explaining language change: An evolutionary approach.* Harlow: Longman.

Durrleman-Tame, S. 2008. *The syntax of Jamaican creole: A cartographic perspective.* Amsterdam: John Benjamins.

Eitler, T. and Westergaard, M. 2014. 'Word order variation in late Middle English: The effect of information structure and audience design', in K. Bech and K. Eide (eds.), *Information structure and syntactic change in Germanic and Romance languages.* Amsterdam: John Benjamins.

Faarlund, J. T. 2000. 'Reanalysis in word order stability and change', in R. Sornicola, E. Poppe and A. Shisha-Halevy (eds.), *Stability, variation and change of word-order patterns over time.* Amsterdam: John Benjamins, pp. 119–32.

Falk, C. 1993. 'Non-referential subjects in the history of Swedish', unpublished PhD thesis, Lund University.

Gregersen, F. and Pedersen, I. L. 1997. 'Hovedsætningsordstilling i underordnede sætninger' [Main clause word order in embedded clauses], *Danske Folkemål* 39: 55–112.

Gupta, A. 1994. *The step-tongue: Children's English in Singapore.* Clevedon: Multilingual Matters.

Haeberli, E. 2002. 'Inflectional morphology and the loss of verb-second in English', in Lightfoot (ed.), pp. 88–106.

Harris, A. C. and Campbell, L. 1995. *Historical syntax in cross-linguistic perspective* (Cambridge Studies in Linguistics 74). Cambridge University Press.

Holmberg, A. and Platzack, C. 1995. *The role of inflection in Scandinavian syntax.* New York: Oxford University Press.

Hróarsdóttir, T. 2004. 'Cues and expressions', *Nordlyd* 32(1): 135–55.

Hyams, N. 1986. *Language acquisition and the theory of parameters.* Dordrecht: Reidel.

Iversen, R. 1973. 'Om sluttstilling av verbet i norsk folkemål' [On the final position of the verb in Norwegian spoken language], in O. T. Beito and I. Hoff (eds.), *Frå norsk målføregransking: Utvalde utgreiingar 1908–1969.* Oslo, Bergen and Tromsø: Universitetsforlaget.

Jonas, D. 2002. 'Residual V-to-I', in Lightfoot (ed.), pp. 251–70.

Kroch, A. 1989. 'Reflexes of grammar in patterns of language change', *Language Variation and Change* 1: 199–244.

1994. 'Morphosyntactic variation,' in K. Beals *et al* (eds.), *Papers from the 30th regional meeting of the Chicago Linguistics Society*, vol. 2: *Parasession on variation and linguistic theory*. Chicago Linguistics Society, pp. 180–201.

2001. 'Syntactic change,' in M. Baltin and C. Collins (eds.), *The handbook of contemporary syntactic theory*. Cambridge, MA, and Oxford: Blackwell, pp. 699–729.

Kroch, A. and Taylor, A. 1997. 'Verb movement in Old and Middle English: Dialect variation and language contact', in A. van Kemenade and N. Vincent (eds.), *Parameters of morphosyntactic change*. Cambridge University Press, pp. 297–325.

Lightfoot, D. W. 1979. *Principles of diachronic syntax*. Cambridge University Press.

1991. *How to set parameters: Arguments from language change*. Cambridge, MA: MIT Press.

1999. *The development of language: Acquisition, change and evolution*. Malden, MA, and Oxford: Blackwell.

(ed.) (2002). *Syntactic effects of morphological change*. Oxford University Press.

2006. *How new languages emerge*. Cambridge University Press.

Lightfoot, D. W. and Westergaard, M. 2007. 'Language acquisition and language change: Inter-relationships', *Language and Linguistics Compass* 1(5): 396–416.

Palmer, F. 1990. *Modality and the English modals*, 2nd edn. London: Longman.

Pintzuk, S. 1999. *Phrase structures in competition: Variation and change in Old English word order*. New York: Garland.

2002. 'Verb-object order in Old English: Variation as grammatical competition', in Lightfoot (ed.), pp. 276–99.

Poletto, C. 2014. *Word order in Old Italian*. Oxford University Press.

Roberts, I. 1985. 'Agreement parameters and the development of English modal auxiliaries', *Natural Language and Linguistic Theory* 3: 21–58.

2007. *Diachronic Syntax*. Oxford University Press.

2010. 'Grammaticalization, the clausal hierarchy and semantic bleaching', in E. C. Traugott and G. Trousdale (eds.), *Gradience, gradualness and grammaticalization*. Amsterdam: John Benjamins, pp. 45–73.

Roeper, T. 1999. 'Universal bilingualism', *Bilingualism: Language and Cognition* 2(3): 169–86.

Snyder, W. 2007. *Child language: The parametric approach*. Oxford University Press.

Sollid, H. 2003. 'Dialektsyntaks i Nordreisa: Språkdannelse og stabilisering i møtet mellom kvensk og norsk' [Dialect syntax in Nordreisa: Language creation and stabilization in a contact situation between Kven-Finnish and Norwegian], unpublished PhD thesis, University of Tromsø.

Traugott, E. C. and Trousdale, G. 2010. 'Gradience, gradualness and grammaticalization: How do they intersect?', in E. C. Traugott and G. Trousdale (eds.), *Gradience, gradualness and grammaticalization*. Amsterdam: John Benjamins, pp. 19–44.

Tsimpli, I., Sorace, A., Heycock, C. and Filiaci, F. 2004. 'First language attrition and syntactic subjects: A study of Greek and Italian near-native speakers of English', *International Journal of Bilingualism* 8(3): 257–77.

Valian, V. 1990. 'Null subjects: A problem for parameter-setting models of language acquisition', *Cognition* 35(2): 105–22.

   1991. 'Syntactic subjects in the early speech of American and Italian children', *Cognition* 40: 21–81.

van Kemenade, A. 1987. *Syntactic Case and morphological case in the history of English*. Berlin: Walter de Gruyter.

van Kemenade, A. and Westergaard, M. 2012. 'Syntax and information structure: Verb-second variation in Middle English', in A. Meurman Solin, M. J. López-Couso and B. Los (eds.), *Information structure and syntactic change in the history of English (Oxford Studies in the History of English 2)*. New York: Oxford University Press, pp. 87–118.

Vittersø, G. 2004. 'Fra *sva* til *sav*: Stabilitet og endring i norske leddsetninger 1200–1875' [From *sva* to *sav*: Stability and change in Norwegian embedded clauses 1200–1875], unpublished cand.philol. thesis, University of Oslo.

Waldmann, C. 2008. 'Input och output: Ordföljd i svenska barns huvudsatser och bisatser' [Input and output: Word order in Swedish children's main and embedded clauses]. *Lundastudier* A 65, unpublished PhD thesis, University of Lund.

Warner, A. 1982. *Complementation in Middle English and the methodology of historical syntax*. University Park: Pennsylvania State Press.

   1983. 'Review of D. Lightfoot, *Principles of diachronic syntax*', *Journal of Linguistics* 19:187–209.

   2007. 'Parameters of variation between verb-subject and subject-verb order in late Middle English', *English Language and Linguistics* 11(1): 81–112.

Westergaard, M. 2008. 'Acquisition and change: On the robustness of the triggering experience for word order cues', *Lingua* 118(12): 1841–63.

   2009a. 'Microvariation as diachrony: A view from acquisition', *Journal of Comparative Germanic Linguistics* 12(1): 49–79.

   2009b. 'The development of word order in Old and Middle English: The role of information structure and first language acquisition', *Diachronica* 26(1): 65–102.

   2009c. *The acquisition of word order: Micro-cues, information structure and economy (Linguistik Aktuell/Linguistics Today 145)*. Amsterdam: John Benjamins.

2009d. 'Many small catastrophes: Gradualism in a microparametric perspective', in P. Crisma and G. Longobardi (eds.), *Historical syntax and linguistic theory*. Oxford University Press, pp. 75–90.

2013. 'The acquisition of linguistic variation: Parameters vs. micro-cues', in T. Lohndal (ed.), *In search of universal grammar: From Old Norse to Zoque*. Amsterdam: John Benjamins, pp. 275–98.

Westergaard, M. and Bentzen, K. 2007. 'The (non-)effect of input frequency on the acquisition of word order in Norwegian embedded clauses', in I. Gülzow and N. Gagarina (eds.), *Frequency effects in language acquisition: Defining the limits of frequency as an explanatory concept* [Studies on Language Acquisition]. Berlin and New York: Mouton de Gruyter, pp. 271–306.

Westergaard, M., Vangsnes, Ø.A. and Lohndal, T. 2012. 'Norwegian *som*: The complementizer that climbed to the matrix Left Periphery and caused Verb Second violations', in V. Bianchi and C. Chesi (eds.), *Enjoy linguistics! Papers offered to Luigi Rizzi on the occasion of his 60th birthday*. Siena: CISCL Press, pp. 329–43.

Wexler, K. 1999. 'Very early parameter setting and the unique checking constraint: A new explanation of the optional infinitive stage', in A. Sorace, C. Heycock and R. Shillock (eds.), *Language acquisition: Knowledge representation and processing, special issue of Lingua* 106: 23–79.

Yang, C. 2002. *Knowledge and learning in natural language*. Oxford University Press.

2010. 'Universal Grammar, statistics or both?', in C. Yang (ed.), *Language acquisition (Critical concepts in linguistics)*, vol. II. London and New York: Routledge, pp. 128–40.

22

Cyclicity

Elly van Gelderen

22.1 Cyclicity: A Definition

Linguistic cycles are used to describe regular patterns of language change taking place in a systematic manner and direction. They involve the disappearance of a particular word and its renewal by another. Perhaps the most well-known cycle is the negative cycle where a negative word may be added to an already negative construction for emphasis after which the first one may disappear. This new negative may itself be reinforced by another negative and may then itself disappear. What I have just described would be a cycle followed by another cycle. This negative cycle is also known as Jespersen's Cycle, after the Danish linguist Otto Jespersen, who may not have been the first to see this change as a cycle (see van der Auwera 2009). Cyclical changes are unidirectional and they typically involve changes where a phrase or word gradually disappears and is replaced by a new linguistic item.

The term 'cyclicity', as in this chapter title, cannot be found in the *Oxford English Dictionary* but 'cycle' has been in the English language since 1387 with the meaning of a 'recurrent period of a definite number of years adopted for purposes of chronology' (*OED* s.v. cycle), as in lunar or solar cycles. A later definition involves a 'period in which a certain round of events or phenomena is completed, recurring in the same order in succeeding periods of the same length'. Its use is then extended to physics, geology and collections of stories, as in the 'Arthurian cycle'. A linguistic use is not mentioned in the *OED*.

One of the most quoted descriptions of the linguistic cycle is the passage in von der Gabelentz (1901: 256). Because new cycles are not identical to the earlier ones, one way of characterizing a cycle is as a spiral, as in (1). Meillet (1912: 140) also uses spiral as a term ('une sorte de développement en spirale') for what I will continue to refer to as a cycle.

Some of the material in this chapter, especially that in §22.1 and §22.2, is based on van Gelderen (2011, 2013).

(1)   The history of language moves in the diagonal of two forces: the
       impulse toward comfort, which leads to the wearing down of
       sounds, and that toward clarity, which disallows this erosion and
       the destruction of the language. The affixes grind themselves down,
       disappear without a trace; their functions or similar ones, however,
       require new expression. They acquire this expression, by the
       method of isolating languages, through word order or clarifying
       words. The latter, in the course of time, undergo agglutination,
       erosion, and in the mean time renewal is prepared: periphrastic
       expressions are preferred ... always the same: the development
       curves back towards isolation, not in the old way, but in a parallel
       fashion. That's why I compare them to spirals. (von der Gabelentz
       1901: 256; my translation, EvG)

In (1), von der Gabelentz states that languages may have affixes that then
require new expression after the grinding down of these affixes. The new
expression may be 'through word order or clarifying words'.

Basing themselves on Givón (e.g. 1971), Heine, Claudi and Hünnemeyer
(1991: 245) make a distinction between three kinds of cyclical change. One
kind refers to 'isolated instances of grammaticalization', as when a lexical
item grammaticalizes and is then replaced by a new word. For instance,
the lexical verb *go* (or *want)* is often used as a future marker and the motion
(or volition) meaning would then need to be renewed. A second kind refers
to 'subparts of language, for example, when the tense-aspect-mood system
of a given language develops from a periphrastic into an inflexional pattern and back to a new periphrastic one' or when negatives change. A third
kind of cyclical change refers 'to entire languages and language types'.
Heine, Claudi and Hünnemeyer (1991: 246) feel there is 'more justification
to apply the notion of a linguistic cycle to individual linguistic developments', for example the development of future markers, of negatives, and
of tense, rather than to changes in typological character, as in from
analytic to synthetic and back to analytic. I shall refer to the former two
kinds as microcycles and to the latter as a macrocycle.

Before concluding this introduction, let me mention another, unrelated
linguistic use of 'cycle', namely as a technical term in a generative derivation,
as in Chomsky (1966) and Evers (1975). In this early model, cycles specified
that transformations applied to certain domains before others. Currently (see
Chomsky 2001), the term 'phase' is more commonly used in that context.

Having given a brief idea of what a linguistic cycle is, in §22.2, I provide
more detail on earlier descriptions of linguistic cycles, of all the kinds
discussed in Heine, Claudi and Hünnemeyer (1991). I also discuss accounts
of what sets them in motion, returning to von der Gabelentz's comfort and
clarity. In §22.3, I provide a description of some (micro)cycles, namely the
agreement and copula cycles. Finally, I argue that the traditional account of
comfort and clarity translates into a contemporary formal account (§22.4).

22.2 The Linguistic Cycle

In this section, I provide more background on work on the cycle that has been done the last two centuries and an example of a microcycle as well as a macrocycle (§22.2.1). I then look into the explanations that have been given to account for the cycle (§22.2.2).

22.2.1 The Microcycle and Macrocycle

There are early advocates of the view that language change is cyclical. Robins (1967: 150–9) provides a useful overview of how, for instance, Condillac (1746) and Tooke (1786–1805) think that abstract, grammatical vocabulary develops from earlier concrete vocabulary. Bopp (1816) similarly argues that affixes arise from earlier independent words and provides many examples of a phenomenon that I have termed a macrocycle.

In the late nineteenth century, work on cyclical change by von der Gabelentz ([1891] 1901) appears. In (1), von der Gabelentz is quoted as saying that languages develop into isolating systems from inflectional and agglutinative ones and then again develop into agglutinating systems. This too involves a macrocycle. Meillet's (1912) work on language change as grammaticalization is an obvious source for ideas on cyclical change. Meillet, as mentioned, also uses the term spiral rather than cycle and describes the addition of words to obtain a more intense meaning and the subsequent weakening of the markers that had been used before (1912: 140f.). For Meillet, the reason for these changes is a loss of expressivity. His examples of grammaticalization are many: the French verb *être* 'to be' going from independent verb to perfective auxiliary, *aller* 'to go' developing grammaticalized future functions, and the Greek *thelô ina* 'I want that' changing to a future marker that is much reduced in phonology, namely *tha*.

Grammaticalization is a process where new grammatical categories are created from lexical categories. This may go hand in hand with a loss of phonological weight and semantic and pragmatic specificity. It is often put as the cline in (2).

(2)   content item > grammatical word > clitic > inflectional affix
       (Hopper and Traugott 2003: 7)

The loss in phonological content is, however, not a necessary consequence of the loss of semantic content (see Kiparsky 2011; Kiparsky and Condoravdi 2006; Hoeksema 2009). For instance, Kiparsky (2011: 19) writes 'in the development of case, bleaching is not necessarily tied to morphological downgrading from postposition to clitic to suffix'. According to Kiparsky, unidirectionality is the defining property of grammaticalization.

Grammaticalization constitutes one step in the cycle. The best-known examples of lexical elements changing to grammatical ones are verbs being reanalysed as auxiliaries, minimizing words such as *nothing* as negatives, and prepositions as complementizers. The grammatical categories may in their turn grammaticalize and new lexical words may be added to substitute for the loss of the original meaning, resulting in a cycle. This is a clear case of Heine, Claudi and Hünnemeyer's (1991) 'first kind' of cyclical change, i.e. what I refer to as a microcycle.

The original lexical element may, however, be kept side-by-side with the grammatical one. For instance, the verb *go* has grammaticalized to an auxiliary, as in (3a), but can still be used as main verb, as in (3b) (this is the same as French *aller*).

(3)   a. I'm going to leave for the summer.
       b. I'm going to Flagstaff for the summer.

Hopper and Traugott (2003: 2f.) famously outline the typical characteristics of grammaticalization. Once the reanalysis from verb to auxiliary has taken place, the new form can undergo processes that typically auxiliaries undergo, such as phonological reduction in (4a). The main verb does not undergo such weakening, as the ungrammaticality of the reduced *gonna* in (4b) shows.

(4)   a. I'm gonna leave for the summer.
       b. *I'm gonna Flagstaff for the summer.

Even if *gonna* in (4a) is now a future auxiliary, it retains some of its earlier flavour of intent to do something but this may also disappear and *be going to/gonna* might become a general future.

Nesselhauf (2012) provides a very precise account of the changes in the various future markers (*shall, will, 'll, be going to, be to* and the progressive) in the last 250 years. She identifies three meanings associated with the future markers-to-be, namely intention, prediction and arrangement. Nesselhauf argues that, as the sense of intention is lost and is replaced by the sense of prediction, new markers of intention will appear. One such candidate is *want* where intention is expressed in (5a) and it is starting to gain the sense of prediction, as in (5b).

(5)   a. The final injury I want to talk about is brain damage ...
          (Nesselhauf 2012: 114)
       b. We have an overcast day today that looks like it wants to rain.
          (Nesselhauf 2012: 115)

A full cycle, i.e. microcycle, involving *go* could be for it to disappear as a motion verb and for a new motion verb to appear, but other scenarios are possible. For instance, the new auxiliary use of 'go' may develop a specialized (often clitic-like) paradigm, such as the use of *gonna* in all persons, whereas the lexical use may continue with the usual, more elaborate morphological forms. A concrete example of this is Catalan where the verb 'go' *anar* has one conjugation for the lexical verb in the present (namely *vaig, vas, va, anem, aneu, van*) whereas in its auxiliary uses (followed by the plain infinitive) as a preterite auxiliary it has, in many persons, a distinct conjugation (e.g. *và(re)ig, và(res), va, và(re)m, và(re)u, và(re)n*), e.g. *anem al mercat* 'we go to the market' vs *và(re)m anar al mercat* 'we went to the market'.[1] Nesselhauf's data on British English *going to* show that its use as a future marker has increased, both in the intention and prediction sense, and that the proportion of pure prediction is increasing. Once the sense of prediction prevails, another verb may be taking over to compensate for the feature of intention.

Another example of a microcycle is the already mentioned negative cycle. The development of negation has become strengthened enormously by the recent publication of the first volume of *The History of Negation in the Languages of Europe and the Mediterranean*, edited by Willis, Lucas and Breitbarth (2013). Early in the past century, Jespersen (1917) had discussed changes in negatives with examples from many languages and talked about weakening and strengthening tendencies. A typical chain of changes is given in (6), from the history of English.

(6)
early OE >	OE/ME	> early ModE >	Colloquial English
no/ne	*(ne) . . . not*	*-n't*	*-n't . . . nothing*

Jespersen (1917: 4) writes that the 'negative adverb is first weakened, then found insufficient and therefore strengthened'. The weakening occurs because 'some other word in the same sentence receives the strong stress of contrast'. Kiparsky and Condoravdi (2006: 5) disagree with the phonetic weakening scenario and argue that it is 'not phonetic weakening of plain negation, but semantic weakening of emphatic negation'.

In Old English, a negative can be expressed as *ne*, as in (7), and this is also possible with indefinite nouns, as with *seldguma* in (8). Frequently, however, an additional negative accompanies the *ne*, as in (9a) and (9b). This is known as negative concord (see Hoeksema 2009 for this as an essential stage in Jespersen's Cycle).

(7)
Men	**ne**	cunnon	secgan	to	soðe . . .	hwa
man	NEG	could	tell	to	truth . . .	who

'No man can tell for certain . . . who'. (*Beowulf* 50–2)

(8)
n-is	þæt	seldguma	wæpnum	geweorðad
NEG-is	that	hall.man	weapons	adorned

'That is not an (ordinary) hall-man, adorned with weapons'. (*Beowulf* 249–50)

---

[1] The Catalan example was pointed out by the volume editors.

(9) a. Forþæmþe hie   hiora **nan wuht** ongietan   **ne** meahton
         because   they their   no   thing understand NEG could
         'because they couldn't understand anything'. (Alfred, *Pastoral
         Care*, Cotton 4/12)

     b. Ac   **nænig mon** in þære mægðe   **ne** heora lif
        But   no   man   in that province   NEG their life
        onhyrgan   wolde ne heora lare   gehyran.
        imitate   would nor their teaching heed
        'And nobody in that province imitated their life or pay heed to
        their teaching.' (Bede 302.21)

The next stage is when the negative argument, e.g. *nan wuht* in (9a), is
reanalysed as a negative adverb. Examples of this are given in (10) and (11),
the latter from early Middle English. The *Pastoral Care* only has non-
argumental *noht/naht* in sentences that are either phrasal or sentential
negation.

(10) **N-æron** **naht** æmetti3e,   ðeah ge   wel **ne** dyden
      NEG-were   not   unoccupied. though you well NEG did
      'You were not unoccupied, though you did not do well' (Pastoral
      Care Hatton, Sweet, 207, 20, from the *OED*)

(11) ne **ne** helpeð **nawiht** eche   lif   to haben
      nor NEG helps not   eternal life to have
      'Nor does it help to have eternal life.' (Katherine 26/6)

What remains controversial is whether the phonological weakening of
the *ne*, as seen from the contraction with the verb in (8) and (10), led to the
reinforcement, or whether the reinforcement was pragmatically conditioned and that the latter led to the loss of *ne*.

Current colloquial English *-n't* is again reinforced by another negative.
As Labov (1972: 176f.) points out, 'negative concord is an optional rule for
almost all dialects of English', one that has 'strongly emphatic character'.
In short, the negative cycle proceeds as in (5). The next stage would be for
-n't to disappear and for another negative to be used for reinforcement.
Prescriptive forces that prohibit two negative markers to mark the negative may stop this development.

Hodge (1970) has done more than anyone to feed recent ideas on the
cycle with his short article entitled 'The Linguistic Cycle'. In it, he examines the overall changes in Egyptian, a macrocycle, and uses lower and
upper case to give a visual representation of full cycles from synthetic 'sM',
i.e. a language with lots of inflectional morphology as indicated by the
capital *M*, and lower-case *s* for less syntax, to analytic Sm, i.e. a language
with a lot of syntax, indicated by the capital *S*, but less morphology,
indicated by lower-case *m*. By more or less syntax Hodge means the degree

Table 22.1 *Developments in Egyptian (from Hodge (1970: 5), where * means the stage is reconstructed)*

Proto-Afroasiatic	analytic	*Sm
Old Egyptian	synthetic	sM
Late Egyptian	analytic	Sm
Coptic	synthetic	sM

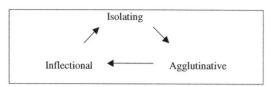

Figure 22.1 Attachment-type cycle

of reliance on function words and word order. His representation is provided in Table 22.1.

Analytic languages have words with few morphemes, with the most analytic showing a one-to-one relationship between word and morpheme. Chinese is often cited as a good example of this. Words in synthetic languages contain more than one morpheme. Languages with verbal agreement are synthetic. As is obvious from this description, it is easy to decide on a purely analytic language but hard to decide on what counts as a synthetic language: is it having words that contain three morphemes or words with five morphemes? Von Humboldt (1836) proposes a third type of language, namely polysynthetic, that is widely accepted.

August Wilhelm von Schlegel seems to be the first in 1818 to use the terms analytic and synthetic where languages are concerned. As Schwegler (1990: 4f.) points out, from the beginning, the terms were not used in precise ways since they include gradations, such as 'elles penchent fortement vers' ['they lean strongly towards'] and 'une certaine puissance de' ['a certain power of']. Since Greenberg (1954), the morphological structure is quantified in terms of degree of synthesis which is measured by dividing the total number of morphemes by the total number of words in a sentence. A value between 1.00 to 1.99 marks an analytic language, one between 2.00 and 2.99 a synthetic language, and one above 3 a polysynthetic language. Modern English is analytic with 1.68, Old English synthetic with 2.12 and Eskimo polysynthetic with 3.72.

Apart from morphemes per word, a second distinction is made as to whether the morphemes in the synthetic languages are agglutinative, as in Korean, or (in)flectional, as in English and Navajo. Sometimes, this is put as a cycle as well, for instance, in Crowley (1992: 170) and reproduced in Figure 22.1.

The attachment cycle is a macrocycle and is similar to what Hodge has in mind but, as mentioned before, it is hard to define what counts as synthetic and the same would hold for inflectional. Therefore, there is scepticism about how practically useful this cycle is.

In addition to Hodge (1970), there is research in the 1960s and 1970s by Greenberg (1978), Givón (1976) and Tauli (1958, 1966) that is relevant for cyclical change and the linguistic cycle. The renewed interest in grammaticalization starting in the 1980s is of course essential to understanding the stages of a linguistic cycle, with work such as Lehmann (1982, 1985), Traugott and Heine (1991) and others. After the 1960s and 1970s, there are sporadic references to cycles but recently work on the negative cycle has started to appear again. For instance, from June 2008 to May 2009, one-day events on the negative cycle took place in Birmingham (www.lhds.bcu .ac.uk/english/cycles-of-grammaticalization), culminating in Ingham and Larrivée (2011); a volume on cyclical change, edited by van Gelderen, appeared in 2009; and the volume edited by Willis, Lucas and Breitbarth (2013), mentioned above, adds much to the empirical coverage of cyclical developments. One section of the *Oxford Handbook on Historical English Linguistics* (Nevalainen and Traugott 2012) is devoted to 'Cycles and Continua' and another workshop on Cyclical Change took place in April 2014 (van Gelderen 2016).

In short, research on the cycle has gone through various stages of renewed interest. One of the reasons it is currently more popular again is that accounts for cycles are easier to formulate in a formal framework, as I show in §22.4.

22.2.2 Clarity and Comfort

Cycles have often received explanations as in von der Gabelentz (1901), namely in terms of a weakening of the endings due to comfort, as in (1) above, and a strengthening of the original idea due to clarity. In the original, he uses 'Deutlichkeit' ('clarity') and 'Bequemlichkeit' ('comfort') as important competing factors. In this section, I provide a bit more background about what the terms mean.

Von der Gabelentz (1901) gives various examples of clarity, namely special exertion of the speech organs (1901: 183), 'Wiederholung' ('repetition', 1901: 239), periphrastic expressions (1901: 239), replacing words like *sehr* 'very' by more powerful and specific words such as *riesig* 'gigantic' and *schrecklich* 'frightful' (1901: 243), using a rhetorical question instead of a regular proposition, and also replacing case with prepositions (1901: 183). He also gives specific examples of comfort and they include the unclear pronunciation of everyday expressions, the use of a few words instead of a full sentence, i.e. ellipsis (1901: 182–4), 'syntaktische Nachlässigkeiten aller Art' ('syntactic carelessness of all kinds', 1901: 184), and loss of gender (1901: 254).

For von der Gabelentz, the course of the spiral is connected with the agglutination theory, as evident in (1), where he says that all affixes were once independent words (1901: 255). The examples he gives of clarity and comfort do not specifically relate to the microcycles, however, and even the cases of words turning into affixes are all pretty general, not specific examples.

Jespersen has reservations about cycles, especially macro ones, and that may be at the bottom of this statement about linguistic change as a tension, a 'tug-of-war' between the speaker's needs and those of the community. Jespersen does not see this 'tug-of-war' resulting in cyclical change and in that way it is different from von der Gabelentz's two tendencies. He writes that 'the correct inference can only be that the tendency towards ease may be at work in some cases, though not in all, because there are other forces which may at times neutralize it or prove stronger than it' (1922: 262) although he mainly gives instances of weakening, i.e. phonetic ease. It is not always easy to decide which sounds are easier and in which contexts. Most examples of ease that Jespersen gives are phonetic, e.g. [h] being an easier fricative than [s] or [f].

So although cyclical change has often been put in terms such as comfort and ease, such a formulation of, for instance, the negative and agreement cycles, is impressionistic. There is, however, an intuitive appeal to the two forces and this view provides an insight that can be translated into a more formal account. First, I describe more contemporary ideas of what sets a (micro)cycle in motion.

There are several different types of answers, language-internal and external ones, namely (a) phonetic or pragmatic reasons for reinforcement and (b) language contact, language attitudes, and matters pertaining to language and identity, among other sociolinguistic issues, respectively. In acknowledging weakening of pronunciation ('un affaiblissement de la pronunciation'), Meillet (1912: 139) writes that what provokes the start of the (negative) cycle is the need to speak forcefully ('le besoin de parler avec force'). Kiparsky and Condoravdi (2006), in examining Jespersen's Cycle in Greek, find no evidence for phonetic weakening and similarly suggest pragmatic and semantic reasons. A simple negative cannot be emphatic; in order for a negative to be emphatic, it needs to be reinforced, e.g. by a minimizer. Adapting ideas from Dahl (2001), they argue that, when emphatic negatives are overused, their semantic impact weakens and they become the regular negative and a new emphatic will appear. Larrivée (2010), examining the history of French negation, argues that a specific pragmatic function, namely accessibility of a proposition to the hearer, plays a role. Language-internal reasons have also been argued as responsible for grammaticalization (and the cycle) in Roberts and Roussou (2003) and van Gelderen (2004, 2011). These authors have suggested that the child in acquiring its language makes choices based on economy principles. I return to this in §22.4, translating the notions of comfort and clarity into more formal terms.

Heine and Kuteva (2005) examine grammaticalization, and cyclical morphological changes, as set in motion by language contact. For instance, if a language does not have a conjunction such as 'because' of its own, it can,

Table 22.2 *Six examples of cyclical change*

Negative cycles
A negative marker is reinforced by a negative indefinite and then lost.
A negative marker is replaced by an aspect marker or verb with negative semantic features.
Subject agreement cycle
Nouns, demonstratives or personal pronouns are reanalysed as agreement on the verb.
Object agreement cycle
Pronouns are used as object markers on verbs.
Copula Cycles
Demonstratives, locative verbs or adpositions come to be used as copula verbs.
Conjunction cycles
Wh-pronouns are used as Y/N markers or as conjunctions.
Adpositions, adpositional phrases or adverbs get to be used as conjunctions.
Nominal cycles
Nouns can be used to mark plurality or gender.

under the influence of a contact language that does have such a grammatical word, use one of its own prepositions to reanalyse as a conjunction. This happened to various American Indian languages that came into contact with Spanish, according to Heine and Kuteva (2005).

To end this section, I present a partial list of cycles in Table 22.2, some of which will be discussed in the next section. As a language reaches the 'zero' stage on the right side, there will already typically be an element that is used for renewal and that may be responsible for the change in the first place. This new lexical element may resemble the one on the left side of the original cline.

22.3 The Cycles

In this section, I provide examples of the subject agreement and copula cycles.

22.3.1 The Agreement Cycle

I now look at the reanalysis of pronouns as agreement markers. Givón, arguing that agreement markers arise from pronouns, says 'agreement and pronominalization ...are fundamentally one and the same phenomenon' (1976: 151). Givón's most recent work on Ute, a Uto-Aztecan language of the US southwest, shows such a change. See (12).

(12) 'úwa >   'úwa >   -'ú   Ute
      demonstrative   pronoun   article/agreement
      invisible-animate   (Givón 2011: 163–5)

Many languages indeed have subject pronouns, as in (13), that look like fuller versions of the inflection on the verb, as in (14) from Tunica, where the correspondence is not perfect but suggestive.

(13) Personal pronouns:
     ʔima [1S],   ma' [2SM],   hɛ'ma [2SF],   ʔu'wi [3SM],   ti'hči [3SF]

(14) Tunica verbal prefixes:
     ʔi- [1S],   wi-[2SM],   hi-/ he-[2SF],   ʔu- [3SM],   ti- [3SF]
                                (Haas 1946: 346f.)

French has gone through a complete agreement cycle. The Modern French data are well known from Lambrecht (1981) and Zribi-Hertz (1994): the current pronoun has been argued to be verbal agreement. In Old French, the emphatic first-person singular subject pronoun is *je*, as in (15), or *jou*, as in (16). *Je* in Old French is not a clitic because it occurs separated from the verb but is possibly being reinforced in this stage because another subject pronoun appears regularly, as in (16). This would suggest the change is triggered by pragmatic strengthening rather than phonological weakening.

(15)   Se **je** meïsme ne   li   di   (Old French)
       If   I   myself   NEG   him   tell
       'If I don't tell him myself.' (Franzén 1939: 20, Cligès 993)

(16)   Renars   respond: **"Jou, je** n'irai"   (Old French)
       Renard   answers   I   I   NEG.go.FUT
       'R answers "Me, I won't go".'
       (*Coronnement Renart*, A. Foulet (ed.) 1929: 598, from Roberts 1993: 112)

Old French is pro-drop and has first- and second-person pronouns *je* and *tu* for nominative forms and *moi* and *toi* for accusative emphatic forms, respectively. Once pro-drop is lost, *je* and *tu* become the regular clitic pronouns and *moi* and *toi* get used emphatically for both nominative and accusative, according to Harris (1978: 117).

In the modern period, the situation is different from (15) because the subject pronoun is obligatorily proclitic to the finite verb, as (17a) shows. If it does not immediately precede the verb, it is ungrammatical, which the deletion of the second *j(e)* in (17b) shows.

(17)   a. Je   lis   et   j'écris   (Modern French)
           I   read   and   I.write
       b. *Je   lis   et   écris
           I   read   and   write

As a result of this obligatory attachment of *je* to the verb, it is no longer possible to separate them, as (18a) shows,[2] whereas a full noun can be separated from the verb, as (18b) shows.

---

[2] As pointed out by the volume editors, there are formulaic exceptions, such as (i). I regard those as archaisms.
   (i)   je,   le   soussigné,   déclare   que . . .
         I   the   undersigned   declare   that
         'I, the undersigned, hereby declare that . . . '

(18) a. *Je heureusement ai   vu   ça   (French)
         I   probably   have seen that
         'I've probably seen that.'
      b. Kurt, heureusement, a   fait beaucoup d'autres choses.
         Kurt fortunately   has done many   other   things
         'Fortunately, Kurt did many other things' (Google search of
         French websites)

Lambrecht (1981: 6) also mentions the elimination of clitic–verb inversion, as in (19). Instead, one hears (20). The reason for this is the increasingly fixed prefixal position of the subject.

(19) Où   **vas-tu**? (Standard French)
      where go.YOU

(20) Où   **tu**   **vas** ? (Colloquial French)
      where YOU go
      'Where are you going?'

Where and why does the agreement cycle start? It could be similar
to the negative cycle in that pragmatic/semantic strengthening, e.g. by
jou in (16), triggers the weakening of the *je*, or the other way round,
namely that the phonetic weakening of *je* triggers the presence of
an emphatic. I come back to this question towards the end of the
chapter.

22.3.2 The Copula Cycles

Li and Thompson (1977) are among the first to examine the change from
demonstrative to copula systematically and Katz (1996) is one of the first to
note its systematic nature and to discuss it as a cycle. Copula cycles occur
in many typologically and genetically different languages: Turkish, Uto-
Aztecan, Chinese, Hebrew, Palestinian Arabic, Maltese, Kenya Luo, Lango,
Logbara, Nuer, Wappo, West Greenlandic and creoles. There are other
sources for copulas, mainly prepositions and verbs (see Hengeveld 1992;
Stassen 1997; Pustet 2003).

In the cycle that involves a pronoun, a third-person subject pronoun or
demonstrative is reanalysed as a copula verb, initially with its person and
number features intact. This change is different from the subject cycle of
the previous section, where first and second person are consistently the
first to change and where all persons participate.

Copulas come in many 'flavours'. This flavour is due to the semantic
features of the source. Let us take an example from English, a language
very rich in copula verbs, e.g. *be, become, go, fall, turn, seem, appear, stay* and
remain, to mention but a few. Verbs such as *remain* and *stay*, when they are
main verbs, have [duration] as a semantic feature and *seem* and *appear* have

[visible]. These features remain active when the main verbs, such as in (21a), are used as copulas in (21b). I have listed some of these features in (22).

(21) a. We want to remain at the forefront of developing and build-
          ing democracy across the region. (COCA *Washington Monthly*
          2012)
      b. You understand, T.J., that you have the right the remain silent
          (COCA *CBS Evening News* 2012)

(22) The semantic features of some English copula verbs:
    be   remain, stay   seem, appear
    [location]   [duration]   [visible]
    [equal]

One of the problems with a representation such as (22) is that it seems rather ad hoc which semantic features we assign to the lexical items.

The way the pronoun to copula cycle has been explained is through the reanalysis of a topic or focus construction (see, for example, Li and Thompson 1977).

(23)   The elephant   that   happy
       TOPIC   SU   VP
                      ↓
       SU   copula   VP

However, if the reanalysis in (23) is correct, the question is why first- (or second-)person pronouns are never reanalysed as copulas since they are frequent topics. I will provide an example of the change of a demonstrative to copula from Egyptian.

Loprieno (1995: 68) explains that in Old Egyptian there are many series of demonstratives. There is a pronominal based one, with a person marker (*p-* for masculine singular, *t* for feminine singular, and *jp-* and *jpt-* for the plural) followed by a deictic element (e.g. *-n* and *-w* for different degrees of closeness). This results in demonstratives such as *pn* 'this' in (24a) and *jpw* 'those' in (24b).

(24) a. rmt   **p-n** (Old Egyptian)
          man   MSG-PROXIMAL
          'this man'
      b. ntr-w **jp-w**
          god-PL   MPL-PROXIMAL
          'those gods' (Loprieno 1995: 68)

According to Loprieno, the masculine *pw*-pronouns become copulas in Middle Egyptian, as in (25), not agreeing in gender or number with the nominal predicate.

(25) a. rmt   **pw** (Middle Egyptian)
         man   be
         'This is a man.' (Loprieno 1995: 68)
      b. ṯmjt   **pw**   jmnt
         city.F be   west.F
         'The West is a city.' (Loprieno 2001: 1752)

In the change from (24) to (25), *pw* loses its deictic and person and number features.

I shall now turn to possible accounts for these cycles.

22.4 Minimalist Cycles

In §22.2, I mentioned several reasons that have been posited to account for cycles. These involved phonetic and pragmatic weakening with subsequent renewal of the lost content. There are, however, different ways of describing cycles as resulting from comfort and clarity. Here, I reformulate the cycle's two tendencies in a minimalist framework. I will argue that grammaticalization finds an account in the Minimalist Programme's reliance on formal features and so do cycles.

Chomsky (1995) focuses on features as the locus for language acquisition. It is only in features that languages differ. Baker (2008) formulates this as in (26).

(26)   All parameters of variation are attributable to differences in the features of particular items (e.g., the functional heads) in the lexicon. (Baker 2008: 156)

This new emphasis makes it possible to see the cycle as a loss of features, followed by a renewal, a conclusion that is not surprising considering traditional work in grammaticalization. First, we need a little more background on features.

In addition to phonological and semantic features, there are formal features which can be interpretable or uninterpretable. The case features on nouns and the agreement features on verbs are uninterpretable (in English) because they are not relevant for the interpretation. The interpretable features are the tense of the sentence, the person and number features on nouns. Interpretable features are relevant for the interpretation of a sentence: the [i-3sG] in (27a) stands for interpretable third person and singular number features on the noun and the [u-phi] for uninterpretable, and as yet unspecified, person and number features on the verb. The latter are deleted in (27b) after having been checked because they are not relevant for the interpretation. In (27), I just show the phi-features.

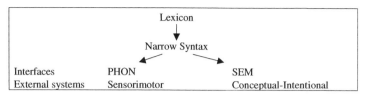

Figure 22.2 Interfaces

(27)   She   eats   beans
  a. before checking   [i-3sɢ]   [u-phi]   [i-3ᴘʟ]
  b. after checking   [i-3sɢ]   ~~[u-phi: 3S]~~   [i-3ᴘʟ]

A category bearing an uninterpretable feature is called a probe and it needs an interpretable feature, i.e. the goal. An interpretable feature is independent of other features and we will see this is important for the cycle.

Chomsky (1995: 230, 381) writes that 'formal features have semantic correlates and reflect semantic properties (accusative Case and transitivity, for example)' and later (Chomsky 2001: 10) he says that semantic and formal features 'intersect'. This intersection was not there in Chomsky (1965: 142) where semantic features are defined as not involved in the syntax. I take the intersection to mean that the Interpretative component does not distinguish between these features and that semantic features may provide the valuation for the uninterpretable ones. Sentences such as (9) show this valuation. My view is a departure from standard assumptions that only interpretable features check/value uninterpretable ones; it provides the reason behind the possibility of the reanalysis from semantic to interpretable.

After the derivation is built, it splits into a part that goes to the sensory-motor interface to be pronounced, and a part that goes to the conceptual interface to be interpreted. Figure 22.2 shows the derivation and the interfaces. Interpretable features end up at SEM, the semantic interface; uninterpretable features are transferred to PHON.

I now return to three cyclical changes, negatives, agreement and copulas, that we have seen before to show that there is a change from semantic/interpretable to uninterpretable features.

Let us start with the negative cycle, described in §22.2. In (9a), we saw a renewal of the Old English negative *ne* by means of *nan wuht* 'no creature'. In the early stages of the renewal, the renewing element can be any negative argument that reinforces the negative *ne*, e.g. **nan** *þing* 'no thing', *nan wuht, na(n)wuht, nan scild* 'no shield', and *na mon* 'no man'. There is not one designated form. The semantically negative features of these arguments aid in the renewal. The next step is for these semantic features to be reanalysed as interpretable ones, as has happened in the Early Middle English (11), where *nawiht* is no longer an argument. The final

step in the cycle is for the *nawiht/noht* to be reanalysed as weak, i.e. uninterpretable, and for renewal to start again.

In tree form, using a Neg(ation)P, the changes are represented in (28).
In (28a), the negative features are analysed by the language learner as
interpretable but they are (re)analysed in (28b) as uninterpretable because
there is an argument that is negative in semantic features.
The uninterpretable negative feature acts as a probe looking for a goal.
In (28c), the *nowuht* becomes the designated negative with interpretable
features which it loses in (28d) and so on.

(28)

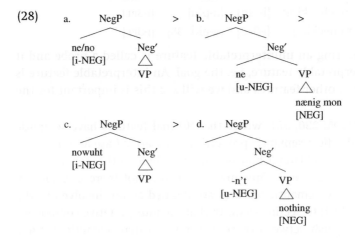

Changes in negatives can be explained by arguing that their (initially)
semantic features are reanalysed as interpretable and then as uninterpretable. So, the pragmatically renewed negative has semantic features that
end up being used grammatically, initially as a full phrase in the specifier
position, as in (28a), and then in the head, as in (28b). Once the phrase is
reanalysed as a head (e.g. Old English *ne* 'not'), another element is required.
Van Gelderen (2008, 2011) formulates these changes as an Economy
Principle, as in (29).

(29) **Feature Economy**
      Semantic features can be reanalysed as interpretable and interpre-
      table features as uninterpretable in, for instance:
      DP in the VP   Specifier of NegP Head Neg   negative affix
      semantic   >   [i-NEG]   >   [i/u-NEG] > [u-NEG]

This means the child in acquiring his/her words will initially connect
these with semantic features but later extrapolate the grammatical ones.

The changes can be represented as in Figure 22.3: semantic features are
reanalysed in the specifier position as interpretable and in the head as
uninterpretable features.

Above, in relation to (22), I mentioned that features are very numerous
and possibly ad hoc. According to Roberts (2009: 47), we need 'an appropriate feature system which breaks down major categories (N, V, etc.) into

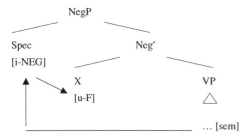

Figure 22.3 The linguistic cycle

smaller ones (count noun, transitive verb, etc.) up to a fairly fine-grained level. In the case of functional categories, which will be the major concern in what follows, we will be dealing with categories such Modal, which can be divided into epistemic, alethic, deontic, etc.' How does the child know which features are available? This will have to be from Universal Grammar (for in-depth discussion, see Chapter 13, this volume). Even as early as 1965, Chomsky writes that 'semantic features … too, are presumably drawn from a universal "alphabet"' (1965: 142). He continues to say, up to the present, 'UG must at least provide atomic elements, lexical items …each a structured array of properties (*features*)' (2007: 6). So, let us assume that the inventory of features is given and that the semantic and phonological interfaces require that their input is legible, this being responsible for the various formal features.

The change represented in (29) occurs in the case of the negative cycle as well as the subject pronoun to agreement cycle: the interpretable person (and gender) features of a full pronoun are reanalysed as uninterpretable when they become agreement, as represented in (30).

(30) **Subject agreement cycle**
emphatic pronouns > full pronoun > head pronoun > agreement
[phi]   [i-phi]   [u-1] [i-2/3] [u-phı]

Let us take the Old French in (15) above, and repeated as (31). In (31), the emphatic pronoun is *je*; it is optional and need not immediately precede the verb *di*. It has first person singular features but these are semantic features,[3] not necessarily involved in checking. If Old French is pro-drop (see Adams 1987; Vance 1997), it is the null subject that provides the interpretable features for the verb's uninterpretable ones to check with.

(31) Se **je** meïsme ne   li   di   (Old French)
      If I   myself not him tell
      'If I don't tell him myself'

---

[3] In the case of English and French pronouns, it is not so obvious that they have semantic person features. Southeast Asian languages show this better. Indonesian *saya* 'I' originates from 'servant, slave', but is now the regular first person. Thai is reported to have over twenty first- and second-person markers, all derived from nouns.

In most languages, pro-drop is lost earlier for first person and later for second and third (van Gelderen 2000) and, hence, my differentiation between first and second/third person in (30). Once pro-drop is lost, the uninterpretable phi-features on the verb need new semantic or interpretable features which they find in the emphatic *je* pronoun of, for example, (31). This stage is then reached for all persons and *je* 'I', *tu* 'you', and *il/elle* 'he/she' and others are reanalysed as valuing the phi-features of the verb. Currently, the last stage of the cycle is taking place because the first and second person pronouns are being reanalysed as agreement on the verb, i.e. as having uninterpretable phi-features in need of another semantic or interpretable phi-marker. This is the reason (32) is frequent.

(32)   **Moi,** je   lis   toujours que .... (Spoken French)
       me,   I   read   always   that
       'I always read that ...'

Now we have come full cycle where a pronoun becomes agreement and is replaced by a new pronoun.

As for the copula cycle, in van Gelderen (2011), I argue the change is due to the deictic features of the demonstrative which translate into locational features on the copula, as in (33) and (34) for Egyptian.

(33)   D   >   V
       semantic   [distance]   [location]
       formal   [i-3sG]   [u-phi]

(34)   Old Egyptian   Middle Egyptian
                     p-w   >   *pw*
       semantic   [proximal]   [i-loc]
       formal   [i-phi]   [u-phi]

In conclusion to this section, I have translated the traditional ideas of comfort and clarity, and phonetic and pragmatic weakening, into minimalist features to account for the cycle(s).

22.5   Conclusions and Future Directions

This chapter has provided background on the linguistic cycle and examples of such cycles. Macrocycles affecting the character of a language are controversial and I have therefore mainly restricted the discussion to microcycles. I have also considered accounts of what starts cycles. The Gabelentzian idea of clarity corresponds to pragmatic strengthening and that of comfort to phonetic weakening. I have argued that one can also look at the two forces in terms of Feature Economy.

The urge of speakers to be innovative may introduce new, loosely adjoined elements into the structure and that may provide evidence to the language learner to reanalyse the older form as uninterpretable. Speakers may want to be explicit and therefore choose full phrases rather than heads. In conclusion, languages change in systematic ways. The only plausible reason for this is that the learners have principles guiding these changes.

In §22.2.1, I listed some current projects on the linguistic cycle. What are some of the challenges that lie ahead? I shall list three questions here and elaborate a little on them without providing an answer. (a) Which are the features that need to be expressed by formal features? (b) why are some changes slow? (c) Why are some categories semi-lexical and unlikely to change? As for question (a), there are features that have to be expressed and some that do not have to. Negatives are needed but a dual number is not. Although von der Gabelentz says in (1) that the 'affixes grind themselves down, disappear without a trace [and that] their functions or similar ones ... require new expression', this requirement is not quite correct for all grammatical features. As for (b), it is well-known that some change is just slow or stops. An example is negative reinforcement in present-day English. Possible reasons for non-renewal are prescriptive pressures present in a particular society. As for (c), it has been documented that certain light verbs remain consistently stable (Butt and Lahiri 2013) and light nouns, such as *pair of* and *couple of* again consistently remain nominal (Wood 2013). The reason may be that certain semantic features cannot be reanalysed further (see Talmy 2001).

References

Adams, M. 1987. 'From Old French to the theory of Pro-drop', *Natural Language and Linguistic Theory* 5: 1–32.

Baker, M. 2008. *The syntax of agreement and concord*. Cambridge University Press.

Bopp, F. 1816. *Über das Conjugationssystem der Sanskritsprache in Vergleichung mit jenem der griechischen, lateinischen, persischen und germanischen Sprachen*. Frankfurt-am-Main.

Butt, M. and Lahiri, A. 2013. 'Diachronic pertinacity of light verbs', *Lingua* 135: 7–29.

Chomsky, N. 1965. *Aspects of the theory of syntax*. Cambridge, MA: MIT Press.
  1966. *Topics in the theory of generative grammar*. Berlin: Mouton.
  1995. *The minimalist program*. Cambridge, MA: MIT Press.
  2001. 'Derivation by phase', in M. Kenstowicz (ed.), *Ken Hale: A life in language*. Cambridge, MA: MIT Press, pp. 1-53.
  2007. 'Approaching UG from below', in H.-M. Gärtner and U. Sauerland (eds.), *Interface + Recursion = Language? Chomsky's minimalism and the view from syntax and semantics*. Berlin: Mouton de Gruyter, pp. 1–29.

Condillac, E. B. de 1746. *Essai sur lórigine des connaissances humaines*. Paris.

Crowley, T. 1992. *An introduction to historical linguistics*, 2nd edn. Oxford University Press.

Dahl, O. 2001. 'Inflationary effects in language and elsewhere', in J. Bybee and P. Hopper (eds.), *Frequency and the emergence of linguistic structure*. Amsterdam: John Benjamins, pp. 471–80.

Evers, A. 1975. 'The transformational cycle in Dutch and German', unpublished PhD thesis, University of Utrecht.

Franzén, T. 1939. *Etude sur la syntaxe des pronoms personnels sujets en ancien français*. Uppsala: Almqvist & Wiksell.

Gabelentz, G. von der [1891] 1901. *Die Sprachwissenshaft: Ihre Aufgaben, Methoden und bisherigen Ergebnisse*, 2nd edn. Leipzig: Weigel (reprint Tübingen: Narr 1972).

Givón, T. 1971. 'Historical syntax and synchronic morphology', *Chicago Linguistic Society Proceedings* 7: 394–415.

1976. 'Topic, pronoun, and grammatical agreement', in C. N. Li (ed.), *Subject and topic*. New York: Academic Press, pp. 151–88.

2011. *Ute reference grammar*. Amsterdam: John Benjamins.

Greenberg, J. 1954. 'A quantitative approach to the morphological typology of language', in R. Spencer (ed.), *Method and perspective in anthropology*. Minneapolis: University of Minnesota, pp. 192–220.

1978. 'How does a language acquire gender markers?', in J. Greenberg (ed.), *Universals of human language*, vol. 3. Stanford University Press, pp. 47–82.

Haas, M. 1946. 'A grammatical sketch of Tunica', in H. Hoijer (ed.), *Linguistic structures of native America*. New York: Viking, pp. 337–66.

Harris, M. 1978. *The evolution of French syntax*. London: Longman.

Heine, B., Claudi, U. and Hünnemeyer, F. 1991. *Grammaticalization: A conceptual framework*. University of Chicago Press.

Heine, B. and Kuteva, T. 2005. *Language contact and grammatical change*. Cambridge University Press.

Hengeveld, K. 1992. *Non-verbal Predication*. Berlin: Mouton de Gruyter.

Hodge, C. 1970. 'The linguistic cycle', *Linguistic Sciences*: 13: 1–7.

Hoeksema, J. 2009. 'Jespersen recycled', in van Gelderen (ed.), pp. 15–34.

Hopper, M. and Traugott, E. 2003. *Grammaticalization*. Cambridge University Press.

Humboldt, W. von 1836. *Über die Verschiedenheit des menschlichen Sprachbaus und seinen Einfluss auf die geistige Entwicklung des Menschengeschlechts*.

Ingham, R. and Larrivée, P. (eds.) 2011. *The evolution of negation: Beyond the Jespersen Cycle*. Berlin: Mouton de Gruyter.

Jespersen, O. 1917. *Negation in English and other languages*. Copenhagen: A. F. Høst (reprinted 1966).

1922. *Language*. London: Allen & Unwin.

Katz, A. 1996. 'Cyclical grammaticalization and the cognitive link between pronoun and copula', unpublished PhD thesis, Rice University.

Kiparsky, P. 2011. 'Grammaticalization as optimization', in D. Jonas, J. Whitman and A. Garrett (eds.), *Grammatical change origins, nature, outcomes*. Oxford University Press, pp. 15–51.

Kiparsky, P. and Condoravdi, C. 2006. 'Tracking Jespersen's Cycle', in M. Janse, B. Joseph and A. Ralli (eds.), *Proceedings of the 2nd international conference of modern Greek dialects and linguistic theory*. Mytilene: Doukas, pp. 172–97.

Labov, W. 1972. *Language in the inner city*. University of Philadelphia Press.

Lambrecht, K. 1981. *Topic, antitopic, and verb agreement in non standard French*. Amsterdam: John Benjamins.

Larrivée, P. 2010. 'The pragmatic motifs of the Jespersen Cycle: Default, activation, and the history of negation in French', *Lingua* 120(9): 2240–58.

Lehmann, C. 1982 [1995]. *Thoughts on grammaticalization*. Munich: Lincom.
  1985. 'Grammaticalization: Synchronic variation and diachronic change', *Lingua e stile* 20(3): 303–18.

Li, C. and Thompson, S. 1977. 'A mechanism for the development of copula morphemes', in C. N. Li (ed.), *Mechanisms of syntactic change*. Austin: University of Texas Press, pp. 414–44.

Loprieno, A. 1995. *Ancient Egyptian*. Cambridge University Press.
  2001. 'From Ancient Egyptian to Coptic', in M. Haspelmath, E. König, W. Oesterreicher and W. Raible (eds.), *Language typology and language universals: An international handbook*, vol. 2. Berlin: de Gruyter.

Meillet, A. [1912] 1921. 'L'évolution des formes grammaticales', in E. Champion (ed.), *Linguistique historique et linguistique générale*. Paris: Librairie Ancienne Honoré Champion, pp.130–48 (reprinted 1958).

Nesselhauf, N. 2012. 'Mechanisms of language change in a functional system: The recent semantic evolution of English future time expressions', *Journal of Historical Linguistics* 2(1): 83–132.

Nevalainen, T. and Traugott, E. (eds.) 2012. *Oxford handbook on historical English linguistics*. Oxford University Press.

Pustet, R. 2003. *Copulas: Universals in the categorization of the lexicon*. Oxford University Press.

Roberts, I. 1993. *Verbs and diachronic syntax*. Dordrecht: Kluwer.
  2009. 'Grammaticalization, the clausal hierarchy, and semantic bleaching', in G. Trousdale and E. Traugott (eds.), *Gradience, gradualness, and grammaticalization*. Amsterdam: John Benjamins, pp. 45–73.

Roberts, I. and Roussou, A. 2003. *Syntactic change: A minimalist approach to grammaticalization*. Cambridge University Press.

Robins, R. H. 1967. *A short history of linguistics*. London: Longman.

Schlegel, A. W. von 1818. *Observations sur la langue et la littérature provençales*. Paris.

Schwegler, A. 1990. *Analyticity and syntheticity*. Berlin: Mouton de Gruyter.

Stassen, L. 1997. *Intransitive predication*. Oxford University Press.

Talmy, L. 2001. *Toward a cognitive semantics*, 2 vols. Cambridge, MA: MIT Press.

Tauli, V. 1958. *The structural tendencies of languages*. Helsinki.

1966. *Structural tendencies in Uralic languages*. The Hague: Mouton.

Tooke, J. H. 1786–1805. *The viversion of Purley*. London.

Traugott, E. C. and Heine, B. 1991. *Grammaticalization*. Amsterdam: John Benjamins.

van der Auwera, J. 2009. 'The Jespersen cycles', in van Gelderen (ed.), pp. 35–71.

van Gelderen, E. 2000. *A history of English reflexive pronouns*. Amsterdam: John Benjamins.

2004. *Grammaticalization as economy*. Amsterdam: John Benjamins.

2008. 'Where did late Merge go? Grammaticalization as feature economy', *Studia Linguistica* 62(3): 287–300.

(ed.) 2009. *Cyclical change*. Amsterdam: John Benjamins.

2011. *The linguistic cycle*. Oxford University Press.

2013. 'The linguistic cycle and the language faculty', *Language and Linguistics Compass* 7: 233–50.

(ed.) 2016. *Cyclical change continued*. Amsterdam: John Benjamins.

Vance, B. 1997. *Syntactic change in Medieval French*. Dordrecht: Kluwer.

Willis, D., Lucas, C. and Breitbarth. A. (eds.) 2013. *The history of negation in the languages of Europe and the Mediterranean*. Oxford University Press.

Wood, J. 2013. 'Quantity nouns and grammaticalisation: Language change and *couple* and *pair*', unpublished MS.

Zribi-Hertz, A. 1994. 'La syntaxe des clitiques nominatifs', *Travaux de Linguistique et Litterature* 32: 131–47.

Part V

Explanations

23

Endogenous and Exogenous Theories of Syntactic Change

David Willis

23.1 Introduction

Historical linguists seeking explanations for syntactic innovation (actuation) in the process of transmission of syntactic systems from one generation to the next encounter the paradox that whatever grammatical property is undergoing change must have been acquired successfully by children in the not too distant past (see also Chapter 18, this volume). If conditions for successful acquisition were present then and if children are swift and efficient acquirers of language, as much research in language acquisition suggests, then it is puzzling why faithful transmission of such a system should have failed to occur. This core question, the logical problem of language change, is particularly central to the standard generative model, which assumes that language change is the result of transmission failure (see discussion in Chapter 24, this volume). It is also of importance to more traditional approaches, which must also address the question of causation in syntactic change, and is central to the actuation question (see Chapter 19, this volume). This chapter looks at different possible solutions to this problem focusing on various approaches which locate the motivation for change with:

- (i) spontaneous innovation;
- (ii) alteration in conditions of acquisition by language use;
- (iii) alteration in conditions of acquisition by other linguistic changes (including typological accounts);
- (iv) imperfect acquisition due to delayed onset or limited access;
- (v) alteration in conditions of acquisition due to coexistence of more than one grammatical system (including speech of non-native speakers).

Any or all of these could be valid scenarios for change and they may exist in combination (for instance, (ii) may be argued to lead to immediate change or may require further random events in the form of (i)). They are arranged broadly from endogenous approaches to exogeneous ones. However, which of them would be classed as 'endogenous' or 'exogenous', and under what conditions, depends on what exactly is meant by 'endogenous' and 'exogenous' approaches to change. This is not as straightforward as may at first appear, since both these terms raise the question 'endogenous or exogenous to what?' Possible answers include 'to the language', 'to the dialect', 'to the speech community', 'to the linguistic system', 'to syntax' and 'to the individual'. Which of these answers is chosen has an enormous impact on whether an account should be classified as 'endogenous' or 'exogenous', and 'internal' or 'external' (cf. discussion by Gerritsen and Stein 1992: 7; Fischer 2007: 30f.), and even whether endogenous change exists at all.

Scenario (i) might be considered the endogenous scenario *par excellence*, since change is motivated purely by some property of the grammatical system itself: by acquisitional ambiguity (see Chapter 18, this volume), by syntactic analogy or extension (see Chapter 5, this volume), or by typological considerations (see Chapter 30, this volume), all of which would traditionally be considered language-internal, endogenous motivations for change. On the other hand, scenario (v), which invokes contact with other languages (see Chapter 8, this volume), would traditionally be considered a language-external, exogenous account of change. However, even canonical endogenous scenarios may be catalyzed by language contact: syntactic analogy may be favoured if the input to acquisition is limited by the presence of another language in the community, and typologically driven change may be the product of language use (production or processing considerations).

In this chapter, we explore various types of explanation from the perspective of the exogenous–endogenous dichotomy. We will mainly (with the exception of multiple actuation) be dealing in this chapter with innovation (actuation and the conditions that lead up to it) rather than transmission or diffusion of innovations (on which, see Chapter 24, this volume).

23.2 Spontaneous Innovation

The classic model of syntactic innovation, as outlined in Harris and Campbell (1995), sees change as initiated by reanalysis of a structure open to two possible analyses during acquisition (see further Chapters 4 and 18, this volume), which we can term 'acquisitional ambiguity' to distinguish it from syntactic or semantic ambiguity, where two interpretations are available to adult speakers. While this approach seeks triggers for change, seeing it, for instance, sometimes as a reaction to other, often non-syntactic, changes or to language contact, and therefore interacts closely with phenomena discussed in §23.4 and §23.5 below, it does not presuppose that change takes place 'only when necessary' (Lightfoot 1979: 124). For this reason, it is treated separately here, being the most endogenous scenario on all conceptions of change.

On this view, there are preconditions for innovation, in that the potential for reanalysis or analogical extension must exist, but that potential need not lead to innovation, either immediately or indeed ever. This leads to perhaps the dominant position in work on syntactic change, and language change more generally, namely that we cannot predict change: all we can do is establish the limits on possible change, setting out the possible pathways that a given linguistic system may go down, and perhaps their relative likelihood, but we cannot state the precise circumstances under which each of those possible futures will materialize (Harris 1984).

An argument that potential innovations do not always turn into actual innovations comes from the fact that languages diverge from one another via syntactic dialect (and hence language) splits (Harris and Campbell 1995: 5). It is unlikely that such splits can always be attributed to the differential impact of syntax-external factors (sound change or language contact affecting only one region) or to limits imposed on diffusion of innovation by social or geographic boundaries. In fact, the view that a potential reanalysis is inevitable once the conditions for it have arisen would suggest that social or geographic boundaries are irrelevant: it would diffuse by being rapidly (re-)innovated wherever the preconditions for it have arisen, but this does not always seem to happen in practice.

A standard example where a purely endogenous approach postulating spontaneous change might be adopted is the reanalysis of *for ... to* in Middle English to create a complementizer marking Case on subjects in non-finite clauses. The standard account, criticized sharply by Garrett (2012: 55–66), claims that *for ... to* arose from the following reanalysis in the early sixteenth century (Fischer 1992: 330–4; Fischer, van Kemenade, Koopman and van der Wurff 2000: 214–20):

(1)   PREDICATE [$_{PP}$ [$_P$ *for*] NP] [$_{TP}$ *to* VP] => PREDICATE [$_{CP}$ [$_C$ *for*] [$_{TP}$ NP *to* VP]]

(2)   It is bad [$_{PP}$ for you] [$_{TP}$ to smoke] => It is bad [$_{CP}$ for [$_{TP}$ you to [$_{VP}$ smoke]]]

Under this reanalysis, a new item, complementizer *for*, is created, distinct from the homophonous preposition. This reanalysis can be identified once its effects begin to be seen, for instance, in the appearance of examples containing non-finite clauses not selected by a benefactive predicate taking a beneficiary marked by *for* (for full discussion and exemplification, see §4.3), as with the example in (3), where the *for ... to* clause follows *than*.

(3)   ... no better remedy or deuise can be found, than [$_{CP}$ [$_C$ for] [$_{TP}$ you to aspire & seeke the Kings fauor and seruice]]

(1567, William Painter, *The palace of pleasure*, vol. II, cited by Garrett 2012: 57)

The acquisitional ambiguity arises only in Middle English: benefactives had typically been expressed with preverbal dative-marked noun phrases in Old English, and these could be parsed accurately with the beneficiary as an argument of the main-clause verb. While Fischer (1992: 332–4) notes syntactic changes (such as fixing of SVO word order) that may have aided the reanalysis of *for*, these only serve to remove obstacles to reanalysis, reducing clear evidence in favour of the older structure. That is, such an account shows how acquisitional ambiguity arose. On this type of approach, once acquisitional ambiguity has arisen, reanalysis becomes a possibility at any time, but is never required. Such approaches are often criticized as lacking explanatory power in failing to explain why the reanalysis actually happens and why it happens when it does (De Smet 2009; Garrett 2012). However, if misparsing by children (leading to reanalysis) is distributed randomly in the population (perhaps with some social contexts, such as population mixing, favouring it), it would be pointless to expect more.

23.3   Typological Approaches

Approaches grounded in language typology also offer the prospect of endogenous innovation, depending on the explanations assumed for the typological generalizations themselves. Such approaches, in the spirit of Greenberg (1963) (see Chapter 30, this volume), place synchronic restrictions on the ways in which languages may combine features, and therefore make system-based predictions about possible and impossible changes. A tradition going back to Lehmann (1973) treats cross-categorical word-order harmony as a target at which all languages 'aim'. This may be instantiated either as a drive towards consistent head-initial order (verbs before their objects, and nouns before their adjectives, possessors, demonstrative, numerals and relative clauses) or towards its exact inverse, consistent head-final order. On this approach the need to achieve more consistent word order across categories is itself a motivation for change. In its most extreme form, such work claimed that languages with disharmonic word order were drifting towards a particular (consistent) word-order type. For instance, English has been drifting from an OV to a VO typology (Vennemann 1975; for further discussion see also §11.5.1, §20.4, §21.3.3). Innovation of postnominal *of*-phrases (*the king of England*), which spread at the expense of prenominal morphological genitives (*England's king*), would thus be attributed to typological drift towards harmonic VO word order (noun–genitive order being harmonic with

VO and genitive–noun order being harmonic with OV; see also discussion in §25.3.2). The changes associated with such drifts may take place over an extended, in fact, indefinite, period of time: the drift that has been observed for English can be traced as far back as Proto-Indo-European and is still far from complete. This means that, at best, this kind of typological approach offers only a pathway for change: it sets out what the possible next changes in word order may be, but does not specify when, or even if, they will actually occur. The individual changes that are permitted occur spontaneously as described in §23.2 above, the drive for cross-categorial harmony creating the possibility of change, but not requiring it.

Typological approaches have been used to propose a connection between case and word order, based around Greenberg's Universal 41 (see also discussion in §30.2):

(4)   Universal 41

> If in a language the verb follows both the nominal subject and nominal object as the dominant order, the language almost always has a case system.   *(Greenberg 1963: 59)*

Vennemann (1975: 287f.) generalizes this universal to make the claim that, if an OV language (typically an SOV language) loses its case system, it changes to a VO language (typically an SVO language). The shift in word order here is endogenously motivated (although of course the original loss of case may be due to any number of factors, including exogenous ones due to language contact). The crucial claim is that, with no other change to the grammar, the loss of case will make SOV either unlearnable or unusable for acquirers and speakers. Viewed from a purely system-based perspective, this approach is endogenous, but it makes little sense on its own, since it does not offer any cause for the change beyond the word-order correlation itself. So, if the correlation does hold (which is itself debatable), then there must be a mechanism that enacts it.

Vennemann (1975: 288f.) himself proposed that caseless SOV languages were difficult to use, because, in a number of environments, it was unclear whether an element was a subject or an object (effectively a recourse to language use, see §23.4). For instance, the noun phrases and relative markers in the SOV German relative clause in (5) are all ambiguous between nominative and accusative, leaving the example as a whole also ambiguous, between a subject and an object relative:

(5)   die   Mutter, die   ihre   Tochter   liebt (German)
        the   mother   REL.FSG her   daughter   loves
        'the mother who loves her daughter', 'the mother whom her daughter loves'

Vennemann proposed that language users can resolve such ambiguity by appending a clarificatory clause at the right edge of the sentence, leading to postverbal clausal constituents. This order is subsequently generalized to nouns by the Principle of Natural Serialization, which states that languages prefer consistent (harmonic) orders across different operator–operand (effectively, head–modifier) pairs. Thus, if clausal complements follow their verbs, then direct objects preferentially do so too. Implementation of this principle is essentially spontaneous on this approach, symmetry being inherently valued by linguistic systems (although the 'why'-question remains).

Hawkins (1983: 211) proposes Universal Consistency in History, namely the principle that 'at each stage in their historical evolution, languages remain consistent with implicational universals derived from current synchronic evidence'. Given a typological implicational universal of the form 'if a language has property P, then it has property Q' (P ⊃ Q), then a language that has neither property may not gain P without either previously or simultaneously gaining Q (Hawkins 1983: 211; 1990b: 97–9). That is, the two diachronies represented schematically in (6) and (7) are both permitted, while the one in (8) is disallowed, because the intermediate state P&-Q (starred) is disallowed by the synchronic universal.

(6)   -P&-Q > -P&Q > P&Q

(7)   -P&-Q > P&Q

(8)   -P&-Q > *P&-Q > P&Q

Thus, given Universal 3, 'Languages with dominant VSO order are always prepositional' (Greenberg 1963: 45), a VSO language may not develop a postposition directly: for whatever reason, speakers or acquirers will never find the reanalysis [[NP noun] adverb] > [PP [NP noun] postposition] appealing. If postpositions are to develop, the language must switch to SVO or some other basic word-order type first.

Consider a concrete example. Among many other complex implicational universals, Hawkins proposes Postp ⊃ (AN ⊃ GN), that is, 'if a language has postpositions, then, if the adjective precedes the noun, then the genitive precedes the noun' (Hawkins 1983: 67f.). He notes that German innovated some postpositions in the sixteenth century, thereby activating this universal, and uses this to motivate an increase in the frequency of genitives preposed to their nouns at that period (Hawkins 1983: 228). The connection between these changes thereby receives a typological, endogenous motivation (at least in so far as the initial innovation of postpositions is considered to be endogenous).

More recently, the Final-over-Final constraint (FOFC; Biberauer, Sheehan and Newton 2010) works in a similar way to restrict possible diachronies, this time by stating that, if a language changes from head-final to head-initial word order, it must follow the pathway in (9), and if it changes from head-initial to head-final order, it must follow exactly the reverse pathway (for further details, see §19.2.1).

(9)   [[[O V] Aux] C] → [C [[O V] Aux]] → [C [Aux [O V]]] → [C [Aux [V O]]]

Thus, English has changed from OV to VO within the verb phrase and from VP–Aux to Aux–VP within the auxiliary phrase (TP), thereby undergoing the final two transitions in (9). FOFC constrains these changes, so the change in auxiliary order must have been innovated earlier and must always have been more advanced that the change in verb–object order, as indeed the historical record of English confirms.

Stated purely in terms of typology of linguistic systems (a change is permitted or prevented because typological universals require this, or a change is motivated by a language's 'desire' to conform to principles of word-order harmony), these are radically endogenous approaches. However, almost all linguists working within this framework have accepted that, while typology may restrict the possible pathways of change, it does not offer any form of explanation unless the universals themselves can be independently motivated (see Hawkins 1990b: 99). Depending on the form this motivation takes, this may make the approach exogenous, at least on some interpretations of the term. Hawkins (1990a, 1994) provides a processing explanation for harmony across different word-order types, arguing that such harmony promotes efficient, early parsing. This effectively means that typology acts as a selection pressure on innovations: children are more likely to or will only posit innovations that result in more efficient parsing, and once they have entered the grammar, the structures produced by these innovations, being more easily processed, will be used more frequently, ultimately driving out the former structures and the grammatical settings that produced them. Conversely, child hypotheses that lead to less efficient parsing will be rapidly rejected.

FOFC, on the other hand, is proposed by Biberauer, Sheehan and Newton (2010: 41) to be part of Universal Grammar, although they also consider the possibility that it might be a processing preference of the same kind that Hawkins proposed, or an extra-linguistic, economy-oriented 'third factor' (Chomsky 2005). If the first interpretation is followed, FOFC would effectively be a cognitive constraint on hypotheses that children could construct about their language. Thus, in the case of Old English, children, having established that their language had VP–Aux order, would simply not consider the possibility that the object might precede the verb within the verb phrase, preventing any innovation in this domain. Conversely, if children were to posit basic VO order for their language early on, this would prevent them from considering VP–Aux as a possible order, leading them to innovate Aux–VP or else to grammaticalize the auxiliary as a suffix.

This is a possible approach to the grammaticalization of the future in Romance (for general discussion of the innovation, see Fleischman 1982; Pinkster 1987; Roberts 1993a; Roberts and Roussou 2003: 48–58; Ledgeway 2012: 134–40). Late Latin made use of a modal periphrasis using the auxiliary *habere* 'have' and an infinitive in the order VP-Aux, for instance *amare habeo* 'I shall love, I am to love', formally [$_{TP}$ [$_{VP}$ *amare*] [$_T$ *habeo*]]. With the fixing of verbal word order as VO in Romance, this structure would become unacquirable, since, if the verb phrase is head-initial, it violates FOFC. However, sequences of this type would necessarily be present in the adult varieties to which children were exposed. Treating the sequence as a single morphologically complex word, thereby innovating an inflected future, would be a natural response to make sense of these sequences in some other way. The result is a radically endogenous (and deterministic, rather than probabilistic) account of the innovation, this time making reference only to other syntactic change and to typological principles (FOFC), on this account encoded in Universal Grammar.

23.4 Language Use

The interaction of language with its conditions of use features prominently in work on grammaticalization (see Chapter 1, this volume), and depending on one's conception of language, may be considered an endogenous or an exogenous account. In work on grammaticalization, frequent use of an expression is claimed to lead to its entrenchment and conventionalization and thus to the loss of internal structure. We see this in the emergence of new quantifiers such as *a bit of* or *a lot of* in English (Traugott 2008), which have plausibly undergone the reanalysis [$_{NP}$ *a lot* [$_{PP}$ *of* [NP]]] > [$_{QP}$ [$_Q$ *a-lot-of*] [NP]]. This reanalysis is favoured by speakers' frequent use of the sequence in exactly this form (without additional modifiers). Once this sequence is rarely varied and of high frequency, acquirers may acquire it as a single unit (constructionalization within Construction Grammar, see discussion of functionalist approaches in §1.3.2 and in Chapter 31 this volume, or simply lexicalization in other approaches) and organize their syntactic structures to match. This process is likely to be probabilistic in the sense that it is not inevitable, merely favoured by certain conditions. Semantic processes (metaphor, conventionalization of implicature) may also bias acquirers away from a compositional analysis where *a lot of* is derived from the noun *lot*.

The 'afterthought' phenomenon has been implicated in mediating the transition from SOV to SVO by increasing the frequency of apparent SVO to a point where it is acquired as a basic pattern rather than being dismissed as a performance error (Gerritsen and Stein 1992: 4). Hyman (1975) proposed such a process as the mechanism by which SOV word order developed into SVO in certain Niger-Congo languages (Yoruba, Igbo, etc.). Afterthought is exemplified in (10), from Kru, a language which has undergone the shift, but retains SOV in negative clauses:

(10) Kru (Hyman 1975: 126)

ɔ́ sé súa tɛ̀, táì kɔ̀
he NEG fish buy and rice
'He did not buy fish ... and rice.'

Failure to establish the performance-related nature of sentences like this could lead acquirers to posit a basic SVO grammar. Such an approach externalizes the explanation for change, shifting it from purely system-internal (typological) to language use.

Even within generative approaches, frequency of use may be invoked as the lead-up to changes in core grammatical properties, as a way that the primary linguistic data for language acquisition may change, without any change in the grammar. Thus, in accounting for the loss of verb-second (V2) in French, Roberts (1993b: 145–8) argues that the set of adverbs that were exceptions to V2 rose during the Middle French period, increasing the frequency of word orders where the verb superficially appeared in third position or later (V>2) from under 5% to 10–15%. Crucially 'children acquiring the French of the first quarter of the 15th century would be exposed to significantly more occurrences of the order Adv XP V than the children of one or two centuries previously' (Roberts 1993b: 148). This allows an essentially deterministic non-spontaneous approach to be maintained, with change nevertheless ultimately attributed to a non-systematic development external to the core grammar.

23.5 Syntactic Change Induced by Other Linguistic Levels

It has long been clear that syntactic change may be the by-product of changes in other parts of the linguistic system, whether phonological, morphological, semantic or pragmatic (see further Chapter 26, this volume). We have seen this in chains of changes suggested already (e.g. innovation of postpositions in German leads to a rise in frequency of preposed genitives; see §23.3 above). Such chains may link different syntactic changes, but may also cross boundaries between linguistic levels.

The impact of sound change on syntax is particularly profound, and will be used here to exemplify this general approach. It may be thought of as an exogenous impact, if we think of syntax as an autonomous system. Sound change also ultimately provides a link to physiological and acoustic factors in language change. These may favour certain sound changes, with unexpected ramifications for syntax.

Sound change may trigger syntactic change either directly, or indirectly through its impact on morphology. Instances where phonological erosion or merger has led to the loss of morphological distinctions used in the syntax are numerous. The general direction of sound change is towards the loss of distinctions, which then has morphosyntactic repercussions: 'Every morphological system is destroyed in time by phonological change' (Vennemann 1975: 293).

Such change reflects the drift towards analyticity (Sapir 1921: 157–82) that is observed to a greater or lesser extent in the histories of many Indo-European languages. For instance, loss of unstressed word-final vowels eroded the Old English case system, which was then lost over several centuries, although the sound changes in and of themselves are not sufficient to bring this about entirely. Traditionally, the development in Middle English of nominative experiencers, (12) developing out of (11), and of indirect passives, as in the modern (14) in place of the Old English pattern with topicalization of the indirect object in (13), is accounted for in this way (Jespersen 1927; Lightfoot 1999).

(11)   Old English (Jespersen 1927: 209)
Þam   cynge   licodon   peran.
the.DAT   king.DAT.SG   like.PST.3PL   pears.NOM
'The king liked pears.'

(12)   The king (SUBJ) liked (SG) pears (OBJ).

(13)   Old English (Allen 1995: 2)
Him   wæs   holpen.
he.DAT   be.PST.3SG   help.PST.PTCP
'He was helped.'

(14)   He was helped.

While many verbs assigned an oblique case to their experiencers in Old English, loss of distinctiveness in the case system meant that learners could not reliably identify the case of these experiencers, and they were reanalysed as nominative. Similarly, the merger of dative and accusative allowed former datives to become the target of passivization.

Although in such cases, one might consider the ultimate cause of the sound change or loss of case to be exogenous (if, for instance, it was triggered or catalyzed by Norse contact), this scenario is essentially endogenous to the linguistic system as a whole, although not to the syntax. Whether the change is deterministic, in the sense that these conditions are sufficient to predict it, is unclear. Lightfoot (1991: 124) takes a fairly deterministic line, stating that 'because the linguistic environment at some point ceased to distinguish accusative and dative, oblique case was no longer triggered', leading to the various consequences outlined above. However, there was still plenty of evidence for learners to correctly acquire the system, which leads to the conclusion that erosion of case morphology increased the probability of change, but did not force it at any given time. Furthermore, as argued extensively by Allen (1995), the reinterpretation of the syntax of dative experiencers was a drawn-out process showing significant differences between individual verbs, again calling into question the role of loss of case morphology as a sufficient condition for change.

Simply declaring the change to be part of the 'drift to analyticity', using drift in the technical sense of 'the unconscious selection on the part of its speakers of those individual variations that are cumulative in some special direction' which may be inferred from the past history of the language (Sapir 1921: 166), is no explanation either, since it raises the question of what motivates the drift in the first place. Parallel problems arise in the use of similar explanations in the histories of other branches of Indo-European (Romance, Celtic, South Slavic, etc.); see Harris (1978) and Ledgeway (2012: 10–28) for discussion of the Romance case.

The role of phonological change is less controversial in the case of the loss of the verb-second rule of Welsh. Middle Welsh had a V2-system in which particles (glossed as PRT below), positioned immediately before and proclitic to the verb, identified the preverbal element that counted as the first element for V2. For instance, when the first element is a subject, as in (15), the particle *a* appears, but, when it is an adverbial, as in (16), the particle *y(d)* appears.

(15) Middle Welsh (Willis 1998: 51)
      A' r   ederyn a   doeth y 'r   ynys   honn.
      and the bird   PRT came to the   island   this
      'And the bird came to this island.'

(16) Middle Welsh (Willis 1998: 51)
      Yn Hardlech y   bydwch   seith   mlyned ar ginyaw ...
      In Harlech   PRT   be.FUT.2PL seven   years   at dinner
      'In Harlech you will be at dinner for seven years ... '

These particles were crucial to identification and acquisition of the V2-system, because, unlike in modern V2 languages such as German, V3, V4 and indeed V5 orders regularly occurred, when adverbials preceded the verb in addition to the topic. The particles nevertheless identified these structures as unambiguously forming part of the V2-system. Thus, in (17), the particle *a* identifies the topic as a subject, the only other preverbal element being an adverbial adjunct that is optionally ignored for the purposes of calculating V2.

(17)   Middle Welsh (Willis 1998: 59)
        Hir bylgeint   Guydyon   a   gyuodes.
        early.morning   Gwydion   PRT   get.up.PST.3SG
        'Early next morning, Gwydion got up.'

These particles merged phonologically in speech in the sixteenth century as schwa, before being eroded entirely. Willis (1998, 2007) argues that, without the help of the particles, acquisition of the V2 system became impossible, because the cases in (16) and (17) could no longer be distinguished. Acquirers hypothesized that (16) was a VSO clause with an initial optional adverbial, and took this as evidence that the language allowed VSO main clauses. Other parallel changes leading to the postulation of basic VSO word order in main clauses, such as the reanalysis of expletive subject pronouns as affirmative particles, can also be attributed to this ultimately phonological source.

Finally, one may note the role of erosion of verbal endings in the loss of null subjects in many Indo-European languages. Phonological change often leads to the loss of distinctions within the verbal paradigm (rich verbal agreement). While it is tempting to link loss of agreement in a deterministic way to the loss of null subjects, Falk (1993) shows that, during the period in the sixteenth century when Swedish was losing null subjects, there was no direct correlation between the verb having a rich agreement form in a given sentence and there being a null subject in the same sentence (see also Roberts (1993b) and Vance (1997) on the loss of null subjects in the history of French). While the general dependence is clear, the diachronic relationship does not seem to be direct and deterministic.

23.6 Language-External Exogenous Approaches

So far we have considered 'exogenous' approaches that are external to syntax or to the construction under consideration, but nevertheless internal to the language. Traditionally, exogenous explanations have been understood above all to refer to explanations that cite language contact as the main motivating factor in a change (see Chapter 8, this volume). Linguists have argued as to whether a given syntactic change should be explained as due to language contact or whether a more endogenous account is to be preferred, witness, for instance, the vigorous debate, summarized and evaluated by van der Auwera and Genee (2002), on whether the development of *do*-support in English is best attributed to any one of a number of language-internal hypotheses or to the substrate effect of Brythonic Celtic (see also discussion in §3.4, §11.5.3, §18.4, §20.4).

There has been a tendency to think of this type of exogenous explanation as a last resort, to be admitted only when no strictly endogenous account can be constructed. On this view, an exogenous explanation may be rejected on the grounds that similar changes have occurred in other languages without evidence of contact, or that there is no exact parallel between the structures in the donor and recipient languages. Such logic would lead one, for instance, to deny the significance of language contact with German for the current tendency towards grammaticalization of an indefinite article based on the numeral 'one' in Czech, Slovene and Upper Sorbian (Reindl 2008: 133–5), since indefinite articles regularly emerge in precisely this way in the absence of contact. An endogenous explanation in terms of language use is thus readily available. Nevertheless, it is telling that only Slavic languages that are in contact with German are undergoing the change.

Lass (1997: 209) exemplifies this position, stating that 'in the absence of evidence, an endogenous explanation of a phenomenon is more parsimonious, because endogenous change *must* occur in any case, whereas borrowing is never necessary'. Parsimony, however, operates at the theoretical level (see Lucas 2009: 38–43), and no linguist would deny that some changes are attributable to language contact and that contact must therefore be included in any list of mechanisms of syntactic change (see Chapter 8, this volume). This is particularly evident when language contact exerts a pressure that directly contradicts a more endogenous factor, as with the shift of some Ethiopian Semitic languages from VSO to SOV under Cushitic influence in violation of their own general typology (Leslau 1945). Denying its role in a given instance does not therefore make one's theory of change more parsimonious.

At the other extreme, Meisel (2011) and Meisel, Rinke and Elsig (2013) have proposed that all core syntactic change (all syntactic change that can be judged parametric) is exogenous. They take the position that core grammatical properties (parameters) of a language are always perfectly acquired provided that children are exposed solely to the output of native speakers of it. They suggest that this is true irrespective of whether the children themselves are monolingual or bilingual, explicitly claiming that 'neither structural ambiguity nor the frequency of occurrence of certain constructions proved to be a sufficient condition triggering changes of core properties of grammars' (Meisel, Rinke and Elsig 2013: 171). This leads to the position that syntactic change can occur only when non-native (L2) speakers form a substantial part of the speech community and when therefore a substantial part of the input to acquisition comes from such speakers. It makes the clear, if controversial, claim that monolingual children can never introduce an innovation to a core grammatical feature of their language. They ultimately conclude that 'core grammatical change requires the agency of L2 learners' (Meisel, Rinke and Elsig 2013: 182).

This approach leads to the problem that, superficially at least, languages undergo changes in their core grammatical properties where second-language acquisition is not suspected of being involved. Meisel, Rinke and Elsig argue that these lie outside the core grammar. For instance, they consider the loss of V2 in French not to involve such a core feature. Instead, they argue that Old/Middle French was not a true V2 language, hence 'loss' of V2 is merely a change in the frequency of different word-order patterns brought about by changes in the pragmatic associations of those patterns. This saves us from being forced to attribute it to indepen-dent lexical changes impacting on frequency of use of certain word-order patterns as Roberts (1993b) does (see §23.4 above). Similarly, the loss of null subjects in French is treated as a decline in the frequency of null subjects brought about by a change in the pragmatic status of subject pronouns.

The idea that Old French was not a V2 language, but merely exhibited isolated V2 phenomena, has been defended elsewhere, for instance, by Kaiser (2002) and Sitaridou (2012). However, this still leaves us a long way from being able to confidently assert that all cases of loss of V2 can be dismissed in the same way, let alone all instances of core syntactic change where there is no obvious evidence of exogenous causation. For instance, it is unlikely that the loss of V2 in Welsh, attributed above all to a response to phonological change in §23.5 above, would be amenable to such a reinterpretation.

23.7 Inertia: A Construction-External Exogenous Approach

A less extreme exogenous approach is the Inertia Principle (Longobardi 2001; see also Chapter 20, this volume), which takes exogenous to mean 'exogenous to the syntactic feature undergoing change', and sets very strict limits on syntactic change (understood as changes in the formal, non-phonetic, non-semantic features of items listed in the lexicon):

> syntactic change should not arise, unless it can be shown to be *caused* – that is, to be a well-motivated consequence of other types of change (phonological changes and semantic changes, including the appearance/disappearance of whole lexical items) or, recursively, of other syntactic changes. *(Longobardi 2001: 278)*

Longobardi specifically rejects any probabilistic element to syntactic change and assumes a deterministic language acquisition device (LAD), stating that 'no such things as "imperfect" learning or "spontaneous" innovation would exist in syntax' (Longobardi 2001: 278).

This approach builds on Keenan's (2002) concept of inertia:

(18) Things stay as they are unless acted upon by an outside force or decay. (Keenan 2002: 327)

Decay in this sense may be phonological or semantic, while an 'outside force' is generally a language-external one (language contact). Phonological decay destroys morphological boundaries, case inflections and so on (as discussed above in §23.5). Semantic decay is essentially the semantic bleaching found in grammaticalization, potentially leading to syntactic change, as with the regular shift of demonstratives to create definite articles (e.g. Lat. *ille* 'that' > Fr. *le* 'the') or the loss of contrastive semantics for *self* leading to the creation of reflexive pronouns in English (Keenan 2002).

Longobardi's example is the grammaticalization of the French preposition *chez* 'at the house of, according to' from Latin *casa(m)* '(hut >) house.NOM(ACC)'. In essence, his argument runs as follows: *chez* develops in the transition from Latin to French as the unstressed counterpart to the stressed form *chiese*. Initially these are different forms of the same noun, the former found when there is a possessor (the construct-state construction) and the latter elsewhere. Acquirers recognize the phonological relationship between the two forms, and therefore successfully continue the system by postulating two realizations of a single noun. The category reanalysis of *chez* from noun to preposition is triggered when the stressed form *chiese* is lost from the language. This is a non-syntactic event (perhaps due to social changes in housing, for instance), and is therefore an exogenous trigger for change (external to the syntactic construction under consideration). Since other Romance languages (with the notable exception of Sardinian) retain their reflex of Latin *casa(m)*, only French develops this new preposition.

The conceptual appeal of this is that it provides a solution to the timing part of the actuation problem (see Chapter 19, this volume): we do not have to explain why a grammatical system was transmitted faithfully at one time but underwent some change during the transmission process somewhat later: reanalysis occurs as soon as *chiese* is lost as a lexical item. Under the Inertia Theory, such a situation simply does not arise: if a grammar undergoes a change, it cannot be the case that it was once successfully acquired under current conditions. The conditions must have changed, in some way, to motivate the change. The linguist's task is to establish what change in conditions led up to the current syntactic innovation. It thus also excludes the possibility of syntactic change initiated by the structure of the syntactic system itself, at least in so far as such changes cannot be motivated opportunistically, and thus implies scepticism of typologically motivated syntactic change of the kind discussed in §23.3 above.

Furthermore, this approach links change to real-world phenomena, whether to sound change, often the result of physiological factors, to semantic change, often the result of negotiation in language use, or to population mixing of whatever kind. It is therefore far less divorced from the approaches discussed in the earlier part of this chapter than Meisel's radically exogenous approach. This is clearly part of its appeal, since it is in harmony with the minimalist idea of syntax as a perfect system: where imperfections occur, they should ideally be motivated by reference to factors external to the grammar.

Less appealing is the fact that this logic also implies that some other areas of linguistic structure should be diachronically inert; for instance, there should be no cognitively based sound changes (hypercorrections) (such as British English intrusive /r/), or spontaneous phonological reorganizations not triggered externally by sound change or language contact. It is even hard to see how the theory permits analogy, whether in the form of morphological analogy or syntactic extension.

Providing a plausible account of how a single change may have been triggered by some other change is not sufficient to demonstrate that all syntactic change arises this way. Such a negative conclusion can never be proved: the best we can hope to do is to fail in successive, serious attempts to disprove it. In the current instance, we should at least attempt to generalize across different language histories. The grammaticalization of adpositions from nouns (or adpositional phrases containing nouns) is in fact a very fruitful area for this kind of enterprise, since examples are very numerous indeed:

(19) $[_{NP}$ N $[_{PP}$ P NP]] > $[_{PP}$ P [NP]]
prepositions: Old Norse *hjá* (Icelandic, Faroese *hjá*, Norwegian (Nynorsk) *hjå*) 'by, near, with; past; compared to' < *hjá* 'household'; Mainland Scandinavian *hos* 'at the house of; at, with' < *hus* 'house'; Swedish/Norwegian *mot* 'to(wards)' < *mot* 'meeting' (Julien and Garbacz 2014); Welsh *chwedl* 'according to' < *chwedl* 'story, tale'; Finnish *kohten* 'towards' < *kohde* 'point' (Aristar 1991: 7).
postpositions: Finnish *vieressä* 'beside' < inessive of *vieri* 'side', *kanssa* 'with' < *kansa* 'people, company' (inessive); Estonian *juurde* 'towards' < *juur* 'root' (illative), *juures* 'at, by, near' < inessive and *juurest* 'from' < elative of the same lexeme; Hungarian *mellet* 'by, beside' < *mell* 'chest' (Tauli 1958: 16; 1973: 27), etc.

(20) $[_{PP}$ P $[_{NP}$ N $[_{PP}$ P NP]]] > $[_{PP}$ P [NP]]
English *instead of* < Old English *stede* 'place', *in front of, behind, beside*; German *aufgrund* 'on the basis' < *auf* 'on' + *grund* 'ground', *anhand* 'with the aid of' < *an* 'on' + *hand* 'hand', *anstatt* 'instead of' < *an* 'on' + *statt* 'place'.

There are four major 'inertial' (i.e. exogenous in the relevant sense) routes to this change:

(i)   lexical loss: the noun is lost (its meaning expressed now by another item), and remaining instances are interpreted as prepositions (perhaps due to some acquisitional bias towards positing functional rather than lexical items);

(ii) sound change affects the item differently in different syntactic environments, leading acquirers to fail to connect, say, reduced and unreduced forms, leading to a split into noun and adposition;

(iii) semantic change leads to a generalization of the meaning of the noun in certain collocations, leading acquirers to treat the item in its generalized and non-generalized uses as a case of homonymy, hence a split into noun and adposition;

(iv) routinization of a collocation (perhaps in combination with other lexical items) leads to an increase in frequency which leads acquirers to posit two separate items.

A combination of these is conceivable in many instances. Longobardi's scenario for *chez* effectively has (ii) occurring but not leading to a split (reanalysis), which is triggered instead by (i), leading to (iii).

Lehmann (1991: 8–11) discusses currently emerging new phrasal prepositions in German and notes that they are non-compositional and cannot be straightforwardly derived from general syntactic rules. For instance, *im Wege* 'by means of (lit. in.the way)' has a metaphorical meaning that is not entirely predictable from the meanings of its component parts. However, the noun from which it derives, *Weg* 'way, path' remains in the language and there is no phonetic reduction. The full nouns corresponding to Old Norse *hjá* and Mainland Scandinavian *hos* (both) 'at the house of' have also survived (as Old Norse *hjá* 'household' and Mainland Scandinavian *hus* 'house'), suggesting that the generalization of meaning is historically primary. These cases look like they are motivated by factor (iii) with elements of factor (iv). Stated in these terms, while the drivers of change (metaphor and routinization) are very different from those proposed by Longobardi for French *chez*, they are nevertheless consistent with inertia. In fact, this is the standard functional approach to grammaticalization, viewing it as primarily a semantic change with (historically later) ramifications for syntax.

The timing of the reanalysis, itself immune to direct observation by definition, is also open to interpretation. All the scenarios in (i)–(iv), in accordance with the inertial hypothesis, treat the reanalysis as secondary (and hence 'caused'), but in scenarios (i) and (iii), the reverse is conceivable: the description in (i) gives historical primacy to lexical loss rather than syntactic reanalysis, but one might ask why, if the noun is lost, it is not also lost from the pre-prepositional construction. An obvious answer is that the lexical loss was bled by the reanalysis: in the French case, this would mean claiming that *chez* was 'saved' from being lost at the same time as its variant *chiese* because it was already a distinct lexical item. Even here,

though, we could save the inertial theory by insisting on the historical
primacy of the semantic generalization:

(21)   (i) semantic generalization (metaphor)
        (ii) reanalysis (lexical split)
        (iii) loss of lexical (ungrammaticalized) item

This would have the advantage of assimilating the case of French *chez*
with that of Old Norse *hjá* and Mainland Scandinavian *hos*, which, on the
face of it, are identical changes except for the fact that loss of the original
lexical item occurs only in French. Thus, while we are led to doubt aspects
of Longobardi's analysis for French, the alternative approach suggested
here itself remains consistent with the inertial theory. This is likely to be
the case of any examples involving grammaticalization, since the standard
functionalist position with historically primary semantic change (see
Chapters 1 and 31, this volume) will always be consistent with the inertial
theory.

Beyond grammaticalization, however, it is less easy to construct narratives consistent with inertia. Waltereit and Detges (2008: 23–8) discuss one
potential problematic case. Spanish has a presentational/existential construction using the verb *haber* 'have', with a single theme argument treated
as a direct object. In many varieties of Spanish, this argument has been
reanalysed as a subject, a reanalysis manifested especially, but not exclusively, in the imperfect tense. The appropriate bridging context is
a sentence with a singular theme, such as (22), where third-person singular
verbal agreement does not allow us to choose between an analysis with *un
soldado* as subject or as object:

(22)   Spanish (Waltereit and Detges 2008: 26)
        Había   un   soldado en   el   patio.
        have.IMPF.3SG a   soldier in   the   courtyard
        'There was a soldier in the courtyard.'

Waltereit and Detges suggest that, in those varieties participating in
the reanalysis, a general principle that single arguments are encoded
as subjects has applied. Once the reanalysis has taken place, evidence
of its actualization is provided by the appearance of third-person
plural agreement in cases where the theme argument is plural:

(23)   American Spanish varieties (Waltereit and Detges 2008: 24)
        Habían   soldados en   el   patio.
        have.IPFV.3PL soldiers in   the   courtyard
        'There were soldiers in the courtyard.'

While Waltereit and Detges favour a usage-based approach, even in
generative terms, this example is challenging for inertia. A grammar
in which existential *haber* took a theme argument in the accusative

(and a null expletive subject) is clearly acquirable (since it once existed and still exists for speakers of other varieties and since such grammars are found in other languages, such as French or German). However, some acquirers failed to acquire it successfully, positing instead a grammar where *haber* took a theme argument in the nominative. We can accept the (reasonable) assumption that the default hypothesis during acquisition is that a single theme argument maps onto subject position (the usual case with unaccusative verbs like existential *haber* in Spanish and beyond). However, we are still faced with the problem that, at one point in time, the counterevidence from sentences such as (24), where absence of verbal agreement shows *soldados* to be a direct object, was sufficient to allow acquirers to reject the default analysis, while at a later time, in some varieties, it was not.

(24) Spanish
  Había   soldados en   el   patio.
  have.IPFV.3SG soldiers in   the   courtyard
  'There were soldiers in the courtyard.'

Overall, then, this looks like 'spontaneous actuation' as outlined in §23.2, that is, a classic instance of the actuation problem (Weinreich, Labov and Herzog 1968: 101) with no solution. We are left considering a probabilistic model of actuation of precisely the type that Longobardi (2001: 278) specifically rejects. On such a view, differences in the frequency with which various structures were used (whether systematic or due to random variation in the experience of individual acquirers) would have led a very small proportion of acquirers (independently) to innovate the new grammar. Once one acquirer establishes the new grammar and actualizes it by producing innovative sentence types compatible only with the new grammar, such as (23), the probability that other acquirers will acquire the new feature will rise sharply (a 'snowball' effect), since there is now positive evidence in its favour. The random distribution of primary actuators and the snowball effect combine, leading to the creation of clusters of innovative usage. If there is an acquisitional bias towards the new grammar (because it is simpler or in some sense a default), it is certain to spread unless some counteracting bias (such as social stigmatization) outweighs the acquisitional bias.

23.8 Conclusion: Determinism in Language Acquisition and Change

Both approaches discussed in the last two sections effectively deny a random element in triggering syntactic innovation, and are radically deterministic in their view of language acquisition (see Walkden's 2012 criticisms of Inertial Theory, particularly his 'thought experiment'). On this view, two children exposed to the output of the same grammar will always converge on the same grammatical system. We cannot say that there is a 99.9 per cent (or whatever) probability that they will converge on grammatical system G_1 and a 0.1 per cent probability that they will converge on grammatical system G_2. Nor can we make reference to day-to-day differences in their experience or to minor genetic differences in either the language-learning component or wider cognitive abilities (such as attention span).

Clearly children acquiring a language are not all genetically identical, and no two children can experience the same linguistic input, whether in terms of the set of sentences they hear or in terms of the timing (or other conditions) of that experience. We are accustomed to the idea that all children acquire their native language perfectly with minimal effort and that all children are equally capable of acquiring their native language. Investigating how this happens is the central research question in first-language acquisition. These are of course useful idealizations for first-language research, and the second in particular has been a necessary counter to the lay view that, say, non-standard English is simply a corrupted (badly acquired) form of standard English. However, idealizations they remain. Not all children replicate all aspects of the grammatical systems of those around them perfectly. In fact, it is hard to see how they could, since there is a degree of variability in all communities and the PLD for each child is formed from the output of a variety of speakers, in different proportions for each child. Perhaps the result is that, in a relatively homogenous speech community (the best conditions for faithful transmission), 99.9 per cent of children will replicate 99.9 per cent of the grammar successfully. Under more challenging conditions for acquisition, where the PLD are limited in quantity (as with minority language maintenance and some other bilingual environments) or varied in quality (as with dialect mixing or sharp generational differences), everyone agrees that faithful transmission will be much less successful (see Trudgill 2011). Change initiated in these scenarios is often treated as exogenous since the factor worsening the conditions for acquisition is often associated with an external language or dialect. Returning to the 'best-case scenario', the question is whether a very low 0.1 per cent failure rate is sufficient to trigger spontaneous, endogenous change.

It has already been hinted that the best-case scenario does not exist. It could only be achieved if a child were raised by one person only, who spoke extensively to the child, but who never interacted with anyone else in the child's presence. It is possible that, under such conditions, transmission would always be perfect, and language would never change. If so, we might conclude that endogenous change does not exist. But this is not a very interesting conclusion, since the scenario described is next to impossible to imagine in the real world. We might come to the conclusion that endogenous change does not exist, but only because truly endogenous transmission does not exist in practice. Acquirers always receive input from a range of speakers with slightly different grammars, and the PLD which they use to construct their grammars are always potentially subject to the impact of the kinds of changes due to language use and interactions with other linguistic levels that we have seen in the course of this chapter.

References

Allen, C. L. 1995. *Case marking and reanalysis: Grammatical relations from Old to Early Modern English*. Oxford: Clarendon Press.

Aristar, A. R. 1991. 'On diachronic sources and synchronic pattern: An investigation into the origin of linguistic universals', *Language* 67: 1–33.

Biberauer, T., Sheehan, M. and Newton, G. 2010. 'Impossible changes and impossible borrowings: The Final-over-Final Constraint', in A. Breitbarth, C. Lucas, D. Willis and S. Watts (eds.), *Continuity and change in grammar*. Amsterdam: John Benjamins, pp. 35–60.

2005. 'Three factors in language design', *Linguistic Inquiry* 36: 1–22.

De Smet, H. 2009. 'Analysing reanalysis', *Lingua* 119: 1728–55.

Falk, C. 1993. 'Pro-drop in Early Modern Swedish', *Folia Linguistica Historica* 13: 115–32.

Fischer, O. 1992. 'Syntax', in N. Blake (ed.), *The Cambridge history of the English language,* vol. II: *1066–1476.* Cambridge University Press, pp. 207–408.

2007. *Morphosyntactic change: Functional and formal perspectives*. Oxford University Press.

Fischer, O., van Kemenade, A., Koopman, W. and van der Wurff, W. 2000. *The syntax of early English.* Cambridge University Press.

Fleischman, S. 1982. *The future in thought and language: Diachronic evidence from Romance*. Cambridge University Press.

Garrett, A. 2012. 'The historical syntax problem: Reanalysis and directionality', in D. Jonas, J. Whitman and A. Garrett (eds.), *Grammatical change: Origins, nature, outcomes*. Oxford University Press, pp. 52–72.

Gerritsen, M. and Stein, D. 1992. 'Introduction: On "internal" and "external" in syntactic change', in M. Gerritsen and G. Stein (eds.), *Internal and external factors in syntactic change*. Berlin: Mouton de Gruyter, pp. 1–15.

Greenberg, J. H. 1963. 'Some universals of grammar with particular reference to the order of meaningful elements', in J. H. Greenberg (ed.), *Universals of language*. Cambridge, MA: MIT Press, pp. 73–113.

Harris, A. C. and Campbell, L. 1995. *Historical syntax in cross-linguistic perspective*. Cambridge University Press.

Harris, M. B. 1978. 'The inter-relationship between phonological and grammatical change', in J. Fisiak (ed.), *Recent developments in historical phonology*. The Hague: Mouton, pp. 159–72.

  1984. 'On the strengths and weaknesses of a typological approach to historical syntax', in J. Fisiak (ed.), *Historical syntax*. Berlin: Walter de Gruyter, pp. 183–97.

Hawkins, J. A. 1983. *Word order universals*. New York: Academic Press.

  1990a. 'A parsing theory of word order universals', *Linguistic Inquiry* 21: 223–61.

  1990b. 'Seeking motives for change in typological variation', in W. A. Croft, K. Denning and S. Kemmer (eds.), *Studies in typology and diachrony: Papers presented to Joseph H. Greenberg on his 75th birthday*. Amsterdam: John Benjamins, pp. 95–128.

  1994. *A performance theory of order and constituency*. Cambridge University Press.

Hyman, L. M. 1975. 'On the change from SOV to SVO: Evidence from Niger-Congo', in Li (ed.), pp. 113–47.

Jespersen, O. 1927. *A modern English grammar on historical principles*, part III: *Syntax*, vol. II. Heidelberg: C. Winters.

Julien, M. and Garbacz, P. 2014. 'Prepositions expressing source in Norwegian', *Nordic Atlas of Language Structures Journal* 1: 191–206.

Kaiser, G. A. 2002. *Verbstellung und Verbstellungswandel in den romanischen Sprachen*. Tübingen: Max Niemeyer.

Keenan, E. L. 2002. 'Explaining the creation of reflexive pronouns in English', in D. Minkova and R. Stockwell (eds.), *Studies in the history of English: A millennial perspective*. Berlin: Mouton de Gruyter, pp. 325–55.

Lass, R. 1997. *Historical linguistics and language change*. Cambridge University Press.

Ledgeway, A. 2012. *From Latin to Romance: Morphosyntactic typology and change*. Oxford University Press.

Lehmann, W. P. 1973. 'A structural principle of language and its implications', *Language* 49: 47–66.

Lehmann, C. 1991. 'Grammaticalization and related changes in contemporary German', in E. Closs Traugott and B. Heine (eds.), *Approaches to grammaticalization*, vol. II. Amsterdam: John Benjamins, pp. 493–535.

Leslau, W. 1945. 'The influence of Cushitic on the Semitic languages of Ethiopia: A problem of substratum', *Word* 1: 59–82.

Li, C. N. (ed.) 1975. *Word order and word order change*. Austin: University of Texas Press.

Lightfoot, D. W. 1979. *Principles of diachronic syntax*. Cambridge University Press.

  1991. *How to set parameters: Arguments from language change*. Cambridge, MA: MIT Press.

  1999. *The development of language: Acquisition, change and evolution*. Oxford: Blackwell.

Longobardi, G. 2001. 'Formal syntax, diachronic minimalism, and etymology: The history of French chez', *Linguistic Inquiry* 32: 275–302.

Lucas, C. 2009. 'The development of negation in Arabic and Afro-Asiatic', unpublished PhD thesis, University of Cambridge.

Meisel, J. M. 2011. 'Bilingual language acquisition and theories of diachronic change: Bilingualism as cause and effect of grammatical change', *Bilingualism: Language and Cognition* 14: 121–45.

Meisel, J. M., Elsig, M. and Rinke, E. 2013. *Language acqusition and change: A morphosyntactic perspective*. Edinburgh University Press.

Pinkster, H. 1987. 'The strategy and chronology of the development of future and perfect tense auxiliaries in Latin', in M. B. Harris and P. Ramat (eds.), *The historical development of auxiliaries*. Berlin: Mouton de Gruyter, pp. 193–223.

Reindl, D. F. 2008. *Language contact: German and Slovenian*. Bochum: Brockmeyer.

Roberts, I. 1993a. 'A formal account of grammaticalisation in the history of Romance futures', *Folia Linguistica Historica* 13: 219–58.

1993b. *Verbs and diachronic syntax*. Dordrecht: Kluwer.

Roberts, I. and Roussou, A. 2003. *Syntactic change: A minimalist approach to grammaticalization*. Cambridge University Press.

Sapir, E. 1921. *Language: An introduction to the study of speech*. New York: Harcourt, Brace & Co.

Sitaridou, I. 2012. 'A comparative study of word order in Old Romance', *Folia Linguistica* 46: 553–604.

Tauli, V. 1958. *The structural tendencies of language*, vol. I: *General tendencies*. Helsinki: Suomalainen Tiedeakatemia.

1973. *Standard Estonian grammar: Phonology, morphology, word-formation*. Uppsala: Acta Universitatis Upsaliensis.

Traugott, E. C. 2008. 'The grammaticalization of NP of NP patterns', in A. Bergs and G. Diewald (eds.), *Constructions and language change*. Berlin: Mouton de Gruyter, pp. 23–45.

Trudgill, P. 2011. *Sociolinguistic typology: Social determinants of linguistic complexity*. Cambridge University Press.

van der Auwera, J. and Genee, I. 2002. 'English do: On the convergence of languages and linguists', *English Language and Linguistics* 6: 283–307.

Vance, B. 1997. *Syntactic change in medieval French: Verb-second and null subjects*. Dordrecht: Kluwer.

Vennemann, T. 1975. 'An explanation of drift', in Li (ed.), pp. 269–305.

Walkden, G. 2012. 'Against inertia', *Lingua* 122: 891–901.

Waltereit, R. and Detges, U. 2008. 'Syntactic change from within and from without syntax: A usage-based analysis', in U. Detges and R. Waltereit (eds.), *The paradox of grammatical change: Perspectives from Romance*. Amsterdam: John Benjamins, pp. 13–30.

Weinreich, U., Labov, W. and Herzog, M.I. 1968. 'Empirical foundations for a theory of language change', in W. P. Lehmann and Y. Malkiel (eds.),

Directions for historical linguistics. Austin: University of Texas Press, pp. 95–195.

Willis, D. 1998. *Syntactic change in Welsh: A study of the loss of verb-second.* Oxford: Clarendon Press.

2007. 'Specifier-to-head reanalyses in the complementizer domain: Evidence from Welsh', *Transactions of the Philological Society* 105: 432–80.

24

Imperfect Transmission and Discontinuity

David W. Lightfoot

24.1   Introduction

If syntacticians walk the 400 miles from Berlin to Amsterdam, covering ten miles a day, it is said that they hear no noticeable difference in the language of local people they meet at breakfast and at dinner. Not even on the day when they cross the border from Germany into the Netherlands. The paradox is that the German of Berlin is different from the Dutch of Amsterdam.

As in space, so in time. The messages that my daughters send are similar to the letters my mother sent. They use different words with different meanings in a few cases, but the syntax is the same and the vocabulary close to identical. And the paradox is similar: local differences are slight but, if we look over larger time spans, we see big differences in the language of Chaucer, Shakespeare, Jane Austen and Toni Morrison.

In many contexts, between neighbouring towns and villages or between generations of a family, language seems to be stable and its transmission frequently seems close to perfect. Change is often gradual to the point of being imperceptible but, when we use a wider-angle lens, we see major discontinuities.

There are many understandings of this paradox, depending on one's broad view of what drives syntactic change. In §§24.2–3 I will sketch some views, leaving it as an exercise for the reader to work out the details of how discontinuities might be treated. In §24.4 I will outline in greater detail a particular 'cue-based', discovery approach to acquisition and consider the paradox through that lens. In §24.5 we will work through some details of discontinuities discussed in Chapter 18 (this volume), considering how children were driven to the discontinuities revealed through the new internal systems, the new I-languages that children grew. And in §24.6 we will think about the spread of new I-languages, using the methods of population biology.

24.2   Discontinuities and Special Events

One view is that generally transmission takes place more or less perfectly and children acquire the same language capacity as their neighbours and parents, unless something special happens. For example, Jürgen Meisel has argued that change takes place only in multilingual contexts, which he takes to involve sociologically distinct languages like German and Turkish (Meisel 2011). Consequently, discontinuities are unusual events provoked by particular social contexts, when people are exposed to multiple languages in the conventional sense of the term. So in recent generations the multilingualism of Turks and Germans in Germany has had effects on the two languages.

However, multilingualism in Meisel's sense does not explain how languages like Icelandic, which have been isolated for a long time, nonetheless undergo changes in their syntactic structures, including major shifts in word order. Furthermore, once one moves beyond conventional definitions of languages as properties of groups, it underestimates the variation and multilingualism found everywhere (Lightfoot 2011). People have their own private systems and there is significant variation among people within the same speech community. In §24.4 we will reject the conventional notion of a socially defined language as the locus of change and distinguish internal and external languages, two quite different kinds of entities.

A similar predilection for stasis in normal times, except for special events, comes from recent ideas about 'inertia', developed by Longobardi (2001) and Keenan (2002) (see Chapter 20, this volume). The central idea is that '[t]hings stay as they are unless acted upon by an outside force or decay' (Keenan 2002: 327) or that 'syntactic change should not arise, unless it can be shown to be *caused* – that is, to be a well-motivated consequence of other types of change (phonological changes and semantic changes, including the appearance/disappearance of whole lexical items) or, recursively, of other syntactic changes' (Longobardi 2001: 278). These ideas were developed in part as a reaction against ideas that changes may be internally motivated by 'UG biases' and cyclical forces (Roberts and Roussou 2003; van Gelderen 2011). Inertia approaches require an external cause for change but the external cause might be a prior change in grammars, internal systems (for critical discussion, see Walkden 2012).

Another view is that sometimes there is 'imperfect learning' (Kiparsky 1968; Trudgill 2002; Mitchener and Nowak 2004): children are exposed to the same linguistic experience as their parents but their learning is imperfect and they converge on a different mature system, yielding imperfect transmission, hence discontinuity. Imperfect learning may be a special event but it is not triggered by new experiences and can take place at any time, yielding discontinuities randomly.

24.3 Acquiring Grammars by Evaluation

In *Syntactic Structures* Chomsky devoted a chapter to outlining the goals of a linguistic theory. He argued that the goals of *discovering* a grammar for a corpus of sentences or of *deciding* whether a particular grammar was correct for that corpus of sentences were too ambitious to be realized. In contrast, a weaker goal of *evaluating* the success of various grammars in generating a corpus and ranking them did seem to be achievable, by measuring their simplicity in a precise way.

The discussion in 1957 was intended to guide analysts as they hypothesized grammars for languages like Chinese and Chichewa. However, by the time of the 1975 publication of the dissertation on which *Syntactic Structures* was based, Chomsky extended the claims to cover language acquisition by children, writing in the introduction:

> We thus have two variants of the fundamental problem of linguistics, as it was conceived in this work: under the methodological interpretation, the problem is taken to be the justification of grammars; under the psychological interpretation, the problem is to account for language acquisition ... Under the methodological interpretation, the selected grammar is the linguist's grammar, justified by the theory. Under the psychological interpretation, it is the speaker-hearer's grammar, chosen by the evaluation procedure from among the potential grammars permitted by the theory and compatible with the data as represented in terms of the preliminary analysis.
> *(Chomsky 1975: 36)*

For the following decades, language acquisition specialists pursued the idea that children were converging on the best analysis for their language by evaluating grammars against a body of data. Chomsky and Halle (1968) devoted considerable attention to the acquisition of their analyses of English phonology from this perspective. Gibson and Wexler (1994) developed a Triggering Learning Algorithm, enabling children to evaluate the success of eight toy, three-parameter grammars in generating sets of word-order patterns.

The most richly elaborated evaluation metric was Robin Clark's (1992) Fitness Metric (see Figure 24.1), which measures precisely the fitness of grammars with respect to a corpus of sentences.

$$\frac{\left(\sum_{j=1}^{n} v_j + b\sum_{j=1}^{n} s_j + c\sum_{j=1}^{n} e_j\right) - (v_i + bs_i + ce_i)}{(n-1)\left(\sum_{j=1}^{n} v_j + b\sum_{j=1}^{n} s_j + c\sum_{j=1}^{n} e_j\right)}$$

Figure 24.1 Clark's (1992) Fitness Metric

where

v_i = the number of violations signaled by the parser associated with a given parameter setting;

s_i = the number of superset settings in the counter; b is a constant superset penalty <1;

e_i = the measure of elegance (= number of nodes) of counter i; c <1 is a scaling factor.

Clark's key idea is that particular grammars provide a means to understand particular sentences and not others; that is, they generate particular sentences. The Fitness Metric quantifies the failure of grammars to parse sentences in a corpus, the 'violations', v. The sum term, sigma, totals all the violations of all grammars under consideration, perhaps five grammars with a total of fifty failures or violations. The linguist/child then subtracts the violations of any single grammar and divides by the total violations (multiplied by $n - 1$). This provides a number that grades candidate grammars. For example, if one candidate has ten violations, its score is 50 – 10, divided by some number; if another candidate has twenty violations, its score is 50 – 20, divided by that same number, a lower score (there are two other factors in the equation, a superset penalty s and a measure of elegance e, but they are subject to a scaling condition and play a lesser role, which I ignore here). Clark's Fitness Metric grades the success of grammars with exquisite precision and I have sketched it here because it is the most sophisticated and precisely worked-out evaluation measure that I know. Such evaluation measures rate grammars against a corpus of sentences, as outlined in 1957.

However, there are huge feasibility problems with such approaches evaluating grammars against sets of data. If there are thirty points of binary choices (a very conservative estimate), there are over a billion grammars to evaluate against the data set; if there are forty points of variation, then over a trillion grammars to evaluate; if there are fifty points of variation, then the numbers become astronomical. And bear in mind that each grammar generates an infinite set of sentences and structural descriptions. In addition, in order to check whether the generative capacity of a grammar matches what the child has heard, s/he will need to retain a memory of everything that has been heard. Such an approach to language acquisition faces great difficulties once one thinks beyond toy systems with just a few parameter settings. For discussion, see my introduction to the second edition of *Syntactic Structures* (Chomsky 2002) and Lightfoot (1999).

Furthermore, this evaluation model of acquisition faces quite different, fundamental problems for people interested in explaining the discontinuities of language change through acquisition. Under this view of acquisition, the child would need to be confronted with the data generated by the new grammar in order to first select the grammar that generates them and this introduces problems of circularity: what comes first, the new grammar to generate the new data or new data that require the child to select the new grammar?

24.4 Acquiring Elements of I-Languages

An alternative stance is to embrace Chomsky's anti-positivist arguments that there is no procedure to guarantee that scientists discover or decide on correct theories; the best they can do is to compare theories and decide which gives a superior account of some predetermined data, is learnable, achieves greater depth of explanation, etc. On the other hand, children are not constructing theories but they subconsciously acquire a system that characterizes their linguistic capacity. They may be following a kind of discovery procedure.

Before we come to the discovery procedure itself, let us identify a key idea that lays the groundwork: Chomsky's abandonment of sociologically defined languages like French and Navajo and his 1986 distinction between external language and internal, individual, intensional languages ('I-languages'). In later sections we will invoke Kroch's extension of Chomsky's emphasis on the individual: Kroch has postulated that individuals use multiple internal systems, invoking the idea of coexisting, competing grammars (Kroch 1989, 1994). This will become important in §24.6, when we consider the spread of new I-languages.

Linguists have never been able to provide a clear definition of a language as distinct from a dialect, because the sentences of, say, English do not constitute a recursively enumerable set. As noted in Chapter 18 (this volume), if one asks if *She might could do it* is a sentence of English, the answer is that it is a sentence of English in Alabama but not in Alaska. Therefore there is no notion of English such that it is something acquired by children growing up in Alabama, Alaska and Alice Springs. Rather, children acquire different capacities, different I-languages, and one needs something more granulated. It is not clear that the sociological notion of English is relevant for an account of people's biological language capacity, but we return to this matter in §24.7.

Wilhelm von Humboldt distinguished languages as the creations of nations from languages as the creations of individuals: language 'is not a mere external vehicle, designed to sustain social intercourse, but an indispensable factor for the development of human intellectual powers ...While languages are ... creations of nations, they still remain personal and independent creations of individuals' (1836/1971: 5, 22). Chomsky (1986) followed in this vein and distinguished external E-language and internal, individual I-languages. E-language refers to language out there in the world, the kind of thing that a child might be exposed to, an amorphous, mass concept. I-language, on the other hand, refers to a biological *system* that grows in a child's mind/brain in the first few years of life and characterizes that individual's linguistic capacity. It consists of items like structures, categories, morphemes and phonemes, and a set of computational operations that copy the items, delete them, assign indices to them, etc. One's I-language is a private object that permits communication with certain other speakers, although is not necessarily identical to the I-languages of those speakers. Indeed, Kroch and his colleagues have shown that individuals operate with more than one I-language and likewise speech communities, his coexisting or competing grammars.

These ideas of E-language and I-languages (also sketched briefly in §18.2) suffice for the purposes of accounting for language acquisition and we do not need the conventional, sociologically defined notion of English or Estonian, it seems. With these notions, one can view children as acquiring their individual I-language on exposure to external E-language. Rather than evaluating systems against a set of data, children can be viewed as paying no attention to what any I-language or grammar generates but instead growing an I-language by identifying its elements (Lightfoot 2006). This is cue-based acquisition, a procedure whereby children parse the E-language they hear and acquire the categories and structures needed to understand what they hear and thereby acquire the elements of their I-language.

Universal Grammar (UG) provides children with the set of structures that they might need in order to understand and parse the E-language that they are exposed to (for discussion, see Chapter 13, this volume); these structures are the cues and robust E-language elicits them. Children are born to parse and at a certain stage of development, after they know that *cat* is a noun referring to a domestic feline and *sit* is an intransitive verb, they may hear an expression *The cat sat on the mat* and recognize that it contains a Determiner Phrase (DP) consisting of a determiner *the* and a noun *cat* and a Verb Phrase (VP) containing an inflected verb *sat* followed by a Preposition Phrase (PP) *on the mat*. The child makes use of the structures needed to parse what is heard and, once a structure is used, it is incorporated into the emerging I-language. In this way children accumulate the structures of their I-language, which are required to parse the ambient E-language; children acquire elements of their I-language, their cues, in piecemeal fashion.

At no stage does the child calculate what his/her current I-language can generate; rather s/he simply accumulates the necessary structures. Furthermore, if UG makes available a thousand possible structures for children to draw from, that raises no intractable feasibility problems comparable to those facing a child evaluating the generative capacity of grammars with thirty possible parameter settings, checking the grammars against what has been heard. It involves no elaborate calculations. Children developing some form of English I-language learn without apparent difficulty irregular past tense and plural forms for a few hundred verbs and nouns. Learning that there is a structure $_{VP}$[V+I PP] seems to be broadly a similar kind of learning, although much remains to be said; for detailed discussion, see Fodor (1998), Dresher (1999) and Lightfoot (1999).

24.5 Discontinuities Revisited

Equipped now with these ideas of E-language and I-language, seeing language acquisition as a procedure to discover the elements of grammars, and I-languages as coexisting in a single speech community and in a single speaker, one can understand discontinuities as new I-languages triggered by new E-language, that is by new primary linguistic data (PLD). Discontinuities do not constitute a special event, rather the normal state of affairs confronting any child. There is no 'imperfect learning' or 'imperfect transmission', just different transmission, new E-language triggering new I-languages. New E-language is the initial locus of change and, furthermore, we can link particular aspects of E-language to new I-languages. Nothing is transmitted and I-languages, in particular, are invented afresh in each generation and each individual.

If work on change provides insight on linking particular aspects of E-language to new I-languages, that constitutes a major contribution to our understanding of children's language acquisition, not achieved so far in experimental work on children. Furthermore, as in so many other domains, seeing how something changes often reveals properties of the object changing.

To see how this works, let us elaborate on two changes in the I-languages of English speakers, discussed preliminarily in Chapter 18, this volume. In that chapter (§18.3) we noted that by Early Modern English, but beginning earlier, I-languages had *can, could, may, might, must, shall, should, will* and *would* categorized as Infl items, whereas they had been verbs for earlier speakers. As a result, they came to have a more restricted syntactic distribution, ceasing to occur in various contexts. There is good reason to believe that this change in I-languages was triggered by a prior change in E-language.

Old English I-languages showed many inflections indicating the tense, person, number and conjugation type of verbs and the number, case and declensional class of nouns. Regular Modern English verbs show up in four forms (*refuse, refuses, refused, refusing*) but Old English verbs had over a hundred forms. However, all of this was vastly simplified over the course of Middle English. The morphological distinctions were eliminated first in the north of England (manifested first in the

Lindisfarne Gospels) and later in London and the south, arguably an effect of widespread English–Scandinavian bilingualism (O'Neil 1978). Individuals with English and Scandinavian I-languages had a rich morphological system, similar to each other but different and not learnable as a single system.

The only aspect of present-tense verb morphology to survive the great Middle English simplification was the third-person singular ending in -s/-eþ, and it is quite unclear why that one element of present-tense verb morphology should have survived. However, the verbs that were to be recategorized as Infl elements had been members of the preterite-present class, which had what were usually past-tense endings for forms of the present tense, a phenomenon that occurs in Latin verbs like *coepi* 'begin', *odi* 'hate' and Greek verbs like *oida* 'know' and *eoika* 'seem', which are present tense in meaning but perfective in form. The crucial fact about the morphology of the preterite-presents is that they never had the -s/-eþ third-person singular ending and therefore now lacked what had become the single morphological property of present-tense verbs. Of the original preterite-presents, some dropped out of the language (e.g. *unnan* 'grant', *benugan* 'suffice'), others assimilated to regular verbal inflections with the third-person -s ending (*witan* 'know', *dugan* 'be of value'), and the remainder were recategorized as Infl items.

Furthermore, with the loss of subjunctive endings as part of the morphological impoverishment, another defining property of verbs came to be that -d forms indicated past tense. However, the -d forms of the items to be recategorized, *could, might, must, would, should,* rarely indicated past tense (**She might lift eighty kilos until yesterday*) but rather retained 'subjunctive meaning'.

One of the tasks of a child developing his/her internal I-language is to identify the words and the categories to which they belong and this is done on the basis of formal and distributional properties. After the simplification of complex verb morphology, having the third-person singular -s ending became a defining property of verbs and *can, could, may,* etc. did not have it. Verbs had past tenses in -d, but *might, would, should* and *must* almost never carried past time meaning and *could* only rarely (*She could lift 75 kilos until she turned thirty*). Therefore, after the great simplification of morphology, the old preterite-presents lacked what had become the defining formal properties of verbs; they could no longer be verbs and were assigned to the only plausible candidate category that could be immediately followed by a VP: Infl or T, depending on one's theory of functional categories. Hence the newly restricted syntactic distribution: if *can, may,* etc. were instances of Infl or T, they could not occur to the right of an aspectual marker, a position restricted to lexical verbs (**She has could gone, *Canning go, she left angrily*), and they cannot occur with the infinitival *to* or another modal verb, which are also instances of Infl/T (taken as a cover term for the relevant functional heads), because there can be only one such element in a clause (**I want to can leave, *She might could read it*).

New E-language resulted from the contact and bilingualism between English and Scandinavian speakers in the north, if O'Neil is right. That new E-language triggered new I-languages with the old verbs *can, may, shall*, etc., recategorized as Infl items, as shown in Chapter 18, this volume. Hence the discontinuity and its explanation. There is no imperfect learning or imperfect transmission, just new E-language triggering a new I-language. The explanation for the change is local and depends on particular changes in the ambient E-language at this time. The equivalent change has not taken place in closely related languages like Dutch and German or slightly more distant languages like French and Italian, because there were no comparable changes in E-language. Furthermore, we are not trapped into circularity by having to claim that the new I-language was triggered by exposure to the new data generated by the new I-language, a problem confronted by proponents of evaluation approaches to acquisition, as noted.

Let us turn now to the second of the reanalyses discussed in Chapter 18 (this volume), the loss of V-in-I structures, $_IV$, resulting from the movement of a verb to an Infl position, another change that has not taken place in closely related languages like Dutch and German. Under the cue-based, discovery approach to acquisition, for such a structure to be acquired by children, it needs to be *expressed* sufficiently in the PLD, i.e. required for the child to be able to understand and parse an utterance. For example, once Chaucer's son knew that *understand* was a verb and could occur in high positions in expressions like *Understands she this chapter?* or *She understands not this chapter*, he would know that the verb could occur in an Infl position and therefore also in a C position for the first of the two utterances. Such sentences in E-language expressed the $_IV$ cue and the first sentence also expressed the $_{C[IV]}$ cue. Similarly, Thomas More, for whom *can* and *may*, etc. were verbs, would also understand *She cannot understand this chapter* as expressing the $_IV$ cue, because the verb *can* occurs to left of the negative *not* and therefore must have moved to the higher Infl position. Similarly, a French-speaking child hears *Elle comprend pas ce chapitre* 'She doesn't understand this chapter' as expressing the $_IV$ cue, and likewise a Dutch child hearing *Begrijpt zij dit hoofdstuk?* 'Understands she this chapter?'; *comprend* has moved to the left of the negative marker, to Infl, and *begrijpt* has moved to an Infl position, from which it can move to a higher C.

However, somebody younger than Thomas More, for whom *can, may*, etc. were not verbs but Infl items, would not parse *She cannot understand this chapter* as expressing the $_IV$ cue, because *can* is an Infl item and therefore not a verb in the Infl position. Given that a clear majority of simple sentences contain a modal auxiliary (Leech 2003), i.e. an Infl item, this means that there was a large reduction in the expression of the ₁V cue.

Alongside the fact that sentences with a modal auxiliary no longer express the ₁V cue, expressions like *Understands she this chapter?* and *She understands not this chapter*, expressing the ₁V cue, were giving way to forms with the periphrastic *do: Does she understand this chapter?* and *She doesn't understand this chapter*, where the ₁V cue is not expressed (*do* is not a verb moved to Infl; in these examples *understand* is the verb). These forms entered the language in the late fifteenth century and spread from the southwest across the rest of the country. Ellegård (1954) provided a remarkably detailed account of that spread and recently McWhorter (2009) has argued that periphrastic *do* arose in the southwest under the influence of Cornish (McWhorter (2009: 164) argues that 'Cornish's auxiliary *do* presents a thoroughly plausible model for English's periphrastic *do*' as a carrier of tense in negated and interrogative contexts. He goes on to show how this provides a good explanation for the spread of periphrastic *do* in Middle English). The spread of periphrastic *do* further reduced the expression of the ₁V cue.

The evidence suggests that new E-language, stemming from the combination of the recategorized Infl items (an I-language change) and the new *do* forms, reduced the expression of the ₁V cue below the threshold that enabled it to be acquired. Again there were changes in E-language, some induced by new I-language and others resulting from forms introduced under Cornish influence, that entailed that children could no longer add the ₁V cue to the structures making up their mature I-languages. As a result of that change in I-languages, there were further changes in E-language, such that expressions like *Understands she this chapter?*, *She understands not this chapter* and *She understood on Tuesday the chapter* no longer occur.

In these two well-understood phase transitions, we see discontinuities that can be explained as responses to new E-language. In the case of the new Infl items, new E-language arose because of a prior change in I-languages, the dramatic simplification of morphological endings resulting from English–Scandinavian bilingualism. In the case of the loss of the operation moving verbs to a higher Infl position, E-language changed as an effect of the new Infl items just mentioned and of contact with Cornish, such that the old ₁V cue was no longer expressed sufficiently to be attained by children at this time. Nothing comparable has happened in the E-language that Dutch or German speakers experience and therefore no comparable change in I-languages. In the case of the loss of the ₁V cue, however, unlike in the case of the recategorization of certain verbs, there are comparative data from other languages. Heycock *et al.* (2012) report the tail end of the loss of ₁V cues in Faroese and Vikner (1995) argues that mainland Scandinavian has lost those cues.

We see changes in I-languages, discontinuities, that can be understood as responses to new E-language and there is nothing imperfect at work.

Of course, no two children have exactly the same PLD; they hear different things. Nonetheless, despite variation in experience, children often attain the same mature I-language in terms of the set of known syntactic structures. Individual experiences may vary indefinitely, but I-languages show structural stability and vary only in limited ways. I-languages emerge in the usual manner on exposure to E-language that has changed in a critical way and we understand the discontinuity naturally enough. Neither E-language nor I-languages get transmitted, neither imperfectly nor perfectly. In particular, I-languages are not transmitted in any sense; rather, they are created afresh by young children on exposure to E-language and they are not shaped by earlier I-languages except indirectly through E-language. I-languages are not objects gliding smoothly through time and space.

24.6 Gradual Change in Languages vs Spread of I-Languages

We have emphasized that grammars, I-languages, exist for people and not for languages; there is no grammar of English in any biological sense. We noted antecedents for this view in the writings of von Humboldt in the early nineteenth century. Hermann Paul (1877: 325) emphasized the individual and biological view of grammars, noting in an early work 'dass die reelle Sprache nur im Individuuum existiert' ('real language exists only in individuals'). Later, as we noted in in §15.4, Paul (1880: 31) attacked the group psychology of Lazarus and Steinthal and wrote that 'Wir müssen eigentlich so viele Sprachen unterscheiden als es Individuen gibt' ('we must in fact distinguish as many languages as there are individuals').

Paul and modern work take a biological view of languages, as opposed to a social view. At a minimum, different questions arise under each view and the same questions take on quite different complexions; for discussion, see Lightfoot (1995; 1999: 79–82).

Everyday common sense rests to some degree on the notion of continuity and gradual change. The basic idea is that if there is little distortion, the patterns, processes and structures of life do not change very much. Similarly with language. The overwhelmingly most common view among historians is that language change is gradual (see Chapter 21, this volume) but things depend on the units of analysis: languages, seen as social entities, change gradually, but I-languages change abruptly.

Fries (1940) found that Old English showed object–verb order 53 per cent of the time around the year 1000 and that it was gradually replaced by verb–object order, reducing to 2 per cent by the year 1500. He provided one set of statistics for each century but offered no analysis. Fries' counts

ignored the distinction between matrix and embedded clauses and he had
no analysis of the fact that the finite verb often appeared in second position in simple clauses. If one makes such distinctions, one sees that Old
English I-languages had object–verb order underlyingly and a system yielding subjects in second and third position and objects 'extraposed' to the
right (but not the widely imitated Dutch/German analysis applied by van
Kemenade 1987, moving finite verbs to a higher C position in matrix
clauses). Consequently we find object–verb order uniformly in embedded
clauses, but only variably in matrix clauses. In fact, at least two distinct
changes took place in I-languages, and took place at different times:
object–verb order was replaced by verb–object and the operation moving
objects to the right of the verb was lost (Haeberli 2002a, b; Kroch and
Santorini 2013). If units of analysis are as gross as Fries', change will look
gradual.

At the other end of the scale, if we use a telescopic lens, the speech of no
two people is identical and change is everywhere; all is in flux and languages are constantly changing in piecemeal, gradual and minor fashion,
and again we see gradual change. Some changes really do progress gradually. Initial experiences are never entirely the same for two speakers and
they may differ in minor and insignificant ways. In that case, if one looks at
them diachronically, they may change gradually. Some construction type
might become more frequent, perhaps as a result of taking on some
expressive function. This would reflect a way in which I-languages are
used, but not in the I-language itself. Such changes in frequency do not
reflect a change in I-languages but they do entail a change in the PLD for
the next generation of speakers.

Not only may PLD change gradually, but the very nature of language
acquisition ensures a kind of gradualness under circumstances where
children draw much of their PLD from their parents and older siblings.
This works against major discontinuities in the class of expressions and
their associated meanings. For example, one does not find an I-language
yielding more or less uniform object–verb order being replaced abruptly
by one yielding uniform verb–object order. Even so, one does find
significant discontinuities, especially in contexts where the output of
a parent's native I-language does not contribute significantly to a child's
PLD. To be sure, there is no reason to believe that there is any formal
relationship between the I-languages of parents and children.
I-languages are created afresh by every individual and may differ in
form from that of the parents, perhaps radically, within the limits of
UG. For discussion, see Lightfoot (1999: ch. 4), who views I-language
changes as Thom-style catastrophes, like a gradual change in the
temperature of water until there are structural changes only at 0° and
100°Celsius (Thom 1989; Casti 1994).

Whether differences between I-languages are small-scale or large-scale,
they do not have temporal properties and cannot be 'gradual'. Apparent

gradualness is a mirage, conjured by a failure to distinguish independent change events. PLD may differ in ways that do not trigger a new I-language. However, a natural way for linguists to think of catastrophic changes is to consider different sets of PLD sometimes crossing thresholds, which entails that a different I-language system is triggered. So the inventory of variable properties given by UG (the cues) constitutes the set of fixed-point attractors, defining the nature of possible changes.

Factoring into thinking about apparent gradualness of change and the diffusion of new I-languages are the ideas of Kroch and his associates on competing grammars. Paul thought that there were as many languages as individuals but Kroch and colleagues maintain that there are more languages than individuals, because people operate with coexisting I-languages in a kind of internalized diglossia, indeed an internalized multiglossia. Their work enriches grammatical analyses by seeking to describe the variability of individual texts and the spread of a grammatical change through a population. In postulating two (or more) coexisting I-languages in an individual, a researcher needs to show not only that the two I-languages together account for a range of expressions used, but also that the two I-languages are learnable under plausible assumptions about children's PLD. Diglossic grammars are subject to exactly the same learnability demands as any other biological grammar.

In fact, this kind of diglossia represents an interesting approach to solving significant learnability problems. It offers a way of eliminating an unlearnable distinction between optional and obligatory operations (Lightfoot 1999: 92ff., and see Chapter 18, this volume). Chomsky (1995) argued that grammars do not permit optional operations. In that case, apparent optionality would be a function of coexisting I-languages. Rather than allowing one I-language to generate forms *a* and *b* optionally, one would argue that a person has access to two I-languages, one of which generates form *a*, the other form *b*; the speaker has the option at any given time of using one or other of the I-languages. This move reduces the class of available grammars, eliminating those with optional operations (see also Wallenberg forthcoming).

This, in turn, entails that, when Old English texts show verb-second phenomena sometimes, that cannot entail that Old English I-languages had a device generating verb-second order optionally. Rather, there must have been competing I-languages, one generating verb-second order and the other not. Certain speakers have access to just one I-language; other speakers have access to the other I-language; and others have access to both systems in an internalized diglossia. This turns out to be a productive analysis (Kroch and Santorini 2013).

On the view developed by Kroch, 'change proceeds via competition between grammatically incompatible options which substitute for one another in usage' (Kroch 1994: 180). One reason for believing that this view of changes through competing systems is along the right lines is that alternating forms cluster in their distribution, and the clustering follows from how sets of I-languages unify the forms. We do not find free variation, but oscillation between two (or more) fixed points. This is reflected in the Constant Rate Effect of Kroch (1989) and was noted in Chapter 18, this volume, in the context of Shakespeare using the old ₁V system as well as the new system without verb movement, alternating between the old and new systems within the same sentence.

Because cues are abstract, changing one structure or one categorization may entail a range of new surface phenomena. The Constant Rate Effect entails that all surface phenomena reflecting the new I-language property show usage frequencies changing at the same rate, but not necessarily at the same time. This is easy to understand if one I-language is replaced over time by another, and if that change takes place in a winner-take-all competition between the two systems. We do not find complex arrays of linguistic data changing randomly. Instead, they tend to converge towards a relatively small number of patterns or attractors, in a kind of 'anti-chaos' in the sense of Kauffman (1995). The points of variation defined by the theory of grammar constitute the attractors and the two competing I-languages define the points of oscillation.

When we view an individual's language capacity as characterized by a private, personal I-language, then the spread of a new I-language across a speech community will be approached through the methods of population biology. An individual may be exposed to PLD that differ from what anybody else has been exposed to. This could happen because of population movements, new patterns of bilingualism, adult innovations, or perhaps because the PLD are truncated in some way, not including earlier expressions or not including them with the same frequency as a generation earlier. One individual might select a structure differently from others in his/her community and, in that event, is likely to produce different utterances. These new expressions, in turn, affect the linguistic environment, and s/he will now be an agent of further change, reinforcing the PLD that might trigger another instance of his/her new I-language in his/her younger siblings. As those younger siblings pick the same structures as their older brother/sister, so other people's PLD will differ and a chain reaction is created. In this way a new I-language may spread analogously to what has been observed in population genetics, replicating aspects of evolutionary change.

Niyogi and Berwick (1995, 1997) produced a computer model that analysed change in this way and derived the trajectory of changes. The model was made richer by Niyogi (2006). They postulate a learning theory with three subcomponents: a theory of grammar; a learning algorithm by which a child generates grammars on exposure to data; and PLD. They postulate a population of child learners, a small number of whom fail to converge on pre-existing grammars. After exposure to a finite amount of data, some children converge on the pre-existing grammar, but others attain a different I-language.

> The next generation will therefore no longer be linguistically homogeneous. The third generation of children will hear sentences produced by the second – a different distribution – and they, in turn, will attain a different set of grammars. Over successive generations, the linguistic composition evolves as a dynamical system.   *(Niyogi and Berwick 1997: 2)*

Language change, in this simulation, is a logical consequence of specific assumptions about the theory of grammar, the learning algorithm and the PLD. Interestingly their model yields different trajectories for different changes. A common trajectory is the familiar S-curve (Weinreich, Labov and Herzog 1968; Kroch 1989): a change may begin gradually, pick up momentum and proceed more rapidly, tailing off slowly before reaching completion. The success of Niyogi and Berwick is to build a dynamical system from a parameterized system and a memory-less learning algorithm. As a result, they *derive* the S-curve rather than build it into their model as a specific assumption. Further, the model entails that changing elements of the theory of grammar or of the learning algorithm may yield different trajectories, including trajectories other than the S-curve. That means that their model may be amended in light of the way that it matches the actual trajectory for specific changes in specific languages. This offers a new empirical demand for theories to meet, in addition to demands of learnability, coverage of data, etc.: theories can be expected to provide the most accurate diachronic trajectories for changes.

Deriving possible trajectories for changes also provides an alternative to flawed attempts to build 'biases' into UG in order to account directly for what are seen as common pathways for change, such as grammaticalization (see Chapter 1, this volume).

Niyogi and Berwick provided a model for how new I-languages progress through a community of speakers. This is a remarkable result, which clearly could not be replicated under a social definition of grammars, which denies the usefulness of individual, biological grammars. There may be slowness and gradualness in the spread of a change through a population but changes in I-languages are instantaneous at the individual level; familiar S-curves generally arise as a function of averaging across groups. The instantaneousness of change follows from an extension of the intuition behind Aronoff's Blocking Constraint, which limits coexisting forms to those that are functionally distinct (Aronoff 1976).

This all strongly suggests that structural changes are rapid and abrupt at the individual level and that they often spread through a population rapidly. The speed of the spread depends on non-grammatical factors relating to social cohesion, facility of communication among different groups, etc.

24.7 Conclusion

The overwhelming consensus among historical linguists is that languages change gradually. Admittedly there are significant discontinuities that happen from time to time, but they are allegedly due to exceptional events.

We have outlined a different approach here in terms of a distinction between amorphous and constantly shifting E-language, constantly in flux and never experienced the same way by any two people, and biological I-languages represented in the mind/brains of individuals, recursive systems that characterize the individual's language capacity. We view an I-language as emerging in a child as its elements are expressed in the ambient E-language and are acquired by the child. I-languages are internal, individual entities and speakers typically operate with more than one I-language. Different I-languages may be attained when children are exposed to different E-language.

Construing a person's language capacity as an individual, private matter, we can understand how different linguistic experience may trigger a different internal system, which may then spread through a speech community in ways that can be understood through the methods of population biology. Under this view, discontinuities, new I-languages are liable to emerge at any time and can be understood as natural phenomena. Nothing is transmitted from one generation to another but children develop an I-language when exposed to E-language that expresses certain structures. A child might develop a novel I-language and that new I-language may spread through a community. That is our understanding of 'language change', a derivative function that is best understood as an individual phenomenon that may affect the linguistic experience of others and lead to a shift in group behaviour. By seeking to understand the emergence of new linguistic patterns through the acquisition of language systems by individuals, we can sometimes explain the new group behaviour.

In this chapter we have emphasized the development of language systems as a property of individuals, sharing Hermann Paul's view that languages belong to individuals. However, a recent paper by Narayanan and Niyogi (2013) takes an intriguing approach, seeking to model how a group of linguistic agents might arrive at a shared communication system through local patterns of interaction, for example developing a shared vocabulary. If successful, this would *derive* the group properties of Navajo, Norwegian and Nubian, and thereby give them some biological reality and cast new light on what we have described here as properties of population biology.

Understanding the emergence of new I-languages as a function of language acquisition leads us to understand the apparent gradualness of change differently, recognizing discontinuities as a natural part of language history. I-languages are created afresh by every individual on exposure to the ambient E-language, which is different for every individual. Nothing gets transmitted and change is an epiphenomenon of individuals acquiring their private I-language.

The study of diachronic syntax is in its infancy and, as it matures, one would expect it to cast new light on lay ideas about languages and on their sociological character. And much more.

References

Aronoff, M. 1976. *Word formation in generative grammar*. Cambridge, MA: MIT Press.

Casti, J. 1994. *Complexification: Explaining a paradoxical world through the science of surprise*. New York: HarperCollins.

Chomsky, N. 1975. *The logical structure of linguistic theory*. New York: Plenum.
 1986. *Knowledge of language: Its nature, origin and use*. New York: Praeger.
 1995. *The minimalist program*. Cambridge, MA: MIT Press.
 [1957] 2002. *Syntactic structures*, 2nd edn. Berlin: De Gruyter.

Chomsky, N. and M. Halle 1968. *The sound pattern of English*. New York: Harper & Row.

Clark, R. 1992. 'The selection of syntactic knowledge', *Language Acquisition* 2: 83–149.

Dresher, B. E. 1999. 'Charting the learning path: Cues to parameter setting', *Linguistic Inquiry* 30: 27–67.

Ellegård, A. 1954. *The auxiliary do: The establishment and regulation of its use in English*. Stockholm: Almqvist & Wiksell.

Fodor, J. D. 1998. 'Unambiguous triggers', *Linguistic Inquiry* 29: 1–36.

Fries, C. 1940. 'On the development of the structural use of word-order in Modern English', *Language* 16: 199–208.

Gibson, E. and Wexler, K. 1994. 'Triggers', *Linguistic Inquiry* 25: 407–54.

Haeberli, E. 2002a. 'Inflectional morphology and the loss of verb second in English', in D. W. Lightfoot (ed.), *Syntactic effects of morphological change*. Oxford University Press, pp. 88–106.
 2002b. 'Observations on the loss of verb second in the history of English', in C. J.-W. Zwart and W. Abraham (eds.), *Studies in comparative Germanic syntax: Proceedings from the 15th Workshop on comparative Germanic syntax*. Amsterdam: John Benjamins, pp. 245–72.

Heycock, C., Sorace, A., Hansen, Z. S., Wilson, F. and Vikner, S. 2012. 'Detecting the late stages of syntactic change: The loss of V-to-T in Faroese', *Language* 88: 558–600.

Humboldt, W. von 1836. *Über die Verschiedenheit des menschlichen Sprachbaues und ihren Einfluss auf die geistige Entwicklung des Menschengeschlechts*. Royal Academy of Sciences of Berlin [*Linguistic variability and intellectual development*, trans. G. C. Buck and F. A. Raven 1971. Philadelphia: University of Pennsylvania Press].

Kauffman, S. 1995. *At home in the Universe: The search for laws of self-organisation and complexity*. Oxford University Press.

Keenan, E. 2002. 'Explaining the creation of reflexive pronouns in English', in D. Minkova and R. Stockwell (eds.), *Studies in the history of the English language: A millennial perspective*. Berlin and New York: Mouton de Gruyter, pp. 325–54.

Kiparsky, P. 1968. 'Linguistic universals and linguistic change', in E. Bach and R. Harms (eds.), *Universals in linguistic theory*. New York: Holt. Rinehart & Winston.

Kroch, A. 1989. 'Reflexes of grammar in patterns of language change', *Language Variation and Change* 1: 199–244.

1994. 'Morphosyntactic variation', in K. Beals *et al.* (eds.), *Papers from the 30th regional meeting of the Chicago Linguistics Society: Parasession on variation and linguistic theory*. Chicago Linguistics Society, pp. 180–201.

Kroch, A. and Santorini, B. 2013. 'What a parsed corpus is and how to use it', paper presented at LSA Summer Institute Workshop on diachronic syntax, www.ling.upenn.edu/~kroch/lsa13ws.html.

Leech, G. 2003. 'Modality on the move: The English modal auxiliaries 1961–1992', in R. Facchinetti, M. Krug and F. Palmer (eds.), *Modality in contemporary English*. Berlin: Mouton de Gruyter, pp. 223–40.

Lightfoot, D. W. 1995. 'Grammars for people', *Journal of Linguistics* 31: 393–9.

1999. *The development of language: Acquisition, change, and evolution*. Oxford: Blackwell.

2006. *How new languages emerge*. Cambridge University Press.

2011. 'Multilingualism everywhere', *Bilingualism: Language and Cognition* 14: 162–4.

Longobardi, G. 2001. 'Formal syntax, diachronic minimalism, and etymology: The history of French *chez*', *Linguistic Inquiry* 32: 275–302.

McWhorter, J. H. 2009. 'What else happened to English? A brief for the Celtic hypothesis', *English Language and Linguistics* 13: 163–91.

Meisel, J. 2011. 'Bilingual language acquisition and theories of diachronic change: Bilingualism as cause and effect of grammatical change', *Bilingualism: Language and Cognition* 14: 121–45.

Mitchener, W. G. and Nowak, M. A. 2004. 'Chaos and language', *Proceedings of the Royal Society of London*, series B, 271: 701–04.

Narayanan, H. and Niyogi, P. 2013. 'Language evolution, coalescent processes, and the consensus problem on a social network', unpublished MS available at http://faculty.washington.edu/harin/LangEvol.pdf.

Niyogi, P. 2006. *The computational nature of language learning and evolution*. Cambridge, MA: MIT Press.

Niyogi, P. and Berwick, R. 1995. 'The logical problem of language change', MIT AI Memo no. 1516.

1997. 'A dynamical systems model of language change', *Complex Systems* 11: 161–204.

O'Neil, W. 1978. 'The evolution of the Germanic inflectional systems: A study in the causes of language change', *Orbis* 27: 248–85.

Paul, H. 1877. 'Die Vocale der Flexions- und Ableitungssilben in den ältesten germanischen Dialecten', *Beiträge zur Geschichte der deutschen Sprache und Literatur* 4: 314–475.

1880. *Prinzipien der Sprachgeschichte*. Tübingen: Niemeyer.

Roberts, I. and Roussou, A. 2003. *Syntactic change: A minimalist approach to grammaticalisation*. Cambridge University Press.

Thom, R. 1989. *Structural stability and morphogenesis: An outline of a general theory of models*. Reading, MA: Addison-Wesley.

Trudgill, P. 2002. *Sociolinguistic variation and change*. Washington, DC: Georgetown University Press.

van Gelderen, E. 2011. *The linguistic cycle: Language change and the language faculty*. Amsterdam: John Benjamins.

van Kemenade, A. 1987. *Syntactic case and morphological case in the history of English*. Dordrecht: Foris.

Vikner, S. 1995. *Verb movement and expletive subjects in the Germanic languages*. Oxford University Press.

Walkden, G. 2012. 'Against inertia', *Lingua* 122: 891–901.

Wallenberg, J. Forthcoming. 'Extraposition is disappearing', *Language*.

Weinreich, U., Labov, W. and Herzog, M. 1968. 'Empirical foundations for a theory of language change', in W. Lehmann and Y. Malkiel (eds.), *Directions for historical linguistics*. Austin: University of Texas Press, pp. 95–189.

25

Social Conditioning

Suzanne Romaine

25.1 Introduction

By abandoning the strict Saussurean dichotomy between synchrony and diachrony in favour of viewing synchronic variation as a stage in long-term change, Weinreich, Labov and Herzog (1968) provided empirical foundations for a theory of language change. Linguistic hetereogenity is not random, but regularly structured along a number of internal linguistic and external social dimensions, including, for instance, linguistic context, speaker position/status, text type (style, genre, etc.), age, gender, etc., displaying directional gradience through social groups, geographic space and time. Through understanding what Weinreich, Labov and Herzog (1968) term the 'embedding problem' (i.e. how this structured heterogeneity is embedded in a social and linguistic matrix) in contemporary speech communities and the social meanings indexed by variants, we can make predictions about the directions and pathways of change moving through a community.

There is no reason to assume that syntax would be an exception to these general principles for a theory of language change, but due to differences in goals, theoretical assumptions and working methods, the study of variation, in particular externally conditioned variability, has had limited impact on the development of syntactic theory. Although the variationist approach is not tied to any particular theoretical framework, most syntactic theories have been reluctant to incorporate variation or optionality as a property of grammars or to consider factors outside the abstract language system internalized by speakers (Henry 2002; Cornips and Corrigan 2005a). Syntacticians tend to rely on grammaticality judgments generally based on standard written varieties, while sociolinguists tend to work with spontaneous spoken data often from non-standard varieties. In addition, the primacy of phonology in variationist sociolinguistics contrasts with the primacy of syntax in theoretical linguistics. This chapter addresses the question of social conditioning as an explanatory mechanism of syntactic change by examining evidence from a variety of languages. §25.2 provides an overview of methodology, followed by discussion of five case studies in §25.3. The final section, §25.4, concludes with a brief discussion of some remaining problems and consideration of new analytical tools, novel data sources and theoretical frameworks.

25.2 Methodology

This section discusses some fundamental methodological prerequisites to defining, identifying and analysing syntactic variation. Addressing these issues presupposes criteria for determining which structural phenomena can properly be called 'syntactic' or 'morphosyntactic', and for deciding when two or more such forms can be considered variants of each other. The answers to these questions are interrelated and theory-dependent, as Sells, Rickford and Wasow (1996: 173) observe: 'Variation theory needs grammatical theory because a satisfactory grammatical characterization of a variable is a prerequisite to decisions about what to count and how to count it, and it is an essential element in the larger question of where variation is located in speakers' grammar.'

The locus of syntactic variation differs not only according to theoretical framework but cross-linguistically as well. The fundamental working method of variationist sociolinguistics is to identify and quantify so-called (sociolinguistic) 'variables' that can be regarded as alternative ways of saying the same thing. A variable represents a class of variants displaying a regular relationship with some external dimension like social class, style, gender, etc. as well as internal linguistic constraints such as the structural environment in which the variable occurs (Tagliamonte 2011). Most of the early work (and even now, the bulk of studies) focus on phonological variables like loss of initial /h/ before vowels in stressed syllables in words such as *heart*, or morphosyntactic variables like the presence or absence of an overt pronominal subject in a finite clause (e.g. It. *parla inglese* speak.PRS.3SG vs *lei parla inglese* she speak.PRS.3SG '(she) speaks English'). Various factors are responsible for the relative neglect of syntactic variables. Firstly, phonological variables occur more frequently. Most conventional synchronic and diachronic multi- and single-genre corpora are still far too small for studying syntactic variables and some of the most interesting variables, particularly recessive or relic features like double modals in some varieties of southern United States English (e.g. *I **might could** help you*), are quite rare and subject to pragmatic constraints limiting their occurrence in the kinds and amounts of data collected by contemporary sociolinguists and historical linguists. After examining a sample of some 15.5 million words of texts spanning six centuries, Kytö and Romaine (2005) found only 123 examples (or on average 7.85 per million words) of a rare construction expressing avertive meaning that became obsolete in standard English in the late nineteenth century (e.g. . . . *if he had not had a good hors he **had be like to haue ben** in joparté of his lyfe*; 1472, *Paston Letters*, Margaret Paston, Letter 217).

Secondly, not everyone agrees that syntactic variation is subject to social influence, or whether socially conditioned syntactic variation can be modelled in the same way as phonological variation. Labov (2001: 28f.) argued that abstract linguistic structures are not likely to become highly socially stratified or strongly evaluated in social perception (although there are exceptions, such as negative concord). In one of the earliest studies of syntactic variation from a sociolinguistic perspective Weiner and Labov (1983) claimed that choice between the active and agentless passive (e.g. *They **broke into** the liquor closet* vs *The liquor closet **was broken into***) was constrained entirely by syntactic factors and carried neither social nor stylistic significance. Thirdly, there is some disagreement about whether the notion of variable itself can be meaningfully extended beyond phonology to syntax. Syntactic variables displaying alternation with a zero form such as deletion of complementizer *that* in English (e.g. *I thought **that**/∅ I'd go*) or *que* in Canadian French (e.g. *Tu veux **que**/∅) je vienne* 2SG want.PRS.2SG COMP 1SG come.SBJV.1SG 'Do you want me to come?) are more directly analogous to the kinds of typical phonological variables most frequently studied. That is, variation consists of alternation between presence or absence of the variable, occurs frequently, is easy to quantify and preserves semantic equivalence. Because phonological variants are typically allophones of the same phoneme and have no semantic content, it is easy to argue, for example, that variation in the pronunciation of the final consonant of a word like *car* does not change its meaning. Syntactic variables, however, form one or more elements in discourse, and may be multifunctional, which makes it difficult to decide which function a syntactic variant has (Romaine 1984).

Weiner and Labov's (1983) study was carried out from the perspective of transformational generative grammar, where semantic equivalence of the two constructions could be defined and defended by virtue of their derivation from the same underlying structure. That is, variation arises from the optional application of the rule deriving alternative surface variants. More recent syntactic theories, however, have abandoned the notion of transformations in favour of parametric approaches to variation. Within the minimalist framework syntactic variation arises primarily from features in the lexicon. Parametric variation reduces to the fact that different languages have different lexicons. Within other theoretical frameworks like cognitive and functional linguistics and construction grammar every grammatical alternative carries some meaning. Indeed, Bolinger (1968: 127) contended that 'a difference in syntactic form always spells a difference in meaning'. Likewise, within construction grammar the 'Principle of No Synonymy' of grammatical forms dictates that 'if two constructions are syntactically distinct, they must be semantically or pragmatically distinct' (Goldberg 1995: 67). Thus, active and passive are instances of two separate constructions rather than alternative ways of saying the same thing. Within construction grammar variation consists of variation in repertoires of syntactic patterns. However, even while acknowledging that meaning should be construed broadly enough to include 'contexts of use' (Goldberg 1995: 229, n.6), opening the way for register to be a critical social variable, construction grammarians have largely ignored social conditioning of variation.

While variation may be easy to find, deciding whether or how to account for it may prove difficult when it is impossible to specify the contexts where the variable could have occurred but did not. Double modals are non-standard syntactic forms with no clear alternates. Although some pairs like *might could* appear equivalent to standard English *might be able to*, other forms like *may can, must can, might should* and *might would* lack clearly identifiable alternatives preserving synonymy. Cases like these typically arise from contact between standard and non-standard varieties or language contact more generally. There are pragmatic and distributional differences in various uses of negators in standard compared to non-standard English as well as in English-lexicon creoles, which may adopt Standard English forms without their function. Trinidadian Creole *ain't* appears superficially identical to non-standard English *ain't*, but is not equivalent to *be + not*. It is used as a tenseless and aspectless negative marker alternating with Standard Eng. *didn't* (e.g. I **ain't/didn't** have). Both variants express negation and show social differentiation (Winford 1996: 183). Muysken (2005: 39–44) observes that in the case of gerunds used as main verbs in Ecuadorian Spanish (e.g. *tranquilo anda-ndo* quiet walk-GER 'I walk quietly'), it would be almost impossible to study the alternative for purely quantitative reasons: one would also need to look at the use of all main finite verbs, which would be quantitatively overwhelming. Quechua-dominant bilinguals tended to use more gerunds than Spanish-dominant bilinguals, while Spanish monolinguals have usage levels intermediate between these two groups. Social class was also important, with the highest social group using fewer gerunds than the lowest, but other social factors like age, gender and education level were not significant. Variation was also grammatically conditioned, with gerunds more likely when adverbial clauses were followed rather than preceded by the main verb, and also when the subjects were identical. Adverbial clauses preceding the main verb may be tied to the influence of Quechua.

Biber *et al.* (1999: 14,6) offer a somewhat less stringent definition when they refer to syntactic variants as optional, in the sense of being 'nearly equivalent in meaning and have roughly the same communicative effect'. This, however, does not entirely resolve problems arising from complex syntactic variables varying along several dimensions. Consider Table 25.1,

Table 25.1 *French* wh-*interrogatives*[a]

	SBJ–V order		Wh		Interrogative marker	
	normal	inverted	*in situ*	fronting	*c'est que*	Inversion *est-ce que*
a. *Tu vas où?* 2sg go.PRS.2sg Q-where	+		+			
b. *Où tu vas?* Q-where 2sg go.PRS.2sg	+			+		
c. *Où vas- tu?* Q-where go.PRS.2sg 2sg		+		+		
d. *Où est- ce que tu* Q-where is.PRS.3sg DEM COMP 2sg *vas?* go.PRS.2sg	+			+		+
e. *Où c' est que tu* Q-where DEM is-PRS.3sg COMP 2sg *vas?* go.PRS.2sg	+			+	+	
f. *c' est où que tu* DEM is.PRS.3sg Q-where COMP 2sg *vas?* go.PRS.2sg	+		+		+	
g. *Où est- ce que* Q-where is.PRS.3sg DEM COMP *c' est que tu vas?* DEM is.PRS.3sg COMP 2sg go. PRS.2sg	+			+	+	+
h. *Où que tu vas?* Q-where COMP 2sg go-PRS.2sg	+			+		

[a] This table considers only interrogatives with pronominal (rather than NP) subjects.

showing the set of contemporary French constructions that can potentially be regarded as variants of *wh*-interrogatives.

The only obligatory element common to all variants is the *wh*-word. Although all are translatable as 'where are you going?', not all speakers use all of them. Despite Elsig's (2009) claim that internal constraints account for most of the variation, studies have revealed social conditioning factors, e.g. register (speech vs writing), social class background, style (formal vs informal) and age. Variants a, b and c could easily be argued to involve semantically vacuous movement: a and b preserve normal subject–verb word order, but c displays inversion and triggers *wh*-fronting (like b), while a preserves *wh*-in-situ. Where inversion occurs, *wh* must be fronted, so variation is ruled out (i.e. **vas-tu où?*). Rowlett (2007: 198) argues that examples of *wh*-in-situ are not semantically equivalent to examples of fronted *wh* because *in-situ* questions are 'strongly presuppositional in a way that [fronted wh are not]'. Other variants, however, despite having normal word order, introduce new lexical material and additional complexity through using various clefting and focus strategies. Variants d, e, f and g contain the cleft *est-ce que/c'est que* 'is it/it is that', with both *c'est* and *est-ce* combined in g. A double cleft construction is also possible, i.e. *où c'est que c'est que tu vas?* Like a, f shows *wh-in-situ* rather than fronting. Variants b *où tu vas?* and h *où que tu vas?* are identical except for the presence of complementizer *que*. In fact, the number of possible variants may not end here, depending on how narrowly or broadly we define the so-called envelope of variation (i.e. delimiting relevant environments), and how much additional material we allow to enter. If we add the invariant informal demonstrative *ça* 'that' to constructions like *où ça tu vas, où ça que tu vas, où ça est-ce que tu vas, où ça c'est que tu vas*, etc., an even more extensive array of variants is possible (see Gadet 1989: 138 for yet a few more possible variants). The interrogative itself is a variable, with *où* 'where', *quand* 'when', and *combien* 'how much/many' preferring the *wh-in-situ* construction, while *comment* 'how/what' and especially *pourquoi* 'why' prefer fronting. There may also be meaning differences for *comment* and *pourquoi* depending on their position in the utterance. Lexical verbs are more compatible with fronted structures while copular verbs are more compatible with the *in-situ* structure (Coveney 2002). In summary then, French allows its *wh* to be fronted (b, c, d, e, g, h), to remain *in situ* (a, f), to be 'reinforced' with various elements (d, e, f, g), to appear bare (a, b, c), to trigger inversion (c), or not (a, b, d, e, f, g, h).

The complexity of the present system reflects diachronic layering, persistence of older variants and emergence of new ones over centuries in the context of syntactic changes tied to more general loss of V2 in French and regularization of SVO word order. Historically, variant c with pronominal subject–verb inversion was the default method of question formation in Old, Late Middle and Early Modern French, but after other alternatives arose in Middle French, inversion steadily declined in favour of other variants preserving canonical word order, especially in colloquial spoken varieties, which have almost completely abandoned inversion (Coveney 2002: 190). Prescriptive grammarians still endorse c as the correct variant for standard written French. Variants with canonical word order (i.e. without inversion) are generally considered more colloquial constructions inappropriate for written French and/or formal registers (Elsig 2009; Rowlett 2011; Adli 2013). The interrogative marker *est-ce que* composed of copula plus clitic (*est-ce/c'est*) appeared in Old French as an inverted interrogative cleft marking grammatical focus, and subsequently grammaticalized during the sixteenth century. After grammaticalization *est-ce que* lost the emphatic properties of a cleft construction, and its independent status. In its phonologically reduced and condensed form /ɛsk(ə)/, it acts more like a morphological affix attached to the *wh*-word (i.e. *wh-est-ce que*) to form a single structural unit or unanalyzable chunk (Druetta 2002, 2003). In clefted interrogatives the question expression may either precede or follow *c'est* (in COMP or *in situ*, respectively, as in d, e, f, g). The clitic *ce* 'it' no longer has semantic content and is dependent on the copula *est* is.PRS.3SG 'is'. Bare *wh* is a lexical variant of *wh-est-ce que*. Subject–verb inversion is incompatible with *est-ce que* (i.e. **où est-ce que vas-tu?*); nor can *est-ce que* appear in situ (i.e. **tu vas où est-ce que?*). The interrogative marker may have originated in the spoken language as a change from below, i.e. below the level of conscious awareness (Labov 1994: 78), appearing first in genres like plays during the fifteenth century and then spreading to other genres during the sixteenth and seventeenth centuries (Elsig 2009).

Variant b with normal declarative word order, but with *wh*-movement not triggering inversion is found marginally as far back as the seventeenth century predating the *in-situ* variant (a) by several centuries. By some accounts, this is the unmarked structure for colloquial spoken French even though grammarians consider it incorrect. The truncated cleft (h) with its additional *que* characteristic of *français populaire* ranks lowest on both social and stylistic continua, dismissed as vulgar by normative grammarians. Middle-class speakers tend not to use it. According to evidence from the *Atlas linguistique de la France* (Edmont and Gilliéron 1902–10), however, this is the most common variant across France at the end of the nineteenth and beginning of the twentieth century. This suggests that it is quite old, but given its vernacular status, it is hard to find in print. The construction appeared first with *où* 'where', followed within fifty years by *combien* 'how much', *comment* 'how' and *pourquoi* 'why', and finally by *quand* 'when'. While this variant took only about 150 years to spread, the interrogative marker *est-ce que* took over 400 years (Tailleur 2013: 35f.). The most recent variant (a) with *wh-in-situ* is not found in the *Atlas linguistique de la France* (Tailleur 2013), but may be spreading. It is difficult to present a coherent overall picture of the French interrogative system because studies are based on different corpora of different sizes, include different structures, quantify the variants in different ways, use different terminology and analyses, and conflate some of the social conditioning factors, e.g. speech vs writing, style, register and class (Coveney 2002: 112). The case studies in the next section, however, focus on simpler variables in order to draw out more clearly the role of some of the major social or external conditioning factors in change: social status, network, gender, age, style and region. Understanding the relationships between these social factors is also important.

25.3 Some Case Studies Illustrating Social Conditioning of Syntactic Change

Innovations in language occur all the time and many will not permanently enter the language system. Once they do, however, they tend to follow predictable paths through social and linguistic structures, which we now know a great deal about, thanks to the research programme articulated by

Weinreich, Labov and Herzog (1968) and five decades of research on socio-linguistic variation. As the case of the French interrogative demonstrated, some changes can be quite rapid while others take many centuries. The chance of an innovation's survival depends partly on where/when it is introduced into the social and linguistic system and by whom.

25.3.1   Two Early Case Studies: Relativization Strategies in English and Word Order in German Subordinate Clauses

The emergence of a research field variously called sociohistorical linguis-tics or historical sociolinguistics, terms often used interchangeably, estab-lished a new framework for applying insights from the synchronic investigation of socially conditioned variation to the analysis of historical texts (Romaine 1982; Nevalainen and Raumolin-Brunberg 2003). Taking account of developments across a broader range of varieties, especially those from geographically or socially peripheral communities or indivi-duals further removed from literate traditions presents opportunities for a richer account of language change because non-standard varieties used in rural and working class communities often preserve older stages of changes already completed and no longer directly observable in the stan-dard. Both of the two early studies examined in this section show the intersection of social and stylistic continua, one of the most important findings of quantitative sociolinguistics: namely, a feature occurring more frequently in lower-class groups, will tend to occur more frequently in the informal styles of all groups.

For example, the *wh*-relativization strategy in English is a later develop-ment historically, superimposed possibly by contact with Latin or French, onto an older system in which relative clauses are marked by the subordi-nator *that*, which may be deleted variably (e.g. *the woman (*whom, that, Ø)
I met*), except in subject position (e.g. **the woman [Ø lives next door] is a doctor*). The infiltration of *wh* pronouns such as *who, whose* and *whom* can be seen as completed in the modern standard written language and some varieties of educated spoken English, but it has not really affected modern spoken vernaculars, which still prefer *that* or zero marking (Romaine 1982; Tagliamonte 2006). The *wh*-relativization strategy entered sixteenth-century Middle Scots in the most syntactically complex styles (as repre-sented by official and legal prose texts) and least frequently relativized syntactic positions, until it eventually spread throughout the system by working its way down a stylistic continuum containing different types of prose and verse texts ranging from the more fully Scottish styles to the most fully anglicized ones. The fact that the *wh*-relativization strategy seems to have 'sneaked in the back door' of the language via the most complex and formal styles and least frequently relativized syntactic posi-tions is a hallmark of so-called 'change from above', i.e. emanating from conscious, more formal speech styles rather than from the vernacular,

often through borrowing from outside the system. *Wh* forms occur more frequently in more formal styles, whether written or spoken, while *that* and zero (absence of a relative marker) occur in the less formal styles of speaking and writing.

Other social conditioning factors like gender also played a role. Typically, women show lower rates of use of stigmatized variants and a higher rate of prestige variants of stable variables than men. Moreover, in cases of linguistic change from above, women adopt prestige forms at a higher rate than men and are a generation ahead of men in terms of change. In this instance, however, zero marking was associated with women, the lower social orders and speech-related genres like letters. Only in the women's correspondence were there instances where relative markers were absent in subject position. The association of women with non-standard vernacular variants does not contradict the typical synchronic sociolinguistic pattern linking women with prestige forms because at earlier times in the history of English (and even today in some societies where literacy rates for women are lower than those for men) women were more isolated, regardless of their social status, from the norms of the written (standard) language. Relativization strategies are also gender-differentiated in the fifteenth-century Paston Letters, written by members of a Norfolk family rising from peasantry to aristocracy in two generations, with male members preferring *wh* pronouns, while women prefer *that* (Bergs 2005).

Other cases of syntactic change in other languages evidence similar embedding of variation and change in both linguistic and social factors. Consider word order in two verb complexes in German subordinate clauses. Contemporary standard German requires fixed ordering with the non-finite followed by the finite verb (1a). This contrasts with the ordering found in main clauses, where the finite verb occupies second position (1b). Earlier stages of German, as well as some contemporary dialects such as Swabian and Austrian German, show considerable variation in word order within the verbal complex, allowing the finite verb to precede the non-finite one (1c).

(1)   a. *Ich weiss   dass, sie   Peter   gesehen   hat.* (subordinate: non-finite + finite)
          I   know that she Peter seen   has
          'I know that she saw Peter.'

       b. *Sie hat Peter   gesehen.* (main: finite + non-finite)
          she has Peter seen

       c. *Ich weiss dass, sie   Peter   hat   gesehen.* (finite + non-finite)
          I   know that she Peter has seen

The variant orderings of finite + non-finite (1–2) and non-finite + finite (2–1) in subordinate clauses coexisted for centuries, subject to morphological, syntactic, pragmatic, and sociolinguistic conditioning, with the eventual loss of finite + non-finite in most varieties as a result of change from above passed down from the prestigious chancery style. The change from 1–2 to 2–1 order is part of a long-term trend toward the fixing of SOV order in the standard language. Linguistic conditioning factors include syntagm type, presence of a stressed separable prefix, and phonological weight of the word preceding the verbs. Examining text types from fourteenth to sixteenth century Nuremberg, Ebert (1981) looked at social factors such as style, education, occupation and class. More formal letters showed higher rates of the 2–1 order. Administrators showed the highest use of 2–1 order followed by merchants, artisans, students, nuns and secular women. This social hierarchy overturns a commonly held view that Latin influence was responsible for the change from 1–2 to 2–1 order. Merchants and artisans, who would not have had much schooling in Latin, used the 2–1 order more frequently than students, whose education was Latin-based and who therefore would have been more likely to follow Latin syntax.

A more recent study focused on verb order in sixteenth-century Nuremberg teenagers, finding that most of those studied increased their usage of 2–1 order over their lifetimes. Increased schooling was also correlated with higher use of 2–1 order, as was gender, with young men ahead of young women. Chancery and other official documents had the lowest rates of 1–2 order, followed by religious texts, technical writings and private letters (Ebert 1998). A similar study of a corpus of sixteenth-century Augsburg texts also revealed a decline in the 1–2 order over time. The text types furthest removed from the spoken language (i.e. chronicles, city ordinances, schoolmasters' letters, official letters and reports and printed pamphlets) had the lowest rates of 1–2 order, while those closest to spoken language (i.e. personal letters and narratives, guild books and flyers) had the highest rates (Reifsnyder 2003). The change to 2–1 order was also variable across geographic space, with southern and eastern dialects such as those of Swabia, Nuremburg, Augsburg, Vienna and Saxony showing higher rates of the 1–2 order than northern and western dialects such as those of Cologne, Alsace, Hesse, Thuringia and Zurich (Sapp 2011).

25.3.2   A Case Study: The English Genitive

Modern English has two syntactically distinct constructions for expressing the relationship between possessor and possessee: the inflectional *s*-genitive and the analytical *of*-genitive, e.g. *the car's window* vs *the window of the car*. As the example illustrates, the order of possessor and possessee differs in the two types, with the possessor preceding the possessee in the *s*-genitive construction and the possessee preceding the possessor in the *of*-genitive. Although both types are attested in Old English, the *of*-genitive was marginal until the twelfth century, after which it steadily increased at the expense of the *s*-genitive. By the fourtheenth century the *of*-genitive was the predominant form. Although the *of*-genitive is clearly of native origin, and other Germanic languages developed similar constructions, some scholars speculate that its spread was possibly reinforced by contact with the corresponding French *de*-genitive construction. Myers (2011), for instance, found that the genitive system of early Middle English Kentish sermons dating from the second half of the thirteenth century was far advanced in terms of the use of the *of*-genitive, which is unexpected given the morphologically conservative nature of southern dialects, especially Kentish. Texts from this region preserved case distinctions the longest. However, Kent was also the first point of contact for the numerous French settlers who crossed the Channel after the Norman conquest, and the Kentish Sermons are a translation of a French text, possibly by a bilingual scribe.

Nevertheless, contrary to what might be expected from the general typological drift in English from a more synthetic SOV language relying on inflections towards a more analytical one with relatively fixed SOV word order, the frequency of the *s*-genitive has been steadily increasing since around the sixteenth century (Rosenbach 2007: 154), continuing through the latter half of the twentieth century in both American and British English (Hinrichs and Szmrecsanyi 2007). The resurgence of the *s*-genitive, *the girl's bicycle*, is unexpected because this direction of change is at odds with the typological tendency whereby languages with VO order tend to have head–modifier (i.e. [N$_{head}$ *of* NP$_{mod}$] or possessee–possessor) order for other constituents. Hence, we would expect modern English possessives to favour the analytical *of*-genitive, i.e. *the bicycle of the girl*, where the genitive modifier follows the head noun.

Alternation between these two types of genitives occurs across a range of contexts in which the variants can be considered semantically equivalent and choice of one over the other is conditioned by semantic-pragmatic, syntactic, phonological and sociolinguistic factors (see, however, Stefanowitsch 2003 for a different point of view). Among the most important of several competing linguistic constraints affecting the linear arrangement of possessive constructions is the interplay between two discourse-pragmatic principles, the animacy scale and the referentiality/thematicity scale, which give preference to animate and thematic over inanimate and non-thematic participants. Because animate participants tend to precede inanimate ones, the *s*-genitive occurs more frequently with animate personal possessors, e.g. *the girl's bicycle* vs *the bicycle of the girl*. Inanimate possessors favour the *of*-genitive, e.g. *the pedal of the bicycle* vs *the bicycle's pedal*. Between the fifteenth and early seventeenth century the *s*-genitive became more frequent with animate possessors. In Early Modern English *s*-genitives were still restricted to animate nouns, and it is only in the Late Modern English period that the *s*-genitive spread to inanimate nouns (Rosenbach 2007: 153–60). Some scholars suggest that this development originated in journalistic prose and diffused from there to other genres (Jespersen 1909–49: VII, 327–8; Potter 1969: 105f.). The animacy effects observed for English genitive variation are not specific to this construction but reflect cross-linguistic principles governing language-internal variability. Where a language has two possessive strategies, the choice between them will be determined by the animacy and/or the giveness (or referentiality) of the possessor, i.e. the so-called animacy/referentiality split (Koptjevskaja-Tamm 2002), which predicts that prenominal possessives are restricted to referents high in animacy and givenness. Referents low in animacy and referentiality tend to be realized postnominally. In addition, the tendency for 'heavier' (i.e. longer and/or more complex) constituents to follow 'lighter' ones can be seen in a trend for long possessees to favour the *s*-genitive (e.g. *the nation's federal welfare chief*), while long possessors favour the *of*-genitive because they put the possessor last (Szmrecsanyi, Rosenbach, Bresnan and Wolk 2013: 5). Another factor is repetition or persistence; that is, usage of one variant in preceding discourse influences the choice of variant in subsequent slots. Other linguistic conditioning factors are phonological. Possessors ending in a sibilant (e.g. *Ross's house*) disfavour the *s*-genitive.

Contemporary varieties of English vary in the extent to which inanimate possessors occur with the *s*-genitive, e.g. *the table's leg*. American English speakers use the *s*-genitive more frequently with inanimate nouns than British English speakers, and overall its popularity is increasing faster in American than British English (Szmrecsanyi *et al.* 2013: 11). Indeed, Leech, Hundt, Mair and Smith (2009: 206) describe the increase in *s*-genitives between 1961 and 1991 in the Brown family of corpora as 'spectacular'. Specifically, they documented a rise of *c.* 43 per cent in American English and *c.* 25 per cent in British English, with the greatest changes found in the information-oriented Press and Learned subcorpora, which showed remarkable increases of 41 and 91 per cent in American English and 36 and 35 per cent in British English, respectively (Leech *et al.* 2009: 223f.). Conversely, the category of Fiction showed the lowest increase in *s*-genitives. Weakening of animacy as a constraining factor on occurrence of the *s*-genitive does not appear to have played the most important role (Hinrichs and Szmrecsanyi 2007: 467f.). Leech *et al.* (2009: 234) explain their findings by way of a trend towards greater information density in the noun phrase, well suited to the requirements of journalism. With modernity triggering an information explosion, the pressure of economy of expression is particularly evident in genres like newspapers that need to compress large amounts of knowledge into short texts for their readers (Biber 2003: 170). Constructions in which nouns are juxtaposed, as in *s*-genitive constructions (N's N), permit condensation of information into a smaller space, so it is unsurprising that newspaper reportage would have played a major role in spearheading this shift. Otherwise, in written English the *of*-genitive tends to be more frequent, while the *s*-genitive is more frequent in spoken

English. Nevertheless, Szmrecsanyi and Hinrichs (2008: 304) contend that the reasons for the greater frequency of the *s*-genitive in spoken English and newspaper writing are different. The effects of animacy, referentiality and possessee length as conditioning factors have different impacts on speech and writing. Possessee length, for instance, does not appear to have any effect on spoken language. Grafmiller (2014), however, found the *of*-genitive to be more frequent in both spoken and written English. The reasons for this difference in findings are unclear, but it is possible they are due to differences in the corpora selected for comparison and the time period between them. Grafmiller compared the written Brown corpus (1961) with the *Switchboard Corpus of Spoken American English* (1992), while Szmrecsanyi and Hinrichs (2008) compared the *Corpus of Spoken American English* (2003) and the *Freiburg Corpus of Spoken English Dialects* with the Brown family of corpora. As Leech *et al.* (2009) show, much has happened in the intervening three decades separating Brown representing American English from 1961 and the matching Frown corpus of American English from 1991. In addition, there is no agreement on the set of possessive categories or different types of possessive relations, so different studies may be operating with different notions of what constitutes a permissible possessive construction. While the effect of animacy as the largest contributor to explaining the results of most studies is overwhelming, it may be the case that animate possessors are generally shorter in length and therefore lighter in weight than inanimate ones (Grafmiller 2014). More work is needed with both synchronic and diachronic corpora representing more genres and varieties of English.

25.3.3 A Case Study: Null Subject Pronouns in Spanish

Null subjects represent an empty, phonologically unrealized definite pronoun (*pro*) in subject position of a finite clause. Compare It. *Ø/io dico* and Sp. *Ø/yo digo* 'Ø/I say.1SG'. The null option (Ø) alternates with overt marking by the first person singular pronoun *io* or *yo*. The original motivation for postulating the null subject parameter within the principles and parameters approach derived largely from evidence from various Romance languages like these, where presence of null subjects tends to be closely correlated with rich agreement inflection on the finite verb. Originally, this difference was captured within the principles and parameters framework by means of a binary parameter: languages were either +Null Subject or –Null Subject, but more recent typological work suggests a more refined typology (Holmberg and Roberts 2010) based on a combination of macro- and microparameters

The null subject parameter has been the focus of extensive cross-linguistic empirical and theoretical work resulting in an impressive body of theoretical research, including developmental data from first and second language acquisition. Variation between null and overt subject pronouns in Spanish has been studied in detail across numerous regional varieties and dialects for more than three decades of empirical research, making this a 'showcase variable in quantitative sociolinguistics' (Bayley, Greer and Holland 2013: 22). Thanks to these studies the constraints on Spanish null subject variation are reasonably well understood and extend across a range of varieties on all five continents where Spanish is spoken. Among the linguistic constraints are person and number, emphasis, position of the subject pronoun in the clause, verb semantics, lexical aspect and discourse connectedness, i.e. agreement of a tensed verb with the preceding verb in person, number, tense and mood. Co-reference with the subject of the preceding tensed verb is widely agreed to be one of the most important factors. Some studies include not only pronominal subjects (e.g. *yo* 'I' *ella* 'she', etc.) but numerous other items appearing in the subject slot like nouns (e.g. *Pedro*, *Carmen*, etc.), or demonstrative pronouns (e.g. *estos/estas* 'those.MPL/FPL') while others consider only pronominal ones as a site for alternation with null subjects. Subjects co-referential with the subject of the preceding tensed verb are less likely to be realized overtly than non-co-referential subjects, but a switch in reference favours an overt pronoun. Singular subject pronouns, especially first person *yo*, are more likely to be realized overtly than plurals. Verbs denoting mental states or activities also tend to favour overt subject pronouns. These factors, however, apply only to certain varieties (Flores-Ferrán 2007; Bayley 2013; Bayley, Greer and Holland 2013).

One area of disagreement, however, concerns the possible effect of morphological ambiguity, with some studies finding support for the 'functional hypothesis', i.e. a tendency to avoid loss of information, while others do not (Nagy, Aghdasi, Denis and Motut 2011). The functionalist requirement of meaning preservation suggests that variable deletion of a meaningful segment would be constrained, depending on the amount of information present elsewhere in the context. This would predict that in instances where the referent is indeterminable from the verbal morphology null subjects would be avoided, e.g. *estaba* 'I/she/he was' or 'you (formal) were', and speakers would introduce overt pronouns to clarify the discourse referent. In Mexican Spanish ambiguity may arise in the first and third person singular imperfect, conditional, and the present subjunctive, which are identical in form. Varieties exhibiting relatively high rates of use of overt pronouns also have high rates of /s/ deletion, which can neutralize the distinction between the second person informal (e.g. *hablas* speak.PRS.2SG 'you speak') and third person verb forms (*habla* speak.PRS.3SG '(s)he speaks') in most tenses, as well as the distinction among all singular forms in some tenses (Bayley 2013: 16f.). Overall, however, most studies of these and similar cases do not provide strong evidence that speakers take preemptive action to preserve distinctions that would otherwise be lost, but they do seem motivated to maintain structural parallelism (Labov 1994: 570).

Social conditioning factors include geographic region, genre, gender, education, social network, age and degree of bilingualism, but different studies have produced different outcomes. Varieties spoken in Madrid, most of Mexico and the Andean region tend to have low rates of overt subject pronoun use, while those spoken in the Caribbean, coastal areas of Colombia and Venezuela, and eastern Bolivia tend to have higher ones (Bayley 2013). Indeed, Dominican Spanish (along with Brazilian Portuguese) are becoming obligatorily overt-subject languages. Contact between a null subject language and a non-null subject language like English, which bars null subjects in all finite clauses (except in specific discourse contexts) may be reflected in increased use of overt subject pronouns. Spanish speakers who arrived in New York City after the age of 16 and had been living there fewer than six years had a significantly lower rate of occurrence of overt subject pronouns than those born and raised in the city or who had arrived before age three (Otheguy *et al.* 2007). The influence of English may, however, be confounded with dialect levelling effects in urban areas like New York City where contact between Spanish speakers of varieties exhibiting different levels of null subject pronouns may be leading to convergence. Recently arrived Dominican speakers use overt pronouns at a rate of 41 compared to 27 per cent for Ecuadorians, 24 per cent for Colombians and 19 per cent for Mexicans (Otheguy *et al.* 2007). Other cross-generational studies, however, found no effects of contact with English. Looking at evidence from Italian, for instance, Nagy *et al.* (2011) found no significant difference in null subjects between Italian-Canadians born in Italy and those born in Canada. The Italian of native speakers under attrition from prolonged exposure to English by dint of long residence in the UK displayed very similar behavior in the spontaneous production of overt pronominal subjects (Tsimpli, Sorace, Heycock and Filiaci 2004).

25.4 Conclusion: Future Directions

Many questions remain unanswered: why does variation exist? Where does optionality or choice reside, in grammar, in speakers, or the community? Why do some languages appear to have more variation than others? Adger and Trousdale (2007: 261) contend there is 'little theoretically significant variation in English as a whole', with core phenomena like *wh*-questions, raising and control constructions, passives, basic clausal structure appearing fairly stable across varieties. Ball (2000: 5), on the other hand, emphasizes the many points on which standard and colloquial French diverge, affecting central areas of grammar (see also Gadet 2007). As indicated in §25.2, the answers to these questions are to some extent theory-dependent, with mainstream syntactic theories and variationist sociolinguistics remaining poles apart.

Accounting for variation in the French interrogative system in Table 25.1 poses challenges not only with respect to defining the envelope of variation, but also to the general minimalist principle disallowing optionality (in this case, optionality of movement; see however Biberauer and Roberts 2005, 2009 for proposals regarding the introduction of optionality into a minimalist grammar). Interrogative constructions have played a central role in the development of modern syntactic theory, with the issue of characterizing constraints on the 'dislocation' of *wh*-phrases at the heart of work on generative grammar since the mid 1960s (Ginzburg and Sag 2000: 1). With its two sites for *wh*, French challenges binary cross-linguistic typologies grouping languages into those with movement vs those without movement. The *in-situ* construction is 'perhaps the most puzzling interrogative structure in contemporary French' (Coveney 2002: 218), especially for traditional analyses regarding French as a *wh*-movement language (see Rowlett 2007). Although Weinreich, Labov and Herzog (1968: 100f.) stress that 'nativelike command of heterogeneous structures is not a matter of multidialectalism or "mere" performance, but is part of unilingual linguistic competence', an alternative solution would be postulating coexistence of competing but invariant grammars (Lightfoot 1999; Kroch 2000) or diglossia between Standard and popular French. Speakers make choices about which grammar to use, subject to sociolinguistic effects and syntactic change proceeds via competition between mutually exclusive grammatical options. This approach does not challenge the basic assumption that grammar and use are separate domains and it does not account for stable variation persisting over centuries. Although Adger and Smith (2007) propose a model capable of handling probabilistic frequencies associated with syntactic variation, at the same time they contend there is no need to incorporate social information on input probabilities into grammar. By locating linguistic variation in the post-spell-out morphology and phonology components, a firm line remains between grammar and use.

Nevertheless, there is considerable difference between postulating two grammars within the individual and a single grammar incorporating optionality. One can distinguish between optionality resulting from lexical choice and optionality resulting from speaker choice of syntactic operations. Another problem is that variability is generally not limited to a single construction, but instead occurs in a range of structures, not all of which are variable for all speakers. If there is grammar competition, then it is between a wide range of grammars, not just two (Henry 2002). Construction grammars and other usage-based approaches drawing on naturally-occurring language data, particularly from large corpora, are better able to handle variation than rule-based approaches assuming abstract categorical rules.

It is also still unclear why some syntactic variables appear sensitive to sociolinguistic constraints while others do not. There is no theoretical framework for determining what constitutes a possible conditioning factor due to a general lack of clarity regarding the distinction between internal and external factors, and the relationship between them in triggering change (for further discussion, see Chapter 23, this volume). What counts as internal or external depends on a particular theory, with external factors often appealed to only as a last resort for anything not explicable internally (Romaine 1996). Some, like Lass (1999: 5f.), insist that

> the structural history of a language ('linguistic history' in the strict sense) is quite independent in principle of its social history. The story of a language 'itself' must be carefully distinguished from the story of its changing uses, users, and social context – just as the changes themselves (as results) must be distinguished from the mechanisms by which they came about (e.g. lexical and social diffusion). The two are related in subtle and complex ways, but the relation is never 'causal' in any philosophically respectable sense … It is a vulgar error to talk about the 'social causation' of changes in linguistic structure.

By contrast, Meillet (1921: 16f.) argued that since language is a social institution, linguistics must be a social science and the only variable that we may appeal to in order to account for a linguistic change is social change. By separating language change from the external conditions on which it depended, Saussure in effect reduced it to an essentially inexplicable abstraction. If languages were not used, there would be no reason for them to change. Likewise, Labov (1994: 3) contends that to 'explain a finding about linguistic change will mean to find its causes in a domain outside of linguistics'. Nevertheless, while making a convincing argument for considering both social and linguistic conditioning as complementary aspects of the embedding problem, Weinreich, Labov and Herzog (1968) do not satisfactorily explain how changes in use get incorporated into abstract language structure because they make no distinction between a change and its propagation, nor between a change itself and an analysis of its mechanism. Meanwhile, Labov's (2001: 29) strategy in searching for causes of language change is 'to transform the traditional question "Why does language change?" into a different form: "Who are the leaders of linguistic change?"' Reposing the question in this way, however, still leaves us one step removed from the original question since the leaders are not necessarily the innovators, but rather those who by virtue of their behaviour and location in social networks advance a change most strongly. Linguistic and social structure are treated as isolated domains that do not interact and the force of social evaluation is attached mainly to superficial aspects of language, i.e. allophonic variation and vocabulary.

As the borderline between what is regarded as internal and external is continually shifting, the role of an innate universal grammar is being progressively reduced by more sophisticated work in pragmatics and cognition with the result that a number of abstract and fundamental grammatical principles are being shown to derive from more general processing constraints and pragmatic considerations. Future studies should shift from analysis of individual constructions to entire networks of constructions, while adding more social variables: dialects, registers, genres and styles. This requires not only large data samples but also increasingly sophisticated statistical models (e.g. logistic regression and mixed effects) allowing for interaction within and across linguistic and social factors will need to replace current models that assume their independence (Johnson 2009). A number of factors typically involved in constraining linguistic variation are correlated with one another to different degrees making it difficult to assess the extent to which an individual factor contributes to the overall result. Some of the variables examined in this chapter, especially those relating to agreement phenomena, indicate that pronouns are more likely to trigger agreement than nominal subjects (Henry 2002). In the case of German word-order variation in subordinate clauses, when the preceding word is a noun, there is no clear preference for either order, but a preceding pronoun is more likely to prefer the 2–1 order (Ebert 1981). Here the difference may be primarily one of stress, with nouns typically stressed, and pronouns unstressed. The emerging field of 'cognitive sociolinguistics' relying on a convergence of method and theoretical frameworks to study cognitive and social constraints on linguistic variation holds promise for building a fruitful alliance between variationists and syntacticians (Gries 2013; Hollmann 2013).

References

Adger, D. and Trousdale, G. 2007. 'Variation in English syntax: Theoretical implications', *English Language and Linguistics* 11: 261–78.

Adli, A. 2013. 'Syntactic variation in French Wh-questions: A quantitative study from the angle of Bourdieu's sociocultural theory', *Linguistics* 51 (3): 473–515.

Ball, R. 2000. *Colloquial French grammar*. Oxford: Blackwell.

Bayley, R. 2013. Variationist sociolinguistics, in R. Bayley, R. Cameron and C. Lucas (eds.), *The Oxford handbook of sociolinguistics*. Oxford University Press, pp. 11–30.

Bayley, R., Greer, K. and Holland, G. 2013. 'Lexical frequency and syntactic variation: A test of a linguistic hypothesis', *University of Pennsylvania Working Papers in Linguistics* 19(2): 21–30.

Bergs, A. 2005. *Social networks and historical linguistics: Studies in morphosyntactic variation in the Paston letters (1421–1503)*. Berlin: Mouton de Gruyter.

Biber, D. 2003. 'Compressed noun-phrase structure in newspaper discourse: The competing demands of popularization vs. economy', in

J. Aitchison and D. Lewis (eds.), *New media language*. London and New York: Longman, pp. 169–81.

Biber, D., Johannsson, S., Leech, G., Conrad, S. and Finegan, E. 1999. *Longman grammar of spoken and written English*. London: Longman.

Biberauer, T. and Roberts, I. 2005. 'Changing EPP parameters in the history of English: Accounting for variation and change', *English Language and Linguistics* 91: 5–46.

2009. 'The return of the subset principle', in P. Crisma and G. Longobardi (eds.), *Historical syntax and linguistic theory*. Oxford University Press, pp. 58–74.

Bolinger, D. 1968. 'Entailment and the meaning of structures', *Glossa* 2(2): 119–27.

Cornips, L. and Corrigan, K. P. 2005a. 'Toward an integrated approach to syntactic variation: A retrospective and prospective synopsis', in Cornips and Corrigan (eds.), pp. 1–27.

Cornips, L. and Corrigan, K. P. (eds.) 2005b. *Syntax and variation: Reconciling the biological and the social*. Amsterdam: John Benjamins.

Coveney, A. B. 2002. *Variability in spoken French: A sociolinguistic study of interrogation and negation*. Bristol and Portland: Elm Bank.

Druetta, R. 2002. '*Qu'est-ce tu fais?* État d'avancement de la grammaticalisation de *est-ce que*. Première partie', *Linguae etc.* 2: 67–88.

2003. '*Qu'est-ce tu fais?* État d'avancement de la grammticalisation de *est-ce que*. Deuxième partie', *Linguae etc.* 1: 21–35.

Ebert, R. P. 1981. 'Social and stylistic variation in the order of auxiliary and non-finite verb in dependent clauses in Early New High German', *Beiträge zur Geschichte der deutschen Sprache und Literatur* 103: 204–37.

1998. *Verbstellungswandel bei Jugendlichen, Frauen und Männern im 16. Jahrhundert*. Tübingen: Niemayer.

Edmont, E. and Gilliéron, J. 1902–10. *Atlas Linguistique de la France*. Paris: H. Champion.

Elsig, M. 2009. *Grammatical variation across space and time – the French interrogative system*. Amsterdam: John Benjamins.

Flores-Ferrán, N. 2007. 'A bend in the road: Subject personal pronoun expression in Spanish after 30 years of sociolinguistic research', *Language and Linguistics Compass* 1(6): 624–52.

Gadet, F. 1989. *Le français ordinaire*. Paris: Armand Colin.

2007. *La variation sociale en français*, 2nd edn. Paris: Ophrys.

Ginzburg, J. and Sag, I. A. 2000. *Interrogative investigations: The form, meaning and use of English interrogatives*. Stanford, CA: CSLI Publications.

Goldberg, A. 1995. *Constructions: A construction grammar approach to argument structure*. University of Chicago Press.

Grafmiller, J. 2014. 'Variation in English genitives across modality and genre', *English Language and Linguistics* 18: 471–96.

Gries, S. Th. 2013. 'Sources of variability relevant to the cognitive socio-linguist, and corpus- as well as psycholinguistic methods and notions to handle them', *Journal of Pragmatics* 52: 5–16.

Henry, A. 2002. 'Variation and syntactic theory', in J.K. Chambers, P. Trudgill and N. Schilling-Estes (eds.), *The handbook of language variation and change*. Oxford: Blackwell, pp. 267–82.

Hinrichs, L. and Szmrecsanyi, B. 2007. 'Recent changes in the function and frequency of standard English genitive constructions: A multivariate analysis of tagged corpora', *English Language and Linguistics* 11(3): 437–74.

Hollmann, W. B. 2013. 'Constructions in cognitive sociolinguistics', in T. Hoffmann and G. Trousdale (eds.), *The Oxford handbook of construction grammar*. Oxford University Press, pp. 491–509.

Holmberg, A. and Roberts, I. 2010. 'Introduction: Parameters in minimalist theory', in T. Biberauer, A. Holmberg, I. Roberts and M. Sheehan (eds.), *Parametric variation: Null subjects in minimalist theory*. Cambridge University Press, pp. 1–57.

Jespersen, O. 1909–49. *A modern English grammar on historical principles*. 7 vols. London: George Allen and Unwin; Copenhagen: Munksgaard.

Johnson, D. E. 2009. 'Getting off the GoldVarb standard: introducing Rbrul for mixed-effects variable rule analysis', *Language and Linguistics Compass* 3(1): 359–83.

Koptjevskaja-Tamm, M. 2002. 'Adnominal possession in the European languages: form and function', *Sprachtypologie und Universalienforschung* 55: 141–72.

Kroch, A. 2000. 'Syntactic change', in M. Baltin and C. Collins (eds.), *Handbook of syntax*. Oxford: Blackwell, pp. 629–39.

Kytö, M. and Romaine, S. 2005. '"We had like to have been killed by thunder & lightening": The semantic and pragmatic history of a construction that like to disappeared', *Journal of Historical Pragmatics* 6(1): 1–35.

Labov, W. 1994. *Principles of linguistic change*, vol. 1: *Internal factors*. Oxford: Blackwell.

2001. *Principles of linguistic change*, vol. 2: *Social factors*. Oxford: Blackwell.

Lass, R. 1999. 'Introduction', in R. Lass (ed.), *Cambridge history of the English language*, vol. III: 1476–1776. Cambridge University Press, pp. 1–12.

Leech, G., Hundt, M., Mair, C. and Smith, N. 2009. *Change in contemporary English*. Cambridge University Press.

Lightfoot, D. W. 1999. *The development of language: Acquisition, change and evolution*. Oxford: Blackwell.

Meillet, A. 1921. *Linguistique historique et linguistique générale*. Paris: La Société Linguistique de Paris.

Muysken, P. 2005. 'A modular approach to sociolinguistic variation in syntax: The gerund in Ecuadorian Spanish', in Cornips and Corrigan (eds.), pp. 31–53.

Myers, S. 2011. 'Innovation in a conservative region: The *Kentish Sermons* genitive system', *English Language and Linguistics* 15: 417–39.

Nevalainen, T. and Raumolin-Brunberg, H. 2003. *Historical sociolinguistics: Language change in Tudor and Stuart England*. London: Longman.

Nagy, N. G., Aghdasi, N., Denis, D. and Motut, A. 2011. 'Null subjects in heritage languages: Contact effects in a cross-linguistic context', *University of Pennsylvania Working Papers in Linguistics* 17(2): 135–44.

Otheguy, R., Zentella, A.C. and Livert, D. 2007. 'Language and dialect contact in Spanish in New York: Toward the formation of a speech community', *Language* 83(4): 770–802.

Potter, S. 1969. *Changing English*. London: Deutsch.

Reifsnyder, K. L. 2003. *Vernacular versus emerging standard: An examination of dialect usage in early modern Augsburg (1500–1650)*. Madison: University of Wisconsin.

Romaine, S. 1982. *Socio-historical linguistics: Its status and methodology*. Cambridge University Press.

  1984. 'On the problem of syntactic variation and pragmatic meaning in sociolinguistic theory', *Folia Linguistica* 18: 409–39.

  1996. 'Internal vs. external factors in socio-historical explanations of change: A fruitless dichotomy?', in *Proceedings of the Twenty-First Annual Meeting of the Berkeley Linguistics Society*. Berkeley: Department of Linguistics, University of California, pp. 478–90.

Rosenbach, A. 2007. 'Emerging variation: determiner genitives and noun modifiers in English', *English Language and Linguistics* 11(1): 143–89.

Rowlett, P. 2007. *The syntax of French*. Cambridge University Press.

  2011. Syntactic variation and diglossia in French', *Salford Working Papers in Linguistics and Applied Linguistics* 1: 13–26.

Sapp, C. D. 2011. *The verbal complex in subordinate clauses from medieval to modern German*. Amsterdam: John Benjamins.

Sells, P., Rickford, J. R. and Wasow, T. 1996. 'Variation in negative inversion in AAVE: An optimality theoretic approach', in J. Arnold, R. Blake, B. Davidson, S. Schwenter and J. Solomon (eds.), *Sociolinguistic variation: Data, theory, and analysis*. Stanford, CA: CSLI, pp. 161–6.

Stefanowitsch, A. 2003. 'Constructional semantics as a limit to grammatical alternation: The two genitives of English', in G. Rohdenburg and B. Mondorf (eds.), *Determinants of grammatical variation in English*. Berlin: Mouton de Gruyter, pp. 413–41.

Szmrecsanyi, B. and Hinrichs, L. 2008. 'Probabilistic determinants of genitive variation in spoken and written English: A multivariate comparison across time, space, and genres', in T. Nevalainen, I. Taavitsainen, P. Pahta and M. Korhonen (eds.), *The dynamics of linguistic variation:*

Corpus evidence on English past and present. Amsterdam: John Benjamins, pp. 291–309.

Szmrecsanyi, B., Rosenbach, A., Bresnan, J. and Wolk, C. 2013. 'Culturally conditioned language change? A multi-variate analysis of genitive constructions in ARCHER', in M. Hundt (ed.), *Late Modern English syntax*. Cambridge University Press, pp. 133–52.

Tagliamonte, S. A. 2006. 'Historical change in synchronic perspective: The legacy of British dialects', in A. van Kemenade and B. Los (eds.), *The handbook of the history of English*. Oxford: Blackwell, pp. 447–506.

2011. *Variationist sociolinguistics*. Cambridge University Press.

Tailleur, S. 2013. 'The French wh interrogative system: Est-ce que, clefting?', unpublished PhD thesis, University of Toronto.

Tsimpli, I., Sorace, A., Heycock, C. and Filiaci, F. 2004. 'First language attrition and syntactic subjects: A study of Greek and Italian near-native speakers of English', *International Journal of Bilingualism* 8(3): 257–77.

Weiner, J. and Labov, W. 1983. 'Constraints on the agentless passive', *Journal of Linguistics* 19: 29–58.

Weinreich, U., Labov, W. and Herzog, M. 1968. 'Empirical foundations for a theory of language change', in W. P. Lehmann and Y. Malkiel (eds.), *Directions for historical linguistics*. Austin, TX: University of Texas Press, pp. 95–189.

Winford, D. 1996. 'The problem of syntactic variation', in J. Arnold, R. Blake, B. Davidson, S. Schwenter and J. Solomon (eds.), *Sociolinguistic variation: Data, theory, and analysis*. Stanford, CA: CSLI, pp. 177–92.

26

Non-syntactic Sources and Triggers of Syntactic Change

Laurel J. Brinton and Elizabeth Closs Traugott

26.1 Introduction

A fundamental question in any study of syntactic change is what causes it to occur and under what linguistic circumstances particular changes may arise (see Biberauer and Roberts 2008: 80), particularly whether these changes occur at the level of the category (e.g. the rise of syntactic auxiliaries or binominal quantifiers) or whether they affect specific individual members of those categories (e.g. *will*, *a lot of*). As has frequently been pointed out, such circumstances are not deterministic since change does not have to take place. In the minimalist model, discussion usually centres on 'triggers' and explanation of changes in terms of changes in parameter settings (see, for example, Chapter 7, this volume). In other frameworks, especially usage-based ones, discussion usually centres on enabling factors for and 'sources' of change. In this chapter we present an overview of some hypotheses concerning non-syntactic ('exogenous') reasons for syntactic change with a focus on enabling factors and on 'motivations' (the 'why' and causes of change) rather than 'mechanisms' (the 'how' and means of change), in other words, what factors in the input may enable the mechanisms of change such as reanalysis and analogy (see Chapters 4 and 5, this volume).[1]

We draw on evidence identified in different frameworks, but most especially in usage-based frameworks. In the discussion that follows it will be important to recognize that different models make different assumptions about change. In UG-based frameworks, it is assumed that what changes is grammar (Kiparsky 1968), or more specifically parameter settings, and that acquisition relevant to syntactic change occurs in early childhood and is essentially passive (see Lightfoot 1991). By contrast, in usage-based frameworks, it is assumed that usage, not grammar, changes (Croft 2000) and that acquisition relevant to syntactic change takes place throughout a speaker's

---

[1] Chapter 23, this volume, addresses the hypothesis of endogenous syntactic change; see also §26.3 below.

lifetime (see e.g. Croft 2000; Bybee 2010). Speakers and hearers are under-stood to be actively engaging in negotiated communication, not passive participants. Acquisition is conceptualized as part of cognitive development in general, not strictly linguistic development, and therefore both analogical thinking leading to analogy and parsing (see e.g. Hawkins 2004) leading to reanalysis are considered to be essential enabling factors in change.[2] In both frameworks, however, abduction by the hearers from input is considered to be the major reason for language change (see Chapter 15, this volume).

Our focus will be on micro-changes and examples of linguistic evidence in the input to change. In §26.2 we introduce the main non-syntactic language-internal sources that have been discussed in the literature and a few language-external ones. In §26.3 we briefly address the hypothesis that syntax is 'inert' (Keenan 2002; see also Chapter 20, this volume) and changes only as a result of non-syntactic changes. §26.4 touches on questions related to the topic of this chapter and elaborated on elsewhere in the volume.

26.2 Examples of Non-syntactic Sources of Syntactic Change

In this section we discuss the role of various types of changes that have been hypothesized to be sources of syntactic change (see also discussion in §23.5). Semantic-pragmatic and discursive factors receive the greatest amount of attention (§26.2.1 and §26.2.2 respectively). Other hypothesized sources are morphology (§26.2.3), phonology, especially prosody (§26.2.4), contact (§26.2.5), changes in the repertoire (§26.2.6) and frequency (§26.2.7). These enabling factors are discussed separately for purposes of exposition. They are not mutually exclusive, nor are they necessarily discrete. In several cases, such as word-order change, some appear to work together cumulatively.

26.2.1 Semantically and Pragmatically Driven Change in Context

One of the longest-lived and most active debates in work on syntactic change has concerned the role of semantics, and most especially of prag-matics. In a Principles-and-Parameters model of grammar that treats syn-tax as the core module, and semantics as interpretative, semantic change appears most naturally to follow from syntactic change. But in other models such as Lexical Functional Grammar and usage-based models, semantics is easily seen as a potential trigger. In most of the studies cited here, close study of textual evidence suggests that pragmatics and/or semantic change precedes syntactic reanalysis.

The issue has largely been discussed in the context of work on gramma-ticalization (see Chapter 1, this volume), where a key observation has been

---

[2] Analogical thinking is sometimes assumed under analogy; see, for example, Fischer (2007).

that there are constraints on the semantics of the lexical sources of grammatical markers, e.g. topological spatial terms may give rise to markers of case and tense, terms for desire to markers of modality, etc. (see e.g. Heine, Claudi and Hünnemeyer 1991; Bybee, Perkins and Pagliuca 1994; Heine and Kuteva 2002). Another key observation has been that bleaching is only part of the semantic change involved in grammaticalization. Bleaching pertains to the contentful components of a lexical item, but at the same time, what was formerly only a pragmatic implicature becomes enriched and semanticized in the new grammatical item (Sweetser 1988). For example, in the case of future tense markers developing from English *go* or French *aller* 'go', the meaning of physical motion is bleached, but a temporal implicature of later time and future is semanticized. In Old Hungarian, the implicature of internal space is conventionalized in the grammaticalization of *bél* 'guts, core' as a locative case marker (Anttila [1972] 1989: 149). In other words, a loss-and-gain model of change is needed.

Most importantly for triggers of syntactic change, grammaticalization has been hypothesized to occur only in specific syntactic contexts. In a much-cited quotation, Bybee, Perkins and Pagliuca (1994: 297) say: '[e]verything that happens to the meaning of a gram happens because of the contexts in which it is used'. Anttila notes that the development of the Old Hungarian noun *bél* into the case marker *-ba* occurs in phrases like *világ bele* 'world core/guts:DIRECTIONAL' > *világbele* 'into the world' > *világba* (inflected N *bele* > case marker *ba*); the relevant contexts here are the relational phrase 'world core' and the directional case marker *-e* ([1972] 1989: 149).

Traugott and König (1991) propose that grammaticalization begins primarily in the context of implicatures in the flow of speech and the potential for enriching these implicatures in processing. Heine, Claudi and Hünnemeyer (1991) refer to such changes as 'context-induced reinterpretation', which evokes interpretation and perception. Hopper and Traugott ([1993] 2003) use the term 'invited inferencing' to emphasize the dual role of speakers/writers and addressees/readers in the dyadic speech event, i.e. of production as well as perception. Invited inferencing is hypothesized to lead to semantic change (see Traugott and Dasher 2002); it is not unique to grammaticalization and is often unconscious (see Keller's 1994 theory of 'invisible hand' change).

Heine (2002) and Diewald (2002, 2006) offer the most complete attempts to understand the role of context in the onset of grammatical change. Both Heine and Diewald consider context (and the inferences that arise in specific contexts) as 'triggers' for grammatical change, but focus on different aspects of context (for comparisons, see Narrog 2012: 66f.; Traugott 2012: 230). For the onset Heine (2002) identifies a 'bridging' context (Evans and Wilkins 2000),[3] which 'triggers' an inferential mechanism whereby

---

[3] In the discussion of grammatical change, 'bridging' contexts are sometimes seen as both structurally and semantically ambiguous (see e.g. Ghesquière and Davidse 2011: 262), although they are conceived as purely semantic by Evans and Wilkins (2000).

a new 'target' or grammatical meaning is foregrounded. Evans and Wilkins argue that in bridging contexts 'speech participants do not detect any problem of different assignments of meaning to the form because both ... interpretations of the utterance in context are functionally equivalent, even if the relative contributions of lexical content and pragmatic enrichment differ' (2000: 550). According to Heine, in the crucial stage of change, the item or construction occurs in a 'switch context', which is incompatible with a salient feature of the source meaning; moreover, '[u]nlike conventional meanings, meanings appearing in switch contexts have to be supported by a specific context (or cluster of contexts)' (Heine 2002: 85). By contrast, the onset contexts that Diewald (2002, 2006) identifies are first the spread of an item to 'untypical contexts' where it has not been used before; new meanings may arise through implicature, but the contexts give no clues as to the preferred reading (Diewald 2002: 106). The actual 'triggering' of the grammatical process occurs in a 'highly marked context' that she calls the 'critical context'. Here there is structural and semantic ambiguity, with several meanings possible, including the pragmatically induced new grammatical meaning. 'The critical context functions as a kind of catalyst' (Diewald 2006: 5) for the development of 'isolating contexts' in which the change is attested.

A well-known example of a context for pragmatically induced new meaning is provided by the onset of the development of auxiliary *BE going to*. Because *BE going to* originated in purposive expressions, it was always associated with an implicature of relative future time – what one purposes is expected to occur at a time that is later than that of the purpose, as in (1a). In particular contexts this implicature was strengthened, specifically when *to V* followed the motion verb directly (not after a directional phrase such as appears in (1a)), and when the agent of motion was demoted in passive purposive clauses. To our knowledge the earliest example of the latter use is (1b):

(1)   a.   **goyng**   to   Cogysbyry   **to gete   Tymbyr**
          going   to   Cogsbury   to   fetch   Timber
          (1447–8 Acc.Yatton in Som.RS 4; MED, s.v. *geten* 3a)
      b.   ther   passed   a theef byfore   alexandre   that   **was**
          there   passed   a thief   before   Alexander   who   was
          goyng   to   be   hanged   whiche   saide ...
          going   to   be   hanged   who   said ...
          'a thief who was going to be hanged passed before Alexander and said'
          (1477 Mubashshir ibn Fatik, Abu al-Wafa', eleventh century; *Dictes or sayengis of the philosophhres*; EEBO; Traugott 2012: 234)

(1b) is a bridging context because both the motion with a purpose and the future meaning can be interpreted from the context. *Passed*, being itself a motion verb, primes the motion meaning, and indeed it is extremely unlikely that the writer of (1b) intended anything but motion. However, in this passage we can with hindsight see a likely onset context that allowed some addressees to pay more attention to the temporal than to the motion meaning.

Both Heine's and Diewald's approaches attribute a decisive role to ambiguous contexts. Also in both, the new grammatical meaning is hypothesized to arise first as a contextually induced meaning, which creates pragmatic ambiguity between the original 'source' meaning and the new 'target' meaning.[4] The ambiguity is resolved in favour of the pragmatic meaning as the grammatical process proceeds, with the pragmatic meaning becoming semanticized as the conventional meaning of the form independent of context. Kuteva (2001: 150) aptly calls this process 'context-absorption'.

Himmelmann (2004: 32f.) views the role of context in grammaticalization somewhat differently, arguing that the context of a grammaticalizing item expands. In his view, not only is there 'semantic-pragmatic expansion' such as arises with the development of polysemies in switch contexts, but after the onset of grammaticalization there is 'host-class expansion' (i.e. the class of elements with which a grammaticalizing element is in construction expands) and syntactic context expansion (i.e. the syntactic contexts in which a grammaticalizing element is used increase).

A much-discussed example is the development of binominal quantifiers out of binominal pseudo-partitives, e.g. *a lot/bit/shred of*.[5] The context in which measure and size terms were reinterpreted as quantifiers is the complex noun phrase *NP of NP*. If both NPs are indefinite and the first denotes a part (e.g. Old English [OE] *dæl* 'part' > 'deal', OE *hlot* 'share' > 'lot', *bite* 'bite, morsel' > 'bit'), there is an inference of quantity from NP1 to NP2. Historical data suggest that initially there was a meaning change, largely in Early Modern English (EModE), allowing host-class expansion of NP1 to nouns in NP2 that are not normally partitioned, e.g. *love, honour*, and resulting in mismatch between form and meaning. In the nineteenth century the mismatch was 'resolved' by a syntactic head-shift, as evidenced by agreement with NP2 (Aarts 1998; Langacker 2009; Brems 2011).[6] Compare non-head-shifted (2a) where *a lot of* means 'a unit for sale' with shifted (2b) where *a lot of* means 'many' and refers to *goods*, not *lot*:

---

[4] The 'ambiguity', being pragmatic, is not a matter of 'true polysemy' (see Diewald 2002: 118), but rather of underspecification.

[5] Pseudo-partitives are indefinite, e.g. English *a N of a N*. In English the distinction between indefinite and definite partitives is not great, but in many other languages there is distinct morphology, e.g. in Swedish the partitive is instantiated by the preposition *av*, while the pseudo-partitive is zero (Koptjevskaja-Tamm 2009).

[6] Focusing on *bunch*, Francis and Yuasa (2008) argue that binominal quantifiers in Present-Day English are still mismatched with respect to the semantics (where NP2 is the head) and the syntax (where NP1 is the head). They reject agreement evidence on grounds that collectives have variable agreement. However, *lot*, *bit* and especially *shred*, all of which are currently attested with agreement with NP2, are not readily construed as collectives.

(2)   a.   [T]he worthy Mr. Skeggs is busy and bright, for **a lot of goods is**
           to be fitted out for auction.
           (1852 Stowe, *Uncle Tom's Cabin*; COHA; cited in Traugott and
           Trousdale 2013: 25)
      b.   I have **a lot of** goods to sell, and you wish to purchase **them**.
           (1852 Arthur, *True Riches*; COHA; cited in Traugott and Trousdale
           2013: 25)

Further evidence for the head shift is provided by phonological changes
reflected in spellings like *allotta*.

   Many examples support the hypothesis that ambiguity is a necessary condition for reanalysis in grammaticalization. For example, pragmatic ambiguity is evidenced in texts for well over a hundred years (from 1477 to 1611) in
the development of the *BE going to* future. However, in other cases, empirical
evidence for ambiguity is scarce and the importance of ambiguous contexts
for triggering syntactic change has recently come under question (see e.g.
Ghesquière 2011: ch. 2). In fact, in the development of *a lot of/lots of*, ambiguous examples appear only after the change has taken place.

26.2.2   The Role of Discursive Contexts

While Heine and Diewald focus on largely clausal contexts, others point to
the importance of discursive interaction and negotiation of meaning in
the development of some syntactic structures (e.g. Detges 2006; Traugott
2010; Waltereit and Detges 2008; Waltereit 2012). Focusing on the obligatorification (syntacticization) of subject pronouns in languages such as
French, Brazilian Portuguese and some varieties of Spanish, Detges
(2006) argues that first-person pronouns lead the change. In Brazilian
Portuguese, first person is realized 82 per cent, second person
78 per cent and third person 45 per cent of the time (Oliveira 2000: 39).
Detges attributes this skewing to interactional language use, in which first
person is used contrastively to 'self-topicalize' and invokes the topicality
hierarchy in which personal pronouns are ranked as follows: 1st > 2nd >
3rd person (see e.g. Silverstein 1976: 122). Over time, this strategy typically
becomes over-used and therefore devalued. The pragmatic force of pronoun use is lost, resulting in the new syntax with obligatory subject
pronouns.

   An example of discursive argumentation as a source of new complex
syntactic structures is the development of clefts of various types.
The context is typically contrastive information structuring (see
Lehmann 2008) and contrastive argumentation (Patten 2012). While information structuring is considered to be syntactic in the minimalist framework (see Rizzi 1997), Hinterhölzl and Kemenade (2012) and Patten (2012),
among others, argue that it is pragmatic. The textual evidence suggests
that historically, clefting has its origins in discourses like the following:

(3)   a. þa   cwædon þa   geleafullan, '**Nis   hit na   Petrus** þæt
           then said   the faithful,   NEG-is it NEG Peter REL
           þær   cnucað, ac is   his   ængel'.
           there knocks but is   his   angel
           'then said the faithful, "it is not Peter who knocks there, but his
           angel"'
           (Ælfric, *Catholic Homilies*, I,_34:474.247.6867; Patten 2012: 172,
           citing Ball 1991: 39)
       b. there is no possibilitie of overthrowing the new election … **all
           you can doe is to do some good for the tyme to come,** which
           if you can doe conveniently, and without much trouble, it wilbe
           woorth your labour. (1624 Oliver Naylor, *Letter to John Cosin*; CEEC;
           cited in Traugott and Trousdale 2013: 141)

In such contrastive contexts, *hit* 'it' and *all* implicate specificational and
exhaustive pragmatics, enabling the development of IT-clefts and pseudo-
clefts respectively. In the case of *all*-pseudo-clefts *all* 'everything' is semanticized as 'only'. These constructions develop in a domain in which the role
of pragmatic inferencing is especially high, but opportunities for ambiguity appear to be low.

A second example of the discursive situation giving rise to a new syntactic structure is the development of metalinguistic comment clauses such
as *if you will/ prefer/choose/wish/like* (Brinton 2014). These arise as the speaker
is negotiating (often out of politeness) with the hearer concerning the
correct choice of words. In the process what would otherwise be
a subordinate conditional 'if' clause (a 'protasis') loses conditional meaning and comes to function syntactically as a parenthetical. Such parenthe-
ticals are what Quirk *et al.* (1985: 1095) call 'indirect conditionals'. They are
dependent not on an explicit apodosis, but on an implicit speech act of the
utterance, which must be inferred (something like 'if you wish {I will call it
X, you can call it X}'). These indirect conditions may develop in contexts in
which the speaker explicitly encourages the hearer to use a particular
expression ('call it X' constructions (4b)):

(4)   a. The humbleness, meanness **if you like,** of the subject, together
           with the homely mode of treating it, brought upon me a world of
           ridicule by the small critics
           (1823 'Everett's new ideas on population', *North American Review*;
           COHA; cited in Brinton 2014)
       b. **Call it** cruelty **if you like,** not mercy
           (1860 Hawthorne, *The marble faun*; COHA; cited in Brinton 2014)

The process known as 'pragmaticalization' is at work here.[7]

---

[7] It is doubtful that pragmaticalization is a separate process from grammaticalization. Pragmatic markers structure
discourse and are at the extreme procedural end of the continuum of less to more pragmatic grammatical markers. For
a summary of the pragmaticalization/grammaticalization debate, see Brinton (2008: 61–3).

In discursive contexts the speaker/writer is always present and the addressee/reader is present at least by implication. Therefore, subjectivity and intersubjectivity are always ambient in communication (Benveniste [1958] 1971) and, like variation, are generally enabling factors in change. Processes of change identified as (inter)subjectification are semantic and metonymic to the communicative event. They accompany a large number of changes, some lexical (e.g. the development of performative verbs such as *promise*), but most grammatical (e.g. the development of scalar expressions such as *only*, quantifiers such as *a lot of*), and syntactic (e.g. the development of focus-marking clefts), and are best considered to be mechanisms rather than sources of change.[8]

26.2.3 Morphology-Driven Change

Morphologically driven syntactic change often involves change due to loss of morphological case. An example is the obsolescence and eventual loss in Middle English (ME) of 'recipient passives', which had dative morphology in OE. Compare the OE in (5) with the modern translation:

(5) buton   him   ðurh   his hreowsung &   ðurh
     unless   he.DAT   through   his penitence and through
     God-es   miltse   **geholpen**   weorðe
     God-GEN   mercy.ACC   helped   be
     'Unless he be helped by his penitence and God's mercy'
     (*Cura Pastoralis* B9.1.3; DOEC)

Roberts (2007) hypothesizes that with the loss of morphological case marking, nominals were ambiguous. A constructed example is 'Unless the man be helped by ...'.[9] As long as dative was available in the trigger there was no ambiguity, but when dative was lost the feature make-up of *v* was reanalysed, i.e. its ability to 'value Case on the object has been switched off' (Roberts 2007: 158). The parametric change resulted in the loss of indirect passives and eventually of all non-subject arguments in subject position.

In this scenario the changes are reanalyses of parametric settings arrived at by abduction (see Chapter 4, this volume, on reanalysis). Roberts (2007: 232f.) argues that 'both ambiguity and opacity of the P(arameter)-expression are required in order for abductive change to take place'.

---

[8] López-Couso (2010) provides an excellent overview of issues in (inter)subjectification, with particular attention to their role in grammaticalization.

[9] Very few such examples appear in the *Middle English Dictionary* (MED), however, as almost all have pronominal subjects; an example with NP (*some syke folk*) from later ME is:

(i) Some   syke   folk   ben   holpen   with   lyghte   medicynes,
    some   sick   folk   are   helped   with   light   medicines
    and   some   folk   ben   holpen   with   sharpe   medicynes.
    and   some   folk   are   helped   with   strong   medicines
    (Chaucer, *Boethius* 4.pr.6.228; MED, s.v. *light* adj 2)

As mentioned in §26.2.1, the importance of ambiguity has, however, been called into question. A further hypothesis is that there is 'a general preference on the part of language acquirers to assign the simplest possible structural representation to the strings they hear' (Roberts 2007: 131). The proposal that there is a cognitive bias toward optimization in acquisition, and indeed in grammars is explored in van Gelderen (2004) within the minimalist framework. Adopting an Optimality rather than minimalist approach to morphosyntactic change, Kiparsky (2012: 49) postulates 'the existence of a type of non-exemplar-based analogy, which projects UG constraints that are not positively instantiated in language use'. This kind of analogy entails reanalysis since projections change, and unidirectionality since it is 'grammar optimisation' (2012: 21) (see also Chapters 5 and 23, this volume).

The development of a syntactic category and with it the crystallization of subordinate structure is illustrated by the development of the category of complementizers in the history of Korean. Prior to the eighteenth century there were no complementizers in Korean. What appears to have triggered their development is the reanalysis of a quotative structure that became univerbated (Rhee 2008). According to Rhee, there were three types of quotative, two paratactic, and a third, which can be said to be embedded because the verb *ha* 'say' appears in final position in the clause, following the quotation, and is past tense, as in (6). After a quotative marker *hAko* came into existence, this 'quotative marker underwent a fusion with the sentential ending of the embedded direct speech' with different forms for declarative (*-ta*), interrogative (*-nya*), imperative (*-la*) and hortative (*-ca*). Rhee gives the constructed example of *tako* in (6), ignoring intermediate stages. In (6a) we find the declarative (DECL) *ta* and *ha* 'say', in (6b) the fused complementizer (COMP) *tako*:

(6) a. *Stage I*

      ku-ka   ka-n-*ta*-*ha*-*ko*   malha-yss-ta

      he-NOM   go-PRS-DECL-say-CONNECTIVE   say-PST-DECL

      (Lit._) 'he said "(I) am going" and said'

      'He said he was going (leaving)'

   b. *Stage II*

      ku-ka   ka-n-*tako*   malha-yss-ta

      he-NOM   go-PRS-COMP   say-PST-DECL

      'He said that he was going (leaving)'

The reanalysis of the declarative quotative summarized in (7) seems to have been the model for the rise of the set of complementizers *-tako*, *-nyako*, *-lako* and *-cako* (Rhee 2008: 203):

(7) -ta   +   ha + ko   >   tako

     Sentential Ending   say   CONNECTIVE COMP

26.2.4 Phonology-Driven Change

Recently there has been considerable interest in syntax–phonology interfaces, especially the complex interaction of pragmatic information structure, prosody and word-order changes in Germanic languages, which
encode focus by prosody rather than morphology (see Hinterhölzl and
Kemenade 2012). The hypothesis is that the OV > VO word-order shift
that occurred during the ME period was enabled not only by morphological case loss (as has traditionally been argued), but also by a shift from
coding of OE information structure primarily by prosody to coding by
determiners. Likewise, Speyer (2012) hypothesizes that the loss of contrastive object topicalization in EModE was an epiphenomenon of the loss in
the fifteenth century of V2, 'but the link between these two processes is
prosodic well-formedness' (2012: 882). Specifically, loss of V2 led to violations of a Stress Clash Avoidance requirement in those utterances where
the contrastive object and the subject both bore focus. Avoiding stress
clash, language users ceased to apply topicalization in these environments. For example, expressions like (8) were possible in OE: here the
topicalized object *oþer* 'the one' is followed by the finite verb (*heold* 'held')
in V2 position, then by *Daniel*, the subject. *Oþer . . . oþer* are contrastive and
are both in focus, as also are the subjects *Daniel . . . Aldhelm*.

(8) oþer   heold   Daniel,   oþer   Aldhelm
     other   held   Daniel   other   Aldhelm
     'Daniel held the one, Aldhelm (held) the other.'
     (cochronA- 1,ChronA_[Plummer]:709.1.428; cited in Speyer 2012: 878)

In Present-Day English (PDE) the object topicalization in (8) is strongly
dispreferred, and the expected word order is as in the translation.

While word-order change has recently been hypothesized to be enabled
by prosody in addition to other factors, the role of phonology in some
other changes has been called into question. For example, it is often
thought (following Jespersen 1917: 4) that Jespersen's cycle of negation
proceeds as follows (see also Willis, Lucas and Breitbarth 2013 and §24.2.1):
a single negator comes to be used very frequently and weakened, then it
comes to be strengthened by a second negator, and the first may be lost.
Hansen (2012) summarizes arguments starting with Meillet ([1912] 1958:
140) that in fact the negator is strengthened first (with addition of a second
negator), resulting in the weakening of the first negator. On this view, the
enabling factor for the syntactic change is not phonological, but pragmatic
and discourse-functional; phonological weakening is a consequence
rather than a cause (Hansen 2012: 576).

Another example in which phonological processes seem to underlie
a morphosyntactic change is the loss of second-person enclitics at the
beginning of the EModE period. In ME, and to some extent in OE, we
find second-person clitics of *thou* (-*tou*, *tow*, -*tu*, -*te*, etc.) attached to
forms of BE, HAVE, DO, modal auxiliaries, and other common verbs (SAY,

KNOW, SEE, etc.) (see Brinton 2004). The loss of these cliticized forms after 1550 has been considered a case of 'decliticization', and hence 'degrammaticalization' by Newmeyer (1998: 270f.). A more plausible explanation is that this change is the result of loss of the sandhi rule assimilating thorn ('th') to the preceding dental, a more general rule that had also affected demonstratives (e.g. *and þat > and tat, and þe > and te, at þe > ate*). The reappearance of full *thou* forms in sixteenth-century English after a period of reduced *-tou/-tow* forms is an instance of 'replacement' by a pre-existing form, one that had continued to exist. Furthermore, the process of subject enclisis itself is not lost in English, later producing encliticized *-ye/-ee* (as is *hearye, lookee, prayee*) from the full form *you.*

26.2.5 Contact-Driven Change

Contact with other languages and dialects is often a major catalyst for change. In ME a word-order change involving V2 syntax is observed in northern dialects. OE, like Yiddish and Icelandic, exhibits V2 in main clauses and also in a broad range of subordinate clauses. This type of V2 syntax persisted in southern and midland dialects of ME, but in the north a V2 syntax developed that is found more commonly in Germanic languages, including Scandinavian languages. It allows V2 in only a very restricted set of subordinate clauses. Kroch and Taylor (1997) hypothesize that the change was triggered by extensive contact in the North resulting from Scandinavian settlements there.

An example of contact-driven syntactic change that Roberts (2007) gives is the development in French spoken on Prince Edward Island (Canada). Standard French does not allow preposition stranding, a cross-linguistically rare option, but English does, and so does Prince Edward Island French. In the latter, preposition stranding occurs with borrowed prepositional phrases (9a) and the preposition *de* 'of, from' (9b). (9b) is ungrammatical in Standard French, which requires pied-piping (9c):

(9) a. Qui   ce-qu'a   eté   layé   off __?
         who that has   been   laid   off?
         'Who has been laid off?' (Roberts 2007: 240, citing King 2000: 142)
     b. Où   ce-qu'elle   vient   de __?
         where that she   comes   from
         'Where does she come from?' (Roberts 2007: 239, citing King 2000: 136)
     c. D'où   vient   elle __?
         from where   comes   she __
         'From where does she come?'

Roberts' hypothesis is that borrowings such as *lay off* combined with the lack of inherent Case in French led to an input that was no longer unambiguously a trigger for preposition stranding.

Contact-induced syntactic change can be difficult to establish. A much-debated instance of such change relates to so-called 'contact-clauses' (clauses with zero relatives, especially those missing subject relatives), and relative clauses with resumptive pronouns in English. These occur in earlier stages of English and in non-standard varieties of Present-Day English. They are common in earlier and Present-Day Welsh (Filppula, Klemola and Paulasto 2008: 88). OE resumptives are exemplified in (10a), Middle Welsh resumptives in (10b):

(10) a. Ther-ynne   wonyþ   a   yȝt,   **þat** wrong   is **his**   name,
          therein   dwells a   creature REL   wrong   is his   name
          'there lives a creature whose name is wrong'
          (*PPl.C* (Hnt 143) 2, 59; cited in Fischer 1992: 309)
      b. Y   coedyd   **y**   foassant v-**dunt**
          the   woods   they   fled   to-them
          'the woods to which they fled'
          (Filppula, Klemola and Paulasto 2008: 89)

Filppula, Klemola and Paulasto (2008: 94) conclude cautiously that there is 'room for a contact-based explanation, especially with regard to structures involving resumptive pronouns, which … are now mainly (though not exclusively) found in dialectal varieties spoken in the formerly Celtic-speaking areas'.

Extreme contact situations such as those which enable the development of creoles frequently give rise to a mixed language that tends to have fewer alternative structures with respect to syntax, morphology, phonology and lexis than the input languages. Creoles tend to be syntactically VO and periphrastic; lexical (contentful) words are derived from a dominant 'lexifier' language. The grammatical structure typically shows aspects of one or more 'substrate' languages. For example, in (11) from Early Sranan, a largely English-based creole of Suriname, the completive marker (COMPL) *kaba* is derived from Portuguese *acabar* 'to complete', but has structural properties that align it to the substrate Gbe languages, which have a VP-final verb meaning 'finish' (Winford and Migge 2007), an unusual feature in an otherwise largely VO language:

(11) Mastra   we   doore   *kaba*
      Master   we   arrive COMPL
      'Master, we have arrived'
      (van Dyk *c.* 1765; Winford and Migge 2007: 83, citing Arends and Perl 1995: 127)

While creoles have been hypothesized to be exceptional, warranting the positing of universal aspects of simplification and even specialized UG principles and parameters (see e.g. Bickerton 1984), the most widely accepted current view is that they are not exceptional. Rather, they reflect different degrees of contact and mixture, depending on the circumstances under which they arose (see e.g. Mufwene 2001; DeGraff 2005). Therefore syntactic changes motivated by creolization are not unique to this type of contact-based change.

26.2.6 The Role of Changes in Repertoire

Contact may result in changes in repertoire. Literacy may be introduced to a non-literate society, as has happened over the millennia worldwide. So may new genres, such as romances (a French genre) in the ME period. Such factors, especially the development of literacy, may play an enabling part in syntactic change. While most change doubtless occurs in spoken contexts, some syntactic changes have been attributed to writing.

For example, with the acquisition of a Christianized literary tradition through conversion, the Anglo-Saxons acquired a number of syntactic structures from Latin. One is the parenthetical apposition marker OE *þæt is* 'that is', which would appear to be either strongly influenced by or directly calqued upon Latin *id est*. Native parenthetical apposition, as used in vernacular OE writing, shows gender, person and number agreement between a nominal in the preceding clause and a pronoun in the parenthetical, as with **me** and **ic** in (12):

(12) Þa   bearn   **me**   on mode *ic*   **truwige ðurh   godes**
      Then   burned me.1.SG   in mind I.1.SG trust   through god's
      gife. þæt   ic   ðas   boc   of   ledenum gereorde to
      gift   that I   this book from Latin   language into
      engliscre spræce awende.
      English   speech should.translate
      'Then I desired passionately in my mind, I trust through god's grace, to translate this book from Latin into English'
      (ÆCHom I (Pref) B1.1.1 0002 (174.48); DOEC; cited in Mitchell 1985: II:943)

The *þæt is* parenthetical is found mainly in scholarly and translated texts such as the Benedictine Rule in (13a):

(13) a. on þisum tid-um   we gereccað lofu   urum
        at this   time-DAT.PL.F   we express   praise our
        sceppende ofor domes his rihtwisnesse
        lord   over glory his righteousness
        þæt   **is** æfter sangum primsang...
        that.NOM.SG.N is   after singing primesong...

      *Ergo his temporibus referamus laudes creatori nostro super judicia justitiae sue **id est** matutino prima ... completorio*
      'At this time we express our praise to the lord for the righteousness of his glory, that is after the singing of the prime song ... '
      (BenRGl C4 0217 (16.46.11); DOEC)

b. Þa   apostol-i   **þæt**   **sind**   godes
   the   apostle-NOM.PL.M   that-NOM.SG.N   are.PRS.PL   god's
   bydel-as   toferdon geond   ealne middaneard
   preacher-NOM.PL.M travelled around   all   earth
   'the apostles, that is the preachers of god, travelled over the entire earth'
   (990–2 ÆCHom I, 1 B1.1.23 0100 (353.236); DOEC; cited in Brinton 2008:105)

What distinguishes this construction as an adaptation of the Latin, rather than a native construction, is the fact that it does not follow OE agreement rules: *þæt* is invariable, irrespective of the number and gender of the antecedent noun (*tidum* in (13a), *apostoli* in (13b)), and the verb is governed by the number of the complement, not by the singular subject *þæt* (13b) (see Mitchell 1985: I:130f.). In the history of English, the imposition of a second literary tradition, that of Anglo-Norman, is likely to have led to the adoption of the longer form, *that is to say*, calqued on French *c'est-à-dire*, during the ME period. Thus, both changes to the appositional resources show the effects of new literary conditions as well as language contact.

26.2.7 The Role of Frequency

One factor in change that has been discussed at length is frequency (Bybee 2003, 2010). Cognitive representations in the language acquirer must be retained in memory and this leads to prototype effects in which some members of a category are considered better or more central than others (Bybee 2010: 18). In this framework analogical extension is conceptualized as involving exemplar matching and more prototypical members are thought to be the source for analogical extension. A key distinction is made between token and type frequency (Bybee 2003). It is type frequency that is expanded by analogy, e.g. once one verb with modal meaning developed pre-auxiliary characteristics in English, others followed (Warner 1993). Once the binominal quantifier *a deal of* 'a part of' > 'a largish quantity of' arose, others like *a bit/lot/shred of* followed (Brems 2011; Traugott and Trousdale 2013: 49). Once Korean *tako* had arisen, other, similar complementizers did too.

In our view, token frequency cannot be a direct trigger of change since it results from other factors, such as routinization in certain discourse strategies (Waltereit and Detges 2008), but the effects of frequency contribute to the nature of the language acquirer's experience. We may note that many of the syntactic changes discussed in Roberts (2007) and Biberauer and Roberts (2008) entail type frequency since they involve categories that gain or lose the members they license one by one. This gradual gain and loss (see Chapter 21, this volume) may eventually trigger parametric change, such as the cascade of changes following the loss of recipient passives, as mentioned in §26.2.3.

26.3   Some Comments on the Hypothesis of Syntactic Inertia

In the minimalist framework as represented by Roberts and his colleagues' work, there has recently been interest in the idea initially put forward by Keenan that syntax is inert and that '[t]hings stay as they are unless acted on by an outside force or decay' (Keenan 2002: 2; see also Chapter 20, this volume). This was restated as '[s]yntactic change should not arise, unless it can be shown to be **caused**' (Longobardi 2001: 278, emphasis original). The assumption behind the hypothesis of syntactic inertia is that the cause of syntactic change is non-syntactic. In the null case language acquirers (children) would acquire grammars that matched those of their parents and there would be no change: 'the task of language acquirers is to set the right parametric values on the basis of the input they are exposed to. This UG along with the appropriate trigger experience yields a particular grammar' (Roberts and Roussou 2003: 9). Change is 'triggered (switched on-off) on the basis of relevant input sentences' (Yang 2000: 233). If the input to children's 'learning device' has become 'obscure or ambiguous' (Roberts and Roussou 2003: 12) then they may set the parameter differently from the way their parents set theirs. According to the syntactic inertia hypothesis, the experience that may lead to syntactic change is the consequence of 'independent phonological, morphological, or lexical change, or from extra-grammatical factors such as contact' (Biberauer and Roberts 2008: 80), but not of syntactic change. The focus of this chapter is motivated by this assumption.

The hypothesis of syntactic inertia has been challenged by Biberauer and Roberts (2008), who suggest that cascade effects may be motivated by syntax, and therefore, syntactic change may be a trigger for further change. A usage approach to change suggests that the hypothesis that '[t]hings stay as they are unless acted on by an outside force or decay' in fact applies to all aspects of language and is equally valid for phonological or semantic change, if one assumes that: (i) speakers have a linguistic system ('grammar') that is entrenched; (ii) that communities of speakers share commonalities; and (iii) that grammar is modular. This is true even if the system is considered to be variable or subject to optimality constraints, since variability and the constraints do not in themselves lead to change, although they make it less likely that things will 'stay the same'. It is even true in a model of grammar that rejects the hypothesis that speakers 'have' a grammar, arguing instead that grammar is always emergent (see Hopper 2011) since on this view only speakers can enable change.

Waltereit and Detges (2008: 14) argue that linguistic systems are systemically inert because they are conventional objects and are modified by 'continuous enactment and re-enactment', in other words, by use. They illustrate with two examples. One is the rise of the French interrogative particle *est-ce que* 'is it that', the second is the rise of Spanish presentational constructions, which introduce new participants into discourse, e.g. *There are apples in the garden* (2008: 25). In Standard Spanish there is no agreement with the presentational verb *haber* 'to have', but in some dialects, especially American Spanish, there is agreement; compare (14a) with (14b) (2008: 24):

(14)   a. Standard Spanish
         Hay   coches   en   el   patio
         There.is   car.PL   in   the   courtyard
         'There are cars in the courtyard'
       b. American Spanish
         Habían   soldados   en   el   patio
         there.were soldier.PL in   the   courtyard
         'There were soldiers in the courtyard'

Waltereit and Detges (2008) analyse *coches* in (14a) as direct object and *soldados* in (14b) as subject, on grounds of agreement, and point out that variation in agreement is common cross-linguistically in presentationals. They posit two conflicting constraints (2008: 26):

(15)   1. Focal information is coded as non-subject
       2. Single arguments are coded as subject

When the subject is singular as in (16), there is ambiguity as to which constraint applies (2008: 26):

(16)   Había   un   soldado   en   el   patio
       there.was a   soldier.SG in   the   courtyard
       'There was a soldier in the courtyard'

The authors argue that the fact that the reanalysis of the presentational occurred primarily in the low-frequency site of past tense (Bentivoglio and Sedano 1989: 72) suggests that the change originates with speakers who are unsure of the conventionality of the construction. If so, the rise of the focal construction may be thought of as an instance of syntactic hypercorrection (see Janda 2001). It is a change originating in a clash of syntactic constraints (Waltereit and Detges 2008: 28) and therefore an example of change within syntax.

Such examples suggest that the source of syntactic change may be change in any part of the linguistic system, including syntax.

26.4   Related Issues

Other chapters in this volume address questions of evolution and what triggered the rise of syntax in the first place (see, for example, Chapter 28, this volume). Here we simply mention that it is possible that design features of syntax have evolved, whether by natural selection (e.g. Pinker and Bloom 1990; Hurford, Studdert-Kennedy and Knight 1998) or adaptation (e.g. Kirby 2000). One such design feature is the transparent match between form and meaning (compositionality) that is assumed in the studies discussed above. Other design features are embedding and cues for it (Shibatani and Givón 2009) and the very categories of which syntactic phrases consist (Denison 2010).

Corpora and databases

CEEC   *Corpus of Early English Correspondence.* 1998. Compiled by Terttu Nevalainen, Helena Raumolin-Brunberg, Jukka Keränen, Minna Nevala, Arja Nurmi and Minna Palander-Collin. Department of English, University of Helsinki. www.helsinki.fi/varieng/domains/CEEC.html.

COHA *The Corpus of Historical American English, 400 million words, 1810–2009.* 2010–. Compiled by Mark Davies. Brigham Young University. Available online at http://corpus.byu.edu/coha/.

DOEC *Dictionary of Old English Corpus.* 2011. Original release 1981 compiled by Angus Cameron, Ashley Crandell Amos, Sharon Butler and Antonette diPaolo Healey. Release 2009 compiled by Antonette diPaolo Healey, Joan Holland, Ian McDougall and David McDougall, with Xin Xiang. University of Toronto. http://tapor.library.utoronto.ca/doecorpus.

EEBO *Early English Books Online*, http://eebo.chadwyck.com/home.

MED   *The Middle English Dictionary.* 1956–2001. Ann Arbor: University of Michigan Press. Available online at www.hti.umich.edu/dict/med.

References

Aarts, B. 1998. 'Binominal noun phrases in English', *Transactions of the Philological Society* 96: 117–58.

Anttila, R. [1972] 1989. *Historical and comparative linguistics*, 2nd edn. Amsterdam: John Benjamins.

Arends, J. and Perl, M. 1995. *Early Surinamese creole texts: A collection of 18th-century Sranan and Saamaka documents.* Frankfurt: Vervuert; Madrid: Iberoamericana.

Ball, C. N. 1991. 'The historical development of the *it*-cleft', unpublished PhD thesis, University of Pennsylvania.

Bentivoglio, P. and Sedano, M. 1989. 'Haber: ¿Un verbo impersonal? Un estudio sobre el español de Caracas', *Estudios sobre el español de América y lingüística afroamericana: Ponencias presentadas en el 45 congreso interna-cional de americanistas*. Bogotá: Instituto Caro y Cuervo, pp. 59–81.

Benveniste, É. 1971. 'Subjectivity in language', in *Problems in general linguis-tics*, trans. M. E. Meek. Coral Gables, FL: University of Miami Press, pp. 223–30. (First published in 1958 as 'De la subjectivité dans le langage', in É. Benveniste, *Problèmes de linguistique générale*. Paris: Gallimard, pp. 258–66.)

Biberauer, T. and Roberts, I. 2008. 'Cascading parameter changes: Internally-driven change in Middle and early Modern English', in T. Eythórsson (ed.), *Grammatical change and linguistic theory: The Rosendal papers*. Amsterdam: John Benjamins, pp. 79–113.

Bickerton, D. 1984. 'The language bioprogram hypothesis', *Behavioral and Brain Sciences* 7: 212–18.

Brems, L. 2011. *Layering of size and type noun constructions in English*. Berlin: De Gruyter Mouton.

Brinton, L. J. 2004. 'Subject clitics in English: A case of degrammaticaliza-tion?', in H. Lindquist and C. Mair (eds.), *Corpus approaches to gramma-ticalization in English*. Amsterdam: John Benjamins, pp. 227–56.

   2008. *The comment clause in English: Syntactic origins and pragmatic develop-ment*. Cambridge University Press.

   2014. '*If you choose/like/prefer/want/wish*: The origin of metalinguistic and politeness functions', in M. Hundt (ed.), *Late Modern English syntax in context*. Cambridge University Press, pp. 271–90.

Bybee, J. 2003. 'Mechanisms of change in grammaticization: The role of frequency', in B. D. Joseph and R. D. Janda (eds.), *The handbook of historical linguistics*. Oxford: Blackwell, pp. 602–23.

   2010. *Language, usage and cognition*. Cambridge University Press.

Bybee, J., Perkins, R. and Pagliuca, W. 1994. *The evolution of grammar: Tense, aspect, and modality in the languages of the world*. University of Chicago Press.

Croft, W. 2000. *Explaining language change*. Harlow: Longman, Pearson Education.

DeGraff, M. 2005. 'Morphology and word order in "creolization" and beyond', in G. Cinque and R. S. Kayne (eds.), *The Oxford handbook of comparative syntax*. New York: Oxford University Press, pp. 293–372.

Denison, D. 2010. 'Category change in English with and without structural change', in E. C. Traugott and G. Trousdale (eds.), *Gradience, gradualness, and grammaticalization*. Amsterdam: John Benjamins, pp. 105–28.

Detges, U. 2006. 'From speaker to subject: The obligatorization of the Old French subject pronouns', in H. Leth Andersen, M. Birkelund and M.-B. Mosegaard Hansen (eds.), *La Linguistique au coeur: Valence verbale, gramma-ticalisation et corpus. Mélanges offerts à Lene Schøsler à l'occasion de son 60e anniversaire*. Odense: University Press of Southern Denmark, pp. 75–103.

Diewald, G. 2002. 'A model for relevant types of contexts in grammatica-lization', in Wischer and Diewald (eds.), pp. 103–20.

2006. 'Context types in grammaticalization as constructions', *Constructions* SV1-9. http://elanguage.net/journals/index.php/construc tions/article/viewFile/24/29.

Evans, N. and Wilkins, D. 2000. 'In the mind's ear: The semantic extensions of perception verbs in Australian languages', *Language* 76: 546–92.

Filppula, M., Klemola, J. and Paulasto, H. 2008. *English and Celtic in contact.* New York: Routledge.

Fischer, O. 1992. 'Syntax', in N. Blake (ed.), *The Cambridge history of the English language*, vol. II: *1066–1476*. Cambridge University Press, pp. 207–408.
   2007. *Morphosyntactic change: Functional and formal perspectives.* Oxford University Press.

Francis, E. J. and Yuasa, E. 2008. 'A multi-modular approach to gradual change in grammaticalization', *Journal of Linguistics* 44: 45–86.

Ghesquière, L. 2011. 'The directionality of (inter)subjectification in the English NP: Identification and intensification', unpublished PhD thesis, University of Leuven.

Ghesquière, L. and Davidse, K. 2011. 'The development of intensification scales in noun-intensifying uses of adjectives: Sources, paths and mechanisms of change', *English Language and Linguistics* 15: 251–77.

Hansen, M.-B. M. 2012. 'Negative cycles and grammaticalization', in H. Narrog and B. Heine (eds.), *The Oxford handbook of grammaticalization.* Oxford University Press, pp. 570–79.

Hawkins, J. A. 2004. *Efficiency and complexity in grammars.* Oxford University Press.

Heine, B. 2002. 'On the role of context in grammaticalization', in Wischer and Diewald (eds.), pp. 83–101.

Heine, B., Claudi, U. and Hünnemeyer, F. 1991. *Grammaticalization: A conceptual framework.* University of Chicago Press.

Heine, B. and Kuteva, T. 2002. *World lexicon of grammaticalization.* Cambridge University Press.

Himmelmann, N. P. 2004. 'Lexicalization and grammaticization: Opposite or orthogonal?', in W. Bisang, N. P. Himmelmann and B. Wiemer (eds.), *What makes grammaticalization – a look from its fringes and its components.* Berlin: Mouton de Gruyter, pp. 21–42.

Hinterhölzl, R. and Kemenade, A. van 2012. 'The interaction between syntax, information structure, and prosody in word order change', in Nevalainen and Traugott (eds.), pp. 803–21.

Hopper, P. J. 2011. 'Emergent grammar and temporality in interactional linguistics', in P. Auer and S. Pfänder (eds.), *Constructions: Emerging and emergent.* Berlin: De Gruyter Mouton, pp. 22–44.

Hopper, P. J. and Traugott, E. C. [1993] 2003. *Grammaticalization*, 2nd, rev. edn. Cambridge University Press.

Hurford, J. R., Studdert-Kennedy, M. and Knight, C. (eds.) 1998. *Approaches to the evolution of language: Social and cognitive bases.* Cambridge University Press.

Janda, R. D. 2001. 'Beyond "pathways" and "unidirectionality": On the discontinuity of transmission and the counterability of grammaticalization', in L. Campbell (ed.), *Grammaticalization: A critical assessment*, special issue of *Language Sciences* 23: 265–340.

Jespersen, O. 1917. *Negation in English and other languages* (Historisk-filologiske Meddeleser 1). Copenhagen: Høst.

Keenan, E. 2002. 'Explaining the creation of reflexive pronouns in English', in D. Minkova and R. P. Stockwell (eds.), *Studies in the history of English: A millennial perspective*. Berlin: Mouton de Gruyter, pp. 325–55.

Keller, R. 1994. *On language change: The invisible hand in language*, trans. B. Nerlich. London: Routledge (first published in 1990 in German).

King, R. 2000. *The lexical basis of grammatical borrowing: A Prince Edward Island case study*. Amsterdam: John Benjamins.

Kiparsky, P. 1968. 'Linguistic universals and linguistic change', in E. Bach and R. T. Harms (eds.), *Universals in linguistic theory*. New York: Holt, Rinehart & Winston, pp. 171–202.

2012. 'Grammaticalization as optimization', in D. Jonas, J. Whitman and A. Garrett (eds.), *Grammatical change: Origins, nature, outcomes*. Oxford University Press, pp. 15–51.

Kirby, S. 2000. 'Syntax without natural selection: How compositionality emerges from vocabulary in a population of learners', in C. Knight, M. Studdert-Kennedy and J. R. Hurford (eds.), *The evolutionary emergence of language: Social function and the origins of linguistic form*. Cambridge University Press, pp. 303–23.

Koptjevskaja-Tamm, M. 2009. '"A lot of grammar with a good portion of lexicon": Towards a typology of partitive and pseudo-partitive nominal constructions', in J. Helmbrecht, Y. Nishina, Y.-M. Shin, S. Skopeteas and E. Verhoeven (eds.), *Form and function in language research: Papers in honour of Christian Lehmann*. Berlin: De Gruyter Mouton, pp. 329–46.

Kroch, A. and Taylor, A. 1997. 'Verb movement in Old and Middle English: Dialect variation and language contact', in A. van Kemenade and N. Vincent (eds.), *Parameters of morphosyntactic change*. Cambridge University Press, pp. 297–325.

Kuteva, T. 2001. *Auxiliation: An enquiry into the nature of grammaticalization*. Oxford University Press.

Langacker, R. W. 2009. *Investigations in cognitive grammar*. Berlin: Mouton de Gruyter.

Lehmann, C. 2008. 'Information structure and grammaticalization', in E. Seoane and M. J. López-Couso (eds., in collaboration with T. Fanego), *Theoretical and empirical issues in grammaticalization*. Amsterdam: John Benjamins, pp. 207–29.

Lightfoot, D. W. 1991. *How to set parameters: Arguments from language change*. Cambridge, MA: MIT Press.

Longobardi, G. 2001. 'Formal syntax, diachronic minimalism, and etymology', *Linguistic Inquiry* 32: 275–302.

López-Couso, M. J. 2010. 'Subjectification and intersubjectification', in A. H. Jucker and I. Taavitsainen (eds.), *Historical pragmatics*. Berlin: De Gruyter Mouton, pp. 127–63.

Meillet, A. [1912] 1958. 'L'évolution des formes grammaticales', in A. Meillet, *Linguistique historique et linguistique générale*. Paris: Champion, pp. 130–48. (Originally published in *Scientia* (*Rivista di scienza*) XXII, 1912.)

Mitchell, B. 1985. *Old English syntax*. 2 vols. Oxford: Clarendon Press,

Mufwene, S. 2001. *The ecology of language evolution*. Cambridge University Press.

Narrog, H. 2012. *Modality, subjectivity, and semantic change*. Oxford University Press.

Nevalainen, T. and Traugott, E. C. (eds.) 2012. *The Oxford handbook of the history of English*. Oxford University Press.

Newmeyer, F. J. 1998. *Language form and language function*. Cambridge, MA and London: MIT Press.

Oliveira, M. de 2000. 'The pronominal subject in Italian and Brazilian Portuguese', in M. A. Kato and E. V. Negrão (eds.), *Brazilian Portuguese and the null subject parameter*. Frankfurt a. M.: Vervuert, pp. 37–53.

Patten, A. L. 2012. *The English IT-cleft: A constructional account and a diachronic investigation*. Berlin: De Gruyter Mouton.

Pinker, S. and Bloom, P. 1990. 'Natural language and natural selection', *Behavioral and Brain Sciences* 13: 707–84.

Quirk, R., Greenbaum, S., Leech, G. and Svartvik, J. 1985. *A comprehensive grammar of the English language*. London: Longman.

Rhee, S. 2008. 'Through a borrowed mouth: Reported speech and subjectification in Korean', in P. Sutcliffe, L. Stanford and A. Lommel (eds.), *LACUS forum 34: Speech and beyond*, pp. 202–10. Available online at www.lacus.org/volumes/34/217_rhee_s.pdf.

Rizzi, L. 1997. *Parameters and functional heads: Essays in comparative syntax*. Oxford University Press.

Roberts, I. 2007. *Diachronic syntax*. Oxford University Press.

Roberts, I. and Roussou, A. 2003. *Syntactic change: A minimalist approach to grammaticalization*. Cambridge University Press.

Shibatani, M. and Givón, T. (eds.) 2009. *Syntactic complexity*. Amsterdam: John Benjamins.

Silverstein, M. 1976. 'Hierarchy of features and ergativity', in R. M. W. Dixon (ed.), *Grammatical categories in Australian languages*. Canberra: Australian Institute of Aboriginal Studies, pp. 112–71.

Speyer, A. 2012. 'Stress clash and word order changes in the left periphery in Old and Middle English', in Nevalainen and Traugott (eds.), pp. 873–83.

Sweetser, E. E. 1988. 'Grammaticalization and semantic bleaching', in S. Axmaker, A. Jaisser and H. Singmaster (eds.), *Berkeley Linguistics Society 14: General session and parasession on grammaticalization*. Berkeley, CA: Berkeley Linguistics Society, pp. 389–405.

Traugott, E. C. 2010. 'Dialogic contexts as motivation for syntactic change', in R. A. Cloutier, A. M. Hamilton-Brehm and W. Kretzschmar (eds.), *Variation and change in English grammar and lexicon*. Berlin: De Gruyter Mouton, pp. 11–27.

    2012. 'The status of onset contexts in analysis of micro-changes', in M. Kytö (ed.), *English corpus linguistics: Crossing paths*. Amsterdam: Rodopi, pp. 221–55.

Traugott, E. C. and Dasher, R. B. 2002. *Regularity in semantic change*. Cambridge University Press.

Traugott, E. C. and König, E. 1991. 'The semantics-pragmatics of grammaticalization revisited', in E. C. Traugott and B. Heine (eds.), *Approaches to grammaticalization*, vol. I. Amsterdam: John Benjamins, pp. 189–218.

Traugott, E. C. and Trousdale, G. 2013. *Constructionalization and constructional changes*. Oxford University Press.

Van Dyk. P. n.d. (*c.* 1765) *Nieuwe en nooit bevoorens geziene onderwyzinge in het Bastert Engels, of Neeger Engels, zoo als het zelve in de Hollandsze Colonien gebruikt word*. Amsterdam: Jacobus van Egmont.

van Gelderen, E. 2004. *Grammaticalization as economy*. Amsterdam: John Benjamins.

Waltereit, R. 2012. 'On the origins of grammaticalization and other types of language change in discourse strategies', in K. Davidse, T. Breban, L. Brems and T. Mortelmans (eds., in collaboration with B. Cornillie, H. Cuyckens and T. Leuschner), *Grammaticalization and language change: New reflections*. Amsterdam: John Benjamins, pp. 51–72.

Waltereit, R. and Detges, U. 2008. 'Syntactic change from within and without syntax: A usage-based approach', in U. Detges and R. Waltereit (eds.), *The paradox of grammatical change*. Amsterdam: John Benjamins, pp. 13–36.

Warner, A. R. 1993. *English auxiliaries: Structure and history*. Cambridge University Press.

Willis, D., Lucas, C. and Breitbarth, A. (eds.) 2013. *The history of negation in the languages of Europe and the Mediterranean*, vol. 1: *Case studies*. Oxford University Press.

Winford, D. and Migge, B. 2007. 'Substrate influence on the emergence of the TMA systems of the Surinamese Creoles', *Journal of Pidgin and Creole Languages* 22: 73–99.

Wischer, I. and Diewald, G. (eds.) 2002. *New reflections on grammaticalization*. Amsterdam: John Benjamins.

Yang, C. D. 2000. 'Internal and external forces in language change', *Language Variation and Change* 12: 231–50.

Part VI

Models and
Approaches

27

Principles and Parameters

Adam Ledgeway and Ian Roberts

27.1 Introduction: Principles and Parameters

The Principles-and-Parameters (P&P) approach to cross-linguistic variation was first developed by Chomsky and his associates in the early 1980s (see in particular Chomsky (1981), and, for more general introductions, Roberts (1996), Baker (2001); see also discussions in §7.2, §13.5, §16.4.1, §28.2). The leading idea is that Universal Grammar (UG) contains an invariant set of principles associated with parameters which define the space of possible variation among actual languages. Taking the principles to be innately given, and the parameters to be triggered by salient parts of the primary linguistic data (PLD) for language acquisition, this approach was held to be a major step in the direction of explanatory adequacy (in the sense of Chomsky 1964), since language acquisition could be seen as setting the parameters of the native language on the combined basis of the innate UG and the triggering aspects of the PLD.

To give a concrete, if rather simplified, example: we know that languages can be divided into those which have unmarked VO order, e.g. English, and those which have OV order, e.g. Japanese (see also the discussion of Romance and Latin in §27.3 below). On the classical P&P view, the notion of 'verb' is given by the universal theory of syntactic categories, the notion of 'object' is given by the universal theory of grammatical functions, and the idea that the two combine to form a VP is given by the universal theory of phrase structure. These are all taken to be reflexes of UG principles. But experience tells the child which order of O and V inside VP is the appropriate one, and so a child hearing Japanese sets the parameter to OV, while the child hearing English sets it to VO. Parameters describe what is variant in natural-language syntax, and as such they predict the dimensions of language typology, predict aspects of language acquisition and predict what can change in the diachronic dimension. A consequence of this setting of a parameter for OV or VO on the basis of experience is a more general and abstract setting of a directionality parameter determining the orders of all heads and complements (with, again, the notion of 'head' and the notion of 'complement' being UG-defined); see Dryer (1992) for typological support for the idea that head–complement order is predicted by the order of V and O.

The P&P approach was seen as a significant step forward for generative grammar, since earlier approaches (Chomsky 1973, 1975, 1977) had defined UG as a grammatical metatheory specifying a broad format for rules and some general principles on rule application (island constraints, etc.), a particular grammar as a system of language-specific, construction-specific rules, and language acquisition as rule induction. This theory offered little hope for insights into either language typology (see Chapter 30, this volume) or language acquisition (see Chapter 18, this volume), and the P&P approach stood in stark contrast to this from its inception.

The immediate consequence of P&P theory in the 1980s was an explosion of formal syntactic work on a wide range of the world's languages. Comparative work became the norm. The stimulus to comparative syntactic research led to the postulation of a number of parameters, without much attention being paid to the format for parameters. This initial conception gave rise to a rather arbitrary-looking collection of parameters: the Null Subject Parameter (Taraldsen 1978; Rizzi 1982), a parameter determining the Case properties of Prepositions (Kayne 1984), the head-directionality parameter (Hawkins 1983; Koopman 1984; Travis 1984), V-movement parameters (Emonds 1978; Pollock 1989; den Besten 1983), the overt vs covert nature of *wh*-movement (English vs Chinese: Huang 1982) and non-configurationality (Hale 1981, 1982, 1983).

Partly inspired by the first postulation of the Minimalist Programme in the early 1990s, with its emphasis on formal features as the driving force behind derivations, a significant shift took place in the conception of the locus for parameters: parameters were thought to be specified in the (functional) lexicon, rather than directly on UG principles (a variant of this proposal had earlier been put forward by Borer 1984: 29). More precisely, Chomsky (1995) proposed that parameters be viewed as being specified by the formal features of functional heads. This view of parameters naturally leads to the concept of microparametric syntax (Kayne 2005b), according to which there is a rather large number of parameters, each responsible for a fairly small point of difference between grammars (e.g. that past participles agree with fronted *wh*-words in French, but not in Spanish; see §27.4.1.1). The microparametric view, although not uncontroversial (see Baker 2008b), has become the dominant one in current formal comparative syntax. This view was enshrined in what Baker (2008b: 156), acknowledging the twin sources of the approach, called the Borer–Chomsky Conjecture:

(1)   All parameters of variation are attributable to differences in the formal features of particular items (e.g. the functional heads) in the Lexicon.

The precise set of formal features of functional heads remains undetermined and in particular no satisfactory intensional definition of this set of elements has been given (but see Biberauer (2011) for a possible intensional characterization of formal features). A partial extensional characterization, however, includes at least categorial features (N, V, etc.), φ-features (person, number, gender, etc.), abstract Case features (NOM, ACC, etc.,) and movement-triggering features (EPP, EF, etc.).

27.2   Macro- and Microparameters

As mentioned above, the Borer–Chomsky Conjecture was taken as defining the microparametric approach: each functional head in each language can be characterized as having its own set of formal features; this approach does not necessarily imply the clustering of surface phenomena that was characteristic of the Government–Binding view of parameters (for very illuminating discussion of this point, see Kayne 2005b). A contrasting approach was pursued by Baker (1996, 2008a) (see also Bošković 2008; Huang 2015), who argued for the existence of macroparameters, parameters which may be directly associated with UG principles (unlike the formal features of the Borer–Chomsky Conjecture) and which profoundly impact on the overall nature of a grammatical system. The Polysynthesis Parameter of Baker (1996) was of this kind, being formulated in relation to a general notion of 'argument visibility', a very general requirement on the formal realization of the semantic arguments of a predicate, and positing two quite distinct ways of satisfying this requirement: one in terms of syntactic configurations, the other in terms of the formation of complex words. As such, the setting of this parameter had deep and ramified consequences for the grammatical system; indeed, Baker (1996: 3) connects this concept of macroparameter with Sapir's (1921) notion of the 'genius' of a language (we will come back to this last idea in §27.5).

Although much recent work in comparative syntax has been largely microparametric in character, with the Borer–Chomsky Conjecture often implicitly or explicitly assumed, the notion of macroparameter has not been conclusively shown to be unfounded (Newmeyer (2005) criticizes the GB notion of parameter in general, and while this could be construed as a criticism of Baker-style macroparameters it does not seem to have been explicitly intended as such). Moreover, in his general discussion and defence of the microparametric approach, Kayne (2005b) explicitly asserts the value of work on macroparameters. In this chapter we follow the lead taken by Kayne (2005b: 10) and developed in particular by the *Rethinking*

Comparative Syntax (ReCoS) project (see note 2 for details and references; see also in particular §§7.3–4) in combining the two approaches (see also Huang and Roberts to appear). We hope to show that this can be valuable in understanding aspects of syntactic change.

27.2.1 The Microparametric Approach

The microparametric approach, as articulated by the Borer–Chomsky Conjecture, has various advantages, which we now briefly review (for further discussion, see Roberts 2012, 2014a).

First, the microparametric approach imposes a strong limit on what can vary. Limiting possible variation to the formal features of functional heads has the consequence that various imaginable parameters, which could have been countenanced under a GB approach, cannot be formulated. One important case is the 'arity' of Merge, i.e. the number of syntactic objects this operation can combine at a time. Merge is standardly taken to be binary, and indeed this may follow from its very nature as an optimal formal operation (Watumull 2015). Most importantly, External Merge at least does not seem to be regulated by formal features of functional heads. Interestingly, early versions of the GB '(non-)configurationality parameter' countenanced exactly the possibility of what we would now call n-ary Merge, in treating non-configurational languages as having 'flat', i.e. n-ary branching, structures (Hale 1981; see §§27.3–4). The nature of (External) Merge is such that the Borer–Chomsky Conjecture could not allow such an option; note that this implies that whatever the intensional characterization of the formal features of functional heads turns out to be, it cannot include a feature such as [±binary Merge].

A second advantage, pointed out by Borer (1984: 29), is that associating parameter values with lexical entries (of functional heads) reduces them to the one part of a language which clearly must be learned anyway: the lexicon. Note that this is true even if, perhaps especially if, the domain-specific innate component of language in first-language acquisition is radically reduced, as frequently suggested in the context of the Minimalist Programme (see Chomsky 2005, 2007).

Third, the Borer–Chomsky Conjecture allows us to formulate parameters in a very simple and appealing way, along the following general lines:

(2)   For some formal feature F and some parameter P, P = ±F.

Note that (2) effectively states the identity of formal features and parameters. We will see various examples of the general schema in (2) as we proceed.

This simplicity of formulation in turn makes possible a statement of parametric variation at the UG level which relies on the logic of underspecification:

(3) a. For some formal feature F, −F is the default value of P.

  b. P has +F when triggered (i.e. under specified conditions), −F elsewhere.

  c. +F is the marked value of P.

By effectively treating formal features/parameters as privative in this way, we are able to derive a very simple formal approach to markedness.

Before looking at examples of microparametric change we need to give a definition of a microparameter. Biberauer and Roberts (2012b) give the following definition:

(4) Definition of a microparameter:
  For a given value v_i of a parametrically variant feature F: a small subclass of functional heads (e.g. modal auxiliaries, pronouns) shows v_i.

An example of microparametric change is the development of the class of English modals in the sixteenth century. It is well known that the class of English modals emerged through grammaticalization at around this time (for discussion and analysis, see Lightfoot 1979; Warner 1993, 1997; Roberts 1985; Roberts and Roussou 2003; and also §15.3, §18.3, §23.3.1). In general, the definition of microparameter in (4), combined with the general characterization of grammaticalization given in Roberts and Roussou (2003) as categorial reanalysis of a member of a lexical category as a member of a functional category (or of one functional category as another; see also van Gelderen 2004, 2011; and discussion in §1.3.1, §4.4 of this volume, and note 1 below), implies that grammaticalization is typically microparametric change.

As observed in Traugott (1972), there is some variation among the modals, but the basic line of development can be summarized as follows: in Middle English modals were lexical verbs taking infinitive clausal complements (in fact, they were probably 'restructuring verbs' since they triggered verb (projection) raising in Old and Middle English; see Biberauer and Roberts 2008). As one would expect of lexical verbs, the Middle English premodals were able to appear in non-finite forms:

(5) I shall not konne answere
  'I shall not can [be able to] answer.' (1386, Chaucer; Roberts 1985: 22)

By around 1550, modals had become restricted to finite contexts and, for the most part, only appear with VP complements. Roberts and Roussou (2003: 40f.) propose that the following structural reanalysis took place at roughly this time:

(6) [$_{TP}$ it [$_T$ may [$_{VP}$ (may) [$_{TP}$ (it) happen]]]] >
  [$_{TP}$ it [$_T$ may [$_{VP}$ happen]]]

Here we see a categorial change: the modal was a V in the earlier grammar, but it is a realization of T (or of some relatively high functional head) in the later grammar.[1]

Roberts and Roussou propose that the change was caused by the loss of the infinitive ending on verbs (formerly *-e(n)*). This took place around 1500. Prior to that time, we find forms like (7) (although they were somewhat rare in the fifteenth century):

(7)   nat can we seen …
        Not can we see
        'we cannot see'
        (*c.* 1400: Hoccleve *The Letter of Cupid* 299; Gray 1985: 49; Roberts
        1993: 261)

Roberts and Roussou propose that the presence of the infinitival ending triggered the postulation of a non-finite T in the complement to the modal. When this ending was lost, there was no evidence for the non-finite T and hence no bar to the reanalysis in (6), which only has a single, main-clause T node. The reanalysis of the modals seems to have taken place within around fifty years of the loss of the infinitival ending (see Roberts and Roussou (2003: 36–48) for more detailed discussion, and Warner (1997) for a careful discussion of the chronology of this change, a matter we have simplified here for the purposes of exposition).

So we see that the class of modals was introduced by a microparametric change. Biberauer and Roberts (2012b) point out that the modals seem to have started to undergo further changes (involving, among other things, conditional inversion; see also Biberauer and Roberts forthcoming b) in the eighteenth century, just 200 years after their creation as a separate class. This kind of diachronic instability, they suggest, is typical of microparametric settings.

27.2.2   The Macroparametric Approach

Baker (2008b) offers a very interesting and, in our view, convincing defence of macroparameters. As he points out, on the microparametric view 'there should be many mixed languages of different kinds, and relatively few pure languages of one kind or the other' (2008: 350). On the other hand, the macroparametric view predicts, falsely, rigid

---

[1] Cinque (2006) argues that restructuring verbs in Italian are functional heads. If West Germanic verb (projection) raising triggers are assimilated to this class (see Wurmbrand 2015), then the OE and ME premodals were already functional heads. In these terms, the sixteenth-century reanalysis can be viewed as reanalysis from one (class of) functional heads to another, placing them higher in the inflectional field than formerly. This higher position is one which is required to be finite, as is generally the case for epistemic modals across languages. On this approach, these finiteness requirements are the consequence of 'high' merger rather than any semantic property. For a cartographic analysis of Modern English modals, see Biberauer and Roberts (2015a). Note that an analysis of the development of the modals of this kind is still consistent both with Roberts and Roussou's approach to grammaticalization and the idea that grammaticalization is typically microparametric change.

division of all languages into clear types (OV vs VO, etc.): every category in every language should pattern in one way or the other (we glossed over this obvious point in our presentation of the directionality parameter in the Introduction). But if we combine the two approaches, as he advocates, then we expect to find a bimodal distribution: languages should tend to cluster around one type or another, with a certain amount of noise and a few outliers from either one of the principal patterns. This is what we find in the case of word order, as the evidence from the *World Atlas of Language Structures* (Dryer 2013a, b) shows.

Biberauer and Roberts (2012b) give the following definition of a macroparameter:

(8)   For a given value v_i of a parametrically variant feature F, all functional heads of the relevant type share v_i.

They suggest that for head-directionality, the 'relevant type' of functional heads is all heads (in fact, assuming the approach to linearization in Kayne (1994), this might extend to all lexical heads too, a complication we leave aside here); for radical pro-drop, the relevant set is all potentially φ-feature bearing probes; for polysynthesis, all potential incorporation triggers (which may amount to all potential probes in terms of the approach to incorporation in Roberts 2010c).

Macroparametric changes, then, may affect properties such as head-directionality, radical pro-drop and polysynthesis. Strikingly, these properties strongly tend to be diachronically quite stable. Harmonic head-final order has been extremely stable throughout the history of the Dravidian languages (Steever 1998: 31), and in both Japanese and Korean. The oldest texts in Japanese date from around AD 700–800 (Frellesvig 2010), and so are over 1,000 years old; these texts show both consistent head-finality and radical pro-drop (see also Yanagida 2005; Yanagida and Whitman 2009). The same is true for the oldest texts in Korean. Lee and Ramsey (2011: 55) in their discussion of the text inscribed on a Silla-period stele, *Imsin sŏgi sŏk*, probably dating from the sixth century, say:

> In this text, all the Chinese characters are used in their original, Chinese meanings, but the order in which they are put together is completely different from that of Classical Chinese. The syntax is almost purely Korean. For example, instead of the Chinese construction 'from now', the order of the two characters is reversed, Korean-style … Sentences end in verbs.

Korean, then, also appears to have been rigidly head-final throughout its recorded history. Lee and Ramsey (2011) also indicate that the same is true for radical pro-drop.

Concerning polysynthesis, Branigan (2014) makes the twin observations that (a) polysynthesis (which he analyses as multiple incorporation) is a 'signature' property of the Algonquian family, and (b) this family is very old and geographically widespread. Regarding (a), Branigan (2014: 22) points out that 'all Algonquian languages appear to make use of multiple head-movement in essentially identical ways'; similarly, Mithun (1991: 338) observes that Algonquian languages are polysynthetic. This property seems to have been strongly conserved over millennia and across a vast geographical area (in which the Algonquian languages were in contact with many other Native American language families).

Of course, it is well known that both Latin/Romance and English have undergone changes in head-directionality in their recorded history (we will say more about the Latin/Romance change in §27.3). In fact, it seems clear from recent work on the older Indo-European languages that these systems conform to a general type in showing non-rigid head-final order, second-position effects, a very active left periphery, sub-extraction from DP, null subjects and objects, synthetic verbal morphology and case inflections (on Latin, see Devine and Stephens 2006; Salvi 2011; Ledgeway 2012a, b, 2014b, 2016a; Dankaert 2012; on Greek, Taylor 1990; on Sanskrit, Hale 1995; Kiparsky 1995; on Old Church Slavonic, Pancheva 2008; on Celtic, Watkins 1963, 1964; Russell 1995: 300–4; Newton 2006; on Germanic, Walkden 2014: 106–12; Ringe 2006: 295; on Old Iranian, Skjærvø 2009: 94f.; and on Anatolian, Garrett 1990). Many of these properties have been lost in the more recent history of the respective branches: on Romance, see below; Greek shows a similar overall development to Romance (although morphological case is retained as an impoverished Nominative–Accusative–Genitive system alongside a very rich article system); West Germanic (aside from the recent history of English) is somewhat conservative, although North Germanic has undergone the OV>VO change (see in particular on Old Icelandic Hroársdóttir 2000) but relatively innovative in DP; Slavic appears to have undergone the same change (Pancheva 2008); Celtic has innovated VS order but is otherwise somewhat similar to Romance, while Indic, presumably as a consequence of long-standing contact with Dravidian (in Matisoff's (1990) terms, these languages belong to the 'Indosphere'), has developed rigid OV order. (The situation in the Iranian languages is more complicated owing in part to contact with Turkic; see Harris and Campbell 1995: 139–41.) But we can observe that (a) evidence from Anatolian in particular suggests that the parent language was head-final and (b) head-final systems tend to be stable. This leads us to ask why several branches of European Indo-European have developed in these rather similar, but, for head-final languages, atypical ways. An important factor may have been the widespread second-position phenomena in these branches of Indo-European. Following the general line of research into these phenomena instigated by den Besten's (1983) account of Germanic verb second, we take these phenomena to involve a combination of head- and XP-movement into the left periphery as part of a general activation of the left periphery. This, combined with the development of initial complementizers (which may have been connected; see Kiparsky 1995), may have 'destabilized' the earlier head-final order. Hence we see what from a wider cross-linguistic perspective may be a rather unusual pattern of OV>VO change in these families.

We thus concur with Baker's conclusion that both microparametric and macroparametric variation must be countenanced. We add to his conclusion that this must hold for diachronic variation (i.e. change) as well as for synchronic variation. Furthermore, there is evidence that microparameters are less diachronically stable than macroparameters. In the next sections, we will provide further support for this view from the diachronic developments in the passage from Latin to Romance.

27.3 Combining Macro- and Microparameters: the Latin–Romance Transition

Even the most cursory of comparisons of Latin and Romance syntax reveals some fundamental changes in the Latin–Romance transition which, in typological terms, can be interpreted as involving some 'large steps' and, at the same time, a series of 'smaller steps' both in the passage from Latin to Romance and in the subsequent developments that have produced considerable differentiation across the many Romance languages and dialects. Changes of the former type have traditionally been modelled in terms of macroparameters (see §27.2.2) which, on most accounts, would include at least the following major dimensions of linguistic variation:

(9)   a. Head directionality (Tesnière 1959; Chomsky 1981; Hawkins 1983; Travis 1984)
       b. Configurationality (Hale 1981, 1982, 1983; Ledgeway 2012a: chs. 3, 5; 2012b)
       c. Nominative/ergative alignment (Comrie 1978; Dixon 1994; Sheehan 2014)
       d. Polysynthesis (Baker 1996)
       e. Topic/Subject prominence (Li and Thompson 1976; Huang 1982)

Of these macroparameters, only the first two are relevant to Latin–Romance developments. In terms of the head parameter, at least in its earliest attestations, Latin was predominantly head-final (10a) whereas modern Romance is head-initial (10b), with Classical Latin representing a transitional stage in which both conservative head-final (11a) and innovative head-initial (11b) orders are found (Adams 1976; Ledgeway 2012a: ch. 5).

(10)   Archaic Latin (CIL 12.7)
       a. quoius forma   uirtutei   **parisuma**   fuit
          whose   beauty.NOM valour.DAT most.equal.NOM   was

Italian

b. la cui bellezza fu **pari** <u>al</u> valore
 the whose beauty was equal to.the valour
 'whose beauty was fully equal to his valour'

(11) Latin (Cic. Diu. 2.113)

  a. <u>constantibus</u>   <u>hominibus</u> **par** erat
   resolute.ABL.PL men.ABL equal.NOM it.was
   '[our apprehension] was equal to that of men of strong character'
   Latin (Cic. Phil. 1.34)

  b. illa   erat uita [. . .] libertate esse **parem** <u>ceteris</u>
   that.NOM was life.NOM freedom.ABL be.INF equal.ACC rest.DAT.PL
   'What he considered life . . . was the being equal to the rest of the
   citizens in freedom'

In terms of structural organization, Latin has also been argued to exhibit a non-configurational syntax in which relationships between individual linguistic items are signalled lexocentrically through the forms of the items themselves (case inflections, agreement), whereas in Romance relationships between related linguistic items are encoded by their fixed positions relative to each other (Vincent 1988: 53f., 62f.; 1997: 149, 163; 1998a: 423f.; Ledgeway 2011: §3; 2012a: ch. 3). Consequently, in Latin not only is it difficult to establish fixed orders for individual heads and their associated complements or modifiers within their given phrase (12a–b), even adjacency between semantically related items is not a requirement (Marouzeau 1949: 42; 1953: 62; Ernout and Thomas 1953: 162; Pinkster 1990: 184–6; Oniga 2004: 101–2; Powell 2010). As a consequence, we frequently find discontinuous structures such as (13a), where the adjectival modifier *celeris* has been fronted under focus to the left edge of the containing DP separating it from its associated nominal *subsidii*. In Romance, by contrast, all elements appear to have pre-established positions (12c) and the languages do not readily license hyperbaton under edge-fronting (13b).

(12) Latin (Caes. *B.G.* 1.22.3)

  a. <u>Caesar</u> **suas** **copias** in proximum collem subducit
   Caesar.NOM his.ACC troops.ACC in next.ACC hill.ACC withdraws
   'Caesar leads off his forces to the next hill'
   Latin (Caes. *B.G.* 1.24.1)

  b. **copias** **suas** <u>Caesar</u> in proximum collem
   troops.ACC his.ACC Caesar.NOM in next.ACC hill.ACC
   subduxit
   withdrew

'Caesar drew off his forces to the next hill'
French

c. César retire **ses** **troupes** (*ses) (*César)
   Caesar withdraws his troops his Caesar

(13) Latin (Caes., *B.C.* 3.69.2)

a. legio   pompeiana, **celeris**   spe   subsidii
   legion.NOM Pompeian.NOM quick.GEN hope.ABL help.GEN
   confirmata
   assured

Romanian

b. legiunea   pomepeiană, întărită   de (*rapid)nădejdea unui
   legion=the Pompeian   strenghtened by quick hope=the of.a
   ajutor **rapid**
   help quick
   'the Pompeian legion, encouraged by the hope of speedy assistance'

However, as observed above (see §27.2.1), over recent decades much work has radically departed from this macroparametric view with a shift of focus on predominantly surface-oriented variation (see Kayne 1996, 2000, 2005a, b; Manzini and Savoia 2005), an approach well suited to modelling the 'smaller steps' in diachronic change. This has led to the proliferation of a remarkable number of local, low-level microparameters interpreted as the (PF-)lexicalization of specific formal feature values of individual functional heads (Borer 1984; Chomsky 1995) in accordance with the Borer–Chomsky Conjecture (Baker 2008b: 353). By way of illustration, consider (14a–d) where we see that, in contrast to Romance, Latin lacks functional categories in that none of the functional heads are overtly lexicalized in accordance with the traditional Latin–Romance synthetic–analytic dichotomy (Ledgeway 2012a: chs. 2, 4; forthcoming d). At the same time, we also observe how across Romance there is significant variation in which of the functional heads are realized and the overt distinctions they mark. For instance, only French lexicalizes all functional heads in (14), including an overt transitive/causative light verb *fait*, whereas Italian only optionally encodes the partitive distinction on D through the partitive article *del* 'of.the'. By contrast, Romanian fails to overtly mark either of these head positions but uniquely displays robust marking on C for the realis/irrealis opposition (*că* vs *să*), otherwise paralleled in the indicative/subjunctive distinction realized on T in the Romance perfective auxiliary, in turn further distinguished by way of the HAVE/BE split (*a* vs *fi*) in Romanian (Ledgeway 2014a). In short, what we see here are minimal differences across otherwise highly homogenous systems which can be read both horizontally and vertically as cases of synchronic and diachronic microvariation, respectively.

(14)

	C		T		*v*		D	
a. Dico/Uolo	Ø	eum	Ø		Ø	coxisse	Ø	panem (Lat.)
b. Je dis/veux	**qu'**	il	**a/ait**		**fait**	cuire	**du**	pain (Fr.)
c. Dico/Voglio	**che**		**ha/abbia**		Ø	cotto	**(del)**	pane (It.)
d. Spun/Vreau	**că/să**		**a/fi**		Ø	copt	Ø	pâine (Ro.)

I.want/say   that$_{(Realis/Irrealis)}$ him/he has$_{IND/(be)sBJV}$ made bake(d) some bread
'I want him to have/I say that he has baked some bread'

Arguably, then, any account of the Latin–Romance transition must make reference to changes of both a macro- and microparametric kind (see §27.2). Approaches couched narrowly in terms of macroparameters would lead us to expect successive stages of languages to rigidly fall into one of a few 'pure' types, while microparametric approaches would lead us *a priori* to expect wildly 'mixed' types. As observed by Roberts (2010b: 24f.), neither scenario correctly captures the relevant facts about the Latin–Romance transition. For example, a purely macroparametric view would incorrectly lead us to expect Romance varieties to present properties like those in (15), in which among the macro-dimensions of variation in (15a–e) some (viz. 15a–b) might show change with respect to Latin, whereas low-level micro-properties such as those in (15f–j) are not expected to diverge at all from Latin, contrary to fact:

(15) a. **Head-initial**: (S)VO, postnominal genitives
   b. **Configurational**: grammatically fixed word order
   c. Nominative–accusative
   d. Non-polysynthetic
   e. Subject prominent
   f. Absence of functional categories: articles, clitic pronouns, auxiliaries, few complementizers (see Ledgeway 2012a: ch. 4; 2016a)
   g. Rich inflectional agreement, null arguments (including objects; see Vincent 2000)
   h. Predominant infinitival complementation, notably accusative with infinitive (see Herman 1989; Greco 2012)
   i. (Imperfective) synthetic passive/middle voice (see Cennamo 2016)
   j. Simple preverbal negation (see Molinelli 1988; Willis, Lucas and Breitbarth 2013)

By contrast, under a purely microparametric view not only do we expect Romance varieties to present those properties which have actually changed with respect to Latin combining small-scale changes (16f–j) with more far-reaching large-scale developments (see 16a–b), but we should also expect the relevant variation to be greater and less constrained, with some Romance varieties displaying unattested clusters of properties which freely mix features of Latin and attested Romance syntax. Yet we do not find fictitious varieties such as *Latinalabrese* (<Latin+(ca)labrese) mixing, for example, head-final order and full configurationality with synthetic passives and articles (17a), or *Latinais* (<Latin+(fra)nçais) combining head-initial order and non-configurationality with the accusative with the infinitive (AcI) and auxiliaries (17b), or even *Latiñol* (<Latin+(espa)ñol) displaying head-initial order and full configurationality alongside case, null objects and determiners, and discontinuous negation (17c).

(16) a. Head-initial: (S)VO, postnominal adjectives/genitives

   b. Configurational: grammatically fixed word order

   c. Nominative–accusative

   d. Non-polysynthetic

   e. Subject prominent

   f. Proliferation of functional categories: articles, pronominal clitic, auxiliaries, complementizers (Vincent 1997; Ledgeway 2012a: chs. 2, 4; 2016a)

   g. Relatively rich inflectional agreement, null subjects (but cf. Modern Fr.), subject clitics (Rizzi 1986; Brandi and Cordin 1989; Poletto 2000; Roberts 2010a)

   h. Predominant finite complementation, viz. *que/che-* clauses (Ledgeway 2016b)

   i. Presence of periphrastic active/passive paradigms (Vincent 1987; Ledgeway 2016, forthcoming c)

   j Preverbal, discontinuous and/or postverbal negation (see Poletto 2016)

(17) a. Ari   nova   du   pizzaiolu   a   pizza   'nfornaður. (*Latinalabrese)
        at.the nine of.the pizzaiolo the pizza place.in.oven.3SG.PRS.PASS
        'At nine o'clock the pizza is placed in the oven by the pizzaiolo.'

   b. Trop   savons   belle   la   femme   avoir   dansé. (*Latinais)
      too.much we.know pretty.FSG the.FSG woman.F have.INF danced
      'We know that the beautiful lady has been dancing too much.'

   c. María   visitó   pueblom   pero   yo   no   conozco   paso. (*Latiñol)
      María   visited village.ACC but   I   NEG know   step.NEG
      'María has visited the village but I don't know it.'

Rather, what we find is a bimodal distribution of macro- and micro-parametric properties (see Baker 2008b; see also §27.2) whereby all Romance varieties tend towards the same basic linguistic 'type', namely head-initial, configurational, accusative, non-polysynthetic (with strong analytic tendencies) and subject-prominent (see 16a–e), but which at the same time allow some degree of low-level deviation from some of these core patterns. For example, although operating in terms of a core nominative–accusative reflexes of split intransitivity

(Bentley 2006, 2016) manifested, among other things, in the distribution of perfective HAVE/BE splits (18a), INDE-cliticization (18b), subject positions (18c), and bare plural DPs (18d).

(18) a. **Avèm**   susat   / **Sem**   arribats   al   mercat. (Occ.)
         we.have   sweated   we.are   arrived   at.the   market
         'We sweated / We arrived at the market.'
      b. *Tres [en]   **en** menjan   (tomàquets) / **N'**   han
         three   of.them=eat   tomatoes   of.them=have
         vingut tres [en]. (Cat.)
         come three
         'Three of them are eating (tomatoes) / Three of them came.'
      c. **Carmine** fumava (la sigaretta) / Sul   tavolo   fumava
         Carmine   smoked the cigarette on.the table   smoked
         una   **tazza**   **di**   **tè**   **verde**. (It.)
         a   cup   of   tea   green
         'Carmine was smoking (the cigarette) / On the table stood a cup of
         steaming green tea.'
      d. ***Animales** han comido (la hierba) / Han   muerto **animales**. (Sp.)
         animals   have eaten   the grass   have died   animals
         'Animals have been eating (the grass) / Animals have died.'

Similarly, alongside core subject-prominent structures a number of Romance varieties also show specific kinds of topical non-nominative subjects with unaccusatives (19a–c), paralleling in many respects topic-prominent structures (see Cardinaletti 2004: 122–6, 136f.; Avelar 2009; Avelar and Galves 2011; de Andrade and Galves 2014).

(19) a. **Essas carros** cabem   muita   gente. (Br.Pt.)
         these cars   fit.3PL much   people
         'Many people can fit into this car.'
      b. **A Gianni** è capitata   una   grande   disgrazia. (It.)
         to Gianni   is happened a   big   misfortune
         'A big misfortune befell Gianni.'
      c. **Me**   faltaban   las   palabras. (Sp.)
         me=   were.missing   the   words
         'I was at a loss for words.'

27.4 Parameter Hierarchies

Above we have seen considerable evidence that any theory of language change, and in particular any account of the Latin–Romance transition, must make reference to changes of both a macro- and microparametric order. So we are led to propose a theory that combines some notion of macroparameters alongside microparameters (Baker 1996, 2008a, b).

Following ideas first proposed by Kayne (2005b: 10) and further developed by Roberts and Holmberg (2010) and Roberts (2012), progress in this direction has recently been made by the Rethinking Comparative Syntax research group;[2] their central idea is that macroparameters should be construed as the surface effect of aggregates of microparameters acting in unison, ultimately as some sort of composite single parameter (see also the discussion in §§7.3–4). On this view, macroparametric effects obtain whenever all individual functional heads behave in concert, namely are set identically for the same feature value, whereas microparametric variation arises when different subsets of functional heads present distinct featural specifications (see the definitions of micro- and macroparameter given in (4) and (8) above). Conceived in this way, parametric variation can be interpreted in a scalar fashion and modelled in terms of parametric hierarchies along the lines of (20). Macroparameters, the simplest and least marked options that uniformly apply to all functional heads, are placed at the very top of the hierarchy, but, as we move downwards, variation becomes progressively less 'macro' and, at the same time, more restricted with choices becoming progressively more limited to increasingly smaller subsets of features, namely, no F(p) > all F(p) > some F(p) (for F a feature and p some grammatical behaviour). More specifically, functional heads increasingly display a disparate behaviour in relation to particular feature values which may, for example, characterize: (i) a naturally definable class of functional heads (e.g. [+N], [+finite]), a case of mesoparametric variation; (ii) a small, lexically definable subclass of functional heads (e.g. pronominals, proper nouns, auxiliaries, unaccusatives), a case of microparametric variation proper; and (iii) one or more individual lexical items, a case of nanoparametric variation.

(20)

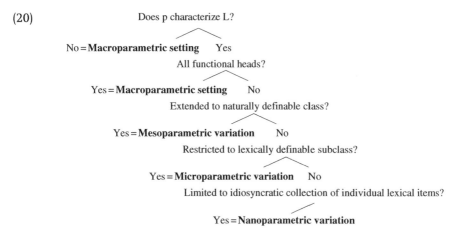

---

[2] Recent publications of the ReCoS project (http://recos-dtal.mml.cam.ac.uk/) include Biberauer, Holmberg, Roberts and Sheehan (2014), Biberauer and Roberts (2012a, b, 2015a, b, forthcoming a, b), Roberts (2012), Biberauer, Roberts and Sheehan (2014), Sheehan (2014). See also Ledgeway (2013, 2015, forthcoming b, d).

In light of these assumptions, consider again the head parameter. In §27.3 above we saw how at the macroparametric level the passage from Latin to Romance is marked by a reversal in the head parameter (see (10)–(11)), from which, following Ledgeway (2012a: ch. 5, 2012b, 2014b, forthcoming a), the perceived effects of configurationality can also be ultimately derived. This development can therefore be modelled by way of the parameter hierarchy in (21).

(21)   Do functional heads license roll-up?

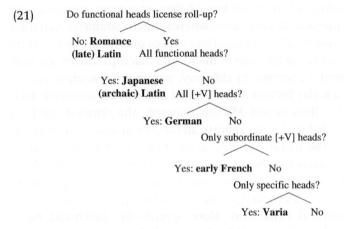

The hierarchy in (21) based on Roberts (2012: 320–3) makes the plausible assumption that head-initiality represents the unmarked and least costly option, as made explicit in many recent structural analyses following Kayne (1994), where head-initiality instantiates the basic underlying order, whereas the derivationally more complex nature of head-finality obtained through roll-up movement of the complement across the head to a derived (inner) specifier represents the more marked option (see Ledgeway 2012a: ch. 5; Biberauer, Holmberg and Roberts 2014). On this view, in Romance the effect of the parameter is unmistakably 'macro' in that all functional heads in Romance are unequivocally aligned with the head-initial setting, whereas in Latin the parameter fluctuates between both settings as a result of its occupying an intermediate position in the gradual shift from head-finality to head-initiality. This oscillation between head-last and head-first structures in the history of Latin can be captured along two axes of variation (see Ledgeway 2012a: 236), the first in terms of diachronic variation (head-last (archaic Latin) ⇒ head-initial (early/late Latin)) and the second in terms of diaphasic (and no doubt diastratic and diamesic) variation (head-final (formal, literary) vs head-initial (subliterary, colloquial)). The facts can therefore be interpreted in terms of a progressive reversal of the head parameter from a regular head-final setting (as in languages like Japanese) towards a head-initial setting, with Classical Latin displaying an ambivalent behaviour on account of its non-uniform characterization in relation to these two dimensions of variation (see 11a–b), namely, non-archaic (predominantly head-first), but formal and literary (predominantly head-final).

As we move down the hierarchy in (21) we come across increasingly more marked and restricted linguistic options of the microparametric type, including those whose effects have been described above as involving meso- and nanoparametric distributions. For example, we find languages like modern German which have been argued to present a 'mixed' (viz. mesoparametric) setting for the head parameter (Biberauer, Holmberg and Roberts 2014), with head-final roll-up orders in the verbal domain (see 22a) but head-initial orders in the nominal domain (see 23b) ultimately statable in terms of a distinction between [±V] heads (we take C to be excluded from this class of [+V] heads). This sort of behaviour also finds a parallel in early Romance (e.g. Old French; see Bauer 1995: 107–11) where it has been observed that (S) OV order exceptionally survives in subordinate clauses (see 23a–b). One natural way to frame this generalization is in terms of a strictly microparametric representation whereby roll-up movement is limited to a particular subclass of V-heads, namely those marked by the lexical specification [+subordinate]. Diachronically, we thus witness a movement down the hierarchy whereby the distribution of roll-up movement in the verbal domain, still systematic in Latin in embedded contexts (Charpin 1989; Ledgeway 2012a: 177–9), becomes increasingly constrained and infrequent before eventually falling out of the hierarchy entirely by the modern Romance period.

(22) German
   a. daß Paul [[das Buch **gelesen**] **hat**]
      that Paul the book read has

   b. **Das** **Buch** von Paul
      the book from Paul

(23) Old French (Strasbourg Oaths)
   a. in quant Deus sauir et podir me **dunat**
      as God wisdom and power me grants

   b. cum om per dreit [[son fradra **saluar**] **dift**]
      as one by right one's brother protect.INF must

Of course, before dropping out of the hierarchy, it is not unusual for once-productive options to persist as isolated or sporadic lexical archaisms on the margins of the system. Arguably, such nanoparametric variation is visible in a small number of individual Romance lexical items which may residually present conservative roll-up orders, including specific (perhaps lexicalized) uses of the Italian prepositions *malgrado* 'despite' (cf. head-final *mio* **malgrado** lit. '1SG.GEN despite (= against my will)' vs head-initial **malgrado** *Gianni* 'despite Gianni (= against Gianni's will)') and the French adposition *durant* 'during' (cf. head-final/-initial *sa vie durant*/*durant sa vie* 'throughout/during his life').

27.4.1 Diachronic Microvariation: Some Romance and Germanic examples

In what follows we examine the development of several phenomena across a number of different Romance and Germanic varieties which show how minimal differences among otherwise highly homogenous 'systems' can be used to investigate microvariation along the diachronic axis in order to better understand what precisely may vary and how such variation may be implicationally structured in relation to the predictions of parametric hierarchies like (20). The overall picture highlights an unmistakable tension between the demands of detailed empirical description on the one hand, which forces us to assume many distinct featural (viz. microparametric) instantiations of different functional heads, and the desire to provide a principled explanation within the limits of a maximally constrained theory of UG on the other.

27.4.1.1 Romance Past Participle Agreement

The distribution of agreement of the active past participle displays a number of patterns across Romance (Smith 1999; Loporcaro 1998, 2016; Manzini and Savoia 2005: II:553–96; Ledgeway 2012a: 317f.), a representative sample of which is exemplified in (24a–g):

(24) a. La   manzana, la   había [$_{vP}$ [$_{Spec}$ ~~la~~] comid$\underline{o}$]   ~~la.~~ (Sp.)
       the.FSG   apple.FSG   it.F=   I.had   eaten.MSG
       'I had eaten the apple.'

   b. pro$_i$ seme [$_{AgrOP}$ [$_{Spec}$ ~~pro$_i$~~] magn$\underline{i}$te] lu
      pro   are.1PL   eaten.MPL the.MSG
      biscotte   / pro$_i$so [$_{vP}$ [$_{Spec}$ ___] magn$\underline{i}$te] li   biscutte. (Ariellese)
      biscuit.MSG/ pro am   eaten.MPL the.MPL biscuits.MPL
      'We have eaten the biscuit. / I have eaten the biscuits.'

   c. Avètz   [$_{vP}$ [$_{Spec}$ ___] pres$\underline{as}$]   de fot$\underline{ò}$s? (Occ.)
      you.have   taken.FPL of photos.FPL
      'Did you take any photos?'

   d. La   clé   que   j'ai   [$_{vP}$ [$_{Spec}$ ~~la clé~~] pris$\underline{e}$] ~~la clé~~ (Fr.)
      the.FSG key.FSG that   I.have   taken.FSG
      'The key which I took'

e. Li/Ci   hanno   [$_{vP}$ [$_{Spec}$ ~~li/ci~~] vist**i**]   ~~li/ci~~ (It.)
them.M/us= they.have   seen.MPL
'They saw us.'

f. Los/Nos   as   [$_{vP}$ [$_{Spec}$ ~~los/nos~~] vist**os**/vist**u**] ~~los/nos~~ (Lula, Sardinia)
them.M/us= you.have   seen.MPL/MSG
'You have seen them/us.'

g. Els/Les   he   [$_{vP}$ [$_{Spec}$ ~~els/les~~] llegit/llegi**des**] ~~els/les~~ (Barcelona Cat.)
them.M/F I.have   read.MSG/FPL
'I've read them.'

Assuming active participle agreement to be the surface reflex of an underlying Agree relation for φ-features between, say, the functional head v_{PtP} and a given nominal, we are forced to recognize at least seven different microparametric specifications for v_{PtP}. The simplest and least constrained system is exemplified by Ibero-Romance varieties such as Spanish (24a), where v_{PTCP} quite simply never displays any agreement, failing to enter into an Agree relation with any DP. Its mirror image is the pattern of participial agreement found in the dialect of Arielli (24b) spoken in eastern Abruzzo, Italy, where the participle, and hence v_{PTCP}, simply agrees with any plural DP, be it the internal or external argument (D'Alessandro and Roberts 2010). Slightly more constrained, though still liberal by general Romance standards, is the conservative pattern found in Occitan varieties (24c) where the participle agrees with all types of DP object, a pattern further constrained in modern Standard French (24d) by the additional requirement that the object DP be overtly fronted (either under object-to-subject fronting as with unaccusative structures, or under relativization and *wh*-fronting). In this respect, Modern Italian (24e) proves even more restrictive in that, in addition to A-moved superficial subjects of unaccusatives and passives, v_{PTCP} only agrees with fronted nominals when they are represented by pronominal clitics, an option taken a stage further in Sardinian dialects (24f) where there is a further requirement that the pronominal clitic also be third person. Finally, there are varieties such as standard Barcelona Catalan (24g), where v_{PTCP} is further restricted to agreeing only with feminine third person pronominal clitics.

Empirically, then, we are forced to assume as many as seven distinct featural (viz. microparametric) instantiations of v_{PTCP} across Romance, the distribution of which can be modelled in terms of a small-scale parametric hierarchy along the lines of (25), ultimately part of a larger hierarchy related to agreement and argument marking (see also Ledgeway 2013: 189–92; Sheehan 2014):

(25)   Do functional heads probe for φ-features?

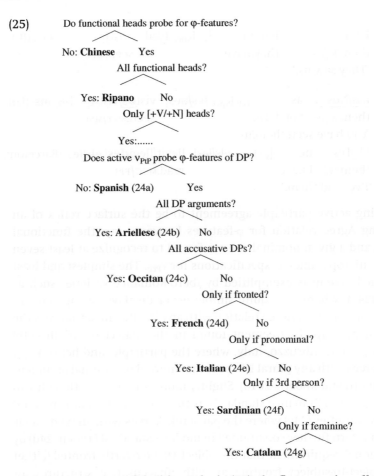

No: **Chinese**   Yes

All functional heads?

Yes: **Ripano**   No

Only [+V/+N] heads?

Yes: ......

Does active v_PtP probe φ-features of DP?

No: **Spanish** (24a)   Yes

All DP arguments?

Yes: **Ariellese** (24b)   No

All accusative DPs?

Yes: **Occitan** (24c)   No

Only if fronted?

Yes: **French** (24d)   No

Only if pronominal?

Yes: **Italian** (24e)   No

Only if 3rd person?

Yes: **Sardinian** (24f)   No

Only if feminine?

Yes: **Catalan** (24g)

Starting at the top of the hierarchy in (25), the first question allows us to draw a simplex – arguably macroparametric – distinction between languages such as Chinese, where all functional heads systematically fail to license any form of overt agreement, and varieties like the central Italian dialect of Ripatransone where, by contrast, gender and number agreement is ubiquitous, surfacing on all categories.[3] Moving down the tree, we can then ask more restrictive questions to identify more marked options regarding the ability of smaller and smaller subsets of functional heads (e.g. just those marked [+N] or [+V]) to probe for φ-features,[4] until we eventually come to isolate the functional head responsible for active participle agreement, viz. v_{PTCP}. This is the portion of the hierarchy with which we are most interested here and where the gradual cascading effect produced by the options presented in (25) not only mirrors the gradual diachronic contraction of Romance participle agreement (for example, as

---

[3] For discussion of the dialect of Ripatransone, see Parrino (1967), Lüdtke (1974, 1976), Mancini (1993), Harder (1998), Ledgeway (2012a: 277–86).

[4] For a recent analysis of parametric variation in relation to the distribution of subject clitics in Tuscan and northern Italian dialects, arguably instances of Agr(ement) markers, see Roberts (2014a).

late as the nineteenth century the distribution of Italian past participle agreement largely mirrored that of Modern French), but also highlights how variation in relation to the ability of v_{PTCP} to probe the φ-features of specific nominals is not uniform but, rather, licenses differing degrees of surface variation in accordance with the growing markedness conditions that accompany the available parametric options as one moves down the hierarchy.

In this respect, we can note that Spanish and Ariellese represent rather simple and relatively unmarked options, in that v_{PTCP} in these varieties either indiscriminately fails to probe all DP arguments or, on the contrary, systematically probes all (plural) DP arguments. Occitan varieties, on the other hand, are slightly more constrained in that v_{PTCP} only probes a subset of DP arguments, namely those marked [+ACC], whereas in French there is the further proviso that the DP$_{\text{ACC}}$ must have also undergone A- or A′-movement. In all four cases, however, we are dealing with a case of mesoparametric variation, in that the four options can be subsumed within a naturally definable class insofar as they exclusively make reference to a single functional head [D], in turn further specified for the feature [+ACC] in Occitan and French (presumably un(der)specified in the case of Spanish and Ariellese) and the relevant A/A′-movement feature in French.

We observe, however, a shift from meso- to microparametric variation as we move down the hierarchy to Italian, insofar as the relevant class of triggers for participial agreement is no longer represented *tout court* by a naturally definable class of functional heads (viz. [D]), but now also makes reference to a small and lexically definable subclass of Ds, namely pronominals. Arguably, in the case of Sardinian and Barcelona Catalan where this lexically definable subclass is today further broken down into the ever more marked pronominal categories of third person and, in turn, feminine, we are now entering nanoparametric territory where the relevant generalizations hold of just a handful of individual lexical items, namely Sardinian *lu* (MSG), *la* (FSG), *los* (MPL) and *las* (MSG) and Barcelona Catalan *la* (FSG) and *les* (FPL).

27.4.1.2   Romance Auxiliary Selection

An area of spectacular diachronic and synchronic microvariation in Romance regards the numerous dimensions of variation characterizing the choice of auxiliary in the formation of various perfective periphrases in conjunction with the past participle. Indeed, work over recent decades in particular has brought to light an unrivalled degree of variation (for relevant bibliography, see Ledgeway 2012a: 292–9, 311–17), the precise empirical limits of which still remain to be defined. While making no claims to exhaustiveness, in what follows we review how some of the major patterns of meso- and microvariation in this area and their inter-relationships can be mapped in terms of parameter hierarchies (for fuller discussion, see Ledgeway forthcoming d). We begin by considering the hierarchy in (26).

(26)   **1. Does L present auxiliary alternation?**

No: *Pescolanciano* (27)   Yes:

Portuguese (28)   **2. Sensitive to mood?**

Yes: *Romanian* (29)   No

3. Sensitive to tense?

Yes: *Sanleuciano* (30)   No

4. Sensitive to person?

Yes: *Ariellese* (31a-b)   No

5. Sensitive to argument structure?

Yes: *Occitan* (32a-b)

(26) reveals five broad dimensions of mesoparametric variation in auxiliary distribution, the markedness and complexity of which grows as we move down the hierarchy. Question (1) serves to draw the simplest and broadest distinction between those varieties which do not show any alternation in the perfective auxiliary on the one hand and all other varieties (the vast majority) that display varying patterns of alternation between BE (B) and HAVE (H) on the other. Clearly, the simplest option is represented by those varieties which generalize one auxiliary to all perfective contexts without further differentiation (see Tuttle 1986: 267–76; Manzini and Savoia 2005: II:759–809; Legendre 2010: 188–9; Ledgeway 2012a: 341–2), be it BE as in many central-southern dialects of Italy (e.g. Pescolanciano in (27a–c)) or HAVE as in many Ibero-Romance and (extreme) southern Italian varieties (e.g. Portuguese in (28a–c)). Although on cross-linguistic and theoretical grounds HAVE has been argued, following Benveniste (1960), Freeze (1992) and Kayne (1993), to be derivationally more marked than BE qua the surface spell-out of an underlying LOC+BE structure (for recent implementations, see Roberts 2013: 20–3; Ledgeway 2014a), the generalization of one or the other auxiliary is non-contrastive in these varieties and ultimately has no bearing on the mesoparametric choice in question.

(27)   a. (mə) **sɔŋgə** / (tə)   **si** /   (ts)
           (me=) I.am   (you.SG=) you.are.SG (self=)
           ε . . . mə'nu:tə/maɲ'ɲɛɐtə (/la'va:tə)
           is   come/eaten   washed
           'I/you/(s)he have/has come/eaten/washed.'

       b. (mə) **jiva** /   (tə)   **jivə** /   (tsə)
           (me=) I.was   (you.SG=) you.were.SG   (self=)
           jiva . . . mə'nu:tə/maɲ'ɲɛɐtə (/la'va:tə)
           (s)he.was come/eaten   washed
           'I/you/(s)he had come/eaten/washed.'

c. (mə / tə / tsə)   **fussə** ...
   (me= you.SG= self=)   I/you.SG/he.be.IPFV.SBJV
   mə'nuːtə/maɲ'ɲɛɐtə (/la'vaːtə)
   come/eaten   washed
   'I/you/(s)he would have come/eaten/washed.'

(28) a. **tenho**(-me) / **tens**(-te) /   **tem**(-se) ...
      I.have(=me) you.SG.have(=you.SG) (s)he.has(=self)
      vindo/comido (/lavado)
      come/eaten   washed
      'I/you/(s)he have/has come/eaten/washed.'

      b. **tinha**(-me) / **tinhas**(-te) /   **tinha**(-se) ...
      I.had(=me) you.SG.had(=you.SG) (s)he.had(=self)
      vindo/comido (/lavado)
      come/eaten   washed
      'I/you/(s)he had come/eaten/washed.'

      c. **teria**(-me) /   **terias**(-te) /   **teria**(-se) ...
      I.have.COND(=me) you.SG.have.COND(=you.SG) (s)he.have.COND(=self)
      vindo/comido   (/lavado)
      come/eaten   washed
      'I/you/(s)he would have come/eaten/washed.'

27.4.1.2.1 Mood and Tense as Determinants of Auxiliary Selection

If a variety does present auxiliary alternation,[5] then as indicated in (26) this variation can, in order of complexity, be determined by mood, tense, person and argument structure. Beginning with mood and tense, we thus find varieties such as: (i) Romanian where auxiliary choice is entirely dictated by the realis (⇒ HAVE) vs irrealis (⇒ BE) mood distinction (Avram and Hill 2007),[6] in that (inflected) HAVE (viz. *am, ai*, ...) is uniquely licensed in the present indicative (29a) and (invariable) BE (viz. *fi*) in the present subjunctive (29b), future and conditional perfect (29c), and the perfect infinitive (29d); and (ii) the Campanian dialect of San Leucio del Sannio (Iannace 1983: 72–80, 88f.; Ledgeway 2012a: 342f.), where auxiliary distribution proves sensitive to tense distinctions, inasmuch as the present perfect (30a) and the future-oriented conditional perfect/pluperfect subjunctive (30b) – henceforth 'counterfactual perfect' – align with HAVE and the pluperfect indicative with BE (30c).

---

[5] For reasons of expository simplicity, in (26) we informally talk of a language presenting a rule of auxiliary alternation. Following Benveniste's (1960) seminal derivational analysis of the BE vs HAVE alternation, according to which forms of copula/auxiliary HAVE are to be interpreted as the superficial manifestation of the incorporation of a(n abstract) locative preposition into an underlying copula/auxiliary BE (see also Freeze 1992; Kayne 1993), this can be formalized by asking whether BE is probed by the locative prepositional head (viz. [TP HAVE (= BE +P°) ... BE [v-VP PTCP]]).

[6] Ledgeway (2014a) argues that the relevant distinction is one of finiteness, with finite forms aligning with HAVE and non-finite forms with BE. However, the differences between the two approaches are irrelevant to the current discussion – and in any case probably amenable to conflation if, following Vincent (1998b: 151–2), mood and finiteness represent subparts of the same overall grammatical category (see also Miller 2002: 1, 68f.) – in that what is crucial here is that both approaches serve to draw the relevant binary split (be it [±realis] or [±finite]) across all verb forms.

(29) a. **Am** /   **Ai**/ **A** /   **Am**   / **Aţi** / **Au**
          I.have you.have (s)he.has we.have you.have they.have
          mâncat / plecat.
          eaten   left
          'I/you/(s)he/we/you/they have(/has) eaten/left (. . . ate/left).'

      b. Vor   / Ar   **fi**   mâncat / plecat.
          they.will they.would be.INF eaten   left
          'They will/would have eaten/left.'

      c. Nu cred   să **fi**   mâncat / plecat.
          not they.believe that be.SBJV eaten   left
          'They don't believe that I/you/(s)he/we/you/they have(/has) eaten/
          left.'

      d. Înainte de a **fi**   mâncat / plecat citeam ziarul.
          before of to be.INF eaten   left   I.read newspaper.DEF
          'Before having eaten/left, I was reading the newspaper.'

(30) a. **Èggio** fatto tutto / **èggio** muorto / M'   **èggio** lavato.
          I.have   done   all   I.have   died   me= I.have   washed
          'I have done everything/died/washed.'

      b. Si nun' **èsse**   muórt' u   marito nun s'
          if not had.SBJV   died   the husband not self=
          èsse   mòssa da llà /
          she.had.SBJV moved from there
          Chi   l'   **èsse**   mai   ditto?
          who   it= had.SBJV   ever   said
          'If her husband hadn't died she wouldn't have ever moved from
          there / Who would have ever thought it?'

      c. **Èrem'** auta dice quéllo / **èra**   venutu /s'   **era**
          we.were had.to say.INF that   he.was   come   self= he.was
          truatu nu   bèllu pòstu
          found a   nice job
          'We had had to say that. / He had come. / He had found himself
          a nice job.'

Auxiliary distribution in both varieties represents the surface reflex of
a relatively simple distinction between naturally definable instantiations
of T_{Aux} (or maybe v_{Aux}): in the case of Romanian the auxiliary system
differentially marks a binary [±realis] distinction, whereas in Sanleuciano
the alternation arguably spells out a binary [±past] temporal distinction in
that [+past] licenses BE in the pluperfect while the [-past] specification on
T_{Aux}, which unites the present and counterfactual,[7] licenses HAVE in the
present and counterfactual perfects. Although both mesoparametric auxiliary options apparently make reference to a binary featural opposition,

---

[7] We follow here, among others Iatridou (2000) and Ritter and Wiltschko (2014), in taking the superficial past-tense
   morphology found in counterfactuals to be 'fake', insofar as it does not receive a past-tense interpretation, but, rather, is
   responsible for the licensing the counterfactual reading. See also the discussion of microparametric variation in
   counterfactual inversion in Biberauer and Roberts (forthcoming b).

sensitivity to mood has been placed higher than tense in (26) in accordance with the assumption that, while the most primitive modal distinction involves a simple binary contrast between realis and irrealis, tense involves, following Vikner's (1985) neo-Reichenbachian analysis, three binary temporal relations as formalized, for example, in Cinque's (1999: 81–3) functional representation T_{Past} (= R_1 ... S) > T_{Future} (R_2 ... R_1) > $T_{Anterior}$ (E ... R_2), according to which the featural specification [+past] arises from the combination of the values R_1_S; R_1,R_2; E,R_2. Furthermore, more general considerations such as the observation that all (Romance) verbs have to be specified at the very least for mood (/finiteness), while not all verbs are necessarily specified for tense, lead us to assign a more basic, and hence less marked, status to mood over tense in (26).

27.4.1.2.2 Person and Argument Structure as Determinants of Auxiliary Selection Below the modal and temporal dimensions in (26) follow those relating to person and argument structure. The former accounts for patterns such as that in (31) for the eastern Abruzzese dialect of Arielli (D'Alessandro and Ledgeway 2010; D'Alessandro and Roberts 2010) where, in the present at least, auxiliaries are distributed along the lines of a simple binary person split in accordance with a [±discourse participant] distinction (see Benveniste [1950] 1966: 228; Harley and Ritter 2002), which yields BE in first/second persons and HAVE in third persons.

(31) a. **So / si /**   **a**   fatecate /   'rrevate.
         I.am you.SG.are have.3 worked.SG arrived.SG

      b. **Seme / sete /**   **a**   fatichite / 'rrivite.
         we.are you.PL.are have.3 worked.PL arrived.PL
         'I/you/(s)he/we/you/they have/has worked/arrived.'

In other varieties such as Lengadocien Occitan we find a conservative binary active–stative split (Ledgeway 2012a: 319–23), where HAVE surfaces in conjunction with A/S_A (transitive/unergative) subjects (32a) and BE with S_O (unaccusative) subjects (32b–c).

(32) a. **Avètz**   fach   bon   viatge?
         you.have made good trip
         'Did you have a good journey?'

      b. **Soi** vengut amb los amics. / L' aiga s' **èra** poirida.
         I.am come   with the friends the water self= was rotten
         'I came with friends. / The water has gone off.'

As shown in some detail in Ledgeway (forthcoming d), auxiliary systems that operate fundamentally in terms of person and argument structure distinctions frequently blend these with modal and temporal restrictions to produce increasingly marked and complex proper subsets of person and verb class combinations. For example, in the southern Lazio dialect of Pontecorvo (Manzini and Savoia 2005: II:701f.) a [±present] temporal restriction limits the person split to the present perfect (33a), with general-ization of BE in the pluperfect (33b) and counterfactual (33c). Similarly, the active-stative split found in many early Romance varieties is frequently sus-pended in [-realis] contexts (Nordahl 1977; Ledgeway 2003; Stolova 2006), where all instances of S_O may exceptionally align with HAVE on a par with A/S_A, witness the old Sicilian and Spanish contrasts in (34a–b), respectively:

(33)   a.   su / si[8] /   **a** /   semǝ / setǝ /   **avǝ**   par'lacǝ/vǝ'nucǝ
            I.   you.   (s)   we.   you.   they.   spoken/come
            am SG.are   he.has are   are   have

       b.   ɛrǝ /   irǝ /   ɛra /   ɛra'vamǝ / ɛra'vatǝ /
            I.was you.SG.were (s)he.was we.were   you.were
            'ɛrǝɲǝ   par'lacǝ/vǝ'nucǝ
            they.were spoken/come

       c.   sa'ria /   sar'rissǝ /   sa'ria /   sa'rissǝmǝ / sar'itǝ /
            I.was   you.SG.were (s)he.was we.were   you.were
            sa'riǝɲǝ   par'lacǝ/vǝ'nucǝ
            they.were spoken/come

(34)   a.   li   pili   ià   li   **eranu** caduti / si killa
            the   hairs   already to.him= were   fallen   if that
            dirrupa **avissi**   caduta
            rock   had.SBJV fallen
            'his hair had already droppd out / if that rock had fallen'

       b.   Si el   sieruo   que   **es**   fuydo   mora   mucho en casa /
            if the   servant that   is   fled   stays   much in house
            si ladrones que furtan
            if thieves   that steal
            de dia   &   de   noche **ouissen** entrado
            of day   and   of   night had.SBJV entered
            'If the servant who has fled remains a long time at home / if thieves who steal by day and night had entered'

It is crucial to note in this respect that the relevant lower-level modal and temporal contrasts introduced into such systems do not override or efface the fundamental person or verb class distinctions – hence we cannot speak of mood- or tense-based systems as in (29)–(30) above – but, rather, are embedded within the categories of person and argument structure to intro-duce more fine-grained person and verb class combinations. It is for this reason that person and argument structure are positioned lower than mood and tense in (26), in that mood and tense as independent determinants of auxiliary variation are not constrained, at least in Romance, by person and argument structure, whereas person and argument structure as independent dimensions of auxiliary selection are frequently augmented by the

---

[8] 2sg. *si* causes initial consonantal lengthening of the following participle not indicated in (33a).

incorporation of restrictions relating to mood and tense. By the same token, auxiliary systems driven by argument structure may, in turn, also incorporate restrictions on person in addition to those on tense and mood. In this way, the hierarchy in (26) correctly models the subset and inclusiveness relations implicit in Romance auxiliary systems, including so-called cases of triple auxiliation (Loporcaro 2007), according to which, for example, person-based systems may embed modal and temporal restrictions (see 33a–c) but not those relating to argument structure, whereas auxiliary systems based on active-stative splits may variously overlay modal, temporal and personal restrictions. As an example of this latter option, consider the Pugliese dialect of Minervino Murge (Manzini and Savoia 2005: III:27–8): in the present all verb classes show free variation in all persons except the third person where BE is only an option (alongside HAVE) with unaccusatives (35a), whereas transitives/unergatives only license HAVE (35b):

(35) a. sɔ(ndə)~jaɟɟə / si~a /   **jɛ~ɔ /**   simmə~a'vimmə /
          I.am~have   you.sɢ.are~have (s)he.is~has we.are~have
          sɛitə~a'vɛitə / **sɔndə~jɔnnə** mə'nɛutə
          you.are~have they.are~have   come

      b. sɔ(ndə)~jaɟɟə / si~a /   ɔ /   simmə~a'vimmə /
          I.am~have   you.sɢ.are~have (s)he.has   we.are~have
          sɛitə~a'vɛitə / **jɔnnə**   dər'mɛutə
          you.are~have they.have   slept

27.4.1.2.3 Diachronic Considerations   To conclude this discussion of Romance auxiliary selection, some general comments about the implications of (26) for syntactic change are in order. We begin by observing that the most conservative pattern of auxiliary distribution of the five mesoparametric options presented in (26), that determined by argument structure (see Bentley 2006) with strong precedents already in Latin (Vincent 1982; Ledgeway 2012a: 130–4; Adams 2013; Roberts 2013: 17–20), is situated at the bottom of the hierarchy. This implies that all deviations from this mesoparametric pattern in the history of Romance involve a movement up the hierarchy towards one of the other four less marked and conceptually simpler options but,[9] significantly, no movements downwards from, say, mood-driven auxiliation to person-auxiliation. There is also no *a priori* reason to assume that movement up the hierarchy must proceed stepwise, as witnessed by the development of Romanian where, following Dragomirescu and Nicolae (2009) and Ledgeway (2014a), the shift from an original active–stative split to a (finiteness-/)mood-driven system (see 29a–d) involves a saltational

---

[9] This upward movement is reflected indirectly in many varieties which, although having abandoned the original active–stative split in the auxiliary system in favour of person-driven auxiliation or the generalization of a single auxiliary, preserve the split in the distribution of participle agreement witnessed in §27.4.1.1 (see Loporcaro 1998: 8–12; 2016: §49.2; Manzini and Savoia 2005: II:§5.6.2).

change, with no evidence of auxiliary variation having first passed through intermediate person- and tense-driven splits (for limited relics of the original active–stative split in modern Romanian, see discussion below). That said, movements up the hierarchy might be motivated by earlier downward microparametric shifts within a given mesoparametric network. This is the case with HAVE generalization found in many modern Ibero-Romance and (extreme) southern Italo-Romance varieties where, as we saw above (see 34a–b), in (late) medieval texts the first extensions of HAVE to unaccusative syntax are licensed uniquely in irrealis modal contexts, from where Ledgeway (2003) demonstrates that it gets a foothold in the system before progressively spreading to realis contexts yielding the generalized extension of HAVE witnessed in these varieties today (see 28a–c). Arguably, in this case the rise of a modally determined extension of HAVE to unaccusative syntax represents a microparametric change, involving a downward movement within the mesoparametric network dedicated to argument structure which will ultimately provide the necessary impetus to trigger the mesoparametric change targeting the top of the hierarchy. Biberauer and Roberts (forthcoming b) describe a similar diachronic development in the history of English involving inversion; see §27.4.1.4.

One final dimension of variation that we have not yet discussed in relation to (26) is the possibility that the core reflex of unaccusativity, viz BE-selection, has become lexically fossilized and is today limited to a synchronically opaque, small number of intransitive predicates. This nanoparametric state of affairs, in which a once productive auxiliary distinction has all but fallen out of the system today precariously surviving in association with particular predicates as a lexical idiosyncrasy (though for potential semantic motivation, see discussion below of the Auxiliary Selection Hierarchy), accurately describes the situation in many *langue d'oïl* varieties. Even French – reflexives aside which today invariably license BE – has witnessed a striking decline in the number of unaccusatives that today may still select BE, ranging from somewhere between twenty and thirty predicates according to most counts (Benveniste 1965: 181; Giancarli 2011: 373f.) and representing a small subset of those which still systematically align with BE in varieties such as Italian, Occitan or Corsican (Maiden and Robustelli 2007: 262; Giancarli 2011). In so-called popular varieties of French the retreat is even greater with HAVE replacing BE in conjunction with most if not all unaccusatives (Bauche 1946: 105; Guiraud 1969: 40f.), a situation replicated in many eastern *langue d'oïl* varieties (Flutre 1955: 59; Remacle 1956: 39–48; Descusses 1986: 126; Hendschel 2012: 177, §166 b).

More striking are those varieties which residually show retention of BE with just one or two unaccusatives. For example, in the Picard patois of Nibas (Vasseur 1996: 52) and Valenciennes (Dauby 1979: 35) BE is today limited to *mourir* 'die' and *aller* 'go', respectively, with HAVE having penetrated all other unaccusatives. Similarly, in the Lorrain variety of Ranrupt all unaccusatives today take HAVE with the sole exception of 'come' which still licenses BE (Aub-Büscher 1962: 84, §107). Here one must not forget various Canadian French varieties where, putting aside some complex sociolinguistic factors (Sankoff and Thibault 1977; King and Nadasdi 2005; Rea 2014), unaccusatives frequently show free alternation of HAVE~BE (including with reflexives), though often with a higher propensity of BE in just a subset of core unaccusatives (e.g. *aller* 'go'). In all cases we are clearly dealing with nanovariation, namely synchronically unpredictable cases of lexical exceptions which residually reflect formerly more widespread and regular patterns of variation.

Arguably also relevant here are those limited cases of resultative BE found in varieties which otherwise have generalized HAVE with unaccusatives. For example, modern Romanian still retains a relic of auxiliary BE with a subset of unaccusatives when interpreted with a resultative value (Avram 1994: 494, 506–8; Motapanyane 2000: 16; Avram and Hill 2007: 49–52; Nevaci and Todi 2009: 142; Dragomirescu 2010: 210; Pană Dindelegan 2013: 228), as illustrated by the relative acceptability of HAVE (36a) and BE (36b) with punctual and resultative temporal adverbials in the following examples taken from Dragomirescu and Nicolae (2009).

(36) a. Ion **a** / *e sosit ieri / de ieri în oraş.
        John has is arrived yesterday since yesterday in city
        'John arrived yesterday/since yesterday in the city.'
      b. Ion **e** /*a sosit de ieri în oraş.
        John is Has arrived since yesterday in city
        'John has been here since yesterday in the city.'

Crucially, as Dragomirescu and Nicolae observe, the distribution of BE in such cases is not indiscriminate, but is limited to a subclass of unaccusatives, namely verbs of directed motion and change of location and verbs of (dis)appearance situated at the top of Sorace's (2000) Auxiliary Selection Hierarchy. Significantly, a similar, if not identical, phenomenon is reported by Manente (2008: 42f.) to have occurred in the recent history of Québécois French, where auxiliary HAVE has been extended to unaccusatives of change of location. Although in such cases HAVE has now replaced original BE to mark punctual events (37a), auxiliary BE survives with these same verbs under the resultant state interpretation (37b).

(37) a. Jean **a** arrivé / parti /entré / tombé à huit heures / en deux
        Jean has arrived left entered fallen at eight hours in two
        minutes.
        minutes
        'Jean arrived / left / came in / fell at eight / in two minutes.'
      b. Jean **est** arrivé / parti / entré / tombé.
        Jean is arrived left entered fallen
        'Jean is here / away / in(side) / on the floor.'

The Québécois French facts thus replicate patterns found in Romanian, inasmuch as relics of auxiliary BE are restricted in both varieties to resultative readings of a similar subclass of unaccusatives (viz. verbs of directed motion), the only difference being that we have documented evidence of the original HAVE–BE transitive–unaccusative split, of which resultative BE is a residue, in the recent history of Québécois French, but not in Romanian.

27.4.1.3 Subject-Clitic Systems of Northwestern Romance

Across a range of varieties of Northwestern Romance spoken in northern Italy, France, Switzerland, and including Standard French, we can observe the development of systems of subject clitics interacting with the null-subject parameter synchronically and diachronically (§22.3.1, §25.3.3). An important aspect of these changes has again featured grammaticalization (again construable as defined by Roberts and Roussou 2003; see the discussion in §27.2.1) of pronouns (D-elements) as functional heads in T and C systems (see Poletto (2000), Roberts (2014a) and in particular Manzini and Savoia (2005) on the synchronic range of systems featuring extreme microparametric variation concerning which clitics have reanalysed from their earlier pronominal status and how). Partly owing to the complexity of the situation in northern Italian dialects, we illustrate the main points here with French.

The basic pattern of development is summarised in (38):

(38) **Pronouns:**
      Stage I: Strong subject pronouns
      Stage II: Weak subject pronouns
      Stage III: syntactic clitics
      Null subjects:
      Stage I: consistent null subjects
      Stage II: restricted null subjects
      Stage III: no null subjects
      Stage IV: consistent null subjects

Stage I is exemplified by Latin and most of the Romance languages outside the Northwestern area under consideration here (with the notable exception of the recent history of Brazilian Portuguese; see Duarte 1995; Roberts 2014b). In all these varieties, we find strong subject pronouns and full-fledged null-subject systems. Old French (see below), Medieval Veneto (Poletto 1995) and probably other medieval northern Italian dialects (Vanelli, Renzi and Benincà 1985) show a combination of restrictions on null subjects along with strong subject pronouns. Standard Literary French and sixteenth-century Veneto are (to a close approximation) non-null-subject systems with weak subject pronouns (in the sense of Cardinaletti and Starke 1999). Finally, many modern northern Italian dialects and, arguably, 'advanced' vernacular varieties of contemporary French have grammaticalized the former subject pronouns as agreement markers (bundles of uninterpretable φ-features) in T (the functional head typically associated with finite agreement) and have thus 'returned' to null-subject status.

Evidence for strong subject pronouns in Old French comes from examples like the following, showing that these pronouns, reflexes of Latin EGO, etc., could appear in elliptical contexts, be coordinated and be modified by *meïsmes* ('self') (see for discussion and documentation, see Roberts 1993: 112–14):

(39)   Old French

    a. Et **je** que sai?
       and I   what know.1SG
       'What do I know?'

    b. e **jo** e vos i   irum
       and I and you there= go.FUT.1PL
       'and you and I will go there'

    c. se **je** meïsmes ne li   di
       if I   self   NEG CL.DAT.3SG= tell.1SG
       'if I myself don't tell him'

It is well known that Old French allowed null subjects, but only in contexts of verb-second, i.e. (to a close approximation) only in main clauses. In (40), we see examples of null subjects in V2 contexts in Old French (taken from Roberts 1993: 124ff.):

(40)   Old French

    a. Tresqu' en la mer **cunquist**   la   tere altaigne.
       until   in the sea conquered.3SG the land high
       'He conquered the high land all the way to the sea.' (*Roland*, 3)

    b. Si   **chaï** en   grant povreté.
       thus fell.1SG into great poverty
       'Thus I fell into great poverty.' (*Perceval*, 441)

    c. Si   en **orent** moult grant merveille
       thus of.it= had.3PL very   great marvel
       'So they wondered very greatly at it.' (*Merlin*, 1)

In non-V2 contexts, null subjects are not found. In (41a) we have an example of an overt pronoun in the subordinate clause coreferential with a null pronoun in the main clause, a situation strongly dispreferred in fully null-subject languages. In (41b) we see an embedded pronominal subject coreferential with an inanimate (*la joie* 'the joy') in the main clause, also strongly dispreferred in fully null-subject languages:

(41)   Old French

    a. Ainsi s'   acorderent que **il**   prendront par nuit.
       thus self= they.agreed that they will.take by   night
       'This they agreed that they would take by night ... '

(*Le Roman du Graal*, B. Cerquiglini (ed.), Union Générale d'Editions, Paris, 1981, 26; Adams 1987: 1; Roberts 1993: 84)

b. dont   la   joye fut tant grant par la   ville qu' **elle** ne
of.which the joy was so   great in   the town that it   NEG
se   pourroit compter
self=   could   count.INF
'the joy concerning which was so great around town that it could not be counted' (*Jehan de Saintré* 160, 5; Sprouse and Vance 1999: 263)

In Modern French, the situation is quite complex owing in large part to the very strong normative tradition which arguably preserves an earlier diachronic stage in the literary language. Based on Roberts (2010a), who follows Zribi-Hertz (1994), we can distinguish at least four varieties. First, there are the 'high' registers, which Zribi-Hertz (1994: 136) calls *français standard moderne* 'modern standard French'. These varieties allow stylistic inversion, complex inversion and subject-clitic inversion (on the various kinds of inversion in French, see Kayne 1972; Rizzi and Roberts 1989); this is the 'highest' register of current literary Standard French. In stylistic inversion, expletive null subjects are allowed in a very narrow range of environments, depending on clause type, hence on the features of C (subjunctive, interrogative and relative, to a close approximation). So this variety represents a highly restrictive form of expletive null-subject language in TP. However, as both Pollock (2006) and Roberts (2010a) argue, subject-clitic and complex inversion constitute a form of *conjugaison interrogative* ('interrogative inflection'), whereby φ-features in C license null subjects in SpecTP. So here we have a system of C-licensed expletive null subjects and, in inversion contexts, argumental null subjects.

Second, there are registers which do not allow any form of stylistic inversion, but allow complex and subject–clitic inversion. This is also a fairly high register of spoken Standard French, certainly very much in use among educated Parisians and in the media. This is a non-null-subject variety in TP. Again, then, this is a restricted null-subject variety with argumental null subjects licensed by the φ-features of argumental C.

Third, there are colloquial registers in which all forms of inversion and are lacking; Zribi-Hertz (1994: 137) designates these as *français parlé courant* ('everyday spoken French'). These are fully non-null-subject systems in which neither C nor T licenses a null argument under any conditions. This is probably the most widely-spoken form of Modern Standard French.

Finally, there are vernacular varieties in which subject proclitics are to be analysed as realising φ-features of T, just as in many northern Italian dialects (according to the analyses in Manzini and Savoia (2005), Roberts (2014a) and the references cited there). Zribi-Hertz (1994: 137) refers to these varieties as *français très évolué* ('very advanced French'). These varieties are fully null-subject in TP, thanks to the presence of the subject clitic in T realizing uninterpretable φ-features in a fashion analogous to the role played by 'rich' verbal agreement inflection in a canonical null-subject language such as Italian. This is shown by the fact that they co-occur with non-referentially quantified subjects (which as such cannot be in dislocated positions) as in the attested examples in (42):

(42) a. Tout le monde **il** est beau,   tout le monde il   est gentil.
         everyone   he is handsome everyone   he is nice
         'Everyone is handsome, everyone is nice.' (film title)
      b. Personne **il** fiche rien,   à Toulon.
         No-one   he does anything at Toulon
         'No-one does anything in Toulon.' (Zribi-Hertz 1994: 137; (42b)
         from P. Mille *Barnavuax et quelques femmes*, 1908)

It is hard to date the changes in the non-standard varieties of French due to the normative influence on written French, but the development of northern Italian dialects, judging from Poletto's (1995) treatment of Veneto, suggests that the various stages were fairly short-lived. Both Veneto and French seem to have gone through the stages listed in (38) in their recorded histories since about 1400. Again, then, we observe relatively rapid microparametric change.

In terms of parameter hierarchies, we can posit a subpart of a larger hierarchy related to agreement and argument-marking dealing with microparametric variation in licensing null arguments along the lines of (43), adapted from Roberts (2012):

(43)

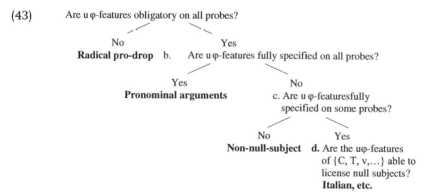

Further down this hierarchy there are options concerning partial null-subject languages (see Holmberg 2010) and expletive null-subject languages, along the following lines (where C[+F] designates a marked clause-typing feature):

(44)   Does C[+φ] license null subjects?

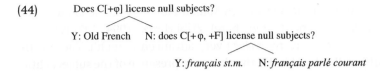

     Y: Old French   N: does C[+φ, +F] license null subjects?

               Y: *français st.m.*   N: *français parlé courant*

(Here we have glossed over the distinction between argumental and expletive null subjects, and hence the distinction between the first two varieties of Modern French described above.)

French and Veneto (and presumably other Northern Italian dialects) have moved progressively down this hierarchy, until they reach the stage of full grammaticalization of subject clitics as agreement markers in T, at which point they 'jump' back up to the position of Italian in (43), somewhat higher up the hierarchy. So again (see the discussion above of HAVE-generalization from examples like (34a–b)) we see a pattern of incremental changes moving a system down a microparametric hierarchy followed by a relatively dramatic reanalysis leading to a 'jump' upwards in the hierarchy.

27.4.1.4   Inversion in the History of English

As we have seen, there is evidence for the parametric taxonomy in (45):

(45)   For a given value v_i of a parametrically variant feature [F]:
    a. Macroparameters: all functional heads of the relevant type share v_i;
    b. Mesoparameters: all functional heads of a given naturally definable class, e.g. [+V], share v_i;
    c. Microparameters: a small sub-class of functional heads (e.g. modals) shows v_i;
    d. Nanoparameters: one/more individual lexical items has v_i.

If parametric change involves acquisition-mediated reanalysis of PLD, macroparameters will be set 'easily', hence resisting reanalysis and being strongly conserved; meso- and microparameters are correspondingly less salient in the PLD, hence less reanalysis-resistant and less strongly conserved. Nanoparameters are, in principle, still less reanalysis-resistant and thus more unstable, aside from the intervention of frequency effects. We have seen evidence for the stability of macroparameters and the relative instability of microparameters in the preceding sections, as well as cases of changes moving a system down a hierarchy followed in some cases by an abrupt 'jump' to a higher position in a hierarchy.

In this section we summarize a case of change from meso to micro to nano involving Conditional Inversion (CI) in the history of English (a full exposition is given in Biberauer and Roberts forthcoming b). We show that the central component of CI has remained unchanged since Old English, in that it involves T-to-C movement where C has a feature marking the clause Irr(ealis) (e.g. *swelte ic, libbe ic* 'die I, live

I' = 'if I live or die'). In Old English, CI was part of a family of operations raising inflected verbs into the C-system (V2). This feature is general to all root and some embedded Cs and holds across Germanic, making it a good candidate for a mesoparameter.

What has changed since Old English is the range of elements undergoing CI, and how CI relates to other forms of inversion. The loss of V2 is usually dated to the fifteenth century (Fischer, van Kemenade, Koopman and van der Wurff 2000), but various forms of 'residual V2' in marked clause-types survived, e.g. interrogative inversion and CI. The shift from full to residual V2 is a shift from meso to micro: the class of T-attracting Cs contracts. In Early Modern English, lexical V-to-T movement was lost (this was probably connected to the grammaticalization of the modals discussed in §27.2.1; see Roberts 1985). Thereafter, only auxiliaries undergo CI, as in interrogative and other kinds of inversion. The shift from residual V2 to subject-aux inversion further restricts the items undergoing inversion, although the T-to-C trigger is unchanged. What changed here is a T-feature, from a meso – all verbs – to a micro – auxiliaries only – value. The most interesting change affecting CI is recent, though: between the seventeenth and the nineteenth centuries, CI was no different to other inversions, featuring with all auxiliaries, including 'dummy' *do*. At this period, then, we find examples of CI with a wider range of auxiliaries than is possible in contemporary English. Here are some early nineteenth-century examples:

(46)   a. *Would* you be really … a man of honour … you would … restore that parchment to Lord Evandale. (1816, Scott, Old Mortality (Tauchn.) 435; Visser 1963–73: III:1730)
       b. This was a very prudential resolution, *could* he have kept it. (1751, Smollett, Peregr. Pickle II, xix; Visser 1963–73: III:1748)
       c. *Might* I kiss those eyes of fire, A million scarce would quench desire. (1807, Byron, Hours of Idleness: To Ellen; Visser 1963–73: III:1778)

From roughly 1850, CI became restricted to *had*, *should* and, more marginally, *were*. This looks like a nanoparameter, as it affects one modal, and specific forms of *have* and *be*. Meanwhile, interrogative inversion has remained fully productive for all auxiliaries. Optative inversion, however, was first limited to *may*, before becoming formulaic (*May you rot!* but **May you eat!*).

On the view of parameters advocated here, then, the parametric taxonomy in (45) allows us to understand how systems may become gradually more marked, requiring ever more specific triggers for operations, until a feature(class) ceases to act as a trigger, and the system radically simplifies. In the case of CI, the last stage is reached in the varieties of vernacular English in which this construction has been entirely lost.

27.5   Conclusion: Speculations on a Further Kind of Parameter

In the foregoing, we have essentially tried to support the general case made by Baker (2008b) that there are different kinds of parameters, using diachronic evidence and at the same time showing how this kind of approach can give insights into syntactic change. We have tried to support our case in terms of a specific, emergentist approach to parameters (see also §7.3, §16.4.2) which is associated with parameter hierarchies and the related taxonomy in (45). Further support, and much detailed evidence and analysis, is given in the references provided, and more examples of parameter hierarchies can be found in the references given in note 2.

There is a further issue that we would like to raise, in a somewhat more speculative vein. The Principles-and-Parameters approach is based on an analogy with genetics. The parametric genotype (e.g. the setting of a putative 'directionality parameter' as head-final vs head-initial) gives rise to the surface phenotype (OV/VO, Pre-/Post-positions, etc.). But an important concept in genetics has gone largely undiscussed and unexploited in work in this tradition: that of pleiotropy. In genetics, pleiotropy occurs when one gene influences multiple, seemingly unrelated phenotypic traits. In terms of the standard Principles-and-Parameters model, we could think of pleiotropic parameters as 'deep' parameters which profoundly influence the overall shape of a grammatical system.

The notion of pleiotropic parameter does not correspond to the concept of 'macroparameter' as discussed above. From that point of view, as we have seen, the notion of macroparameter is epiphenomenal, arising when a class of microparameters, characterized as formal features of functional heads act 'in concert' to produce an emergent macroparametric effect. The notion of pleiotropic parameter, on the other hand, is a novel one: distinct from both the primitive GB concept and the derivative emergentist one. Taking seriously the idea that parameters are nothing more than optional, emergent formal features (i.e. not innately prespecified by Universal Grammar, and possibly not domain-specific; see Biberauer 2011; Biberauer, Roberts and Sheehan 2014), it is possible that a small subset of these features act as 'master features', determining the ways in which many other features manifest themselves (to use a further useful concept from genetics, the latter features are epistatic; epistasis is a phenomenon that consists of the effect of one gene being dependent on the presence of one or more 'modifier genes' in the genetic background). Pleiotropic parameters have a disproportionate and profound effect on the parametric phenotype as it can be observed in surface variation. We may be witnessing the effect of pleiotropic features/parameters in cases of convergent patterns of diachronic change of the kind documented above from the history of Latin/Romance. We leave this potentially important new research area open for further elaboration here, merely noting that it may prove as fruitful as the approach described here and, indeed, as the original notion of parameter of Universal Grammar itself.

References

Adams, J. 1976. 'A typological approach to Latin word order', *Indogermanische Forschungen* 81: 70–99.

2013. 'Past participle + *habeo*', in *Social variation and the Latin language*. Cambridge University Press, pp. 615–51.

Adams, M. 1987. 'From Old French to the theory of pro-drop', *Natural Language and Linguistic Theory* 5:1–32.

Andrade, A. de and Galves, C. 2014. 'A unified analysis of subject topics in Brazilian Portuguese', *Journal of Portuguese Linguistics* 13: 117–47.

Aub-Büscher, G. 1962. *Le parler rural de Ranrupt (Bas Rhin)*. Paris: Klincksieck.

Avelar, J. 2009. 'Inversão locativa e sintaxe de concordância no português brasileiro', *Matraga* 16: 232–52.

Avelar, J. and Galves, C. 2011. 'Tópico e concordância em português brasileiro e português europeu', in A. Costa, I. Falé and P. Barbosa (eds.), *Textos seleccionados, XXVI Encontro nacional da associação portuguesa de linguística*. Lisbon: APL, pp. 49–65.

Avram, L. 1994. 'Auxiliary configurations in English and Romanian', *Revue roumaine de linguistique* 5–6: 493–510.

Avram, L. and Hill, V. 2007. 'An irrealis *BE* auxiliary in Romanian', in R. Aranovich (ed.), *Split auxiliary systems: A cross-linguistic perspective*. Amsterdam: John Benjamins, pp. 47–64.

Baker, M. 1996. *The polysynthesis parameter*. Oxford University Press.

2001. *The atoms of language: The mind's hidden rules of grammar*. Oxford University Press.

2008a. *The syntax of agreement and concord*. Cambridge University Press.

2008b. 'The macroparameter in a microparametric world', in T. Biberauer (ed.), *The limits of syntactic variation*. Amsterdam: John Benjamins, pp. 351–74.

Battye, A. and Roberts, I. (eds.) 1995. *Clause structure and language change*. Oxford University Press.

Bauche, H. 1946. *Le langage populaire: Grammaire, syntaxe et dictionnaire du français tel qu'on le parle dans le peuple avec tous les termes d'argot usuel*. Paris: Payot.

Bauer, B. 1995. *The emergence and development of SVO patterning in Latin and French*. Oxford University Press.

Bentley, D. 2006. *Split intransitivity in Italian*. Berlin and New York: Mouton de Gruyter.

2016. 'Split intransitivity', in Ledgeway and Martin (eds.), pp. 821–32.

Benveniste, E. 1950. 'Actif et moyen dans le verbe', *Journal de Psychologie* 43: 119–27. (Reprinted in Benveniste, E. 1966. *Problèmes de linguistique générale I*. Paris: Gallimard, pp. 168–75.)

1960. '"Être" et "avoir" dans leurs fonctions linguistiques', *Bulletin de la Société linguistique de Paris*, 55: 113–34. (Reprinted in Benveniste, E. 1966. *Problèmes de linguistique générale I*. Paris: Gallimard, pp. 187–207.)

1965. 'Structure des relations d'auxiliarité', *Acta Linguistica Hafniensia* 9: 1–15.

Besten, H. den. 1983. 'On the interaction of root transformations and lexical deletive rules', in W. Abraham (ed.), *On the formal syntax of the Westgermania*. Amsterdam: John Benjamins, pp. 47–131.

Biberauer, T. 2011. 'In defence of lexico-centric parametric variation: Two 3rd factor-constrained case studies', paper presented at the Workshop on Formal Grammar and Syntactic Variation: Rethinking Parameters (Madrid).

Biberauer, T., Holmberg, A. and Roberts, I. 2014. 'A syntactic universal and its consequences', *Linguistic Inquiry* 45: 169–225.

Biberauer, T., Holmberg, A., Roberts, I. and Sheehan, M. (eds.) 2010. *Parametric variation: Null subjects in minimalist theory*. Cambridge University Press.

2014. 'Complexity in comparative syntax: The view form modern parametric theory', in F. Newmeyer and L. Preston (eds.), *Measuring Linguistic Complexity*. Oxford University Press, pp. 103–27.

Biberauer, T. and Roberts, I. 2008. 'Cascading parameter changes: Internally-driven change in Middle and Early Modern English', in T. Eythórsson (ed.), *Grammatical change and linguistic theory: The Rosendal papers*. Amsterdam: John Benjamins, pp. 79–114.

2012a. 'Towards a parameter hierarchy for auxiliaries: Diachronic considerations', in J. Chancharu, X. Hu and M. Mitrović (eds.), *Cambridge Occasional Papers in Linguistics* 6: 209–36.

2012b. 'The significance of what hasn't happened', paper presented at the 14th conference on Diachronic Generative Syntax, Lisbon, 4 July.

2015a. 'Rethinking formal hierarchies: A proposed unification', in J. Chancharu, X. Hu and M. Mitrović (eds.), *Cambridge Occasional Papers in Linguistics* 7: 1–31.

2015b. 'Clausal hierarchies', in U. Shlonsky (ed.), *Beyond functional sequence*. Oxford University Press, pp. 295–313.

forthcoming a. 'Towards a parameter hierarchy for auxiliaries: Diachronic considerations', in A. Kroch (ed.), *Proceedings of the XII Diachronic Generative Syntax Meeting*. Oxford University Press.

forthcoming b. 'Conditional inversion and types of parametric change', in B. Los and P. de Haan (eds.), *Verb-second languages: Essays in honour of Ans van Kemenade*. Amsterdam: John Benjamins.

Biberauer, T., Roberts, I. and Sheehan, M. 2014. 'No-choice parameters and the limits of syntactic variation', in R. Santana-LaBarge (ed.), *Proceedings of WCCFL 31*. Somerville, MA: Cascadilla Press, pp. 46–55.

Borer, H. 1984. *Parametric syntax*. Dordrecht: Foris.

Bošković, Ž. 2008. 'What will you have, DP or NP?', in E. Elfner and M. Walkow (eds.), *Proceedings of the thirty-ninth annual North Eastern Linguistic Society*. Amherst, MA: GLSA, pp. 101–14.

Brandi, L. and Cordin, P. 1989. 'Two Italian dialects and the null subject parameter', in O. Jaeggli and K. Safir (eds.), *The null subject parameter*. Dordrecht: Kluwer, pp. 111–42.

Branigan, P. 2014. 'Macroparameter learnability: An Algonquian case study', unpublished MS, Memorial University Newfoundland.

Calboli, G. (ed.) 1989. *Subordination and other topics in Latin: Proceedings of the third colloquium on Latin linguistics, Bologna, 1–5 April 1985*. Amsterdam: John Benjamins.

Cardinaletti, A. 2004. 'Toward a cartography of subject positions', in L. Rizzi (ed.), *The structure of CP and IP*. Oxford University of Press, pp. 115–65.

Cardinaletti, A. and Starke, M. 1999. 'The typology of structural deficiency: A case study of the three classes of pronouns', in H. van Riemsdijk (ed.), *Clitics in the languages of Europe*. Berlin: de Gruyter, pp. 145–235.

Cennamo, M. 2016. 'Voice', in Ledgeway and Maiden (eds.), pp. 967–80.

Charpin, F. 1989. 'Etude de syntaxe énonciative: L'ordre des mots et la phrase', in Calboli (ed.), pp. 503–20.

Chomsky, N. 1964. *Current issues in linguistic theory*. The Hague: Mouton.
  1973. 'Conditions on transformations', in S. Anderson and P. Kiparsky (eds.), *A festschrift for Morris Halle*. New York: Holt, Rinehart and Winston, pp. 232–86.
  1975. *Reflections on language*. New York: Pantheon.
  1977. *Essays on form and interpretation*. Amsterdam: North-Holland.
  1981. *Lectures on government and binding*. Dordrecht: Foris.
  1995. *The minimalist program*. Cambridge MA: MIT Press.
  2005. 'Three factors in language design', *Linguistic Inquiry* 36(1): 1–22.
  2007. 'Approaching UG from below', in H.-M. Gärtner and U. Sauerland (eds.), *Interfaces + recursion = language?* Berlin: Mouton de Gruyter, pp. 1–29.

Cinque, G. 1999. *Adverbs and functional heads: A cross-linguistic perspective*. Oxford University Press.
  2006. *Restructuring and functional heads: The cartography of syntactic structures*, vol. 4. Oxford University Press.

Comrie, B. 1978. 'Ergativity', in W. P. Lehmann (ed.), *Syntactic typology: Studies in the phenomenology of language*. Austin: University of Texas, pp. 329–94.

D'Alessandro, R. and Ledgeway, A. 2010. 'The Abruzzese T-*v* system: Feature spreading and the double auxiliary construction', in D'Alessandro, Ledgeway and Roberts (eds.), pp. 201–9.

D'Alessandro, R., Ledgeway, A. and Roberts, I. (eds.) 2010. *Syntactic variation: The dialects of Italy*. Cambridge University Press.

D'Alessandro, R. and Roberts, I. 2010. 'Past participle agreement in Abruzzese: Split auxiliary selection and the null-subject parameter', *Natural Language and Linguistic Theory* 28: 41–72.

Dankaert, L. 2012. *Latin embedded clauses: The left periphery*. Amsterdam: John Benjamins.

Dauby, J. 1979. *Le livre du 'rouchi': Parler picard de Valenciennes*. Amiens: Musée de Picardie.

Descusses, M. 1986. *Le patois ardennais de Gespunsart*. Paris: Société d'études linguistiques et anthropologiques de France.

Devine, A. M. and Stephens, L. D. 2006. *Latin word order: Structured meaning and information*. Oxford University Press.

Dixon, R. 1994. *Ergativity*. Cambridge University Press.

Dragomirescu, A. 2010. *Ergativitatea: Tipologie, sintaxă, semantică*. Bucharest: Editura Universității din București.

Dragomirescu, A. and Nicolae, A. 2009. 'Relics of auxiliary selection in Romanian', unpublished MS, Iorgu Iordan – Al. Rosetti Institute of Linguistics, Bucharest and University of Bucharest.

Duarte, E. 1995. 'A perda do princípio "evite pronome" no português brasileiro', unpublished PhD thesis, Unicamp.

Dryer, M. S. 1992. 'On the Greenbergian word-order correlations', *Language* 68: 81–138.

  2013a. 'Relationship between the order of object and verb and the order of adposition and noun', in Dryer and Haspelmath (eds.). Available online at http://wals.info/chapter/95. Accessed 20 September 2015.

  2013b. 'Relationship between the order of object and verb and the order of relative clause and noun', in Dryer and Haspelmath (eds.). Available online at http://wals.info/chapter/96. Accessed 20 September 2015.

Dryer, M. S. and Haspelmath, M. (eds.) 2013. *The world atlas of language structures online*. Leipzig: Max Planck Institute for Evolutionary Anthropology. Available online at http://wals.info.

Emonds, J. 1978. 'The verbal complex V-V′ in French', *Linguistic Inquiry* 9: 151–75.

Ernout, A. and Thomas, F. 1953. *Syntaxe latine*. Paris: Klincksieck.

Fischer, O., van Kemenade, A., Koopman, W. and van der Wurff, W. 2000. *The syntax of early English*. Cambridge University Press.

Flutre, L.-F. 1955. *Le Parler picard de Mesnil-Martinsart (Somme)*. Geneva: Droz.

Fodor, J. D. and Sakas, W. G. Forthcoming. 'Learnability', in Roberts (ed.).

Freeze, R. 1992. 'Existentials and other locatives', *Language* 68, 3: 553–95.

Frellesvig, B. 2010. *A history of the Japanese language*. Cambridge University Press.

Garrett, A. 1990. 'The syntax of Anatolian pronominal clitics', unpublished PhD thesis, Harvard University.

Giancarli, P.-D. 2011. *Les auxiliaires être et avoir: Étude comparée corse, français, acadien et anglais*. Rennes: Presses Université de Rennes.

Gray, D. 1985. *The Oxford book of late medieval prose and verse*. Oxford University Press.

Greco, P. 2012. *La complementazione frasale nelle cronache latine dell'Italia centro-meridionale (secoli X-XII)*. Naples: Liguori.

Guiraud, P. 1969. *Le Français populaire*. Paris: Presses Universitaires de France.

Hale, K. 1981. *On the position of Warlpiri in a typology of the base*. Bloomington, IN: Indiana University Linguistics Club.

  1982. 'Preliminary remarks on configurationality', in J. Pustejovsky and P. Sells (eds.), *Proceedings of the twelfth annual meeting of the North-Eastern Linguistic Society*. Amherst, MA: GSLA, pp. 86–96.

  1983. 'Warlpiri and the grammar of non-configurational languages', *Natural Language and Linguistic Theory* 1: 5–47.

Hale, M. 1995. 'Wackernagel's Law in the Rigveda', unpublished MS, University of Concordia.

Harder, A. 1998. 'La declinazione dei verbi in un dialetto di transizione nelle Marche', in G. Ruffino (ed.), *Atti del XXI congresso internazionale di linguistica e filologia romanza. Centro di studi filologici e linguistici siciliani, Università di Palermo 18–24 settembre 1995. Volume V, sezione 5, Dialettologia, geolinguistica, sociolinguistica*. Tübingen: Niemeyer, pp. 389–99.

Harley, H. and Ritter, E. 2002. 'A feature-geometric analysis of person and number', *Language* 78(3): 482–526.

Harris, A. C. and Campbell, L. 1995. *Historical syntax in crosslinguistic perspective*. Cambridge University Press.

Hawkins, J. 1983. *Word order universals*. New York: Academic Press.

Hendschel, L. 2012. *Li Croejhete walone: Contribution à une grammaire de la langue wallonne*. http://home.base.be/vt6134585/croejhete.pdf.

Herman, J. 1989. '*Accusativus cum infinitivo* et subordonné à *quod, quia* en latin tardif: Nouvelles remarques sur un vieux problème', in Calboli (ed.), pp. 133–52.

Holmberg, A. 2010. 'Null subject parameters', in Biberauer, Holmberg, Roberts and Sheehan (eds.), pp. 88–124.

Hroársdóttir, Þ. 2000. *Word order change in Icelandic: From OV to VO*. Amsterdam: John Benjamins.

Huang, C.-T. J. 1982. 'Logical relations in Chinese and the theory of grammar', unpublished PhD thesis, MIT.

  2015. 'On syntactic analyticity and parametric theory', in A. Li, A. Simpson and W.-T. Dylan Tsai (eds.), *Chinese syntax in a crosslinguistic perspective*. Oxford University Press, pp. 1–50.

Huang, C.-T. J. and Roberts, I. Forthcoming. 'Principles and parameters of universal grammar', in Roberts (ed.).

Iannace, G. 1983. *Interferenza linguistica ai confini fra Stato e Regno: Il dialetto di San Leucio del Sannio*. Ravenna: Longo.

Iatridou, S. 2000. 'The grammatical ingredients to counterfactuality', *Linguistic Inquiry* 31: 231–70.

Kayne, R. 1972. 'Subject inversion in French interrogatives', in J. Casagrande and B. Saciuk (eds.), *Generative studies in Romance languages*. Rowley, MA: Newbury House, pp. 70–126.

1984. *Connectedness and binary branching*. Dordrecht: Foris.

1993. 'Toward a modular theory of auxiliary selection', *Studia Linguistica* 47: 3–31.

1994. *The antisymmetry of syntax*. Cambridge, MA: MIT Press.

1996. 'Microparametric syntax: Some introductory remarks', in J. Black and V. Montapanyane (eds.), *Microparametric syntax and dialectal variation*. Amsterdam: John Benjamins, pp. ix–xviii.

2000. *Parameters and universals*. Oxford University Press.

2005a. *Movement and silence*. Oxford University Press.

2005b. 'Some notes on comparative syntax, with special reference to English and French', in G. Cinque and R. Kayne (eds.), *Handbook of comparative syntax*. Oxford University Press, pp. 3–69.

King, R. and Nadasdi, T. 2005. 'Deux auxiliaires qui voulaient mourir en français acadien', in P. Brasseur and A. Falkert (eds.), *Français d'Amérique: Approches morphosyntaxiques*. Paris: L'Harmattan, pp. 103–11.

Kiparsky, P. 1995. 'Indo-European origins of Germanic syntax', in Battye and Roberts (eds.), pp. 140–69.

Koopman, H. 1984. *The syntax of verb-movement: From verb movement rules in the Kru languages to Universal Grammar*. Dordrecht: Foris.

Ledgeway, A. 2003. 'L'estensione dell'ausiliare perfettivo *avere* nell'antico napoletano: Intransitività scissa condizionata da fattori modali', *Archivio glottologico italiano* 88: 27–71.

2011. 'Syntactic and morphosyntactic typology and change in Latin and Romance', in M. Maiden, J. C. Smith and A. Ledgeway (eds.), *The Cambridge history of the Romance languages*. Cambridge University Press, pp. 382–471, 724–34.

2012a. *From Latin to Romance: Morphosyntactic typology and change*. Oxford University Press.

2012b. 'From Latin to Romance: The rise of configurationality, functional categories and head-marking', in J. Barðdal, M. Cennamo and E. van Gelderen (eds.), *Variation and change in argument realisation*. Oxford: Blackwell. Special Issue of the *Transactions of the Philological Society* 110: 422–42.

2013. 'Greek disguised as Romance? The case of southern Italy', in M. Janse, B. D. Joseph, A. Ralli and M. Bagriacik (eds.), *Proceedings of the 5th international conference on Greek dialects and linguistic theory*. Laboratory of Modern Greek Dialects, University of Patras, pp.184–228. Available at http://lmgd.philology.upatras.gr/en/research/downloads/MGDLT5_proceedings.pdf.

2014a. 'Romance auxiliary selection in light of Romanian evidence', in G. Pană Dindelegan, R. Zafiu, A. Dragomirescu, I. Nicula and A. Nicolae (eds.), *Diachronic variation in Romanian*. Newcastle upon Tyne: Cambridge Scholars Publishing, pp. 3–35.

2014b. 'Parametrului poziției centrului și efectele sale pragmatice în trecerea de la latină la limbile romance', in R. Zafiu, A. Dragomirescu and A. Nicolae (eds.), *Diacronie și sincronie în studiul limbii române*. Bucharest: Editura Universității din București, pp. 11–26.

2015. 'Parallels in Romance nominal and clausal microvariation', *Revue roumaine de linguistique* 60: 105–27.

2016a. 'Functional categories', in Ledgeway and Maiden (eds.), pp. 761–71.

2016b. 'Sentential complementation', in Ledgeway and Maiden (eds.), pp. 1013–28.

Forthcoming a. 'From Latin to Romance: The decline of edge-fronting', in A. Cardosa and A. M. Martins (eds.), *Word order change*. Oxford University Press.

Forthcoming b. 'Parameters in Romance adverb agreement', in M. Hummel and S. Valera (eds.), *Adjective–adverb interfaces in Romance*. Amsterdam: John Benjamins.

Forthcoming c. 'Syntheticity and analyticity', in A. Dufter and E. Stark (eds.), *Manual of Romance morphosyntax and syntax* (to appear in series *Manual of Romance linguistics*, edited by G. Holtus and F. Sánchez Miret). Berlin: De Gruyter.

Forthcoming d. 'From Latin to Romance syntax: The great leap', in P. Crisma and G. Longobardi (eds.), *The Oxford handbook of diachronic and historical linguistics*. Oxford University Press.

Ledgeway, A. and Maiden, M. (eds.) 2016. *The Oxford guide to the Romance languages*. Oxford University Press.

Lee, K.-M. and Ramsey, S. R. 2011. *A history of the Korean language*. Cambridge University Press.

Legendre, G. 2010. 'A formal typology of person-based auxiliary selection in Italo-Romance', in D'Alesssandro, Ledgeway and Roberts (eds.), pp. 186–200.

Li, C. and Thompson, S. 1976. 'Subject and topic: A new typology of language', in C. Li (ed.), *Subject and topic*. New York: Academic Press, pp. 457–89.

Lightfoot, D. W. 1979. *Principles of diachronic syntax*. Cambridge University Press.

Loporcaro, M. 1998. *Sintassi comparata dell'accordo participiale romanzo*. Turin: Rosenberg & Sellier.

2007. 'On triple auxiliation', *Linguistics* 45: 173–222.

Loporcaro, M. 2016. 'Auxiliary selection and participial agreement', in Ledgeway and Maiden (eds.), pp. 802–18.

Lüdtke, H. 1974. 'Die Mundart von Ripatransone – ein sprachtypologisches Kuriosum', *Acta Universitatis Carolinae – Philologica* 5: 173–77.

1976. 'La declinazione dei verbi in un dialetto di transizione marchigiano-abruzzese', *Abruzzo* 14: 79–84.

Maiden, M. and Robustelli, C. 2007. *A Reference grammar of modern Italian.* London: Hodder Arnold.

Mancini, A. M. 1993. 'Le caratteristiche morfosintattiche del dialetto di Ripatransone (AP), alla luce di nuove ricerche', in S. Balducci (ed.), *I dialetti delle Marche meridionali.* Alessandria: Edizioni dell'Orso, pp. 111–36.

Manente, M. 2008. 'L'aspect, les auxiliaires 'être' et 'avoir' et l'hypothèse inaccusative dans une perspective comparative français/italien', unpublished PhD thesis, Universities of Venice and Paris VIII.

Manzini, M. R. and Savoia, L. 2005. *I dialetti italiani e romanci: Morfosintassi generative,* 3 vols. Alessandria: Edizioni dell'Orso.

Marouzeau, J. 1949. *L'ordre des mots dans la phrase latine. III. Les articulations de l'énoncé.* Paris: Les Belles Lettres.

1953. *L'ordre des mots en latin: Volume complémentaire.* Paris: Les Belles Lettres.

Matisoff, J. 1990. 'On megalocomparison', *Language* 66(1): 106–20.

Miller, G. 2002. *Nonfinite structures in theory and change.* Oxford University Press.

Mithun, M. 1991. *The languages of North America.* Cambridge University Press.

Molinelli, P. 1988. *Fenomeni della negazione dal latino all'italiano.* Florence: La Nuova Italia.

Motapanyane, V. (ed.) 2000. *Comparative studies in Romanian syntax.* Amsterdam: Elsevier.

Nevaci, M. and Todi, A. 2009. 'The grammaticalization of perfect auxiliaries in Romanian. historical and dialectal aspects', *Revue roumaine de linguistique* 54: 137–50.

Newmeyer, F. J. 2005. *Possible and probable languages: A generative perspective on linguistic typology.* Oxford University Press.

Newton, G. 2006. 'The development of the Old Irish system of verbal inflection', unpublished PhD thesis, University of Cambridge.

Nordahl, H. 1977. 'Assez avez alé: Estre et avoir comme auxiliaires du verbe aler en ancien français', *Revue romane* 12(1): 54–67.

Oniga, R. 2004. *Il latino: Breve introduzione linguistica.* Milan: FrancoAngeli.

Pană Dindelegan, G. 2013. 'The participle', in G. P. Dindelegan (ed.), *The grammar of Romanian.* Oxford University Press, pp. 222–32.

Pancheva, R. 2008. 'Head-directionality of TP in Old Church Slavonic', in A. Antonenko, J. Bailyn and C. Bethin (eds.), *Formal approaches to Slavic linguistics 16: The Stony Brook meeting, 2007.* Ann Arbor: Michigan Slavic Publications, pp. 313–32.

Parrino, F. 1967. 'Su alcune particolarità della coniugazione nel dialetto di Ripatransone', *L'Italia dialettale* 30: 156–66.

Pinkster, H. 1990. *Latin syntax and semantics*. London: Routledge.

Poletto, C. 1995. 'The diachronic development of subject clitics in North Eastern Italian dialects', in Battye and Roberts (eds.), pp. 295–24.

2000. *The higher functional field*. Oxford University Press.

2016. 'Negation', in Ledgeway and Maiden (eds.), pp. 833–46.

Pollock, J.-Y. 1989. 'Verb movement, Universal Grammar and the structure of IP', *Linguistic Inquiry* 20: 365–424.

2006. 'Subject-clitic inversion, complex inversion and stylistic inversion in French', in M. Everaert and H. van Riemsdijk (eds.), *The Blackwell companion to syntax*. Oxford: Blackwell, pp. 601–59.

Powell, J. 2010. 'Hyperbaton and register in Cicero', in E. Dickey and A. Chahoud (eds.), *Colloquial and literary Latin*. Cambridge University Press, pp. 163–85.

Rea, B. 2014. 'Aspects of pronoun and auxiliary morphology in French, with particular reference to spoken Montréal French', unpublished MPhil thesis, University of Oxford.

Remacle, L. 1956. *Syntaxe du parler wallon de La Gleize*. Paris: Les Belles lettres.

Ringe, D. 2006. *A history of English*, vol. I: *From Proto-Indo-European to Proto-Germanic*. Oxford University Press.

Ritter, E. and Wiltschko, M. 2014. 'The composition of INFL: An exploration of Tense, tenseless languages, and tenseless constructions', *Natural Language and Linguistic Theory* 32: 1331–86.

Rizzi, L. 1982. *Topics in Italian syntax*. Dordrecht: Foris.

1986. 'On the status of subject clitics in Romance', in O. Jaeggli and C. Silva-Corvalan (eds.), *Studies in Romance linguistics*. Dordrecht: Foris, pp. 391–419.

Rizzi, L. and Roberts, I. 1989. 'Complex inversion in French', *Probus* 1: 1–30. (Reprinted in A. Belletti and L. Rizzi (eds.) 1996. *Parameters and functional heads*. Oxford University Press, pp. 91–118.)

Roberts, I. 1985. 'Agreement parameters and the development of English modal auxiliaries', *Natural Language and Linguistic Theory* 3: 21–58.

1993. *Verbs and diachronic syntax: A comparative history of English and French*. Dordrecht: Kluwer.

1996. *Comparative syntax*. London: Edward Arnold.

2010a. 'Varieties of French and the null subject parameter', in Biberauer, Holmberg, Roberts and Sheehan (eds.), pp. 303–26.

2010b. 'The pronominal domain: DP-NP structure, clitics and null subjects', in D'Alessandro, Ledgeway and Roberts (eds.), pp. 3–27.

2010c. *Agreement and head movement: Clitics and defective goals*. Cambridge MA: MIT Press.

2012. 'Macroparameters and minimalism: A programme for comparative research', in C. Galves, S. Cyrino, R. Lopez and J. Avelar (eds.), *Parameter theory and linguistic change*. Oxford University Press, pp. 320–54.

2013. 'Some speculations on the development of the Romance peri-phrastic perfect', *Revue roumaine de linguistique* 58(1): 3–30.

2014a. 'Subject clitics and macroparameters', in P. Benincà, A. Ledgeway and N. Vincent (eds.), *Diachrony and dialects: Grammatical change in the dialects of Italy*. Oxford University Press, pp. 177–201.

2014b. 'Taraldsen's generalisation and diachronic syntax: Two ways to lose null subjects', in P. Svenonius (ed.), *Functional structure from top to toe: The cartography of syntactic structures*, vol. 9. Oxford University Press, pp. 115–48.

(ed.) Forthcoming. *The Oxford handbook of Universal Grammar*. Oxford University Press.

Roberts, I. and Holmberg, A. 2010. 'Introduction: Parameters in minim-alist theory', in Biberauer, Holmberg, Roberts and Sheehan (eds.), pp. 1–57.

Roberts, I. and Roussou, A. 2003. *Syntactic change: A minimalist approach to grammaticalization*. Cambridge University Press.

Russell, P. 1995. *An introduction to the Celtic languages*. London: Longman.

Salvi, G. 2011. 'A formal approach to Latin word order', in R. Oniga, R. Iovino and G. Giusti (eds.), *Formal linguistics and the teaching of Latin: Theoretical and applied perspectives in comparative grammar*. Newcastle upon Tyne: Cambridge Scholars, pp. 23–50.

Sankoff, G. and Thibault, P. 1977. 'L'alternance entre les auxiliaires *avoir* et *être* en français parlé à Montréal', *Langue française* 34: 84–108.

Sapir, E. 1921. *Language: An introduction to the study of speech*. New York: Harcourt, Brace and Company.

Sheehan, M. 2014. 'Towards a parameter hierarchy for alignment', in R. E. Santana-LaBarge (ed.), *Proceedings of WCCFL 31*. Somerville, MA: Cascadilla Press, pp. 399–408.

Skjærvø P. O. 2009. 'Old Iranian languages', in G. Windfuhr (ed.), *The Iranian languages*. London and New York: Routledge, pp. 43–195.

Smith, J. C. 1999. 'Markedness and morphosyntactic change revisited: The case of Romance past participle agreement', in S. Embleton, J. Joseph and H.-J. Niederehe (eds.), *The emergence of the modern language sciences: Studies on the transition from historical-comparative to structural linguistics in honour of E. F. K. Koerner*, vol. 2: *Methodological perspectives and applications*. Amsterdam: John Benjamins, pp. 203–15.

Sorace, A. 2000. 'Gradients in auxiliary selection with intransitive verbs', *Language* 76: 859–90.

Sprouse, R. and Vance, B. 1999. 'An explanation for the decline of null pronouns in certain Germanic and romance dialects', M. DeGraff (ed.), *Language creation and language change: Creolization, diachrony, and development*. Cambridge, MA: MIT Press, pp. 257–84.

Steever, S. B. 1998. *The Dravidian languages*. Cambridge University Press.

Stolova, N. 2006. 'Split intransitivity in Old Spanish: Irrealis and negation factors', *Revue roumaine de linguistique* 2: 301–20.

Taraldsen, T. 1978. 'On the NIC, vacuous application and the *that*-trace filter', unpublished MS, MIT.

Taylor, A. 1990. 'Clitics and configurationality in Ancient Greek', unpublished PhD thesis, University of Pennsylvania.

Tesnière, L. 1959. *Eléments de syntaxe structurale*. Paris: Klincksieck.

Travis, L. 1984. 'Parameters and effects of word order variation', unpublished PhD thesis, MIT.

Traugott, E. 1972. *A history of English syntax*. New York: Holt, Rinehart and Winston.

Tuttle, E. 1986. 'The spread of ESSE as universal auxiliary in central Italo-Romance', *Medioevo romanzo* 11: 229–87.

van Gelderen, E. 2004. *Grammaticalization as economy*. Amsterdam: John Benjamins.

   2011. 'Grammaticalization and generative grammar: A difficult liaison,' in B. Heine and H. Narrog (eds.), *The Oxford handbook of grammaticalization*. Oxford University Press, pp. 43–55.

van Kemenade, A. and Vincent, N. (eds.) 1997. *Parameters of morphosyntactic change*. Cambridge Universiy Press.

Vanelli, L., Renzi, L. and Benincà, P. 1985. 'Typologie des pronoms sujets dans les langues romanes', in *Actes du XVIIe congrès international de linguistique et philologie romanes*, vol. 3: *Linguistique descriptive, phonétique, morphologie et lexique*. Aix-en-Provence: Université de Provence, pp. 163–76.

Vasseur, G. 1996. *Grammaire des parlers picards du Vimeu (Somme) avec considération spéciale du dialecte de Nibas*. Abbeville: F. Paillart.

Vikner, S. 1985. 'Reichenbach revisited: One, two, or three temporal relations', *Acta Linguistica Hafniensia* 19: 81–8.

Vincent, N. 1982. 'The development of the auxiliaries *habere* and *esse* in Romance', in N. Vincent and M. Harris (eds.), *Studies in the Romance verb: Essays offered to Joe Cremona on the occasion of his 60th birthday*. London and Canberra: Croom Helm, pp. 71–96.

   1987. 'The interaction of periphrasis and inflection: Some Romance examples', in M. Harris and P. Ramat (eds.), *The historical development of auxiliaries*. Berlin and New York: Mouton de Gruyter, pp. 237–56.

   1988. 'Latin', in M. Harris and N. Vincent (eds.), *The Romance languages*. London: Routledge, pp. 26–78.

   1997. 'The emergence of the D-system in Romance', in van Kemenade and Vincent (eds.), pp. 149–69.

   1998a. 'Tra grammatica e grammaticalizzazione: Articoli e clitici nelle lingue (italo-)romanze', in P. Ramat and E. Roma (eds.), *Sintassi storica. Atti del XXX congresso internazionale della Società di linguistica italiana, Pavia, 26–28 settembre 1996*. Rome: Bulzoni, pp. 411–40.

   1998b. 'On the grammar of inflected non-finite forms (with special reference to old Neapolitan)', in I. Korzen and M. Herslund (eds.), *Clause combining and text structure* (Copenhagen Studies in Language 22). Copenhagen: Samfunds-litteratur, pp. 135–58.

2000. 'Competition and correspondence in syntactic change: Null arguments in Latin and Romance', in S. Pintzuk, G. Tsoulas and A. Warner (eds.), *Diachronic syntax: Models and mechanisms*. Oxford University Press, pp. 25–50.

Walkden, G. 2014. *Syntactic reconstruction and Proto-Germanic*. Oxford University Press.

Warner, A. 1993. *English auxiliaries: Structure and history*. Cambridge University Press.

1997. 'The structure of parametric change, and V movement in the history of English', in van Kemenade and Vincent (eds.), pp. 380–93.

Watkins, C. 1963. 'Preliminaries to a historical and comparative analysis of the syntax of the Old Irish verb', *Celtica* 6: 1–49.

1964. 'Preliminaries to the reconstruction of Indo-European sentence structure', in H. Lunt (ed.), *Proceedings of the 9th international congress of linguists*. The Hague: Mouton, pp. 1035–42.

Watumull, J. 2015. 'The linguistic Turing machine', unpublished PhD thesis, University of Cambridge.

Willis, D., Lucas, C. and Breitbarth, A. 2013. 'Comparing diachronies of negation', in D. Willis, C. Lucas and A. Breitbarth (eds.), *The History of negation in the languages of Europe and the Mediterranean*, vol. I: *Case studies*. Oxford University Press, pp. 1–50.

Wurmbrand, S. 2015. 'Restructuring cross-linguistically', unpublished MS, University of Connecticut.

Yanagida, Y. 2005. 'Word order and clause structure in Early Old Japanese', *Journal of East Asian Linguistics* 15: 37–67.

Yanagida, Y. and Whitman, J. 2009. 'Alignment and word order in Old Japanese', *Journal of East Asia Asian Linguistics* 18: 101–44.

Zribi-Hertz, A. 1994. 'La syntaxe des clitiques nominatifs en français standard et en français avancé', in G. Kleiber and G. Roques (eds.), *Travaux de linguistique et de philologie*. Strasbourg-Nancy: Klincksieck, pp. 131–47.

28

Biolinguistics

Cedric Boeckx, Pedro Tiago Martins and Evelina Leivada

28.1 Introduction

Coming across a contribution that deals with the biological foundations of the human language faculty in a handbook that is dedicated to historical syntax is likely to surprise many. Is the human language faculty not uniform? And is historical change not a cultural process, rather than a biological one?

We would like to use this introduction to make a few things clear. First, although our chapter is located next to those dealing with theoretical frameworks like Principles and Parameters, we insist on biolinguistics being taken not as an alternative framework (synonymous with, say, Minimalism), but as an orientation for linguistic studies, within which choice of framework is appropriate.

Second, we follow the generative tradition that takes language change to be closely tied to language acquisition and typology. And in this context biolinguistic considerations lead us to an important and surprising conclusion: natural language syntax is invariant. It is not subject to variation, and therefore not subject to change. At least within our species. We could, of course, talk about syntactic change in a biolinguistic context by focusing on differences between natural language syntax and birdsong syntax. There, of course, there has been a significant syntactic change. But we feel that this topic is not what readers of this handbook might expect, and so we will leave it aside (interested readers can turn to Boeckx 2012; Berwick *et al.* 2012).

Third, there is a sense in which the much discussed 'Darwin problem' in the recent biolinguistic literature really pertains to language change. As is well known, Darwin did not really discuss the origin of species in his most famous book, if by that we mean 'emergence of form': he focused on historical changes *once* the relevant form had emerged. As such, we agree with Koji Fujita (p.c.) that Darwin would have been more interested in the emergence of specific grammatical systems (language change) rather than in the emergence of a species with a language-ready brain (the latter problem may have interested Turing far more, so we could call it Turing's problem).

That said, we do not want to suggest that biolinguistics has nothing to contribute to studies of language change. Quite apart from establishing that syntactic change is non-existent, biolinguistic considerations help refine our understanding of notions like I(nternal)-language and E(xternal)-language (Chomsky 1986) that have figured prominently in the literature on (alleged) syntactic change.

In line with the aforementioned state of affairs, we will review the arguments in favour of the claim that syntax (narrow syntax or s-syntax in Hale and Keyser 1993), is invariant and that the 'syntactic' variation (and change) that one observes across languages is in reality reducible to aspects of a 'post-syntax' (Boeckx 2014b), that is, to varying patterns of morphophonology (externalization strategies). Second, we will argue that grammars or I-languages (i.e. patterns that correspond to l-syntax) are in part shaped by the environment. They are then expected to vary, however, within the limits imposed by s-syntax. We suggest that change, variation and the emergence of complex, grammatical markers reflect environmental needs and, relying on Deacon's (2006) distinction between various levels of emergence and attendant complexity, we are inclined to think that I-languages display traces of cumulative complexity (Deacon's third level); this being the area of intersection between I- and E-language (Boeckx *et al.* 2013).

Focusing on instances of recent (sign) language emergence, and evidence from birdsong, we conclude that biolinguistics should not operate on the basis of a strong I-/E-language divide. It should instead take a lesson from biology on why it would be wrong to ignore what it can learn from how sociocultural factors affect the linguistic phenotype.

28.2   Principles, Parameters and Variation in Syntax

Human beings are biologically equipped with the capacity to acquire language. The faculty of language is innate to humans and the initial state of it, Universal Grammar (UG), 'may be thought of as some system of principles, common to the species and available to each individual prior to experience' (Chomsky 1981a: 7). In the same work, establishing a link between UG and language acquisition, Chomsky defined UG, placing it in a typical acquisition scenario, as 'a characterization of children's prelinguistic initial state' (1981a: 7). Since that publication, UG is usually conceptualized in terms of an architecture that involves principles and parameters (for in-depth discussion, see Chapter 13, this volume). The so-called Principles and Parameters (P&P) version of UG probably stands for the most articulate conception of it. Because biolinguistic considerations have led us to reject this model, we think it is important to expand on some of its properties and see how problematic they are.

The P&P architecture, and more specifically the part of it that corresponds to parametric variation, has been related to language change through a diachronic perspective. This perspective seeks to answer whether linguists are in a position to identify clear pathways of change (probably through processes of grammaticalization; see Chapter 1, this volume) across languages that make them 'converge on certain parametric settings' and in this sense they create 'a space of possible variation within which grammatical systems are distributed' (Roberts and Roussou 2003: 3).

Over the years, several hypotheses have been entertained regarding the locus of variation. Perhaps the most well known is the so-called Chomsky–Borer conjecture, based on the following two statements:

(1) Variation is restricted to possibilities that the inflectional component makes available (Borer 1984: 3).
(2) Variation is restricted to the lexicon; to a narrow category of (primarily inflectional) morphological properties (Chomsky 2001: 2).

But there are at least two other visions or 'conjectures' that one can discern in the literature, though they have not been named as such. We will do so here. The first one could be called the Chomsky–Baker conjecture. This one takes the view that there are 'parameters within the statements of the general principles that shape natural language syntax' (Baker 2008), a view that arguably was the one in Chomsky's original (1981b) formulation of Principles and Parameters.

The second conjecture is of more recent vintage. It is one that takes variation to be confined to morphophonological variants. This is a view endorsed in Berwick and Chomsky (2011), so in the present work it is referred to as the Chomsky–Berwick conjecture. It corresponds to Bocckx's (2011) Strong Uniformity Thesis: 'Principles of narrow syntax are not subject to parametrization; nor are they affected by lexical parameters.' All variation is then post-syntactic.

To be sustainable, the Chomsky–Berwick conjecture must rely on another conjecture, implicitly assumed for many years in the field, though rarely defended in a systematic fashion (but see Ramchand and Svenonius 2008): there cannot be any semantic parameter. Given the transparency of the syntax–semantics mapping (so transparent that it has led some to entertain an Identity thesis; e.g. Hinzen 2006), if there are semantic parameters, there must be syntactic parameters. But if 'principles of narrow syntax are not subject to parametrization; nor are they affected by lexical parameters', and syntax 'carves the paths that semantics must blindly follow' (Uriagereka 2008), then, it follows that if there is no syntactic variation, there will not be any semantic variation either. In other words, the 'no semantic parameter' conjecture directly conflicts with the

Chomsky–Baker conjecture. Quite apart from these architectural considerations, the question, of course, is which conjecture is correct, empirically.

Before we adduce arguments in favour of the Chomsky–Berwick conjecture (building, in part, on previous work of ours, such as Boeckx 2011, 2014a, b; Boeckx and Leivada 2013), we would like to note that in fact the Chomsky–Borer conjecture arguably decomposes into either the Chomsky–Baker conjecture or the Chomsky–Berwick conjecture. This has to do with the evolving notion of the lexicon. In a conception of the lexicon of the sort advocated in a theoretical framework like Distributed Morphology (DM), or other realizational models like Nanosyntax, there is no lexicon in the sense familiar from generative grammar. Instead, the tasks assigned to the component called the lexicon in earlier theories are scattered across various other components. DM assumes that syntax itself generates and manipulates an unordered hierarchy of abstract syntactic features devoid of phonological content, the so-called 'morphemes' (Halle and Marantz 1993). Once generated, phonological content is inserted into these abstract feature bundles (a step called vocabulary insertion). Accordingly, the 'inflectional component' or the '(primarily inflectional) morphological properties' referred to in Borer's and Chomsky's statements (1)–(2) could either refer to the pre-syntactic component of the lexicon (what Marantz 1997 dubbed the narrow lexicon or List A) or the post-syntactic morphological component (the Vocabulary or List B in DM).

If one looks at the recent literature dealing with variation, one cannot avoid being struck by the fact that numerous proposals converge in re-analysing points of syntactic variation in morphophonological terms. These analyses are indications of the existence of a substantially greater degree of syntactic (and semantic) invariance than previously thought. Representative examples include Acedo-Matellán (2010), Jenks (2012), Real-Puigdollers (2013) and Safir (2014). The conclusion raised based on these works (to which we could add models like the one in Richards 2010 or Boeckx 2014b) is that (morpho)phonology has a much larger impact on the final form of a linguistic utterance than is generally thought.

Even empirical considerations, then, point to the existence of an invariant syntactic component (Boeckx 2014b takes this as an argument for a feature-free, Merge-only syntax model), with variation confined to the margin of the faculty of language, in the externalization component (in the literature on variation we are aware of only a few works explicitly denying that all points of variation are reducible to morphophonological decisions; they are discussed and refuted in Boeckx and Leivada 2013).

If syntactic operations are not subject to variation, they are not subject to change either. Of course, we could still continue talking about syntactic change if by syntax we mean 'post-syntax', or 'morphosyntax' or 'l-syntax' in the sense of Hale and Keyser (1993), on which we are about to the expand for the purpose of clarification. But contrary to recent claims that frameworks like DM reduce morphology to syntax, Hale and Keyser were well aware that the notions of 'l(exical)-syntax' and 's(yntactic)-syntax' should not be conflated. Here is what they wrote:

> We have proposed that argument structure is a syntax, but we have also separated it from s-syntax, … probably an onerous distinction, perhaps nothing more than a temporary terminological convenience. [BUT]
>
> We must nevertheless assume that there is something lexical about any verbal/lexical entry … What is it that is lexical about the entry correspond-ing to shelve? Clearly, it is a lexical fact that shelve exists as a simple transitive verb in English.
>
> … in reality all verbs are to some extent phrasal idioms, that is, syntac-tic structures that must be learned as the conventional 'names' for various dynamic events.

In effect, Hale and Keyser are pointing out that their 'l-syntax' is a syntax in the representational sense (a post-syntax, a morphology, in our terminology), whereas 's-syntax' is a syntax in the dynamic, derivational sense (narrow syntax, for us). It is syntax in the latter sense that we claim cannot change.

Although linguists often refer to the varying l-syntax patterns as corre-sponding to syntactic variation, it might be the case that these patterns can be reconstructed in morphophonological terms instead of syntactic terms. For example, Longobardi and Guardiano (2009) make reference to *syntactic* parameters in the nominal domain. According to their description, these are parameters that correspond to various grammatical relations inside the DP module: for example, the status of various features (person, number, gender), definiteness, and the position of the head noun with respect to various elements of the DP and the different kinds of movements it undergoes. A closer inspection of these syntactic parameters, however, renders their characterization as 'syntactic' dubious. For instance, parameter 5 corre-sponds to feature spread on N, parameter 19 to feature spread from cardinals, and parameter 57 to feature spread on possessives. These parameters seem to be instantiations of morphological concord, thus more related to morphology than syntax. Moreover, the parameters that correspond to head movement patterns instead of viewed as the result of syntactic movement can be ana-lysed as varying realizations of copies which according to Bošković and Nunes (2007) are determined by conditions that come from the phonological com-ponent and not from syntax (i.e. syntactic movement) per se. In this context, it seems that many of the parameters in Longobardi and Guardiano (2009) can be reconstructed in morphophonological terms; a fact that suggests that these are not syntactic parameters but, rather, are realizational variants.

28.3 Language Change: on the Emergence of Complexity

Complexity is a notion recurrently showing up in the literature on the evolution of language and as such it is of great importance when one discusses the emergence of certain aspects of I-language through change.

Assuming the cross-linguistically uniform character of language acquisition in typically developing populations, and given that all humans are equipped with the same linguistic endowment, it has been traditionally concluded that all languages are equal in terms of complexity, despite the surface variation observed between them. As Fromkin and Rodman (1974) put it, '[a]ll languages are equally complex and equally capable of expressing any idea in the universe'. Our claim that syntax is invariant may suggest to some that we subscribe to this statement, but we do not. We crucially distinguish between an invariant syntax and grammatical systems that vary and change. Some of these may be more complex than others, precisely because of their past.

But what exactly is meant by complexity? Deacon (2006) usefully distinguishes between various notions or levels of emergence (and attendant complexity), and we think that they could be useful in the context of biolinguistics. Specifically, Deacon's notions of second- and third-order emergence are worth distinguishing. Deacon argues that many thermodynamic effects correspond to first-order emergent relationships. These arise when relational properties of systems amplify intrinsic material properties, eventually resulting in a reduction in complexity. Deacon's second level involves the self-organization of systems; what he calls 'autopoietic' sets. Self-organization gives rise to what one might call spontaneous complexity. Deacon's third level encloses the additional factor of 'recursive causality' of self-organized systems, arising from interaction among agents. As he notes, this type of emergence inevitably carries a flavour of cumulative complexity since it entails an evolutionary, historical character.

Traditionally, this latter type of complexity has not been given much attention in the generative literature: social phenomena are often relegated to 'E-language', a notion distinct from what Chomskyan linguists focus on (i.e. I-language). 'I-language' and 'E-language' were first defined in Chomsky (1986) along the following lines: E-language treats language 'independently of the mind/brain' (1986: 20), and I-language 'is some element of the mind of the person who knows the language, acquired by the learner, and used by the speaker-hearer' (1986: 22). Different definitions of these terms exist in the literature; however, most definitions reach a point of agreement on assuming that E-language entails a sociocultural perspective, whereas I-language entails a cognitive/biological perspective. This state of affairs is taken by some to suggest that I-language and the environment factor can be kept far apart, probably to the extent of arguing that internalists give a negative answer as to whether (i) 'some ontology of "language" [exists] outside of individuals' mind/brain' and (ii) 'we can ever construct a serious scientific theory of such "language"' (Lohndal and Narita 2009: 325).

While we generally agree with this broad distinction, it seems to us that recognizing the influence of environmental factors on the range of properties grammatical systems manifest may be of interest in the context of complexity issues (specifically, Deacon's levels 2 vs 3). Here we review recent work in biolinguistics that bears directly on this.

In biology, it is standardly recognized that there is a mutual relation between what counts as the genetic make-up of an organism and the environmental influences it undergoes. Genes determine the capacities of organisms, yet the limits of these capacities are subject to environmental triggers. Eventually these limits may never be explored, depending on how adequate the environmental factor proves to be; in the case of language, this basically means that, 'human beings can speak because they have the right genes and the right environment' (Lewontin 2000: 28).

We suggest that the theoretical argument that the environment factor makes an impact on the development of certain I-properties can receive empirical support from cases of recently emerged languages. The reference here is to those cases where a sufficient period of development time has not yet elapsed and the emergence of (complex) I-properties is still in its earliest stages. The underlying assumption is that if language emergence is in its early stages, time is not enough for it to have already undergone significant environmentally driven adaptations (i.e. cumulative complexity, or third-order emergence in Deacon's terms). One such case of recent language emergence is that of Al-Sayyid Bedouin Sign Language (ABSL), which will be discussed next. The facts reported below are generally in line with the predictions made by approaches such as those in Kirby (2001), Kirby and Hurford (2002) and Kirby *et al.* (2008).

28.3.1 Complexity in Language

ABSL is a language now in its third generation of speakers that emerged in the last 70–75 years within a small Bedouin community in southern Israel. The presence of a gene for non-syndromic, genetically recessive, profound pre-lingual neurosensory deafness (Scott *et al.* 1995) coupled with consanguineous marriage patterns within the tight-knit Bedouin community have resulted in the birth of a proportionately large population of deaf individuals in a relatively short period of time (Sandler *et al.* 2011). ABSL is unique in that it can be treated as a case of truly spontaneous language emergence (Providence Island Sign Language was a similar case; once known by the majority of the people on Providencia Island off the Nicaraguan coast (Washabaugh 1986), it is now nearly extinct (Lewis 2009)). Given its uniqueness, its study can offer valuable insights into the core properties of a grammatical system when the time factor did not allow for much impact from the environment.

The gradual development of complex grammatical markers in this language is a well-documented fact. According to Meir *et al.* (2010), ABSL first-generation signers have the tendency to break an event that requires two arguments into two clauses which come along with two verb signs, each predicates of a different argument. For example, a description of a girl feeding a woman could be realized with two SV clauses rather than a single SOV (e.g. WOMAN SIT, GIRL FEED instead of GIRL WOMAN FEED), which would be the prevalent word order among ABSL signers. The conclusion these authors draw based on such data is that language takes time to develop grammatical markers such as the ones that facilitate distinguishing between the subject and the object phrases in a clause. If this observation is on the right track, it suggests that grammaticalization is an environmentally driven process and it is no accident that its occurrence coincides with the period of language development during which morphosyntactic and phonological structural properties of language need to develop as a means to meet environmental needs. By observing complexity in emergent language or in primary, spontaneously developed child or adult gestural systems of communication (i.e. home-signs), one can distinguish between those properties of I-language that are innate and those that have come to be internalized, but encompass an interplay between innate, biological predisposition and the influences of the environment.

Both types of properties would be properties of I-language; therefore, first the role of the environment is already smuggled into a discussion that has 'I-language' or 'the ontology of language' as its object of study and second the sharp distinction between I- and E-language in reflection of internalist and externalist inquiries respectively, is destabilized from the moment the boundaries between the two become blurred in cases like ABSL or Providence Island Sign Language. The emergence of complexity does instantiate this interplay in the sense that in home-signs or in recently emerged languages, complexity is reasonably expected to be less advanced compared to its manifestations in extensively grammaticalized languages, though not totally absent. In other words, its existence does not depend solely on the environment: biology provides a seed from which a capacity evolves, with its development being subject to environmental factors.

28.3.2 Complexity in Birdsong

Discussing the ontology of human language through approaching certain properties such as development of complex (grammatical) markers as environmentally driven adaptations of an innate capacity is nothing more than extending to human language what biologists do for the systems of communication of other animals.

Complexity considerations are not only relevant when one discusses human language. As a matter of fact, the emergence of complex markers in the latter displays strong parallels with what one observes in birdsong. Song quality in Bengalese finches 'partially reflects early ontogenetic conditions', whereas 'considering that song syntactic complexity is subject to female preference in the Bengalese finch, it is likely that maternal resource allocation strategies play a role in song evolution' (Soma *et al.* 2009: 363), such strategies obviously being a component of the environment factor. Moreover, it has been argued that long-domesticated Bengalese finches display a phonologically and syntactically more complex courtship song compared to their cousins that live in the wild (Okanoya 2012). Evidently, the path to deriving complexity goes through the environment and this happens not only in the case of human language. It seems that the existence of properties like varying complexity in what gets externalized is not restricted to humans and, more importantly, the factors that affect these properties are quite alike across species in that they are environmentally driven adaptations.

Leaving communication systems aside, the genotype–environment interaction is present in a plethora of studies that deal with the development of biological traits in organisms. The 'genotype-by-environment interaction' refers to the contributions to the phenotypic variation of differing effects of different genotypes across environments (West-Eberhard 2003: 15). The degree to which environmental choices affect the way genetic blueprint is expressed depends on the specific genotype–environment interaction in each case. This view is consistent with what Lupyan and Dale (2010) propose for language structure being determined in part by social structure. Having conducted a statistical analysis of over 2,000 languages, their results suggest that language structures adapt to the environment just as biological organisms are shaped by ecological niches.

According to their Linguistic Niche Hypothesis, there exists a relationship between social structure and linguistic structure such that 'the level of morphological specification is a product of languages adapting to the learning constraints and the unique communicative needs of the speaker population' and 'the surface complexity of languages arose as an adaptation to the esoteric niche' (Lupyan and Dale 2010: 7). Apart from reflecting statistical correlations, these predictions map nicely onto the findings elicited by comprehension task which aimed to examine interpretations of spatially modulated verbs in Nicaraguan Sign Language. More specifically, Senghas (2003) notes a mismatch in form that is observed from one age cohort to the cohort that follows and suggests 'that each age cohort ... transforms the language environment for the next, enabling each new cohort of learners to develop further than its predecessors' (2003: 511). Of course the notion of time/age cohort is only one subpart of the 'environment' factor. There are more: for instance, the proportion of deaf to hearing members in the community, the gestural practices of hearing members (in different terms, the richness of raw materials), and many others (Senghas 2005). It seems that another subcomponent of the 'environment' factor cluster is the distribution of speakers/signers within a community as well as the need to communicate using shared resources or not.

Wray and Grace (2007) argue that the nature of the communicative context affects the (surface) structure of language. According to these authors, esotericity allows for grammatical and semantic complexity, whereas exoteric, intergroup communication leads language towards rule-based regularity and semantic transparency. In Bolender (2007), the link between exoteric communication and enhanced linguistic complexity is related to syntax. He suggests that the increase of intergroup communication, due to population expansion, is what triggered the realization of an up to then dormant linguistic operation: syntactic movement, or, as it is now called, internal merge. We think that attention ought to be paid to such considerations, as archaeological evidence traditionally taken to point to the emergence of language goes back to periods of important demographic changes (see Mellars 2006).

Incidentally, the possibility of environmental influences on the emergence of complex aspects of language was acknowledged in Chomsky (1980: 176), when he wrote that the development of some complex structures is subject to the degree of stimulation they receive from their external environment. In his own words:

> it is entirely conceivable that some complex structures just aren't developed by a large number of people, perhaps because the degree of stimulation in their external environment isn't sufficient for them to develop. That wouldn't be too surprising. If we really look into the details of the development of this particular system we might find successive thresholds of this kind, but I would expect to find exactly the same thing in the study of any physical organ.   *(Chomsky 1980: 176)*

Finally, Deacon (2010) observes that numerous organisms delegate to their environments properties that they once encoded in their genes. Such situations arise in the context of relaxed selection. The structural aspects of language, as they grow more complex and interlinked, relax the process of selection, with its natural tendency to hone particular functional adaptations. In turn, this opens up new evolutionary spaces for the evolution of complexity. In the case of language, this relaxed selection opens up language to greater epigenetic influence and social and experiential learning. In Deacon's words, 'the relaxation of selection at the organism level may have been a source of many complex synergistic features of the human language capacity, and may help explain why so much language information is "inherited" socially'. We think that this could be the main source of what linguists call parametric variation (points of underspecification in Universal Grammar), and the seeds of change.

References

Acedo-Matellán, V. 2010. 'Argument structure and the syntax-morphology interface: A case study in Latin and other languages', unpublished PhD thesis, Universitat de Barcelona.

Baker, M. 2008. 'The macroparameter in a microparametric world', in T. Biberauer (ed.), *The Limits of Syntactic Variation*. Amsterdam: John Benjamins, pp. 351–73.

Berwick, R.C., Beckers, G.J.L., Okanoya, K. and Bolhuis, J.J. 2012. 'A bird's eye view of human language evolution', *Frontiers in Evolutionary Neuroscience* 4, doi:10.3389/fnevo.2012.00005.

Berwick, R.C. and Chomsky, N. 2011. 'The Biolinguistic Program: The current state of its development', in Di Sciullo and Boeckx (eds.), pp. 19–41.

Boeckx, C. 2011. 'Approaching parameters from below', in Di Sciullo and Boeckx (eds.), pp. 205–21.

2012. 'The emergence of the language faculty, from a biolinguistic point of view', in M. Tallerman and K. Gibson (eds.), *Oxford handbook of language evolution*. Oxford University Press, pp. 492–501.

2014a. 'What principles & parameters got wrong', in C. Picallo (ed.), *Linguistic variation and the minimalist program*. Oxford University Press, pp. 155–78.

2014b. *Elementary syntactic structures*. Cambridge University Press.

Boeckx, C. and Leivada, E. 2013. 'On the particulars of Universal Grammar: Implications for acquisition', unpublished MS, ICREA & Universitat de Barcelona.

Boeckx, C., Leivada, E. and Martins, P.T. 2013. 'Language and complexity considerations: A biolinguistic perspective', *Llengua, Societat i Comunicació* 11: 20–6.

Bolender, J. 2007. 'Prehistoric cognition by description: A Russellian approach to the upper paleolithic', *Biology and Philosophy* 22: 383–99.

Borer, H. 1984. *Parametric syntax: Case studies in Semitic and Romance languages*. Dordrecht: Foris.

Bošković, Ž. and Nunes, J. 2007. 'The copy theory of movement: A view from PF', in N. Corver and J. Nunes (eds.), *The copy theory of movement*. Amsterdam: John Benjamins, pp. 13–74.

Chomsky, N. 1980. 'Discussion of Putnam's comments', in M. Piattelli-Palmarini (ed.), *Language and learning: The debate between Jean Piaget and Noam Chomsky*. Cambridge, MA: Harvard University Press, pp. 310–24.

1981a. 'On the representation of form and function', *The Linguistic Review* 1: 3–40.

1981b. *Lectures on government and binding*. Dordrecht: Foris.

1986. *Knowledge of language: Its nature, origin and use*. New York: Praeger.

2001. 'Derivation by phase', in M. Kenstowicz (ed.), *Ken Hale: A life in language*. Cambridge, MA: MIT Press, pp. 1–52.

Deacon, T.W. 2006. 'Emergence: The hole at the wheel's hub', in P. Clayton and P. Davies (eds.), *The re-emergence of emergence: The emergentist hypothesis from science to religion*. Oxford University Press, pp. 111–50.

2010. 'A role for relaxed selection in the evolution of the language capacity', *Proceedings of the National Academy of Sciences* 107: 9000–6.

Di Sciullo, A.M. and Boeckx, C. (eds.) 2011. *The biolinguistic enterprise: New perspectives on the evolution and nature of the human language faculty.* Oxford University Press.

Fromkin, V. and Rodman, R. 1974. *An introduction to language.* New York: Holt, Rinehart and Winston.

Hale, K. and Keyser, S.J. 1993. 'On argument structure and the lexical expression of grammatical relations', in Hale and Keyser (eds.), *The view from building 20: Essays in linguistics in honor of Sylvain Bromberger.* Cambridge, MA: MIT Press, pp. 111–76.

Halle, M. and Marantz, A. 1993. 'Distributed morphology and the pieces of inflection', in Hale and Keyser (eds.), pp. 111–176.

Hinzen, W. 2006. *Mind design and minimal syntax.* Oxford University Press.

Jenks, P. 2012. 'Definite spans and blocking in classifier languages', unpublished MS, University of California, Berkeley.

Kirby, S. 2001. 'Spontaneous evolution of linguistic structure – an iterated learning model of the emergence of regularity and irregularity', *IEEE Transactions on Evolutionary Computation* 5(2): 102–10.

Kirby, S., Cornish, H. and Smith, K. 2008. 'Cumulative cultural evolution in the laboratory: An experimental approach to the origins of structure in human language', *Proceedings of the National Academy of Sciences* 105: 10681–6.

Kirby, S. and Hurford, J. 2002. 'The emergence of linguistic structure: An overview of the Iterated Learning Model', in A. Cangelosi and D. Parisi (eds.), *Simulating the evolution of language.* London: Springer, pp. 121–48.

Lewis, M.P. (ed.) 2009. *Ethnologue: Languages of the world,* 16th edn. Dallas, TX: SIL International.

Lewontin, R. 2000. *The triple helix: Gene, organism, and environment.* Cambridge, MA: Harvard University Press.

Lohndal, T. and Narita, H. 2009. 'Internalism as methodology', *Biolinguistics* 3: 321–31.

Longobardi, G. and Guardiano, C. 2009. 'Evidence for syntax as a signal of historical relatedness', *Lingua* 119: 1679–706.

Lupyan, G. and Dale, R. 2010. 'Language structure is partly determined by social structure', *PLoS ONE* 5: e8559.

Marantz, A. 1997. 'No escape from syntax: Don't try morphological analysis in the privacy of your own lexicon', in A. Dimitriadis, L. Siegel, C. Surek-Clark and A. Williams (eds.), *Proceedings of the 21st annual Penn linguistics colloquium.* Philadelphia: University of Pennsylvania, pp. 201–25.

Meir, I., Sandler, W., Padden, C. and Aronoff, M. 2010. 'Emerging sign languages', in M. Marschark and P.E. Spencer (eds.), *The Oxford handbook of deaf studies, language, and education,* vol. 2. Oxford University Press, pp. 267–80.

Mellars, P. 2006. 'Why did modern human populations disperse from Africa ca. 60,000 years ago? A new model', *Proceedings of the National Academy of Sciences* 103(25): 9381-6.

Okanoya, K. 2012. 'Behavioural factors governing song complexity in Bengalese finches', *International Journal of Comparative Psychology* 25: 44-59.

Ramchand, G. and Svenonius, P. 2008. 'Mapping a parochial lexicon onto a Universal Semantics', in T. Biberauer (ed.), *The Limits of Syntactic Variation*. Amsterdam: John Benjamins, pp. 219-45.

Real-Puigdollers, C. 2013. 'Lexicalization by phase: The role of prepositions in argument structure and its cross-linguistic variation', unpublished PhD thesis, Universitat de Barcelona.

Richards, N. 2010. *Uttering trees*. Cambridge, MA: MIT Press.

Roberts, I. and Roussou, R. 2003. *Syntactic change: A minimalist approach to grammaticalization*. Cambridge University Press.

Safir, K. 2014. One true anaphor, *Linguistic Inquiry* 45(1): 91-124.

Sandler, W., Meir, I., Dachkovsky, S., Padden, C. and Aronoff, M. 2011. 'The emergence of complexity in prosody and syntax', *Lingua* 121: 2014-33.

Scott, D.A., Carmi, R., Elbedour, K., Duyk, G.M., Stone, E.M. and Sheffield, V.C. 1995. 'Nonsyndromic autosomal recessive deafness is linked to the DFNB1 locus in a large inbred Bedouin family from Israel', *American Journal of Human Genetics* 57: 965-8.

Senghas, A. 2003. 'Intergenerational influence and ontogenetic development in the emergence of spatial grammar in Nicaraguan Sign Language', *Cognitive Development* 18: 511-31.

2005. 'Language emergence: Clues from a new Bedouin sign language', *Current Biology* 15: R463-R465.

Soma, M., Hiraiwa-Hasegawa, M. and Okanoya, K. 2009. 'Early ontogenetic effects on song quality in the Bengalese finch (*Lonchura striata* var. *domestica*): Laying order, sibling competition, and song syntax', *Behavioral Ecology and Sociobiology* 63: 363-70.

Uriagereka, J. 2008. *Syntactic anchors*. Cambridge University Press.

Washabaugh, W. 1986. *Five fingers for survival: Deaf sign language in the Caribbean*. Ann Arbor, MI: Karoma Press.

West-Eberhard, M.J. 2003. *Developmental plasticity and evolution*. Oxford University Press.

Wray, A. and Grace, G. 2007. 'The consequences of talking to strangers: Evolutionary corollaries of socio-cultural influences on linguistic form', *Lingua* 117(3): 543-78.

29

Lexical-Functional Grammar

Kersti Börjars and Nigel Vincent

29.1 Introduction

Lexical-Functional Grammar (LFG) is frequently referred to as a theory but, as Bresnan, Asudeh, Toivonen and Wechsler (2015: 39) put it: 'the formal model of LFG is *not* a syntactic theory in the linguistic sense. Rather, it is an architecture for syntactic theory. Within this architecture, there is a wide range of possible syntactic theories and sub-theories, some of which closely resemble syntactic theories within alternative architectures, and others of which differ radically from familiar approaches' (emphasis theirs). The same of course may be said for other approaches: when he launched it, Chomsky dubbed Minimalism a 'program', while Sag, Boas and Kay (2012) discuss recent developments in the domain of Construction Grammar in terms of 'research communities'. Like most of these approaches, LFG was conceived in the first place on synchronic grounds and does not contain a specific theory of linguistic change and it does not in and of itself aim to answer questions such as 'Why does language change?' or 'Does language change only at the point of first acquisition?' However, as with other approaches, the design of LFG makes it easier to state some theories of change rather than others, and as we shall show, the design principles also have implications for how historical change is captured and accounted for.

LFG is a parallel-correspondence architecture, which means that different types of linguistic information are represented separately, each with its own formal representation. The dimensions generally recognized are p(rosodic)-structure, m(orphological)-structure, c(onstituent)-structure, f(unctional)-structure, a(rgument)-structure, s(emantic)-structure and i(nformation)-structure. The different dimensions are connected by mappings which permit – even expect – non-one-to-one relations. For an excellent brief account of all dimensions and how they are connected, see Asudeh and Toivonen (2009: §5) and for more extended accounts of LFG, see Bresnan *et al.* (2015) and Dalrymple (2001). We will use c-structure and f-structure to illustrate the basic principles of LFG. C-structure is represented as category-labelled tree structures constrained by a form of X-bar syntax which may appear somewhat unconventional compared to other current implementations of the basic principles. C-structure is motivated by syntactic properties only, trees need not be either binary branching or endocentric, and functional categories are used in a restricted way. A ditransitive verb in English would, for instance, be assumed to have two sisters, as illustrated in (1a). A clause in a language like Latin, where word order is relatively free, and there are no clear arguments in favour of an articulated clause structure, would be assumed to be headed by an exocentric category S and would not contain a VP, as in (1b). Functional categories are assumed only where a functional feature is associated with a specific structural position (Kroeger 1993; Börjars, Payne and Chisarik 1999). An example is what are often referred to as verb-second languages, but which may more appropriately be called 'finite-second' languages. Here the feature [+FIN] is associated with second position, and hence a functional node I is assumed in LFG. In English, the special positional properties of finite auxiliaries provide additional motivation for an I node, as in (1c). Non-projecting categories are also permitted in c-structure (Toivonen 2003).

(1)   a.   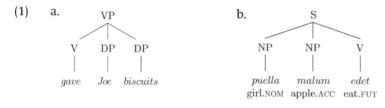   b.

   c.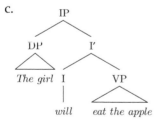

F-structure takes the shape of an unordered set of feature-value pairs. There are three types of features: grammatical relations, functional features and PRED. Grammatical relations such as SUBJ(ect), COMP (finite clausal complement) or ADJ(unct) take as their value an f-structure. In languages where information-structural functions such as TOPIC or FOCUS are identified by means of their structural position, these are part of the f-structure and are referred to as grammaticalized discourse functions. The functional features have atomic values, for example [DEF +], [ASPECT *progressive*] or [PERS 3]. PRED has a semantic value which also lists any grammatical relations required by the element, as mapped from its a-structure, for example [PRED '*meatball*'] or [PRED '*eat* ⟨SUBJ, OBJ⟩'].

Each constituent in the c-structure is linked to some f-structure, and the f-structure of a phrase is built up from the f-structures associated with its constituent parts in a monotonic fashion. In a language like English, which relies heavily on structure for identifying grammatical relations, the mapping between c-structure and f-structure links a particular structural position to a grammatical relation, for instance SUBJ is linked to the specifier of IP and the OBJ to the sister of the verb. This is captured through annotated rules as exemplified in (2a), where ↑ should be read as 'the f-structure associated with the mother node' and ↓ as 'the f-structure associated with this node', hence the annotation under DP is read as 'the f-structure associated with the mother node – that is the IP – has a feature SUBJ and the value of that feature is the f-structure associated with this node – that is the DP'. Similarly, in a language like English that has a grammaticalized sentence-initial FOCUS position – as in *Horseradish, I hate more than celery* – this would be captured through a rule such as (2b). The annotation under I′ and C′ indicates that all f-structure information is shared between the f-structure associated with the daughter and that of its mother. This is a typical head relationship.

(2)   a. IP →   DP   I′
                  (↑SUBJ) = ↓   ↑=↓

       b. CP →   DP   C′
                  (↑FOCUS) = ↓   ↑=↓

In a language where case is the main marker of grammatical relations, on the other hand, the mapping is directly between the case and the grammatical relation, without reference to the element's structural position. The equation in (3) does exactly this, and would be appropriate for Latin. It states that 'if the f-structure associated with this node contains the feature CASE with the value *nom*, then the f-structure associated with its mother node contains the feature SUBJ and the value of that feature is the f-structure associated with this node'. If the element marked as [CASE *nom*] is embedded inside an NP, then the feature and its value will also attach to the NP by means of the sharing of f-structure between a constituent and its head daughter, indicated by ↑=↓ as we saw in (2).

(3)   (↓CASE) = *nom* ⇒ (↑SUBJ) = ↓

In a similar way, a verb's subject agreement features can identify the SUBJ function in f-structure. This is illustrated in (4a), which states that if an element's *agr* features – which are features such as PERS, NUM and GEND – are identical to the features specified as a (SUBJ *agr*) feature by the verb, then that element will be the subject. A verb in a language that relies on verb agreement for the identification of grammatical relations would have a third person singular feminine verb specified as in (4b), and the verb's feature, in combination with (4a), would identify a third person singular feminine noun phrase as its subject.

(4)   a. $(\downarrow agr) = (\uparrow \text{SUBJ } agr) \Rightarrow (\uparrow \text{SUBJ}) = \downarrow$
        b. $(\uparrow \text{SUBJ PERS}) = 3$
           $(\uparrow \text{SUBJ NUM}) = sg$
           $(\uparrow \text{SUBJ GEND}) = fem$

It is of course common for case and agreement features to work in conjunction to identify a particular grammatical relation, as with the Latin SUBJ, for example. Crucially, however, structure need not play a role in identifying the SUBJ. The link from c-structure to the f-structure feature SUBJ in English and in Latin can then be illustrated as in (5).

(5)

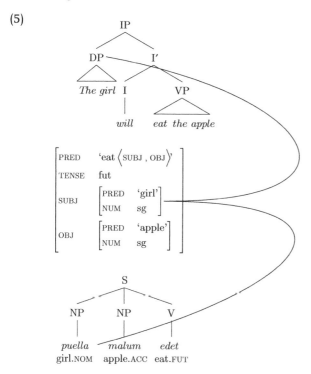

The design of the LFG architecture has a number of consequences for the analysis of historical change, since, as we noted above, different architectures more readily accommodate different accounts in the diachronic domain just as they do in synchrony. The approach to c-structure allows lexical categories that do not project. This means that the development of a category can be captured as a stepwise progression, from the emergence of a category as a set of elements with similar morphosyntactic behaviour, but with no evidence of a projection, to a category that shows the characteristics of an element that heads its own phrasal category. We shall look at just such an example in §29.2 below.

Changes to the syntactic organization of a language can be captured as changes in c-structure. A change from a flexible word order with little evidence of VPs or other headed constituents to one with evidence of constituency and headedness can be captured as a change from a relatively flat c-structure involving exocentric categories to one based on an articulated hierarchical structure. Such a change may occur without any clear changes to other dimensions, in which case the mapping principles are realigned accordingly. However, a change to clausal organization can be connected to changes in other dimensions. For instance, the history of the Germanic languages has been argued to involve a change from word order being determined to a great extent by information-structural considerations to one where syntactic constraints have a greater role (see for instance articles in Hinterhölzl and Petrova (2009) and Bech and Eide (2014) and references therein). In an LFG account, this would involve capturing the firmer syntax in the c-structure and realigning the mapping to i-structure. If information-structural roles have been grammaticalized, then the c-structure will involve rules similar to (2b). Furthermore, as the role of word order in signalling discourse organization is reduced, prosody may play a bigger role, in which case p-structure and its mappings would also need to be revised.

The separation of the different dimensions has as a logical consequence that change may happen in one dimension but not in another. This is a desirable outcome since it is well-known that changes to form and function frequently occur at different pace, so that at one stage only one or the other has changed. As Dahl (2001: 102) puts it: 'the grammaticalization process may halt for a long time, maybe several centuries. In fact, many complexities of grammar are due to such halted processes of grammaticalization.' In what follows we will provide examples of this.

29.2 Case Studies

29.2.1 Definiteness in North Germanic and the Growth of a Configurational DP

It is recognized in the literature that functional categories may develop over time, both at clausal and at noun-phrase level (e.g. Kiparsky 1995; Bošković 2008, 2009; Lander and Haegeman 2013). These analyses tend to assume that the change in the grammar is essentially a one-step process from a lexical projection to a full functional projection, in the case of the noun phrase from an NP to a DP. This is the assumption not only in analyses within the Chomskyan tradition, but van de Velde (2010: 293) within a Construction Grammar framework concludes from the fact that a D category has emerged that there is also a DP projection. LFG's approach to c-structure, on the other hand, can capture intermediate steps in this development. Börjars, Harries and Vincent (2016) use LFG to analyse the development of a DP from Old Norse to modern Faroese in terms of the emergence of a functional category combined with increased configurationality.

Old Norse had markers of definiteness, both morphological and syntactic; the different markers could co-occur and also co-occurred freely with possessive pronouns as illustrated in (6). In (6a), the free definiteness marker occurs with a noun without a bound definiteness marker, whereas in (6b), the two co-occur. In (6c) the free definiteness marker co-occurs with a demonstrative and in (6d) with a possessive pronoun. There is then at this stage no evidence of competition for one D slot.[1]

(6)   a. Inn   nýi   átrúnaðr
        DEF   new.WK   faith
        'the new faith' (ON, BN, 255:12)

     b. inna   feitu   hestanna
        DEF.PL   fat.WK.PL   horse.DEF.PL
        'the fat horses' (ON, BN, 62: 23)

     c. sá   inn   mikli   maðr
        DEM   DEF   great.WK   man
        'this great man' (ON, BN, 59:18)

     d. þessi   þinni   meðferð
        DEM   POSS.2SG   co-operation
        'your co-operation' (ON, VG 25:25)

However, an explicit marker of (in)definiteness was not required for a noun phrase to be referential. The example in (7a) occurs when the Norwegian has just been introduced, and hence the reference is definite. In (7b), on the other hand, the woman appears for the first time, and the reference is indefinite. The fact that there can be (in)definite reference without any overt marking further supports the conclusion that there is no category D and hence no DP at this stage (a conclusion also reached by Lander and Haegeman 2013).

(7)   a. Austmaðr   svarar ...
        east.man   answers
        'The Norwegian answers ... ' (ON, Gunnl 2.62)

     b. Ok   gekk   kona   fyrir   útibúrsdyrrin
        and   went   woman   in front of   outhousedoor.DEF
        'A woman passed in front of door of the outhouse.' (ON, ER, 203:25)

The only definiteness marking that is obligatory is that associated with the adjective. An adjective always carries marking for weak or strong, which largely (but not completely) corresponds with definite and

---

[1] We will only gloss for features related to definiteness here and will generally not include case or number. For explanation of the Old Norse sources, see Harries (2015: 5).

indefinite, and in addition, with a small number of exceptions, a weak adjective must be preceded by the syntactic definite element (h)*inn*. This leads Börjars, Harries and Vincent (2016) to analyse (h)*inn* as a non-projecting category which specifies adjectives, a conclusion which is in line with a number of traditional analyses of adjectives in early Germanic.

At this stage, word order within the noun phrase is syntactically quite free; demonstratives, adjectives and possessors can precede or follow the noun. Compare the examples in (8) with those in (6).

(8) a. fjǫrðinn   þenna   inn   mikla
         fjord.DEF   DEM   DEF   big.WK
         'this big fjord' (ON, GRþ, 277:3)

     b. þenna   bæ   hinn   nýja
         DEM   building   DEF   new.WK
         'this new building' (ON, LX, 68:2)

     c. skipi   sínu
         ship   his.REFL
         'his ship' (ON, LX, 5:16)

     d. andlát Gellis
         death Gellir.GEN
         'Gellir's death' (ON, LX, 229:18)

It is generally claimed for Old Norse that the neutral position of the adjective was postnominal, but that it could occur prenominally for emphasis. In (9a), the adjective *laungetna* 'illegitimate' involves a contrast with the legitimate children referred to later in the sentence. In (9b), the contrast involves two possessives. In Börjars, Harries and Vincent (2016) we argue that this is evidence of a prenominal information-structurally privileged position.

(9) a. hann   átti   **tvá**   **laungetna**   **sonu,**   Hriflu   ok
         he   had   two   illegitimate   sons,   Hfriflu   and
         Hrafn,   en   síðan
         Hrafn   and   since
         hann   kvángaðist, áttu   þau   Jófríðr   tíu   börn.
         he   married had   they   Jófríðr   ten children
         'He had two illegitimate sons, Hriflu and Hrafn, and after his marriage with Jófríðr ten children.' (ON, Egil 167.25)

     b. at   **minn**   **faðir**   væri   eptirbát   **þins**   **fǫður**
         that   POSS.1SG   father   was   after.boat   POSS.2SG   father
         'that my father trailed in the wake of yours' (ON, Gunnl 9.33)

Within LFG, freedom of word order is seen as evidence of a flat, rather than articulated hierarchical, structure, since a structural position associated with a particular information-structural status can be captured as a grammaticalized discourse function. With these assumptions, the noun phrases of Old Norse can then be represented as in (10), where Ŝ stands for 'specifier' and the circumflex indicates a non-projecting category (see Toivonen 2003), and we have used FOCUS for the information-structurally privileged position without wishing to commit to a particular approach to information-structural categories.

(10)

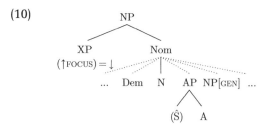

Though limited Medieval Faroese material has been preserved, some clear changes to noun phrase structure can be detected. There is still no indefinite article (11a), but for a noun phrase to have definite reference, there needs to be explicit marking. If the noun phrase consists of just a noun, this noun carries the bound definiteness marker as in (11b), but if there is a demonstrative, then the noun occurs without the definiteness marking as in (11c). The texts also provide examples of the syntactic definiteness marker *hinn* used with modifiers, as in (11d), but it can no longer co-occur with the demonstrative.

(11)   a. Ef **sauðr** gengi j   annars haga, ... (MedFa)
          if sheep goes in other's field
          'If a sheep goes into another man's field ... '
       b. Bardr Peterson war ritade **brefet**. (MedFa)
          Bardr Peterson was written letter.DEF
          'Barður Peterson had written the letter.'
       c. Nu   gengr **þessi saiðr** aptr í **þann haga** (MedFa)
          now   goes   DEM   sheep   back in DEM   pen
          'Then this sheep goes back into his pen.'
       d. hin   kærazste win (MedFa)
          DEF   dearest   friend
          'the dearest friend'

Evidence is then emerging that there is a category D, for which definite elements compete. Word order is still relatively flexible; adjectives and possessors can still occur before or after the noun. As in the earlier stage, information-structural properties play a role, but the information-structurally privileged position is less clearly marked. In LFG this can be represented as a flat structure similar to the one assumed for Old Norse in (10), but now with a category D. We further assume that at this stage, the requirement for the definiteness to be explicitly marked is not yet a structural constraint, but a featural constraint; if the noun is marked as being definite, no element of the D category is required.

(12)

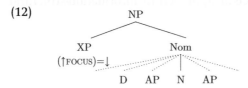

Turning now to Modern Faroese, as (13) shows, an indefinite article has developed.

(13) a. *(Ein) ungur   maður (ModFa)
          INDEF   young.STR man

      b. *(Eitt) nýtt   dagtilhald (ModFa)
          INDEF   new.STR   day.residence

When a definite noun phrase includes postmodification, definiteness marking takes the form of the bound definiteness marker, as in (14). However, when there is premodification, a syntactic definiteness marker is required, as in (15).

(14) a. borðinum,   sum høvuðspersónarnir skuldu sita við (ModFa)
          table.DEF   REL head.person.PL   would   sit   at
          'the table that the main people would sit at'
      b. maðurin   í   bilinum (ModFa)
          man.DEF   in   car.DEF
          'the man in the car'

(15) a. *(tann) hvíta   fiskin (ModFa)
          DEF   white.WK   fish.DEF

      b. *(tey) stóru   børnini (ModFa)
          DEF   big.WK.PL   CHILD.PL

What we see here is the emergence of a requirement that definiteness be marked on the left edge of the noun phrase, which means that the definiteness constraint is now structural and can be satisfied either by a definite noun or by a syntactic definite element. It is exactly this type of association between a functional feature and a structural position that motivates the assumption of a functional projection within LFG. Hence we now have evidence of a DP. Word order is firm at this point, with adjectives preceding the noun, with exceptions similar to those in English, relating to weight for instance, which means that post-modified adjectives follow the noun. Thus we assume that Faroese has an articulated structure as represented in (16).

(16)

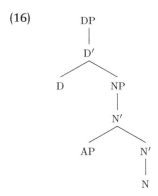

Though one can argue about the detailed interpretation of the data, there are evidently three stages to the structural development: stage 1 with no unified category D and flexible word order; stage 2 with a category D emerging and still relatively flexible word order; and stage 3 with firm word order and definiteness marking associated with a structural position. In LFG, these stages can be represented as structurally different. As the structure changes, the mapping to f-structure also changes, though the f-structure itself remains constant. In the early stages with relatively free word order, the mapping relied on case and verbal agreement, whereas in modern Faroese the mapping is structural. Similarly, the mapping between c-structure and i-structure will have changed over time.

29.2.2 Causatives in Romance and the Development of Complex Predicate Constructions

Our first case study concerned a diachronic trajectory in which the functional and informational structures remained stable over time but the c-structure and the mapping onto it changed. In this second study, by contrast, the key changes are at the level of f-structure. Although there are also changes in m-structure and c-structure they arise in the main for independent reasons.

To begin at the end, all the Romance languages, except for Daco-Romanian, have both in their modern and in their earliest attested stages a causative construction built out of the verb meaning 'do' plus an infinitive. A selection of examples is given in (17) (for more examples and more detailed philological discussion see Vincent 2016):

(17) a. Je ferai   réparer   la   voiture à   Marie. (Fr.)
          I   do.FUT.1SG repair.INF the car   to Mary
          'I will have Mary repair the car.'

      b. He   fet   veure el problema al   director. (Cat.)
          have.PRS.1SG make.PST.PTCP see.INF the problem   to.the director
          'I made the director see the problem.'

      c. Il professore glielo   fa   leggere. (It.)
          the teacher   he.DAT.SG=it.ACC.SG= do.PRS.3SG read.INF
          'The teacher makes him read it.'

    d. Faz   tomar   grave   vindita (OPt.)
       do.PRS.3SG take.INF harsh   revenge
       'he makes (them) take harsh revenge/harsh revenge be taken'
    e. ... fichili   chamari (OSic.)
         do.PST.3SG=they.ACC.PL call.INF
       'he had them summoned'

A variety of tests show that these structures are monoclausal and constitute a complex predicate construction with the light 'do' verb (*faire, fare*, etc.) combining with a lexical infinitive. Thus, if the arguments are pronominal they must cliticize to the 'do' verb (as in 17c, e). If the infinitival verb is intransitive (either unergative or unaccusative), then its subject occupies the object position directly after the verb as in (17d). If the infinitival verb is transitive, which implies that this object slot is already occupied, then its subject is marked with the preposition *a/à* 'to', that is to say the marker which would be usual for an indirect object (17a, b), or the relevant clitic is dative (17c). In addition, structures such as these cannot be iterated in contrast to the biclausal English causative in an example such as *Bill made his son make the dog stop barking.*

    Complex predicate constructions like this are a good example of a structure that is better handled in a constraint-based framework such as LFG, where the light verb contributes the theta-role of the subject and the infinitive those of the direct and indirect objects without recourse either to syntactic movement or to an otherwise unmotivated functional head (Abeillé and Godard 2010; Butt 2010). The contents of a-structure gets mapped to f-structure (for details, see Lexical Mapping Theory in, for instance, Dalrymple 2001), which in turn maps to c-structure as illustrated in (18), which represents example (17a).

(18)

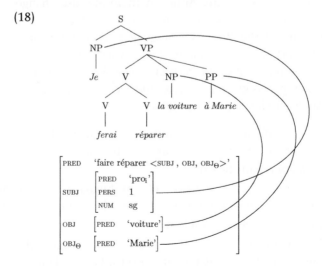

This structure shows the surface organization of the clause with a complex verb head and three associated arguments. That the OBJ$_\theta$ in a structure of this kind has the semantic value of causee is determined by the mapping between the f-structure and the a-structure (for details of one mechanism by which this may be achieved, see Alsina 1996: ch.6).

When we track the origins of this construction back to Latin we encounter structures that at first sight look very similar such as the examples in (19):

(19) a. ventus   ... fecit   ... spissescere   nubem
          wind.NOM.SG   make.PFV.3SG   thicken.INF   cloud.ACC.SG
          'the wind caused the cloud to thicken' (Lucretius 6.176)

      b. hoc   me   ... telum   flere   facit
          this.NOM.SG   me.ACC.SG   dart.NOM.SG   cry.INF   make.PRS.3SG
          facietque   diu
          make.FUT.3SG=and   long time
          'this dart makes me cry and will make me cry for a long time' (Ov. *Met.* 7.690–1)

      c. purpureamque   uvam   facit   albam   pampinum
          purple.ACC=and   grape.ACC   make.PRS.3SG   white.ACC   vine shoot.ACC
          habere
          have.INF
          'and it (the sun) causes the pale vine-shoot to have purple grapes' (Lucilius 1224, trans. Warmington)

      d. quae   faciunt   ignis   interstingui   atque
          REL.NOM.PL   do.PRS.3PL   fire.ACC.PL   extinguish.INF.PASS   and
          perire
          go.out.INF.ACT
          'which (places) cause the fires to be extinguished and go out' (Lucretius 5.761)

Yet, the Latin pattern here is clearly biclausal as witnessed by the fact the complement clause has an independent subject marked with the accusative case (*nubem* in (19a), *me* in (19b), *albam pampinum* in (19c), *ignis* in (19d)). If the infinitival verb is transitive, as in (19c), then there will be a second accusative to mark its object *purpureamque uvam*, just as with any main clause object. In addition, the infinitival verb can bear its own voice marking as seen with the conjoined passive and active infinitives in (19d). In short, the examples in (19) are instances of the well attested Latin accusative and infinitive construction, in which the embedded accusative subject is the result of a clause internal case assignment rule as proposed in Jøhndal (2012), which overrides the normal main clause rule assigning nominative to the subject as set out in (3). The relevant c- to f-structure mapping is shown in (20), which depicts example (19c):

(20)

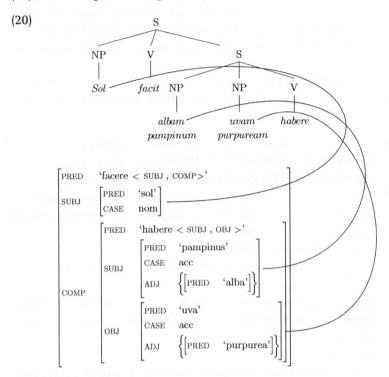

When we compare the structures in (18) and (20) we see that at the semantic level we have continuity: there is on the one hand a main verb expressing causation and introducing as its subject argument the semantic role of agent and causer and on the other a dependent infinitival verb with its own argument structure expressing as appropriate the agent, patient or experiencer of the caused action or state. The difference lies in the point at which the arguments are combined: in Latin this is a consequence of one clause serving as the c-structure complement of the causative predicate which is situated in a higher clause, whereas in Romance the arguments are combined into a derived lexical item within a single clause. Moreover, the verb is the same lexical item – Latin *facere* and its Romance reflexes *faire, fare, hacer, fer*, etc. – despite its having undergone a range of locally different phonological and morphological changes. This is consistent with the claim by Butt and Lahiri (2013) that light verbs, despite having developed into new constructions such as the one exemplified in (17), continue to be linked with their associated lexical verbs. This fact in turn argues for the basic transitive uses such as *Piero ha fatto il pane* 'Piero made the bread' (It.) to be connected to the use in a complex predicate construction via a single underspecified semantic representation (Butt 2010). Nonetheless, at the morphosyntactic level there has been a reorganization as is evidenced in the different ways the f-structures and c-structures are linked in the representations in (18) and (20). This new mapping is what defines the emergent causative construction.

There are of course also differences between the c-structures in these two examples, but these are independently motivated and apply outside the specific contexts of the complex predicate construction. Thus, as noted in §29.1, Latin exhibits flat clause structure without a VP node or an I head, whereas the Romance languages have developed a more configurational syntax both in simple and complex sentences (Ledgeway 2012). Similarly, the consistent head-initial word order of Romance is also evidenced here in the sequence *faire/fare* + V_{INF} rather than the free ordering between these elements which is to be seen in the Latin examples in (19). And as new paradigmatic structures emerge such as periphrastic perfects, these too apply to the causative construction as much as they do elsewhere: see for example (17b).

Note finally that this new causative, which emerges in the sixth or seventh century AD, is itself diachronically stable, and has remained mono-clausal up to the modern day in Catalan and in Italian and many Italo-Romance dialects (although in Spanish and French there is some evidence of a tendency to revert to a biclausal structure; see Vincent (2016) and references therein). This is in contrast to the gradual semantic and syntactic development that temporal and aspectual auxiliaries display over time, and is consistent with the arguments advanced by Butt and Lahiri (2013) that the creation of a complex predicate is different in kind from the standard grammaticalization mechanism which yields auxiliaries (see Chapter 1, this volume). If the latter process is to be characterized via the growth of functional heads, as many have argued and as seems correct, it is a point in favour of the LFG account that such a mechanism is not required here. This formal difference in the synchronic analysis of light verbs and auxiliaries then corresponds to a difference in the diachronic profile.

29.2.3 Pronouns to Copulas and Lateral Grammaticalization

Our third case study represents a qualitatively different kind of development from the previous two. In Faroese we saw how the marking of the typically nominal category of definiteness emerged, whereas the Romance example showed the emergence of a structure marking the typically verbal category of causativity. Here, instead, we see a different development in which a marker in the nominal domain appears to shift sideways into the verbal domain, hence the label 'lateral grammaticalization' which has been given to this type of change (Simpson and Wu 2002). The relevance of this phenomenon for contemporary theories of change was first discussed by Li and Thompson (1977) who pointed out that the modern Chinese copula *shì* exemplified in (21a) derives from a demonstrative in Archaic Chinese, as in (21b):

(21) a. nèi-ge   rén   **shì**   xuéshēng (ModCh.)
          that-CLASS man   be   student
          'that man is a student'

      b. **shì** yè   yě   zhaò-mèn jī   zǐ-xī míng (Arch.Ch.)
          this   night PART zhao-men and zi-xi ally
          'this night, Zhao-men and Zi-xi formed an alliance' (*Zhuǒ Zhuàn*,
          sixth century BC)

The crucial context for reanalysis is a topic-comment structure like (22), in which either the copula interpretation, the only one permitted in the modern language, or the demonstrative interpretation is possible.

(22)   zhī   ér   shǐ   zhǐ   **shì** bù   rèn   yě
        know   then   use   him   this   not   kind   PART
        'to use him knowing (that he would rebel), that was unkind' (Ch.,
        Mencius, fourth century BC)

This shift is by no means unique to Chinese. Li and Thompson go on to observe similar developments in a number of Semitic languages, including Hebrew, Palestinian Arabic and the Ethiopian language Zway, as well as in the Californian language Wappo. Further instances from Iranian languages are adduced by Korn (2011), so what we have here is a change which recurs across a number of periods and language families in a way that is reminiscent of those changes that have been extensively discussed in the grammaticalization literature. Indeed, as we have seen, it is often referred to as a sub-type of grammaticalization although strictly speaking this label is inappropriate since it is not clear that the input to the change is any less grammatical than the outcome (see the discussion of secondary grammaticalization in §2.3).

It is generally agreed, following Li and Thompson's original insight, that the categorial change here betokens a larger move from a Topic–Comment to a Subject–Predicate organization of the clause, as shown in (23), where we assume that on the demonstrative reading the item *shì* constitutes the head of a DP:

(23)   zhī   ér shǐ zhǐ   shì   bù rèn ye
        topic   DP   comment
                             ∨
        subject   V_cop   predicate

The question is how to model such a development, which in LFG terms involves changes at both f-structure and c-structure. The earlier stage can be accommodated if we assume that *shì* fulfils the function of SUBJ of the comment part of the clause, and is linked to the topic by a functional equation of the form ↑TOPIC = ↑SUBJ. When it comes to the remainder of the comment, there are, as Nordlinger and Sadler (2007) demonstrate, two possible analyses for such an overtly verbless pattern, corresponding to two different typological groups of languages. We adopt here the analysis which they dub 'single-tier' and which constitutes in their words 'the default hypothesis for verbless clauses cross-linguistically'. This involves an f-structure in which there is no verbal element at any level and the requirement for a clausal subject is straightforwardly stated as part of the PRED value of the adjective: [PRED '*rèn* ⟨SUBJ⟩']. Crucially, on this account since there is no covert 'be' verb as part of the c-structure of the clause, the change to the modern structure involves the emergence of a new copular element with its own PRED value: [PRED '*shì* ⟨SUBJ⟩'] and its own place under a V head within the clause. Thus, in a different context and with different ingredients, we observe a similar phenomenon of syntax 'growing' as we saw in the case of the Nordic NP/DP.

A further development attested in some northern Mandarin dialects is to be seen in what Simpson and Wu (2002) call the *shi-de* construction exemplified in (24):[2]

(24)   a.   wo   shi   zuotian   mai   piao   de (ModCh.)
             I   be   yesterday buy   ticket DE
             'It was yesterday that I bought the ticket'
       b.   wo   shi   zuotian   mai   de   piao (Northern Mandarin)
             I   be   yesterday buy   DE   ticket
             'It was yesterday that I bought the ticket'

In the standard language, sentences (24a) and (24b) are alternative ways of constructing a cleft sentence using the nominalizing particle *de*, which Simpson and Wu analyse as a D head. In the northern dialects, however, the version (24b), in which *de* occurs next to and cliticized onto the copula *shi*, is now associated with the past temporal meaning of the phrase, and thus on their account has changed category from D to T. In the broader context of the typology of such changes, this is striking because, as Li and Thompson (1977: 131) had already noted, the copulas that emerge in this way are not typically verb-like insofar as they tend not to inflect for tense or aspect even when they occur in languages where such inflections are to be found. What the *shi-de* example shows, then, is that the copula *shì* in the relevant dialects is becoming more verb-like in its behaviour. Within the Minimalist model that Wu and Simpson assume, the only way for a change like this to be represented is categorially via the postulation of the functional heads D and T. In similar vein, van Gelderen (2011: ch. 4) also argues for an account of the determiner-to-copula shift based on syntactic heads. At the same time, Wu and Simpson (2002: 199) are surely right to observe that the motivation behind the shift is to be sought not in the categorial status of the item involved but in its semantic content and thus constitutes an instance of 'a functional element with a basic deictic orientation from

---

[2] We follow here Simpson and Wu, who, unlike Li and Thompson, refrain from marking the tones in the examples they cite.

one domain effectively just reapplying its underlying deictic/referential function in/to a new second type of domain'. In LFG, properties such as definiteness and tense are located within the f-structure, so that the change in question becomes one of realignment of the relevant feature from the verbal to the nominal part of the clause, but with no need to postulate any intermediate and otherwise unmotivated categorial bearer of that feature.

Given the reapplication of featural content from one domain to another that Wu and Simpson posit, it is natural to ask whether the change could go in the other direction with a former copula coming to assume a pronominal value. Some possible cases of this kind are proposed by Korn (2011). For example the Northwest Iranian language Laki has a second-person plural clitic pronoun *-ino(n)* whose source seems to be the verbal ending *-in(o)*, and Western Iranian varieties that have a first-person singular clitic *-n* also display a homophonous verbal ending for the same person. The philological details of the argument are complex and cannot readily be summarized here but in her words: 'If the interpretations suggested above are correct, Iranian would present evidence for both the change of pronouns to copula and of copula / verbal ending to pronominal clitic' (Korn 2011: 67). The fact that this kind of change can go in both directions is consistent with Simpson and Wu's designation of 'lateral' for this phenomenon and marks it out as being rather different in kind from the types of change in which the shift is from a lexical category such as N or V to a grammatical one such as P or T. We return to the question of how formally to model grammaticalization in the next section.

29.3 Conclusion and Comparison

So far, then, we have considered three different types of morphosyntactic change and have demonstrated how they would be handled within LFG, at the same time making occasional comments about the differences between the LFG account and others that have been offered of the same or similar material. By way of conclusion, let us now attempt a more systematic comparison of different approaches in respect of a number of general issues that have emerged in the literature on diachronic morphosyntax over the years (see also for more detailed discussion of some of these points Vincent 2001). In order to do so we adopt the classification proposed by Francis and Michaelis (2003), who divide grammatical models into three broad classes: (a) derivational (for example, minimalism), (b) licensing (for example, Construction Grammar) and (c) level-mapping. LFG is an instance of this third category in which, as we have seen, each level of structure is expressed in terms of its own primitive notions and the relations between the levels are stated in terms of correspondences. One immediate benefit of such an approach is that no one level is privileged above all others, either synchronically or diachronically. In particular, syntax is a dimension of its own that interacts with and links to morphology and information structure but there is no compulsion to represent every property of a phrase or clause in syntactic terms, and hence no need to proliferate either functional heads or empty categories, nor to model morphology in syntactic terms as happens with Distributed Morphology. LFG's move away from a universal configurationality of structure and its consequences for change are particularly evident in our examples here of the Nordic noun phrase and the Chinese pronoun-to-copula shift.

By contrast, as we have seen, a core role is played by f-structure and this implicitly raises the issue of the unfortunately polyvalent term 'functional'. Within LFG the term is used both in the sense of a grammatical function such as SUBJ, COMP and TOPIC and that of a mathematical function, which is what defines the formal operations within the model that apply both to grammatical functions and to features such as tense and definiteness. Crucially, however, it does not imply 'functionalist' in the sense of explanations for change that appeal to external factors of language processing and use (for which see Chapter 31, this volume). Rather, LFG is neutral on this question and thus demonstrates the misplaced nature of the debate to be found in the literature on formalist vs functionalist approaches to language and language change. LFG is a formal system in the mathematical sense of that term and can, but does not have to, be deployed as part of a functionalist explanation for a given change such as the one standardly advanced for the shift from topic–comment to subject–predicate structure in the history of Chinese.

Such differences come clearly to the fore when we consider the historical phenomenon of grammaticalization in which, as is well known, shifts tend to be from lexical to grammatical rather than vice versa (see Chapter 1, this volume). Within a derivational framework, this directionality has been claimed to follow from the fact that grammaticalization involves an upward path from the lexical to the functional layers of the clause, while a corresponding downward movement is ruled out by the principles of Universal Grammar (Roberts and Roussou 2003: 205–9; see also §1.3.1); hence the apparently exceptional nature of a 'lateral' shift from D to T or vice versa. There is no equivalent notion of structural directionality within LFG, and in consequence such preferred patterns have to be ascribed to external properties of human cognition and of language in use, as in much of the existing literature on the topic (see Börjars and Vincent 2011 for a review). At the same time the detail of the stages in the grammaticalization process can be straightforwardly modelled through gradually accumulating modifications in the entries of the lexical items, which, as the name of the framework implies, are a key component. This may well involve the postulation of emergent functional heads, but crucially only when there is evidence that such positions are overtly realized, and, as we saw with the Romance causatives, lexical entries may change without the item in question starting off down a grammaticalization path.

One aspect of grammaticalization processes in particular and language change in general which is especially compatible with a framework like LFG is the way changes proceed at different paces within different domains of language so that form–function mismatch is a common outcome. For example, Börjars and Burridge (2011) show how the Pennsylvania German element *fer*, cognate with English *for*, has retained the categorial status and structural position of a complementizer while its function has changed from a purposive marker to that of a semantically bland infinitival marker. Similarly, the Romance verbs *faire/fare*/etc. retain many of the properties of the full lexical verb while serving the causative function and do not need to be analysed as having moved to an appropriate functional head. In addition, there are many instances in the literature where an item can retain a degree of syntactic independence in one language while having become fully morphologized in a sister language. For example, the Romance adverbial suffix *-ment/mente*, which derives from Latin *mente* 'mind.ABL.SG', is a simple derivational suffix in French and Italian but in Spanish behaves like a nominal head in co-ordinated structures, hence the contrast between Spanish *ni política ni económicamente* lit. 'neither political nor economically' and Italian *né politicamente né economicamente* 'neither politically nor economically'. In this respect LFG is different on the one hand from derivational models in which form–function parallelism is retained through the postulation of additional, and frequently covert, syntactic heads, and on the other from an approach such as Construction Grammar, which is built around the notion that constructions involve a link between form and function somewhat along the lines of the Saussurean conception of the linguistic sign (Closs Traugott and Trousdale 2013: 4). The intrinsic link between form and function that such a conceptualization implies is belied by the evidence of change and suggests that level-mapping models such as LFG, which allow the different levels of language to work in their own terms and at their own diachronic speeds, are to be preferred.

In the recent literature, and particularly in the work of van Gelderen (2011, 2014), the cross-linguistically recurrent grammaticalization paths have come to be known as cycles (for full discussion, see also Chapter 22, this volume). The term itself is misleading since it seems to imply a change which returns to the point of origin, as with cyclical processes in the natural world. While this may be a plausible assumption in the case of negation, where it is reasonable to assume that all languages have to have a means of expressing negation so that if one falls out of use, for instance as a consequence of sound change, another item will come to serve the same function (see §22.2.1). However, this argument cannot be extended to domains like tense, aspect, definiteness and the like where languages differ in their grammatical inventories and where whole subdomains such as tense or definiteness may go unexpressed in the grammar. In van Gelderen's work, the driving force behind the changes she discusses are the so-called economy principles (see §22.4), which are argued to guide learners and which determine a preference for example for them to postulate heads rather than full phrases in contexts where there is no evidence to the contrary. This in turn may lead items that start life as specifiers to develop into heads and thus to start off on a grammaticalization path. This line of thought continues the long tradition of work within the Chomskyan framework that sees language acquisition as the principal locus of change (see Chapters 6, 7, 15, 18, 24 and 27, this volume). Here is not the place for a detailed critique of this approach but it is important, in concluding, to underline the point we made in our introduction, namely that a framework like LFG does not have any such inbuilt principles, and is therefore open to explanations both deriving from acquisition and to those that emerge from the mounting body of evidence for change as driven by contact (see Chapter 8, this volume) and other external factors, or conversely by the view that an important locus of change is indeed at the point of acquisition but that the conditioning factors are external and depend on things like frequency in context rather than any inherent and innate properties of the language faculty (see Chapters 25 and 26, this volume). The exact balance between such factors remains of course a matter of ongoing investigation (for discussion, see also Chapter 23, this volume).

References

Abeillé, A. and Godard, D. 2010. 'Complex predicates in the Romance languages', in D. Godard (ed.), *Fundamental issues in the Romance languages*. Stanford, CA: CSLI Publications, pp. 107–70.

Alsina, A. 1996. *The role of argument structure in grammar: Evidence from Romance*. Stanford, CA: CSLI Publications.

Asudeh, A. and Toivonen, I. 2009. 'Lexical-functional grammar', in Heine and Narrog (eds.), pp. 425–58.

Bech, K. and Eide, K. G. 2014. *Information structure and syntactic change in Germanic and Romance languages*. Amsterdam: John Benjamins.

Börjars, K. and Burridge, K. 2011. 'From preposition to purposive to infinitival marker: The Pennsylvania German *fer … zu* construction', in M. T. Putnam (ed.), *Studies on German-language islands*. Amsterdam: John Benjamins, pp. 385–411.

Börjars, K., Payne, J. and Chisarik, E. 1999. 'On the justification for functional categories in LFG', in M. Butt and T. Holloway King (eds.), *Proceedings of the LFG99 conference*. Stanford, CA: CSLI Publications. Available at: http://web.stanford.edu/group/cslipublications/cslipublications/LFG/LFG4-1999/.

Börjars, K., Harries, P. and Vincent, N. 2016. 'Growing syntax: The development of a DP in North Germanic', *Language* 92: e1–e37.

Börjars, K. and Vincent, N. 2011. 'Grammaticalization and directionality', in Heine and Narrog (eds.), pp. 163–76.

Bošković, Ž. 2008. 'What will you have, DP or NP?', in E. Elfner and M. Walkow (eds.), *Proceedings of the North Eastern Linguistic Society meeting 37*, vol. 1. Amherst, MA: GLSA, pp. 101–14.

2009. 'More on the no-DP analysis of article-less languages', *Studia Linguistica* 63(2): 187–203.

Bresnan, J., Asudeh, A., Toivonen, I. and Wechsler, S. 2015. *Lexical-functional syntax*, 2nd edn. Oxford: Wiley: Blackwell.

Butt, M. 2010. 'The light verb jungle: Still hacking away', in M. Amberber, B. Baker and M. Harvey (eds.), *Complex predicates: Cross-linguistic perspectives on event structure*. Cambridge University Press, pp. 48–78.

Butt, M. and Lahiri, A. 2013. 'Diachronic pertinacity of light verbs', *Lingua* 135: 7–29.

Dahl, Ö. 2001. 'Grammaticalization and the life cycles of constructions', *RASK – Internationalt Tidsskrift for Sprog og Kommunikation* 14: 91–134.

Dalrymple, M. 2001. *Lexical functional grammar*. New York: Academic Press.

Francis, E. J. and. Michaelis, L. A. 2003. 'Mismatch: A crucible for linguistic theory', in E. J. Francis and L. A. Michaelis (eds.), *Mismatch: Form-function incongruity and the architecture of grammar*. Stanford, CA: CSLI Publications, pp. 1–27.

Harries, P. 2015. 'The distribution of definiteness markers and the growth of syntactic structure from Old Norse to Modern Faroese', unpublished PhD thesis, University of Manchester.

Heine, B. and Narrog, H. (eds.), *The Oxford handbook of linguistic analysis*. Oxford University Press.

Hinterhölzl, R. and Petrova, S. (eds.) 2009. *Information structure and language change*. Berlin: Mouton de Gruyter.

Jøhndal, M. 2012. 'Non-finiteness in Latin', unpublished PhD thesis, University of Cambridge.

Kiparsky, P. 1995. 'Indo-European origins of Germanic syntax', in I. Roberts and A. Battye (eds.), *Clause structure and language change*. Oxford University Press, pp. 140–67.

Korn, A. 2011. 'Pronouns as verbs, verbs as pronouns: Demonstratives and the copula in Iranian', in A. Korn, G. Haig, S. Karimi and P. Samvelian (eds.), *Topics in Iranian linguistics*. Wiesbaden: Ludwig Reichert, pp. 53–70.

Kroeger, P. R. 1993. *Phrase structure and grammatical relations in Tagalog*. Stanford, CA: CSLI Publications.

Lander, E. and Haegeman, L. 2013. 'ON as an NP language, with observations on the common Norse and Northwest Germanic Runic inscriptions', *Transactions of the Philological Society* 111: 1–40.

Ledgeway, A. 2012. *From Latin to Romance: Morphosyntactic typology and change.* Cambridge University Press.

Li, Ch. N. and Thompson, S.A. 1977. 'A mechanism for the development of copula morphemes', in Ch. N. Li (ed.), *Mechanisms of syntactic change.* Austin: University of Texas Press, pp. 419–45.

Nordlinger, R. and Sadler, L. 2007. 'Verbless clauses: Revealing the structure within', in A. Zaenen (ed.), *Architectures, rules, and preferences: Variations on themes by Joan W. Bresnan.* Stanford: CSLI, pp. 139–60.

Roberts, I. and Roussou, A. 2003. *Syntactic change: A Minimalist approach to grammaticalization.* Cambridge University Press.

Sag, I., Boas, H. and Kay, P. 2012. 'Introducing sign-based construction grammar', in H. Boas and I. Sag (eds.), *Sign-Based construction grammar.* Stanford, CA: CSLI Publications, pp. 1–29.

Simpson, A. and Wu, Z. 2002. 'From D to T: Determiner incorporation and the creation of tense', *Journal of East Asian Linguistics* 11: 169–209.

Toivonen, I. 2003. *Non-projecting words: A case study of Swedish particles.* Dordrecht: Kluwer.

Traugott, E. C. and Trousdale, G. 2013. *Constructionalization and constructional changes.* Oxford University Press.

van de Velde, F. 2010. 'The emergence of the determiner in the Dutch NP', *Linguistics* 48: 263–99.

van Gelderen, E. 2011. *The linguistic cycle: Language change and the language faculty.* Oxford University Press.

2014. 'Generative syntax and language change', in C. Bowern and B. Evans (eds.), *The Routledge handbook of historical linguistics.* London: Routledge, pp. 326–42.

Vincent, N. 2001. 'LFG as a model of syntactic change', in M. Butt and T. Holloway King (eds.), *Time over matter: Diachronic perspectives on morphosyntax.* Stanford, CA: CSLI, pp. 1–42.

2016. 'Causatives in Latin and Romance', in J. Adams and N. Vincent (eds.), *Early and late Latin: Continuity or change?* Cambridge University Press, pp. 294–312.

30

Typological Approaches

Sonia Cristofaro and Paolo Ramat

30.1 Introduction

Diachrony is at the theoretical core of the typological approach that developed from the work of Joseph Greenberg. In this approach, the cross-linguistic distribution of grammatical properties, which represents the primary object of linguistic investigation, is the combined result of diachronic processes that lead to the development of the relevant constructions in particular languages and processes of transmission whereby these properties are passed on from one speaker to another over time, both during language acquisition and through sociohistorical mechanisms leading to the conventionalization of these constructions in the language (see, for example, Greenberg 1978, 1995; Bybee 1988, 2006, 2008; Newmeyer 1998, 2002, 2005; Croft 2000; Dryer 2006b). In principle, then, the study of syntactic change and language change in general is crucial to the typological approach, both in the sense that it sheds light on the principles that lead speakers to create the constructions described by typological generalizations in the first place (Bybee 1988, 2006, 2008; Aristar 1991; Dryer 2006b) and in the sense that it sheds light on the factors that determine the cross-linguistic distribution of these constructions (such as, for example, transition probabilities from one language type to another: see among others Nichols 1992; Maslova 2000; Bickel 2007).

In practice, however, typological investigations of syntactic change and language change in general have been relatively unsystematic to date. Over the past decades, several large-scale cross-linguistically oriented studies of syntactic change have been produced within the grammaticalization framework (see Chapter 1, this volume) and historical linguistics in general, for example, Heine, Claudi and Hünnemeyer (1991), Harris and Campbell (1995), Gildea (1998), Hopper and Traugott (2003) and Hendery (2012). More and more studies of syntactic change in individual languages or language families also adopt a typological perspective, and there has been renewed interest in the interaction between synchronic variation (both intralinguistic and cross-linguistic) and language change, as witnessed, for example, by several edited volumes in the Benjamins series Studies in Language Companion and Typological Studies in Language (Seoane and Lopez-Couso 2008; Givón and Shibatani 2009; Yap, Grunow-Hasta and Wrona 2011; Davidse, Breban, Brems and Mortelmans 2012; Giacalone Ramat, Mauri and Molinelli 2013; van Gelderen, Barðdal and Cennamo 2013; Viti 2015). In spite of this, the explanatory generalizations proposed for typological universals are still usually based on synchronic, rather than diachronic, data. This is probably partly due to the fact that, while there are a number of recurrent cross-linguistic patterns that are easily captured at the synchronic level, detailed diachronic data for these patterns are often unavailable for many of the (sometimes sketchily described) languages usually included in typological studies. As a result, in spite of the theoretical evidence placed on diachrony, typological studies have mainly remained synchronically oriented.

Furthermore, the typological approach has never developed a specific theory of either syntactic change or syntax in general. Rather, the attitude of typologists towards these topics has always been rather heterogeneous, and there is widespread agreement that syntactic patterns and syntactic change can be accounted for in whatever terms seem appropriate. Typological descriptions and explanations are often based on categories and concepts originally developed within traditional grammar and historical linguistics, rather than within the typological approach itself (see, among others, Dryer 2006b; Nichols 2007).

This is in contrast with formally oriented theories of grammar, particularly theories specifically addressing the cross-linguistic patterns identified by typological research, such as Optimality Theory. In these theories, the ultimate explanation for individual syntactic patterns lies in a speaker's mental representation of the grammar of their language, which includes a number of constraints leading speakers to produce precisely the relevant constructions (see, for example, Aissen's 2003 model of differential object marking). This implies that any explanatory theory of syntax should provide a model of a speaker's mental grammar, and how this grammar is altered when a syntactic change takes place. Such a model, however, is unnecessary in the typological approach, because syntactic patterns are ultimately explained in terms of principles that lead speakers to create particular constructions diachronically, but need not play any role in a speaker's synchronic production and use of these constructions once they are part of the language. These principles, then, need not be part of a speaker's mental grammar (Newmeyer 1998, 2002, 2004, 2005; Dryer 2006b; Cristofaro 2011).

For example, several cross-linguistic word-order correlations have been related in the typological literature either to various principles pertaining to processing ease, or to the fact that the relevant constructions develop from one another and maintain the same word order throughout the process. In particular, the latter explanation has been proposed to account for the correlation between the order of adposition and noun and that of possessor and possessed item (Bybee 1988; Aristar 1991; more on this in §30.3), that is, prepositions and postposed possessors, as illustrated by English constructions such as *the President of the United States*, and postpositions and preposed possessors, as illustrated by the German examples in (1):

(1)   German
      a. Gottes   Wort
         God.GEN   word
         'God's word'
      b. des   Vaters   wegen
         the.GEN   father.GEN   because
         'because of the father'

In discussing this correlation, Dryer (2006b; see also Newmeyer 1998) argues that, once the relevant constructions become established in a language, a speaker's production of these constructions is a result of the conventions of the language and the inferences that children make from input sentences during the learning process, not processing ease or the factors originally leading to the reinterpretation of the source constructions.

Syntactic change, however, has been investigated in typology with regard to two major issues. First, it has been assumed that the results of cross-linguistic investigation can contribute to a general theory of language change, including syntactic change, in that they point to universally valid constraints and motivations for possible changes. Second, some typologists, most notably Bybee (1988, 2006, 2008; see also Aristar 1991), have raised the point that the actual processes of change that lead to the patterns described by typological universals (particularly word-order patterns) suggest alternative explanations for these universals to those traditionally proposed on synchronic grounds. In what follows, a critical assessment of these two perspectives will be provided, and some distinctive features and theoretical implications of typological treatments of syntactic change will be discussed.

30.2   Constraints and Motivations for Syntactic Change

While diachronic syntax has never been a central focus of investigation in typology, there has always been a general idea in the field that the study of cross-linguistic syntactic patterns can provide crucial insights into syntactic change, both with regards to what types of syntactic change are possible or more frequent in the world's languages, and with regards to why syntactic change happens in the first place.

A first manifestation of this idea is an assumption that the patterns described by typological universals, particularly implicational ones, point to both constraints on and motivations for possible changes. Typological universals are empirically established generalizations that capture the fact that certain logically possible language types are attested with statistically significant frequency, while others are rare or (in a limiting and less frequent case) unattested. Such skewed distributions suggest that there should not be changes leading to patterns that are unattested or rare at the synchronic level. Also, the fact that certain types are significantly more frequent than others has been taken as evidence that there are general language preferences for those types, while unattested or rare types are dispreferred. These preferences are assumed to motivate possible changes from one type to another, either in the sense that languages will evolve from one preferred type to another, or in the sense that changes can be triggered by the need for a language to shift from a dispreferred to a preferred type.

This view, which goes back to Greenberg's own work (see, for example, Greenberg 1963, 1978), is particularly apparent in John Hawkins's work on word order. For example, Hawkins (1990: 97–9) observes that, given Greenberg's (1966) universal VSO → Prepositions, no language can arise that has VSO order and postpositions, because this pattern is ruled out by the universal. Implicational universals such as this one also constrain the sequence of possible changes. Given an implication of the type A → B, A and B may be present in a language from the beginning, or they can develop later in the evolution of the language. In the latter case, however, A and B can develop simultaneously, or B can develop before A, but it is not possible for A to develop before B, because this would lead to the type A → ~ B, which is ruled out by the universal. For example, if a language has no VSO order and no prepositions, it can develop the two simultaneously, or prepositions can develop before VSO order, but VSO order cannot develop before prepositions, because this would lead to the type VSO → ~ Prepositions, which is ruled out by Greenberg's universal.

On a similar note, Hawkins (1990: 102) argues that, given Greenberg's (1966) universal SOV/OVS → Case, if phonological processes erode the case system of an SOV language, then this provides a motivation for the language shifting from SOV to SVO, because languages with SVO and case are allowed by the universal. It is worth noting that this analysis assumes that the triggering factors for the relevant syntactic changes are non-syntactic, for example language contact or phonological change. This is a natural consequence of the idea that the types predicted by a universal

reflect general preferences for those types. This implies that these preferences should not be violated, so, if they are, this is assumed to be an
accidental result of factors independent of the grammar of the language,
such as language contact or phonological erosion.

The idea that syntactic change is triggered by the need for
a language to evolve from dispreferred to preferred types, as defined
by typological universals, is also inherent in Hawkins' (1994, 2004)
Early Immediate Constituents principle. This principle is based on an
assumption that languages prefer those types of word order that allow
faster recognition of the constituent structure of the sentence. This is
the case, for example, with prepositions in a VO language and postpositions in an OV language, because these combinations make it
possible to minimize the amount of words needed in order to construe
the immediate constituents of the verbal phrase (see Dryer 1992 and
Hawkins 1994 for details). Hence Hawkins argues that word-order
types that do not optimize immediate constituent recognition will be
diachronically unstable and evolve into types where recognition is
optimized.

Explanations in terms of preferred language types are goal-oriented,
in the sense that syntactic change is assumed to be triggered by some
need for the language to develop the relevant constructions (for example, because in this way it will comply with some assumed principle of
optimization of grammatical structure). These explanations, however,
have mainly been proposed on synchronic grounds, that is, based on the
synchronic cross-linguistic distribution of particular syntactic patterns,
rather than the actual diachronic processes that give rise to these
patterns. Another strand of typologically oriented research on syntactic
change, mainly carried out within the grammaticalization framework,
has concentrated instead on actual instances of change in individual
languages, either in order to place these particular changes in
a general cross-linguistic context, or in order to collect cross-linguistic
data that could contribute to a general theory of syntactic change.
Practioners of this approach generally adopt a different, non-goal-
oriented view, drawing on insights from traditional historical linguistics and grammaticalization studies. On this view, as outlined for example by Mithun (2003), syntactic change is largely determined by the
circumstances of language use and the contexts of occurrence of particular source constructions, rather than the properties of the resulting
constructions.

Sometimes, for example, syntactic change is assumed to be a result of
language contact (see Chapter 8, this volume). In particular, this has been
argued with regard to several word-order changes (Harris and Campbell
1995: 136–41 and references therein), as well as the presence of the same
types of grammaticalized patterns in geographically contiguous languages
(Heine and Kuteva 2005). While the fact that a pattern is introduced into

a language through contact does not rule out that the process may be driven by some principle of optimization of the grammatical structure of the receiving language, most accounts usually relate contact processes to sociohistorical factors, rather than any specific need for the receiving language to develop the relevant patterns (see, for example, the discussion in Heine and Kuteva 2005: ch. 4).

Alternatively, syntactic change is assumed to originate in processes of context-induced reinterpretation of pre-existing constructions in the language, which lead to changes in the syntactic structure of these constructions, as well as processes of extension of individual constructions from one context to another. The latter are based on perceived similarities between the relevant contexts and ultimately lead to the replacement of the constructions originally used in the target context. As the same processes of reinterpretation and extension occur over and over cross-linguistically, different languages will recurrently display the same syntactic changes (Bybee 2008, among others).

This is illustrated, for example, by a case often discussed in the typologically oriented literature involving the development of direct object markers from 'take' verbs and a series of related syntactic changes. In many languages initially displaying SVO order, including for example Mandarin Chinese (Li and Thompson 1981, among others) and several West African languages (Lord 1993), 'take' verbs are used in serial verb constructions of the type 'take X and Verb (X)'. As the taking event is accessory to the event described by the other verb, the 'take' verb is desemanticized and reinterpreted as merely indicating the direct object role that the entity being taken plays both in the taking event and in the event described by the other verb. This leads to the 'take' verb becoming an adposition, as well as to changes in both the constituent structure and the word order of the sentence. While the source construction consists of two independent clauses, the 'take' clause' and another clause, the former 'take' verb and its direct object become part of a single constituent functioning as the direct object argument of the verb in the other clause. As a result, the former SVOV pattern where the first verb is the 'take' verb gives rise to an SOV pattern in the resulting sentence.

This process is illustrated by the Ga (Niger-Congo) examples in (2) below. The sentence in (2a) displays the original SVO order of the language. In (2b), which has SOV order, the direct object is introduced by the preposition kɛ̀, formerly a verb meaning 'take', as shown by a number of cognate forms in related languages (e.g. Yoruba ká, kò, Fon *kple*, Ewe *kè*, 'pick, take, gather, collect': Lord 1993: 120). This preposition cannot be used for direct objects incompatible with taking events, for example objects of 'see' verbs, as shown by the ungrammaticality of (2c). This is the phenomenon that scholars of grammaticalization refer to as persistence, the fact that the distribution of a grammaticalized form is constrained by its original lexical meaning (Hopper and Traugott 2003). Over time, however, adpositions derived from 'take' verbs can be extended also to direct objects whose referents are not usually involved in taking events, as was for example the case in Mandarin Chinese (Li and Thompson 1981: ch. 15).

(2)   Ga (Niger-Congo)
       a. è   wò   tó   lὲ   mlî̀   nù
          she put   bottle the   inside water
          'She put water in the bottle.' (Lord 1993: 119)
       b. è   kὲ   nù   wò   tó   lὲ   mlî̀
          she OBJ   water put   bottle the   inside
          'She put water in the bottle.' (Lord 1993: 119)
       c. *tὲtὲ   kὲ   kɔkɔ́   nà
          tete   OBJ   Koko   saw
          'Tete saw Koko.' (Lord 1993: 120)

Context-induced reinterpretation and extension have also been argued to be responsible for several types of changes in alignment systems, that is, the systems used to encode the two arguments of transitive verbs and the only argument of intransitive verbs (henceforth, following a standard practice in typology, A, P and S arguments). A considerable body of typologically oriented studies is now available, for example, on different processes that can give rise to ergative systems cross-linguistically (more on this in §30.3). One such process has been described by Rude (1991, 1997) for Sahaptian languages (Sahaptin and Nez Perce). In these languages, as can be seen from (3a–b), a Proto-Sahaptian suffix *-nɨm (possibly derived from a verb 'come' in a serial verb construction) gave rise to a directional marker used on both verbs and nouns to indicate an action directed towards the speaker or the hearer. When attached to the A argument of a transitive clause, as in (3c), the suffix was reinterpreted as a marker of the A role. As A, S and P arguments were previously undifferentiated, this gave rise to a system with a dedicated marker for A arguments and no markers for P and S arguments, that is, an ergative system. Due to its original semantics, the use of the marker was initially restricted to clauses with third-person A arguments and first or second-person P arguments, but in Nez Perce, as can be seen from (4), it was later extended to all cases of transitive clauses with third-person A arguments.

(3)   Sahaptin (Penutian)
       a. áw   i-q'ínum-**im**-a   wínš
          now   3.NOM-see/look-CSL-PST   man
          'Now the man looked *this way*' (Rude 1991: 41)
       b. áw-naš   i-q'ínun-a   wínš-**nɨm**
          now-1SG 3NOM-see/look-PST man-ERG
          'Now the man looked at me.' (Rude 1991: 41)

c. áw-naš   x̣wisaat-**nim**   i-twána-m-aš
now-1sg   old.man-erg   3nom-follow-csl-ipfv
'Now the old man is following me.' (Rude 1991: 41)

(4)   Nez Perce (Penutian)
wewúkiye-ne   pée-'wi-ye   háama-**nm**
elk-obj   3/3-shoot-pst   man-erg
'The man shot an elk.' (Rude 1991: 25)

A third, well-known process that has been accounted for in terms of
context-induced reinterpretation and extension is the development of
various types of tense, aspect and mood constructions (Bybee, Perkins
and Pagliuca 1994, among others). A classical example of this process is
the development of perfect constructions from possessive constructions, which has been described in detail for Romance and Germanic
languages by a number of historical linguists (Benveniste 1968; Vincent
1982; Pinkster 1987; Ramat 1987: ch. 8; Harris and Campbell 1995:
182–7; Adams 2013, among others; see Heine 1997: ch. 4 for examples
of the process in other languages). This is illustrated in example (5) for
Latin. The starting point are constructions of the type in (5a–b), where
the possessed item functions as the object of a possession verb.
The possessed item is in a state described by a co-occurring participial
form, and resulting from a past action which may or may not have been
performed by the possessor ('X has Y Verbed', meaning 'X has a Y to
which something has been done'). Over time, this gives rise to a perfect
construction, 'X has Verbed Y', as in (5c). At this point the former
possession verb and the participle form a single unit, so they have
a single subject, they must usually be adjacent to each other, and the
participle usually no longer agrees with the object. Linguists working in
a functional-typological perspective (Ramat 1987: ch. 8; Bybee, Perkins
and Pagliuca 1994: 68f.; Heine 1997: ch. 4) have emphasized that this
process is related to two major, context-driven meaning changes. First,
the meaning of past action, which is part of the global meaning of the
possessive construction since the beginning, is reinterpreted over time
as the central meaning of the construction, as the meaning of possession
is bleached. Bybee, Perkins and Pagliuca (1994: 68f.) suggest that the
reintepretation may have been favoured by contexts where the past
action sets the stage for a subsequent action, and hence is particularly
relevant. Second, one of the possible interpretations of the possessive
construction, the one in which the action described by the participle is
performed by the possessor, becomes conventionalized. This may have
been triggered by the fact that there are a number of contexts, for
example contexts where the participle describes a cognitive or sensory
state, as in (5c), where this is the only possible interpretation
(Benveniste 1968; Vincent 1982; Ramat 1987: ch. 8). Once the shift

from possession to perfect is completed, the construction can be extended to intransitive verbs incompatible with the original possessive meaning, as in (5d).

(5)   Latin
    a. multa bona   bene   parta   habemus
       many properties honestly obtained   have.1PL
       'We possess much property, honestly obtained.' (Plautus, *Trinummus* 347)

    b. fidem   meam   habent ... cognitam
       faith.ACC my.ACC have.3PL   known
       'My good faith is known to them.' (Cicero, *Divinatio in Q. Caecilium* 11)

    c. haec   omnia   probatum habemus
       those.ACC.PL all.ACC.PL   Tried   have.1PL
       'We have tried all those things.' (Oribasius, *Synopsis* 7.48)

    d. sicut   parabolatum   habuistis
       as   spoken   have.PRF.2PL
       'As you had spoken.' (*Formulae Merkelianae* 260, 7; Cennamo 2008: 124)

Explanations in terms of context-induced reinterpretation and extension imply that the properties of the constructions resulting from a syntactic change play no role in triggering the change. Rather, the change is an epiphenomenal result of the fact that particular contexts (often indicated as bridging contexts, see for example Traugott and Dasher 2005) allow for multiple interpretations of the same construction, as well as a result of perceived similarities between different contexts, which lead speakers to extend particular syntactic patterns from one context to another. For example, the changes in word order and constituent structure associated with the development of direct object markers from 'take' verbs ultimately originate from the fact that the 'take' meaning is peripheral in the context and is eventually obliterated, leading to the reinterpretation of the 'take' verb as a direct object marker and its subsequent extension to different types of contexts involving direct objects. Likewise, the development of an ergative system from a directional marker originates from the fact that the directional marker is sometimes used in association with an A argument, and can therefore be interpreted as indicating the A role, at which point it is extended to other contexts also involving A arguments. The shift from possession to perfect and the related syntactic changes originate from the fact that the original possessive construction involves the meaning of past action and can be interpreted to the effect that the possessor is the agent performing this action. Syntactic change, then, is ultimately motivated by the factors that lead speakers to adopt alternative interpretations for some particular construction, or establish a connection between different contexts. These factors are often semantic and pragmatic, and they are assumed to be related to the specific circumstances of language use, for example the availability of particular context-induced inferences. To the extent that these circumstances are the same from one language to another, they will lead to the same types of changes, but these changes are determined by the properties of particular source constructions, rather than the properties of the resulting constructions.

30.3 Syntactic Change and Explanations for Synchronic Cross-Linguistic Patterns

Syntactic change has also been discussed in the typological literature in relation to the issue of possible explanations for the syntactic patterns described by typological universals.

As was mentioned in §30.2, these explanations are usually proposed on synchronic grounds: if the synchronic distribution of particular syntactic phenomena, as described by some universal, can plausibly be related to particular principles, then these principles are assumed to be responsible for that distribution, independently of how the relevant phenomena actually originated in individual languages. For example, the functionalist principle whereby languages evolve towards structures that allow faster constituent recognition has been proposed by Hawkins (1994, 2004), based on the synchronic distribution of particular word-order patterns, not the actual diachronic processes leading to the development of these patterns from one language to another.

To the extent that typological universals are regarded as a result of specific diachronic processes that give rise to the relevant distributional patterns, however, explanations for individual universals should in principle also account for these processes, not just the distributional patterns in themselves. This point, originally raised by Bybee (1988), has prompted a body of research on the actual diachronic processes that gives rise to the patterns described by several major typological universals; in many cases, diachronic evidence for different explanations for these universals than those proposed on synchronic grounds.

For example, Bybee (1988) and Aristar (1991) discuss the bidirectional implicational universal whereby the order of adposition and noun correlates with that of possessor and possessed item in possessive constructions, that is, if a language has prepositions, then the possessor follows the possessed item and, if the possessor follows the possessed item, then the language has prepositions, as illustrated in §30.1. In the typological literature, this universal has been accounted for in terms of various principles related to processing ease, such as Cross-Categorial Harmony (Hawkins 1983) and the Branching Direction Theory

(Dryer 1992, 2006b). Adpositions, however, often originate from nouns referring to the possessed item in a possessive construction, and maintain the order of these nouns within the construction: when the possessed item precedes the possessor, this will yield prepositions, as in example (6), while when the possessed item follows the possessor this will yield postpositions, as in example (7). In such cases, then, the correlation between the order of adposition and noun and that of possessor and possessed item is motivated by the fact that the two constructions were originally one and the same, rather than any more general processing preference.

(6)   Neo-Aramaic (Semitic)
       qaama di beetha > **qaamid** beetha
       front   GEN house   in.front.of house
       'in front of the house' (Aristar 1991: 6)

(7)   Finnish (Uralic)
       poja-n **kansa-ssa** > *poja-n* **kanssa**
       boy-GEN company-IN   boy-GEN with
       'with the boy' (Aristar 1991: 6)

Aristar (1991) also addresses a universal pertaining to the order of relative clause and noun and that of possessor and possessed item. In languages where the possessor follows the possessed item, the relative clause follows the noun. In an influential proposal by Hawkins (1983, 1994, 2004), this pattern too has been related to the need to optimize immediate constituent recognition. When a modifier is preposed to the noun, this delays the recognition of the phrasal head until the modifier is processed, and the more structurally complex the modifier (in terms of number of syllables, words and constituents involved), the longer the delay, and the heavier the burden that the whole process will place on working memory. As a result, structurally complex modifiers will tend to be postposed, rather than preposed to the noun, and, if less complex modifiers such as possessors are postposed, so are more complex modifiers such as relative clauses.

Aristar (1991) shows, however, that in several languages relative clauses and constructions used to encode possessors both originate from a demonstrative phrase. This is for example the case in Luo, where both of these constructions, illustrated in (8a) and (8b) below, are postposed to the noun. The relative clause marker and the possessive marker have the same form as the demonstrative, illustrated in (8c). This suggests that the two developed from the same construction, one where an anaphoric demonstrative in combination with a modifying expression was in apposition to a head noun, that is, 'X, that (who) Verbed' and 'X, that (of) Y', which gave rise, respectively, to 'The X who Verbed' and 'the X of Y'.

(8) Luo (Nilo-Saharan)
     a. ji   **m**-o-biro
         men   REL-COMPL-come
         'the men who have just come' (Stafford 1967: 29)
     b. duong'   **ma**-r   piny
         greatness GEN-SG   land
         'the greatness of the land' (Stafford 1967: 29)
     c. i-dwaro   **ma**?
         2SG-want   this
         'Do you want this?' (Stafford 1967: 34)

In such cases too, the correlation between the order of relative clauses and that of possessor constructions is naturally accounted for by the fact that these constructions maintain the order of the demonstrative phrase from which they both derive, so there is no evidence for any more general motivating principle such as processing ease.

Similar points have been made in relation to alignment systems. The various alignment systems attested in the world's languages (accusative, ergative and active systems, that is) are traditionally accounted for in terms of a variety of synchronically established functional principles, some of which are meant to explain a number of recurrent similarities between these systems. For example, all alignment systems usually distinguish between A and P arguments. This is assumed to be because these arguments co-occur in transitive clauses, and need therefore to be disambiguated. Also, it is usually assumed that arguments that share semantic or pragmatic properties will be encoded in the same way. For example, A and S arguments will be encoded in the same way (in accusative and active systems) because they correspond to agentive participants, topical participants or, more generally, participants that represent a starting point in discourse. S and P arguments will be encoded in the same way (in ergative or active systems) because they typically correspond to participants introduced for the first time in discourse, because certain types of S arguments correspond to non-agentive participants, or, in some analyses, because the participants most immediately involved in the state of affairs being described occur in S or P role (see, among others, Moravcsik 1978; Dixon 1979, 1994; DeLancey 1981; Du Bois 1985; Mithun 1991; Mithun and Chafe 1999; Givón 2001; Song 2001).

Diachronic work on the origins of alignment systems has shown, however, that they typically develop from processes of reinterpretation of pre-existing constructions, along the lines described in §30.2 (Harris 1985; Garrett 1990; Rude 1991, 1997; Bubeník 1998; Creissels 2008; Holton 2008; König 2008; Mithun 2008; Verbeke and De Cuypere 2009; Verbeke 2013). These processes are plausibly motivated in terms of a number of often highly specific properties of the source constructions, rather than more general principles pertaining to the properties of particular arguments, as assumed on synchronic grounds.

For example, ergative systems have been argued to sometimes arise from intransitive constructions of the type 'X is done by Y' as these become functionally equivalent to transitive ones, 'Y has done X'. In the resulting transitive constructions, X, the P argument, is marked in the same way as S arguments, because it originates from the S argument of the source construction, while Y, the A argument, has dedicated marking, because it maintains the oblique marking of the agent of the source construction, from which it originates. This process has been postulated, for instance, for the Hindi perfective construction in (9), whose presumed Sanskrit antecedent is reported in (10) (for recent comprehensive reviews of the issues involved, see Verbeke and De Cuypere 2009; Stroński 2011; Verbeke 2013).

(9)   Hindi (Indo-European)
        laṛk-**e=ne**   bacch-e=ko   mār-a   hai
        boy-OBL-ERG   child-OBL-ACC   hit-PRF.M.SG   be.AUX
        'The boy has hit the child.' (Verbeke and De Cuypere 2009: 5)

(10)   Sanskrit (Indo-European)
        devadatt-**ena**   kaṭa-ḥ   kṛ-taḥ
        Devadatta-INS   mat-NOM   make-NOM.PST.PTCP
        'The mat is made by Devadatta.' (Verbeke and De Cuypere 2009: 3)

Another source for ergative systems, extensively documented by Gildea (1998) for a number of Carib languages, are biclausal constructions involving nominalized clauses, e.g. 'It will be Y's Verbing', or 'To Y will be the Verbing of X'. Over time, these are reinterpreted as monoclausal structures, e.g. 'Y will Verb', or 'Y will Verb X'. In the resulting structures, P and S arguments have the same marking, because they derive from the possessor of the nominalized verb, while A arguments are marked differently, because they derive from a dative NP in the original construction. This pattern is illustrated in (11) below for Carinã.

(11)   Carinã (Carib)
        a. i-woona-ri-ma
            1-cultivate-NMZ-3.be
            'I will cultivate.' (from a nominalized structure of the type 'It will be my cultivating'; Gildea 1998: 169)
        b. a-eena-ri-ma   i-**'wa**
            2-have-NMZ-3.be   1-DAT/ERG
            'I will have you.' (from a nominalized structure of the type 'To me it will be your having'; Gildea 1998: 170)

Active systems have been argued to develop from transitive clauses with unexpressed third-person A arguments, which are reinterpreted as intransitive ones, e.g. '(It) Verbed me' becomes 'I am Verbed' (see, among others, Harris 1985; Malchukov 2008; Mithun 2008). In the intransitive clause, the verb describes the state resulting from the action described by the transitive clause.

Direct diachronic evidence of this process is provided by Holton (2008) for Galela. In this language, the undergoer prefixes used to cross-reference S arguments on stative intransitive verbs, illustrated in (12a), are also used to cross-reference P arguments on transitive verbs. This is a result of the fact that intransitive clauses with stative verbs were originally transitive clauses with a third-person non-human A argument cross-referenced by a verbal prefix *i-*. In the late nineteenth century, this prefix became optional, as can be seen from the comparison between (12b) and (12c), and it eventually disappeared. This loss led to the reinterpretation of the transitive clause as a corresponding intransitive one.

(12)   Galela (Austronesian)
   a.   ni-kiolo
        2SG.UNDG-asleep
        'You are asleep.' (Modern Galela; Holton 2008: 261)
   b.   **i**-mi-tosa
        3SG.A.NON-HUM-3F.SG.UNDG-angry
        'She is angry.' (nineteenth-century Galela; Holton 2008: 272)
   c.   mi-pereki
        3F.SG.UNDG-old
        'She is old.' (nineteenth-century Galela; Holton 2008: 272)

To the extent that particular alignment systems originate from the reinterpretation of pre-existing constructions, their structure is a result of the original structure of the source construction, and their development is directly motivated in terms of whatever factors give rise to the reintepretation process, for example, the conceptual similarity between passive clauses and the corresponding active ones, that between certain types of complex sentences and the corresponding monoclausal structures, or the processes of inference that lead speakers to reinterpret transitive clauses as signalling a state resulting from an action rather than the action itself. This provides alternative explanations to the more general functional principles usually postulated to account for alignment systems on synchronic grounds, such as the need to disambiguate co-occurring arguments or the tendency to encode in the same way semantically or pragmatically similar arguments (Garrett 1990; Harris and Campbell 1995: 251–5; Gildea 1998; Creissels 2008; Cristofaro 2012, 2014).

Similar points have also been raised in relation to so-called split ergativity phenomena, the fact that ergative alignment is sometimes found in only a subset of the NPs of a language, such as inanimate nouns as opposed to animate nouns and pronouns, nouns as opposed to pronouns, or nouns and third-person pronouns as opposed to first- and second-person pronouns. This pattern has been explained in terms of a general assumption that overt case marking for particular NP types is only used when those NPs are less likely to occur in a particular role, and hence that role needs to signalled explicitly. As in most ergative systems A arguments are marked overtly, while S and P arguments are zero marked, it is assumed that such systems will only be used for the NP types that are less likely to occur as A arguments, as is the case with inanimate nouns as opposed to other NP types, or nouns and third-person pronouns as opposed to first- and second-person pronouns (see, among others, Dixon 1979, 1994; Comrie 1989; DeLancey 1981; Song 2001).

A number of linguists working on the origins of ergative systems in a typological perspective have shown, however, that, when these systems are limited to particular NP types, this is naturally accounted for in terms of their origins, rather than the relative likelihood of those NPs occurring in A function. For example, Garrett (1990) shows that in some languages, such as Hittite, specific markers for A arguments are likely to have developed through the reinterpretation of an instrumental marker in sentences with no overt third-person A arguments, that is, sentences such as '(X) opened the door with the key' were reinterpreted as 'The key ERG opened the door'. As instrumentals usually do not apply to animates or pronouns (particularly first- and second-person ones), the resulting A markers are restricted in the same way.

McGregor (2006, 2008) shows that, in a number of Australian languages where ergative systems are not used with pronouns, the ergative marker can be transparently related to an indexical element, that is, a demonstrative or a third-person pronoun. This is illustrated in (13) for Bagandji.

(13) Bagandji (Australian)
      yaḍ-u-ḍ-**uru**   gāndi-d-uru-ana
      wind-DEM/ERG   carry-FUT-3SG.SBJ-3SG.OBJ
      'This wind will carry it along / The wind will carry it along.' (Hercus 1982: 63)

McGregor (2006, 2008) accounts for this pattern by assuming that indexicals are initially used in apposition to nouns occurring in the A role to emphasize that these nouns exceptionally encode new or unexpected information. As a result, they are subsequently reanalysed as encoding the A role. Thus, for example, sentences such as 'This one, X, did Y' or 'He, X, did Y' become 'X ERG did Y'. Indexicals, McGregor (2006) argues, are not used with pronouns because pronouns represent given information, and this explains why the resulting A markers are not used with pronouns either.

While diachronic work on the syntactic patterns captured by typological universals is still very much in its infancy, this line of research fills a crucial gap in traditional approaches to these universals and their relationship with syntactic change. Typological universals are usually viewed as a product of syntactic change insofar as they describe syntactic patterns that developed through specific diachronic processes at some point in the evolution of the relevant languages. As a result of this view, the principles postulated to account for individual universals on synchronic grounds, for example processing ease or the need to disambiguate particular arguments, are also implicitly or explicitly assumed to trigger the changes that give rise to the patterns described by the universal. This, however, is in contrast with a generalized view that syntactic change originates in processes largely independent of these principles, such as context-induced reinterpretation and extension, as described in §30.2. By integrating these processes into the explanation of individual universals, diachronically oriented approaches provide a solution to this contrast and make it possible to establish a more direct connection between the results of typological research and those of disciplines specifically concerned with syntactic change, such as grammaticalization studies and historical linguistics in general.

30.4 Concluding Remarks

While no specific theory of syntax or syntactic change has been developed within the typological approach, typologically oriented linguists have investigated syntactic change in relation to the issue of possible explanations for the synchronic patterns captured by typological universals. In the typological approach, these patterns are a result of recurrent diachronic processes leading to the development and conventionalization of the relevant constructions in individual languages (rather than principles inbuilt in a speaker's mental grammar independently of these processes, as argued in formally oriented approaches). Consequently, the factors that motivate the changes that give rise to particular synchronic patterns also provide the ultimate motivation for these patterns.

In some analyses, these factors are drawn from the synchronic patterns themselves. Individual patterns are assumed to comply with some general language preferences, that is, principles of optimization of grammatical structure, and it is further assumed that these preferences operate at the diachronic level by leading speakers to create the constructions involved in the pattern as opposed to others. For example, some word-order configurations are assumed to be easier to process, and it is then assumed that, because of this, syntactic chance will lead to the creation of these configurations as opposed to others. Likewise, particular alignment patterns are assumed to optimize functional principles such as the need to disambiguate co-occurring arguments or the tendency to associate arguments with similar semantic or pragmatic properties. It is then assumed that these principles will lead to the creation of the relevant alignment patterns in individual languages.

The idea that the grammatical patterns attested synchronically comply with general language preferences leading to the creation of these patterns has a long history in linguistics (for discussion, see, for example, McMahon 1994: ch. 12; Harris and Campbell 1995: chs. 2, 11; Newmeyer 1998: ch. 3; Mithun 2003). This idea is in fact at the heart of functionally oriented approaches to the study of language (Haiman 1983, 1985; Du Bois 1985; Givón 2001; see also Chapter 31, this volume), and similar ideas are also manifested in formal approaches to syntactic change, as shown for example by Roberts and Roussou's (2003) hypothesis that the syntactic changes involved in grammaticalization lead to the creation of structures associated with simpler syntactic representations (in terms, for example, of movement and feature syncretism).

Diachronic evidence shows, however, that many syntactic changes (for example, changes in word order or constituent structure, or the development of new alignment systems) originate through processes of reinterpretation and extension of pre-existing constructions, triggered by often highly particularized contextual factors. This has led some typologically oriented linguists to argue that the development of the syntactic patterns captured by typological universals is best accounted for in terms of the properties of particular source constructions and the contexts in which they are used, rather than any general property of the resulting patterns in themselves (such as the fact that these patterns comply with some assumed principle of optimization of grammatical structure).

While this approach has not been pursued systematically in typology, it makes it possible to address some general problems with existing explanations of typological universals and the processes that give rise to the patterns captured by these universals. Most typological universals are implicational ones allowing for different patterns; for example, the implicational relationship between postposed possessors and posposted relative clauses, described in §30.3, allows for languages where both relative clauses and possessors are postposed to the noun, languages where both are preposed, and languages where relative clauses are postposed but possessors are preposed. The principles traditionally proposed to account for individual universals, however, usually provide a direct explanation for some of these patterns only. If these principles lead to optimization of grammatical structure, then it is not clear why some languages develop alternative patterns. For example, Hawkins' (1983, 1994, 2004) idea that structurally complex modifiers should be postposed to the noun accounts for why some languages have postposed relative clauses and postposed possessors, but is in contrast with the fact that other languages have preposed possessors and preposed relative clauses, or postposed relative clauses and preposed possessors.

Another problem is that typological universals usually have a varying number of exceptions, that is, several languages display patterns ruled out by the universal. As a matter of fact, typological universals are statistical tendencies, rather than universals proper. This is in contrast with the assumption that (at least some of) the patterns captured by the universals reflect principles of optimization of grammatical structure that are valid for all languages, because in this case one has to account for why these principles are violated in some languages. A similar problem is in fact faced by models where typological universals are a result of universal constraints inbuilt in a speaker's mental grammar, because exceptions to a particular universal mean that the assumed constraints are violated in a number of languages.

These problems have been addressed in a number of ways in the literature, for example, by postulating competitions between different functional principles leading to different grammatical outputs (as in competing motivations models; see, most recently, the papers collected in MacWhinney, Malchukov and Moravcsik 2014) or between universal grammatical constraints that are specifically represented in the speaker's mind and can be ranked differently in different languages, also leading to different grammatical outputs (as in Optimality Theory treatments of typological universals; see e.g. Aissen 2003). Attempts have also been made to redefine the formulation of particular universals so as to make them exceptionless (Hawkins 1983; Baker and McCloskey 2007). In general, however, these proposals are faced with two major problems: the fact that there usually is no independent evidence for the assumed competition between different functional principles or grammatical constraints (Newmeyer 1998: 145–53, among others) and the fact that in most cases it is not possible to identify exceptionless universals.

If synchronic syntactic patterns arise through the reinterpretation and extension of pre-existing constructions, then it is to be expected that not all languages should have some particular pattern or conform to a particular universal, because not all languages have the same source constructions, individual constructions need not undergo the same processes of reinterpretation or extension, and some of the constructions that give rise to a particular pattern may disappear after the pattern has been created, leading to exceptions to particular implicational universals. For example, the implicational correlation between the order of the adposition and noun and that of possessor and possessed item will be manifested in languages where adpositions derive from possessive constructions, but not necessarily in languages where they originate from other sources, or where possessive constructions undergo a word-order change after giving rise to adpositions (Dryer 2006a).

These facts point to a new way to deal with the syntactic patterns captured by typological universals and the changes that give rise to these patterns. In both functionally and formally oriented approaches, explanations for individual patterns are usually proposed based on particular synchronic properties of the pattern. These properties are also implicitly or explicitly assumed to account for the syntactic changes that gave rise to the pattern in individual languages. The actual diachronic evidence for these changes, however, suggests shifting the focus of attention from the synchronic properties of individual patterns to what source constructions can give rise to what patterns from one language to another, through what mechanisms, and possibly why some of these processes are more frequent than others.

References

Adams, J. N. 2013. *Social variation and the Latin language*. Cambridge University Press.

Aissen, J. 2003. 'Differential object marking: iconicity vs economy', *Natural Language and Linguistic Theory* 21: 435–83.

Aristar, A. R. 1991. 'On diachronic sources and synchronic patterns: An investigation into the origin of linguistic universals', *Language* 67: 1–33.

Baker, M. C. and McCloskey, J. 2007. 'On the relation of typology to theoretical syntax', *Linguistic Typology* 11(1): 285–96.

Benveniste, E. 1968. 'Mutations of linguistic categories', in W. P. Lehmann and Y. Malkiel (eds.), *Directions for historical linguistics*. Austin: University of Texas Press, pp. 83–94.

Bickel, B. 2007. 'Typology in the 21st century: Major current developments', *Linguistic Typology* 11(1): 239–51.

Bubeník, V. 1998. *A historical syntax of late middle Indo-Aryan (Apabrahṃśa)*. Amsterdam: John Benjamins.

Bybee, J. 1988. 'The diachronic dimension in explanation', in J. A. Hawkins (ed.), *Explaining language universals*. Oxford: Blackwell, pp. 350–79.

  2006. 'Language change and universals', in R. Mairal and J. Gil (eds.), *Linguistic universals*. Cambridge University Press, pp. 179–94.

  2008. 'Formal universals as emergent phenomena: The origins of structure preservation', in J. Good (ed.), *Linguistic universals and language change*. Oxford University Press, pp. 108–21.

Bybee, J., Perkins, R. and Pagliuca, W. 1994. *The evolution of grammar*. University of Chicago Press.

Cennamo, M. 2008. 'The rise and development of analytic perfects in Italo-Romance', in Þ. Eyþórsson (ed.), *Grammatical change and linguistic theory: The Rosendal papers*. Amsterdam: John Benjamins, pp. 115–42.

Comrie, B. 1989. *Language universals and linguistic typology*, 2nd edn. Oxford: Blackwell.

Creissels, D. 2008. 'Direct and indirect explanations of typological regularities: The case of alignment variations', *Folia Linguistica* 42: 1–38.

Cristofaro, S. 2011. 'Language universals and linguistic knowledge', in J. J. Song (ed.), *Handbook of linguistic typology*. Oxford University Press, pp. 227–49.

   2012. 'Cognitive explanations, distributional evidence, and diachrony', *Studies in Language* 36: 645–70.

   2014. 'Competing motivations and diachrony: What evidence for what motivations?', in B. MacWhinney, A. Malchukov and E. Moravcsik (eds.), *Competing motivations in grammar and usage*. Oxford University Press, pp. 282–98.

Croft, W. 2000. *Explaining language change: An evolutionary approach*. Harlow: Longman.

Davidse, K., Breban, T., Brems, L. and Mortelmans, T. (eds.) 2012. *Grammaticalization and language change: New reflections*. Amsterdam: John Benjamins.

DeLancey, S. 1981. 'An interpretation of split ergativity and related patterns', *Language* 57: 626–57.

Dixon, R. M. W. 1979. 'Ergativity', *Language* 55: 59–138.

   1994. *Ergativity*. Cambridge University Press.

Dryer, M. 1992. 'The Grenberghian word order correlations', *Language* 68: 81–138.

   2006a. 'Descriptive theories, explanatory theories, and basic linguistic theory', in F. Ameka, A. Dench and N. Evans (eds.), *Catching language: The standing challenge of grammar writing*. Berlin and New York: Mouton de Gruyter, pp. 207–34.

   2006b. 'Functionalism and the metalanguage – theory confusion', in G. W. G. Libben, T. Priestly, R. Smyth and S. Wang (eds.), *Phonology, morphology, and the empirical imperative: Papers in honour of Bruce Derwing*. Taipei: Crane, pp. 27–59.

Du Bois, J. A. 1985. 'Competing motivations', in J. Haiman (ed.), *Iconicity in syntax*. Amsterdam: John Benjamins, pp. 343–66.

Garrett, A. 1990. 'The origin of NP split ergativity', *Language* 66: 261–96.

Giacalone Ramat, A., Mauri, C. and Molinelli, P. (eds.) 2013. *Synchrony and diachrony: A dynamic interface*. Amsterdam: John Benjamins.

Gildea, S. 1998. *On reconstructing grammar: Comparative Cariban morphosyntax*. Oxford University Press.

Givón, T. 2001. *Syntax: An introduction*. Amsterdam: John Benjamins.

Givón, T. and Shibatani, M. (eds.) 2009. *Syntactic complexity: Diachrony, acquisition, neurocognition*. Amsterdam: John Benjamins.

Greenberg, J. H. 1963. 'Some universals of language, with particular reference to the order of meaningful elements', in J. H. Greenberg (ed.), *Universals of language*. Cambridge, MA: MIT Press, pp. 73–113.

1966. *Language universals, with particular reference to feature hierarchies.* The Hague: Mouton.

1978. 'Diachrony, synchrony and language universals', in J. H. Greenberg, C. H. Ferguson and E. A. Moravcsick (eds.), *Universals of human language*, vol. 1: *Method and theory.* Stanford University Press, pp. 62–91.

1995. 'The Diachronic typological approach', in M. Shibatani and T. Bynon (eds.), *Approaches to language typology.* Oxford: Clarendon Press, pp. 145–66.

Haiman, J. 1983. 'Iconic and economic motivation', *Language* 59: 781–819.

1985. *Natural syntax.* Cambridge University Press.

Harris, A. C. 1985. *Diachronic syntax: The Kartvelian case.* New York: Academic Press.

Harris, A. C. and Campbell, L. 1995. *Historical syntax in cross-linguistic perspective.* Cambridge University Press.

Hawkins, J. A. 1983. *Word order universals.* New York: Academic Press.

1990. 'Seeking motives for change in typological variation', in W. Croft, K. Denning and S. Kemmer (eds.), *Studies in typology and diachrony: Papers presented to Joseph H. Greenberg on his 75th birthday.* Amsterdam: John Benjamins, pp. 95–128.

1994. *A performance theory of word order and constituency.* Cambridge University Press.

2004. *Efficiency and complexity in grammars.* Oxford University Press.

Heine, B. 1997. *Possession.* Cambridge University Press.

Heine, B., Claudi, U. and Hünnemeyer, F. 1991. *Grammaticalization.* University of Chicago Press.

Heine, B. and Kuteva, T. 2005. *Language contact and grammatical change.* Cambridge University Press.

Hendery, R. 2012. *Relative clauses in time and space: A case study in the methods of diachronic typology.* Amsterdam: John Benjamins.

Hercus, L. 1982. *The Bagandji language* (Pacific Linguistics. Series B-67). Canberra: Australian National University.

Holton, G. 2008. 'The rise and fall of semantic alignment in Northern Halmahera, Indonesia', in M. Donohue and S. Wichmann (eds.), *The typology of semantic alignment.* Oxford University Press, pp. 252–76.

Hopper, P. J. and Traugott, E. C. 2003. *Grammaticalization*, 2nd edn. Cambridge University Press.

König, C. 2008. *Case in Africa.* Oxford University Press.

Li, C. and Thompson, S. A. 1981. *Mandarin Chinese: A functional reference grammar.* Berkeley and Los Angeles: University of California Press.

Lord, C. 1993. *Historical change in serial verb constructions.* Amsterdam: John Benjamins.

MacWhinney, B., Malchukov, A. and Moravcsik, E. (eds.) 2014. *Competing motivations in grammar and usage.* Oxford University Press.

Malchukov, A. 2008. 'Split intransitives, experiencer objects and "transimpersonal" constructions: (Re-)establishing the connection', in M. Donohue and S. Wichmann (eds.), *The typology of semantic alignment*. Oxford University Press, pp. 76–101.

Maslova, E. 2000. 'A dynamic approach to the verification of distributional universals', *Linguistic Typology* 4: 307–33.

McGregor, W.B. 2006. 'Focal and optional ergative marking in Warrwa (Kimberley, Western Australia)', *Lingua* 116: 393–423.

  2008. 'Indexicals as sources of case markers in Australian languages', in F. Josephson and I. Söhrman (eds.), *Interdependence of diachronic and synchronic analyses*. Amsterdam: John Benjamins, pp. 299–321.

McMahon, A. S. 1994. *Understanding language change*. Cambridge University Press.

Mithun, M. 1991. 'Active/agentive case marking and its motivation', *Language* 67: 510–46.

  2003. 'Functional perspectives on syntactic change', in B. D. Joseph and R. D. Janda (eds.), *The handbook of historical linguistics*. Oxford: Blackwell, pp. 552–72.

  2008. 'The emergence of agentive systems in core argument marking', in M. Donohue and S. Wichmann (eds.), *The typology of semantic alignment*. Oxford University Press, pp. 297–333.

Mithun, M. and Chafe, W. 1999. 'What are S, A, and O?', *Studies in Language* 23(3): 569–96.

Moravcsik, E. A. 1978. 'On the distribution of ergative and accusative patterns', *Lingua* 45: 233–79.

Newmeyer, F. J. 1998. *Language form and language function*. Cambridge, MA: MIT Press.

  2002. 'Optimality and functionality: A critique of functionally-based optimality theory', *Natural Language and Linguistic Theory* 20: 43–80.

  2004. 'Typological evidence and Universal Grammar', *Studies in Language* 28: 526–48.

  2005. *Possible and probable languages*. Oxford University Press.

Nichols, J. 1992. *Linguistic diversity in space and time*. University of Chicago Press.

  2007. 'What, if anything, is typology?', *Linguistic Typology* 11(1): 231–8.

Pinkster, H. 1987. 'The strategy and chronology of the development of future and perfect tense auxiliaries in Latin', in M. Harris and P. Ramat (eds.), *Historical development of auxiliaries*. Berlin: Mouton de Gruyter, pp. 193–223.

Ramat, P. 1987. *Linguistic typology*. Berlin: Mouton de Gruyter.

Roberts, I. and Rossou, A. 2003. *Syntactic change: A minimalist approach to grammaticalization*. Cambridge University Press.

Rude, N. 1991. 'On the origin of the Nez Perce Ergative NP suffix', *International Journal of American Linguistics* 57: 24–50.

  1997. 'On the history of nominal case in Sahaptian', *International Journal of American Linguistics* 63: 113–43.

Seoane, E. and Lopez-Couso, M.J. 2008. *Theoretical and empirical issues in grammaticalization*. Amsterdam: John Benjamins.

Song, J. J. 2001. *Linguistic typology: Morphology and syntax*. Harlow, Essex: Longman.

Stafford, R. 1967. *An elementary Luo grammar. With vocabularies*. Nairobi: Oxford University Press.

Stroński, K. 2011. *Synchronic and diachronic aspects of ergativity in Indo-Aryan*. Poznan: Uniwersytet Adama Mickiewicza.

Traugott, E. C. and Dasher, R.B. 2005. *Regularity in semantic change*. Cambridge University Press.

van Gelderen, E., Barðdal, J. and Cennamo, M. (eds.) 2013. *Argument structure in flux: The Naples-Capri papers*. Amsterdam: John Benjamins.

Verbeke, S. 2013. *Alignment and ergativity in New Indo-Aryan languages*. Berlin: Mouton de Gruyter.

Verbeke, S. and De Cuypere, L. 2009. 'The rise of ergativity in Hindi: Assessing the role of grammaticalization', *Folia Linguistica Historica* 30: 1–24.

Vincent, N. 1982. 'The development of the auxiliaries *habere* and *esse* in Romance', in N. Vincent and M. Harris (eds.), *Studies in the Romance verb*. London: Croom Helm, pp. 71–96.

Viti, C. (ed.) 2015. *Perspectives on historical syntax*. Amsterdam: John Benjamins.

Yap, F. H., Grunow-Hårsta, K. and Wrona, Y. (eds.) 2011. *Nominalization in Asian languages: Diachronic and typological perspectives*. Amsterdam: John Benjamins.

31

Functional Approaches

Marianne Mithun

31.1 Introduction

Functionalist work on syntactic change is much like work in other traditions in the methodologies employed and the mechanisms cited. Change is tracked through corpora from different periods, comparison of cognate constructions in related languages, and examination of coexisting forms within a language at different stages of development. It is typically described in terms of such classical notions as reanalysis, analogy, routinization, extension and renewal (see Chapters 4 and 5, this volume). Differences are generally subtle but foundational. For most functionalists, synchrony and diachrony are tightly intertwined, each playing an integral role in shaping the other. Synchronic systems and the myriad complexities of their use set the stage for possible changes. Diachronic changes produce the results that become synchronic systems. Explanations for the grammatical patterns we find are thus couched in terms of the sequences of cognitive, social and communicative processes which bring them into being and strengthen them.

This point of view has certain theoretical consequences. Universals are sought less in predetermined categories and structures and more in the processes that create and shape the categories and patterns over time, often in sequences of small steps. Apparent irregularities and fuzzy boundaries become more interesting, providing clues to the points at which particular innovations first enter the grammar, pathways over which they progress, and factors which speed or impede their progress. The following sections illustrate this perspective with examples from several core areas of syntactic structure: alignment, argument structure, constituent order and dependency.

31.2 Alignment

A fundamental difference among languages is their categorization of core arguments as nominative/accusative, ergative/absolutive, agent/patient, etc. We could simply declare that each represents a language type, or we could ask what makes them this way.

It has been proposed that alignment is highly stable over time (Nichols 1992). Yet there are related languages that differ in just this way. There is now a sizable literature on pathways by which these patterns can develop. For the majority of languages, there is no ancient documentation which would allow us to trace the developments of new patterns step-by-step through time, but comparisons of modern forms across and especially within languages provide clues.

31.2.1 Synchronic Clues to Diachrony

Hanis Coos, a language indigenous to the Oregon coast of North America, shows ergative patterning in noun case. The last speaker died in 1972, but there are published texts in Frachtenberg (1913) and Jacobs (1939, 1940), and a grammar in Frachtenberg (1922). Ergative case is marked with a clitic x̣, attached before nouns, and absolutive case is unmarked, as in most languages of this type.

(1)   Hanis Coos ergative/absolutive case (Frachtenberg 1913: 80.19, 64.13, 80.20)

    a. Emí:hel   **lə**   **hu:mik-ša**.
       blind   the   old.woman.ENDEARMENT
       'The old woman [ABS] was blind.'

    b. A:yu   ił   sisí:nt   lə   winqas **hú:mik**.
       indeed they visit   the   spider   old.woman.ENDEARMENT
       'Indeed, they went to see Spider **Old Woman** [ABS].'

    c. Sqats   hə   wálwal   **lə=x̣**   **hu:mik-ša**.
       seize.TR the   knife   the=ERG   old.woman-ENDEARMENT
       'The old woman [ERG] seized the knife.'

In many languages with ergative patterning, the ergative case marker has the same shape as some other case. In Hanis it matches an oblique which marks instruments and sources.

(2)   Hanis instrument (Frachtenberg 1913: 22.16)

    K'win-t   x̣=mil:aqətš.
    shoot-TR INS=arrow
    '(He) shot at him **with** an arrow.'

(3)   Hanis ablative (Frachtenberg 1922: 323)

    X̣=kwiléƛe:i-tš   n̩=dji:.
    ABL=sweathouse-in   1SG=came
    'I came **from** the sweathouse.'

When, as here, third-person referents need not be expressed overtly, instrumental constructions like that in (2) are ripe for reanalysis. The marked instrument is interpreted as an agentive core argument of the transitive clause.

(4)   Hanis reanalysis (Frachtenberg 1913: 32.8)
       X̣=qainé:s ka:s   tsx̣áu:w-at heł   tó:miȴ.
       ERG=cold   almost lie-CAUS   that old.man
       'That old man died from the cold [OBL].'
               >   'Cold weather [ERG] nearly killed that old man.'

Once the reanalysis of instruments as ergatives had occurred in Hanis, ergative marking apparently spread to other agents of transitive events, even those that would not be considered instruments, as in 'The old woman [ERG] seized the knife' in (1c) above. It has not, however, been extended to pronouns.

Hanis also contains clues to another pathway of development to ergativity. Passive constructions are marked with a suffix on the verb: *-u:* for perfectives and *-i:ł* for imperfectives. Hanis passives function much like those in other languages, maintaining topic continuity over stretches of discourse, as below.

(5)   Hanis passive (Frachtenberg 1913: 58.8)
       ['Spider Old Woman had five children. One morning she was travelling outside. She walked somewhat far off. Her children were given battle [by the people] from below. Spider Old Woman was not at home. They began to fight.']
       His   i:n łhení:yeəs ił   aiai?w-á:y-**u**.
       Also   not long   3PL   RDP.kill-PAST-**PASS**
       'Not long afterward they were killed.'

This passage is about the children, not the killers, who were not identified beyond the reference 'from below' and then never mentioned again.

Pronominal subjects in Hanis are identified by proclitics before the verb.

(6)   Hanis subject proclitics (Frachtenberg 1922)
       n=ȴowitat   '**I** ran'
       e?=ȴowitat   '**you** ran'
          ȴowitat   '(he/she/it) ran'

       n=qáqał   '**I** sleep'
       e?=qáqał   '**you** sleep'
          qáqał   '(he/she/it) sleeps'

Since third persons are unmarked, transitive clauses with third-person patients show the same clitics as intransitives.

(7)   Hanis transitives (Frachtenberg 1922)
    n=tó:hits   '**I** hit (him/her/it)'
    eʔ=tó:hits   '**you** hit (him/her/it)'
    tó:hits   '(he/she/it) hit (him/her/it)'

It is well known that speakers tend to select certain participants over others for the role of subject. Semantic agents tend to be chosen over patients; identifiable (definite) referents over unidentifiable ones; given referents over new; and first and second persons over third. English speakers are more likely to say 'Did you see George?' than 'Was George seen by you?' In Hanis the preference for first and second persons over third has become crystallized in the grammar. It is no longer possible to say 'he hit me' (*3>1) or 'he hit you' (*3>2). The only grammatical option is a passive: 'I was hit' or 'You were hit'.

(8)   Hanis Coos obligatory passivization (Frachtenberg 1922: 351)
    n=tó:hits=**u:**   'he hit me'   (= 'I was hit')
    eʔ=tó:hits-**u:**   'he hit you'   (= 'you were hit')

Clauses with first or second persons acting on third (1>3, 2>3) cannot be passivized.

Third-person agents can be identified with an oblique nominal if desired. In (9) below, the second clause is passive, because it was framed with a third-person agent acting on a second person (3>2) 'Crow tells you'. Here the passive was clearly required by the grammar rather than the discourse: the second person was used for generic reference 'one'.

(9)   Hanis passive with oblique agent (Frachtenberg 1913: 15.1)
    Xti:tš   he   **eʔtšinéheni:**,
    what   customarily   you.are.thinking
    'Whatever one contemplates (doing)

    laʷ   xwendž   he   **eʔ**=kwiskwí:-**i:ɬ**   lə=**x̣**   má:qal.
    this   that.way   customarily   2=inform-PASS   the=OBL   crow
    'Crow is able to tell it.'   (*lit.* 'you can be told by Crow')

The marker of oblique agents is the same as that used for instruments and ablatives: the clitic x̣.

If passive constructions are the only option for describing a situation involving a third person acting on a first or second (3>1, 3>2), it is no surprise that they would eventually be reanalysed as basic transitives. The oblique x̣ on passive agents has been reanalysed as ergative. The unmarked patient subject of the erstwhile passive, which matches the unmarked subjects of other intransitives, has been reanalysed as absolutive.

The Hanis ergative case marking thus apparently arose via two pathways, reanalysis of passive agents as ergatives and reanalysis of instruments as ergatives. It is likely that one facilitated the other. The pattern has now been extended to all nouns representing transitive agents.

It appears that there was still another factor involved in the development. When Europeans arrived on the Pacific coast, speakers of languages of three small families, Coosan, Siuslawan and Alsean, were living along adjacent 10–20-mile stretches of the beach. There was extensive contact, multilingualism and intermarriage (Zenk 1990a, b). In the second half of the nineteenth century, groups from all three were moved to the same reservations, where contact was even more intense. The three families are not considered demonstrably related, though they share numerous features. Similar lexical items are generally so close in form that they have been attributed to borrowing. Languages in all three families have crystallized a preference for speech-act participants as subjects into a grammatical requirement: all prohibit transitive clauses with third persons acting on first or second (*3>1, *3>2) and require passivization in such situations. It is easy to imagine how a stylistic preference for the framing of clauses could be transferred from one language to the next. Bilinguals could simply replicate the frequency and contexts of their use in one of their languages when speaking the other (Mithun 2005).

The fine details of the Hanis system, including the restriction of ergative patterning to lexical nominals, the ergative and oblique case homophony, the unmarked absolutive case, and the transitive and passive suffix homophony, all make sense in terms of the sequences of processes which produced it, processes which occurred under such social circumstances as intense contact, and such linguistic circumstances as the absence of overt third persons where reference is clear and reanalysis of oblique clitics as ergatives in coexisting constructions.

31.2.2 Alignment Splits

It has long been recognized that many languages show splits in alignment patterns. Early on, Silverstein (1976) proposed that pattern splits can be captured with a referential hierarchy like that in Figure 31.1. Essentially, if members of a category show nominative/accusative patterning, so will all members of categories to its left on the hierarchy; if members of a category show ergative/absolutive patterning, so will all members of categories to its right.

1, 2 PRONOUNS < 3 PRONOUNS < HUMANS < ANIMATES < INANIMATES
ACCUSATIVE   ERGATIVE

Figure 31.1   Hierarchy of case marking

Silverstein's predications are often borne out, as in Hanis. We can go further and ask why.

31.2.2.1   Referential Splits

Some answers come from work by Garrett (1990). Proto-Indo-European is generally reconstructed with accusative patterning, but the Anatolian branch, including Hittite, shows some ergativity. Ergative case marking is restricted to neuter nouns, however.

The Anatolian languages, like many others, do not require overt mention of third persons if reference is clear. Instruments are identified with an ablative case suffix.

(10)   Hittite (Garrett 1990: 278)
    šamuḫann=a ...   alwanzešn-**aza**   šer   šunništa
    šamuha.ACC=and   witchcraft-ABL   PREVERB   fill.PRET.3SG
    'and (he) filled Samuha with witchcraft'

The situation is exactly as in Hanis Coos. Such sentences were structurally ambiguous. In the absence of an overt third-person subject, the marked instrument, here 'witchcraft', was apparently interpreted as a core argument, an ergative.

(11)   Hittite reanalysis (Garrett 1990: 278)
    šamuḫann=a ...   alwanzešn-**aza**   šer   šunništa
    šamuha=and   witchcraft-ERG   PREVERB   fill.PRET.3SG
    'and witchcraft filled Samuha'

This situation reveals the point of entry of the reanalysis: neuter gender nouns. Ergativity was never extended further.

Garrett (1990) discusses similar splits in the Eastern Highlands family of Papua New Guinea. The family has two branches, Garokan and Kainantu. All Garokan languages show ergativity, but no Kainantu languages do. The Proto-Garokan ergative singular case suffix is reconstructed as *-moʔ/*-muʔ. Some languages in the Garokan branch contain instrumental suffixes which match their ergatives. All eight languages in the other branch, Kainantu, contain instrumental case suffixes reconstructed as *-moʔ/*muʔ. Using the comparative method, it is possible to reconstruct a Proto-Eastern-Highlands suffix *-moʔ/*muʔ with only instrumental function. The suffix apparently developed into an ergative in the Garokan branch. In the Garokan languages, ergative case marking is now obligatory for inanimates but optional for animates, evidence for its point of entry into the grammar and also the direction of its incipient extension. In at least one Garokan language, Hua, stressed third-person pronouns are also inflected for ergativity. Verbal affixes in all Garokan languages show accusative patterning.

31.2.2.2 Independent and Dependent Clauses

Alignment splits along other dimensions are also common cross-linguistically. In many languages, independent clauses show one pattern and dependent clauses another. Such splits were discussed early on by Larsen and Norman (1979) for Mayan. The thirty Mayan languages are spoken primarily in Guatemala, southern Mexico and Belize in Mesoamerica. The comparative method indicates that Proto-Mayan had ergative patterning in pronominal affixes on verbs. Third-person absolutives are zero. There is no noun case. The pattern can be seen in Quiche.

(12)   Quiche ergative pattern (Larsen and Norman 1979: 349)
   a. x-**a**-ch'ay-oh
      PFV-**2SG.ERG**-hit-TR
      'You (ERG) hit (him).'
   b. x-**at**-war-ik
      PFV-**2SG.ABS**-sleep-INTR
      'You (ABS) slept.'
   c. x-**at**-**u**-ch'ay-oh
      PFV-**2SG.ABS**-**3SG.ERG**-hit-TR
      'He (**ERG**) hit you (**ABS**).'

In languages of the Kanjobalan branch of Mayan, main clauses show the original ergative pattern, but complements are accusative. All subjects in complements, both transitive and intransitive, are identified the same way, with forms that match the ergative markers.

(13)   Jacaltec main and complement clauses (Craig 1977: 288, 294, 302)
   a. Ch-**a**-watxe-'   kap   camixe.
      ASP-**2.ERG**-make-FUT.TR   the   shirt
      '**You** (**ERG**) will make the shirt.'
   b. Ch-**ach**   oc-i
      ASP-**2.ABS**   enter-INTR
      '**You** (ABS) enter.'
   c. xc-**ach**   y-iptz-e
      ASP-**2.ABS**   3.ERG-force-TR
      'He forced **you** (ABS)
      naj **ha**-tuci **ha**-bey yulaj   finca.
      he   **2**-stop   **2**-go   to   plantation
      [to stop [going to the plantation]].'

The ergative prefixes in Jacaltec main verbs and the subject prefixes on complements also match the possessive prefixes on nouns: *chaon* **ha**-*colo* '**you** help us', *ha-mam* '**your**-father'. A common strategy for forming complements cross-linguistically is nominalization. The strategy can be seen as a kind of analogical extension. Complement clauses function syntactically much like nouns, as arguments of clauses. When clauses are nominalized, one of their core arguments may be expressed as a possessor. Often this is the subject, as in English: *He dislikes [**your** going to the plantation]*. The alignment split in Jacaltec now makes sense in light of the developments behind it. The subject prefixes in complement clauses are the descendants of possessive prefixes on nominalized clauses.

31.2.2.3 Aspect Splits

Larsen and Norman describe other kinds of alignment splits in other Mayan languages. In Yucatecan languages such as Mopan, perfective aspect clauses show the original ergative pattern, but imperfectives show accusative patterning.

(14) Mopan ergative perfectives (Larsen and Norman 1979: 353)
    a. **a**-lox-aj-**en**
        2SG.ERG-hit-SUF-1SG.ABS
        'You (ERG) hit me (ABS).'
    b. lub'-**eech**
        fall-**2SG.ABS**
        'You (ABS) fell.'
    c. **in**-lox-aj-**ech**
        1SG.ERG-hit-SUF-**2SG.ABS**
        'I (ERG) hit you (ABS).'

(15) Mopan accusative imperfectives (Larsen and Norman 1979: 354)
    a. tan   **a**-lox-ik-en
        PROG   **2SG**-hit-SUF-**1SG**
        'You (SBJ) are hitting me (OBJ).'
    b. tan   **a**-lub'-ul
        PROG   **2SG**-fall-SUF
        'You (SBJ) are falling.'
    c. tan   **in**-lox-ik-**ech**
        PROG   **1SG**-hit-SUF-**2SG**
        'I (SBJ) am hitting you (OBJ).'

Similar splits occur in Chol, Ixil and Pocomam.

Larsen and Norman note that 'the tenses or aspects which trigger split ergativity are always morphologically marked by the presence of some auxiliary verb or particle preceding the verb. Some of these aspect markers are historically verb roots' (1979: 355). It is likely that the clauses they mark originated as complements of those verbs, nominalized sentences. In fact in Pocomam, Aguacatec and Quiche, they still contain recognizable nominalizing suffixes. The subject prefixes in imperfective clauses are thus descendants of possessive prefixes.

(16) Pocomam (Smith-Stark 1976: 629, cited in Larsen and Norman 1979: 356)
    a. ?ih-wir-i
        PFV-3SG.ABS-sleep
        'He slept.'
    b. nu-ru-wir-**iik**
        IPFV-3SG.ERG-sleep-**NMZ**
        'He is sleeping.'

All of these kinds of splits, by gender, animacy, person, dependency and aspect, appear in numerous unrelated languages, the results of common processes of language change.

31.3 Argument Structure

Languages often provide speakers with alternative argument structures, such as passives, antipassives, causatives and/or applicatives. In Navajo, an Athabaskan language of the North American Southwest, core arguments are identified in the verb with pronominal subject and object prefixes. Another core argument can be added with an applicative prefix like *-taa-* 'among' in (17b) below, where the added argument is identified by the third-person pronominal prefix *bi-*.

(17) Navajo[1] (Melvatha Chee, speaker p.c.)
    a. naashniih
        naa-sh-niih
        around-1SG.SBJ-act.with.hand.IPFV
        'I pass it around.'
    b. **bi**taashniih
        bi-taa-sh-niih
        3-among-1SG.SBJ-act.with.hand
        'I pass it out to **them**.'

The verb in (17b) occurred in the remark below.

(18) Navajo applicative (NAV002.185)
    Bi-taa-sh-niih   ayóo   yídaneedlį́į   łeh.
    3-among-1SG.SBJ-distribute   very   they.all.enjoy.it   usually
    'I give it out **to them** and they really enjoy it.'

Additional lexical nominals may be added to further identify referents. The pronominal prefixes remain in the verb.

---

[1] Unless otherwise indicated, Navajo material cited here is drawn from a corpus of conversation compiled with funding from NSF grant BCS-0853598.

(19) Navajo applicative with lexical argument (Young, Morgan and
      Midgette 1992: 471)
      Shik'éi   **bi-taa**-sh-áa-go   shééshį́.
      my.relatives **3-among**-1SG.SBJ-SG.go-SUB   I.summered
      'I spent the summer visiting my relatives.'

Based on our knowledge of the kinds of diachronic processes that produce affixes, we would suspect that the applicative prefixes might have
originated in separate words. In fact the source of this applicative still
exists in the language as a postposition.

(20) Navajo postposition (NAV007.46)
      Áádóó   shi-naaltsoos **bi-tah**   díńsh'į́'...
      then   my-paper   **3-among**   I was looking
      'Then I was looking **through** my papers...'

Navajo postpositions, like verbs, are obligatorily inflected for their
objects.
   The original postposition, complete with pronominal prefix, amalga-
mated with the following verb, by familiar processes of structural reanalysis and grammaticalization.

[(NOUN) PRO-POSTPOSITION] VERB > (NOUN) [PRO-APPLICATIVE-VERB]

Navajo also contains a number of other postposition:applicative pairs at
earlier and later stages of development.

(21) Navajo Postpositions Applicative prefixes
              -'ąą   -'ą-   'over and beyond'
              -k'i   -k'i-   'on'
              -ka   -ka-   'for'
              -lááh   -lá-   'beyond, surpassing'
              -t'ah   -t'a-   'under the cover of'
              -ts'ą́ą́   -tsą́-   'away from'
              -yah   -ya(a)-   'under'

Where there is a difference in shape, the applicative form is more
eroded, not surprising given that it represents a further stage of development. But not all such forms come in pairs. Young, Morgan and Midgette
(1992: 922) list 37 Navajo forms that occur only as postpositions, 21 pairs of
related postpositions and applicatives, and 17 forms that occur only as
applicative prefixes on verbs. Furthermore, those in the middle group
show varying degrees of attachment to the verb when serving as applicatives. We thus have categories with intersecting and fuzzy boundaries. We
could simply declare that language is messy, or we could explain the
pattern in terms of changes in progress.
   The differences in attachment are not unmotivated. They have
developed out of usage patterns. While the postpositions can follow any

lexical noun that makes sense, the applicative prefixes occur only with specific verb stems, those with which they have apparently co-occurred especially frequently. Some are highly productive, appear with large numbers of stems, and are semantically transparent, such as *-á* 'for' in **b-á-** *'díshgéésh* 'I'm cutting off a piece **for him**'. Many are relatively idiomatic, such as *-taa-* ... *-áa* 'among-go' = 'visit' above. Some have meanings that are now difficult to isolate, such as *-ch'a-* in *shi-**ch'a**-hóóshkeed* 'he scolded me' (verb stem *-keed* 'be mean, fierce'), a prefix listed by Young, Morgan and Midgette as 'meaning obscure' (1992: 923). Strings of frequently co-occurring words have become routinized chunks, stored and selected as units.

The development of the Athabaskan applicatives was shaped by a common cognitive process, the automation of frequently occurring sequences. This routinization was stimulated by both linguistic factors (adjacent positions within the clause) and communicative factors (frequency of use). An understanding of the circumstances behind this development helps explain the fuzziness of the formal categories and the fact that while postpositions can in principle occur with any noun, the applicatives are associated with particular lexical verbs to varying degrees.

31.4 Basic Word Order

One of the most commonly cited typological features in linguistic descriptions is the order of constituents in a clause: SOV, SVO, etc. But some languages show no basic, syntactically defined order: all orders reflect the status of the information conveyed within the larger discourse context. Several approaches could be taken to these apparent outlaws. Attempts could be made to fit them into one of the familiar types. Alternatively, we could ask why they are the way they are.

An example is Mohawk, a Iroquoian language indigenous to northeastern North America. As in most languages, transitive clauses with multiple lexical arguments are rare in Mohawk spontaneous speech: speakers normally introduce one new idea at a time. But constituents occur in all relative orders. The passage below is from a conversation about mysterious occurrences. The speaker cited is Konwakeri McDonald. Each line represents a separate intonation unit or prosodic phrase. Constituents comparable to subjects appear before predicates in (a, b, c, d), but after them in (e, f). The location 'in the sand' appears before the predicate in (b), but after it in (e, f).

(22) Mohawk SV and VS

	S	V	O
a. Wahón:nise'	rake'níha	rakká:ratonhs	ki:.
long.ago	my.father	he story tells me	this

'A long time ago my father was telling me this story,

             S   LOC   V

b. thí:ken   ótia'ke   o'nehsaronhkwà:ke í:we's.
   that   other   sand place   it goes around
   about something strange living in the sand.'

             S   V

c. Thò:ne   raksa'okòn:'a   ronatswa'tòn:ne.
   there   children   they used to play
   'That's where the kids used to play.'

             S   V

d. Rake'níha tanon' ro'kèn:'a   sahiahtén:ti'.
   my father and   his younger brother they went back there
   'My father and his younger brother went back there.'

         V   LOC   S

e. Ronatswà:ton'   onehsaronhkwà:ke   ratiksa'okòn:'a.
   they.were.playing sand.place   boys
   'The children were playing in the sand.'

f.   V   LOC   S
   Thó   taiokè:tohte'   o'nehsaronhkwà:ke ne   thi:.
   there it was peeking out   sand place   the   that
   'It was peeking out from the sand, that thing.'

Later in the conversation talk shifted to another strange happening. In the first clause in (23) the counterpart of the English object 'something scary' appeared before the predicate; in the second it appeared after.

(23)   Mohawk OV and VO

    a. O   V
      Néne iótteron   nahò:ten'   wahatkáhtho'.
      that   it.is.frightful something he.saw
      'He saw something very scary.'

    b. V
      Rohnekì:ren,   ó:nen tóka'
      he.was.drinking now   Maybe
      'He'd been drinking maybe,

      TEMP   V
      teiahia'kserà:ke shihohnekì:ren,
      two.weeks   as.he.was.drinking
      for about two weeks,

      O
      ohné:ka'.
      hard liquor.'

Mohawk word order essentially reflects the relative newsworthiness of major constituents at that point in the discourse. More significant information appears earlier in the clause (often after various orienting particles), while more predictable or incidental information appears later.

Understanding the principles behind the ordering is crucial to understanding the syntax of this language. But we can go further and ask why it is the way it is. For the Iroquoian languages, there are no written records dating back to a time when ordering principles were any different than they are today. All of the modern languages show similar patterns, so the comparative method yields no clues. But common processes of language change provide a likely explanation.

Core arguments are represented by pronominal prefixes in the verb, whether coreferential lexical nominals are also present in the clause or not.

(24) Mohawk pronominal prefixes
    a. **rak**ká:ratonhs
       rak-kar-aton-hs
       M.SG>1SG-story-say-HAB
       'He tells **me**.'
    b. *Thò:ne*   ***raksa'okòn:'a***   *ron*atswa'tòn:ne.
       tho=hne   ra-ksa'=okon'a   **ron**-at-hswa't-on-hne
       there   M-child=DISTR   M.PL.PAT-MDL-play-STAT-PST
       there   **children**   **they** used to play
       'That's where **the kids** used to play.'

It is well known that frequent combinations of words can come to be processed as chunks, and, over time, amalgamate (univerbation). The pronominal prefixes were ripe for this: highly frequent, unstressed morphemes that occurred systematically before the verb in most clauses, apparently in SOV order. We see the same process in modern spoken French: sequences like *je te le donne* (*je* 'I', *te* 'you,SG', *le* '3MSG', *donne* 'give.1SG') are now pronounced as single words: [ʃtlədɔn] 'I give it to you'; *je l'aime, mon fils* [ʒlɛm mõ fis] 'I love my son' (*l'* 'him', *aime* 'love.1SG', *mon* 'my.MSG', *fils* 'son').

Once they were part of the verbal morphology, pronominal prefixes could not be stressed for contrast. That function is now served by newer independent pronouns. The comment below followed another exchange in the conversation about monsters.

(25) Mohawk pronominal contrast
      Ketshà:nihs **ní:**   nakwé   aonkwaterièn:tarake'.
      I am afraid **myself** all   I would know
      'I **myself** am afraid to know all of that.'

The Mohawk independent pronouns are not ancestral to the pronominal prefixes; they represent a renewal. They are entirely different in shape. While most of the pronominal prefixes are cognate throughout the family, the independent pronouns are not. The sources of the third-person independent pronouns *raónha* 'he himself', *akaónnha* 'she herself' etc. are still transparent, verbs based on the stem 'be alone'.

In modern Mohawk, lexical nominals are conspicuously rare in spontaneous speech. Many ideas expressed by lexical nouns in other languages are invoked by incorporated noun stems in the verb. The verb *rakká:ratonhs* 'he tells me' actually has the incorporated stem *-kar-* 'story'. The verb *rohnekì:ren* 'he was drinking' contains the incorporated stem *-hnek-* 'liquid', also the foundation of the noun *o-hné:k-a'* 'liquid, liquor'. Many other ideas expressed in nouns in other languages are conveyed by verbs in Mohawk. The word translated 'two weeks' above is morphologically a verb: *teiahia'kserà:ke*, literally 'it week numbers doubly'.

Mohawk clause structures containing more than a verb reflect earlier information structure. Lexical nominals may introduce a new referent (presentative), shift the topic (topicalization), highlight information (focus), or reiterate a continuing topic when reference might be unclear (antitopic). In the first three, the lexical nominal generally precedes the predicate; in the last, it follows. Modern basic sentence structure continues earlier information structure with a reduction in markedness. Such sentences show a prosodic contour that is common cross-linguistically, beginning with a pitch reset, then gradual declination to a final, terminal fall.

(In Mohawk, every major word has just one primary stress. The stressed syllable has one of two distinctive tones, one marked with an acute accent (*í:we's*), the other a grave accent (*o'nehsaronhkwà:ke*). The tone marked with a grave accent consists of an extra steep rise, visible here in the last section of Figure 31.2, followed by a plunge to below the baseline. It is unrelated to information structure.)

Additional constructions are available for indicating marked information structure. Following (25), the speaker continued her

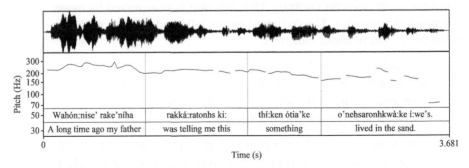

Figure 31.2 Unmarked prosody over Mohawk sentence

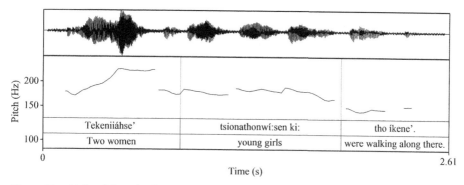

Figure 31.3 Mohawk introduction of new topic

story: 'He was coming home from the bar. He came to the cemetery on the hill.'

(26)   Mohawk presentative
        Tekeniiáhse' tsionathonwí:sen ki: thó   íkene'.
        two women   young girl   this   there they two are walking
        'There were two girls walking along there.'

The prosodic contour of this presentative is different from that in Figure 31.2. The new characters, the women, were introduced with extra high pitch.

Other constructions convey other special information structures, typically with special intonation patterns, some involving various particles. During the same conversation, people were asking who it was who had seen footprints in the graveyard.

(27)   Mohawk focus (Konwákeri McDonald)
        Ro'níha.
        'Her father.'
        Né: rotkáhthon   wahétken'.
        that   he saw it   it is bad
        'He's the one who saw it, that awful thing.'

The particle *né:* was pronounced on high pitch and drawn out (see Figure 31.4).

The initially surprising word order of Mohawk and other Iroquoian languages is explicable in terms of a sequence of common processes of language change: routinization of the most frequent SOV word order, with subsequent loss of word boundaries between unstressed pronouns and the following verbs; routinization of word orders involving lexical nominals in pragmatically marked constructions, resulting in constituent ordering reflecting newsworthiness; and finally renewal of pragmatically marked information structures via distinctive prosody and special constructions like clefts.

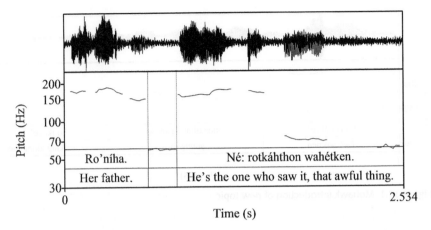

Figure 31.4 Mohawk focus construction

31.5 Dependency and Beyond

The sentence has typically been taken as the fundamental unit of syntax, the object of study. Syntactic theory seeks to specify the structure of sentences. An assumption inherent in most work is that the sentence is a clearly delineated structural unit. But languages vary in the clarity of sentence boundaries, and spontaneous speech often fails to meet our expectations.

The delineation of sentences appears especially clear in languages of the Eskimo-Aleut family. Every verb contains an inflectional mood suffix. Some mood suffixes mark independent sentences and have meanings comparable to mood distinctions in many other languages. In Central Alaskan Yup'ik, spoken in southwestern Alaska, the independent moods include an indicative (for statements and yes/no questions), interrogative (for content questions) and optative (for tentative statements and commands). The dependent moods include a participial, subordinative and others with meanings such as 'when in the past', 'while', 'if, when in the future', 'although', etc. The sentence in (28) consists of a main indicative clause 'we began to wander', with a participial clause 'getting lost' which simply provides supplemental information, and a subordinative clause 'as we were travelling'.

(28)   Yup'ik complex sentence with participial (Elizabeth Ali, speaker p.c.)
        Tuai-ll'   ayainanemegeni
        tuai=llu   ayag-**inaner**-megni
        and=too   go-**CONTEMPORATIVE**-1DU
        'And **as** we two were traveling (**CONTEMPORATIVE**),

Pellaangukuk
pellaa-nge-**u**-kuk
lose.way-INTR.IND-1DU
we began to wander (IND),
Cunawa   tama**lria**kuk.
Cunawa   tamar-**lria**-kuk
So   lose-INTR.PTCP-2DU
gett**ing** lost (PTCP).'

The sentence in (29) consists of an indicative main clause 'My father would sit like this at the table' and a subordinative clause 'facing his friend'.

(29) Yup'ik complex sentence with subordinative (Elizabeth Ali, speaker p.c.)
      Aataka   waten   aqumtullru**u**q,
      aata-ka   waten   aqume-tu-llru-**u**-q
      father-1SG>3SG like.this sit-CUST-PST-INTR.IND-3SG
      'My father would sit like this (IND),
      estuulumi,
      estuulu-mi
      table-LOC
      at the table,
      ilurani   cau**lu**ku.
      ilura-ni   cau-**lu**-ku
      friend-3 R>3   face-SUB-R>3SG
      fac**ing** his friend (SUB).'

Subordinative clauses describe closely associated events or states. Subjects of these adverbial subordinatives must be coreferential with the subjects of their matrix clauses.

Elicited complex sentences show these patterns robustly. The examples above were from spontaneous speech, but a further look at unscripted speech quickly reveals something unexpected: numerous instances of both participial and subordinative clauses do not appear to be syntactically dependent at all. There is often no indicative clause in the vicinity they could be dependent on. And their prosody is often that of an independent sentence.

The sentence in (29) above, 'My father used to sit at the table like this facing his friend', was followed by the account below. Punctuation reflects prosody, with a capital letter indicating a pitch reset, a comma a non-terminal fall in pitch and a period a final, terminal fall.

(30) Yup'ik participials (Elizabeth Ali, speaker p.c.)
      Waten qanrutellr-**u**-a, ilurani-gguq, aká-gguq, nitelleq-gguq,
      'He told his friend (IND), what he had heard,
      kass'at tekipailegata, nunamtenun.
      long ago, before the arrival of white men.'

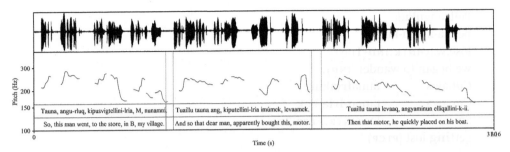

Figure 31.5 Yup'ik participial sentences

Tauna-gguq, angukaraúrluq, kipusvigtellini-**lria**, Mamterillermi,
nunamni.
'This little old man apparently went to the store (PTCP) in Bethel, my
village.'
Tuaillu-gguq tauna angukaraúrluq, kiputellini-**lria** imúmek,
levaamek.
'And then that dear little man apparently bought this motor (PTCP).'
Tuaillu-gguq tauna levaaq, angyaminun elliqallini-**k**-ii.
'Then he apparently quickly placed that motor on his boat (PTCP).'
Elirrarlukullu-gguq, aya-**lria**.
'After he put it on (SUB), he travelled (PTCP).'

The grammatically dependent participial construction is now used
pervasively as an independent sentence, with complete sentence intonation. The pitch traces of the first three participial sentences in (30) are
in Figure 31.5. Each begins after a pause with a pitch reset and ends with
a terminal fall.

As syntactically dependent clauses, participials are typically descriptive,
adding extra information, elaboration. They can function much like relative
clauses in other languages. As independent sentences, they supply extra
information to the discourse, such as background, parenthetical comments,
explanation, evaluation, etc. In (30) above, they provide background to the
story. The construction has been extended from the syntax to the discourse.

The story continued as below. Again, punctuation indicates prosody.

(31)   Yup'ik subordinatives (Elizabeth Ali, speaker)
        Kuigkun anelrar-**lu**-ni,
        'He went downriver (SUB),
        Kusquqvamun ayag-**lu**-ni,
        he went towards the Kuskokwim River (SUB),
        tuai-ll'ayaumallini-**lria**,
        apparently traveling for a very long time (PTCP),
        yakcaara-**lu**-ni.
        traveling with pleasure (SUB).'

Tuaillu-gguq, An'arciimun, tekil-**lu**-ni.
'Then he arrived at the Johnson River (SUB).'

There are four subordinative clauses here, but no indicative matrix clause they could be subordinate to. There are at least two complete prosodic sentences. The subordinative, like the participial, has been extended from marking syntactic relations among clauses within a sentence to marking discourse relations among independent sentences. In its discourse function, it links closely-related aspects of a single event, or, more abstractly, closely related ideas, components of a larger idea.

Autonomous subordinatives, those that function as independent sentences, have developed a rich range of additional functions; they are frequent in conversation, for example, as speakers mark that their comment is pertinent to what has just been said by others. An example is the exchange in (32), part of a telephone conversation. (The suffix takes a different form in negatives.)

(32)　Yup'ik subordinative (Elizabeth Ali, Elena Charles, speakers p.c.)
　　EA　Anngacayaqa　　　　　　　tamaantuq?
　　　　anngaq-cayaq-ka　　　　　　tamaante-u-q
　　　　older.brother-little-1 SG>SG　be.there-INT-3s
　　　　'Is my older brother there?'
　　EC　Anngacayan　　　　　　　　tua-i,
　　　　anngaq-cayaq-n　　　　　　　tuai
　　　　older.brother-little-2 SG>SG　then
　　　　'Your older brother,
　　　　Ayayui**na**ni　　　　　　　　maantauralalria.
　　　　ayag-yuite-na-ni　　　　　　　maante -aurar-lar-lria
　　　　leave-NEG.HAB-**SUB**-3SG　　be.here-continue-HAB-PTCP
　　　　he's not leaving (SUB), just staying here.'

The subordinative mood indicates that the answer is pertinent to what has gone before, here the question posed by the other participant. In some genres, participial and subordinative sentences now greatly outnumber indicative ones.

Much work in diachronic syntax has focused on the reduction of larger structures into smaller, tighter ones. The development of the Eskimo-Aleut mood markers has progressed in the opposite direction. Both the Yup'ik participial and the subordinative suffixes developed from nominalizers. The nominalizer -*lria* is still a highly productive word-formation device in Yup'ik.

(33)　Yup'ik nominalizer -*lria* (George Charles, speaker p.c.)
　　　Taiqata**lria**
　　　tai-qatar-**lria**
　　　come-about.to-NMZ
　　　'**one who** is coming'

The source of the subordinative *-lu* is no longer productive, but its earlier use as a derivational nominalizer can still be detected in Yup'ik nouns.

(34) Yup'ik nominalizer *-lu*

tam-**lu**	'chin'	tamu-	'chew'
kum-**lu**	'thumb'	kumeg-	'scratch'
cur-**lu**	'nostril, sinus'	cur-	'be murky'
u-**lu**	'tongue'	uig-	'taste'

The suffix is reconstructed for Proto-Eskimo-Aleut as *-lu(r)* 'place or thing for performing action X' by Fortescue, Jacobson and Kaplan (1994: 408).

The seemingly fuzzy category of the Yup'ik sentence can now be understood in terms of a common process: extension. Extension of constructions marking dependency from the syntax into discourse can be seen in unrelated languages around the world, though the precise functions of the constructions themselves differ (Mithun 2008).

31.6 Motivation and Teleology

Syntactic change can be stimulated by a wide array of structural and communicative circumstances and goals. Individual changes may be teleological: speakers may extend a pattern for greater expressivity, or automate a frequently recurring string of forms for ease of production. Sequences of changes do not necessarily show the same teleology, however. Each change is motivated only locally, though of course multiple changes may share the same local motivation. We are now in a position to consider the crooked path behind another ergative system, that of Yup'ik.

Ergative case is marked on Yup'ik nouns by a suffix *-m*; absolutives are unmarked.

(35) Yup'ik noun case (George Charles, Elena Charles, speakers p.c.)
  a. Absolutive
      Nayagaq   ulligcinaurtuk.
      Nayagaq   ulligte-naur-tu-k
      younger.sister   cut.fish-HAB-INTR.IND-3DU
      'Nayagaq (ABS) would cut fish.'
  b. Absolutive
      Nayagaq   qanercuuteqsailkeka
      Nayagaq   qanercuute-awaite-ke-ka
      younger.sister   telephone-not.yet-TR.PTCP-1SG>3SG
      'I haven't telephoned Nayagaq (ABS) yet.'

   c. Ergative

      Nayaga**m**   aqvallruakuk,

      nagayaga-**m**   aqva-llru-a-kuk

      younger.sister-ERG   fetch-PST-TR.IND-3SG>1DU

      'Nayagaq (ERG) came and got us.'

The pronominal suffixes on indicative verbs also show ergative patterning. The forms have undergone phonological change, but the first- and second-person suffixes on intransitive verbs generally match those of patients on transitive verbs.

(36)   Yup'ik pronominal suffixes on indicatives

INTRANSITIVE		TRANSITIVE			
1SG	**-nga**	2SG>1SG	**-vnga**	3SG>1SG	**-anga**
2SG	**-ten**	1SG>2SG	**-mken**	3SG>2SG	-aten
1DU	**-kuk**	2SG>1DU	**-vkuk**	3SG>1DU	-akuk
2DU	**-tek**	1SG>2DU	**-mtek**	3SG>2DU	-atek
1PL	**-kut**	2SG>1PL	**-vkut**	3SG>1PL	-akut
2PL	**-ci**	1SG>2PL	**-mci**	3SG>2PL	-aci etc.

The system is thoroughly ergative.

The path to this system was not straightforward, however. Internal reconstruction provides clues to this route. The ergative case suffix *-m* on nouns matches the genitive in form.

(37)   Yup'ik genitive case *-m* (Elena Charles, speaker p.c.)

      Aturpakaamki,

      atur-pakar-a-mki

      use-so.long-CONSEQUENTIAL-1SG>3PL

      'Since I have been using so much of

Nayaga**m**-ll'	akiuturlui	tuai, ...
nayagaq-**m**=llu	akiun-urlu-i	tuai
younger.sister-GEN=also	money-dear-3SG>3PL	then

      poor dear Nayagaq's (GENITIVE) money, ... '

Possession is actually doubly marked in Yup'ik: once on the possessor noun if there is one, and once on the possessed noun by a suffix identifying both the possessor and the possessed. This can be seen above in *akiuturlu-i* 'her dear money', with the suffix *-i* 3sg>3pl on 'money' ('money' is plural in Yup'ik). Additional examples of possessive suffixes are below with *nuna* 'land, village, place, country' in the absolutive case: *nunaka* 'my land', *nunan* 'your land', *nunavut* 'our land', *nunait* 'their lands', etc.

(38) Yup'ik possessive suffixes on nouns (George Charles, speaker p.c.)

	SG	DU	PL
	nuna	nunak	nunat
1SG	nunaka	nunagka	nunanka
2SG	nunan	nunagken	nunaten
3SG	nunaa	nunak	nunai
1DU	nunavuk	nunagpuk	nunapuk
2DU	nunasek	nunagtek	nunatek
3DU	nunangak	nunagkek	nunakek
1PL	nunavut	nunagput	nunaput
2PL	nunasi	nunagci	nunaci
3PL	nunangat	nunagket	nunait

The transitive pronominal suffixes on indicative verbs match these possessive suffixes.

(39) Possessive noun suffixes and transitive verb suffixes

    a. angya**qa**   aqvallrua**qa**
        anyar-**ka**   aqva-llru-ar-**ka**
        boat-**1SG>3SG**   fetch-PST-TR.IND-**1SG>3SG**
        'my boat'   'I came and got him'

    b. amira**gka**   aqvallrua**gka**
        amirar-**gka**   aqva-llru-ar-**gka**
        sealskin.boot-**1SG>3DU** fetch-TR.IND-PST-**1SG>3DU**
        'my sealskin boots'   'I went and got them (two).' etc.

A match between the subjects of dependent clauses and possessors is not uncommon cross-linguistically: we saw this situation in Jacaltec Mayan earlier. Dependent clauses are often formed by nominalization, and their subjects cast as possessors. But here it is the ergatives that match genitives, and the match is in main clauses. The modern system is the result of a multi-stage development.

Some Yup'ik moods, including the indicative, distinguish intransitive and transitive clauses.

(40) Indicative mood

    a. Pellaang**u**kuk
        pellaa-nge-**u**-kuk
        lose.way-INTR.IND-1DU
        'we got lost' (INTRANSITIVE)

    b. Aqvallrua**a**qa
        aqva-llru-**ar**-ka
        fetch-PAST-**TR.IND**-1SG>3SG
        'I came and got him' (TRANSITIVE)

We can still see the source of the transitive indicative mood suffix. Jacobson (1984: 606) lists it as +'(g)ar- for first and second persons, and +'(g)a- for third, to capture its complex morphophonemic behaviour. (The symbol + indicates that the final consonant of the preceding base is retained when this suffix is added, the ' that the final suffix of a base of the form (C)VCe- is geminated when it is added, and the *(g)* that a velar fricative occurs after bases ending in two vowels. In the conventional orthography, <g> represents a velar fricative and <r> a uvular fricative. There are regular *g/k* and *r/q* alternations, whereby the fricatives occur medially and the stops finally.)

Yup'ik also contains a derivational nominalizer of exactly the same shape, with exactly the same complex phonological behavior. Jacobson translates it 'that which has been V-ed' (1984: 431). It attaches only to transitive verbs: *pite-* 'to capture', *pit-aq* 'caught game, quarry'. Like many other nominalizers, it occurs in derived forms with specialized meanings: *mumigte-* 'to turn over', *mumigt-aq* 'pancake, translation'. Possessive pronominal suffixes can be added to the nominalized forms, as to other nouns.

(41) Yup'ik nominalization
  a. keni**r**aqa
     kenir-**ar**-ka
     cook-TR.NMZ-1SG>3SG
     'my cooked thing, my stew, what I have cooked'
  b. Nayagam   Keni**r**aa
     nayagaq-m   kenir-**a**-a
     younger.sister-ERG   cook-TR.NMZ-3SG>3SG
     'Nayagaq's stew'

The modern transitive indicatives have apparently developed from nominalized transitive clauses in which the subjects were expressed as possessors, but these were only *transitive* subjects. The intransitive indicative mood suffix comes from a different source. This fact explains why it is the ergative that matches the genitive, and not all subjects.

But nominalization is typically used for forming dependent clauses. The final step in the development of the modern ergative system can be inferred from the processes seen in the previous section, the extension of dependent clause constructions to independent sentences. Modern indicatives are apparently the result of an extension much like that currently underway with participials and subordinatives, whereby erstwhile syntactically dependent clauses have been extended to use as independent sentences, then gradually replaced an earlier indicative.

The modern Yup'ik ergative system thus developed through a sequence of steps: formation of transitive dependent clauses via nominalization, with their (transitive) subjects cast as possessors; subsequent extension of this dependent structure into discourse; increase in frequency of its autonomous use; and finally replacement of an earlier indicative construction. The development was not teleological: the initial step of nominalizing dependent clauses was not undertaken with the ultimate goal of creating an ergative system. Each step exemplifies a well-known type of change, but each had its own local motivation.

31.7 Change and Explanation

Functional approaches to syntactic change are much like other approaches in methodology and in the mechanisms of change investigated. Their main difference from some is the primary role accorded change in explanation, their focus on the myriad cognitive, social, structural and communicative factors that shape language over time. All kinds of changes, large and small, are viewed as relevant to understanding why language is the way it is: those which occur when children first make sense of their inheritance during acquisition, those which occur as speakers communicate throughout the lifespan and those which occur as adults learn new languages. The increasing availability of corpora is making it possible to look in closer detail at the minute steps involved in changes, from their point of entry into the grammar, complete with linguistic and extralinguistic contexts, through their pathways of development.

Good science is shaped by its subject matter. Optimal methodologies for physics necessarily differ from those for understanding language. Syntactic change need not happen, but when it does, it can go in many directions, because so many factors can affect it. The best evidence of this is the constant divergence of related languages over time. The kinds of processes we see at work in language after language, such as reanalysis, analogical levelling, extension, routinization, abstraction, renewal, etc., are viewed as results of universal cognitive processes, tied to the circumstances in which language is used and the motivations of its speakers.

The preceding sections have shown how some basic types of alignment patterns, argument structure, basic word order and dependent clauses can be understood in terms of the processes which shape them. The development of ergative systems has been traced through the reanalysis of instruments as agentive core arguments (Hanis, Hittite, Garokan languages), of passive clauses as transitives (Hanis), and of possessed nominalizations as basic clauses (Yup'ik). The development of applicatives has been traced to the routinization of recurring postposition – verb sequences, the reanalysis of constituent structure and dissolution of word boundaries, all stimulated by frequency of use (Navajo). The development of pragmatically based word order has been traced from the routinization of unstressed pronoun–verb sequences, through renewal of devices for expressing marked information structure (Mohawk).

In some cases, different pathways of development have converged on similar patterns, such as the ergativity examined here. The convergence could be taken as evidence for at least two hypotheses regarding the nature of syntactic change: (i) that it is essentially shifts around a finite set of universally available structures; or (ii) that the functionality of the outcome affects the directionality of changes and the stability of their results.

The first hypothesis becomes less plausible when syntactic change is observed more closely and seen in many cases to be composed of sequences of small steps. Each step is motivated, but the first step is not taken with a view towards a later endpoint: sequences of change are not teleological. Several such sequences leading to ergativity were seen here. In Hanis Coos, contact with neighbouring languages resulted in an increased tendency for speakers to cast speech-act participants as subjects, as they transferred patterns of topic choice from one of their languages to another. Next, automation of the tendency resulted in crystallization of the pattern, such that if a third person acted on a first or second (3>1, 3>2), passivization was obligatory. Once this became the only way to express such a transitive event, the passives were reinterpreted as basic transitives. Oblique agent nouns were reanalysed as ergatives. Perhaps stimulated by this development, oblique instruments in transitive clauses without overt third-person agents were reanalysed as ergatives. Finally, the ergative pattern was extended to all nouns. It would be difficult to maintain that the original increase in the frequency of first- and second-person subjects was motivated by a push towards ergativity.

A completely different sequence of steps led to ergativity in Yup'ik. Transitive dependent clauses were formed by nominalization, a common strategy cross-linguistically of analogical extension, whereby whole clauses are treated much like lexical arguments, with their subjects as possessors. In Yup'ik, only transitive dependent clauses were formed this way, so only transitive subjects were cast as possessors. Intransitive dependent clauses developed from a different source. At some point, these dependent constructions were extended to independent sentences to indicate larger discourse relations. Over time their frequency increased until they ultimately replaced some earlier indicative construction. Again, it would be difficult to maintain that the motivation behind the original use of nominalization to form syntactically dependent clauses was the creation of an ergative case system.

The second hypothesis proposed to account for the convergence of developments towards certain structures was that constructions that serve useful functions in speech are more likely to be the target of innovating speakers, more frequent in speech and accordingly more stable over time. Ergative systems, like accusative systems, aid in the disambiguation of the roles of arguments in transitive clauses. Certain states are found more frequently cross-linguistically because they are functional resting points. Under this view, the variation in detail we find across similar pattern types is not problematic. Ergative patterns in Hanis, Hittite, the Garokan languages, the Mayan languages and the Eskimo-Aleut languages entered their grammars at different points and were extended analogically to different degrees. In fact the differences among the systems provide our best clues to the processes which shape the development of the various pattern types over time.

Ultimately, what may distinguish functional approaches to syntactic change is a greater focus on the common human cognitive, social and communicative factors which enter into the shaping of linguistic categories and structures.

References

Craig, C. G. 1977. *Jacaltec: The structure of Jacaltec*. Austin: University of Texas Press.

Fortescue, M., Jacobson, S. and Kaplan, L. 1994. *Comparative Eskimo dictionary with Aleut cognates*. Fairbanks, AK: Alaska Native Language Center.

Frachtenberg, L. 1913. *Coos texts* (Columbia University Contributions to Anthropology 1). Reprinted 1969, New York: AMS Press.

1922. 'Coos', in F. Boas (ed.), *Handbook of American Indian languages*, part 2 (Bureau of American Ethnology Bulletin 40). Washington, DC: Government Printing Office, pp. 297–429.

Garrett, A. 1990. 'The origin of NP split ergativity', *Language* 66: 261–96.

Jacobs, M. 1939. 'Coos narrative and ethnologic texts', *University of Washington Publications in Anthropology* 8(1): 1–126.

1940. 'Coos myth texts', *University of Washington Publications in Anthropology* 8(2): 127–360.

Jacobson, S. A. 1984. *Yup'ik Eskimo Dictionary*. Fairbanks, AK: University of Alaska, Alaska Native Language Center.

Larsen, T. and Norman, W. 1979. 'Correlates of ergativity in Mayan grammar', in F. Plank (ed.), *Ergativity*. New York: Academic Press, pp. 347–70.

Mithun, M. 2005. 'Ergativity and language contact on the Oregon Coast: Alsea, Siuslaw, and Coos', *Proceedings of the Berkeley Linguistics Society*, pp. 77–95.

2008. 'The extension of dependency beyond the sentence', *Language* 83: 69–119.

Nichols, J. 1992. *Linguistic diversity in space and time*. University of Chicago Press.

Silverstein, M. 1976. 'Hierarchy of features and ergativity', in R. M. W. Dixon (ed.), *Grammatical categories in Australian languages*. Canberra: Australian institute of Aboriginal Studies, pp. 112–71.

Suttles, W. 1990. *Handbook of North American Indians*, vol. 7: *Northwest coast*. Washington, DC: Smithsonian Institution.

Young, R., Morgan, W. and Midgette, S. 1992. *Analytical lexicon of Navajo*. Albuquerque: University of New Mexico Press.

Zenk, H. 1990a. 'Siuslawans and Coosans', in Suttles (ed.), pp. 572–9.

1990b. 'Alseans', in Suttles (ed.), pp. 568–71.

Index